The Hardball Times Season Preview 2009

Featuring contributions by THT's staff writers and some of the best baseball bloggers on the Internet:

Sal Baxamusa • John Beamer • Brian Borawski
Larry Borowsky • John Brattain • Derek Carty
Alex Carver • Scott Christ • Bradford Doolittle
Cork Gaines • Lisa Gray • Brandi Griffin
Patrick Hageman • Justin Inaz • Ben Jacobs
Eric Johnson • Pat Lackey • Rich Lederer
Scott Lucas • Larry Mahnken • Jim McLennan
Chris Neault • Chris Needham • Harry Pavlidis
Mike Pindelski • Ryan Richards • Eric Seidman
Eric Simon • Sean Smith • Jeff Sullivan • Tuck
Steve Treder • Geoff Young • Victor Wang

Produced by David Gassko
Edited by Joe Distelheim, Carolina Bolado,
Ben Jacobs and Bryan Tsao

The Hardball Times Season Preview 2009
New articles daily at www.hardballtimes.com

Edited by Joe Distelheim, Carolina Bolado, Ben Jacobs and Bryan Tsao
Projections developed by David Gassko and Chris Constancio
Cover design by Tom Wright
Typesetting by Dave Studenmund

Published by: ACTA Sports
                 5559 W. Howard Street
                 Skokie, IL 60077
                 1-800-397-2282
                 info@actasports.com
                 www.actasports.com

ISBN: 978-0-87946-370-0
ISSN: 1940-798X
Printed in the United States of America by Versa Press.
Year: 16 15 14 13 12 11 10 09
Printing: 10 9 8 7 6 5 4 3 2 1

What's Inside

**After you've read the Season Preview,
follow fantasy baseball throughout 2009...**

...on the web with:

THT Fantasy

Your best source for coverage of Major League Baseball is now also your best source for coverage of fantasy baseball. Join David Gassko, Derek Carty (2008 FOX Sports Experts Fantasy Baseball League), Victor Wang (2007 recipient of SABR's Jack Kavanagh Memorial Youth Baseball Research Award), and other experts as they apply the cutting-edge sabermetrics of THT to fantasy baseball player analysis, drafting tactics, trading philosophy, and more!

Read our experts' daily commentary and analysis everyday by visiting...

www.hardballtimes.com/thtfantasy

...in print with:

Heater Magazine

It's 2009—why are you still visiting a newsstand to get your baseball stats? Read Heater and get 60+ pages of goodness every Tuesday morning in a smartly designed PDF. Players are sorted both by team and by position, so you can study them in whichever context you need. It's like getting a Draft Day package every week! Subscribers also get The Rundown—a neat PDF with fantasy-oriented box scores for all the previous day's games, sent to you every morning.

For more information, including a free full sample issue, visit...

www.HeaterMagazine.com

**The fantasy season is a marathon.
We'll make sure you keep running.**

The Book Starts Here

Hello all, and welcome to *The Hardball Times Season Preview 2009*. If you bought the *Season Preview* last year, I'd like to welcome you back, and if you didn't, well, I'm glad you've come around. Whether you've previously owned the *Season Preview* or not, I think you'll find this is exactly the book you need to get ready for the upcoming baseball season.

The structure of the *Season Preview* is simple: The bulk of the book consists of projections and player comments for just about every player who might play any kind of role in the 2009 major league baseball season, more than 1,000 players in all. We've added one feature to our projections this season—a reliability score—which ranges from "very high" to "very low." The score is based mostly on the amount of data we have for each player, and it tells you how much you should trust the projection. When the reliability score is "very low," we freely admit that the projection is just our best guess, but we don't have all that much confidence in it. If you're wondering about the definitions of any other statistics listed in this book, just head over to the glossary, which is printed right after this introduction.

The player comments are written by authors who have obsessively watched and written about these players, meaning that you'll get the kind of information from our authors that you would not be able to get anywhere else. The authors have also written team essays, which take a look back at the 2008 season and tell you what to expect in 2009. The essays and player comments ensure that you know exactly what to look for in this upcoming season.

I know, I know, you're already smitten, but we're not done yet. We've added a ton of content to make sure that the fantasy baseball fans reading this book are given a huge head start over their competitors. Most importantly, we have projected fantasy values for every player of any value starting on page 263. We also have essays from Derek Carty, Chris Neault and Victor Wang that will give you plenty of things to think about as you head into your fantasy draft.

Derek has written about rookies to watch in 2009—these players are notoriously hard to project (though my research has shown that our system does a slightly better job than most), but they also can be huge fantasy breakouts. Derek will tell you which rookies represent good risks, and which ones are overrated.

Chris, meanwhile, covers just about every injury you need to know heading into 2009. Injuries can wreak havoc on your fantasy season, but they are extraordinarily difficult to factor into a statistically-based projection system. Chris' work is a great supplement to our projections.

Finally, Victor will tell you how to handle another important consideration heading into your fantasy draft: risk. We know that some players are riskier than others, and of course, we know that high risk can mean high reward, but Victor will explain how you should balance that fact with the knowledge that taking on too much risk can result in your fantasy team crashing and burning (the current state of our economy being a good example).

Sandwiched between the fantasy values and the essays, you'll find a list of career projections for all major league hitters, aged 21-41 in 2009, who are projected to gather 1,500 hits before they retire or 150 home runs, and all major league pitchers (same age restriction) who are projected to win at least 50 games in their career. The career projections are based on a system I developed in last year's *Season Preview*. These are included cause we think they're fun. Don't take them too seriously.

That about covers it. There are a lot of people who deserve a thank you for helping make this book a reality, but I'll just do it in list form, since to truly thank them would require more space than I'm being afforded. Those people are, Dave Studenmund, Joe Distelheim, Chris Constancio, "SG" from the "Replacement Level Yankees Weblog," Bryan Tsao, Charles Fiore, Tuck—whose fun cartoons are sprinkled throughout this book—and all of our fantastic authors. They have all made producing this book a fantastically fun time.

And finally, I'd like to thank you, the reader. Looking at my introduction from last year, I see I ended that essay in the exact same way, but I don't think I'm being redundant. Rather, you should know that without you, there would be no book—why produce something no one is going to read? So thank you for purchasing *The Hardball Times Season Preview 2009*. I hope you enjoy the book, and I hope you're back again next year, when I'll probably get stuck in another creative rut and end the Intro in the exact same way for a third year in a row. Oh well.

-     David Gassko

Some Notes about our Numbers, or, The Glossary

There are a lot of statistics in the *Preview*. Hopefully, that's not a surprise to you. As you read through the essays and comments, you may come across some statistics you haven't seen before. For instance, FIP stands for Fielding-Independent Pitching, and it represents a pitcher's ERA based only on his strikeouts, walks and home runs. In other words, only those things that fielders don't affect.

Our writers also like to refer to some advanced fielding systems, such as "Plus/Minus" (a system developed by John Dewan) and UZR (Ultimate Zone Rating, from Mitchel Lichtman). Both of these stats express a fielder's performance as the number of plays or runs he made above or below average at his position.

When you see a line like this—.270/.340/.440—that stands for the batter's batting average, on base percentage and slugging percentage.

WHIP stands for walks and hits allowed per inning, and GB% is the percentage of batted balls that are ground balls (the major league average for that one was 44 percent last year).

There may be a few other stats we haven't mentioned. For clarification, you can always visit our online statistics glossary, at http://www.hardballtimes.com/main/statpages/glossary/.

It's tough to keep a printed book current with player movements, so we won't have all players listed with their projected 2009 teams by the time you read this. To help you sort it out, there's an index of all 1,050 players and their listed teams in the back.

Here's a rundown of all the statistics that are included in our player projections.

Batter Statistics

PA – Plate appearances. This projection is based on a player's past playing time and does not take into account his projected major league role.

Runs – The listed runs projection is based on a player's basic statistics, unadjusted for lineup or playing time.

Hit – Hits.

2B – Doubles.

3B – Triples.

HR – Home runs.

RBI – Runs batted in. As with runs, we use a basic formula to calculate a player's projected RBI from his basic statistics without adjusting for lineup position or playing time.

SO – Strikeouts.

BB – Walks.

HBP – Hit-by-pitch.

SB – Stolen bases.

CS – Caught stealing.

BA – Batting average: Hits/At-bats.

OBP – On-base percentage: (Hits + Walks + Hit-by-pitch)/(Plate appearances – Sacrifice hits).

SLG – Slugging average: (Hits + Doubles + 2*Triples + 3*Home Runs)/At-bats.

OPS – On-base plus slugging: OBP + SLG.

3-Year Ch. – The projected change in a hitter's OPS in the next three years. A positive number indicates that the hitter is expected to improve from 2008 to 2010, while a negative number indicates he is expected to get worse. Very old players are difficult to project over long periods of time, so we don't list this statistic for them.

Fielding – We project how many runs above or below average each fielder will be, but because fielding ratings contain some uncertainty, we've listed grades to avoid any false precision. The scale ranges from "A+" to "F-." An "A+" fielder should be winning Gold Gloves most years, while an "F-" fielder should probably be moved to an easier position. Fielders with an "A" rating are very good; "B" fielders are above average; "C" fielders are average; "D" fielders are below average; and "F" fielders are pretty bad.

Reliability – The reliability score tells you how reliable a hitter's projection is, based mostly on how much data we had to work with for that player. The score ranges from "very high" to "very low," with "high," "average," and "low" in between.

Pitcher Statistics

Wins – Wins as listed in our projections are not adjusted for a player's team or projected role.

Losses – See above.

TBF – Total batters faced.

Hit – Our hits projection takes into account each team's projected defensive strength. In fact, a ground-ball pitcher's hits total will benefit more from a good infield than a flyball pitcher's, and vice-versa.

HR – Home runs.

SO – Strikeouts.

BB – Walks.

HBP – Hit-by-pitch.

IP – Innings pitched. This projection is based on a player's past playing time and does not take into account his projected major league role.

ERA – Earned run average. This projection takes each team's projected defensive ability into account.

3-Year Ch. – The projected change in a pitcher's ERA in the next three years. A positive number indicates that the pitcher is expected to decline from 2008 to 2010, while a negative number indicates he is expected to improve. Very old players are difficult to project over long periods of time, so we don't list this statistic for them.

Reliability – The reliability score tells you how reliable a pitcher's projection is, based mostly on how much data we had to work with for that player. The score ranges from "very high" to "very low," with "high," "average," and "low" in between.

Note: The projections printed in this book, as well as fantasy values and career projections, are available in Excel spreadsheets for all purchasers of the *Season Preview*. We've even included projections for players not listed in the *Preview*. They can be downloaded at http://www.hardballtimes.com/THT2009Preview/. The username for this page is "thtpreview09" and the password is "affeldt". As we get closer to the beginning of spring training and drafting season, we'll post updates to the projections. Be sure to visit often.

Projected 2009 Standings

American League

East	W	L	RF	RA	DIV	WC
New York Yankees	100	62	884	702	56.0	31.0
Boston Red Sox	98	64	842	677	43.0	40.0
Tampa Bay Rays	90	72	806	706	1.0	27.0
Toronto Blue Jays	73	89	698	769	0.0	0.0
Baltimore Orioles	67	95	769	921	0.0	0.0
Central	W	L	RF	RA	DIV	WC
Cleveland Indians	86	76	829	767	50.8	1.0
Minnesota Twins	83	79	727	716	22.0	1.0
Kansas City Royals	79	83	744	773	15.8	0.0
Chicago White Sox	79	83	786	820	10.8	0.0
Detroit Tigers	74	88	793	850	0.5	0.0
West	W	L	RF	RA	DIV	WC
Los Angeles Angels	82	80	742	722	52.5	0.0
Oakland Athletics	79	83	781	789	25.0	0.0
Texas Rangers	77	85	813	865	17.5	0.0
Seattle Mariners	73	89	682	747	5.0	0.0

National League

East	W	L	RF	RA	DIV	WC
New York Mets	88	74	830	767	35.8	15.5
Philadelphia Phillies	87	75	841	794	42.3	10.0
Atlanta Braves	84	78	763	725	19.3	10.0
Florida Marlins	75	87	750	805	2.5	2.8
Washington Nationals	66	96	721	858	0.0	0.0
Central	W	L	RF	RA	DIV	WC
Chicago Cubs	89	73	801	719	41.5	14.5
Milwaukee Brewers	89	73	807	746	39.0	20.8
St. Louis Cardinals	81	81	757	758	7.5	4.5
Cincinnati Reds	80	82	726	735	8.0	5.8
Houston Astros	80	82	740	753	4.0	2.0
Pittsburgh Pirates	72	90	687	779	0.0	2.0
West	W	L	RF	RA	DIV	WC
Colorado Rockies	85	77	806	764	44.5	4.5
Arizona Diamondbacks	83	79	733	714	30.0	2.5
Los Angeles Dodgers	79	83	721	757	13.0	2.5
San Francisco Giants	79	83	680	700	11.5	1.5
San Diego Padres	73	89	695	759	1.0	1.0

Notes

- The projected standings are based on 100 computer simulations of the 2009 season, including individual player projections.
- Projected team wins (W) and losses (L), runs scored (RS) and runs allowed (RA) are the average outcome of the 100 simulations.
- The "DIV" and "WC" columns represent the number of times, out of the 100 simulations, that the team won the division title or qualified for the wild card. In other words, these numbers can be interpreted as the percentage chance each team will win its division or wild card title, respectively.

Arizona Diamondbacks

by Jim McLennan of AZ Snakepit (azsnakepit.com)

2009 Diamondbacks Projections

Record: 83-79
Division Rank/Games Behind: 2nd, 2 games back
Runs Scored: 733, 10th in league
Runs Allowed: 714, 2nd in league
Park Factor: 1.05, a hitter's park

What Happened Last Year:

Though they scored more runs, and conceded fewer, the Diamondbacks couldn't quite repeat their 2007 triumph, despite a blistering start to the season—they had a lead of 6.5 games on April 25 and finished the month at 20-8. The division race looked all but over, with starting pitchers Brandon Webb, Dan Haren and Micah Owings having a combined record of 14-1. But the team never was able to recapture anything like its early-season form, and had only one more winning month. The D-backs limped into the All-Star break with a losing record. Still, in the weak NL West, that was good enough for first place.

Arizona held on to the division lead through the end of August, but even a post-deadline trade for slugger Adam Dunn couldn't help the team turn the corner. The pivotal series took place in Los Angeles from Sept. 5-7. The Diamondbacks went into Chavez Ravine with a 1.5-game lead over the Dodgers, and aces Webb and Haren starting the first two games. They were swept out of town by a total score of 19-5, turning the lead into a 1.5-game deficit. This was, effectively, the end of their hopes: Arizona didn't get any closer the rest of the way, finishing two games behind the Dodgers—though it felt like a lot more—with eight fewer wins than the previous season.

The rotation was, by some standards, the best in the majors last year. At 45, Randy Johnson stayed mostly healthy, and, despite falling short of his 300th victory, was an admirable No. 3. Perennial Cy Young candidate Webb started the season by winning his first nine starts on his way to a league-leading 22 victories. Haren proved to be everything the team expected when it got him from Oakland by trade, and had an ERA almost the equal of Webb's.

On the hitting side, Conor Jackson demonstrated his versatility by switching to the outfield; Stephen Drew became one of the best-hitting shortstops in the league

and catcher Chris Snyder improved all aspects of his game.

One reason for the decline in wins was the revenge of Pythagoras: The team couldn't repeat 2007's amazing record in one-run games. The Diamondbacks went 22-23 in one-run contests, a drop of 6.5 games from the year before. Indeed, the bullpen had a record of 17-28, and the team lost 15 games in which it led after six innings. The team did well enough against division rivals; it was outside the NL West where the D-backs struggled badly, going only 38-52. The Diamondbacks also failed to handle good opposition, with a 28-44 record against teams above .500.

Injuries to Eric Byrnes and Orlando Hudson helped expose a severe lack of offensive depth. Third baseman Mark Reynolds led the league in errors and set an all-time major-league record with 204 strikeouts. Center fielder Chris Young wasn't far behind, and struggled to get on base; Justin Upton played like the 20-year-old kid he is, alternating brilliance and idiocy with mercurial frequency.

Players Lost from Last Year's Team:

Juan Cruz, Adam Dunn, Orlando Hudson, Randy Johnson, Brandon Lyon, Robby Hammock, Jeff Salazar, Wil Ledezma, Chris Burke.

Players Acquired:

Felipe Lopez, Scott Schoeneweis.

Management Is:

The trade for Haren before 2008 made it look like the Diamondbacks were entering a "win now" cycle, but events since have cast doubts. The player losses all figure to have a significant impact and as this is being written, there has been little sign of them being replaced in any credible fashion. The team appears to have around $10-15 million to spend to fill the holes, but when Arizona didn't offer Johnson more than $3 million, it led to questions about its commitment.

Some point to the contract extension to Byrnes late in 2007 as a key negative moment. It was largely responsible for the loss of Carlos Quentin, and perhaps, by tying up $11 million of payroll this year, the failure to re-sign Johnson. Certainly, the honeymoon period for GM Josh Byrnes is over. While an extension to Haren's contract already has been negotiated, talks on something similar for Webb broke down. He is signed through 2010, including a team option, but if nothing is worked out and the team drops out of contention, Arizona may look to trade him. Byrnes will find no shortage of takers.

The Minor League System Is:

There's limited hope for immediate renewal, with a number of the top prospects traded away and others still some distance from being ready. Max Scherzer will get his shot at a rotation spot in 2009, but the two generally regarded as the next best, Jarrod Parker and Daniel Schlereth, were no higher than A-ball last season. Schlereth may be on a fast track that would get him to the big club in the second half of '09.

The bonus picks from departing free agents Cruz, Hudson and Lyon mean the Diamondbacks probably will have six selections before the start of the second round in June's draft. Even if not of immediate help to the major-league club, those picks will help restock the system.

Due For a Change:

Twenty-year-old position players do not get regular starting jobs in the major leagues these days—before Justin Upton, the last to appear in 90-plus games was Adrian Beltre, back in 1999. There's generally good reason for this: They're not ready for the big leagues. In this light, Upton's season has to be regarded as a success, with his .250 average likely foreshadowing greater success to come. He showed flashes of brilliance, both at the plate and with the glove. On July 6, he hit a home run estimated at 484 feet—the second longest in Chase Field history. He proved equally capable of butchering simple plays in right field, where he led the league in errors (11).

A strained oblique in his rib cage sent Upton to the DL at the All-Star break, and an extended rehab in Tucson meant he didn't come back to the majors until the end of August. The final stretch was thoroughly impressive, with Upton posting a .922 OPS over the last 25 games—12 of his last 16 hits were for extra bases. That may not be an accurate predictor of what to expect from him in 2009, but the improvement in his approach at the plate over the season was palpable. If he can avoid the bone-headed mistakes that infected his play last season, he could have the most productive season of anyone on the team. Twenty-five home runs and an .850 OPS are far from impossible. Not your average 21-year-old, it's safe to say.

Reasons to be Optimistic:

Even beyond Upton, this is still a young team. The Diamondbacks' position players had the lowest aver-

age age in the National League last year and, other than Chad Tracy and Javier Lopez, everyone in the likely starting eight will have fewer than 500 games in the majors on Opening Day 2009. So, there's plenty of room for natural improvement, simply through age and experience.

The departure of Johnson drops the average age of the pitching staff about two years, and the team turns to a pair of 24-year-olds. Scherzer was the team's first-round pick in the 2006 draft, and arrived with a splash, throwing 4.1 perfect innings in his major-league debut, and finishing with 66 strikeouts in 56 innings. He gets to replace Johnson in the rotation this season; Yusmeiro Petit, who probably will get the No. 5 spot, allowed only 45 hits in 56.1 innings last season.

The bullpen needs to be more reliable. Jon Rauch is probably the key there; he'll see plenty of high-leverage innings, and can prove that his performance for the team in 2008 was an aberration, while Chad Qualls gets to show he can close consistently, as he did in September. The team's new second baseman, Felipe Lopez, has a lot of upside and all but admitted he wasn't trying for the Nationals last season. He tore it up after the Cardinals acquired him, batting .385 in 43 games for St. Louis, and seems only to need motivation to become a solid replacement for Hudson (at the plate, if not defensively). His middle-infield partner, Drew, had a great second half and has All-Star potential.

Reasons to be Pessimistic:

The paragraph above is strangely familiar—I think I wrote much the same in last season's volume. The hoped-for improvement from the Diamondbacks' young players proved patchy, to say the least. Young, in particular, seemed to go backwards, and especially if manager Bob Melvin puts him in the top half of the order, he needs to get on base at a much better clip. Reynolds needs to improve his contact rate—his rate of swings and misses was among the highest in the majors and if he doesn't put the ball in play, 200 strikeouts is certainly possible. Potential will take the team only so far, and a number of the players need to start turning that into production, on a more consistent level than last year.

This is not a team with a lot of depth, and the dropoff from the front-row roster to replacements is huge. In particular, if Webb or Haren goes down, it's almost impossible to see the team competing. Byrnes' fitness remains a big question; he could be the richest bench player in the division now that the Dodgers have released Andruw Jones. His contract might end up being a complete waste of money for Arizona by the time it expires after 2010.

The team lost a lot of players, including some whose output is going to be difficult to replace. A limited budget and the financial crisis hamstrung ownership further, leaving the D-backs struggling to keep up with the Dodgers, who could outspend Arizona by $40 million or more.

Still Left to Do:

The bench spot open at the time this is written looks most likely to go to Tony Clark—the logic of getting a left hander who can play only first base, when your first baseman is left-handed, beats me, but the franchise seems to be in love with Clark's veteran presence. Another back-up infielder behind Augie Ojeda might be nice, though the pick of catcher James Skelton in the Rule 5 draft could block this; he has to remain on the roster all season or be offered back to Detroit.

The tail end of the bullpen is the main area that still remains to be addressed, or at least solidified, since the team has plenty of candidates internally who could be used in mop-up roles. Juan Gutierrez impressed in winter ball, and might be the long reliever and spot starter. The batting order needs to be established, though given Melvin's apparent use of lineup dice to construct it last season, that probably isn't too important to his plans.

Most Likely Team Outcome:

The Dodgers are likely marginal favorites in the NL West, a division that remains fairly even, with everyone except the Padres conceivably in contention. If Scherzer can replace Johnson effectively, the rotation should remain among the best in the majors, and it only would need the bullpen to be a little more effective to give the Diamondbacks a significant number of additional wins. As noted above, the offense is young, and should be good for a few extra runs. I can see the team improving a game or two, but I suspect the impact of those lost players is going to prove too much to overcome. I'd give the Diamondbacks 85 games and second place again, behind Los Angeles, assuming everyone stays reasonably healthy.

Player Projections

Batters

Chris Burke (Shortstop)

PA	R	H	2B	3B	HR	RBI	SO	BB	SB	CS	BA	OBP	SLG	OPS	3-Year	Fielding	Reliability
328	38	72	16	2	6	31	51	29	8	1	.251	.330	.384	.714	-0.04	D	Average

Burke must have some incriminating photos of manager Bob Melvin. That's the only way to explain how he appeared in 86 games while barely batting his weight. Flexibility is part of it—he started games at six different positions—but will that be enough to get him on a major-league roster? It won't be in Arizona, as the team mercifully declined to offer him a deal for 2009.

Eric Byrnes (Left Field)

PA	R	H	2B	3B	HR	RBI	SO	BB	SB	CS	BA	OBP	SLG	OPS	3-Year	Fielding	Reliability
399	53	95	21	3	12	48	63	30	17	3	.263	.324	.437	.761	-0.04	B	Very High

After he signed a fat contract, much was expected of Byrnes; instead, the season was an unmitigated disaster. His hamstring troubles ended his year in June, but he hit only .140 over his last 30 games before that. His speed, a crucial part of his game, was non-existent and he may start 2009 as a highly paid fourth outfielder.

Tony Clark (First Base)

PA	R	H	2B	3B	HR	RBI	SO	BB	SB	CS	BA	OBP	SLG	OPS	3-Year	Fielding	Reliability
266	32	57	11	0	11	37	68	32	0	1	.248	.342	.439	.781	—	C	Low

One of the more pointless acquisitions of the season was Clark—rejected by the D-backs before the season, he returned in a deadline deal. He was almost invisible, however, with a .671 OPS in 38 games. "Clubhouse presence" will take the 36-year-old veteran only so far next season, but it looks like the team may bring him back onto the roster as a PH/1B backup.

James D'Antona (Third Base)

PA	R	H	2B	3B	HR	RBI	SO	BB	SB	CS	BA	OBP	SLG	OPS	3-Year	Fielding	Reliability
469	62	130	30	2	19	74	78	33	1	1	.302	.352	.514	.866	+0.08	C	Very High

I wrote a piece on how the rookie might be a good, cheap option to man the hot corner if Mark Reynolds moves to second, having hit .365/.405/.604 for Triple-A Tucson. However, the D-backs, somewhat inexplicably let him go to Japan. Go figure.

Stephen Drew (Shortstop)

PA	R	H	2B	3B	HR	RBI	SO	BB	SB	CS	BA	OBP	SLG	OPS	3-Year	Fielding	Reliability
589	75	150	33	7	17	77	97	46	4	1	.282	.338	.465	.803	+0.02	F	Very High

Drew was, arguably, the best offensive player Arizona had last year. His OPS was better than any other full-time SS in the majors, except Hanley Ramirez, and he had a great second half, going .326/.372/.556. More walks would be nice, especially if he leads off again, but Arizona will simply want him to justify his first-round draft position.

Adam Dunn (Left Field)

PA	R	H	2B	3B	HR	RBI	SO	BB	SB	CS	BA	OBP	SLG	OPS	3-Year	Fielding	Reliability
592	86	127	27	1	36	100	150	100	3	1	.263	.392	.547	.939	-0.02	F	Very High

Chalked up his fifth consecutive 40-homer, 100-walk season—something only Bonds (2000-04) has ever done before. Batted .236, but the walks made up for that, and his OBP was 17th in the majors. A free agent this winter, he'll be expensive, but he should be among the most productive left-handed sluggers for some time to come.

David Eckstein (Shortstop)

PA	R	H	2B	3B	HR	RBI	SO	BB	SB	CS	BA	OBP	SLG	OPS	3-Year	Fielding	Reliability
428	47	112	20	2	2	38	33	29	4	1	.296	.358	.376	.734	-0.05	D	High

Eckstein came to Arizona as a replacement for Orlando Hudson, but did nothing down the stretch to suggest he'll be a credible fit there in 2009. I'd say the prediction here of a .734 OPS is overly optimistic for a 34-year old with a career figure of .712. He'll remain a decent leadoff option, and should find a spot somewhere as the classic scrappy white guy.

Robby Hammock (Catcher)

PA	R	H	2B	3B	HR	RBI	SO	BB	SB	CS	BA	OBP	SLG	OPS	3-Year	Fielding	Reliability
322	37	76	14	2	9	38	57	27	2	1	.265	.332	.422	.754	-0.04	C	Average

It's been four years since Hammock was even Arizona's backup catcher, but he always seems to find a way to reach the majors. Unlikely to see much playing time except in the event of injury/trade of Miguel Montero and Chris Snyder, he was non-tendered, but may end up in the minors again.

Orlando Hudson (Second Base)

PA	R	H	2B	3B	HR	RBI	SO	BB	SB	CS	BA	OBP	SLG	OPS	3-Year	Fielding	Reliability
493	61	126	26	5	9	55	71	48	5	1	.289	.360	.434	.794	-0.03	C	Very High

Hudson will be, by quite some distance, the best second baseman available on the free-agent market this winter, and looks likely to cash in, despite an injury ending his season prematurely for the second year in a row. It may be a case of "buyer beware," however: While his offense is still good, most metrics agree his defense has been in decline for several years. How long before his hitting goes the same way?

Conor Jackson (Left Field)

PA	R	H	2B	3B	HR	RBI	SO	BB	SB	CS	BA	OBP	SLG	OPS	3-Year	Fielding	Reliability
537	72	142	30	3	18	74	64	54	6	2	.302	.379	.493	.872	+0.07	F	Very High

Hard to say whether Jackson will play mainly first base or left field. The latter seems a more natural fit, but it would relegate Eric Byrnes to being an $11 million fourth outfielder. He will likely see time at both. Certainly, getting his bat into the lineup as often as possible will be the aim for manager Bob Melvin, especially against left-handed pitching. Jackson's power outage—no homers in 200 AB after July 27—is somewhat worrying.

Felipe Lopez (Second Base)

PA	R	H	2B	3B	HR	RBI	SO	BB	SB	CS	BA	OBP	SLG	OPS	3-Year	Fielding	Reliability
545	68	134	26	4	9	52	88	49	21	9	.275	.343	.401	.744	-0.02	F	Very High

He doesn't field well enough to hold an everyday middle-infield job, but he hits much better than your average utility guy. I like him as a pinch-hitter/spot-starter/jack-of-all-trades.

Augie Ojeda (Second Base)

PA	R	H	2B	3B	HR	RBI	SO	BB	SB	CS	BA	OBP	SLG	OPS	3-Year	Fielding	Reliability
328	33	74	12	2	1	24	35	31	1	0	.261	.343	.328	.671	-0.03	C	Average

Helped by one of the smaller strike zones in baseball, Ojeda had more walks than Ks. He also played solid defense in a utility infield role, starting 52 games at three positions and making only three errors in 522 innings. Though he'll never hit for power—six career homers since his 2000 debut—expect more of the same from Ojeda in 2009.

Mark Reynolds (Third Base)

PA	R	H	2B	3B	HR	RBI	SO	BB	SB	CS	BA	OBP	SLG	OPS	3-Year	Fielding	Reliability
544	71	124	25	3	26	81	157	53	6	1	.257	.333	.484	.817	+0.02	D	Very High

Reynolds was nicknamed "Special K" by fans, since his at-bats tended to be either special or Ks. He led the team in homers and RBI, yet set a major league record with 204 strikeouts, and had more errors than any other player, too. He may move to second, but that seems unlikely. Still raw—this was his first full year in the majors—but needs to improve his contact rate and his defense to become truly effective.

Jeff Salazar (Center Field)

PA	R	H	2B	3B	HR	RBI	SO	BB	SB	CS	BA	OBP	SLG	OPS	3-Year	Fielding	Reliability
385	48	88	19	5	8	41	70	43	6	2	.264	.350	.423	.773	-0.02	D	High

Salazar saw plenty of action as a late-inning replacement—after June 27, he appeared in 36 games, starting just twice. His left-handedness may help, since the D-backs are heavily right-handed, but hitting .211 with a .675 OPS isn't getting it done. Assuming Eric Byrnes stays healthy, his playing time will likely be slim at best.

Chris Snyder (Catcher)

PA	R	H	2B	3B	HR	RBI	SO	BB	SB	CS	BA	OBP	SLG	OPS	3-Year	Fielding	Reliability
396	49	89	21	1	16	55	85	47	0	1	.263	.357	.474	.831	+0.01	B	High

Despite landing on the DL with a testicle injury (I'll pause for you to wince), Snyder improved in all aspects of his game. Beyond an .830 OPS and 16 homers, he impressed with his defense, throwing out 31 percent of base-stealers; Snyder's game calling won plaudits from the pitching staff too. He'll be Arizona's front-line catcher, and 130-plus games is not impossible—if he can avoid more unfortunate injuries.

Chad Tracy (First Base)

PA	R	H	2B	3B	HR	RBI	SO	BB	SB	CS	BA	OBP	SLG	OPS	3-Year	Fielding	Reliability
362	43	90	22	2	10	47	64	30	0	1	.276	.337	.447	.784	-0.02	B	High

It was his recovery from knee surgery that limited his 2008 season, but Tracy's future is looking more and more like a platoon player: His career OPS is 229 points better against right handers. With Arizona desperately needing lefties, he should still see playing time at first and, if his knee is up to it, at third.

Justin Upton (Right Field)

PA	R	H	2B	3B	HR	RBI	SO	BB	SB	CS	BA	OBP	SLG	OPS	3-Year	Fielding	Reliability
507	64	115	26	5	17	64	132	53	5	4	.258	.341	.454	.795	+0.11	C	Very High

Twenty-year olds who can hold their own in the majors are few and far between. Upton, though, performed admirably for his age, despite 11 errors in right field. Particularly encouraging was his performance late in the season: After returning from the DL on Aug. 29, Upton had a .922 OPS over his last 25 games. I think the projected numbers here are on the cautious side, and he could be a breakout star in 2009.

Chris Young (Center Field)

PA	R	H	2B	3B	HR	RBI	SO	BB	SB	CS	BA	OBP	SLG	OPS	3-Year	Fielding	Reliability
601	78	136	33	5	25	83	130	51	14	4	.253	.320	.473	.793	+0.01	B	Very High

If he deserved a Gold Glove— well, much more than Nate McLouth—for his work in center, Young struggled elsewhere. His OBP was little above .300 for most of the year, he hit 10 fewer homers and stole half as many bases as in 2007, and his K total would have been a franchise record except for the sterling efforts of teammate Mark Reynolds. That OBP needs to get up nearer .350 this season, though his defense certainly helps balance this.

Pitchers

Billy Buckner (Starter)

W	L	ERA	TBF	IP	Hit	HR	SO	BB	HBP	3-Year	Reliability
5	10	6.37	611	131	164	23	66	64	7	+0.09	Very High

Buckner did see some action (14 IP) and performed credibly. Did, but he allowed rather too many hits in Triple-A to be encouraged (136 in 116.1 IP). But with the likely loss of Brandon Lyon and Juan Cruz from the bullpen, he is a contender for an expanded role in 2009.

Juan Cruz (Reliever)

W	L	ERA	TBF	IP	Hit	HR	SO	BB	HBP	3-Year	Reliability
4	3	4.27	262	60	52	7	69	31	4	+0.21	Low

He's been among the best relievers in the league over the past two years, and has a K/9 rate of 12.62, unsurpassed by anyone in the majors with 50-plus innings. Given this, he seemed criminally underused by Bob Melvin, with most of his appearances in the seventh inning or earlier. A free agent, he should get a multi-year deal from someone, and it probably won't be Arizona.

Doug Davis (Starter)

W	L	ERA	TBF	IP	Hit	HR	SO	BB	HBP	3-Year	Reliability
8	9	4.91	685	153	171	17	104	71	5	+0.27	Very High

One of the feel-good stories of 2008, Davis was diagnosed with cancer before the season, and underwent surgery to remove his thyroid. Remarkably, he started a game less than seven weeks later, and pitched well, with a 107 ERA+. He's never going to overpower hitters, but is the epitome of the "crafty lefty." His starts are usually littered with baserunners, but fans are largely used to that by now.

Edgar Gonzalez (Reliever)

W	L	ERA	TBF	IP	Hit	HR	SO	BB	HBP	3-Year	Reliability
4	5	4.90	345	79	87	12	48	26	4	+0.03	High

Gonzalez missed most of 2008 with a strained elbow, and was taken off the 40-man roster in early November. He's been a long reliever and spot-starter since coming to the majors in 2003, but has only once pitched more than 50 innings. A high HR rate (1.8/9 IP career) means Chase Field is likely not the best fit for him.

Dan Haren (Starter)

W	L	ERA	TBF	IP	Hit	HR	SO	BB	HBP	3-Year	Reliability
12	9	4.06	802	192	197	24	165	45	6	+0.33	Very High

Haren proved to be everything the D-backs wanted, and probably more. He racked up career bests in strikeouts and ERA+ and made the All-Star game. There was something of a fall-off in the second-half, but he still ended with an ERA almost the equal of Brandon Webb. With a bit more luck (his ERA was 2.79 in the nine no-decisions) he could have won twenty, too. His contract was extended, and he may end up eventually becoming the staff ace if Webb is not extended, too.

Randy Johnson (Starter)

W	L	ERA	TBF	IP	Hit	HR	SO	BB	HBP	3-Year	Reliability
10	8	4.02	688	164	163	20	145	44	6	—	Very High

There was no win No. 300 for Johnson in 2008, as the Big Unit ended five short. He should get it in 2009, just not in Arizona, after they decided not to pay the $7-8 million he wanted. That decision may bite them, as there were few better pitchers after the All-Star break, when he posted a 2.41 ERA. Even at age 45, and after multiple back surgeries, Johnson should still be an effective pitcher: His K:BB ratio was almost 4:1 last season.

Wilfredo Ledezma (Reliever)

W	L	ERA	TBF	IP	Hit	HR	SO	BB	HBP	3-Year	Reliability
4	4	5.07	331	73	76	9	58	40	3	+0.25	Average

A late-season pick-up by Arizona, Ledezma pitched most of the season for the Padres, as a mop-up reliever and spot starter. There'll always be a market for lefties like him, though with a career ERA of 5.10, he's likely going to end up being one of the last men picked.

Brandon Lyon (Reliever)

W	L	ERA	TBF	IP	Hit	HR	SO	BB	HBP	3-Year	Reliability
4	3	4.47	284	66	72	7	41	20	2	+0.40	Average

Lyon started as the closer but hit a horrible patch mid-season and was replaced by Qualls. He declined arbitration, a risky move, since he'd likely have gotten $4 million or so there—hard to see anyone paying a decent, rather than brilliant, set-up man that much money. While it's hard to see him as a bargain for any team, or becoming an elite closer, he probably won't be terrible, and has a good variety of pitches on which to survive.

Tony Pena (Reliever)

W	L	ERA	TBF	IP	Hit	HR	SO	BB	HBP	3-Year	Reliability
5	3	3.89	311	74	72	8	51	23	3	+0.11	Average

In the absence of Lyon, Pena will probably slide into a set-up role in front of Qualls. He is one of those pitchers who, in any given outing, will be almost unhittable, or so bad you wonder how he reached the majors. Probably more of the former, with a career ERA+ of 115, and he should be a solid member of the Arizona bullpen. If Qualls falters, he would likely be next in line for the closer's spot.

Yusmeiro Petit (Starter)

W	L	ERA	TBF	IP	Hit	HR	SO	BB	HBP	3-Year	Reliability
6	8	5.08	528	122	128	23	89	40	4	-0.14	Very High

Petit looks likely to be the No. 5 starter, but needs to control his home runs. So far, he's allowed almost two per nine innings, and last season 12 of the 45 hits he allowed left the park. He held opponents to a .216 average, which is great, but too many long balls could kill his career prospects. Still, he is only 24, and while he won't be an ace, could become a decent back- of-the-rotation starter.

Chad Qualls (Reliever)

W	L	ERA	TBF	IP	Hit	HR	SO	BB	HBP	3-Year	Reliability
5	3	3.67	307	73	72	7	60	23	3	+0.19	Average

Pitched 16.2 innings in 2008 before allowing an earned run, and ended the year with a 14.2 innings scoreless streak. Had some struggles in the middle, especially with inherited runners, but was among the team's most reliable relievers and replaced Lyon as closer for the last month, going 7-for-7 in save opportunities. He'll start 2009 in that role, and is likely the best choice for the job.

Jon Rauch (Reliever)

W	L	ERA	TBF	IP	Hit	HR	SO	BB	HBP	3-Year	Reliability
4	4	4.22	306	72	71	10	61	23	2	+0.21	Average

Surely Rauch can't be as bad as in 2008, when he went 0-6 with a 6.56 ERA after a trade from Washington. That's the hope in Arizona, where a contract quirk meant the team had to invoke the 2010 option before 2009 started. Certainly, the signs suggest that was an aberration: His career ERA+ is still 113. However, Arizona fans will be holding their breath until Rauch proves he is not who they thought he was.

Leonel Rosales (Reliever)

W	L	ERA	TBF	IP	Hit	HR	SO	BB	HBP	3-Year	Reliability
3	4	5.43	279	62	69	9	39	29	3	+0.26	Low

A fringe candidate for the Arizona bullpen in the coming year, whether Rosales makes it probably depends on what signings are made by the team in this area. Finally reaching the majors at age 27, he was OK, but walked almost as many as he struck out. He might see some action in the event of injury to a regular reliever.

Doug Slaten (Reliever)

W	L	ERA	TBF	IP	Hit	HR	SO	BB	HBP	3-Year	Reliability
3	2	4.78	213	48	50	6	36	21	2	+0.37	Very Low

The LOOGY of choice for Arizona in 2008, but the team has been sniffing around a number of southpaw relievers this winter, so his situation may be tenuous. Was fairly consistent performance-wise in 2007 and 2008, but his ERA was more than two runs higher this year—probably a more accurate reflection of his skills. Could be used, if no one better can be found.

Brandon Webb (Starter)

W	L	ERA	TBF	IP	Hit	HR	SO	BB	HBP	3-Year	Reliability
14	8	3.30	836	202	196	14	148	58	7	+0.21	Very High

Webb won more games than anyone in the NL for some time but was beaten to the Cy Young by Tim Lincecum. He has still finished first or second three years running, and looks set to remain among the league's elite pitchers for some time to come. He has a low-impact delivery and should be good for 200 innings with an ERA not much above three. If Arizona doesn't extend him, he'll be a very rich man when he hits free agency in 2010.

Atlanta Braves

by John Beamer of The Hardball Times

2009 Braves Projections

Record: 84-78
Division Rank/Games Behind: 3rd, 4 games back
Runs Scored: 763, 6th in the league
Runs Allowed: 725, 4th in the league
Park Factor: 1.00, neutral

What Happened Last Year:

2008 was not a good year for the Braves.

Before a ball was pitched, many thought the Braves would contend for the division. In previous years Atlanta was an offensive juggernaut and, despite the loss of Andruw Jones, there was little reason to suspect any change. Chipper Jones, Mark Teixeira, Brian McCann and Jeff Francoeur were all supposed to let rip with the bat once more.

Among those four, Frenchy Francoeur was the biggest disappointment, hitting an emaciated .239/.294/.349—and to think *Baseball Prospectus* pegged him as its top breakout candidate in baseball in January! Although the other three performed admirably—Jones was knocking on the door of .400 in June and romped to the batting title—there was little else to get excited about in the lineup. The Braves clocked just 4.4 runs per game, the second-worst offensive record in the East. A deeper analysis shows it was a power issue rather than an on-base problem. Park adjusted, Atlanta had the third-best OBP but the fourth-worst isolated power (ISO) in the NL.

The rotation, which had more gray hair than any other starting staff, suffered frequent injuries. Only Jair Jurrjens, a putative fifth starter in spring training, and Jorge Campillo, a 29-year-old journeyman, pitched more than 150 innings. Veterans John Smoltz, Mike Hampton and Tom Glavine managed to total only that number among them.

Actually, the rotation performed admirably, all things considered. Jurrjens, Tim Hudson and Campillo, who collectively started more than half the games, all had sub-4.00 ERAs. It was the relief corps with the issues. Rafael Soriano got injured and pitched only 14 innings; Peter Moylan lasted six. Mike Gonzalez came back after a year out of the game but couldn't rediscover his pre-injury form—he still led the staff with 14 saves, 11 more than the next highest. Behind them, guys like Jeff Bennett, Will Ohman and Manny Acosta were left to mop up.

When the chips were counted, the Braves had a 72-90 record and a fourth-place finish. That was their worst record since 1990, when they lost 97 games. There are two bright spots. One, in 2008 the Braves were unlucky—Pythagoras projected 79 wins. Two, the last time they played this badly they went on to win the World Series the following year.

Players Lost from Last Year's Team:

At the trade deadline, Teixeira, who was weeks away from becoming a free agent, was traded to the Angels. A bat as productive as his is a big loss to any team, and at this point his 30 or so fence hoppers have yet to be replaced.

Hampton joined Houston as a free agent. Few Braves fans will shed a tear, as Hampton pitched only 78 innings in three seasons—all of them last year. If he can overcome his injury woes, he could provide the Astros with some league-average pitching. I'm surprised they took the risk.

Also released by the Braves was Chuck James. When James burst on the scene a couple of years ago, he projected as the No. 3 starter. Last year, he had serious command issues and pitching coach Roger McDowell decided he'd seen enough to jettison the southpaw.

After 21 years, future Hall of Famer John Smoltz is a Brave no more. He signed with the Red Sox.

Players Acquired:

The Braves are hunting for starters. It is no secret that GM Frank Wren has tried to acquire Jake Peavy, but the Padres keep asking too high a price. Yunel Escobar would be the centerpiece of the deal—given how light the Braves are at shortstop, the odds are that Peavy will remain a Friar. The Braves also had a crack at A.J. Burnett, but he took the Yankees' money.

Wren was more successful in picking up Javier Vasquez from the White Sox for a bushel of prospects. Vasquez is an innings-eater who has never quite fulfilled his potential at the major league level. Five years ago, in the middle of the Braves' dynasty with John Schuerholz at the helm, Vasquez would have been a good bet for the next Cy Young award. Given the current regime, expect a season on the DL.

There have been few other significant acquisitions. Catcher David Ross, is a career .222/.309/.435 hitter—although he is an upgrade over Clint Sammons, that isn't anything to boast about. The Braves also have picked up a few journeymen and minor leaguers like Eric O'Flaherty, Diory Hernandez and Stephen Marek.

Management Is:

Last season was a watershed year for the Braves as Wren took the reins from uber-GM Schuerholz. By all accounts, Wren did a nice job despite suffering some bad luck with injuries. Picking up Glavine was a seen as a smart move, as was adding Mark Kotsay after Andruw Jones defected to the Dodgers.

Bobby Cox remains at the helm as manager and shows no sign of retiring. After last year's losing record, some Braves fans have started to turn against Cox. Despite a record that is second to none, there is a question as to whether he is the right man for the job after having been in charge for 18 years. Cox has incredible man-management skills. He demands and shows unswerving loyalty to players and he never fails carries the team with him. That in itself can cause problems, as evidenced by his patience with Francoeur's inability to hit. The players and fans would be devastated if he left.

The Minor League System Is:

Braves watchers are reasonably bullish about the farm, but reality is a little different. The system is nowhere near as stacked as it has been in the past. In fact only Jason Heywood, who was the Braves' first pick in 2007, has superstar potential.

There are a couple of other standout prospects, like Frederick Freeman and Jordan Schafer, but behind them the farm is light. Schafer had his own problems after failing a drug test, but he still played well after forfeiting the juice. Freeman produced a creditable .316/.374/.521 in A-ball as a 19-year-old. Although he needs to work on his plate discipline, he could be a looking at a major league spot in 2011 if all goes well.

There are few ace pitchers in the Braves' minor league system, which is part of the reason they are keen to snap up Peavy. Tommy Hanson is the best the Braves have and he projects as a No. 3 starter. Other guys like Cole Rohrbough and Brett DeVall have potential but are some way from the bigs.

Due For a Change:

Francoeur has been dismal for a couple of seasons now. Sure, he looks like the real deal with his swimmer-esque physique, but he can't hit. Actually he can hit, sort of; the problem is he can't walk.

If the pitcher knows that the batter will hack away come what may, he'll throw a lot of balls wide of the plate. A more discerning hitter will lay off these pitches and manage the count. In response, the pitcher will try to locate his pitches and force the batter into an error.

Our Favorite Braves Blogs:

For a high-spending and popular team, Braves blogs are a little thin on the ground. For everyday news there are three to recommend. Braves Journal (http://www.bravesjournal), an independent blog, is run by the inestimable Mac Thomason and attracts the largest following of any Braves blog.

Chop-n-change (http://mvn.com/chopnchange) and Talking Chop (http://www.talkingchop.com) are the other two and both are part of a blogging network. Chop-n-change is in the MVN family while Talking Chop belongs to Sporting Nation. Talking Chop sometimes goes to spring training and games and frequently features interviews with Braves players and management.

Others worth a read are Sabernomics (http://www.sabernomics.com) and Rain Delay (http://rain-delay.com/).

Unfortunately Frenchy is the biggest swinger in the East. This needn't be an issue provided the player acknowledges the problem and moderates his approach.

Francoeur seems to know he needs to lay off more pitches—every interview he gives he mentions it—but he seems incapable of doing so. Last year he registered 475 outs and only 39 walks. If he doesn't change, he's not going to fulfill his considerable potential.

Reasons to be Optimistic:

On paper, the Braves are probably an 82- or 84-win team, and it takes only a little luck for an 84-win team to win 88 and get within spitting distance of the postseason.

The addition of Vasquez helps stabilize the rotation and if one more top line starter is acquired, the Braves could elevate themselves into playoff contention. Despite Glavine being injured, a front five of Jurrjens, Glavine, Vasquez, Peavy and Jo-Jo Reyes would be extremely useful.

Behind a solid rotation is a reliable pen anchored by Gonzalez and Soriano. Despite being injury-plagued in recent years, each can hurl 80 relief innings and save 45 games between them. These two are backed up by an able relief corps including Moylan, Ohman and Bennett.

And don't forget the batting. Chipper Jones is coming off a batting title and will undoubtedly produce another .300 season. Kelly Johnson, McCann and Escobar are all capable of hitting .300 and provided the power of Teixiera is replaced, Atlanta figures to be above average with the timber. Who knows—maybe Heywood could contribute down the stretch in a pennant or wild card race.

Reasons to be Pessimistic:

Give me a break! Peavy ain't coming and the odds of the first-choice five staying healthy are nil. And if one or more breaks down, who will step in to the breach? Buddy Carlyle? Bennett? Anthony Lerew? There is zero depth.

Aside from Soriano and Gonzalez, both of whom are perennially injured, it's impossible to finger a decent relief pitcher in the state of Georgia. What was the team's Achilles' heel in 2008 will remain so in 2009.

And apart from Chipper Jones, the Braves' lineup is distinctly average. McCann is capable of an explosive season, as is KJ, but Escobar isn't a power hitter and the rest of the team struggles to clear an OPS of .750—that's poor. Crikey, if Jones or McCann gets injured, 2010 won't come soon enough.

Add in the fact that the East is probably the strongest division in the NL and the Braves' prospects dim further. The Mets, Phillies and resurgent Marlins are all better than the Braves.

Still Left to Do:

Quite a lot if the team is to challenge. At least one top-of-the-order starter is needed—Peavy would do nicely, but failing that the Braves still need both front- and back-end pitching.

Without a couple of extra power bats, the Braves' offense starts to look vulnerable. The good news is that based on the noises coming from the front office and the media, the Braves have a little spare cash to splurge. It needs to be invested wisely.

Most Likely Team Outcome:

If recent history is any guide, expect another season of mediocrity. On talent alone the Braves are an 82- or 84-win team, and even the addition of a stud pitcher like Peavy won't propel them into the stratosphere. Moreover, there is downside to that win target. The bench, both for hitting and pitching, is simply abysmal. For instance, look at the current crop of outfielders: Josh Anderson, Gregor Blanco, Matt Diaz, Francoeur and Brandon Jones.

Let me prognosticate. The Braves will come out of the blocks quickly and over the first couple of months will regularly swap the division lead with the Mets and Phillies. The Mets will start a streak in mid/late May, which will put some clear blue water between them and the rest of the division. A Braves slump around the All-Star break will put them firmly out of contention for not only the division but also the wild card. From there on, the fans and players will retool for 2010. It's Groundhog Day.

Player Projections

Batters

Josh Anderson (Center Field)

PA	R	H	2B	3B	HR	RBI	SO	BB	SB	CS	BA	OBP	SLG	OPS	3-Year	Fielding	Reliability
602	74	156	22	4	9	55	96	31	29	5	.281	.326	.384	.710	+0.07	C	Very High

Anderson isn't quite Andruw Jones, in fact he's better than Jones is, at least over the last two years. In 2008 Anderson posted a creditable .294/.338/.426. However, he's incredibly light on power, with three long balls last year. The projection of nine homers appears a stretch, but he's young and improving.

Gregor Blanco (Center Field)

PA	R	H	2B	3B	HR	RBI	SO	BB	SB	CS	BA	OBP	SLG	OPS	3-Year	Fielding	Reliability
511	57	113	16	4	2	36	95	64	12	5	.260	.359	.329	.688	+0.02	C	Very High

The good news for Blanco is that he's only 24. The bad news is that he's not particularly good, hitting a miserly .251/.366/.309. Yes, he gets on base at a fair clip, but he struggles to make contact and has little power. By age 24, Albert Pujols had more than 120 career home runs and regularly slugged over .650.

Matt Diaz (Left Field)

PA	R	H	2B	3B	HR	RBI	SO	BB	SB	CS	BA	OBP	SLG	OPS	3-Year	Fielding	Reliability
284	34	77	13	1	7	35	53	14	4	1	.293	.335	.429	.764	-0.02	B	Average

Diaz is a bit of an enigma. Despite having zero plate discipline—he's walked just 36 times in 1,000 plates appearances—in 2006 and 2007 he made contact frequently and showed a little power. Last year it went to pot with a .244/.264/.304 line. We project a stronger line than that based on his record. That walk rate is worrisome.

Yunel Escobar (Shortstop)

PA	R	H	2B	3B	HR	RBI	SO	BB	SB	CS	BA	OBP	SLG	OPS	3-Year	Fielding	Reliability
534	64	137	24	2	11	60	74	49	4	3	.291	.363	.421	.784	+0.08	C	Very High

Escobar is good-hitting shortstop, makes frequent contact, shows plate discipline and hits for a little power. Although he's prone to the odd error with the glove, at 26 he still has some time to improve that aspect of his game.

Jeff Francoeur (Right Field)

PA	R	H	2B	3B	HR	RBI	SO	BB	SB	CS	BA	OBP	SLG	OPS	3-Year	Fielding	Reliability
602	68	149	31	2	17	75	109	37	2	1	.269	.321	.425	.746	+0.03	C	Very High

Unless Francoeur can master the art of walking, his career will remain underwhelming. He has all the tools but is unable to use them at the same time. The recipe for 2009 is discipline and focus. A trade may do him good; Bobby Cox will stop playing him and a better hitting coach may teach him how to hit.

Omar Infante (Shortstop)

PA	R	H	2B	3B	HR	RBI	SO	BB	SB	CS	BA	OBP	SLG	OPS	3-Year	Fielding	Reliability
339	38	86	18	3	5	35	52	23	2	1	.279	.332	.406	.738	0.00	D	Low

With a line of .293/.338/.416, Infante overperformed last year. His career line is .260/.304/.391. He has moderated his approach at the plate slightly—he strikes out a little less—and that has helped. He's a good bench player but no more.

Kelly Johnson (Second Base)

PA	R	H	2B	3B	HR	RBI	SO	BB	SB	CS	BA	OBP	SLG	OPS	3-Year	Fielding	Reliability
561	74	140	29	6	17	71	105	58	9	4	.287	.364	.475	.839	+0.07	D	High

KJ is only 26 but seems to have been around for ages. He is much underrated at the plate: He has a .300 AVG in him, he walks a lot and he has power. Braves fans bemoan a lack of consistency, but as you THT fiends know, that means little.

Brandon Jones (Left Field)

PA	R	H	2B	3B	HR	RBI	SO	BB	SB	CS	BA	OBP	SLG	OPS	3-Year	Fielding	Reliability
508	57	111	22	4	12	54	110	44	8	4	.243	.311	.388	.699	+0.02	B	Very High

Despite sharing an illustrious name, Brandon doesn't share the same stage as the other, more famous, Jones boys. Given the paucity of talent in the outfield, Jones will get some playing time. It should be limited. Not only is he a weak hitter but also his glovework is sub-par.

Chipper Jones (Third Base)

PA	R	H	2B	3B	HR	RBI	SO	BB	SB	CS	BA	OBP	SLG	OPS	3-Year	Fielding	Reliability
515	76	141	28	2	22	81	72	74	3	1	.325	.422	.550	.972	—	A	Very High

One word. Legend. Chipper is the 2008 batting champion after missing out by a whisker in 2007. Many analysts have projected him to slide down the age curve but have been proved resoundingly wrong. A 2009 line of .325/.422/.550 will again see him contend for the batting title. Lightening cannot strike again. Can it?

Brian McCann (Catcher)

PA	R	H	2B	3B	HR	RBI	SO	BB	SB	CS	BA	OBP	SLG	OPS	3-Year	Fielding	Reliability
526	71	141	35	1	22	82	68	48	3	1	.301	.367	.521	.888	+0.03	C	Very High

At the tender age of 24, McCann is a tremendous hitting catcher. Problem is, his dodgy knees may limit his time behind the plate—he may move to first but his value will go down. Offensively he'll get better; the upside in the projections is questionable.

Corky Miller (Catcher)

PA	R	H	2B	3B	HR	RBI	SO	BB	SB	CS	BA	OBP	SLG	OPS	3-Year	Fielding	Reliability
247	28	52	10	0	9	31	46	25	1	1	.244	.338	.418	.756	-0.04	B	Low

Every team needs a backup catcher or two. Frankly, Miller doesn't cut the mustard. In eight seasons he's had just 59 hits. Miller has a good eye and walks a fair bit. He also has a little power. Problem is he can't bat for toffee, as a .244 AVG projection attests.

Martin Prado (Shortstop)

PA	R	H	2B	3B	HR	RBI	SO	BB	SB	CS	BA	OBP	SLG	OPS	3-Year	Fielding	Reliability
367	40	93	16	3	3	34	50	25	4	2	.278	.330	.371	.701	+0.02	F	High

Last season was a breakout year for Prado, who hit a healthy .320/.377/.461 in 230 AB. Our 2009 projection would have felt toppy a year ago but now feels justified. It's a tough one to call, but upside in those numbers is probably marginal.

David Ross (Catcher)

PA	R	H	2B	3B	HR	RBI	SO	BB	SB	CS	BA	OBP	SLG	OPS	3-Year	Fielding	Reliability
291	35	61	13	0	12	40	67	35	0	1	.249	.345	.449	.794	-0.03	A	Average

Ross has good power and patience, but that's about it. When he does swing the bat, if he doesn't hit it hard, he usually doesn't hit it at all. He's a good backup catcher because his defense is good and he at least brings a couple skills to the plate, but his propensity to strike out and flirt with the Mendoza line would likely make him a liability as an everyday player.

Jordan Schafer (Center Field)

PA	R	H	2B	3B	HR	RBI	SO	BB	SB	CS	BA	OBP	SLG	OPS	3-Year	Fielding	Reliability
502	58	108	23	6	12	52	126	40	9	6	.238	.301	.394	.695	+0.08	D	High

Schafer is one of the top prospects in the Braves system. Unfortunately, he tested positive for HGH last year and was banned for 50 games. On his return he hit well and, given the dearth of talent in the outfield, could get a game or two in 2009. Our forecast line is probably on the low side if he does break through. Odds are, though, that he won't.

Pitchers

Manny Acosta (Reliever)

W	L	ERA	TBF	IP	Hit	HR	SO	BB	HBP	3-Year	Reliability
3	4	4.61	268	59	60	6	42	36	3	+0.19	Low

Acosta's had two years of above-average relief but thrown only a smattering of innings. His strikeout rate isn't high enough to dominate hitters, but he figures to remain a useful addition to the Braves' bullpen. There is upside in these numbers.

Jeff Bennett (Reliever)

W	L	ERA	TBF	IP	Hit	HR	SO	BB	HBP	3-Year	Reliability
5	5	4.25	382	87	90	7	53	41	6	+0.24	Low

Bennett had a breakout year in 2008—if you can call it that—his ERA was 3.70. Statistically similar to Acosta, Bennett hasn't tossed many innings but has been reasonably effective. Regression is expected.

Blaine Boyer (Reliever)

W	L	ERA	TBF	IP	Hit	HR	SO	BB	HBP	3-Year	Reliability
4	4	4.44	312	71	70	8	57	34	3	+0.21	Low

When he burst onto the scene in 2005, Boyer was seen as a future star. An injury-ridden 2006 and 2007 interrupted those dreams, but at least 2008 was healthy. Unfortunately, he was also ineffective, with an ERA of 5.88. Are his best days behind him?

Jorge Campillo (Starter)

W	L	ERA	TBF	IP	Hit	HR	SO	BB	HBP	3-Year	Reliability
7	9	4.85	608	140	156	19	82	44	5	+0.24	High

Campillo had pitched only 17 innings in three years in the bigs before hurling 158 for the Braves last year. He put up some useful numbers, too, with a K/9 of 6 and an ERA of 3.91. Regression is likely in 2009, but he's still a useful addition to the staff. Now may be a good time to trade him.

Buddy Carlyle (Reliever)

W	L	ERA	TBF	IP	Hit	HR	SO	BB	HBP	3-Year	Reliability
4	4	4.39	303	71	70	10	57	26	3	+0.20	Average

In his age-30 season Carlyle was effective, recording a 3.59 ERA, although that was partly the result of switching to relief. His starter days are over and he'll make a cheap addition to the Braves' bullpen. He could be a trade chip, too—if someone is desperate.

Tom Glavine (Starter)

W	L	ERA	TBF	IP	Hit	HR	SO	BB	HBP	3-Year	Reliability
5	8	5.06	507	114	131	15	58	45	4	—	Very High

After making his pilgrimage back to Turner Field, Glavine pitched only 63 innings before landing on the DL. Apart from his first season in the bigs, his second-lowest total was 160 innings during the strike-shortened 1994 season. Although his best days are behind him, let's hope he has one last hurrah in a Braves uniform.

Mike Gonzalez (Reliever)

W	L	ERA	TBF	IP	Hit	HR	SO	BB	HBP	3-Year	Reliability
3	2	3.57	202	48	40	4	50	22	2	+0.19	Very Low

Gonzalez is a power pitcher who can strike out more than one an inning. Problem is, he spends too much time on the surgeon's table. Failure to have an effective 2009 could spell the end of his career.

Tim Hudson (Starter)

W	L	ERA	TBF	IP	Hit	HR	SO	BB	HBP	3-Year	Reliability
9	8	3.93	651	153	164	14	86	46	6	+0.23	Very High

The jury is still out on whether Tim Hudson has been value for money in his stint in Atlanta. There is little doubt he underachieved in his first couple of seasons, but in 2007 he was a stud. Unfortunately, he has undergone Tommy John surgery, so 2009 will be a lost season. Shame.

Chuck James (Starter)

W	L	ERA	TBF	IP	Hit	HR	SO	BB	HBP	3-Year	Reliability
6	9	5.43	591	132	140	25	90	60	6	+0.28	Very High

James was a disaster last year. Touted as a potential No. 3 starter, he proceeded to get blitzed by hitters of all stripes. An ERA of 9.10 followed. He was released by the Braves in the winter.

Will Ohman (Reliever)

W	L	ERA	TBF	IP	Hit	HR	SO	BB	HBP	3-Year	Reliability
4	3	3.96	263	61	57	6	53	26	3	+0.19	Low

Ohman is yet another journeyman reliever. He first pitched in the bigs way back in 2001, but before 2008 had fewer than that 200 innings to his name. Last year was a good one for Ohman—his ERA was 3.68. Our ERA forecast for 2009 suggests 3.96. Seems optimistic to me.

Jo-Jo Reyes (Starter)

W	L	ERA	TBF	IP	Hit	HR	SO	BB	HBP	3-Year	Reliability
7	9	5.16	663	147	155	21	103	77	7	-0.20	Very High

If Reyes makes the Braves' starting rotation, count them out of contention. He strikes out a lot of batters but has no control. We peg him to have a 5.16 ERA in 2009. That is more than 70 points higher than his 2008 record. Yikes.

John Smoltz (Starter)

W	L	ERA	TBF	IP	Hit	HR	SO	BB	HBP	3-Year	Reliability
7	4	3.47	410	100	94	10	90	25	3	—	Very High

Smoltz is nothing short of a legend. His 2008 was blighted by ill health and now, entering his age 42 season, Smoltz's future is uncertain. At his best he will lead the rotation—the last time his ERA surfaced over 4.00 was 1994.

Rafael Soriano (Reliever)

W	L	ERA	TBF	IP	Hit	HR	SO	BB	HBP	3-Year	Reliability
3	2	3.59	181	44	36	5	43	16	2	+0.28	Low

If Soriano were to remain injured for 2009, his acquisition from Seattle for Horacio Ramirez still would go down as a blinding trade for the Braves. Soriano strikes out a batter per inning with pinpoint control. His ceiling figures to be one of the finest closers in the game. All that is required is for him to stay healthy. If he delivers his projected ERA, many will be disappointed.

Baltimore Orioles

by Scott Christ of Camden Chat (camdenchat.com)

2009 Orioles Projections

Record: 67-95
Division Rank/Games Behind: Last, 33 games back
Runs Scored: 769, 9th in the league
Runs Allowed: 921, last in the league
Park Factor: 1.01, pretty much neutral

What Happened Last Year:

With disastrous results expected out of a talent-bereft, rebuilding team, the Orioles surprised a few people by not chasing any records for bad play. Instead, they were your typical Orioles of the last decade: They started out playing some inspired ball, won a few games despite not having the players to compete, and in the end, took a nosedive for two months and wound up at 68-93.

It was bad, but it could and perhaps should have been a lot worse. With a pitching staff ranking better than only Texas in the American League, the Orioles stayed watchable thanks to the bat work of Nick Markakis, Brian Roberts and the stunningly excellent rebound year from Aubrey Huff, and they had a little fun doing it. Clubhouse leader Kevin Millar legitimately taught the Orioles to loosen up and have fun, inspiring a reworking of the famous early '80s "Orioles Magic" song, accompanied by a new video of some of the O's goofing around. It wasn't a wasted year, as Adam Jones got some significant playing time and the Birds were forced to give Garrett Olson and Radhames Liz trials by fire in the rotation. But there remains a ton of work to do.

Players Lost from Last Year's Team:

Daniel Cabrera, Ramon Hernandez, Lance Cormier, Fernando Cabrera, Juan Castro, Alex Cintron, Kevin Millar, Jay Payton

Players Acquired:

Ryan Freel

Management Is:

Stable, for the time being. Andy MacPhail has given Orioles fans a short burst of cautious hope, and field manager Dave Trembley is both a realist and a guy who keeps it all in perspective. One day, he questions whether Daniel Cabrera really has it, or if it's just a lost pipe dream that the big righty truly has great stuff, and then the next, he's lighting a victory cigar at the press conference after the team ends its inexplicable and ridiculous Sunday losing streak.

MacPhail says all the right things about building for the future, even though he seems somewhat reluctant to wash his hands of the veterans and really let the young'uns take their knocks. Owner Peter Angelos could swoop in at any time and tire of this combination of losing **and** not drawing fans, which has come about in the last three years, but for the time being, all is calm on the management side, which is something new.

The Minor League System Is:

On the rise. What once was one of the most laughable by way of depressing systems in baseball has been resurrected with a bevy of good young arms and arguably the best baseball prospect on the planet.

Last year's top draft pick Brian Matusz, Chris Tillman and Jake Arrieta lead the way for the pitchers, and catcher Matt Wieters was dominant at High-A and Double-A ball in his first pro season. There are plenty of other decent prospects on the farm clubs, too, though nobody eye-popping. Still, the solid prospect is a big improvement over the disastrous mess that Syd Thrift and Co. made of the system in their reign(s) of terror.

Due For a Change:

A pitching staff can't be so bad forever, can it? If anything is truly due for a change, it's that. Rick Kranitz is now the man in charge of the hurlers, and he earned some nice praise from the team and the media in his first year, but this is an organization that ran through the highly respected Leo Mazzone and Ray Miller as if they were nobodies, because their pitchers made them look like they didn't know what they were doing. The first thing that needs to change there is talent, because nobody can squeeze orange juice out of a lemon. Otherwise, as bad as the team's record was in '08, things are pretty set in Baltimore for the time being.

Reasons to be Optimistic:

Young outfielders Markakis and Jones are at the heart of the youth movement that's already hit Baltimore, and while Jones wasn't exactly amazing in his first full year in the majors, he showed a lot of progress over the season and still looks like a potential impact player. Markakis continues to exceed projections all over the place, which he's done almost his entire professional career. The contracts of guys like Melvin Mora are coming to their end. MacPhail seems to "get it." For the first time in a decade, there's more than a fool's hope that this team might actually get better.

Reasons to be Pessimistic:

Angelos looms. As hinted at before, there may be a legitimate concern that Ol' Petey will tire of seeing his team at the bottom of the standings in the hyper-competitive AL East, as well as near the bottom of the standings in American League attendance. The last three years the team has finished 10th, 11th and 10th in AL attendance, with 2008 marking the first time the Birds failed to draw two million to Camden Yards. The park opened in 1992, and it took 14 years and some horrible teams for them to fall out of the top five in fan turnout. It's still a beauty and one of baseball's best stadiums, but the park itself can't be counted on to get people out for the games anymore. If Angelos makes any power plays, they run the risk of being disasters, as many have before.

Still Left to Do:

The Orioles, somehow, have to figure out how to stabilize the rotation in 2009 and beyond. Young arms like Matusz, Tillman and Arrieta are nice to have in the system, but nobody is a guarantee. Arms blow out, prospects fail, and sometimes you simply just get a back-end starter or good reliever where you think you have a future ace. Jeremy Guthrie is not so good that he can carry an entire rotation, and with the failures of Olson and Liz in 2008, one might worry about a short leash for both of them, though the organization showed

a first-rate loyalty to the always-dreadful Daniel Cabrera. The answers likely won't come in 2009, but maybe a few of them can. Without even a passable rotation, any rebuilding is going to be a massive uphill climb, no matter how many good young hitters there are.

Most Likely Team Outcome:

Every time a team "rebuilds," the new guy(s) in charge tell the fans to be patient. They're hoping the owners listen, too. Because when they say it's not easy, they're right. It's a hard thing to watch happen, because in most cases, it doesn't come easy at all. Games will be lost the same as before, but the hope is that you're building for a truly better tomorrow, and a better tomorrow that will stick around for a while.

MacPhail has made a lot of great decisions thus far, but the team is still a couple years, at least, from competing in any division, let alone the hyper-competitive AL East. Expect another distant fifth-place finish in 2009. The Orioles aren't yet good enough to leapfrog anyone, and nobody else has gotten bad enough to be jumped.

Player Projections

Batters

Freddie Bynum (Shortstop)

PA	R	H	2B	3B	HR	RBI	SO	BB	SB	CS	BA	OBP	SLG	OPS	3-Year	Fielding	Reliability
286	32	62	11	3	3	23	66	21	9	2	.242	.303	.344	.647	-0.02	C	Very Low

He's got speed and versatility and every now and again he puts a charge into one, and it's always a feel-good moment. Freddie Bynum is one of those players who smiles a lot, so much that you wonder if he's trying to sell you a used car. He is not in any way a major league shortstop, but the fact that he's pretended to be one gives him an extra wrinkle when he negotiates.

Juan Castro (Shortstop)

PA	R	H	2B	3B	HR	RBI	SO	BB	SB	CS	BA	OBP	SLG	OPS	3-Year	Fielding	Reliability
242	22	53	10	1	2	21	38	14	1	0	.238	.284	.319	.603	—	D	Very Low

Castro wound up as the shortstop who stuck in 2008, a fine fielder who has a quiet reputation as a great clubhouse guy. Though it's difficult to watch him take his hacks at the plate, his glove is real and it's hard to not respect a guy who's stuck around this long with essentially one strength.

Alex Cintron (Shortstop)

PA	R	H	2B	3B	HR	RBI	SO	BB	SB	CS	BA	OBP	SLG	OPS	3-Year	Fielding	Reliability
285	29	71	11	1	4	28	42	13	2	1	.269	.306	.363	.669	-0.02	F	Low

The best hitter of the 2008 Baltimore shortstops. If that can't explain how bad the shortstop situation was in Baltimore, nothing can.

Michael Costanzo (Third Base)

PA	R	H	2B	3B	HR	RBI	SO	BB	SB	CS	BA	OBP	SLG	OPS	3-Year	Fielding	Reliability
526	55	107	22	1	15	59	146	47	2	1	.227	.301	.374	.675	+0.01	C	Very High

It seems a decent bet that if Costanzo got enough plate appearances in the majors, he'd obliterate that new strikeout record. In his first season in the Baltimore system, after being part of the Miguel Tejada deal, Costanzo struggled mightily in Triple-A and downgraded his prospects pretty significantly. He's most likely exactly where he'll be for the majority of his career.

Brandon Fahey (Shortstop)

PA	R	H	2B	3B	HR	RBI	SO	BB	SB	CS	BA	OBP	SLG	OPS	3-Year	Fielding	Reliability
399	39	87	13	4	3	30	71	26	5	3	.239	.294	.322	.616	+0.02	D	Average

The Orioles' fascination with stick-thin Fahey is puzzling. He doesn't really do anything well besides have a can-do attitude, but he's got such a can-do attitude that it's hard for even the coldest-hearted of stats geeks to get too worked up when he plays. Fahey is the type of guy who'll play wherever you want him to. When the subject of emergency catcher came up, he was the first to volunteer, followed by the goofy Kevin Millar, both of which would have been awkward and likely hilarious situations. The only position he's really suited to play is second base, where his arm strength isn't an issue. At short or in the outfield, it becomes one. And he obviously can't hit for beans. Fahey is more likely to be mistaken for the bat boy than a player most nights.

Ryan Freel (Center Field)

PA	R	H	2B	3B	HR	RBI	SO	BB	SB	CS	BA	OBP	SLG	OPS	3-Year	Fielding	Reliability
289	34	69	13	1	2	22	44	21	13	3	.266	.329	.347	.676	-0.03	B	Average

Freel's time in Cincinnati ended officially this offseason in the Ramon Hernandez trade, but he's seemingly been a non-factor since 2006. Freel's primary offensive weapon has always been the walk, and his walk rates have plummeted below average in recent years. He has suffered leg injuries and a concussion over the past few years—does he have anything left?

Luis Hernandez (Shortstop)

PA	R	H	2B	3B	HR	RBI	SO	BB	SB	CS	BA	OBP	SLG	OPS	3-Year	Fielding	Reliability
388	34	85	12	3	2	28	52	13	4	3	.233	.259	.299	.558	+0.04	C	High

Luis Hernandez is in large part responsible for the "Orioles Magic" craze that washed out once the team went in the tank late in the year. While it lasted, though, it was fun for everyone. He kicked it all off with a stunning walk-off hit against the Mariners early in the year, capping a remarkable comeback by the Orioles. Coming back to beat the 2008 Mariners might not seem remarkable to those who follow good teams, but the Orioles and their fans take what they can get. He cannot hit, period, and his glove appears to have been seriously overstated.

Ramon Hernandez (Catcher)

PA	R	H	2B	3B	HR	RBI	SO	BB	SB	CS	BA	OBP	SLG	OPS	3-Year	Fielding	Reliability
476	55	114	23	1	15	62	71	39	0	1	.267	.335	.432	.767	-0.04	—	Very High

Some fans may become annoyed by talk of "hustle," but seriously, Hernandez hasn't hustled since Barack Obama was an unknown state senator in Illinois. His complete indifference to the defensive aspects of catching made his bad-luck hitting even harder to tolerate in 2008. Like predecessor Javy Lopez, he turned out to be a moderately priced free agent signed for a three-year deal that was only good for one.

Aubrey Huff (Designated Hitter)

PA	R	H	2B	3B	HR	RBI	SO	BB	SB	CS	BA	OBP	SLG	OPS	3-Year	Fielding	Reliability
576	73	146	33	2	22	83	84	49	2	2	.281	.344	.480	.824	-0.03	C	Very High

All is forgiven. After raising the ire of Orioles fans with his now-infamous radio show appearance in the 2007-08 offseason, Huff did his best to make amends by hammering the ball all year and becoming the first Oriole to hit 30 home runs since Miguel Tejada in 2004, and just the third Bird to do it this decade. He probably won't do it again, since it came as an honest shock to just about everyone that Huff still had that much gas in the tank. Even if he just has the one big year with the O's, at least they can say he wasn't a complete waste of money like so many of their aging-free-agent signings have been.

Adam Jones (Center Field)

PA	R	H	2B	3B	HR	RBI	SO	BB	SB	CS	BA	OBP	SLG	OPS	3-Year	Fielding	Reliability
554	71	144	26	5	19	74	113	31	9	3	.283	.332	.466	.798	+0.05	C	Very High

He impressed in center field, he got better hitting the breaking stuff as the season went on, and his charming, happy-go-lucky personality made him an immediate fan favorite. Now where's the power? It'll come. He's never going to put up a good K-to-BB ratio, which is the only real knock on his skill set. He's got the speed to become a good base stealer if he learns how to be one. He's got Gold Glove potential in center field. And he should hit 20-30 homers a year in his prime. Teamed with Nick Markakis and Matt Wieters, Jones gives the Orioles a fantastic young base to build upon, and the trade that brought him to Baltimore is the first feather in the cap for Andy MacPhail.

Nick Markakis (Right Field)

PA	R	H	2B	3B	HR	RBI	SO	BB	SB	CS	BA	OBP	SLG	OPS	3-Year	Fielding	Reliability
613	81	159	34	2	19	80	96	67	9	3	.295	.374	.472	.846	+0.01	C	Very High

Is Markakis such a huge favorite in Baltimore because he's so good, or because he's so much better (including age numbers) than everyone else on the team? Probably a bit of both. For a young player becoming a star, Markakis showed a healthy willingness to just take the free pass early in 2008, before Aubrey Huff was moved up to hit behind him and it wasn't so easy to simply pitch around Markakis anymore. He's got legitimate Gold Glove defense in right field, good plate discipline and good power, runs the bases well, and hits for average. Barring injuries or a departure as soon as he gets the chance, Markakis could go down as one of the Oriole greats, and he's the anchor of the rebuilding project.

Kevin Millar (First Base)

PA	R	H	2B	3B	HR	RBI	SO	BB	SB	CS	BA	OBP	SLG	OPS	3-Year	Fielding	Reliability
545	62	119	25	0	16	65	86	64	1	2	.253	.347	.409	.756	—	C	Very High

Both Millar's strengths and weaknesses stick out more as he ages. His power has become a weakness, even though he hit 20 homers last year for the first time since jacking 25 in 2003. He doesn't hit the doubles like he used to, partially because he can't run a lick, but also because he just doesn't hit the ball hard anymore. His home runs tended to be high fly balls that carried out. And while he still works a count like a champ (71 free passes), his dreadful contact numbers contributed to his OBP plummeting to .323. Still, he plays an underrated first base and does have actual positive effects as a clubhouse guy. But that can't mask that 2008 was his worst year. The end is near.

Luis Montanez (Left Field)

PA	R	H	2B	3B	HR	RBI	SO	BB	SB	CS	BA	OBP	SLG	OPS	3-Year	Fielding	Reliability
512	60	129	22	2	18	68	80	27	3	2	.272	.315	.440	.755	+0.01	C	Very High

Getting worked up over Montanez's great year at Bowie is a bit much, though you can't blame people for getting excited. He was once the No. 3 pick in the draft, then washed out hard with the Cubs before winding up with the O's. Finally, he hit. Of course, he should have, since it was his umpteenth try at hitting in Double-A ball. He acquitted himself nicely in a late-season call-up, but then so do a lot of guys. The jury remains out, but Montanez is really guilty until proven innocent at this stage.

Melvin Mora (Third Base)

PA	R	H	2B	3B	HR	RBI	SO	BB	SB	CS	BA	OBP	SLG	OPS	3-Year	Fielding	Reliability
536	63	134	24	1	15	66	74	40	5	3	.278	.340	.426	.766	—	D	Very High

Most people weren't aware, but Barry Bonds actually did play baseball in 2008. He showed up disguised as Melvin Mora in August, and played through September. He was a bit rusty that first month, hitting just .311/.373/.533, but he found his groove in September to the tune of .418/.455/.765 with eight home runs. Mora reached 100 RBI for the second time in his career thanks to those two months, and because of that outrageous hot streak there remains some optimism about the veteran third baseman, who will be 37 in 2009. Given his age and recent decline, we're far more likely to see the Mora who played the first half of last year than we are the guy who went bananas for two months. Most probable is that he hits like he did in 2007, which isn't good enough, but he's not exactly blocking anyone in the system, either.

Jay Payton (Left Field)

PA	R	H	2B	3B	HR	RBI	SO	BB	SB	CS	BA	OBP	SLG	OPS	3-Year	Fielding	Reliability
423	45	105	18	2	6	41	51	22	6	1	.267	.307	.369	.676	—	C	High

As Sebastian Bach wailed in Skid Row's "Youth Gone Wild," Jay Payton's nasty reputation has taken him everywhere. In his first season with the Orioles, he got into a nearly physical spat with old friend Melvin Mora. Sure, it was resolved quickly and really meant nothing, but it was hardly the first "bad attitude" news brief of Payton's career. He's still a decent left fielder, still hits lefties a little bit, still runs OK, and still can handle center in a pinch. He'll find work, because he does enough things well to be useful off the bench. But getting more than spotty at-bats will be nothing but pain anymore, and what's worse is Payton, like all proud players, still believes he's a starter.

Guillermo Quiroz (Catcher)

PA	R	H	2B	3B	HR	RBI	SO	BB	SB	CS	BA	OBP	SLG	OPS	3-Year	Fielding	Reliability
262	26	59	12	0	6	29	53	16	1	0	.244	.295	.368	.663	+0.01	D	Low

Quiroz's starts in the fool's gear were a relief defensively, as he at least appeared to care that he had a job to do back there. Long gone are the days when Quiroz might have been a hitter.

Nolan Reimold (Right Field)

PA	R	H	2B	3B	HR	RBI	SO	BB	SB	CS	BA	OBP	SLG	OPS	3-Year	Fielding	Reliability
475	54	101	20	1	18	60	88	40	3	3	.237	.308	.416	.724	+0.02	—	High

Reimold overcame a miserable start in Bowie to have his best season since being drafted out of Bowling Green, aided heavily by the fact that he stayed healthy enough to play 139 games. He looks, in many ways, like he could be a right-handed version of Luke Scott with more injury problems and better fielding range. He's got good power, but it's not outstanding. He won't be hitting 30 homers a year, but 20 seems a fair bet. He'll never be a star, but he could, in some year, for some team, be an All-Star. He's also getting to the point where it's time to kick this career into the next gear.

Brian Roberts (Second Base)

PA	R	H	2B	3B	HR	RBI	SO	BB	SB	CS	BA	OBP	SLG	OPS	3-Year	Fielding	Reliability
625	84	154	36	5	9	58	87	67	35	5	.281	.357	.414	.771	-0.03	B	Very High

After not getting traded to the Cubs or anyone else, Roberts simply went out and did his job all year. Most surprising was that he hit better right-handed (.851 OPS) than he did left-handed (.818) for the first time ever. Counting 2008's numbers, he still hits righties 100 points of OPS better than lefties, and he has had such struggles that some have wondered why he doesn't stop switch-hitting. You'd be forgiven for not expecting the career he's had if you watched him in the early part of the decade, when he looked like just another run of the mill middle infielder who couldn't hit but had some wheels. His 2005 breakout will never be repeated, but he's been among the league's best second baseman the last four years.

Oscar Salazar (First Base)

PA	R	H	2B	3B	HR	RBI	SO	BB	SB	CS	BA	OBP	SLG	OPS	3-Year	Fielding	Reliability
539	63	134	30	2	17	71	78	31	6	2	.267	.310	.437	.747	-0.03	B	High

Had the Orioles played Salazar at first base every day in 2008, there's a pretty fair chance he would have outperformed Millar. Signed by the A's in 1994 and given his first (and until last year, only) cup of coffee in 2002 with the Tigers, Salazar was part of the late-season roster additions and had a nice 81 at-bats, hitting .284/.372/.506 with five homers and 12 walks. Small sample sizes are what they are, but his was pretty enjoyable to watch. Lots of teams could do worse for a first baseman than the projection here.

Luke Scott (Left Field)

PA	R	H	2B	3B	HR	RBI	SO	BB	SB	CS	BA	OBP	SLG	OPS	3-Year	Fielding	Reliability
497	65	119	26	3	21	73	96	53	2	1	.273	.354	.491	.845	-0.02	C	Very High

Would Luke Scott for Miguel Tejada straight up have been a winning trade for the O's? While Tejada was miles ahead of the horrifying mess the Orioles made of the shortstop position in his absence, his 2008 wasn't very good, either. And if you put Tejada on the '08 Orioles and take Scott away, who's playing left field? Jay Payton? It might be sort of a wash, but that ignores the fact that Scott became an easy fan favorite in Baltimore and didn't complain for half the season, piling up all those distracting headlines that sportswriters love to come up with and later decry. Scott's no spring chicken, so his time as a starter might not be too lengthy, but he can hit a little bit, which can go a long way. He was also the first playable starting left fielder in Baltimore since Larry Bigbie in 2004, or if you want to be more harsh, B.J. Surhoff in 1999.

Luis Terrero (Outfield)

PA	R	H	2B	3B	HR	RBI	SO	BB	SB	CS	BA	OBP	SLG	OPS	3-Year	Fielding	Reliability
447	54	105	20	2	15	55	98	27	8	5	.257	.314	.426	.740	-0.01	—	High

The "Quad-A" tag is thrown around a lot, but it's just about the only way to describe Terrero, who is closing in rapidly on 30 years of age and has no real prospects of making any major league splash. Whatever team he's technically employed by, he'll help its_ Triple-A club, and it's comforting to know that a guy who might not embarrass the organization and its fans is just a phone call away if someone goes down.

Matt Wieters (Catcher)

PA	R	H	2B	3B	HR	RBI	SO	BB	SB	CS	BA	OBP	SLG	OPS	3-Year	Fielding	Reliability
541	72	137	23	1	25	83	96	62	1	2	.291	.374	.503	.877	+0.08	—	Low

Whenever Wieters does make his first trip from the on-deck circle to the batter's box at Camden Yards, fan expectation is now such that they might as well play Enrique Iglesias' "Hero." His first pro season was even better than most could have expected, as he torched Frederick for 69 games before earning a promotion to Bowie, where he actually hit better. When it was all said and done in '08, he was called a mix of Joe Mauer and Mike Piazza. There is little doubt he could step in immediately and play in Baltimore, and likely outhit almost everyone on the team. He's got power, he's got patience, he hits for average, and he does it all as a catcher, and a pretty good one at that. Wieters is the best prospect in baseball, but he probably won't stay that way for long. Instead, he'll soon just be one of the best catchers in baseball.

Pitchers

Matt Albers (Reliever)

W	L	ERA	TBF	IP	Hit	HR	SO	BB	HBP	3-Year	Reliability
4	4	4.98	327	73	79	10	41	34	4	+0.02	Very High

Before suffering a season-ending injury that threatens the bulk of 2009 as well, Albers was earning some nice marks for his work both out of the bullpen and in a couple of starting appearances. The hope is his arm will recover enough that he can contribute down the line, which is a gamble worth taking in a system relying on guys to pan out and even start filling out a rotation.

Brian Bass (Reliever)

W	L	ERA	TBF	IP	Hit	HR	SO	BB	HBP	3-Year	Reliability
4	6	4.73	379	87	96	12	44	31	4	+0.12	High

Having failed to impress in 44 games as a rookie reliever for the Twins, Bass was acquired by the Orioles in early September, and he came in and wound up getting four starts in five appearances. He, along with roughly 47 other guys, will be in the running for a rotation spot in the spring.

Randor Bierd (Reliever)

W	L	ERA	TBF	IP	Hit	HR	SO	BB	HBP	3-Year	Reliability
3	3	4.50	242	55	58	6	41	22	3	-0.13	Very Low

An interesting Rule 5 pick from the Tigers with a good arm, Randor Bierd struggled with control and got whacked around pretty good, but he did show some flashes of real hope. He's something of a wild card, but it's not like the world is resting on his shoulders, either. He's one of those guys where he either works out or doesn't, and the organization isn't going to lose sleep about it, which is kind of cold and mean to say, but it's the reality of his situation.

Brian Burres (Starter)

W	L	ERA	TBF	IP	Hit	HR	SO	BB	HBP	3-Year	Reliability
5	9	5.82	578	126	152	20	70	56	6	+0.30	Very High

In a good year, Brian Burres could be a perfectly capable fifth starter, maybe even a No. 4. In most years, he's useful mostly as a long reliever or swing man, given that he's left-handed and can give you some innings. He's a battler, his biggest problem being that he just lacks the natural stuff to be a reliable starter.

Daniel Cabrera (Starter)

W	L	ERA	TBF	IP	Hit	HR	SO	BB	HBP	3-Year	Reliability
8	11	5.10	765	170	181	21	108	88	10	+0.25	Very High

Cabrera is among baseball's most frustrating players, and has been for years now. It's past time to fully leave behind any notion that he'll ever be a star. It's now a battle for Cabrera to simply stay in the league. With his strikeout rates having fallen off the cliff and his walk rates not really getting any more acceptable, he's valuable only as the famed "innings eater," and even then you're accepting that some days you need to get him out of there before the third inning is over. Rick Kranitz took every pitch but the fastball out of his arsenal last year, and it worked briefly, but when a pitching coach demands that a starter throw only one pitch, that sort of raises the red flag, doesn't it? He'll do his familiar song-and-dance routine in '09, and you'd be wise to not waste one of your final fantasy draft picks on him.

Lance Cormier (Reliever)

W	L	ERA	TBF	IP	Hit	HR	SO	BB	HBP	3-Year	Reliability
4	5	4.99	364	82	94	11	43	35	2	+0.32	High

After washing out in Arizona and Atlanta, Cormier worked his way down the alphabetical ladder and found himself in Baltimore. He had by far his best season, and became one of the team's more reliable bullpen arms, doing a lot of multi-inning work after starters imploded. He was non-tendered after the year. Next stop Boston?

Jeremy Guthrie (Starter)

W	L	ERA	TBF	IP	Hit	HR	SO	BB	HBP	3-Year	Reliability
9	10	4.55	729	170	177	24	106	57	7	+0.41	Very High

A nice anchor to build on, but not quite a dominant ace. Every year, he's going to be projected to put up worse numbers than he has the last two seasons, because his stuff isn't exceptional and he doesn't dominate. He simply gets guys out and pitches deep into games. Even if he did regress some, you couldn't ask for more from a guy who came so cheaply after being an early failure, highly touted out of Stanford.

David Hernandez (Starter)

W	L	ERA	TBF	IP	Hit	HR	SO	BB	HBP	3-Year	Reliability
4	11	6.79	628	133	156	26	100	79	9	-0.24	Very High

As a 23-year-old, Hernandez dominated at Double-A Bowie in '08, moving up the Orioles' prospect chart by a fair amount and becoming a legitimate prospect. His change has gotten better, complementing his fastball and power slider nicely as a third pitch. Still young, he's got some time to develop further. So far, as a 16th-round pick given better money than that, he's paying off.

Jim Johnson (Reliever)

W	L	ERA	TBF	IP	Hit	HR	SO	BB	HBP	3-Year	Reliability
3	5	5.28	339	75	86	10	40	33	5	+0.02	Very High

Tell us more about yourself, Jim. Johnson, a starter prospect, injected the Oriole bullpen with a much-needed shot of reliability in the eighth inning, shutting down opposing hitters and doing his job as the bridge man. Chances of a true repeat aren't great if you look only at his lackluster strikeout and K-to-BB numbers, but he's a sinkerballer and is more likely to get away with underwhelming heat. There's been talk of trying him in the big league rotation, and it's hardly as if the experiment could hurt.

Radhames Liz (Starter)

W	L	ERA	TBF	IP	Hit	HR	SO	BB	HBP	3-Year	Reliability
5	12	6.38	707	151	171	29	111	90	10	+0.08	Very High

Yet another Orioles arm from the last decade who appears to either be a lot of empty promise or better suited for a bullpen role, Radhames Liz got to take his lumps for 84 innings in Baltimore, and the results weren't pretty. At 25, he still has time, but not a ton of it with the influx of young pitching talent in the system.

Bob McCrory (Reliever)

W	L	ERA	TBF	IP	Hit	HR	SO	BB	HBP	3-Year	Reliability
3	3	4.78	248	55	58	6	33	30	3	+0.13	Very Low

McCrory throws four pitches (fastball, change, curve, slider) and has good movement on them, but because of that lacks even average command. There aren't many relievers with his variety, but there are plenty of relievers with decent arms and bad control. He's got set-up man potential if not quite closer potential, but it may be an uphill climb.

Kameron Mickolio (Reliever)

W	L	ERA	TBF	IP	Hit	HR	SO	BB	HBP	3-Year	Reliability
3	4	4.49	277	63	61	7	46	32	4	-0.12	Very Low

One of the three prospect arms received for Erik Bedard, Mickolio was predicted to be the first to reach the majors and did so late in the season. He's a huge guy, at 6-foot-9 and with a listed weight of 255, and as such is expected to both strike out batters and have some early trouble with the strike zone. If he finds a groove, there's no reason he can't be a very good reliever and reach his ceiling soon. He probably has the best fastball in the system.

Jim Miller (Reliever)

W	L	ERA	TBF	IP	Hit	HR	SO	BB	HBP	3-Year	Reliability
4	4	4.94	309	70	67	11	61	34	4	+0.17	Average

Considering Miller came over as part of the Rodrigo Lopez deal, anything positive that might happen is a genuine win for the O's. Miller throws a low-90s fastball, with a splitter and a curve for changes of pace. He's run up a nice K-rate over his minor league career, and has spent time closing here and there, including last season in Norfolk for a spell. Some expected he would have been a real piece of the Baltimore bullpen in '08, but he pitched in only eight games after a call-up. This could be his real break-in year.

Garrett Olson (Starter)

W	L	ERA	TBF	IP	Hit	HR	SO	BB	HBP	3-Year	Reliability
7	11	5.54	721	159	181	25	105	73	10	+0.08	Very High

Well, that wasn't easy. No one thought Olson was going to be an ace or anything, but the former Cal Poly Mustang was pressed into active duty after the 900th injury to Adam Loewen, and he wound up sticking in the rotation for the rest of the season. With that time, Olson had some flashes of competence, but usually found himself taking a beating from major league hitters. The jury is still out on whether his "eh, it happens" comments near the end of the year mean he doesn't care or mean he's got a good head on his shoulders.

Hayden Penn (Starter)

W	L	ERA	TBF	IP	Hit	HR	SO	BB	HBP	3-Year	Reliability
4	8	5.88	496	109	133	20	56	45	5	-0.30	Average

Still fairly young, Hayden Penn seems a lot older. That's because he first started getting major league talk in 2005, when he was rumored as part of an A.J. Burnett deal that never came to pass, and also the year when he debuted in Baltimore. He got another short stint in '06, and both times failed to impress. The last two seasons have been rough and far removed from the lights of the big cities, as he's battled injuries and performed at a level you'd expect of a journeyman, not a prospect.

Dennis Sarfate (Reliever)

W	L	ERA	TBF	IP	Hit	HR	SO	BB	HBP	3-Year	Reliability
4	4	5.06	349	75	74	9	69	53	4	+0.21	High

Sarfate knows one speed, and that one speed is "fast." He's a fastball pitcher, period, and suited for a bullpen role. Out of desperation and maybe a smidgen of hope, Sarfate was given a chance to start, which made people appreciate his erratic, gas-pumping bullpen efforts. Control is a problem, as it is for many O's hurlers.

George Sherrill (Reliever)

W	L	ERA	TBF	IP	Hit	HR	SO	BB	HBP	3-Year	Reliability
4	3	3.85	255	60	49	7	60	30	2	+0.18	Very Low

As a throw-in in the Erik Bedard trade, George Sherrill is hard to argue with. As the full-time closer, it becomes a bit easier to start building your case. He still got lefties out, but righties predictably beat him up a little bit, a year after he posted sensational numbers against northpaw hitters in Seattle. Sherrill also always will be able to say that he not only represented the Orioles in an All-Star Game, but that he played a key role. He's not really a closer, but he's a valuable guy to have around, either as a LOOGY or as trade bait as a LOOGY.

Jamie Walker (Reliever)

W	L	ERA	TBF	IP	Hit	HR	SO	BB	HBP	3-Year	Reliability
3	3	4.56	234	55	58	8	35	17	2	—	Low

When a player has a reputation as being a gritty, hard-working overachiever, he usually winds up having a year like Walker's near the end of their line. Dave Trembley insisted on running Walker out there 59 times despite the fact that he couldn't get anyone out. Lefties torched him to the tune of a .304 average and seven home runs in 21.2 innings, so he didn't even do that right. He turns 37 in the middle of 2009. As nice a guy as he is, the Orioles can't be spending their time messing about with players his age if he can't perform.

Boston Red Sox

by Ben Jacobs of The Hardball Times

2009 Red Sox Projections

Record: 98-64
Division Rank/Games Behind: 2nd, two games back
Runs Scored: 842, 2nd in the league
Runs Allowed: 677, 1st in the league
Park Factor: 1.04, a hitter's park

What Happened Last Year:

The Red Sox were consistent, winning 16-18 games in five of the six months of the season. Only in July did Boston struggle, going 11-13. After a slow first two weeks, the Red Sox were in first place, by as many as 3.5 games, most of the time until the end of June.

Tampa Bay took over first place on June 29 and held the lead all but one day the rest of the season. The Red Sox had two chances in the final month to move ahead of the Rays by winning a head-to-head series, but Tampa Bay took two of three both times. Still, the Red Sox made the playoffs easily, finishing six games ahead of the New York Yankees to win the wild card.

In the postseason, the Red Sox dispatched the Los Angeles Angels in four games to reach the ALCS for the third time in five seasons. After shutting out Tampa Bay in the first game, the Red Sox lost three in a row to fall into a 3-1 hole for the fifth time in their last six ALCS appearances.

After falling behind 7-0 in Game 5, Boston's season appeared to be just about over, but the Red Sox rallied for eight runs in the final three innings and then won Game 6 to even the series. The team's fourth comeback from 3-1 down in the ALCS was not to be, however, as Tampa Bay prevailed 3-1 in the seventh game.

The biggest individual bright spots for Boston were second baseman Dustin Pedroia, who followed up his Rookie of the Year season by hitting .326/.376/.493 to win the MVP award, and first baseman Kevin Youkilis, who hit .312/.390/.569 and finished third in the MVP voting.

Starting pitchers Jon Lester (16-6 with a 3.21 ERA in 210.1 innings) and Daisuke Matsuzaka (18-3 with a 2.90 ERA in 167.2 innings) both had fantastic seasons, and closer Jonathan Papelbon (41 saves with a 2.34 ERA) was his usual dominant self.

The Red Sox also got nice contributions from rookies Jacoby Ellsbury (.280/.336/.394 with 50 steals in 61 attempts and excellent defense in center field), Jed Lowrie (.258/.339/.400 while filling in capably at shortstop and third base) and Justin Masterson (a 3.16 ERA in 88.1 innings split between the rotation and the bullpen).

Players Lost from Last Year's Team:

Center fielder Coco Crisp, catcher Jason Varitek, pitchers Mike Timlin, Paul Byrd and Bartolo Colon.

Players Acquired:

Pitchers John Smoltz, Brad Penny, Takashi Saito, Ramon Ramirez and Junichi Tazawa, outfielder Rocco Baldelli and catcher Josh Bard.

Management Is:

The Red Sox have one of the most cohesive management units in baseball. Whether it's true or not, everybody in the organization always seems to be on the same page and general manager Theo Epstein and manager Terry Francona work very well together.

Epstein is adept at finding bargains and always active in free agency and on the trade market. While he knows that sometimes you need to spend big on free agents, he would prefer to develop talent from within the organization. His commitment to making sure Boston has a steady supply of talented players coming through the system, either to play in Fenway or be used in trades, is evident from recent drafts. Now that the hysteria has died down over him becoming the youngest GM in baseball and then leading the team to its first championship in 86 years, he keeps a pretty low profile.

Francona has placed himself firmly in any discussion of the best managers in the history of the Red Sox with his work in the past five seasons. A player's manager, he does a great job of balancing the various egos and wishes of a 25-man major league roster. His in-game decisions have improved since he took over the team and while he's not the best strategist in baseball history, he's unlikely to make a boneheaded decision that costs his team a game.

The Minor League System Is:

The Red Sox have promoted several prospects in the past few seasons (Ellsbury, Pedroia, Clay Buchholz, Masterson, Lowrie), but they still have one of the deepest farm systems in baseball thanks to a willingness to pour money into the amateur draft.

Boston has players such as first baseman Lars Anderson and pitchers Michael Bowden and Daniel Bard in the high minors ready to make an impact in the next year or two. In the lower minors, the Red Sox have outfielder Josh Reddick, shortstop Yamaico Navarro, shortstop/pitcher Casey Kelly and outfielder Ryan Westmoreland among their talented prospects.

Due For a Change:

After a fantastic debut performance at the end of 2007, Ellsbury struggled mightily at times on offense in 2008. However, he had an excellent September and is talented enough to improve upon a rookie season that was solid but not spectacular.

David Ortiz struggled with injuries all season and even when he was able to play, he wasn't the same hitter he usually is. Assuming he's healthy in 2009, he should improve on his 2008 campaign both by playing more games and being more productive at the plate.

Buchholz is too good to not bounce back after posting a 6.75 ERA that limited him to just 76 innings in 2008. Three of Buchholz's five starts in April were very good, but then he fell apart and didn't have another quality start the rest of the season. The Red Sox will almost certainly give the talented righty another shot to prove himself in the 2009 rotation, but they probably can't afford to give him too long a leash considering how competitive the division figures to be.

Josh Beckett went 12-10 with a 4.03 ERA in 174.1 innings in 2008, which is far from a terrible season. As he showed in 2007, however, he's capable of much more than that. He pitched right around 200 innings in both 2006 and 2007, and will have a shot to do so again if he can avoid the nagging injuries that plagued him in 2008. Also, although he didn't have a great ERA, his strikeout (172) and walk (34) rates were both excellent, roughly the same as in 2007, so his higher batting average allowed was probably partially due to bad luck. He did allow home runs at a slightly higher rate, but ultimately he didn't pitch much worse in 2008 than in 2007, and he should bounce back at least somewhat in 2009.

On the flip side are a few pitchers who might not be quite as good in 2009 as they were in 2008.

Daisuke Matsuzaka is very talented, but he's very unlikely to keep his ERA below 3.00 again if he leads the AL in walks for a second season in a row. Even if he is able to cut his walk rate somewhat, it's likely that his ERA will rise by up to half a run just because it's really hard to allow so few runs consistently in the AL.

Tim Wakefield has been a consistently above-average pitcher the last eight seasons, but he's 42 years old and coming off his best season (4.13 ERA in 181 innings) since 2003. While he's unlikely to be a terrible pitcher in 2009, the odds are good that his ERA will be closer to 5.00 than 4.00.

As rotation insurance, the Red Sox took fliers on a couple of free agent right handers, hoping at least one can

> **Our Favorite Red Sox Blogs:**
>
> Keys to the Game (http://keystothegame.blogspot.com/)
>
> Over the Monster (http://www.overthemonster.com/)
>
> Feeding the Monster (http://www.sethmnookin.com/blog/)
>
> Yanksfan vs. Soxfan (http://yanksfansoxfan.typepad.com/ysfs/)

provide some starts reminiscent of their glory days. All-timer John Smoltz was injured last season, pitched just 28 innings for the Braves, and will be 42 before the summer. Brad Penny was immensely ineffective as a Dodger.

Javier Lopez has been a good reliever over his three seasons in Boston, and 2008 was his best performance yet (2.43 ERA in 59.1 innings). However, he seems to be getting by with smoke and mirrors: He doesn't strike out very many people and issues quite a few walks. Even if he manages to avoid having a bad season, another dominant campaign seems unlikely.

Reasons to be Optimistic:

If everybody stays relatively healthy, the Red Sox have a very strong lineup even without knowing who the catcher will be. Ortiz, Youkilis, Pedroia, Jason Bay, J.D. Drew and Mike Lowell are all capable of being excellent offensive players and Ellsbury and Lowrie can at least hold their own. It's also a strong defensive lineup: There probably isn't a bad fielder in the bunch.

The pitching staff has four starters who were above average in 2008, including two who were very good, and two young pitchers who could fill the fifth spot in Buchholz and Masterson. If Buchholz rounds into form and Beckett, Lester and Matsuzaka all pitch up to their potential, Boston's front four could be the best in baseball. The bullpen also appears to be a strength yet again, especially if Buchholz can stick in the rotation, allowing Masterson to help Hideki Okajima and Manny Delcarmen set up for Papelbon.

Reasons to be Pessimistic:

The catcher position is a big question mark. If Varitek returns, it means the Red Sox will likely be carrying an abysmal hitter in the lineup. If they bring in somebody else, it will be a big shakeup for a team that has taken its cues from Varitek's leadership, whether overrated or not, for a long time. Either option could be detrimental, whether it's by upsetting the offense or upsetting the team chemistry.

The Red Sox also have several players (Lowell, Ortiz, Drew, Beckett, Matsuzaka) who had injuries in 2008. If any of those injuries linger into 2009, it could be difficult to replace the production they expect to get from those players.

Boston also figures to rely on at least three young players (Ellsbury, Lowrie and Buchholz) who have yet to completely prove themselves in the big leagues. If none of the three make positive strides in 2009, or even worse, if all three backtrack, the Red Sox could find themselves with unexpected weak spots on the team.

Still Left to Do:

The most important thing for Boston to do is resolve the catcher situation, whether it's re-signing Varitek, trading for one of Texas' surplus backstops or acquiring a catcher somewhere else.

Most Likely Team Outcome:

With the arrival of the young talent in Tampa Bay and the big money being spent in New York, the AL East figures to be an extremely tough division in 2009. The Red Sox are likely to be very good again, but to say they're more likely than not to win the division probably would be optimistic. The most likely outcome is that they're at least in contention for a playoff spot right up until the end of the season, but it's certainly conceivable that they could win 90-95 games and not earn a spot in the October tournament.

Player Projections

Batters

Jeff Bailey (First Base)

PA	R	H	2B	3B	HR	RBI	SO	BB	SB	CS	BA	OBP	SLG	OPS	3-Year	Fielding	Reliability
481	59	106	25	2	16	60	101	50	4	3	.254	.343	.438	.781	-0.02	B	Very High

Bailey saw some action in a late-season call-up and, just as throughout his minor league career, showed that his best attribute is his eye. He has some power, but he struggles to make contact too much to ever be more than a backup first baseman.

Jason Bay (Left Field)

PA	R	H	2B	3B	HR	RBI	SO	BB	SB	CS	BA	OBP	SLG	OPS	3-Year	Fielding	Reliability
598	80	143	32	3	24	85	128	68	7	1	.275	.361	.487	.848	-0.02	C	Very High

After struggling through 2007, maybe because of a lingering knee injury, Bay bounced back nicely in 2008 and concerns about lost bat speed appear to have been unfounded. He can be pitched to, as his high strikeout totals attest, but he will make you pay if you throw him too many fastballs. He's also better on the basepaths than you might expect, thanks to decent speed, smart decisions and constant hustle.

Sean Casey (First Base)

PA	R	H	2B	3B	HR	RBI	SO	BB	SB	CS	BA	OBP	SLG	OPS	3-Year	Fielding	Reliability
348	37	89	23	0	2	32	42	29	1	1	.284	.348	.377	.725	-0.05	D	High

Never a slugger, Casey has lost what little power he did have as he's moved into his mid-30s. He can still hit for average and shows good patience, but a poor defensive first baseman who can't hit the ball out of the park isn't going to see much playing time. He's strictly a backup at this stage of his career.

Kevin Cash (Catcher)

PA	R	H	2B	3B	HR	RBI	SO	BB	SB	CS	BA	OBP	SLG	OPS	3-Year	Fielding	Reliability
261	24	50	12	1	4	23	66	23	1	1	.215	.289	.326	.615	-0.03	C	Low

Cash's calling card is defense, and it's a good thing he's a top-notch defensive catcher because he can't hit a lick. As bad as those projected BA/OBP/SLG are, they would all be significantly better than his career averages. He simply doesn't make much contact, and even when he does, he doesn't make particularly hard contact.

Alex Cora (Shortstop)

PA	R	H	2B	3B	HR	RBI	SO	BB	SB	CS	BA	OBP	SLG	OPS	3-Year	Fielding	Reliability
272	28	63	13	2	1	22	31	20	1	1	.262	.334	.345	.679	-0.04	C	Low

A fine utility player, Cora isn't good enough to play every day. He's a suitable defender at both middle infield positions, and he's developed enough patience at the plate that he's not a complete loss on offense. Still, he has minimal power, doesn't hit for a high average and isn't particularly good on the basepaths.

J.D. Drew (Right Field)

PA	R	H	2B	3B	HR	RBI	SO	BB	SB	CS	BA	OBP	SLG	OPS	3-Year	Fielding	Reliability
481	63	111	27	4	13	59	85	71	3	1	.275	.385	.459	.844	-0.04	B	Very High

After a healthy but disappointing first season in Boston, Drew went back to being an excellent hitter who has trouble staying in the lineup. He has a sweet swing with more power than his career home run numbers suggest. Drew is also very patient at the plate, sometimes to a fault. When he's healthy and locked in, there are few better hitters.

Jacoby Ellsbury (Center Field)

PA	R	H	2B	3B	HR	RBI	SO	BB	SB	CS	BA	OBP	SLG	OPS	3-Year	Fielding	Reliability
553	72	140	24	6	4	43	74	37	34	4	.278	.333	.373	.706	+0.02	C	Very High

One of the fastest players in baseball, Ellsbury is still working on developing his offensive game. He has a nice swing that produces moderate power. When he's playing at his best, he also shows good patience and makes consistent contact, but his big midsummer slump happened when he started swinging at everything and wasn't taking enough pitches or making enough contact.

Mark Kotsay (Center Field)

PA	R	H	2B	3B	HR	RBI	SO	BB	SB	CS	BA	OBP	SLG	OPS	3-Year	Fielding	Reliability
414	43	102	26	2	3	38	46	32	2	1	.272	.328	.375	.703	-0.05	D	High

A solid player most of his career, Kotsay looked terrible in his brief time in Boston in 2008. Normally, he's the kind of player who's solid at just about everything (hitting for contact, power, patience, defense) but not great at anything. He is getting up there in age, though, and perhaps all those years of diving all over the place are starting to take their toll.

Mike Lowell (Third Base)

PA	R	H	2B	3B	HR	RBI	SO	BB	SB	CS	BA	OBP	SLG	OPS	3-Year	Fielding	Reliability
506	61	131	32	1	15	67	65	40	2	2	.286	.344	.459	.803	-0.06	C	Very High

Coming off a career year, Lowell struggled through 2008 with first a thumb injury and then a hip problem. In between, when he was healthy, he had two months where he was pounding out doubles as usual, but by the end of the season it seemed to be a struggle for him even to move. At 35 and coming off a pretty serious injury, it's questionable whether he'll ever have another season like 2007.

Jed Lowrie (Shortstop)

PA	R	H	2B	3B	HR	RBI	SO	BB	SB	CS	BA	OBP	SLG	OPS	3-Year	Fielding	Reliability
511	55	111	33	5	5	47	96	53	3	1	.247	.326	.376	.702	+0.04	D	Very High

Lowrie was a pleasant surprise for the Red Sox in 2008 and should be in line to play nearly every day in 2009. He shows good plate discipline, although he struck out significantly more than in the minors, and power to the gaps. With his frame and swing, though, he'll probably never be much of a home run hitter. His defense at shortstop was better than advertised.

Julio Lugo (Shortstop)

PA	R	H	2B	3B	HR	RBI	SO	BB	SB	CS	BA	OBP	SLG	OPS	3-Year	Fielding	Reliability
416	47	95	22	1	3	33	64	35	17	3	.255	.320	.344	.664	-0.04	C	High

Once an above-average hitter and average fielder, Lugo has become an anemic hitter and below-average fielder. He's still a smart, efficient basestealer, but only a decent batting eye has prevented him from becoming a total loss at the plate since leaving Tampa Bay. With the emergence of Jed Lowrie, his playing time appears to be in jeopardy unless the Red Sox can find a team that wants him.

David Ortiz (Designated Hitter)

PA	R	H	2B	3B	HR	RBI	SO	BB	SB	CS	BA	OBP	SLG	OPS	3-Year	Fielding	Reliability
524	75	127	32	1	27	87	86	79	1	1	.290	.398	.553	.951	-0.04	—	Very High

Hampered by a knee injury early and a wrist injury late, Ortiz was never 100 percent in 2008 and it showed in his swing. When healthy, Ortiz has a ferocious power stroke, although he's also able to make consistent contact. He strikes out a lot, but some of that comes from taking too many two-strike pitches on the corners. The patience and batting eye that results in some looking strikeouts, however, also helps him by forcing pitchers to get closer to the middle of the plate or risk walking him.

Dustin Pedroia (Second Base)

PA	R	H	2B	3B	HR	RBI	SO	BB	SB	CS	BA	OBP	SLG	OPS	3-Year	Fielding	Reliability
610	77	170	42	2	10	70	47	45	12	1	.310	.365	.448	.813	+0.02	C	Very High

Pedroia is a very unusual hitter. He's tiny, but he has good power because he takes vicious hacks. Despite his big swings, he rarely strikes out. His constant hustle and all-out effort help his production both offensively and defensively, and his baseball intelligence helps make up for some of the raw athletic ability he's missing. His intelligence also shows up on the basepaths, where he's an effective basestealer despite not being a speedster.

Jason Varitek (Catcher)

PA	R	H	2B	3B	HR	RBI	SO	BB	SB	CS	BA	OBP	SLG	OPS	3-Year	Fielding	Reliability
473	52	99	21	1	13	52	109	54	0	1	.241	.334	.392	.726	—	C	Very High

Varitek always has had a big, slow swing, but it got even slower in 2008. He still has a good batting eye and still can hit the ball out of the park when he catches up to a pitch, but at 36 years old and with nearly 1,700 professional games under his belt, he may be near the end of the line. He looked like he may be slowing down in 2006 before bouncing back in 2007, but this time around the decline is even more pronounced.

Kevin Youkilis (First Base)

PA	R	H	2B	3B	HR	RBI	SO	BB	SB	CS	BA	OBP	SLG	OPS	3-Year	Fielding	Reliability
576	75	145	37	2	19	78	101	64	3	2	.292	.380	.490	.870	-0.03	B	Very High

Youkilis has a reputation as a walking machine, but his walk total actually has declined each year in the majors and his ability to hit the ball, for average and power, has improved. Maybe pitchers know he won't swing at balls and started coming over the plate more because they weren't scared of his hitting, but he's shown he's not just a product of a strong batting eye. In addition to an ever-improving offensive game, he's a good defensive first baseman, especially when it comes to scooping bad throws.

Pitchers

David Aardsma (Reliever)

W	L	ERA	TBF	IP	Hit	HR	SO	BB	HBP	3-Year	Reliability
3	4	4.62	269	61	59	6	56	32	2	+0.23	Average

Aardsma's best pitch is a fastball that he throws very hard (around 97 mph) but not very accurately. If he could command his fastball, he'd be a good reliever. Instead, he issues so many walks that there are always people on base, and he pitches much worse with men on base, so the walks hurt him twice. He actually does pretty well considering how many people he walks because it's hard to make good contact with his fastball.

Josh Beckett (Starter)

W	L	ERA	TBF	IP	Hit	HR	SO	BB	HBP	3-Year	Reliability
11	8	3.95	715	172	170	20	153	42	6	+0.31	Very High

The biggest problem Beckett has had in his career has been staying healthy for an entire season. When he is healthy, there are few better pitchers as he has a good fastball, curve and change and controls the strike zone very well. Not only does he have excellent stuff, he's earned a reputation as a bulldog on the mound who doesn't get frazzled by tough situations. Since a tough first season in the AL, he's cut down on his home runs and walks allowed while increasing the strikeouts, and there's no reason to think he won't keep pitching well as long as he stays healthy.

Michael Bowden (Starter)

W	L	ERA	TBF	IP	Hit	HR	SO	BB	HBP	3-Year	Reliability
7	8	5.06	595	135	147	17	84	51	6	-0.49	Very High

Bowden has been almost exclusively a starter in the minors and has had success at every level, but with the depth of Boston's rotation he may need to move to the bullpen if he doesn't get traded. He has three quality pitches—a four-seam fastball, a 12-6 curveball and a circle change—and he doesn't walk too many. However, while some reports have his fastball in the low to mid-90s, others have seen a slower version and report somewhat less command.

Paul Byrd (Starter)

W	L	ERA	TBF	IP	Hit	HR	SO	BB	HBP	3-Year	Reliability
8	11	5.25	731	168	210	24	73	31	5	—	Very High

Byrd throws a mediocre fastball, but he supplements it with a variety of offspeed pitches that have made him effective throughout his career. At some point, he may be better off moving to the bullpen, where managers can make better use of the fact that while he struggles mightily against lefties, he's very good against righties. Until then, he'll just have to continue to hope that he doesn't put too many guys on base before a lefty gets to him.

Bartolo Colon (Starter)

W	L	ERA	TBF	IP	Hit	HR	SO	BB	HBP	3-Year	Reliability
6	6	4.66	449	104	114	13	63	30	4	—	Average

Colon pitched well as a fill-in until he suffered a back injury, then made one start in September before leaving the team rather than move to the bullpen. He can still bring a low-90s fastball complemented by a nice sinker, OK slider and average change, but endurance and health are big concerns at this point. His potential makes him a worthwhile gamble for some team that's short on pitching.

Manny Delcarmen (Reliever)

W	L	ERA	TBF	IP	Hit	HR	SO	BB	HBP	3-Year	Reliability
5	3	3.56	304	72	66	5	66	28	3	+0.09	Average

Delcarmen throws a hard fastball, a nice curveball and an average change. He's settled in as a very nice reliever over the past two seasons, although it's still not entirely clear whether Terry Francona trusts him all the time. His combination of good stuff and decent control are enough to make him an above average set-up man, although he does occasionally lose his mechanics and get roughed up a bit.

Jon Lester (Starter)

W	L	ERA	TBF	IP	Hit	HR	SO	BB	HBP	3-Year	Reliability
10	9	4.32	756	174	182	16	125	68	7	-0.13	Very High

After his battle back from cancer, Lester's stuff is about back to full strength. He throws a mid-90s fastball, a nice change, a curveball and a slider. He's not an overpowering strikeout pitcher, but he doesn't walk too many batters and he got a lot of ground balls in 2008, which was a change from the previous two seasons. His stuff is very good, but he'll need either need to keep the groundball rate high or improve the strikeout rate to continue to be a top-notch pitcher.

Javier Lopez (Reliever)

W	L	ERA	TBF	IP	Hit	HR	SO	BB	HBP	3-Year	Reliability
4	3	3.97	270	62	63	3	40	28	3	+0.19	Low

The side-arming lefty has flip-flopped the last two seasons, dominating righties in 2007 while struggling against lefties, then dominating lefties in 2008 while getting hit hard by righties. With his fastball/slider combo and difficult arm angle, the 2008 result is definitely the expectation, and he will likely continue to be used primarily against left handers. He doesn't throw hard and he can struggle with control, so he relies heavily on movement and his tricky arm motion.

Justin Masterson (Reliever)

W	L	ERA	TBF	IP	Hit	HR	SO	BB	HBP	3-Year	Reliability
6	7	4.59	525	119	126	11	75	52	7	-0.24	High

Masterson was solid as a fill-in starter for the Red Sox, but his future may be in the bullpen. He has four pitches, but two of them are significantly better than the others. His low 80s-slider is very good, and his big out pitch is a heavy sinker that he can throw at a variety of speeds. His near-sidearm delivery makes him that much tougher, especially for righties. His control was also less of a problem as a reliever than as a starter. He can be a dominant reliever right now, but he'll need to greatly improve at least one other pitch to be a reliably good starter.

Daisuke Matsuzaka (Starter)

W	L	ERA	TBF	IP	Hit	HR	SO	BB	HBP	3-Year	Reliability
9	9	4.45	712	163	155	18	147	77	7	+0.35	High

Matsuzaka has a wide variety of quality pitches and he's comfortable throwing any of them at any time, so it's difficult for hitters to know what's coming. His high walk total doesn't necessarily indicate poor control so much as that Matsuzaka pitches away from contact too much, trying to throw a perfect pitch every time. The result is high pitch counts and quite a few baserunners, but he was able to avoid giving up a lot of runs in 2008 because his stuff is so hard to hit when he does throw strikes.

Hideki Okajima (Reliever)

W	L	ERA	TBF	IP	Hit	HR	SO	BB	HBP	3-Year	Reliability
5	2	3.62	279	67	61	6	59	24	2	+0.22	Very Low

With a funky delivery and three good pitches, Okajima has become a quality reliever in two seasons in Boston. He throws a high-80s fastball as well as a curveball and change-up, and will occasionally mix in a slider or splitter. He frequently throws the change out of the zone when he's ahead and makes hitters chase it. He has decent control, but because he doesn't throw with much velocity, he gets hit hard when he's not on his game.

Jonathan Papelbon (Reliever)

W	L	ERA	TBF	IP	Hit	HR	SO	BB	HBP	3-Year	Reliability
6	2	2.66	279	70	56	5	77	16	2	+0.18	Low

Papelbon's bread and butter is a mid-90s fastball that is constantly around the plate. He'll mix in a splitter, slider, change or slurve, but not very often. When he gets in trouble, it's usually because he's relying too much on the fastball, sometimes throwing as many as 30 in a row in 2008. Still, even when the hitter knows it's coming, his fastball is so good that it's not easy to hit. He not only has the stuff of a dominant closer, he acts the part as well, with an intensity that borders on insanity at times.

David Pauley (Starter)

W	L	ERA	TBF	IP	Hit	HR	SO	BB	HBP	3-Year	Reliability
6	10	5.70	659	145	181	19	71	56	8	+0.05	Very High

Pauley has been hit hard in his brief stints in the majors, and he hasn't been a dominant pitcher in the minors, either. He throws a sinker, fastball, change and curveball, but he doesn't have particularly impressive stuff. His control is OK, but certainly not great. Even in the minors, he's had trouble putting hitters away because of his lack of a go-to out pitch.

Kyle Snyder (Reliever)

W	L	ERA	TBF	IP	Hit	HR	SO	BB	HBP	3-Year	Reliability
3	5	5.32	316	71	81	9	45	28	4	+0.24	Average

After a solid 2007 season, Snyder spent most of 2008 in Triple-A and wasn't even good there. He throws a fastball, curveball and change, but he doesn't have very good control. He's been used as both a starter and a reliever in his career, but he tends to get hit harder the longer he pitches, making him more suited to pitching out of the bullpen. At this stage of his career, he's not somebody who should be pitching significant innings on a good team.

Mike Timlin (Reliever)

W	L	ERA	TBF	IP	Hit	HR	SO	BB	HBP	3-Year	Reliability
3	4	4.57	258	59	64	7	36	20	2	—	Low

Timlin has had a very nice major league career, but he'll be 43 years old at the start of the 2009 season and is probably just about done. Even if he doesn't retire, he won't be back with the Red Sox, who suffered through the worst season of his career in 2008. Timlin works mainly with a fastball/slider combo, but neither pitch is what it once was and his control, which used to be a strength, seemed to abandon him as well. Maybe he knew his stuff wasn't good enough to challenge hitters anymore, so he was nibbling around the corners more than he used to.

Tim Wakefield (Starter)

W	L	ERA	TBF	IP	Hit	HR	SO	BB	HBP	3-Year	Reliability
9	10	4.61	716	167	169	22	101	57	7	—	Very High

Wakefield is at the mercy of the most unpredictable pitch in baseball, so it's always tough to tell what you're going to get with him. He throws his knuckleball most of the time and when it's fluttering like it's supposed to, it's nearly impossible to hit, but it can also be tough to keep in the strike zone. When it's not moving around, Wakefield gets hammered. He'll occasionally mix in a high-70s fastball and he's added a curveball as well, but the knuckleball is the key to everything. That he's been a league average pitcher or better eight seasons in a row shows that he's come about as close as you can to mastering the knuckler.

Chicago Cubs

by Harry Pavlidis of Another Cubs Blog (anothercubsblog.net)

2009 Cubs Projections

Record: 89-73
Division Rank/Games Behind: Tied for first
Runs Scored: 801, 5th in the league
Runs Allowed: 719, 3rd in the league
Park Factor: 1.04 on average, but it depends on the way the wind is blowing.

What Happened Last Year:

The Cubs won a second straight NL Central title but were swept out of the first round. Again. The 2008 team was far better than the 2007 version, but collapsed in nearly identical fashion, again to an underwhelming NL West champ.

Carlos Zambrano threw a no-hitter on the road against the Houston Astros. In Milwaukee, which folks in Houston really seemed to appreciate. We have Hurricane Ike to thank for the change in venue, and a sleepy and distracted "home" team.

Zambrano was brilliant in the no-hitter, and pitched well in a gut-kick NLDS Game 2 defeat against Los Angeles. Cubs fans got to experience another brilliant pitcher in Rich Harden, acquired midseason from Oakland. Unfortunately, Harden and Zambrano both managed to provide opportunities for spot starters and long relievers. Shoulder issues came up for both aces, along with command issues that got both out of games early.

Geovany Soto won the NL Rookie of the Year, the first catcher since Mike Piazza to do so. He joins an elite class of catchers to achieve the honor, including Johnny Bench and Carlton Fisk. Soto has bright future and could be the Cubs' best weapon in 2009.

Players Lost from Last Year's Team:

Jim Edmonds, a crucial pick-up off the Padres' scrap heap, was not invited back, and was considering retiring. Jimmy Ballgame lost a step in the outfield, but he still showed good instincts, with a bit of showboating, and some pop at the plate.

Kerry Wood finally moved on from the only organization he's known as a professional. Wood's cost was too high, and the years too long, for the Cubs—but not for the Indians. Carlos Marmol is ready to step in as closer, with Kevin Gregg replacing the also-departed Bob Howry.

Mark DeRosa was traded to Cleveland on New Year's Eve. While the prospects the Cubs acquired may not get everyone excited, DeRosa was one of the few right-handed bats Hendry could trade.

Jason Marquis was shipped to Colorado, moving Sean Marshall up a notch in the depth chart.

Also departed: Daryle Ward, Jon Lieber, Henry Blanco, Carmen Pignatiello, Felix Pie

Players Acquired:

Milton Bradley signed a three-year deal and was met with immediate questions about his health, attitude and ability to play right field. Bradley could turn out to be a bargain, as most projections have the switch-hitter valued in excess of his new $10 million base salary. The Cubs became even more left-handed when they signed switch-hitting utility man Aaron Miles and good-speed, no-bat outfielder Joey Gathright.

Gregg came in Florida's regularly scheduled fire sale. The cost was Jose Ceda, a flame-throwing, high-upside prospect. In effect, the Cubs got Gregg for Todd Walker, who was sent to San Diego straight-up for Ceda in 2006. Gregg will set up for Marmol. David Patton was picked-up for cash after the Reds took him in the Rule 5 Draft. He'll start the year in Iowa. Mark Johnson was signed to a minor-league deal and could be Soto's backup or the starter in Iowa. In exchange for Marquis, the Cubs got reliever Luis Vizcaino. For DeRosa, three pitchers came over from the Indians: Jeff Stevens, Chris Archer and John Gaub.

Management Is:

Set for a few years, although ownership is not. Jim Hendry has signed on for four more years, and has given Lou Piniella an extension. The organization is looking at a "two-year window to win."

The Tribune Company (now owned by Sam Zell) filed for Chapter 11, but the Cubs are not part of the bankruptcy proceedings. The sale will move forward, possibly more quickly, despite the Trib's financial woes. Even the down economy won't stop this one. The Cubs' budget for payroll may be as high as $140-145 million in 2009.

The Minor League System Is:

Not producing many bats. The Cubs do have a lot of catching prospects, some middle infielders and lots of pitchers. They keep it fresh from all corners of the globe, including Italy, Korea and Latin America.

41

Catchers Steve Clevenger and Wellington Castillo aren't major league ready. Clevenger has shown he can hit in the Arizona Fall League, which also has given him valuable experience working with quality pitching prospects. Castillo rode the pines in the Dominican Winter league, but will see some time in spring training.

Darwin Barney, Tony Thomas, Nate Spears and Marquez Smith all are infield prospects, but none are blue-chips. Barney is a fan favorite from Oregon (they love him) and may be the second coming of Ryan Theriot. Spears could be a decent 25th man some day, while Smith and Thomas have shown promise, but aren't ready.

Tyler Colvin is the big name in the outfield. Colvin had elbow surgery but should bounce back in 2009. He still has a shot at the 2010 roster.

If there's one thing you'll see this spring, it will be a lot of young pitching. The bullpen is unsettled and there are lots of candidates. The list includes Jose Ascanio, Esmalin Caridad, Mitch Atkins, Jesse Estrada, Randy Wells and on and on. Angel Guzman and Jeff Samardzija will get stretched out in Mesa, but both are leading candidates for set-up jobs in 2009.

Due For a Change:

Guzman may finally cash in on his potential. A year and half after Tommy John surgery, he's out of options and has to stick with the club. He's got starter stuff, but may be headed for the pen.

Marmol will have to become more consistent to handle the (unnecessary and unnatural) pressure of being a closer in Chicago. For a team that hasn't won the prize in 101 years. No biggie.

The shine started coming off Ryan Theriot—he spent more time at the bottom of the line-up as 2008 progressed. Derrek Lee is also on the decline. Kosuke Fukudome could end up in center field full time, but will be on a short leash from the fans' perspective.

Soto could explode into a Piazza-like threat in 2009. I think Piazza had more natural hitting talent, but Geo has managed to reach higher levels than expected each of the last few years.

Reasons to be Optimistic:

The core of the team that has won two straight titles remains. Starting pitching again will be a strength, and the relief corps is stocked with young arms. The division rivals aren't radically improved, so the 97-win team of 2008 will be expected to approach that number once again.

The offense will be powered by Soto and Aramis Ramirez, with support from Alfonso Soriano, and, the Cubs hope, others. The shift to a more left-handed roster should take pressure off the big righties, and Bradley could be as good as any hitter on the club in 2009.

Reasons to be Pessimistic:

Soto and Theriot were the only regulars under 30 last season, and that doesn't look to change in 2009. The Cubs don't look to get any younger by acquisition, either. This could be a drag on team production, as many players may be in a decline phase. Possibly, only Soto stands to develop. This is the flip side of "the core of the team that has won two straight titles remains" optimism. This is a team built to win "now," so this is not actually a major weakness.

Despite the quality of the pitching, there are enough health concerns to make the depth of the staff a key to the club's success. Pitching's a funny thing, and I don't want to go all Forrest Gump here. But you just don't know what you've got in a bullpen year-to-year until you play the games.

Still Left to Do:

Blanco's option was not picked up, so Koyie Hill could be the backup to Soto in 2009, reprising his role in Iowa from 2007. Expect competition in camp for the job, with a veteran type most likely to prevail. Paul Bako also could show up, if rumors are true.

Neal Cotts is the only lefty reliever with big league stuff, unless you count Marshall as part of the bullpen. There are plenty of LOOGYs on the free-agent market, and the Cubs probably will find help there. There could be an open competition for a second lefty spot behind Cotts. I'd still expect the typical "I'm OK with one lefty" line from Piniella, but I still won't believe it.

The Cubs left the winter meetings without Jake Peavy, and talks are apparently over—for the time being. It is possible that, by the time you read this, things will have changed. Adding Peavy would give the Cubs one of the best rotations I can think of, ever. On paper, at least.

Most Likely Team Outcome:

The Cubs should contend and be favorites for a third straight division title. Beyond that, it is hard to imagine anything "likely" when it comes to the Cubs and the postseason. Other than getting there. The offense needs to improve to make a postseason run happen, but the pitching and defense shouldn't hold them back. Ninety wins would be disappointing.

Player Projections

Batters

Henry Blanco (Catcher)

PA	R	H	2B	3B	HR	RBI	SO	BB	SB	CS	BA	OBP	SLG	OPS	3-Year	Fielding	Reliability
220	24	53	11	1	5	25	37	14	1	1	.266	.315	.407	.722	—	A	Very Low

Hank White recovered from neck issues to be a dependable back-up for Geovany Soto. He still threw guys out—nailing 10 of 22 would-be base stealers. While his .292 average was a mirage, he'll be a quality back-up for someone, but probably not the Cubs. His 2009 option was declined.

Ronny Cedeno (Second Base)

PA	R	H	2B	3B	HR	RBI	SO	BB	SB	CS	BA	OBP	SLG	OPS	3-Year	Fielding	Reliability
352	41	89	16	2	7	38	63	22	5	1	.277	.324	.404	.728	+0.02	C	High

Long protected on the 40-man roster, Cedeno has not met expectations. Surpassed by Ryan Theriot and Mike Fontenot, the athletic middle infielder was supposedly dangled in the Jake Peavy bid. Cedeno will continue to play a back-up role, and is a serviceable major leaguer. He's not likely to crack the starting line-up for the Cubs or any other team.

Mark DeRosa (Second Base)

PA	R	H	2B	3B	HR	RBI	SO	BB	SB	CS	BA	OBP	SLG	OPS	3-Year	Fielding	Reliability
546	68	137	29	2	15	68	98	56	4	1	.287	.368	.451	.819	-0.05	C	Very High

Last season was a career year for this super utility man. Getting most of the starts at second base, and more than his share in right, DeRosa posted career highs in nearly every offensive category. His ability to change positions created at-bats for Mike Fontenot, and spared the Cubs from even more at-bats for Kosuke Fukudome—particularly against lefties. DeRosa will almost certainly post numbers more like his career line.

Jim Edmonds (Center Field)

PA	R	H	2B	3B	HR	RBI	SO	BB	SB	CS	BA	OBP	SLG	OPS	3-Year	Fielding	Reliability
415	53	95	20	2	18	60	86	50	1	2	.265	.355	.483	.838	—	D	High

Edmonds was released by the Padres in May, and the Cubs scooped him up at a prorated league minimum. He ended up supplanting Felix Pie and providing the primary, and powerful, piece of an outstanding center field platoon. Edmonds has lost a couple of steps out there, but still made a few highlight moments. Naturally. In the beginning, Piniella was patient, allowing the veteran time to regain his swing—and it paid off. Edmonds became a free agent and, at this writing, may retire.

Mike Fontenot (Second Base)

PA	R	H	2B	3B	HR	RBI	SO	BB	SB	CS	BA	OBP	SLG	OPS	3-Year	Fielding	Reliability
376	47	96	22	3	8	44	63	35	4	1	.289	.357	.445	.802	-0.01	C	High

Ron Santo's "Little Babe Ruth" came over from Baltimore in the Sammy Sosa deal. Getting a good amount of time at second base, Fontenot proved to be an above-average defender and an excellent platoon hitter. Helpless against lefties in 2007, he fared freakishly well in a miniscule sample of at-bats against southpaws in 2008. Fontenot showed some power against right-handed pitching and could be the main piece of a good platoon at second.

Jake Fox (Left Field)

PA	R	H	2B	3B	HR	RBI	SO	BB	SB	CS	BA	OBP	SLG	OPS	3-Year	Fielding	Reliability
520	66	123	27	1	27	82	111	29	5	1	.259	.314	.490	.804	+0.07	—	Very High

He's got nowhere to play, but can swing the bat. A trade to the AL would probably be a good thing—he could DH and sub at first. He'd also be a decent emergency catcher. Fox has been productive for Licey, traditionally the premier team in the Dominican Winter League. He put up an OBP near .400 in Double-A. He could find himself in another organization before camp breaks in April.

Kosuke Fukudome (Right Field)

PA	R	H	2B	3B	HR	RBI	SO	BB	SB	CS	BA	OBP	SLG	OPS	3-Year	Fielding	Reliability
540	65	123	24	3	10	54	96	68	10	3	.265	.360	.394	.754	-0.03	A	Low

By the time George Sherrill faced Fukudome in June, the shine was starting to come off the eventual All-Star and eventual bust. Kosuke swung wildly at sliders away—two feet away—after getting his chin buzzed by a fastball. It seemed Sherrill was on to something—Fukudome couldn't handle the inside game and would swing wildly at garbage away. That basically describes the rest of Fukudome's season. He started out as a phenomenal acquisition from abroad, and turned into a $48 million defensive replacement.

Sam Fuld (Center Field)

PA	R	H	2B	3B	HR	RBI	SO	BB	SB	CS	BA	OBP	SLG	OPS	3-Year	Fielding	Reliability
457	47	96	17	3	4	35	68	42	7	4	.238	.314	.325	.639	+0.02	—	High

As a September call-up in 2007, Fuld made a splash with his defense, and showed enough offense in the Arizona Fall League to compete for a job in spring training. The AFL's MVP showed, however, that he was not even up to Felix Pie's level, played most of his games in Double-A, and never got a call from Chicago. He played well in Venezuela this winter, but Fuld is basically Ryan Theriot with an outfielder's glove.

Koyie Hill (Catcher)

PA	R	H	2B	3B	HR	RBI	SO	BB	SB	CS	BA	OBP	SLG	OPS	3-Year	Fielding	Reliability
371	42	85	19	1	11	46	73	29	3	1	.255	.317	.416	.733	-0.02	C	Average

A possible backup to Geovany Soto in 2009, Koyie has shown himself to be a dependable backstop and a dependably bad hitter. Considering he lost most of his fingers on his right hand in a farm accident, the fact that he's even playing is impressive. I'd look for the Cubs to find a more experienced—and better hitting—option than Hill.

Micah Hoffpauir (First Base)

PA	R	H	2B	3B	HR	RBI	SO	BB	SB	CS	BA	OBP	SLG	OPS	3-Year	Fielding	Reliability
406	56	108	26	2	21	70	76	29	2	1	.291	.343	.542	.885	-0.02	B	High

With Daryle Ward out of the way, Micah Hoffpauir will probably take over as the slow-moving lefty stick off the bench. Able to make it on a jog to right field from either dugout, he'll surely be able to take a few innings in the outfield and first base—assuming someone with significant range is playing beside him, or the game is out of hand. All kidding aside, Hoffpauir can hit, and likes to swing the bat. Ward is a patient hitter, and drew a lot of walks, but Hoffpauir is younger, may improve and will be a lot cheaper.

Reed Johnson (Center Field)

PA	R	H	2B	3B	HR	RBI	SO	BB	SB	CS	BA	OBP	SLG	OPS	3-Year	Fielding	Reliability
395	45	101	21	1	6	42	69	24	4	2	.287	.351	.404	.755	-0.04	D	High

Another cheap pick-up by Jim Hendry after his release by the Blue Jays, Johnson combined with Jim Edmonds for one of the most productive center fields in baseball. Johnson's defense wasn't always great, but he did make the best catch I've ever seen. Re-signed for $3 million, he'll probably share the same job, this time with Fukudome.

Derrek Lee (First Base)

PA	R	H	2B	3B	HR	RBI	SO	BB	SB	CS	BA	OBP	SLG	OPS	3-Year	Fielding	Reliability
578	74	148	34	1	18	77	107	61	6	2	.291	.369	.468	.837	-0.05	B	Very High

The king of the hit-into double play, D(P)-Lee has become an average first basemen. His defense is not Gold Glove caliber anymore. That just makes the slide in Lee's offense the second shoe dropping. Projections seem friendly, but continued decline is probably in order. Lee needs to adjust to the outside pitches he sees almost exclusively. If it weren't for his no-trade clause, Lee might be history.

Felix Pie (Center Field)

PA	R	H	2B	3B	HR	RBI	SO	BB	SB	CS	BA	OBP	SLG	OPS	3-Year	Fielding	Reliability
539	69	137	26	7	14	64	106	37	13	6	.280	.334	.448	.782	+0.06	D	High

With the young center fielder out of minor league options, the Cubs traded Pie. Unable to handle left-handed pitching in Triple-A, Pie is unlikely to contribute full-time in the majors in 2009. While his strike zone judgment seemed to improve during his stint with the Cubs, there weren't many signs of hope in that area in Triple-A—or in Dominican Winter League play, for that matter. Pie's defense and speed may not be enough to justify a spot on the 25-man roster.

Aramis Ramirez (Third Base)

PA	R	H	2B	3B	HR	RBI	SO	BB	SB	CS	BA	OBP	SLG	OPS	3-Year	Fielding	Reliability
575	78	148	35	2	27	93	82	55	1	1	.292	.367	.529	.896	-0.03	C	Very High

In each of his five full seasons as a Cub, Ramirez has posted an OPS+ between 126 and 138. While he struck out nearly 100 times in 2008, he still didn't reach his Pittsburgh totals and set a career high in walks. On defense, he makes more of the routine plays now, but still has limited range. And he runs harder than people give him credit for. He'll be 31 and has yet to show signs of decline—but it will happen within his current contract.

Alfonso Soriano (Left Field)

PA	R	H	2B	3B	HR	RBI	SO	BB	SB	CS	BA	OBP	SLG	OPS	3-Year	Fielding	Reliability
524	78	136	30	2	29	88	112	40	18	5	.287	.344	.542	.886	-0.03	C	Very High

Always a hop away from the DL, Soriano was your typical Soriano in 2008. With his legs getting worse, the stolen bases virtually disappeared, but the power remained. Despite playing just over 100 games, Soriano led the Cubs in home runs. Streaky as ever, the leadoff man who shouldn't be a leadoff man would carry the team for stretches. He simply can't lay off the breaking stuff down and away, and, when he's not on his game, he looks lost. A trip down the order won't happen unless the Cubs acquire an established leadoff hitter.

Geovany Soto (Catcher)

PA	R	H	2B	3B	HR	RBI	SO	BB	SB	CS	BA	OBP	SLG	OPS	3-Year	Fielding	Reliability
506	68	133	31	1	22	80	108	53	0	1	.299	.374	.522	.896	+0.02	C	Very High

The 2008 Rookie of the Year now has two playoff defeats under his belt, and a full season working with the mercurial Carlos Zambrano. Soto handled a veteran staff on a division champion while under tremendous scrutiny. He may swing and miss at too many pitches in the zone, but Soto is a formidable hitter, and has shown the ability to catch 130 games but still be a threat with the bat. If other hitters, like Soriano, stay healthy, expect manager Lou Piniella to rest Soto more often in 2009.

Ryan Theriot (Shortstop)

PA	R	H	2B	3B	HR	RBI	SO	BB	SB	CS	BA	OBP	SLG	OPS	3-Year	Fielding	Reliability
572	68	147	24	4	3	47	62	54	17	5	.290	.359	.370	.729	-0.03	D	Very High

He may be over-rated, but he managed to be mildly effective. His high batting average was hollow, and his 58 multi-hit games featured just two multi-XBH games. His defense is just below league average, by most measures, despite looking far worse to me. If he can't produce another .300 batting average, he may approach replacement level.

Daryle Ward (First Base)

PA	R	H	2B	3B	HR	RBI	SO	BB	SB	CS	BA	OBP	SLG	OPS	3-Year	Fielding	Reliability
217	27	51	13	0	8	30	42	28	0	1	.274	.369	.473	.842	-0.03	B	Very Low

Other than one big home run and a bunch of walks, Ward disappointed in 2008. Given his patience at the plate, he should bounce back well. The Cubs are letting him move on to make room for a cheaper and younger facsimile of Daryle Ward.

Pitchers

Jose Ascanio (Reliever)

W	L	ERA	TBF	IP	Hit	HR	SO	BB	HBP	3-Year	Reliability
3	4	5.66	283	62	69	10	49	30	5	-0.23	Average

A long shot to make the team in 2009, Ascanio has shown decent stuff with a good 95 mph fastball and three off-speed pitches. His command is lacking; even in winter ball, he was sporting just a 2:1 K:BB ratio while setting up for Caracas closer Jorge Julio. Ascanio is young and should contribute more in 2010.

Neal Cotts (Reliever)

W	L	ERA	TBF	IP	Hit	HR	SO	BB	HBP	3-Year	Reliability
4	3	4.50	283	64	64	8	59	31	3	+0.31	Low

Cotts was thrust into a LOOGY role (50 games, 35.2 innings) when Scott Eyre and Carmen Pignatiello didn't work out. He has a very good fastball that misses an unusually high number of bats. But he's a left-handed Bob Howry with less command and, sometimes, more velocity. Cotts is relatively cheap, set to make just $1.1 million in 2009.

Ryan Dempster (Starter)

W	L	ERA	TBF	IP	Hit	HR	SO	BB	HBP	3-Year	Reliability
10	8	4.03	707	165	160	17	137	65	6	+0.19	High

The Man Who Fed us Crow. Very few people, myself included, thought moving Dempster to the rotation was a good idea. So he ends up finishing sixth in the NL Cy Young vote, which sounds about right. Working quickly, with a flip of the mitt in the midst of his delivery, Dempster became the most reliable starter for the Cubs in 2008. The deal he signed with the Cubs for the next four seasons pays him for expected performance, not a few repeats of 2008. It was his career year, but he will continue to be a solid mid-rotation man.

Chad Gaudin (Reliever)

W	L	ERA	TBF	IP	Hit	HR	SO	BB	HBP	3-Year	Reliability
5	6	4.54	416	95	97	11	78	42	4	+0.03	High

Supposedly he fell and hurt his back, involving a curb and a dumpster somehow, and barely pitched at the end of 2008. A big piece of the Rich Harden deal, Gaudin was re-signed for $2 million and adds valuable depth and flexibility to the pitching staff. He has the stuff to be rotation depth and a good middle/late inning set-up guy.

Rich Harden (Starter)

W	L	ERA	TBF	IP	Hit	HR	SO	BB	HBP	3-Year	Reliability
8	7	3.89	560	133	111	17	154	57	5	+0.21	Low

This is one of the more interesting pitchers in baseball. Working with two pitches (including a change-up that he can move a few ways), Harden showed he could be the ace of an All-Star team, or too wild to get out of the early innings. Despite needing extensive rest between starts to rest his fragile shoulder, the midseason acquisition shut down the opposition almost every time out for the Cubs. In 2009, more of his walks will come home to score. Harden is not going to make 32 starts, and he's not going to get past the fifth or sixth very often.

Kevin Hart (Reliever)

W	L	ERA	TBF	IP	Hit	HR	SO	BB	HBP	3-Year	Reliability
4	6	5.72	416	91	102	15	66	46	6	+0.20	Very High

Hart has an impressive curveball and a 92-93 mph fastball, and was a big surprise in 2007. A September call-up, he made the post-season roster and was expected to make a bigger splash in 2008. He didn't. With a sky-rocketing walk rate, Hart spent most of the year in Iowa. He'll get a look, but probably will be organizational depth in Triple-A again.

Bob Howry (Reliever)

W	L	ERA	TBF	IP	Hit	HR	SO	BB	HBP	3-Year	Reliability
5	3	3.93	309	74	74	8	56	18	2	—	Average

He was signed by the Giants after an off year with the Cubs, and Chicagoans sighed in relief. Howry lost a few mph off his fastball, which generally caught too much of the plate. He had too many outings where he threw at basically one speed—and it isn't 95 anymore. Howry maintained a good K:BB ratio, but gave up one fewer home run than Ryan Dempster, in 130 fewer innings.

Jon Lieber (Reliever)

W	L	ERA	TBF	IP	Hit	HR	SO	BB	HBP	3-Year	Reliability
4	3	4.53	285	67	75	9	39	15	3	—	High

The last 20-game winner for the Cubs came back, mostly in relief, for another lap. In his only start, he gave up four home runs in a single inning. Eventually, Lieber left the club saying he was too hurt to continue. I'll always appreciate his career as a Cub, particularly since he came to Chicago in exchange for Brant Brown.

Ted Lilly (Starter)

W	L	ERA	TBF	IP	Hit	HR	SO	BB	HBP	3-Year	Reliability
10	10	4.44	779	183	181	29	151	61	6	+0.23	Very High

Bulldog ended 2007 with a temper tantrum but came back in 2008 as a stopper. He led the club in starts, but also gave up nearly twice as many homers as any of his fellow starters. As a fourth starter, he's well above average, and should perform near the same level in the last half of his contract as he has in the first two, although some age-related decline is expected. Noted for his unusual willingness to throw his change-up inside to right handers, Lilly certainly has earned his nickname.

Carlos Marmol (Reliever)

W	L	ERA	TBF	IP	Hit	HR	SO	BB	HBP	3-Year	Reliability
5	4	3.79	350	82	64	9	96	41	5	+0.12	High

The Rubberband Man has some of the nastiest stuff around. His fastball can go above 95 and moves and sinks from his low-three-quarters delivery. The slurve is one of the best in the business. When he's off, the fastball is what misses and hitters can sit on the slurve. In July and August, he struggled and ended up throwing many more breaking pitches than heaters and got punished. If Marmol throws you a first-pitch fastball for a strike, you're probably toast. If you need to speed up your bat for the heat, your chances of adjusting to the slurve are almost gone.

Jason Marquis (Starter)

W	L	ERA	TBF	IP	Hit	HR	SO	BB	HBP	3-Year	Reliability
8	10	5.08	719	162	180	23	82	65	9	+0.24	Very High

Marquis ended up having a solid season—for a No. 5 starter. He gave the Cubs a few high-quality outings, a few dogs, and it all added up to a good contribution. Once again, he was left out of a postseason rotation. Since he's not comfortable as a reliever, the Cubs traded him (and ate part of his nearly $10 million salary) in favor of Sean Marshall or a bigger name from the free agent market. He produced an alarmingly low K:BB ratio, so he may be on his last legs. Moving to Colorado won't help.

Sean Marshall (Reliever)

W	L	ERA	TBF	IP	Hit	HR	SO	BB	HBP	3-Year	Reliability
6	6	4.55	451	104	108	14	73	40	4	+0.12	Very High

When Scott Eyre was hurt and eventually released, when Carmen Pignatiello couldn't cut it, Marshall was called upon to work with Neal Cotts out of the bullpen. Typically a starter, he managed to convert himself into a LOOGY/long reliever/swingman. The Cubs could end up using him as the fifth, and not seventh, starter now that Jason Marquis was sent packing and if they don't make a major pitching acquisition.

Carmen Pignatiello (Reliever)

W	L	ERA	TBF	IP	Hit	HR	SO	BB	HBP	3-Year	Reliability
3	3	4.90	236	53	56	7	39	25	3	+0.15	Low

One believed by many to be superior to Cotts—OK, believed by me—Pignatiello had a fastball in the mid-80s and not much luck with his slider. He ended up pitching twice for the Cubs—getting a total of two outs while allowing four men to reach base. He was sent to Iowa on April 9, and wasn't recalled. He became a minor-league free agent at the end of the season.

Jeff Samardzija (Starter)

W	L	ERA	TBF	IP	Hit	HR	SO	BB	HBP	3-Year	Reliability
5	9	6.40	597	127	157	22	63	71	6	-0.45	High

The former wide receiver ended up being a key piece of the Cubs bullpen. Eventually taking Bob Howry's seventh-inning job, he displayed a good moving fastball and the fortitude to get outs in tough situations. Samardzija still projects as a starter, but his secondary pitches need a lot of work. He could be bound for a big improvement in 2009, despite the pessimistic projections. The tall righty has managed to move up the ladder more quickly than most observers expected, so far.

Randy Wells (Starter)

W	L	ERA	TBF	IP	Hit	HR	SO	BB	HBP	3-Year	Reliability
5	8	5.40	524	117	133	19	84	50	5	+0.18	High

Wells was taken by the Blue Jays in the 2007 Rule 5 Draft, and made his major league debut for Toronto. He didn't stick, and eventually returned to the Cubs. He posted impressive numbers in Triple-A, and looked pretty good during his cup of coffee. He'll compete for a spot in the back of the bullpen.

Kerry Wood (Reliever)

W	L	ERA	TBF	IP	Hit	HR	SO	BB	HBP	3-Year	Reliability
4	3	3.49	262	63	54	5	62	23	3	+0.17	Very Low

Throwing smoke with his fastball, along with a tight, hard slurve and a cutter, Wood looked very good in 2008. He did miss time, and the All-Star game, with a blister problem. He still has the knack of losing his feel for an at-bat or three, but the problem isn't nearly what it was in the past, when he'd implode in the middle of a good outing. His slurve has snap, and his fastball still explodes. Talking about snap and explode, the health of Woody's arm is still a concern.

Michael Wuertz (Reliever)

W	L	ERA	TBF	IP	Hit	HR	SO	BB	HBP	3-Year	Reliability
4	4	4.11	294	68	64	7	65	32	2	+0.21	Average

A bit of a disappointment in 2008, Wuertz was demoted in July. He worked on his stuff in Iowa and was recalled in September. Wuertz had one of the best sliders around in 2007 but didn't have the same command of his pitches in 2008. The Cubs tendered him a contract for 2009, and he'll be given another shot for a middle relief job. He'll have to improve, as indicated by his increased line drive rate and decreased strikeout rate.

Carlos Zambrano (Starter)

W	L	ERA	TBF	IP	Hit	HR	SO	BB	HBP	3-Year	Reliability
11	9	4.11	760	177	167	20	126	77	8	+0.17	Very High

El Toro. Big Z. Owner of a no-hitter. A man who needs extra potassium in his diet. Questions will ring about his shoulder if he continues to be wild. I remind folks that he has always been wild—effectively so, but wild nonetheless. I would also suggest a moratorium on arm angle analysis from the bleachers. There is no doubt Zambrano's shoulder has become an issue, but his general lack of command is his real problem.

Chicago White Sox

by Mike Pindelski of The Bard's Room (mvn.com/mlb/whitesox/)

2009 White Sox Projections

Record: 79-83
Division Rank/Games Behind: 3rd, 7 games back
Runs Scored: 786, 7th in the league
Runs Allowed: 820, 11th in the league
Park Factor: 1.04, a home run hitting park

What Happened Last Year:

Though it took them 163 games to do it, the 2008 Chicago White Sox pulled a major surprise, winning the American League Central after being projected to finish near the bottom of the division.

Just about every big question the Sox had to begin the season was answered in the best possible way. Talented young pitchers John Danks and Gavin Floyd had above-average seasons. Carlos Quentin played like an MVP candidate until a season-ending injury in September. Alexei Ramirez showed why many believed he was one of the top players in Cuba before defecting. They won big must-win games at the end of the regular season and finished the year off defeating the Twins in a one-game playoff.

Sure, they were limping into the postseason, but it felt a little like 2005 again: The pitching was stellar, they were getting big hits when they needed, and they were winning the big games. Then the playoffs started and just like that, the White Sox lost their swagger, losing three games to one in the ALDS to the eventual American League champion Rays. It wasn't the perfect storybook ending, but for a team that wasn't supposed to sniff the postseason, the White Sox were awfully successful in 2008.

Players Lost from Last Year's Team:

Orlando Cabrera and Juan Uribe departed via free agency. Nick Swisher and Boone Logan were traded to the Yankees. Perhaps the most significant loss, starter Javier Vazquez, was traded to Atlanta for prospects.

Players Acquired:

Wilson Betemit and Jeff Marquez were the return the Sox received for Swisher. Dayan Viciedo, a 19-year-old third baseman and Cuban defector who likely will begin the season in the minors, signed a four-year, $10 million deal.

Management Is:

Looking to get the White Sox younger and trim payroll. By year's end, the Sox already had traded Vazquez and Swisher and there are whispers Jermaine Dye could be moving in exchange for a young pitcher as well. You usually don't see a team coming off a division championship trade so many quality players, but the Sox are doing a little rebuilding.

The Minor League System Is:

Vastly improved from last season. Infielders Gordon Beckham, Dayan Viciedo, Brandon Allen, Chris Getz and Jon Gilmore all have major league potential. Top pitching prospect Aaron Poreda has one of the best left arms in the minors, but currently lacks secondary stuff, indicating a future in the bullpen might be his fast track to the majors. Fellow lefty Clayton Richard doesn't have nearly as much upside as Poreda, but likely will pitch in the back end of the Sox rotation next year. Keep an eye on Tyler Flowers as well. Acquired in the Vazquez trade, he's a big catcher who isn't going to stick behind the plate, but has serious power potential.

Due For a Change:

His stuff is top-notch and his confidence is higher than it's ever been, but if Floyd pitches with the same peripherals next season, it's very difficult to project a sub-4.00 ERA. A 145-to-70 strikeout-to-walk ratio isn't going to cut it in the majors and he gave up 30 home runs last year, which is why it's confusing that he had a season as good as he did. The .256 BABIP from last season probably isn't going to stick, either.

Reasons to be Optimistic:

Even with the losses of Cabrera and Swisher, the Sox still have an above-average lineup. They led the American League in home runs last season and could do the same again, health enabling their big boppers, of course. The back end of the bullpen is loaded with potential, especially with power arms like Bobby Jenks, Matt Thornton, Octavio Dotel and Scott Linebrink. They failed to convert on their fair share of save opportunities last year, but you'd be hard-pressed to find many bullpens with more raw talent.

Reasons to be Pessimistic:

As was the case last season, the back end of the starting rotation is a huge question mark. Outside of Buehrle, Floyd and Danks, you don't know what you're going to get from the pitcher who starts the game. If the Sox don't acquire a major league-ready arm, the final two spots in the rotation probably will be won in spring training. Even with the youth movement Williams is trying to create, they're still an old team and you never know when the injury bug is going to bite. Paul Konerko, Jim Thome and Dye aren't by any means the most dependable players and they need to stay healthy if the Sox want to reach the postseason again. I'm not necessarily implying each will make a trip to the DL, but there's a distinct possibility.

Still Left to Do:

With Vazquez gone and Jose Contreras shelved until midseason (or possibly longer) the Sox have several choices to fill the back end of their rotation. Among

Jeff Marquez, Richard and possibly even Poreda, the Sox could hand two very inexperienced pitchers spots in the starting rotation. I believe they will find someone within the system to fill one spot, but they'll acquire someone to fill the other.

Most Likely Team Outcome:

They surprised us all winning the Central last season and I think they're going to contend in 2009, but it'll come down to the wire again. I'm taking the pessimistic route and saying they'll finish in either second or third place, but given the unpredictability among teams in their division, they might surprise us again.

Player Projections

Batters

Brandon Allen (First Base)

PA	R	H	2B	3B	HR	RBI	SO	BB	SB	CS	BA	OBP	SLG	OPS	3-Year	Fielding	Reliability
541	60	111	24	3	23	72	139	32	6	2	.223	.276	.422	.698	+0.07	C	Very High

The top White Sox position player prospect outside of 2008 draftee Gordon Beckham, the 22-year-old Allen had a monster 2008 season, punishing High-A pitchers during the first half of the season and equally crushing Double-A pitchers in the second half. He has the most raw power of anyone in the Sox minor league system; he hit 14 home runs in 153 Double-A at-bats. As a true first baseman who played the outfield in high school, he'll have to hit his way into the majors, but he's already being talked about as Paul Konerko's eventual replacement.

Brian Anderson (Center Field)

PA	R	H	2B	3B	HR	RBI	SO	BB	SB	CS	BA	OBP	SLG	OPS	3-Year	Fielding	Reliability
288	34	65	14	1	11	38	63	20	5	1	.248	.304	.436	.740	+0.08	B	Average

Though he provides very little offensive or defensive value, Anderson showed some serious pop against left-handed starters last season, hitting eight home runs in just 80 at-bats against them. That alone will get him some at-bats in the Sox lineup in 2009, but that isn't to say last season wasn't an outlier; before 2008 he had two career home runs against lefties in 179 at-bats.

Wilson Betemit (Shortstop)

PA	R	H	2B	3B	HR	RBI	SO	BB	SB	CS	BA	OBP	SLG	OPS	3-Year	Fielding	Reliability
302	36	70	15	0	13	44	76	25	1	1	.258	.323	.457	.780	-0.01	F-	Average

Betemit looked like a steal when the Yankees traded Scott Proctor for him—a young middle infielder with good pop who could be an interim solution at first or might even be a solution at third base should A-Rod opt out. He turned out to be a terrible defensive player who couldn't buy a hit, and wouldn't take a walk. The Yankees traded him to the White Sox for Nick Swisher ... which looks like a steal!

Jason Bourgeois (Second Base)

PA	R	H	2B	3B	HR	RBI	SO	BB	SB	CS	BA	OBP	SLG	OPS	3-Year	Fielding	Reliability
519	62	126	20	4	9	49	74	30	20	5	.266	.312	.381	.693	+0.08	D	High

After an impressive 2007 season split between Double-A and Triple-A, the 26-year-old second basemen took a step back in 2008, hitting just .284/.327/.402 in his first full year at Triple-A. He makes a ton of contact and has plenty of speed on the bases, so he could make it to the majors playing a position like second base, but time is running out.

Orlando Cabrera (Shortstop)

PA	R	H	2B	3B	HR	RBI	SO	BB	SB	CS	BA	OBP	SLG	OPS	3-Year	Fielding	Reliability
639	71	160	31	1	7	59	65	47	17	4	.275	.330	.368	.698	-0.05	C	Very High

Though he took a step back offensively last year, Cabrera still managed to have a very good year for the Sox largely based on Gold Glove-caliber defense at shortstop. Though his OPS+ dropped from 95 in 2007 to 84 in 2008, Cabrera was a top-five defender in the league based on Ultimate Zone Rating. As a shortstop who still provides a little offensive value, terrific defense at short and a little speed around the basepaths, it's easy to see why he was a Type A free agent this winter.

Joe Crede (Third Base)

PA	R	H	2B	3B	HR	RBI	SO	BB	SB	CS	BA	OBP	SLG	OPS	3-Year	Fielding	Reliability
378	44	89	19	0	16	55	51	26	0	1	.259	.315	.454	.769	-0.03	A	High

Even after going under the knife in 2007 with hopes of healing his ailing back, Crede managed to find the DL last season with more back troubles. Despite those troubles, he still played above average defensively, but he struggled offensively, hitting just .248/.314/.460; his batting average was his lowest since 2004. His days with the White Sox are done, but since he's a guy who has a little pop and plays well at the hot corner, he's going to draw interest. Everything will hinge on the health of his back, which may be a chronic problem in the future.

Jermaine Dye (Right Field)

PA	R	H	2B	3B	HR	RBI	SO	BB	SB	CS	BA	OBP	SLG	OPS	3-Year	Fielding	Reliability
571	75	144	32	1	30	95	104	46	2	1	.280	.342	.521	.863	-0.05	D	Very High

From the conventional fan's point of view, Dye had a very good season for the White Sox, hitting .292/.344/.541 with 34 home runs last year, but looking a little deeper we see he was merely average among outfielders in Win Shares. Defensively, he continues to decline and was one of the worst fielders in the game based on Ultimate Zone Rating. Word is, the White Sox are looking to deal him, but he's scheduled to make $11.5 million in 2009, which isn't a very appealing price given his age or production.

Josh Fields (Third Base)

PA	R	H	2B	3B	HR	RBI	SO	BB	SB	CS	BA	OBP	SLG	OPS	3-Year	Fielding	Reliability
431	55	98	20	2	19	61	120	43	5	2	.258	.336	.471	.807	+0.05	D	Very High

It was a lost season for Fields, who lost the starting third base job to Joe Crede to begin the season and hit just .156/.229/.188 in 32 major league at-bats after he was recalled when Crede was injured. Fields battled injury problems himself in Triple-A all year and finished with a .246/.340/.431 batting line, striking out in 30.8 percent of his trips to the plate. Now, Crede's gone and the Sox do not have many attractive alternatives at the position, assuming 19-year-old Dayan Viciedo begins the year in the minors. He'll have to beat out Wilson Betemit for the job, but if he has a good spring training, there's a definite chance he starts the season in the majors.

Christopher Getz (Second Base)

PA	R	H	2B	3B	HR	RBI	SO	BB	SB	CS	BA	OBP	SLG	OPS	3-Year	Fielding	Reliability
440	46	99	14	2	6	38	57	34	8	3	.250	.312	.341	.653	+0.01	D	High

The 25-year-old second baseman put himself on the organizational map last season by hitting .302/.364/.448 at Triple-A, even earning himself a cup of coffee with the big league club at the end of the year. With Alexei Ramirez likely moving to shortstop to fill Orlando Cabrera's void, Getz will have an opportunity to win the starting second base job in spring training, assuming the Sox don't make an acquisition. Given the club's alternatives, chances are he starts Opening Day.

Ken Griffey (Right Field)

PA	R	H	2B	3B	HR	RBI	SO	BB	SB	CS	BA	OBP	SLG	OPS	3-Year	Fielding	Reliability
537	64	118	24	1	20	70	88	65	2	1	.254	.347	.439	.786	—	F-	Very High

The chances Junior wins a starting job somewhere in 2009 have been severely damaged following a rough 2008 with Cincinnati and Chicago. Offensively, he took a step back just about everywhere, particularly in the power department, where his home run per fly ball ratio decreased for the third year in a row. Defensively, he struggled greatly in both right and center field, indicating the best move for him at 39 may be the designated hitter spot.

Toby Hall (Catcher)

PA	R	H	2B	3B	HR	RBI	SO	BB	SB	CS	BA	OBP	SLG	OPS	3-Year	Fielding	Reliability
236	23	53	11	0	5	25	33	13	0	0	.244	.290	.363	.653	-0.03	F-	Low

Hall can't hit right-handed pitching whatsoever, but with career batting stats of .283/.326/.407 against lefties, he makes a fine platoon partner. Defensively, he's no great shakes, but he would make a good backup catcher on many teams.

Paul Konerko (First Base)

PA	R	H	2B	3B	HR	RBI	SO	BB	SB	CS	BA	OBP	SLG	OPS	3-Year	Fielding	Reliability
525	67	123	25	0	24	78	87	59	1	1	.270	.356	.482	.838	-0.04	C	Very High

When the White Sox signed Konerko to a five-year extension following their 2005 championship season, many skeptics argued the slow-footed first baseman would age greatly into the latter years of his contract. Today, those skeptics are nodding sagely. Konerko battled injuries all year, landing on the DL with an oblique strain in June and his performance clearly suffered. He hit just .240/.344/.438 in 514 plate appearances, posting an OPS+ of 102, his lowest since his dismal 2003 season. At times he looked overwhelmed at the plate and struggled to catch up to the fastball. His defense at first base took a step back as well. A healthy season may lead to a bit of resurgence, but his days as a force in the White Sox lineup are almost certainly over.

Jerry Owens (Center Field)

PA	R	H	2B	3B	HR	RBI	SO	BB	SB	CS	BA	OBP	SLG	OPS	3-Year	Fielding	Reliability
463	52	105	14	2	3	31	76	38	24	7	.251	.315	.316	.631	+0.01	D	High

Owens took a huge step back in 2008, hitting just .276/.344/.316 at Triple-A after a 2007 season that featured 356 big league at-bats. His power is nonexistent and, as a 27-year-old center fielder whose only true asset is speed, he's likely going to play in the majors as a bench player and a bench player only.

A.J. Pierzynski (Catcher)

PA	R	H	2B	3B	HR	RBI	SO	BB	SB	CS	BA	OBP	SLG	OPS	3-Year	Fielding	Reliability
522	56	132	26	0	13	62	73	26	1	1	.274	.318	.408	.726	-0.04	F	Very High

A decent catcher all-around, Pierzynski is a serviceable player who has developed a reputation around the organization as a guy who handles his pitching staff well, particularly his young arms. He made a little resurgence last year thanks to a boost in his BABIP. For a catcher good for 10-plus home runs a year, he's well worth the $6.25 million he'll be taking home this next season.

Carlos Quentin (Left Field)

PA	R	H	2B	3B	HR	RBI	SO	BB	SB	CS	BA	OBP	SLG	OPS	3-Year	Fielding	Reliability
505	71	121	28	1	26	81	80	49	4	2	.280	.377	.531	.908	+0.07	D	Very High

A steal in a trade with the Diamondbacks last December, Quentin proved to be the White Sox's most productive hitter until a disappointing season-ending wrist injury. Quentin's unique batting stance allows him to crowd the plate and generated 20 HBPs, which helped boost his .394 OBP. For the most part, he's a pull-happy hitter, but he can spray balls all over the field and he proved he can handle fastballs, off-speed pitches and breaking balls well. Saying Quentin is a sure fire MVP candidate in 2009 may be a stretch, but his bat is essential to any success the White Sox may experience this season.

Alexei Ramirez (Infield)

PA	R	H	2B	3B	HR	RBI	SO	BB	SB	CS	BA	OBP	SLG	OPS	3-Year	Fielding	Reliability
494	63	128	22	2	19	69	72	25	11	4	.280	.320	.461	.781	+0.01	—	Low

"The Cuban Missile" became an instant fan favorite in Chicago following an impressive rookie season, highlighted by a rookie-record four grand slams. As a hitter, he showed little discipline and often looked like he would swing at anything within 10 feet of home plate, but the power he showed was for real. He has a small frame, but generates a ton of torque with a quick swing that even the best fastball can't get by. Defensively, he was considered among the worst second baseman in baseball based on Ultimate Zone Rating. Now he's likely moving to a more demanding position at shortstop, and one wonders if he can handle the workload. The White Sox are apparently willing to find out.

Jim Thome (Designated Hitter)

PA	R	H	2B	3B	HR	RBI	SO	BB	SB	CS	BA	OBP	SLG	OPS	3-Year	Fielding	Reliability
546	76	120	23	0	32	91	131	86	1	1	.266	.387	.530	.917	—	—	Very High

For the third year in a row, Thome eclipsed the 30-home run mark for the White Sox, but his age is starting to show. His batting average dipped below .250 for the first time since his injury-plagued 2005 season and he struggled mightily against breaking balls. His fly balls left the yard with far less frequency than in his past two seasons with Chicago. Despite the fact that he avoided the DL, he's at the age where health is anything but certain.

Juan Uribe (Second Base)

PA	R	H	2B	3B	HR	RBI	SO	BB	SB	CS	BA	OBP	SLG	OPS	3-Year	Fielding	Reliability
426	45	94	21	1	13	52	78	25	1	3	.242	.290	.402	.692	-0.02	C	Very High

Uribe's days as a starter are over and if not for Joe Crede's back problems, he wouldn't have been in the lineup last season nearly as often as he was. Filling in for Crede at third, he played great defense, but he just can't hit. A free agent this winter, Uribe might find a major league bench role.

Dewayne Wise (Center Field)

PA	R	H	2B	3B	HR	RBI	SO	BB	SB	CS	BA	OBP	SLG	OPS	3-Year	Fielding	Reliability
349	46	80	15	4	12	41	71	23	13	3	.255	.311	.442	.753	-0.02	D	Average

Because of Paul Konerko's injury, Nick Swisher's struggles and Carlos Quentin's season-ending injury, Wise managed to sneak into the lineup for 129 at-bats, hitting .248/.293/.450 with six home runs. He played all three outfield positions and held his own at each position defensively. As a hitter, Wise is an interesting case. He handled breaking balls and off-speed pitches relatively well, but was dismal against fastballs. By no means is he a starter, but he's a versatile outfielder and a fine bench player, which is why the White Sox have brought him back on a one-year, $550,000 contract.

Pitchers

Lance Broadway (Starter)

W	L	ERA	TBF	IP	Hit	HR	SO	BB	HBP	3-Year	Reliability
6	10	6.09	662	144	176	27	68	66	8	+0.03	Very High

The White Sox's 2005 first-round pick, Broadway and his marginal stuff struggled at both Triple-A and the majors last season. His fastball, which usually sits in the high 80s, breaking ball and change-up are merely average pitches that aren't going to generate too many swings and misses at the big league level. He could find a role in the bullpen this season, but he'll really have to earn it.

Mark Buehrle (Starter)

W	L	ERA	TBF	IP	Hit	HR	SO	BB	HBP	3-Year	Reliability
11	10	4.42	808	190	210	26	110	48	6	+0.37	Very High

Buehrle isn't supposed to be as effective as he is, but every year he proves the skeptics wrong. Mixing and matching a mid-to-high-80s fastball that he cuts and runs all over the plate, along with a couple of breaking balls and a change-up, Buehrle was once again the Sox's most dependable starter. He pitched at least 200 innings for the eighth year in a row, posting a 121 ERA+. He was a bit more aggressive last season, which led to more hits against him, but more strikeouts as well. Though most projection systems will probably object, expect another 200-plus-inning season from Buehrle with an ERA below 4.00.

D.J. Carrasco (Reliever)

W	L	ERA	TBF	IP	Hit	HR	SO	BB	HBP	3-Year	Reliability
4	4	5.04	330	74	80	9	47	34	4	+0.22	Average

Carrasco pitched in the majors for the first time since 2005 last year, pitching 38.2 innings for the Sox, posting a 3.96 ERA and striking out 30 hitters. He was a bit hit-lucky last season with a .262 BABIP. He builds his repertoire around a so-so breaking ball, so it's difficult to imagine him dominating many major league hitters. Nonetheless, he'll have the opportunity to win a spot in the Sox bullpen come spring training.

Jose Contreras (Starter)

W	L	ERA	TBF	IP	Hit	HR	SO	BB	HBP	3-Year	Reliability
8	8	4.30	621	146	153	17	83	44	7	—	Very High

As if you haven't heard this one before, it was another roller coaster season for Contreras. Sent to the DL in July after struggling to pitch with elbow tendinitis, he returned to the rotation to start against the Red Sox in August. For an inning and two-thirds, he looked great. His fastball was moving and his forkball was biting. Then, while running to cover first base on a groundball, he ruptured his Achilles tendon. Just like that, his season was over. It's tough to know what to expect from Contreras this year; he's expected to return midseason.

John Danks (Starter)

W	L	ERA	TBF	IP	Hit	HR	SO	BB	HBP	3-Year	Reliability
10	9	4.37	724	170	169	23	137	59	6	-0.12	Very High

The addition of a cut fastball to his repertoire as well as a few miles per hour to his heater turned Danks into one of the better pitchers in the American League. He might not be as good as his 138 ERA+ indicates, but he struck out hitters at a greater frequency than in 2007, walked fewer, developed better groundball tendencies and cut his home run rate by a whopping 58 percent. Expecting another Cy Young-caliber season might be pushing it, but it's probably safe to say Danks is turning into a reliable above-average starter.

Octavio Dotel (Reliever)

W	L	ERA	TBF	IP	Hit	HR	SO	BB	HBP	3-Year	Reliability
4	3	3.68	267	64	52	7	71	27	3	—	Very Low

Signed to a two-year, $11 million deal, Dotel paid immediate dividends to the Sox, posting an eye-popping strikeout rate of 15.6 per game. He throws a fastball with very good sink and an occasional breaking ball, but it's his unusual delivery that creates so much deception. It makes his low- to mid-90s heater look quicker than it is, leading to plenty of swings and misses. His control isn't pinpoint and, yes, he does get a little home run happy at times, but, healthy, he's one of the game's better set-up men.

Jack Egbert (Starter)

W	L	ERA	TBF	IP	Hit	HR	SO	BB	HBP	3-Year	Reliability
6	9	5.31	605	135	153	19	88	58	9	+0.06	Very High

Last year was a crucial season for Egbert. Unfortunately, his strikeout rate plummeted, his walk and home run rates jumped and his ERA ballooned in his first season at Triple-A. Egbert isn't going to overpower anyone and builds his arsenal around a sinker, which isn't going to make reaching the majors an easy task. He'll get another shot at Triple-A, but he's 26 and time is running out.

Gavin Floyd (Starter)

W	L	ERA	TBF	IP	Hit	HR	SO	BB	HBP	3-Year	Reliability
9	11	4.88	777	179	186	29	120	65	10	+0.05	Very High

Gavin Floyd finally turned in a quality season seven years after he was drafted as the fourth overall pick, but that isn't to say there weren't a few signs of overachievement and regression. For starters, he tailed off terribly near the end of the year and finished with a strikeout-to-walk ratio of nearly 2:1. It's tough to understand how he managed a sub-4.00 ERA. Regardless of the negatives, Floyd's stuff is still good and if he can develop a bit more stamina and use his pitches more efficiently, he could have another big season in 2009.

Franklyn German (Reliever)

W	L	ERA	TBF	IP	Hit	HR	SO	BB	HBP	3-Year	Reliability
3	3	4.88	248	55	50	7	43	36	3	+0.36	Very Low

A fastball/changeup relief pitcher, German spent the year pitching for the Texas Rangers, Triple-A Indianapolis and Triple-A Charlotte before becoming a free agent following the season. It's a shame he suffers from control problems, because his arm is electric. His fastball usually sits in the mid to high 90s with good life. His change-up is a very effective pitch given his 6-foot-7 stature. An arm like his is going to get plenty of chances, but mastering his control is a must.

Lucas Harrell (Starter)

W	L	ERA	TBF	IP	Hit	HR	SO	BB	HBP	3-Year	Reliability
4	5	5.69	377	82	94	12	32	44	5	-0.45	Low

Once dubbed a sleeper in the White Sox farm system, Harrell missed all of 2007 recovering from elbow surgery. Little scouting has been done to analyze his post-surgery performance, but the 24-year-old still managed to generate plenty of ground balls, indicating that power sinker is still there. He's still young and after a good return to baseball at Double-A, Harrell could find himself as one of the top prospects in the system if he regains all of his arm strength.

Bobby Jenks (Reliever)

W	L	ERA	TBF	IP	Hit	HR	SO	BB	HBP	3-Year	Reliability
5	2	2.94	269	66	56	5	51	21	2	+0.12	Low

Though he was once again an efficient closer, going 30-for-34 in save opportunities in 2008, Jenks wasn't the dominant power pitcher of his reputation. He still throws a mid-90s heater, but his K/9 dropped for the third year in a row, going from 8.0 in 2007 to just 6.0 in 2008. He's starting to resort to secondary pitches other than his curveball that aren't very effective. He did make a trip to the DL in late June with a left scapula bursitis that may have hindered his performance.

Scott Linebrink (Reliever)

W	L	ERA	TBF	IP	Hit	HR	SO	BB	HBP	3-Year	Reliability
3	3	4.18	247	58	58	8	45	18	2	+0.22	Low

Sent to the DL in July with right shoulder inflammation, Linebrink missed a solid chunk of the year, but when available, he was one of the team's more effective bullpen arms. As expected, his home run rate jumped a bit pitching at cozy U.S. Cellular Field against American League hitters, but he still struck out 8.3 hitters per game and walked only 1.9 hitters per game in 46.1 innings. When healthy, Linebrink was nasty, featuring a mid-90s fastball with good sink along with a good change-up and occasional breaking ball.

Jon Link (Reliever)

W	L	ERA	TBF	IP	Hit	HR	SO	BB	HBP	3-Year	Reliability
3	4	5.23	270	60	64	9	45	31	3	-0.15	Low

Acquired from the Padres in exchange for Rob Mackowiak at the trade deadline of 2007, the 24-year-old Link had another good year in the White Sox minor league system, striking out 66 hitters in 56.2 innings while posting a 3.02 ERA at Double-A. Link has the best slider in the White Sox system, according to *Baseball America*, and figures to start 2009 at Triple-A.

Boone Logan (Reliever)

W	L	ERA	TBF	IP	Hit	HR	SO	BB	HBP	3-Year	Reliability
3	3	4.11	244	56	57	6	50	22	3	-0.06	Low

Control is Logan's biggest issue. Though he walked only 2.7 hitters per game, Logan often found himself behind in the count early, causing him to give in to hitters. That led to gaudy hit totals and a .552 slugging percentage against. His overall stuff is better than the 2008 ERA of 5.95 indicates. He throws a good slider, a solid low- to mid-90s heater and an occasional change-up. He's much better against lefties than righties and if he cannot correct the platoon split, his ceiling may be as a LOOGY.

Mike MacDougal (Reliever)

W	L	ERA	TBF	IP	Hit	HR	SO	BB	HBP	3-Year	Reliability
4	3	4.34	291	65	64	5	56	38	3	+0.21	Very Low

Control problems continue to prevent MacDougal from showcasing some real nasty stuff at the major league level. He spent just about all of the season at Triple-A Charlotte experiencing control issues before a September call-up in which he walked as many as he struck out in 17 innings. He still has a fastball and a breaking ball, both with excellent life, that generate many swings and misses, but when you can't control your pitches in the majors, you aren't going to get many chances.

Brian Omogrosso (Reliever)

W	L	ERA	TBF	IP	Hit	HR	SO	BB	HBP	3-Year	Reliability
3	4	5.64	291	63	67	9	30	39	5	-0.34	Average

A former Indiana State University closer and Tommy John survivor, Omogrosso has moved steadily through the White Sox system, reaching Double-A as a 24-year-old last year. A sidearm right-handed pitcher, Omogrosso throws a four-seam fastball, a two-seam fastball and a slider. He gets his heater into the low 90s, which is rare from a pitcher who throws from such an unusual arm angle. Expect him to start the season at Triple-A.

Horacio Ramirez (Reliever)

W	L	ERA	TBF	IP	Hit	HR	SO	BB	HBP	3-Year	Reliability
4	4	4.94	328	74	89	7	28	26	3	+0.36	Average

He'd had a hot start in the Royals' bullpen, and the White Sox traded for Ramirez in August. Then, he was lit up for 11 earned runs in 13 innings. He doesn't have the stuff to miss bats, making it awfully difficult to succeed as a starter or reliever in the majors. The Royals signed him this past winter intending to give him a chance to start again.

Clayton Richard (Starter)

W	L	ERA	TBF	IP	Hit	HR	SO	BB	HBP	3-Year	Reliability
6	10	5.75	663	146	181	24	56	59	8	+0.05	Very High

The No. 3 prospect in the system according to Baseball America, the 25-year-old left-hander struggled in his major league debut (6.04 ERA in 47.2 innings), but has good enough stuff to contribute at the big league level. At 6-foot-4, 225 pounds, Richard has a repertoire that includes a low-90s fastball, a slider and a changeup. Richard isn't going to win any Cy Young Awards, but he's ready to assume a prominent role in the rotation.

Adam Russell (Reliever)

W	L	ERA	TBF	IP	Hit	HR	SO	BB	HBP	3-Year	Reliability
3	5	5.81	333	72	84	11	36	39	5	0.00	Very High

A 6-foot-8 right hander, Russell pitched 26 innings in the majors least season, showcasing a powerful arsenal but struggling with control. Russell has a very good mid- to high-90s fastball with good sink along with a breaking ball and a change-up, though his secondary pitches aren't very useful. If he starts using his non-fastball pitches effectively, and harnesses his stuff, Russell could be a real force out of the Sox bullpen.

Matt Thornton (Reliever)

W	L	ERA	TBF	IP	Hit	HR	SO	BB	HBP	3-Year	Reliability
5	2	3.23	277	67	57	6	66	25	2	+0.18	Low

A big lefty with arguably the best arm in the Sox bullpen, Thornton had his best season last year with Chicago, posting a 2.67 ERA while striking out 77 hitters in 67.1 innings. He's a two-pitch pitcher, but each is excellent: He features a heater with good movement that he can get into the upper 90s and a tight slider. As one would expect, he was more effective against left-handed hitters, but he was quite good against righties as well. If Bobby Jenks struggles or gets injured, Thornton may be the No. 1 candidate to replace him as the team's closer.

Javier Vazquez (Starter)

W	L	ERA	TBF	IP	Hit	HR	SO	BB	HBP	3-Year	Reliability
12	9	3.95	799	191	183	22	179	55	9	+0.21	Very High

Traded to Atlanta over the winter for prospects, Vazquez pitched much better than his numbers of 2008 may indicate. Despite the 4.67 ERA, he placed among the top 10 in the American League in xFIP ERA at 3.96, thanks to great strikeout numbers, good control and a decreased home run rate. Vazquez throws four pitches, a fastball that usually sits in the low to mid-90s with excellent life, a low-80s changeup, a slider and an occasional curveball, each of which can generate strikeouts. He's a very aggressive pitcher, meaning he develops a case of gopheritis from time to time, but there aren't too many pitchers in baseball who can match his pure talent.

Ehren Wassermann (Reliever)

W	L	ERA	TBF	IP	Hit	HR	SO	BB	HBP	3-Year	Reliability
3	4	4.45	276	62	63	6	41	30	4	+0.30	Low

Funky delivery included, the 27-year-old sidearm right hander pitched most of the year at Triple-A Charlotte, experiencing great success as he posted a 1.15 ERA in 39 innings, striking out 42. He made two trips to the big leagues, once to replace the injured Scott Linebrink and the other as a September call-up, but was torched, giving up 17 earned runs in 19.2 innings. Historically, he's been tough against right-handed hitters and you can't help but see a little Chad Bradford in him, so chances at a major league career are still there.

Cincinnati Reds

by Justin Inaz of On Baseball & the Reds (jinaz-reds.blogspot.com)

2009 Reds Projections

Record: 80-82
Division Rank/Games Behind: 4th, 9 games back
Runs Scored: 726, 11th in the league
Runs Allowed: 735, 5th in the league
Park Factor: 1.02, a slight hitter's park.

What Happened Last Year:

A lot of the things I had hoped for came true last year: Joey Votto had an excellent first season and finished second in the Rookie of the Year voting, Jay Bruce arrived midseason and held his own, Edinson Volquez looked like the second coming of Johan Santana during the first half and (strangely) received consideration for Rookie of the Year, and Johnny Cueto turned in an acceptable 175 innings after essentially skipping Triple-A. Even Chris Dickerson made a splash by playing well above his head for the last month of the season. It was the year of rookies, and they all did everything we could reasonably hope for.

And yet, the Reds still sucked. Bad. They reached last place by April 22, and while they did "battle back" to pull ahead of the hapless Pirates for good by late August, those first few weeks of April were pretty much the most interesting of the season. They had a below-average offense (especially after losing Adam Dunn and Ken Griffey Jr.), below-average fielding (this was helped, but not fixed, by jettisoning Dunn and Griffey), and below-average pitching. Their Pythagorean record indicates that they were actually three games "lucky," and other data indicate that they were even more fortunate. The 2008 Reds were just a really bad team.

On top of all of that, the Reds fired their general manager, Wayne Krivsky, and replaced him with owner Bob Castellini's favorite, Walt Jocketty. And they traded away two of the team's most recognizable "stars" in Dunn and Griffey. It's not a fun time to be a Reds fan.

Players Lost from Last Year's Team:

Jeremy Affeldt, Josh Fogg, Matt Belisle, Gary Majewski, Javier Valentin, Paul Bako, Corey Patterson, Jerry Hairston (maybe), Ryan Freel, Jolbert Cabrera and Andy Phillips.

Players Acquired:

Willy Taveras, Ramon Hernandez and Arthur Rhodes.

Management Is:

Jocketty was subject to a great analysis by Brian Gunn in the 2006 *Hardball Times Annual*. His reputation is that of a shrewd negotiator and a man who is fairly traditional in his approach—the scuttlebutt is that he was ousted from St. Louis because he was resistant to the sabermetric movement in that organization. He's made three big deals with the Reds: trading away Dunn and Griffey and acquiring Ramon Hernandez. In all cases, the deals he's made have been relatively fair in appearance, but he's yet to do a deal—trade or otherwise—to bring in someone who can make a substantial positive impact on the team.

Despite those three big moves, Jocketty's tenure has seemed extremely quiet on the transaction front. At the very least, he's proven far more approachable and interactive with the media than the notoriously secretive Wayne Krivsky.

As for manager Dusty Baker, he came with a reputation for (1) prejudice against rookies, (2) abuse of starting pitchers, and (3) really bad lineup construction. I think we can put the first to rest—Votto started almost immediately last season, as did Volquez, Cueto, and Bruce once he arrived. I also thought he did an excellent job of managing Edwin Encarnacion, among other young players.

No. 2 probably has some truth to it—the Reds had four pitchers in the top 30 in Pitcher Abuse Points (not necessarily a bad thing, but it's something to watch), and Baker's overuse of Aaron Harang early in the season is blamed by many as a reason for his struggles. And No. 3 is definitely true: Corey Patterson batted leadoff 32 times and started 82 games despite a magnificent .238 OBP. But Baker also showed good leadership, a tendency to talk up his players in the press, and what seemed to be favorable relations with both players and media. Those aren't worthless qualities, but they also don't make him a good manager.

The Minor League System Is:

The Reds' system still has good depth despite graduating most of its top prospects last season. Newly drafted Yonder Alonso has been impressive in his brief time with the team, while guys like Todd Frazier, Chris Valaika and Neftali Soto made excellent progress last season. Pitching is a bit thin right now, especially after an injury of unknown seriousness to Kyle Lotzkar. But

Homer Bailey's still hanging around, as are guys like Daryl Thompson and Matt Maloney.

Due For a Change:

Bruce was the No. 1 prospect in the nation last offseason, so you have to expect continued improvements from him, especially if he can learn some patience. Harang seems likely to have pitched through hidden (and unhidden) injuries at least some of last season, and Johnny Cueto may be ready to take the next step into No. 2/No. 3 starter territory. On the other side of the coin, Jerry Hairston Jr. exceeded every possible expectation last season and seems very unlikely to repeat. Similar things can be said about Chris Dickerson. I'm also still a little skeptical about Edinson Volquez, mostly because his walk rate scares me.

Reasons to be Optimistic:

The Reds have a core of quality young players to build around: Votto, Bruce, Volquez and Cueto all will be 25 years old or younger next season. The rotation looks like it could be solid if not excellent: Volquez, Harang, Bronson Arroyo, Cueto, and one from among Bailey, Daryl Thompson, Micah Owings or Matt Maloney. The defense should be better now that the terribleness of Dunn and Griffey in the outfield has been relieved. The bullpen has a nice core of people: Francisco Cordero, Jared Burton and Bill Bray make for a nice set up and closing trio. Ramon Hernandez should be an upgrade over Paul Bako, right? And Patterson, Gary Majewski, and Josh Fogg won't be on next year's team.

Reasons to be Pessimistic:

How often does a team that has lousy offense, lousy defense and lousy pitching one year make the playoffs the next season? Most of the time, they don't. The Reds have some good pieces, but they're far more than a part or two away.

Still Left to Do:

As I write this, the Reds have four outfielders on their 40-man roster. Until they added Willy Taveras

Our Favorite Reds Blogs:

Red Reporter (redreporter.com)

Redleg Nation (redlegnation.com)

Reds Minor Leagues (redsminorleagues.com/)

John Fay, beat writer (news.cincinnati.com/apps/pbcs.dll/section?category=blog07)

Chris Sabo's Goggles (chris-sabos-goggles.com)

Dunn and Dunner (www.dunnanddunner.com)

Hal McCoy, beat writer (www.daytondailynews.com/blogs/content/shared-gen/blogs/dayton/cincinnatireds/)

RedLegs Baseball (redlegsbaseball.blogspot.com)

Redlegs Rundown (mvn.com/redlegsrundown)

Red-Hot-Mama (www.red-hot-mama.com)

The Reds Rocket (theredsrocket.blogspot.com)

just before the new year, they had only one (Bruce) who was a sure shot to start full time next season. So that's clearly a need. Shortstop looks like a disaster unless Alex Gonzalez can come back full strength after missing a full season with a leg injury ... and how much is a "full strength" Alex Gonzalez worth anyway? Next door, the Reds desperately need to get Edwin Encarnacion off of third base ... it's just that they don't have any good alternatives there—maybe Jeff Keppinger.

The only hitters on the team with projectable ability to get on base at a good clip are Votto and Encarnacion. The only genuinely plus defensive player is Brandon Phillips (and maybe Dickerson if he starts). It's hard to get better when you have a roster that looks like this. The good news is that the Reds have some budget flexibility, so they may yet sign some impact players before spring training.

Most Likely Team Outcome:

With a few breakout seasons by the young players, improved team fielding, and rebounds by the veteran starters, this could be a solid .500 team this season. But a contender? I just don't see it. Most likely outcome is another 70-something-win season. I hope I'm wrong.

Player Projections

Batters

Paul Bako (Catcher)

PA	R	H	2B	3B	HR	RBI	SO	BB	SB	CS	BA	OBP	SLG	OPS	3-Year	Fielding	Reliability
328	32	67	12	1	5	29	82	32	0	2	.232	.311	.332	.643	—	B	Low

Bako had the month of his life in April, slugging .310/.388/.507. He ended up .217/.229/.328. The definition of a replacement player, Bako played solid defense at a premium position but was an automatic out for most of the season. And somehow, that made him good enough to lead the Reds in starts at catcher. He's not a terrible use of the 25th roster spot, but a team that uses him as a starter is in trouble.

Jay Bruce (Right Field)

PA	R	H	2B	3B	HR	RBI	SO	BB	SB	CS	BA	OBP	SLG	OPS	3-Year	Fielding	Reliability
543	74	140	28	5	26	86	128	38	6	3	.281	.333	.514	.847	+0.13	B	Very High

The 2007 minor league player of the year began the year in Triple-A and hit predictably well there. He also went 5-for-5 and, rumor has it, floated a foot above the ground during his stunning May debut. Afterward, he struggled for a few months before seemingly finding his stroke over the last two months of the season. Bruce is not a particularly patient hitter at this point, but has tremendous power and seems a sure bet to continue to improve. Similarly, while he at times made mistakes in the outfield, he also has the range and arm to be an excellent corner outfielder. He doesn't turn 22 until April. Watching him develop will be one of the few joys of 2009 for a Reds fan. Why haven't they signed him to an extension already?

Jolbert Cabrera (Shortstop)

PA	R	H	2B	3B	HR	RBI	SO	BB	SB	CS	BA	OBP	SLG	OPS	3-Year	Fielding	Reliability
363	40	84	18	3	7	38	69	20	5	2	.252	.304	.388	.692	—	F	Low

In his return from Japan, Orlando's older brother performed admirably in the superutility role last season. He isn't really a shortstop, but he seemed reasonably competent there in short spells. He played around the infield as well as in the outfield corners. At 36, though, it seems unlikely that he has a whole lot left. The Reds thanked him kindly for his service and sent him on his way.

Wilkin Castillo (Shortstop)

PA	R	H	2B	3B	HR	RBI	SO	BB	SB	CS	BA	OBP	SLG	OPS	3-Year	Fielding	Reliability
426	42	95	18	2	7	39	69	18	6	4	.240	.278	.349	.627	+0.03	C	Average

He is the rarest of catchers—he can play shortstop too! An uberutility player among superutility players, the only problem with Castillo is that he hasn't shown much evidence that he can hit yet: his career minor league numbers are .279/.319/.391. Still, Reds GMs love some flexibility, and if it means that the team can avoid carrying three catchers again next season, I'm all for sticking him in the 25th-man roster slot.

Chris Dickerson (Center Field)

PA	R	H	2B	3B	HR	RBI	SO	BB	SB	CS	BA	OBP	SLG	OPS	3-Year	Fielding	Reliability
503	69	108	19	6	18	60	144	58	19	3	.250	.343	.446	.789	+0.05	D	High

Dickerson's debut last year is what every marginal prospect dreams about: He got his shot, absolutely dominated, and they couldn't take him out of the lineup. He has shown substantial L/R splits, both in the majors and minors, and so there's a question about whether he really can handle a full time starting role—especially when his performance returns to earth. He's currently the Reds' No. 2 outfielder, though, so he may get a chance to prove his doubters wrong.

Edwin Encarnacion (Third Base)

PA	R	H	2B	3B	HR	RBI	SO	BB	SB	CS	BA	OBP	SLG	OPS	3-Year	Fielding	Reliability
529	67	128	28	1	20	74	90	48	3	1	.275	.354	.468	.822	+0.02	F-	Very High

At this point, I think he is what he is: a decent hitter who is clearly playing out of position at third base. He may continue to improve on offense, but the days of dreaming that he'll somehow become adequate at that position are past. The Reds need to take a cue from the Brewers and move him to the outfield.

Jerry Gil (Center Field)

PA	R	H	2B	3B	HR	RBI	SO	BB	SB	CS	BA	OBP	SLG	OPS	3-Year	Fielding	Reliability
258	29	55	12	1	11	36	70	9	3	0	.226	.261	.420	.681	+0.06	—	Low

Gil missed all of 2007 and much of last season with Tommy John surgery, and he didn't hit particularly well upon his return. Known before the injury for his throwing arm and the potential for plus power from the middle infield, Gil's window of opportunity may have closed.

Jerry Hairston (Shortstop)

PA	R	H	2B	3B	HR	RBI	SO	BB	SB	CS	BA	OBP	SLG	OPS	3-Year	Fielding	Reliability
352	43	86	18	2	8	38	50	25	10	2	.275	.334	.422	.756	-0.05	C	Low

If you look back on all of the free agent signings in 2008, there may have been no better value for money than Jerry Hairston Jr. He was the Reds' salvation last year, filling in at shortstop and in the outfield, and was probably the Reds' second most valuable position player. Two questions. Can he repeat? And can he stay healthy? He made frequent visits to the DL last season, and his projection line is a far cry from what he did when he played last year.

Ryan Hanigan (Catcher)

PA	R	H	2B	3B	HR	RBI	SO	BB	SB	CS	BA	OBP	SLG	OPS	3-Year	Fielding	Reliability
396	41	91	15	1	6	37	60	37	1	1	.262	.343	.363	.706	-0.04	B	Average

Hanigan did a nice job as a September call-up, playing good defense and showing the excellent batting eye he was known for in the minor leagues. Before the Ramon Hernandez trade, Hanigan was the de facto starter next season. Now, he'll get a chance to prove his debut wasn't a fluke as Hernandez's alternate, which would seem to be an ideal situation for him. He's already 28, but could be a decent player for a few years.

Scott Hatteberg (First Base)

PA	R	H	2B	3B	HR	RBI	SO	BB	SB	CS	BA	OBP	SLG	OPS	3-Year	Fielding	Reliability
271	32	66	14	1	6	31	30	33	0	1	.283	.374	.429	.803	—	C	High

As good as Hatteberg had been, it was a surprise when he was extended, given the emergence of the also left-handed Joey Votto. Sure enough, he was released in May. Hatteberg had substantial home/away splits in Cincinnati, so there has been some concern that his '06-'07 performance was a creation of GABP. I think he's still a solid left-handed bat off the bench, but I doubt he gets to start again.

Norris Hopper (Center Field)

PA	R	H	2B	3B	HR	RBI	SO	BB	SB	CS	BA	OBP	SLG	OPS	3-Year	Fielding	Reliability
271	28	63	10	1	3	23	33	17	5	88	.281	.331	.374	.705	-0.03	C	Average

Hopper missed most of last year due to Tommy John surgery, which probably bothered him all season. His game is his legs, and he makes the best use he can of them by chopping the ball on the ground and push-bunting his way on base. He's not a starter, but if healthy he can be a nice reserve with good speed, range and some ability to get on base.

Paul Janish (Shortstop)

PA	R	H	2B	3B	HR	RBI	SO	BB	SB	CS	BA	OBP	SLG	OPS	3-Year	Fielding	Reliability
481	48	96	18	2	11	48	92	35	3	1	.225	.294	.355	.649	+0.07	F	Very High

Janish's value is his defense. The Fan Scouting Report agrees that he's a plus defender, but he's no Adam Everett (or even Brandon Phillips)— and therefore isn't likely ever to be a starter. As a defensively oriented infield utility guy, though, he might stick on a big league roster.

Jeff Keppinger (Shortstop)

PA	R	H	2B	3B	HR	RBI	SO	BB	SB	CS	BA	OBP	SLG	OPS	3-Year	Fielding	Reliability
498	55	132	23	2	6	50	39	35	3	2	.294	.346	.394	.740	-0.02	F	Very High

Keppinger won a lot of fans when he took over at shortstop and knocked the cover off the ball in 2007. Unfortunately, he lost a lot of them in 2008. The truth is that while Keppinger is a fine contact hitter with a good eye and ability to get on base, his 2007 power was way out of line with his minor league performances. And his defense isn't good enough to play at short. The Reds hope to use him as a utility guy next season and not a starter.

Corey Patterson (Center Field)

PA	R	H	2B	3B	HR	RBI	SO	BB	SB	CS	BA	OBP	SLG	OPS	3-Year	Fielding	Reliability
434	55	102	19	3	11	45	67	22	25	6	.255	.297	.400	.697	-0.02	B	High

I stated—and still believe —that signing Patterson was a smart move. He was still reasonably young, and with his defense he needed to hit only marginally above replacement level to be a good value for his money. Smart moves sometimes don't work out, though, and Patterson was an unmitigated disaster—one of the worst players in baseball. Can he recover?

Brandon Phillips (Second Base)

PA	R	H	2B	3B	HR	RBI	SO	BB	SB	CS	BA	OBP	SLG	OPS	3-Year	Fielding	Reliability
576	79	149	25	4	22	77	91	35	22	5	.282	.332	.469	.801	+0.01	A	Very High

Phillips predictably declined from his power surge in 2007, but was still a decent hitter in a ballpark that seems to suit him well. More of a supporting hitter than the cleanup hitter he was asked to be last season, he is probably too aggressive for his own good. But we've known that for years, and he's shown no indication that he's going to change his approach. Ultimately, Phillips' most valuable attribute is his defense, for which he received his first Gold Glove award last year. It makes him an above-average player, worth a good 10 runs a season in value.

Adam Rosales (Third Base)

PA	R	H	2B	3B	HR	RBI	SO	BB	SB	CS	BA	OBP	SLG	OPS	3-Year	Fielding	Reliability
478	54	100	22	5	13	53	101	30	5	2	.232	.296	.396	.692	+0.01	D	High

Rosales got some attention from dedicated fans for his excellent 2007 season, but he wasn't as impressive in Triple-A or the majors last year. He is versatile defensively, though, and might use that to score a utility position. But there are a lot of players competing for those jobs, and so it may take a few injuries for Rosales to get a chance.

Chris Valaika (Shortstop)

PA	R	H	2B	3B	HR	RBI	SO	BB	SB	CS	BA	OBP	SLG	OPS	3-Year	Fielding	Reliability
570	61	136	24	2	16	67	119	23	5	3	.255	.292	.398	.690	+0.05	—	Average

Valaika rebounded after a so-so 2007 with an excellent 2008 that saw him rise to Double-A. While he's primarily played shortstop thus far, his future is probably at second or third base. If he continues to develop offensively, he could arrive by the end of the season. Best case scenario is that he'll be an offensive-oriented second basemen with enough power and on-base skills to be a starter.

Javier Valentin (First Base)

PA	R	H	2B	3B	HR	RBI	SO	BB	SB	CS	BA	OBP	SLG	OPS	3-Year	Fielding	Reliability
257	28	62	14	1	6	29	38	21	0	1	.267	.327	.413	.740	-0.05	B	Low

Sometime a few years ago, Javier Valentin was designated as one of those guys who can get it done off the bench as a pinch hitter. That, combined with fairly poor defense, resulted in pinch hitting becoming his only real job last season: He appeared in 94 games but got only 144 PAs. This makes it a little hard to know what he could do if he were allowed to play in games like a normal player.

Joey Votto (First Base)

PA	R	H	2B	3B	HR	RBI	SO	BB	SB	CS	BA	OBP	SLG	OPS	3-Year	Fielding	Reliability
561	75	141	29	2	23	82	108	59	7	4	.285	.362	.492	.854	+0.02	B	Very High

Votto outperformed every realistic expectation last year. He was the Reds' most valuable player and runner-up Rookie of the Year, turning in an excellent offensive season and defense that by many accounts was above-average at his position. The question now is whether what we saw last year is what he can do, or whether he'll take the next step.

Pitchers

Jeremy Affeldt (Reliever)

W	L	ERA	TBF	IP	Hit	HR	SO	BB	HBP	3-Year	Reliability
5	3	3.73	319	75	71	6	59	32	2	+0.26	Average

After failing to make the starting staff out of spring training, Affeldt turned in a heck of a season as a left-handed reliever. The strange thing about his season was that Affeldt was used far more often than one would expect in low-leverage situations. It's as if manager Dusty Baker decided early on that he was a mop-up reliever and couldn't change his mind.

Bronson Arroyo (Starter)

W	L	ERA	TBF	IP	Hit	HR	SO	BB	HBP	3-Year	Reliability
10	11	4.67	799	185	200	26	132	59	8	+0.21	Very High

Arroyo's strikeout rate, my bellwether for his success, was the highest it's ever been in 2008. He did have a very rough start, but he rebounded well and finished strong, ultimately setting a career high in wins. He's no ace, but he's a quality major league starting pitcher. He's also not getting any younger, and you have to wonder if he'll still be a capable pitcher when the rest of the team is in a position to contend some years down the line. If he has a good first half, I can see him being dealt.

Homer Bailey (Starter)

W	L	ERA	TBF	IP	Hit	HR	SO	BB	HBP	3-Year	Reliability
6	10	5.45	641	141	157	22	98	72	7	-0.51	Very High

It's amazing how quickly a prospect's stock can fall. While he's still only 22 years old, some are now questioning whether he'll ever pan out as a major league pitcher. And not without reason. The issue with Bailey hasn't really been wildness (that's still a factor, though it was better last year). It's more an issue of hit-ability. The supposed fireballer's fastball averaged under 92 mph last year, and he's seemingly using his lauded curve ball less now in favor of a slider. Some scouting-types think he's feeling a lot of pain. You have to wonder.

Matt Belisle (Reliever)

W	L	ERA	TBF	IP	Hit	HR	SO	BB	HBP	3-Year	Reliability
4	6	5.06	414	94	112	13	56	29	5	+0.40	High

Belisle's frustrating tenure with the Reds finally ended this offseason. From a statistical perspective, he certainly looks interesting, largely due to his excellent walk rates. Those who watched him over the past few seasons, however, noted that he was prone to big innings and meltdowns. I have to think that someone is going to give him a good shot this spring, though, and when they do he might just stick as a solid No. 4 or No. 5 starter.

Bill Bray (Reliever)

W	L	ERA	TBF	IP	Hit	HR	SO	BB	HBP	3-Year	Reliability
3	3	4.08	249	58	54	7	57	24	2	+0.04	Low

While slowed by injuries since his arrival in 2006, Bray finally broke out with a great season as a left-handed setup specialist. He throws in the low 90s with a hard slider, and in his career has shown ability to get righties out as well as lefties. Whether by design or not, Dusty Baker did seem to use him more as a LOOGY as the season went on. I expect that he'll continue to share setup duties next season.

Jared Burton (Reliever)

W	L	ERA	TBF	IP	Hit	HR	SO	BB	HBP	3-Year	Reliability
4	3	4.19	274	63	61	8	54	29	3	+0.17	Low

The other Rule 5 pick from 2007, Burton firmly cemented his role as a setup-caliber reliever during the first half of the year. But he hurt a lat muscle in early July, and ultimately missed most of the second half. Assuming he's healthy—and there's no reason to think he will not be—Burton should vie with David Weathers for the setup job next season.

Francisco Cordero (Reliever)

W	L	ERA	TBF	IP	Hit	HR	SO	BB	HBP	3-Year	Reliability
5	3	3.66	301	71	61	7	75	30	3	+0.22	Low

Coco was the big offseason acquisition, solving what had been perceived as the team's biggest problem—the bullpen. His acquisition pushed everyone back a notch, and the result was a much better bullpen. Cordero himself was not what he was in '07—his strikeout rates were down and walk rates were up (a lot). His fastball velocity hasn't dipped, however, so he should continue to be capable.

Johnny Cueto (Starter)

W	L	ERA	TBF	IP	Hit	HR	SO	BB	HBP	3-Year	Reliability
8	10	5.04	709	162	168	27	131	61	13	-0.40	Very High

Cueto essentially skipped Triple-A to start the season with the Reds last year, so through that lens he had a heck of a season. He had a nice K/BB ratio, though his walk rate was inconsistent—sometimes he had razor precision, and other times he didn't know where it was going. His biggest problem was a propensity to give up the big fly, but if he can get his walk rate down that won't hurt him as much. He's very promising.

Josh Fogg (Starter)

W	L	ERA	TBF	IP	Hit	HR	SO	BB	HBP	3-Year	Reliability
6	8	5.45	564	127	148	21	67	45	7	+0.27	Very High

After a feature performance in the 2007 playoffs, Fogg signed for pennies on the dollar to play with the Reds... but even then wasn't a good value. His peripherals weren't really any different than in prior years. It's just that Fogg will always be a guy who walks a tightrope in a windstorm, and last year, more often than not, he fell off. I'm still not sure how he got 14 starts.

Aaron Harang (Starter)

W	L	ERA	TBF	IP	Hit	HR	SO	BB	HBP	3-Year	Reliability
10	10	4.34	760	180	184	27	148	47	6	+0.21	Very High

The explanation you'll hear for what happened to Harang in 2008 is that Dusty Baker had him pitch three times in eight days (239 pitches), and that this ultimately caused him to get hurt and have a bad season. Whether that's the cause or not, all his peripherals slipped last year. Nevertheless, his best streak was at the end of the season, so I think he's a good bet to rebound next year. That said, the days of Cy Young contention may be behind him.

Daniel Herrera (Reliever)

W	L	ERA	TBF	IP	Hit	HR	SO	BB	HBP	3-Year	Reliability
4	3	4.41	288	66	67	8	51	28	4	-0.13	Low

The 5-foot-8, 140-pound Herrera throws all of 84 mph, but has been effective in the minors because he is one of the few remaining practitioners of the screwball. In theory, it should allow him to be effective against right handers, as it breaks the same direction as a right-handed breaking ball. Whether it works at the major league level, though, is still an open question.

Mike Lincoln (Reliever)

W	L	ERA	TBF	IP	Hit	HR	SO	BB	HBP	3-Year	Reliability
4	4	3.96	306	72	69	8	56	27	3	+0.23	Very Low

Coming off of multiple elbow surgeries and an incredibly long rehab period, Lincoln pitched his way onto the team in spring training and turned in an impressive comeback season. He throws in the low 90s, and mixes in a curve ball. The Reds surprisingly re-signed him to a modest two-year deal, apparently convinced that he'll continue to perform at this level over the next few seasons.

Gary Majewski (Reliever)

W	L	ERA	TBF	IP	Hit	HR	SO	BB	HBP	3-Year	Reliability
3	4	4.76	298	67	76	8	42	26	3	+0.34	Average

Majewski was finally let go after serving as a three-year reminder of the folly of trading starting position players for relievers. He has lost a bit of velocity, but I think the story of the Maj-ek man is that he just was never all that good. He doesn't strike many guys out, and he's not exactly a master of control. He still does induce ground balls at a good clip, so perhaps he could be successful with a good defense and a park that isn't so homer-prone.

Nick Masset (Reliever)

W	L	ERA	TBF	IP	Hit	HR	SO	BB	HBP	3-Year	Reliability
3	5	5.00	306	68	77	8	46	31	3	+0.14	High

Masset may turn out to be the primary return from the Ken Griffey Jr. deal. That he's not particularly impressive says more about Griffey's value than Masset. He induces ground balls at a good clip, but his control is bad and his strikeout rate isn't good.

Micah Owings (Starter)

W	L	ERA	TBF	IP	Hit	HR	SO	BB	HBP	3-Year	Reliability
6	8	4.97	544	124	129	19	91	47	10	+0.19	Very High

Owings appeared in four games with the Reds last year, but has yet to throw a pitch. They used him as a pinch hitter: he sports a career .319/.355/.552 line in 126 plate appearances. The Reds' outfield situation is so desperate that many fans have suggested just letting Owings play out there instead of pitch. As a pitcher, Owings is prone to fly balls and doesn't throw particularly hard, so a Rick Ankiel-type move may indeed turn out to be his best option.

Joshua Roenicke (Reliever)

W	L	ERA	TBF	IP	Hit	HR	SO	BB	HBP	3-Year	Reliability
3	4	4.56	272	61	60	7	56	31	3	+0.14	Very Low

The hard-throwing Roenicke has risen quickly since arriving in the organization. The Reds' bullpen is a bit full, and so would seem to be a longshot to make the team out of spring training. But he seems likely to spend at least some time with the Reds in 2009 as a middle reliever.

Daryl Thompson (Starter)

W	L	ERA	TBF	IP	Hit	HR	SO	BB	HBP	3-Year	Reliability
6	9	5.71	599	133	151	25	77	54	7	-0.34	High

Thompson ascended quickly last season and aroused some optimism among fans before hurting his shoulder at the end of the season. Assuming he heals well, he has a decent fastball and changeup, good control, and a decent shot at taking the No. 5 rotation slot out of spring training.

Edinson Volquez (Starter)

W	L	ERA	TBF	IP	Hit	HR	SO	BB	HBP	3-Year	Reliability
10	9	4.23	748	172	155	21	162	86	9	+0.06	Very High

After years of untapped promise, Volquez finally delivered with the Reds. In him, they seemingly have a legitimate ace with substantial experience and yet, at just 25 years old, lots of life left on his arm. He throws hard, but counters the heat with an excellent change-up. The Reds hope he can keep it up—they want to build their rotation around him.

Sean Watson (Reliever)

W	L	ERA	TBF	IP	Hit	HR	SO	BB	HBP	3-Year	Reliability
3	4	5.68	288	63	65	11	53	38	4	-0.18	Average

This college closer was moved out of the starting role last season and seemed to have some success, judging from his ERA, but his control was beyond horrible. Watson needs a strong Double-A/Triple-A season with much improved command to retain his prospect status.

David Weathers (Reliever)

W	L	ERA	TBF	IP	Hit	HR	SO	BB	HBP	3-Year	Reliability
4	4	4.29	308	71	70	8	45	29	3	—	Average

In last year's Preview, I wrote this: "I've been predicting Stormy Weathers' decline for years now, but he keeps proving me wrong." Same story this year. Weathers actually showed some improvement last year, with a better groundball percentage and slightly better strikeout rate, but both were still below his career norms. After some fairly negative parting comments, Weathers ultimately accepted the Reds' offer of arbitration and will be back for one last year with the team.

Cleveland Indians

by Ryan Richards of Let's Go Tribe (letsgotribe.com)

2009 Indians Projections

Record: 86-76
Division Rank/Games Behind: 1st by 3 games
Runs Scored: 829, 3rd in the league
Runs Allowed: 767, 7th in the league
Park Factor: 1.00, perfectly neutral

What Happened Last Year:

All the main contributors from the previous year's 96-win team returned for 2008, but trouble started early. Victor Martinez got hurt on Opening Day, played injured for a couple of months, then had surgery in June; he wasn't healthy until the end of the season. Jake Westbrook injured his elbow just five starts into the season, undergoing Tommy John surgery in June. Travis Hafner couldn't hit, and eventually missed a significant part of the season due to a bad shoulder; he eventually had to have surgery. Fausto Carmona missed two months with a strained left hip, and even when healthy couldn't throw strikes.

Beyond the injuries, the team just plain didn't hit for the first half of the season. Outstanding pitching kept the Indians competitive through mid-May, but the bottom fell out of the season after that. A 10-game losing streak in late June/early July erased all doubt: 2008 was a lost cause. The past year's Cy Young winner, CC Sabathia, was traded on July 7, and three months of painful baseball loomed. Only it didn't: the offense finally came around and several young players started living up to their potential. The Indians improbably finished 81-81, with a record of 13 games above .500 in the second half.

Cliff Lee and Grady Sizemore were two constants during this bipolar season. Lee had the best season by an Indians starter in a quarter-century—one season after the Indians demoted him to Buffalo while the team was on its way to the playoffs. And Sizemore continued to excel in all phases of the game, setting a career high with 33 home runs and stealing 38 bases in 43 attempts.

Players Lost from Last Year's Team:

By the time the season ended, the Indians had traded any pending free agents of value, so even though they technically will lose only a couple of marginal players from the roster that ended the season, several key players left the club in 2008.

Sabathia was set to head toward richer pastures even before the season began, so it was an easy call to deal him after the Indians fell out of it. During his last years with the Indians, the big left hander combined outstanding stuff with excellent control to go deep into games, saving the bullpen in the process. Replacing his production with one pitcher will be impossible.

In 2003, the cash-strapped Indians signed Casey Blake to a minor-league contract, hoping he'd do until top prospect Corey Smith replaced him. Six years of decent production later, Blake's poised to sign a multi-year contract with the Dodgers and the Indians again are looking for a third baseman. The Indians got a good return when they dealt Blake to Los Angeles in July, but Andy Marte didn't produce during a late-season audition.

Paul Byrd was traded to Boston in August, ending a productive three-season run with the Tribe. Byrd combined outstanding control with, well, not much else as he sprinkled an occasional gem among the usual lot of six-inning tightrope acts. The Indians are not likely to bring him back.

A year after leading the league in saves despite mediocre peripherals, Joe Borowski fell apart completely in 2008. His first outings of the season were atrocious; his stuff had degraded to the point where he wasn't able to get by even by guile. The Indians placed him on the DL in mid-April hoping that rest would bring his effectiveness back, but after one last turn as closer, the Indians finally released him as part of their July purge.

Players Acquired:

The Indians displayed one of baseball's worst bullpens in 2008, and it was a key part of the team's awful first half. Fortunately for the Indians, it was a buyers' market for closers. Over the winter they signed Kerry Wood to a two-year contract. Wood's first season as a closer was a success, if only in that he remained healthy throughout it; his stuff, now packaged into one-inning outings, proved a perfect fit for him. The deal, believe it or not, is the richest free agent contract of the Mark Shapiro Era, speaking to both the Indians' recent timidity in free agency and the desperate need the club had for a good closer.

During the winter meetings, the Indians leveraged their outfield depth for help in two areas of need. They traded Franklin Gutierrez to the Seattle Mariners as part of a three-team trade. In turn, they received Joe Smith, a right-handed sidearmer, from the New York Mets and second baseman Luis Valbuena from Seattle. Smith will go into the bullpen as a matchup right hander, while Valbuena likely will spend much of the season in Columbus.

The Indians traded for everyday utility man Mark DeRosa in late December, giving up Triple-A reliever Jeff Stevens and two lower-level prospects. Although DeRosa can play several positions, the Indians likely will play him mainly at third base, meaning that Jhonny Peralta will remain at shortstop for another season. With DeRosa's contract expiring after this season, the Indians can revisit the infield situation next winter.

Management Is:

Of the four main methods of player acquisition, Mark Shapiro primarily has used two of them to build his teams: trades, and the Latin American academies. Of the other two, free agency and the draft, the first has been largely neglected due to payroll constraints, while the other has been a disappointment despite considerable investment.

On the field, manager Eric Wedge's teams always have played hard, and he seems to work best with younger players. Wedge isn't prone to emotional outbursts on either side of the spectrum, though he is a very good motivator. He likes defined roles in a bullpen, and will follow them religiously, which works well in a consistently good bullpen but horribly in inconsistently good or consistently bad bullpens.

The Minor League System Is:

Improved, thanks mostly to last summer's trades. Catcher Carlos Santana, acquired for Blake, and first baseman-outfielder Matt LaPorta, received for Sabathia, are the system's best prospects. Perennial top prospect Adam Miller, a right-handed pitcher, is still highly regarded, but hasn't been able to stay on the field; he should see some action in the Cleveland bullpen this season if healthy. Outfielder Nick Weglarz has plate discipline and prodigious power at 21 years of age. Left-hander David Huff and outfielders Trevor Crowe and Michael Brantley all could contribute to this season's major-league club.

Due For a Change:

For the worse: Ben Francisco, after posting an .832 OPS in the first half, dropped down to .703 after the All-Star break. It was his first real action in the majors, and it looked like opposing pitchers started to pitch away from his strength (hitting inside fastballs) as the season wore on.

For the better: Martinez didn't hit a home run until the month of September, but that was mainly due to injuries (knee, elbow) that took away his power. After returning from surgery, he began hitting for extra bases again, and should be good to go for 2009.

Reasons to be Optimistic:

Martinez, Hafner, Westbrook and Carmona all spent considerable time on the DL and the team still finished 81-81 last season. On paper, the Indians have drastically improved the back of their bullpen, and have good depth in the rotation and the outfield.

Reasons to be Pessimistic:

The Indians will have to fill three of the five spots in the rotation that started the 2008 season, using players from within the system. And when you start looking at the innings load that Sabathia, Westbrook and Byrd filled over the course of the last couple of seasons (585.1 innings in 2007, for example), the task of replacing them seems even more daunting. Getting power from the four corner positions is going to be a problem, and no one knows what Hafner is going to contribute.

Still Left to Do:

Even though the Indians have good young depth in their rotation, they could use another starter to eat some innings.

Most Likely Team Outcome:

The Indians tread water and finish a few games under .500; too many things have to go right for them to win the division in a normal year.

Player Projections

Batters

Michael Aubrey (First Base)

PA	R	H	2B	3B	HR	RBI	SO	BB	SB	CS	BA	OBP	SLG	OPS	3-Year	Fielding	Reliability
390	42	91	20	1	10	46	64	22	1	1	.253	.301	.398	.699	+0.07	B	Low

Once upon a time, Aubrey was going to be the Indians' first baseman of the future. That was before injury after injury delayed his progress. Last year marked Aubrey's first major league season, and the first in many years in which he was largely healthy. Because of his injuries, the Indians have been given another option year on him, which they'll use. Whether he gets another shot with the Indians depends on whether Kelly Shoppach is still with the team (meaning more Victor Martinez at first), how well Ryan Garko plays, and the progress of Matt LaPorta, assuming he moves to first base. In other words, Aubrey is now a backup plan.

Josh Barfield (Second Base)

PA	R	H	2B	3B	HR	RBI	SO	BB	SB	CS	BA	OBP	SLG	OPS	3-Year	Fielding	Reliability
397	44	97	20	2	8	42	73	18	8	2	.261	.298	.391	.689	+0.07	D	High

Barfield is in much the same situation as Michael Aubrey. While the Indians are thinking of moving Asdrubal Cabrera to shortstop, theoretically giving Barfield another shot, they've also just acquired a young second baseman (Luis Valbuena) who might need a season until he's ready for the majors. That could mean that Barfield may have one more opportunity with the Indians, or it could mean that he's gone. Barfield had a golden opportunity last season when Asdrubal Cabrera was sent to Triple-A, but he got injured shortly after his recall and by the time he returned Cabrera had regained his hitting stroke.

Asdrubal Cabrera (Second Base)

PA	R	H	2B	3B	HR	RBI	SO	BB	SB	CS	BA	OBP	SLG	OPS	3-Year	Fielding	Reliability
572	64	136	27	3	9	56	99	48	7	3	.270	.338	.389	.727	+0.05	C	Very High

Like the rest of the offense, Cabrera struggled the first few months of the year, hitting an anemic .184/.282/.247 in the first half. He was sent down to Buffalo to work on his hitting stroke. He came back with a modified batting stance and a rejuvenated bat, hitting .320/.398/.464 after his return. The defense had always been there, even at a fairly new position for him. Going into his age-23 season, everything seems set for a breakout.

Jamey Carroll (Second Base)

PA	R	H	2B	3B	HR	RBI	SO	BB	SB	CS	BA	OBP	SLG	OPS	3-Year	Fielding	Reliability
402	42	93	15	3	0	27	60	37	7	3	.267	.343	.327	.670	-0.04	B	High

Carroll came in handy for the Indians, what with Asdrubal Cabrera's struggles and Josh Barfield's injury. Carroll filled in at second and third throughout the season, and was a competent everyday starter at second for about two months. As a bonus, Carroll had a good offensive season. Picking up his option was a no-brainer, especially with the unsettled infield situation.

Shin-Soo Choo (Right Field)

PA	R	H	2B	3B	HR	RBI	SO	BB	SB	CS	BA	OBP	SLG	OPS	3-Year	Fielding	Reliability
389	52	100	21	3	13	52	77	40	5	1	.291	.368	.484	.852	+0.06	B	High

In what was his last opportunity to win a starting job, Choo took full advantage of the at-bats, hitting a torrid .343/.424/.614 in 243 second-half plate appearances. He had missed most of 2007 with an elbow injury, and the Indians were out of options on him. Even after elbow surgery, Choo's arm is among the strongest in the game, making right field his best position. He's the starter in right, especially now that Franklin Gutierrez has moved on.

Trevor Crowe (Left Field)

PA	R	H	2B	3B	HR	RBI	SO	BB	SB	CS	BA	OBP	SLG	OPS	3-Year	Fielding	Reliability
445	46	92	18	3	4	33	81	41	11	6	.232	.307	.323	.630	+0.01	B	High

The player who gained the most from Franklin Gutierrez being traded was Crowe; the Indians now need a backup center fielder and pinch runner, and Crowe fits both bills. He rebounded from a poor 2007 by hitting a combined .274/.350/.486 for Akron and Buffalo, and while that line doesn't justify a starting major league job, he's ready to be a fourth outfielder. Michael Brantley, acquired in the Sabathia deal, has a similar skill set, but Crowe's a better defender in center.

David Dellucci (Left Field)

PA	R	H	2B	3B	HR	RBI	SO	BB	SB	CS	BA	OBP	SLG	OPS	3-Year	Fielding	Reliability
360	42	82	17	3	9	41	69	29	3	1	.255	.325	.410	.735	—	C	Average

Platoon mate Jason Michaels was dealt away during the spring offensive swoon, and although Dellucci hit down the stretch, he likewise should be on a short leash. His best defensive position is DH because of a very weak arm, and if he isn't hitting for power, there won't be any justification in keeping him around.

Ben Francisco (Left Field)

PA	R	H	2B	3B	HR	RBI	SO	BB	SB	CS	BA	OBP	SLG	OPS	3-Year	Fielding	Reliability
537	63	128	28	2	14	63	98	41	7	4	.264	.325	.417	.742	+0.01	C	Very High

After the Indians dealt Jason Michaels in early May, they brought up Francisco, hoping for an offensive spark. He immediately paid dividends, hitting .294/.355/.477 in the first two months after the call-up. For a while, he seemed the only player in the lineup hitting with any consistency. His production tailed off in the second half, though, as opposing pitchers started pitching him down and away.

Ryan Garko (First Base)

PA	R	H	2B	3B	HR	RBI	SO	BB	SB	CS	BA	OBP	SLG	OPS	3-Year	Fielding	Reliability
532	63	128	25	1	17	69	89	42	0	1	.272	.348	.438	.786	+0.01	C	Very High

When Garko isn't hitting, as happened early last season, his deficiencies are on display for all to see: He's not a good defender at first and is one of the slowest base runners in the American League. Like the rest of the team, he hit in the second half, but if the Indians keep Kelly Shoppach, his playing time is going to be curtailed dramatically, as that will mean more Victor Martinez at first.

Travis Hafner (Designated Hitter)

PA	R	H	2B	3B	HR	RBI	SO	BB	SB	CS	BA	OBP	SLG	OPS	3-Year	Fielding	Reliability
393	51	87	18	1	16	55	79	57	1	1	.265	.379	.472	.851	-0.03	—	Very High

On a team that's lacking power at the normal power positions, getting the old Travis Hafner back for 2009 is almost essential if the Indians are to contend. Hafner was never right in 2008, and had to have offseason surgery to strengthen his right shoulder. The Indians still owe Hafner $51.75 million over the next four seasons, so his health has a large financial impact as well.

Andy Marte (Third Base)

PA	R	H	2B	3B	HR	RBI	SO	BB	SB	CS	BA	OBP	SLG	OPS	3-Year	Fielding	Reliability
368	38	81	18	1	10	43	72	22	1	1	.243	.291	.392	.683	+0.02	B	High

At this point, the chances of Marte ever playing for the Indians are pretty slim. His last chance was this past season, but it really wasn't much of a chance, as he started only 11 games in April and May. He played more regularly after Casey Blake was dealt, but couldn't take advantage of the playing time and ended the season with a 74 OPS+.

Victor Martinez (Catcher)

PA	R	H	2B	3B	HR	RBI	SO	BB	SB	CS	BA	OBP	SLG	OPS	3-Year	Fielding	Reliability
426	50	109	24	0	10	52	55	40	0	1	.288	.359	.431	.790	-0.02	C	Very High

On Opening Day, Martinez strained his hamstring and had to miss several games. He tried to play through the injury, in addition to a sore elbow that wasn't disclosed at the time in order to prevent teams from running on him. Finally, the elbow flared up again in early June, and he underwent surgery. During his time playing through the injuries, Martinez slugged just .333, though he continued to hit for a decent average; it was obvious in retrospect that the elbow injury completely took away his power. After he returned late in the season, his power returned, so it looks like there will be no long-term effects. That being said, Kelly Shoppach's offensive emergence should allow the Indians to play Martinez more at first and reduce the strain that the body of a full-time catcher goes through.

Jhonny Peralta (Shortstop)

PA	R	H	2B	3B	HR	RBI	SO	BB	SB	CS	BA	OBP	SLG	OPS	3-Year	Fielding	Reliability
596	74	151	30	2	22	83	122	50	3	1	.281	.343	.468	.811	+0.07	D	Very High

With both Victor Martinez and Travis Hafner out of commission most of the season, Peralta partially helped fill the middle-of-the-order void; he slugged 69 extra-base hits, good for 10th in the league, and his .473 slugging percentage far outpaced that of any other AL shortstop. He also had a pretty decent defensive year, still limited in range, yes, but was good at turning double plays and committed just 14 errors, a career low. Peralta is playing some third base in the winter ball in case the Indians decide to move him. As it stands, Peralta isn't hurting the team at shortstop, but the Indians could move a better defensive player there while filling the third base hole.

Kelly Shoppach (Catcher)

PA	R	H	2B	3B	HR	RBI	SO	BB	SB	CS	BA	OBP	SLG	OPS	3-Year	Fielding	Reliability
362	45	85	20	0	17	55	103	30	0	1	.265	.337	.487	.824	-0.03	C	Average

Victor Martinez' injuries gave Kelly Shoppach an opportunity to play every day for four months; previously, even though he was playing more than a typical backup catcher, he'd get only a couple starts a week. As he played regularly from June on, he not only provided offense from the catching position, he became one of the team's most consistent power hitters, finishing third on the team with 21 home runs (the two ahead of him, Grady Sizemore and Jhonny Peralta, also played positions teams usually don't get much power from). It makes all kinds of sense to deal Shoppach for an area of need; the Indians have a couple of good catching prospects in Carlos Santana and Wyatt Toregas, and good, relatively young catchers are hard to come by.

Grady Sizemore (Center Field)

PA	R	H	2B	3B	HR	RBI	SO	BB	SB	CS	BA	OBP	SLG	OPS	3-Year	Fielding	Reliability
660	101	160	36	5	29	94	125	82	27	4	.285	.383	.523	.906	+0.07	C	Very High

Sizemore just keeps getting better. In 2008 he stole 38 bases in 43 opportunities while setting a career high with 33 home runs and reducing his strikeouts at the same time. His 77 extra-base hits ranked second in the American League. He also won his second Gold Glove, and earned his first Silver Slugger Award. Had the Indians been a contender, he probably would have won the AL MVP. There aren't many things he can't do well, and I don't think he's reached his career peak.

Luis Valbuena (Second Base)

PA	R	H	2B	3B	HR	RBI	SO	BB	SB	CS	BA	OBP	SLG	OPS	3-Year	Fielding	Reliability
556	59	125	20	4	7	48	84	47	10	5	.253	.317	.352	.669	+0.05	C	Very High

Not much of a prospect before, Valbuena broke out in a big way in 2008, putting himself on the map by catching fire in West Tennessee and holding his own in Tacoma. His combination of a compact, line drive swing and above-average discipline make him a constant threat to reach base, and while he's not known for his power, he could knock ten out of the park without all that much trouble. What's most impressive about Valbuena, though, is his defense around second base, where he possesses solid range and outstanding instincts. He made some plays in

Seattle that Jose Lopez wouldn't dream of completing. Valbuena's not quite ready yet, but with a few more months of Triple-A seasoning, he could and should be set to begin a long and successful major league career.

Pitchers

Rafael Betancourt (Reliever)

W	L	ERA	TBF	IP	Hit	HR	SO	BB	HBP	3-Year	Reliability
4	4	3.91	301	72	67	8	64	21	2	+0.22	Low

Although Joe Borowski's collapse got the headlines, Betancourt's bad season was more devastating to the bullpen. His WHIP almost doubled from the season before, indicative of a loss of control in and out of the strike zone. The velocity on his fastball remained in the low 90s, but his previously pinpoint location wasn't there. His K/BB ratio, normally among the best in baseball, tilted to around league average. For a reliever whose bread and butter is an accurate fastball, that dropoff was critical.

Joe Borowski (Reliever)

W	L	ERA	TBF	IP	Hit	HR	SO	BB	HBP	3-Year	Reliability
2	3	4.55	197	45	46	6	34	17	1	—	Low

The Indians knew they were taking a chance when they signed Borowski after the 2006 season. The Phillies had some interest, but pulled their two-year offer after looking at the health of his shoulder. That allowed the Indians to ink him to a one-year deal, and while he didn't look good doing it, he was healthy and effective enough to close games in 2007. But he had nothing left after that season, which was readily apparent as the 2008 campaign got under way.

Fausto Carmona (Starter)

W	L	ERA	TBF	IP	Hit	HR	SO	BB	HBP	3-Year	Reliability
8	8	4.04	619	143	150	11	80	58	8	-0.01	Very High

Blessed with natural movement on his fastball, Carmona had an outstanding 2007 season. But that natural movement showed its other side in 2008, when he couldn't get his pitches consistently in the strike zone. Even though his ERA looked good early in the season, it was deceiving; groundball double plays were getting him out of jams. He was still getting his ground balls, but he was also walking batters at a disturbing rate: In April, he walked 26 and struck out 13 in 34.2 innings. Unfortunately, he didn't have the opportunity to work himself out of it—he went on the DL in May with a hip injury. After he came back in late July, the walks continued to haunt him through the end of the season. Getting his mechanics in order will be one of the keys to the 2009 season.

Brendan Donnelly (Reliever)

W	L	ERA	TBF	IP	Hit	HR	SO	BB	HBP	3-Year	Reliability
2	2	4.11	172	40	38	4	29	18	2	—	Very Low

The Indians signed Donnelly knowing that he'd miss most of the season recovering from Tommy John surgery, but betting on having him available for the stretch run. That stretch run never happened, but the Indians did get him on the mound for 13.2 innings at the end of the season. Donnelly doesn't have enough service time to become a free agent, but he had his free agent eligibility negotiated into his 2008 contract.

David Huff (Starter)

W	L	ERA	TBF	IP	Hit	HR	SO	BB	HBP	3-Year	Reliability
7	8	4.47	570	133	135	18	95	47	6	-0.13	Average

Huff hasn't thrown a major-league pitch, but he has a good shot at winning a spot in the rotation this season. The Indians didn't call him up in September because he'd thrown over 80 more innings than in 2007, not because he wasn't a part of the future. The 2006 sandwich pick broke out in 2008, striking out 143, walking 29, and allowing 112 hits in 145.1 innings between Akron (Double-A) and Buffalo (Triple-A). The southpaw throws a low 90s fastball, an outstanding change-up, and a slider.

Zach Jackson (Starter)

W	L	ERA	TBF	IP	Hit	HR	SO	BB	HBP	3-Year	Reliability
6	9	5.50	592	131	157	18	60	54	8	+0.05	Very High

Jackson came to the Indians as a minor part of the Sabathia deal, and made nine starts for Cleveland, pitching much better than his recent minor league numbers would indicate. Jackson's out of options and will have a tough time making the club, so he probably won't be with the organization come Opening Day.

Masahide Kobayashi (Reliever)

W	L	ERA	TBF	IP	Hit	HR	SO	BB	HBP	3-Year	Reliability
4	3	4.00	279	65	67	6	44	22	2	+0.14	Very Low

Kobayashi was one of five Indians relievers to record a save in 2008, doing a decent job in the first half but faltering after the All-Star break to the point that he was barely used after July. His secondary pitches (slider, change-up) were clocked in the mid-80s, not enough difference from his fastball (about 90 mph) to keep hitters off balance.

Aaron Laffey (Starter)

W	L	ERA	TBF	IP	Hit	HR	SO	BB	HBP	3-Year	Reliability
8	9	4.65	677	153	177	16	77	55	10	-0.34	Very High

After starting the year in Buffalo, Laffey was recalled in late April after Jake Westbrook injured a side muscle. He made 16 straight starts, but began to struggle in July and was optioned back to Buffalo at the end of the month. The main culprit for Laffey's problems was that he wasn't getting the same ground ball rates as earlier in the season. Laffey tops out in the high 80s, but when his pitches are darting down in the strike zone, he can cruise through an outing. He'll be a frontrunner for a rotation spot this spring.

Cliff Lee (Starter)

W	L	ERA	TBF	IP	Hit	HR	SO	BB	HBP	3-Year	Reliability
11	9	4.13	777	184	192	20	132	50	7	+0.21	Very High

In this space last year I called for the Indians to trade Lee while he still had some value. Whoops. Lee strengthened his core over the winter, cleaned up his delivery, and proceeded to have one of the best pitching seasons in franchise history, posting a 175 ERA+ and walking just 34 batters in a career-high 223.3 innings. In the process, Lee transformed himself from a fly-ball pitcher with only average control to a control pitcher with groundball tendencies. In 2008 Lee consistently pitched ahead of hitters, not only spotting his fastball for strikes but putting those fastballs on the corners. Even assuming Lee's turned a corner in his career, he's not going to touch what he did last season, but if he falls off, it's going to be based on the new Cliff Lee career path, not the old one.

Jensen Lewis (Reliever)

W	L	ERA	TBF	IP	Hit	HR	SO	BB	HBP	3-Year	Reliability
4	5	4.90	349	79	82	10	63	34	5	-0.12	High

Lewis was one of the bright spots of last year's bullpen, and he ended the season as the closer, not blowing a save during his tenure. Now that the Indians have spent $20 million on Kerry Wood, Lewis will go back to a setup role, but should be a credible backup in case he's needed.

Tom Mastny (Reliever)

W	L	ERA	TBF	IP	Hit	HR	SO	BB	HBP	3-Year	Reliability
3	4	4.36	273	62	60	6	58	30	3	+0.21	Low

Mastny was up and down all season, filling in when the Indians needed an extra reliever, but never getting a consistent look. He'll be playing in Japan next season; the Indians sold him to Yokohama of the Japanese Central League in December.

Rafael Perez (Reliever)

W	L	ERA	TBF	IP	Hit	HR	SO	BB	HBP	3-Year	Reliability
5	4	3.43	324	78	71	7	72	27	3	+0.10	High

"Raffy Left" was for a time the only consistent reliever in the bullpen. In all, he made 73 appearances, nearly all of them in close games. And those weren't just one-or-two-batter matchups; he threw 76.3 innings, one of the higher workloads for a reliever in the AL. As his inning totals indicate, Perez can get righties out, using a back-foot slider to jam right-handed hitters, but he's especially tough on left handers (.599 OPS against). He'll again be counted on in crucial late-inning spots in 2009.

Anthony Reyes (Starter)

W	L	ERA	TBF	IP	Hit	HR	SO	BB	HBP	3-Year	Reliability
6	8	4.97	555	126	134	19	80	50	7	+0.24	Very High

In the midst of the July trade-fest, the Indians took a flier on Reyes, who had fallen out of favor with St. Louis management because of a difference in pitching philosophies. The Indians were shedding starting pitchers, so Reyes joined the rotation and pitched very well before missing his last few starts with elbow soreness; perhaps all he needed was a change of scenery. If he's healthy, he'll be in the rotation.

Jeremy Sowers (Starter)

W	L	ERA	TBF	IP	Hit	HR	SO	BB	HBP	3-Year	Reliability
8	10	4.88	727	166	190	21	80	56	6	+0.06	Very High

Sowers needs to have everything working for him in order to be effective; if he's behind hitters, his outings will be short. The finesse left-hander throws three pitches, including a high-80s fastball, and although he generally has a good plan of attack, he can't get away with mistakes. Opposing hitters batted .291/.345/.481 against him in 2008, which isn't a great sign.

Jake Westbrook (Starter)

W	L	ERA	TBF	IP	Hit	HR	SO	BB	HBP	3-Year	Reliability
6	5	4.21	424	98	111	8	55	31	3	+0.19	Very High

He landed on the disabled list twice in 2008, the second time with serious ligament damage in his right elbow. He underwent Tommy John surgery in June, and won't be back until the middle of this season. Before the injury, Westbrook was one of the more durable starters in the AL, and was normally good for 30 starts and 200 innings of groundball-filled pitching. Between Westbrook and Travis Hafner, who was also injured most of 2008, the Indians have invested $21.5 million of their 2009 payroll. That means about 25 percent of their projected payroll is tied up in two players who will be coming off major surgeries.

Colorado Rockies

by Brandi Griffin of Purple Row (purplerow.com)

2009 Rockies Projections

Record: 85-77
Division Rank/Games Behind: 1st by 2 games
Runs Scored: 806, 4th in the league
Runs Allowed: 764, 11th in the league
Park Factor: 1.09, heaven for hitters

What Happened Last Year:

The 2007 NL Champs stumbled severely out of the gate in 2008, falling to 16 games below .500 by the end of May. That should have eliminated even thinking about another late-season miracle run, but it turned out the rest of the NL West was just about as pathetic, and the Rockies harbored hopes for another comeback as late as August. The Dodgers mercifully put that foolishness to rest.

Players Lost from Last Year's Team:

Matt Holliday, Brian Fuentes, Willy Taveras, Matt Herges and some Livan Hernandez-sized scraps.

Players Acquired:

Huston Street, Greg Smith, Carlos Gonzalez, Alan Embree.

Holliday's loss from the lineup will have some impact, no doubt, but replacing Taveras' .308 OBP in the leadoff slot in 2008 with Ryan Spilborghs will have a greater positive effect than the downgrade from Holliday to Seth Smith.

The bullpen's major loss will be Fuentes, who performed about as well as he ever has in 2008. The Holliday trade to Oakland tried to address this with the acquisition of Street to compete with Manny Corpas for the 2009 closer job. The club hopes the loser of that battle will be a dominant set-up man. Added to Taylor Buchholz, so the plan goes, the Rockies will have a trio of quality high-leverage relievers, and Luis Vizcaino, Jason Grilli and Embree should provide stability in the middle innings. The issue is that neither Street nor Corpas had a 2008 that leaves a whole lot of confidence in his ability to return to an elite level in 2009. The Rockies are gambling that the injuries and underperformance of last season are in the past.

Management Is:

A constant beacon in the swirling darkness. Oh wait, maybe management is the constant darkness around the swirling beacon. It's constant, let's just leave it at that.

The Minor League System Is:

Thinned a bit for the moment, but still with a couple of intriguing prospects. Dexter Fowler should emerge as the Rockies' starting center fielder by the end of the 2009 season, while right-handed pitcher Jhoulys Chacin had a huge season in 2008 and hopes to build upon it. Chris Nelson could be the Rockies' most interesting disappointment if he isn't able to regain some of the luster he once had as a first-round draft pick. He's still being counted on to emerge as the second baseman of the next wave of talent that the Rockies are forming around Fowler, Troy Tulowitzki, Ian Stewart, Gonzalez and Chris Iannetta, but a poor showing and a broken hand in Tulsa in 2008 have many observers souring on his chances to be a productive major leaguer. His infield mate in Tulsa, Eric Young Jr., also suffered a broken hand during the season, but didn't suffer nearly the ill effects, and could emerge as an important utility player for the Rockies in the near future.

Due For a Change:

The projections are seeing a considerable improvement for Tulowitzki, but what if last season's .263/.332/.401 line is closer to reality for the young shortstop? There are reasons to trust the figures and expect otherwise, starting with some inexplicably poor lines for Tulo at home.

Reasons to be Optimistic:

The 2007 season provided a prototype for a successful Rockies team in the post-humidor era. Modeling off that playoff run, a ratio of 850 runs scored to 750 runs allowed could be seen as targets that the team needs to hit or exceed to be safely competitive. That would imply around a 90-win team, which should be enough in a weak division such as today's NL West. As the division improves, the Rockies will have to find ways to score more, but without significant changes to the team's revenue stream, shooting for too much lower on the run prevention scale might prove a problem.

At any rate, scoring more than 850 requires around 5.25 runs a game, and by establishing that target, we can start seeing what it would take for the Rockies to get to that level. Using simulators with THT's projections of the most likely Opening Day lineups still leaves the Rockies a bit shy, but considerably better than they performed in 2008, right around five runs per game, or 810 for the season. The reason they are likely to perform so well is due to OBP projections that are above average (even with a Coors Field adjustment for half the games) for every position except second base and left field. While I wouldn't hold out much hope for Clint Barmes breaking into the positive category in 2009, either Smith or Ian Stewart could be plus players in terms of avoiding outs in 2009.

So, just living up to expectations should get the Rockies part of the way there on offense, and if Spilborghs and Iannetta can hit closer to their 2008 results than their 2009 projections, the Rockies will have a much easier time reaching that 850-run level.

What reason is there to expect that these two might? To begin with, both display exceptional plate discipline. When it comes to laying off pitches outside the strike zone, according to stats compiled at FanGraphs.com, they rank in the NL's top 10 players (Iannetta No. 6, Spilborghs No. 9) with at least 250 plate appearances. Adding Todd Helton (No. 7), the Rockies' projected 2009 lineup boasts an unrivaled trio in this department.

While this will help drive up the team OBP, just laying off bad pitches doesn't necessarily equate to being able to produce when strikes are thrown. After all, that discipline list is topped by lightweight Luis Castillo and includes such luminescent bats as Doug Mientkiewicz and Carlos Ruiz as well as proven hitters like Helton and Chipper Jones.

Thankfully for the Rockies, Iannetta and Spilborghs have been able to perform at that higher level of hitting thanks to solid line drive rates and being able to recognize strikes as well as balls. Iannetta's exceptionally keen understanding of the strike zone might get overlooked due to his relatively high strikeout numbers and because he plays for Colorado, but the spread between the percentage of pitches he swung at in the strike zone (72.3 percent) and those that he swung at outside the zone (16.2 percent) was the largest in the majors by a substantial margin in 2008. It's a good thing Iannetta lays off junk so often, because unlike Jones and other standout hitters, he can't seem to connect when he goes reaching. He was one of just three players last season who didn't connect with swung-at pitches outside the

strike zone at least 40 percent of the time. The other two were masters of the whiff, Kelly Shoppach and Mark Reynolds, with Ryan Howard being next down the list. So while Iannetta did strike out 27 percent of the time, things could have been a whole lot worse without the pitch recognition.

On the run prevention front, once again the Rockies won't have the aces of their division rivals, but they are hoping they can trump the NL West with three kings, a jack and a joker in the rotation instead. Ubaldo Jimenez and Aaron Cook both registered an ERA+ in the 110-119 range for each of the past two seasons, and while THT is pessimistic about their chances of repeating that success, other projections are a bit more sanguine. The Rockies also feel that Jeff Francis can bounce back from an injury-plagued year to pitch the way he did in 2007.

Extending the poker analogy, Jorge De La Rosa might be the team's surprise card. The once-promising hurler, who has been passed around like a hot potato among Arizona, Boston, Milwaukee and Kansas City, finally lived up to his potential from June onward in 2008, and looked particularly strong after the All-Star break (7-3, 3.08 ERA, 68/38 K/BB, 73 IP). His continued high walk numbers are going to lead some to see that run as a fluke, but there was one very strong piece of evidence that there may have been something more to JDLR's renaissance. According to FanGraphs, while he was struggling with the Royals in 2007, De La Rosa's fastball averaged 91.4 mph. In May of 2008, after he had been traded for Ramon Ramirez and had an 8.39 ERA for the Rockies, his velocity was even less, at 90.8 mph. After some mechanical tweaks, his fastball velocity increased in each subsequent month, until it was averaging 93.7 mph in five September starts in which he registered a 2.67 ERA. The added velocity didn't result in many more swings and misses, but it did result in his BABIP dipping from .363 in May to .264 in September. If he starts well and his velocity is still up, it could be an indicator that the Rockies are in for a special season from him.

The final piece to the rotation could be Greg Smith, Greg Reynolds, Jason Hirsh, Franklin Morales or a late free agent pickup like Tim Redding. These hurlers all project to see varying degrees of pain for the Rockies in 2009, so the team is looking for at least one of them to come to camp with some hitherto unseen ability to create more outs and allow fewer runners to cross the plate. It's not a terrible strategy—all have shown minor league dominance at times—but the risk that none of the youth live up to their promise would be why the Rockies would target a stable presence like Redding for insurance.

Reasons to be Pessimistic:

For starters, Helton's .264/.391/.388 line from last season must be improved upon if the Rockies hope to sniff the playoffs again in the remainder of his contract. The projections seem as hopeful as Rockies fans are, but is this realistic? Helton, with a referral from Randy Johnson, visited and then underwent the knife of spinal specialist Dr. Robert Watkins at the end of last season to repair an irritated disc. Reports in the offseason have been encouraging, but back injuries are notoriously fickle. The Rockies don't necessarily need a lot of power from Helton and can probably be competitive in the division if he just reaches that .292/.401/.445 projection, but even if he does return to hit like that, he's likely to need plenty of rest and bench time, and the expected downgrade to the offense that takes place when Helton's out of the lineup makes first base a potential liability for 2009.

Across the diamond, Garrett Atkins' slide over the last two seasons eroded his trade value to the point that the Rockies seem inclined to keep him for at least the start of the 2009 season in hopes that he can bring his numbers back up. A .300/.359/.492 line as projected would be a solid start, particularly if he could perform a little better than the projected F- on defense. As long as he's a Rockie, Atkins will be an important part of the team's offense. If he is in a third straight season of decline out of the gate and doesn't rebound as projected, the Rockies' chances will suffer greatly.

Speaking of defense, we might as well also bring up Brad Hawpe, who could have been the worst defending outfielder in the game last season. Added to Atkins and

Our Favorite Rockies Blogs:

RoxHead (http://www.roxhead.com/)

Rockies Magic Number (http://rockiesmagicnumber.blogspot.com)

Up in the Rockies (http://mvn.com/mlb-rockies/)

Spilborghs as a projected liability in center, the Rockies will have some serious defensive issues.

Still Left to Do:

With Spilborghs expected to start in center until Fowler or Gonzalez proves ready, and with Atkins expected to see most of the time at third until he's traded, the Rockies are faced with a decision on replacing Holliday in left field: Seth Smith or Ian Stewart? (Expect the ascension of one of those center fielders and an Atkins trade at roughly the same time during the 2009 season.)

Smith's a quality hitter, projects well, and would be a solid defender; Stewart is younger and has more upside at the plate, but would be in an unfamiliar position. If the team decides to go with Smith as a starter, look for Stewart to be rotated around second, third, left, right and first until Atkins is moved, essentially taking the left-handed version of Jeff Baker's job.

Most Likely Team Outcome:

I'm an eternal Rockies optimist. I see the team being around 810 runs for, and 780 runs against, or about 84-78 right now, but Colorado could be better if De La Rosa and Jimenez are capable of full seasons like their second half performances and if Iannetta continues to break out. The team could be worse if Helton and Atkins continue to slide.

Player Projections

Batters

Garrett Atkins (Third Base)

PA	R	H	2B	3B	HR	RBI	SO	BB	SB	CS	BA	OBP	SLG	OPS	3-Year	Fielding	Reliability
607	78	164	35	2	22	88	91	51	2	1	.300	.359	.492	.851	-0.03	F-	Very High

Atkins probably will need to be traded relatively early in 2009 for the Rockies to make the most out of their roster, but it will be interesting to see if the team is brave enough to do it if he starts strong. Rockies fans in general did not take well to the departure of Matt Holliday, so losing another of their favorite hitters early in the season will look like a quick white flag and salary dump.

Jeff Baker (Second Base)

PA	R	H	2B	3B	HR	RBI	SO	BB	SB	CS	BA	OBP	SLG	OPS	3-Year	Fielding	Reliability
358	45	89	19	2	14	51	83	28	2	1	.275	.336	.477	.813	+0.00	D	High

Baker's perhaps the Rockies' streakiest hitter: For every month like September (1.008 OPS) or June (1.033) there will be one or two like August (.392) and April (.477). I wish there were some sort of flashing light we could attach to him to tell us when he's on. It would make filling out winning lineup cards for Clint Hurdle so much easier.

Clint Barmes (Second Base)

PA	R	H	2B	3B	HR	RBI	SO	BB	SB	CS	BA	OBP	SLG	OPS	3-Year	Fielding	Reliability
443	51	108	23	4	10	49	69	21	8	3	.267	.313	.417	.730	-0.03	B	High

Clint Barmes in 2008 showed that his pre-deermeat-injury rookie self maybe wasn't the complete mirage it was made out to be—he turned in his best season since falling down the stairs with Todd Helton's game. The trouble is that the best aspects of this performance were entirely at Coors Field. Plenty of middle infielders aren't able to take advantage of the beneficial aspects of altitude, so having a guy like Barmes who does isn't bad. The bad thing is when it's assumed that the Denver Barmes will be the same player in San Diego.

Dexter Fowler (Center Field)

PA	R	H	2B	3B	HR	RBI	SO	BB	SB	CS	BA	OBP	SLG	OPS	3-Year	Fielding	Reliability
513	64	124	24	7	7	49	99	48	12	6	.277	.355	.409	.764	+0.09	C	High

No pressure or anything, but Fowler could be the key to the Rockies' whole season. A trip to China for the Olympics in 2008 put the brakes on what had been a breakout season. I wonder if the government kidnapped him and replaced him with a clone; on his return to Triple-A and in a September call-up he did not look like the same player who had left to play for Team USA. At any rate, he shows that there is still room for development, but the Rockies could use his impact bat and plus glove in center field sooner rather than later.

Carlos Gonzalez (Center Field)

PA	R	H	2B	3B	HR	RBI	SO	BB	SB	CS	BA	OBP	SLG	OPS	3-Year	Fielding	Reliability
550	64	137	32	4	15	68	119	30	6	3	.268	.310	.434	.744	+0.05	C	High

As much as I want to see Alex Rios, I can't help but see Juan Encarnacion. The evidence that says he'll be a star is based almost entirely upon projectability, and that's becoming an issue now that he's 23 years old. Everything about him is aesthetically pleasing—the sweet left-handed stroke, the long strides in the field and on the basepaths, and the cannon arm—but it hasn't translated to performance either in the majors or the high minors. The upshot is that if he can even be average at the plate while playing plus defense in center, he'll still be a valuable player.

Brad Hawpe (Right Field)

PA	R	H	2B	3B	HR	RBI	SO	BB	SB	CS	BA	OBP	SLG	OPS	3-Year	Fielding	Reliability
538	74	132	27	3	24	81	122	69	1	1	.285	.378	.512	.890	-0.03	F	Very High

Hawpe's bat barely covers his atrocious defense, but with Todd Helton firmly planted at first with a no-trade clause, the Rockies don't have many alternatives. In a perfect world, the Rockies would have Dexter Fowler and either Seth Smith or Carlos Gonzalez develop into contending-caliber outfielders in 2009 so that the team could ship Brad while his value is still relatively high. For this next season, though, Hawpe will need to show at least a little more range if the Rockies want to compete.

Todd Helton (First Base)

PA	R	H	2B	3B	HR	RBI	SO	BB	SB	CS	BA	OBP	SLG	OPS	3-Year	Fielding	Reliability
461	58	112	25	2	10	53	60	71	0	1	.292	.401	.445	.846	—	A	Very High

Helton's back problems led to a woeful year for him and the Rockies in 2008. He had his lowest output since taking over the starting first baseman job from Andres Gallaraga in 1998. Helton's career at this point turns to his legacy, and while the Hall of Fame is unlikely, it might not be out of the question if he can find a few more late-career flowers like his 2007 campaign.

Chris Iannetta (Catcher)

PA	R	H	2B	3B	HR	RBI	SO	BB	SB	CS	BA	OBP	SLG	OPS	3-Year	Fielding	Reliability
404	53	95	20	2	15	55	80	49	1	0	.278	.378	.480	.858	+0.02	C	High

Iannetta seized control of the Rockies' catching job with his standout performance in 2008. The next step would be to establish himself as one of the NL's bright lights at the position. If he does continue to hit like he did last season, expect to see the Rockies aggressively pursue an extension for this core piece next winter.

Joseph Koshansky (First Base)

PA	R	H	2B	3B	HR	RBI	SO	BB	SB	CS	BA	OBP	SLG	OPS	3-Year	Fielding	Reliability
513	69	124	26	2	28	86	141	51	2	1	.273	.347	.523	.870	+0.06	B	Very High

Koshansky is the safety in the system in case a lot of things go wrong. He's got a powerful, but slow bat, and will be good for a Rob Deer-like line at the MLB level, but there won't be much more besides a few well-struck baseballs to show for it.

Christopher Nelson (Shortstop)

PA	R	H	2B	3B	HR	RBI	SO	BB	SB	CS	BA	OBP	SLG	OPS	3-Year	Fielding	Reliability
518	52	106	23	4	9	48	106	32	8	2	.224	.279	.346	.625	+0.05	F	High

A disappointing campaign in Tulsa was followed by a high note as Nelson was able to turn things around a little in the hitter-friendly Arizona Fall League. He's going to be playing in another accommodating hitting environment in Colorado Springs next season, and it may be difficult to know whether he's truly rediscovered his groove or is just using altitude effects to his advantage. Keep an eye on the ISO. Nelson should be a power threat, and if it's around .200—high for a middle infielder but about right at that altitude, it will be a sign that a comeback is legit.

Jayson Nix (Second Base)

PA	R	H	2B	3B	HR	RBI	SO	BB	SB	CS	BA	OBP	SLG	OPS	3-Year	Fielding	Reliability
409	49	93	19	1	14	50	85	28	11	2	.252	.309	.422	.731	+0.07	C	High

Nix was one of the first offseason victims of the Rockies' depth in middle infielders. He was given a shot to stick with the club as the starting second baseman in 2008, but a miserable first month gave him a quick trip back to Triple-A. He had one more brief opportunity in the summer, but the next demotion to The Springs was his last. He was cut after the season and signed with the White Sox.

Scott Podsednik (Center Field)

PA	R	H	2B	3B	HR	RBI	SO	BB	SB	CS	BA	OBP	SLG	OPS	3-Year	Fielding	Reliability
314	37	75	15	3	2	25	51	27	10	3	.268	.337	.365	.702	-0.04	D	Average

The Rockies relied on Podsednik as a defensive outfielder/left-handed pinch hitter off the bench, and since he wasn't really good at either job, it's sort of surprising that they are thinking about bringing him back.

Omar Quintanilla (Shortstop)

PA	R	H	2B	3B	HR	RBI	SO	BB	SB	CS	BA	OBP	SLG	OPS	3-Year	Fielding	Reliability
386	42	94	22	2	4	37	67	31	3	1	.275	.338	.386	.724	+0.02	D	Average

Quintanilla's glove is good enough for an everyday MLB job, but his bat thus far hasn't been. He would get more playing time if he showed a regular platoon advantage or an ability to make some solid contact on the road, but he's never hit RHPs much better than he's hit southpaws, and if he's not producing in Coors Field, there's probably not much chance that he'll produce elsewhere. With Chris Nelson, Eric Young and Corey Wimberly at Triple-A, expect 2009 to be Quintanilla's last with the Rockies unless he has a major—and unforeseen—breakout.

Seth Smith (Left Field)

PA	R	H	2B	3B	HR	RBI	SO	BB	SB	CS	BA	OBP	SLG	OPS	3-Year	Fielding	Reliability
458	61	114	25	3	17	63	79	44	6	1	.281	.354	.483	.837	+0.07	C	Very High

Smith has a solid shot at winning the Opening Day left field spot, but he'll probably be back on the bench sometime in the summer without a banner year. Thus far in limited play he's shown an ability to hit well away from Coors Field (.325/.381/.481). An unsustainable BABIP says that number will be going down, but his home numbers should be going up.

Ryan Spilborghs (Center Field)

PA	R	H	2B	3B	HR	RBI	SO	BB	SB	CS	BA	OBP	SLG	OPS	3-Year	Fielding	Reliability
371	48	96	18	2	10	45	60	38	6	2	.293	.367	.451	.818	-0.03	D	High

Spilborghs was a rare bright spot early in the season for the Rockies, but injuries limited his playing time throughout the summer and his bat came back a little cold. He will be given the starting center field post, which the Rockies hope he can keep warm until Dexter Fowler is ready. If he continues to hit as he did in 2008, it could be safe to assume that he would then take over as the starter in left.

Ian Stewart (Third Base)

PA	R	H	2B	3B	HR	RBI	SO	BB	SB	CS	BA	OBP	SLG	OPS	3-Year	Fielding	Reliability
571	74	133	30	5	21	77	142	54	6	2	.263	.340	.467	.807	+0.05	C	Very High

Stewart rose to the occasion early at Colorado Springs and didn't disappoint when he was called up to the Rockies until the last five weeks of the season. With the team unable to find a satisfactory return for Garrett Atkins in the offseason, Stewart's easiest road to the Opening Day lineup will be in left field. His bat should be in Denver to stay, though, and the Rockies will need to develop it into an elite weapon if they wish to keep up with the Dodgers and Diamondbacks.

Willy Taveras (Center Field)

PA	R	H	2B	3B	HR	RBI	SO	BB	SB	CS	BA	OBP	SLG	OPS	3-Year	Fielding	Reliability
491	66	125	17	3	3	33	72	31	44	5	.285	.339	.358	.697	+0.01	A	High

Taveras' inability to get on base consistently and the emergence of Dexter Fowler led the Rockies to cut the speedy center fielder. While an asset on the basepaths, Taveras will need to revive his ability to bunt for base hits and improve his plate discipline if he hopes to see a starting job in the majors again.

Yorvit Torrealba (Catcher)

PA	R	H	2B	3B	HR	RBI	SO	BB	SB	CS	BA	OBP	SLG	OPS	3-Year	Fielding	Reliability
342	37	81	18	1	8	39	58	22	1	2	.262	.320	.405	.725	-0.01	C	Average

Torrealba's time with the Rockies probably will be limited to the duration of his contract, or less if they find a suitable trade partner. He's not bad as a backup to Iannetta, but he's an expensive backup. That's a luxury that mid-market teams typically try to avoid.

Troy Tulowitzki (Shortstop)

PA	R	H	2B	3B	HR	RBI	SO	BB	SB	CS	BA	OBP	SLG	OPS	3-Year	Fielding	Reliability
484	60	122	26	3	14	62	74	42	3	3	.283	.351	.455	.806	+0.04	C	Very High

Part of the Rockies' early-season collapse was due to a poor start from Tulo, which was magnified with a quadriceps tear in late April. He never fully recovered from that. He took out his frustration by slamming a bat into the ground in July, lacerating his hand, his index finger and a considerable chunk of his pride. Tulowitzki reports that he's back to full health and looking forward to a rebound in 2009. The Rockies will need the bat, the head and the glove to be at 100 percent to compete in 2009.

Corey Wimberly (Shortstop)

PA	R	H	2B	3B	HR	RBI	SO	BB	SB	CS	BA	OBP	SLG	OPS	3-Year	Fielding	Reliability
435	52	104	11	2	3	29	55	24	27	5	.265	.322	.327	.649	+0.01	D	High

Wimberly doesn't have the glove of Jonathan Herrera or Omar Quintanilla; he doesn't have the bat of Chris Nelson or perhaps even Eric Young. He has speed, and some contact abilities, but he's been crowded out of the depth chart with Colorado and probably will have more opportunity with another club.

Eric Young (Outfield)

PA	R	H	2B	3B	HR	RBI	SO	BB	SB	CS	BA	OBP	SLG	OPS	3-Year	Fielding	Reliability
555	65	119	17	6	5	38	98	43	27	9	.241	.310	.330	.640	+0.06	—	Very High

Young has been shorted by scouts every step of the way, even though he's continued to put up solid numbers. After last season's successful jump to Double-A, even his most stubborn critics started to admit that he would have some offensive value to a club, even if the D remains a bit of a question. The Rockies will be using him in the outfield extensively at Colorado Springs, hoping he will be a multi-position utility player for them down the road.

Pitchers

Taylor Buchholz (Reliever)

W	L	ERA	TBF	IP	Hit	HR	SO	BB	HBP	3-Year	Reliability
4	4	4.18	305	72	73	9	52	22	2	+0.20	High

Buchholz emerged as a quality set-up man in 2008, filling a role that Luis Vizcaino and Manny Corpas couldn't. Still, he struggled in higher-leverage or closer situations. These were few, so I'd like to think it was only a small-sample fluke and that he could be called on to close in a pinch, but don't expect Buchholz to challenge Huston Street or Corpas for the closer role.

Aaron Cook (Starter)

W	L	ERA	TBF	IP	Hit	HR	SO	BB	HBP	3-Year	Reliability
10	10	4.42	783	181	215	17	71	47	6	+0.34	Very High

Cook's THT projection before last season was for a similar 4.43 ERA. He beat it with a much better performance at Coors Field than he's given in the past. For example, he walked just 3.6 percent of the batters he faced at Coors, compared to a career rate over 6 percent. The bad news is that he was probably lucky when it came to damage caused by balls in play, even for a sinkerball pitcher. I wouldn't be surprised if he beats his projection again—he's learned to use his home park to his advantage—but we probably won't see another sub-4.00 ERA from him this year.

Manny Corpas (Reliever)

W	L	ERA	TBF	IP	Hit	HR	SO	BB	HBP	3-Year	Reliability
4	4	4.34	319	74	83	7	48	22	3	+0.13	Average

The official excuse for Corpas' disappointing sophomore season was that he came to camp out of shape, and you'll note that this was a recurring theme with several of the Rockies pitchers (Franklin Morales, Luis Vizcaino, the traded Ramon Ramirez) in 2008's spring training camp. The front office has hired a coach who's helping with the winter programs of pitchers this year to avoid a replay of the massacre of '08. Without Brian Fuentes around to save his back, Corpas' condition will be more important than most.

Jorge De La Rosa (Starter)

W	L	ERA	TBF	IP	Hit	HR	SO	BB	HBP	3-Year	Reliability
7	9	5.00	626	141	152	20	114	63	5	+0.27	Very High

I wrote about De La Rosa in the team essay, but I do want to re-emphasize that the pitcher the numbers see is far different than the pitcher Rockies fans saw at the end of last year. It showed in his poise on the mound as well as on the radar gun. I think JDLR will be a much better pitcher than most people realize in 2009.

Jeff Francis (Starter)

W	L	ERA	TBF	IP	Hit	HR	SO	BB	HBP	3-Year	Reliability
9	9	4.81	707	162	182	21	103	53	6	+0.25	Very High

Did Francis' career-high workload in 2007 lead to his arm troubles in early 2008? And if not, what did? The scary possibility of a recurrence is another source of pessimism for Rockies fans. I take the optimistic look and hope he returns in 2009 to perform as he did in August and September, but Francis remains a bit of an enigma. I think the rest of a long playoff-less winter will do him about as much good as it will Todd Helton or Troy Tulowitzki.

Brian Fuentes (Reliever)

W	L	ERA	TBF	IP	Hit	HR	SO	BB	HBP	3-Year	Reliability
5	2	3.57	274	65	55	7	68	25	3	+0.21	Low

Fuentes' great strength might be in knowing his limitations and knowing his opponent. He knows which hitters to challenge and which to avoid. That frequently leads to him creating more trouble than he enters the game with, but he's been remarkably successful at parlaying this strategy into the one-inning world of relief work. He's never going to be a dominant 1-2-3-and-you're-done closer—he's going to give fans a lot of gray hairs with baserunners—but you're going to look back at the season and wonder at his success rate. He's prone to falling apart for two to three games in a row, usually just once a season.

Jason Grilli (Reliever)

W	L	ERA	TBF	IP	Hit	HR	SO	BB	HBP	3-Year	Reliability
4	4	4.23	314	72	71	7	56	32	3	+0.23	Average

Grilli was 2008's version of Matt Herges for the Rockies—another team's refuse turned into gold in the Colorado bullpen. That was fine, since Herges was no longer that version of himself. GM Dan O'Dowd did well in acquiring him from Detroit. The key to his turnaround was to scrap his curveball and change-up and just use a fastball/slider mix.

Livan Hernandez (Starter)

W	L	ERA	TBF	IP	Hit	HR	SO	BB	HBP	3-Year	Reliability
8	11	5.77	768	171	220	28	66	55	4	+0.30	Very High

Picking up Hernandez was a misguided attempt by the Rockies front office to light a fire under the team. He actually worked more like an extinguisher, a great big oxygen-sucking extinguisher that drowned what little life the team had left. Giving him starts was bad, taking them away from a hot hand in Jorge De La Rosa was much worse.

Jason Hirsh (Starter)

W	L	ERA	TBF	IP	Hit	HR	SO	BB	HBP	3-Year	Reliability
5	8	5.94	549	120	136	22	57	61	5	+0.18	Very High

Hirsh will be competing with a handful of other candidates for the Rockies fifth starter position, a position he had, but lost to a broken leg in 2007. Hirsh has yet to show the stuff necessary to get it back. He'll be running out of opportunities as a starter with the Rockies soon if he doesn't show it in 2009.

Ubaldo Jimenez (Starter)

W	L	ERA	TBF	IP	Hit	HR	SO	BB	HBP	3-Year	Reliability
10	9	4.65	773	173	174	18	138	93	10	-0.12	Very High

Jimenez had the majors' fastest fastball for a starter in 2008, his other pitches continued to show their nastiness most of the time, and his second half was as sharp as De La Rosa's. In short, he's getting close to being at a level where he should be mentioned alongside Chad Billingsley and Tim Lincecum as the division's top young RHPs, but he'll need to show a full season of dominance before the Rockies can consider him truly a staff ace.

Juan Morillo (Reliever)

W	L	ERA	TBF	IP	Hit	HR	SO	BB	HBP	3-Year	Reliability
3	4	6.08	302	63	69	9	44	48	4	+0.04	High

Morillo throws hard, really hard, but that's about the extent of his skill right now, and the Rockies were willing to include him in a trade with Willy Taveras for Tim Redding during the offseason. It's rumored that the health of Morillo's arm might have been what led to that deal falling apart, so I'm skeptical about how much he'll contribute for the Rockies in 2009.

Mark Redman (Starter)

W	L	ERA	TBF	IP	Hit	HR	SO	BB	HBP	3-Year	Reliability
6	8	5.68	583	128	160	19	53	52	5	+0.18	Very High

Redman's luck with the Rockies ran out early in 2008, and after a demotion to Triple-A, he couldn't find his way back up the depth chart.

Steven Register (Reliever)

W	L	ERA	TBF	IP	Hit	HR	SO	BB	HBP	3-Year	Reliability
3	4	6.17	290	63	78	11	34	28	4	+0.03	High

Register had only two clear appearances out of 10 in 2008— his MLB debut and his last appearance of the season. Both were one out long and consisted of him striking out the batter (Lastings Milledge and Chris Young). Those were the high points, and in between were various shades of ineffectiveness. He's young and promising; he could be better in 2009.

Gregory Reynolds (Starter)

W	L	ERA	TBF	IP	Hit	HR	SO	BB	HBP	3-Year	Reliability
5	9	5.82	556	122	153	18	49	49	6	-0.45	Average

Reynolds' spectacular flop in his MLB debut had to be discouraging for the Rockies' 2006 first-round pick, particularly considering that a guy he faced off against in the Pac-10, who was chosen a few picks after him, won the NL Cy Young. It will be an interesting test of character to see how he responds, as the comparisons to Tim Lincecum are likely to dog him as long as both remain major league pitchers.

Glendon Rusch (Starter)

W	L	ERA	TBF	IP	Hit	HR	SO	BB	HBP	3-Year	Reliability
5	7	5.28	460	104	119	17	60	40	3	+0.17	Average

Rusch rattled off a string of six pretty decent starts for the Rockies in July, didn't totally embarrass himself otherwise, and provided a decent amount of innings for the team when it was under some pretty severe injury duress. For this reason, the Rockies are asking him to come back in the same sixth starter/swing role in 2009.

Ryan Speier (Reliever)

W	L	ERA	TBF	IP	Hit	HR	SO	BB	HBP	3-Year	Reliability
3	4	4.79	285	64	70	7	42	28	3	+0.38	Very Low

Speier was the Rockies' quiet yeoman in middle relief last season. Nothing flashy, he's never going to be confused with a closer, just 50 innings of getting the job done. Another season like that would be just fine.

Luis Vizcaino (Reliever)

W	L	ERA	TBF	IP	Hit	HR	SO	BB	HBP	3-Year	Reliability
4	3	4.40	256	59	56	8	52	27	2	+0.16	Low

Luis Vizcaino proved why it's never good to sign free agent relievers for more than one year, although there could be a question of how much of his problem was him slacking off and how much was the product of overuse in the Yankees bullpen the season before. Given that he'll once again be pitching for a paycheck next winter, expect a rebound.

Detroit Tigers

By Brian Borawski of The Hardball Times

2009 Tigers Projections

Record: 74-88
Division Rank/Games Behind: Last by 12 games
Runs Scored: 793, 6th in the league
Runs Allowed: 850, 12th in the league
Park Factor: 1.00, no longer a pitcher's park

What Happened Last Year:

After making moves before the 2008 season for players like Miguel Cabrera, Dontrelle Willis, Jacque Jones and Edgar Renteria, the Tigers were favored by many to contend for a World Series berth. It didn't take long for attitudes to change after the team started off 2-10. The Tigers did recover by the end of the month, but May and early June didn't treat them any better and on June 6, the Tigers sat at 24-36 before catching fire.

By the end of June, the Tigers had turned things around, going from 24-36 to 42-40 by month's end. They had gone from 9.5 games back to 4.5 games behind and vaulted over the struggling Cleveland Indians to move into third place in the division. At the break, they were 47-47 and still poised to make a second-half run at a division title.

They continued to play .500 ball through the end of the month, when they made an unusual move. Despite being just five games out, the Tigers dealt future Hall of Fame catcher Ivan Rodriguez to the New York Yankees for relief pitcher Kyle Farnsworth. Although the Tigers won their first game after the trade, they then went on a six-game skid that effectively put them out of contention by mid-August.

The reasons for the Tigers' disappointing season are many. Three of the four big names the Tigers picked up during the offseason, Willis, Renteria and Jones, never panned out. Jones' performance was so bad that he was off the team by mid-May. While Edgar Renteria had a decent season at the plate, his lack of range at shortstop showed. Willis was a complete bust and spent most of the season at the Tigers' Low-A minor league affiliate, trying to get the ball over the plate. That left Cabrera, who became the first Tiger since Cecil Fielder in 1991 to win a home run title, but after a mediocre first half. Cabrera also failed miserably at third base, prompting manager Jim Leyland to move him to first base. He was equally bad there, just at a less critical spot on the field.

The rotation was decimated by injuries. Many thought the Tigers would have a formidable rotation in Justin Verlander, Jeremy Bonderman, Willis, Nate Robertson and Kenny Rogers, but by season's end, only one of those five would still be a starter. Bonderman was shut down in early June with a blood clot in his throwing shoulder. Rogers was shut down in mid-September, but that was after losing eight of his past nine starts. Nate Robertson lost his spot in the rotation in late August because he couldn't keep his ERA under 6.00. Even the lone survivor, Verlander, didn't have a banner season and he finished with the first losing record of his career.

Several hitters also had poor seasons. Gary Sheffield, recovering from offseason shoulder surgery, never found his hitting stroke and finished with a .225 batting average. Carlos Guillen never hit the disabled list, but nagging injuries cost him and he played in just 113 games. His .436 slugging percentage wasn't a career low, but it was the lowest since his last injury-filled season in 2005. Brandon Inge also struggled at the plate and his batting average at season's end was barely over .200.

There were some pleasant surprises. Armando Galarraga was the team's best pitcher. Cabrera, despite his slow start, led the league in home runs and came close to an RBI title. Magglio Ordonez, just one year removed from winning his first batting title, competed for another into the final weeks of the season.

The good news is that the Tigers have a solid core of players intact from last year that should help them bounce back in 2009. GM Dave Dombrowski made several moves to help fill holes at shortstop and catcher, and traded reserve outfielder Matt Joyce for one-time top prospect Edwin Jackson to help out in the rotation. Still, the Tigers have their work cut out for them in 2009.

Players Lost from Last Year's Team:

Edgar Renteria, Dane Sardinha, Todd Jones, Aquilino Lopez, Matt Joyce, Kenny Rogers, Freddy Garcia.

Players Acquired:

Adam Everett, Edwin Jackson, Gerald Laird.

Management Is:

Striking out more than it's hitting a home run. On the one hand, Dombrowski has helped put the Tigers back on the map, but the further the Tigers get from 2006, the more you wonder if that season was a fluke.

Unfortunately, Dombrowksi's transaction record hasn't been in his favor: For every Galarraga, there's been a Renteria and Jones. Still, I like the minor moves the Tigers made this offseason; perhaps with some small tweaks instead of a yearly overhaul, the Tigers can get back to competing for a playoff spot.

The Minor League System Is:

Thin but improving. The Tigers literally dealt away the farm the past couple of seasons and they're working on building the system back up. Rick Porcello, the 2007 first-round pick, is one of the best pitching prospects in baseball after being named the Florida State League player of the year. The team's 2008 first-round pick, Ryan Perry, could be the future closer.

Outside of Porcello and Perry, there are few players who will compete immediately for a spot on the major league team. While this is in part because the Tigers are a veteran team with several former All-Stars, it's also indicative of the fact that the Tigers have traded away a lot of major league-ready talent for guys like Cabrera and Renteria. The Tigers also didn't waste much time in trading their breakout prospect from 2008: Guillermo Moscoso, who struck out 122 batters in 86.2 innings between High-A and Double-A, was shipped to Texas as part of the deal for Laird.

Cale Iorg is probably the best position player prospect. He's been tagged as the Tigers' shortstop of the future, but he hasn't played above High-A, and that was after missing two years while on a Mormon mission. Wilkin Ramirez is probably close to major league-ready after hitting 24 homers at Double-A Erie, but he's pretty far down the outfield depth chart.

Due For a Change:

While it's hard to argue that Sheffield won't end up in the Hall of Fame, his time in Detroit has hardly been fruitful. The Tigers have basically gotten two good months from the guy who was supposed to put the Tigers over the top after making it to the World Series in 2006. Sheffield will be playing for a lot of things in 2009. He'll be a free agent at the end of the year, so he's playing for a contract. He's near the end of the career, so he's also playing for his legacy.

Once one of the most feared hitters in baseball, Sheffield could put it all together for one last hurrah in 2009. He'll blow through the 500 home run mark in April and while it's unrealistic to expect 30 homers, something along the lines of his first season in Atlanta (.307/.404/.512) sure would go a long way.

Our Favorite Tigers Blogs:

The Detroit Tigers Weblog (http://www.detroit-tigersweblog.com)

Bless You Boys (http://www.blessyouboys.com)

Take 75 North (http://mvn.com/take75north)

The Daily Fungo (http://www.dailyfungo.com)

Reasons to be Optimistic:

People tend to forget that the 2008 Tigers should have been a good team and heading into 2009, they have several pieces of that team intact. If guys like Sheffield and Guillen can put together productive and relatively injury-free seasons, the Tigers should have one of the best offenses in baseball. The Tigers also vastly improved their defense by shifting Inge back to third base and the combination of Everett and Ramon Santiago at shortstop. While the pitchers are still going to have to pitch, the 2009 defense should give them a lot more help than the 2008 defense did.

Reasons to be Pessimistic:

The Tigers have failed to address one of their biggest flaws last year, their starting rotation. They're hoping Verlander bounces back and that Bonderman returns from his blood clot surgery in good form. They're also hoping that Galarraga can repeat his solid 2008 season and Jackson can repeat the first and only productive season of his big league career. That's a lot of "hope fors," and there's just as good a chance that the Tigers will underperform in 2009, despite an exceptional offense, if their starting pitchers can't get it done.

Still Left to Do:

The Tigers need to address the holes in their pitching staff. While four of their five rotation spots appear set, their bullpen is a patchwork of established names like Fernando Rodney and Triple-A pitchers. They failed to procure a closer at the winter meetings and chances of Joel Zumaya are a crapshoot. The Tigers probably have a pitching staff that's good enough, but there's little depth in the event that a perfect storm like 2008 happens again.

Most Likely Team Outcome:

There's little reason why the Tigers shouldn't compete in a weak American League Central. It should take only 90 wins to take the division, and while the Tigers aren't a lock to get to that total, it's not out of the question. Still, I see a Cleveland Indians resurgence: I'd say the Tigers come in second to Cleveland in 2009.

Player Projections

Batters

Miguel Cabrera (First Base)

PA	R	H	2B	3B	HR	RBI	SO	BB	SB	CS	BA	OBP	SLG	OPS	3-Year	Fielding	Reliability
614	87	171	36	2	30	104	106	60	2	2	.314	.383	.552	.935	+0.02	C	Very High

Cabrera made a big splash in his first season in Detroit and became the first hitter since Cecil Fielder in 1991 to win a home run title. He did so despite a mediocre first half of the season (.489 slugging compared to .601 in the second half). If there was one knock to a great season at the plate, it was that he drew fewer walks than in any of his full seasons in the majors. Cabrera will never win a Gold Glove, but that's not what the Tigers are paying him for. While he played most of the season at first base, he did find his way into 14 games as a third baseman.

Adam Everett (Shortstop)

PA	R	H	2B	3B	HR	RBI	SO	BB	SB	CS	BA	OBP	SLG	OPS	3-Year	Fielding	Reliability
283	27	61	13	2	2	23	36	18	2	1	.241	.294	.332	.626	-0.03	A	Average

A one-time defensive authority at short, Everett has now spent portions of the past two seasons injured and unable to provide the one service that made him a valued commodity. The most recent ailment was a shoulder injury to his throwing arm making his tosses across the diamond look and feel painful before he was mercifully placed on the DL in May. To Twins fans in 2008 he became akin to an Adam Ant lyric: Can't hit, can't throw, what do you do? The 32-year-old Everett has entered the stage of his career where he will split time at short and other infield positions receiving a paycheck on his glovework alone.

Curtis Granderson (Center Field)

PA	R	H	2B	3B	HR	RBI	SO	BB	SB	CS	BA	OBP	SLG	OPS	3-Year	Fielding	Reliability
588	83	149	28	11	20	77	115	57	12	2	.286	.356	.497	.853	+0.01	A+	Very High

For the third straight season, Granderson improved his strikeout-to-walk ratio, a good sign for a player who leads off for a top-tier offensive team. Granderson didn't match his fantastic 2007 season, but he led the league in triples for the second straight season and his 112 runs were second in the American League despite his missing most of the first month of the season. The most important thing about Granderson's 2008 season was that he was finally given a chance against left-handed batters and eventually got better there after posting a league-leading platoon split in 2007.

Carlos Guillen (Third Base)

PA	R	H	2B	3B	HR	RBI	SO	BB	SB	CS	BA	OBP	SLG	OPS	3-Year	Fielding	Reliability
511	66	129	29	4	12	60	75	54	9	5	.288	.365	.451	.816	-0.05	C	Very High

Guillen will be playing his fourth position in three seasons as he makes the jump from infielder to outfielder. His biggest problem has been injuries; when he's been able to stay healthy, he's been very effective. The question will be whether he can give the Tigers a boost as their first everyday left fielder since Bobby Higginson in 2002. Age isn't on Guillen's side—he'll turn 34 by the end of the season, so if he does go on the shelf, you can't expect a quick recovery.

Freddy Guzman (Center Field)

PA	R	H	2B	3B	HR	RBI	SO	BB	SB	CS	BA	OBP	SLG	OPS	3-Year	Fielding	Reliability
534	69	122	17	8	3	33	72	42	40	6	.253	.314	.340	.654	+0.01	C	Very High

Guzman has spent parts of the last four seasons at Triple-A and has just 89 big league at-bats as he awaits his chance to get extended time with a major league team. He has 324 career minor league steals and while he's never hit more than five home runs in a season, he does have some value as a speedy switch hitter. The Tigers don't really have room for him so he'll most likely spend most of next season in Toledo.

Brandon Inge (Catcher)

PA	R	H	2B	3B	HR	RBI	SO	BB	SB	CS	BA	OBP	SLG	OPS	3-Year	Fielding	Reliability
463	52	98	20	2	14	53	104	40	5	2	.241	.317	.403	.720	-0.03	C	Very High

Inge took another step back at the plate and after two subpar seasons, even for him, you have to wonder if he'll ever get back to the level of his breakout season in 2006. He'll be the Tigers' everyday third baseman after a one-year hiatus, once again surviving a trade or free agent signing that cost him his starting job. Inge's .241 projected batting average seems high, but he'll probably flirt with 20 home runs since he'll likely get the nod in 155-plus games.

Gerald Laird (Catcher)

PA	R	H	2B	3B	HR	RBI	SO	BB	SB	CS	BA	OBP	SLG	OPS	3-Year	Fielding	Reliability
401	43	94	22	1	8	43	74	26	3	1	.258	.312	.390	.702	-0.03	C	Average

In six years with Texas, Laird never quite established himself as the unquestioned #1 catcher. Now a Tiger after being traded for two pitching prospects, he'll finally be The Man. He's a capable backstop and particularly skilled at gunning down baserunners. He's also a hacker at the plate, offering a little power and not much patience, with the results turning on the fickle nature of BABIP. Overall, he's an average catcher, roughly worth the $7-8 million he'll earn in his final two arbitration years.

Jeff Larish (First Base)

PA	R	H	2B	3B	HR	RBI	SO	BB	SB	CS	BA	OBP	SLG	OPS	3-Year	Fielding	Reliability
522	61	106	20	2	22	70	124	54	3	2	.231	.316	.427	.743	+0.07	B	Very High

Larish may be the Tigers' best hitting prospect. He just doesn't play a position that would give him consistent at-bats. He did get some time at third base last season and he continued to work on the move in the Arizona Fall League, but he'll probably make the team because he provides the Tigers with a left-handed option at the plate. He showed a good eye in the minors, but he wasn't nearly as effective in the big leagues with a 34/7 strikeout-to-walk ratio.

Magglio Ordonez (Right Field)

PA	R	H	2B	3B	HR	RBI	SO	BB	SB	CS	BA	OBP	SLG	OPS	3-Year	Fielding	Reliability
583	75	163	33	1	19	83	75	52	2	3	.312	.374	.488	.862	-0.06	D	Very High

Ordonez' 30-homer seasons may be a thing of the past, but three straight seasons with 100-plus RBIs and the fact that he can keep his strikeouts under 80 means he'll probably keep his batting average north of .300. As long as Curtis Granderson and Placido Polanco continue to hit well in front of him, I'd expect Ordonez to top his projected 83 RBIs even if he sees a tick or two down in his power numbers.

Placido Polanco (Second Base)

PA	R	H	2B	3B	HR	RBI	SO	BB	SB	CS	BA	OBP	SLG	OPS	3-Year	Fielding	Reliability
567	64	159	28	2	5	57	41	31	5	1	.305	.350	.395	.745	-0.05	A	Very High

With Polanco, you know what you're going to get. That's a .300 batting average without a lot of strikeouts and not a lot of power. Along with that, you get a solid, yet unspectacular, glove at second base. Polanco's projected line of .305/.350/.395 is a pretty safe bet but it would be nice if he finally played in 150-plus games, which he's never done in a season.

Ryan Raburn (Second Base)

PA	R	H	2B	3B	HR	RBI	SO	BB	SB	CS	BA	OBP	SLG	OPS	3-Year	Fielding	Reliability
350	44	82	17	3	12	45	76	31	5	2	.262	.330	.451	.781	+0.01	D	High

Raburn found his way into 92 major league games despite a .666 OPS, but a lot of those were as a defensive replacement. With Brandon Inge fortifying third base and the Tigers' signing of Adam Everett as a mostly everyday shortstop, guys like Ramon Santiago will probably find their way onto the big league roster before Raburn does. His big plus is he can play just about any position, so he could sneak onto the big league team as the 25th man.

Wilkin Ramirez (Left Field)

PA	R	H	2B	3B	HR	RBI	SO	BB	SB	CS	BA	OBP	SLG	OPS	3-Year	Fielding	Reliability
531	61	119	20	5	15	58	145	25	15	8	.239	.279	.390	.669	+0.04	—	High

One of the Tigers' top prospects, Ramirez had a breakout season at Double-A with a .522 slugging percentage in 433 at-bats. Like a lot of the Tigers' fringe outfielders, he's probably going to spend most of his time at Triple-A but if he rakes like he did in Erie in 2008, he might be one of the first hitters the Tigers look at if there's an injury or if someone like Marcus Thames is traded.

Dusty Ryan (Catcher)

PA	R	H	2B	3B	HR	RBI	SO	BB	SB	CS	BA	OBP	SLG	OPS	3-Year	Fielding	Reliability
379	40	76	14	2	12	43	107	31	1	1	.222	.291	.380	.671	+0.03	C	Average

Ryan is probably the best of a mediocre lot of catching prospects the Tigers have in their system. Ryan hit .318 in 44 at-bats in a September call-up. He's most likely going to start the season in the minors after the Tigers signed Matt Treanor to back up Gerald Laird.

Ramon Santiago (Shortstop)

PA	R	H	2B	3B	HR	RBI	SO	BB	SB	CS	BA	OBP	SLG	OPS	3-Year	Fielding	Reliability
296	31	68	12	3	3	26	45	18	4	2	.259	.317	.362	.679	-0.03	D	Low

Santiago was one of the pleasant surprises for the Tigers in 2008. While he played in just 58 games and logged just 124 at-bats, he gave the Tigers a solid fielding option at both shortstop and second base. He's never going to top 15 homers in a season, but if he can hit his projected .259 and continue to play solid defense, Santiago probably will press the newly signed Adam Everett for playing time all season.

Dane Sardinha (Catcher)

PA	R	H	2B	3B	HR	RBI	SO	BB	SB	CS	BA	OBP	SLG	OPS	3-Year	Fielding	Reliability
309	27	59	12	1	7	30	78	15	1	0	.208	.251	.331	.582	-0.02	C	Average

Sardinha eventually became the backup catcher when the Tigers traded Ivan Rodriguez to the Yankees. His batting average was south of .150 for most of the season and after Dusty Ryan's impressive September, the Tigers cut Sardinha loose.

Gary Sheffield (Designated Hitter)

PA	R	H	2B	3B	HR	RBI	SO	BB	SB	CS	BA	OBP	SLG	OPS	3-Year	Fielding	Reliability
465	59	102	18	1	17	57	70	55	10	2	.254	.349	.431	.780	—	C	Very High

Sheffield will be 40 when he begins the season. He began to show his age this past year with one of the worst seasons of his career. He struggled early because he was still recovering from shoulder surgery, but had his best month in September. He's playing for what will probably be his last contract as well as his legacy as his Hall of Fame career winds down.

James Skelton (Catcher)

PA	R	H	2B	3B	HR	RBI	SO	BB	SB	CS	BA	OBP	SLG	OPS	3-Year	Fielding	Reliability
513	54	103	14	3	4	36	102	65	11	5	.235	.334	.308	.642	+0.05	—	Low

Lost in the Rule 5 draft to the Arizona Diamondbacks, Skelton should get a chance to prove his skeptics wrong. The 5-foot-11, 165-pound catcher has a nice eye at the plate (181 minor league walks versus 179 strikeouts) to go along with his .292 career batting average. He hasn't played above Double-A, though, so he has as good of a chance of getting shipped back to the Detroit system as he does of sticking with the Diamondbacks as a backup catcher.

Marcus Thames (Left Field)

PA	R	H	2B	3B	HR	RBI	SO	BB	SB	CS	BA	OBP	SLG	OPS	3-Year	Fielding	Reliability
367	48	85	17	1	24	66	90	27	1	1	.254	.311	.526	.837	-0.03	D	High

Thames is again the odd man out, but the Tigers felt good enough about him to not deal him away. With Thames, you know what you're going to get, namely a .250 batting average, a number of home runs and a lot of strikeouts. He'll begin the season as the Tigers' fourth outfielder while Carlos Guillen moves to left field, but he also should see some time at designated hitter.

Clete Thomas (Center Field)

PA	R	H	2B	3B	HR	RBI	SO	BB	SB	CS	BA	OBP	SLG	OPS	3-Year	Fielding	Reliability
493	52	100	20	4	6	38	110	39	17	6	.226	.290	.330	.620	+0.01	C	Very High

Thomas had a solid showing with the Tigers when he filled in for Curtis Granderson in April and he eventually was part of the revolving door in left field. Still, he's probably just Detroit's fifth outfielder. There's a little bit of extra hope for him because he's left-handed, but if given a choice between the more versatile Ryan Raburn and Thomas, it'll probably be Raburn who makes the team.

Pitchers

Jeremy Bonderman (Starter)

W	L	ERA	TBF	IP	Hit	HR	SO	BB	HBP	3-Year	Reliability
7	6	4.36	519	121	127	14	89	41	3	+0.16	Very High

It's been a rough couple of years for Bonderman. He had a breakout 2006 season and looked to be on track as a Cy Young contender in 2007 before being shut down in a disastrous second half. After a decent start in 2008, he was once again shut down because of a blood clot in his throwing arm. He's expected to be ready for Opening Day. On the one hand, the improved circulation should help tremendously but Kenny Rogers never really bounced back after he had similar surgery in 2007. Unlike Rogers, though, Bonderman has age on his side.

Eddie Bonine (Starter)

W	L	ERA	TBF	IP	Hit	HR	SO	BB	HBP	3-Year	Reliability
5	10	5.72	602	135	169	23	43	40	8	+0.27	Very High

Bonine provided five unspectacular starts when the Tigers gave up on Dontrelle Willis. Bonine is a control pitcher with just 474 strikeouts in 663 minor league innings, but he's been able to finesse his way to a 41-29 career minor league record. At this point, he has little to prove in the minors but has little chance of getting a spot with the Tigers, so he'll probably spend another season at Triple-A Toledo.

Kyle Farnsworth (Reliever)

W	L	ERA	TBF	IP	Hit	HR	SO	BB	HBP	3-Year	Reliability
4	3	4.40	278	64	63	8	57	26	2	+0.23	Low

Farnsworth was in the middle of his third straight mediocre season for the New York Yankees before the Tigers picked him up in a deal for Ivan Rodriguez. He was even less effective in his second stint with the Tigers, but that didn't deter the Royals from signing him to a two-year deal. Odds are his dominant days are behind him.

Casey Fossum (Reliever)

W	L	ERA	TBF	IP	Hit	HR	SO	BB	HBP	3-Year	Reliability
4	5	5.07	376	84	93	10	57	37	5	+0.25	High

Fossum played for his fourth major league team in six seasons after a nice minor league stint for the Mud Hens. While he was talked about as a potential starter throughout 2008, he never did get a turn in the rotation. Fossum gave up five runs in his first third of an inning and that kept his ERA high all season. He could see time with the Tigers, but only because he's been there before.

Armando Galarraga (Starter)

W	L	ERA	TBF	IP	Hit	HR	SO	BB	HBP	3-Year	Reliability
7	10	5.27	670	151	166	24	99	61	10	+0.19	Very High

One of the few pleasant surprises for the Tigers in 2008, Galarraga won a team-high 13 games and finished fourth in the American League Rookie of the Year vote. He was death on right-handed hitters (.174/.252/.291) and while he doesn't strike out many batters, he tends to keep the ball down so he doesn't get burned much. His projection looks a bit grim, but it's just as likely that Galarraga will flame out as that he will repeat what he did in 2008. For now, though, he's been handed a spot in the rotation.

Freddy Garcia (Starter)

W	L	ERA	TBF	IP	Hit	HR	SO	BB	HBP	3-Year	Reliability
4	5	4.51	354	83	87	12	54	23	3	+0.24	High

After he missed most of the 2007 season with an injury, no team was willing to give Garcia a chance in 2008 until the Tigers did. After a late-season call-up, he was solid in two starts and roughed up in another. He wanted to further showcase his comeback in winter ball, but eventually was shut down because of shoulder soreness. An MRI showed no structural damage, but who'll take the risk of signing Garcia to a major league deal?

Chris Lambert (Starter)

W	L	ERA	TBF	IP	Hit	HR	SO	BB	HBP	3-Year	Reliability
5	11	6.09	644	141	167	25	82	65	6	+0.08	Very High

The Tigers traded Mike Maroth for Chris Lambert in 2007 and after a solid season at Triple-A (124 strikeouts/48 walks in 149.1 innings with a 3.50 ERA), he was given a late-season call-up. Unfortunately, he was shelled in his eight games. Lambert might have an outside shot at the fifth spot in the rotation, but he's going to need a spectacular spring to get noticed. Odds are he'll find himself back at Toledo, waiting for an injury to give him another chance in the big leagues.

Aquilino Lopez (Reliever)

W	L	ERA	TBF	IP	Hit	HR	SO	BB	HBP	3-Year	Reliability
4	4	5.06	322	74	80	12	56	25	2	+0.28	Average

After saving 26 games for the Toledo Mud Hens in 2007, Lopez made the Tigers out of camp in 2008 and gave up just one run in his first 18.1 innings. He cooled off a bit and even got sent back down to the minors when the Tigers flirted with turning him into a starter, but he set a career high in innings pitched (78.2). Detroit didn't offer Lopez a deal at the non-tender deadline so he's a free agent.

Zach Miner (Reliever)

W	L	ERA	TBF	IP	Hit	HR	SO	BB	HBP	3-Year	Reliability
6	6	4.53	467	107	113	11	59	44	4	+0.13	High

A 5-2 record and a 4.30 ERA in 13 starts in the final two months of the season make Miner the favorite to begin the season as the fifth starter. He'll have to fend off Nate Robertson and Dontrelle Willis in spring training— the Tigers' trade for Edwin Jackson probably leaves just one spot open for those three hurlers. If Miner does get the spot, he can keep it by continuing to give the Tigers six solid innings every game.

Nate Robertson (Starter)

W	L	ERA	TBF	IP	Hit	HR	SO	BB	HBP	3-Year	Reliability
8	10	4.73	711	163	180	22	101	58	4	+0.22	Very High

Robertson was one of the Tigers' big disappointments in 2008 and he's probably on the outside looking in at the rotation. One thing he has going for him is that he's left handed and it looks like the Tigers will have an all right-handed rotation. He'll need a top-notch spring to make the rotation and he's tough to trade because he's set to get paid $17 million over the next two seasons. That means he could start the season in the 'pen.

Fernando Rodney (Reliever)

W	L	ERA	TBF	IP	Hit	HR	SO	BB	HBP	3-Year	Reliability
4	2	3.55	240	56	47	4	55	28	3	+0.17	Low

Rodney missed the first two-and-a-half months of the season. Less than two months after that, he found himself as the de facto closer after Todd Jones went down with an injury. Rodney had a tough final month of the season, but he'll be the closer unless the Tigers either sign one via free agency or trade for one. It'd be nice if Rodney could get over the injury bug he's had the past couple of years, but recent history shows he'll probably miss some time.

Bobby Seay (Reliever)

W	L	ERA	TBF	IP	Hit	HR	SO	BB	HBP	3-Year	Reliability
4	3	3.96	259	61	57	6	52	25	2	+0.20	Low

Seay took a small step back in 2008 after a breakout 2007 season, but he did strike out more than a batter an inning over a season for the first time in his career. He'll be the Tigers' primary left-handed option out of the bullpen barring an offseason move despite the fact that he struggled against left-handed hitters last season (.303 batting average against).

Justin Verlander (Starter)

W	L	ERA	TBF	IP	Hit	HR	SO	BB	HBP	3-Year	Reliability
10	10	4.25	788	183	183	20	144	67	10	+0.03	Very High

Verlander struggled like a lot of Tigers did in 2008, and it's hard to tell why. He wasn't injured, but his normally high velocity seemed tempered most of the season. His strikeout rate was down from 2007 while his walk rate was up. You have to wonder if Verlander just wore down. If you count the 2006 postseason, Verlander topped the 200 innings mark in his first two big league seasons and he wasn't used to that kind of workload. He didn't get a break in 2008 and once again topped 200 innings. With an improved defense, I like Verlander's projection here. He's probably more apt to pitch to contact, so you should see his walk rate normalize and his ERA come down to his projected 4.25.

Dontrelle Willis (Starter)

W	L	ERA	TBF	IP	Hit	HR	SO	BB	HBP	3-Year	Reliability
5	8	5.36	549	121	139	16	64	59	6	+0.17	Very High

It's hard to know where to start with Willis. He was the other guy the Tigers picked up in the deal that brought Miguel Cabrera to Detroit and to say he had a rough season is a huge understatement. When he wasn't hurt or pitching in the low minors working on his location, he was walking 35 batters in just 24 innings. While it's hard to believe Willis could go Cliff Lee anytime soon, he's had success in the past. His projections are pretty fair, but at this point, it's kind of like throwing darts while blindfolded. It's safe to say he'll have another rough season, but you could always hit the bulls eye.

Joel Zumaya (Reliever)

W	L	ERA	TBF	IP	Hit	HR	SO	BB	HBP	3-Year	Reliability
3	2	4.02	201	46	40	5	42	25	1	-0.03	Low

Two injury-filled seasons have made Zumaya a major question mark. Many thought that Zumaya would be the unquestionable closer for the team by now, but his shoulder injury before the 2008 season forced the Tigers to re-sign Todd Jones. He did get into 21 games that were sandwiched between a pair of injuries and while he struck out 22 he also walked 22. The good news is, his velocity was back up around 100 mph, but that was before the latest injury that shut him down for the season. He hasn't logged more than 40 innings since his breakout season in 2006.

Florida Marlins

By Alex Carver of Marlins Today (mvn.com/mlb/marlins)

2009 Marlins Projections

Record: 75-87
Division Rank/Games Behind: 4th, 13 games back
Runs Scored: 750, 8th in the league
Runs Allowed: 805, 15th in the league
Park Factor: .98, a slight pitcher's park

What Happened Last Year:

The Marlins defied the odds in 2008 by staying competitive for most of the year and edging closer to their first playoff berth since 2003. Coming into the season, many predicted Florida would lose at least 90 games and finish behind the Washington Nationals.

Before the All-Star break, though, Florida disproved both of those theories, leading the division at 50-45. However, while the Mets (namely Carlos Delgado) and the Phillies (namely Ryan Howard) turned on the juice in the second half, the Marlins' offense sputtered. Production dropped from 4.87 runs per game to 4.66, helping drop the Fish to an 11-16 August and third place. Even though the postseason would've been nice after such a good start, taking another step in that direction by posting the Marlins' best non-playoff record (84-77) with a team that wasn't 100 percent healthy until mid-August was an overall success.

Players Lost from Last Year's Team:

Scott Olsen, Mike Jacobs, Josh Willingham, Mark Hendrickson, Joe Nelson, Paul Lo Duca, Matt Treanor, Luis Gonzalez, Doug Waechter, Kevin Gregg, Arthur Rhodes

Players Acquired:

Right-handed pitcher Leo Nunez came from Kansas City in a trade for the surplus bat of Mike Jacobs. Nunez held his ERA under 3.50 in his eight-year minor league career. In 48 innings in the bigs last year, he posted a 2.98 ERA, struck out 26 and held a VORP near 9.0. The team hopes Nunez can become a late-inning setup guy.

Left-handed pitcher Jose Ceda was brought in from the Cubs for troubled closer Kevin Gregg and the $5 million he was set to make in arbitration. In 180 minor league innings, he posted a 3.54 ERA. He'll likely begin his Marlins career in Double-A.

Left-handed pitcher Dan Meyer was claimed off waivers from the A's. Meyer is a power lefty with plus velocity on his fastball and good command over his still-improving second pitch change-up. In his minor league career, including four seasons in the hitter-friendly Pacific Coast League, he held down a sufficient 3.80 ERA.

Left-handed pitcher Zachary Kroenke, if you throw away the four starts he made in High-A in 2006, hasn't had an ERA over 3.09 since high school. Last year, between Double-A and Triple-A, he worked exclusively as a reliever, posting a 2.85 ERA in 41 appearances with 28 walks and 54 strikeouts. With Arthur Rhodes gone, Meyer and Kroenke will battle Taylor Tankersley for the second left-handed bullpen spot.

Infielder Emilio Bonifacio was the centerpiece of the Scott Olsen-Josh Willingham trade with Washington. He is a second baseman by trade, but with Dan Uggla currently there and with Chris Coghlan (.825 OPS in Double-A last year), poised to replace him, the team likely will give Bonifacio a look at third. Bonifacio is a defensive-minded infielder who used his tremendous speed to post an above-average 4.68 range factor over his six-year minor league career. His biggest flaw is his plate discipline. Coming up, he had an egregious 2.5-1 strikeout-to-walk ratio. However, if Bonifacio does get on base, he's a threat to steal.

Management Is:

On top of trying to field a winning team in 2009, the front office will have to try to find the Marlins a place to play in 2011: The opening of the club's new stadium on the grounds of the Orange Bowl was delayed by a lawsuit until 2012. The Marlins' lease with Wayne Huizenga at Dolphin Stadium is up in 2010. They are optimistic that Huizenga will allow them to remain at Dolphin Stadium, the place they have called home for 15 years, but the relationship between Huizenga and owner Jeffrey Loria is tepid at best. If an agreement with Huizenga is not reached, and with no other venues in the area capable of hosting a major league game, the club may find it hard to house the team.

The Minor League System Is:

The Marlins have a couple of prospects bound for a big league berth in 2009. Outfielder John Raynor, 24, looks the most intriguing. He has had a fantastic minor league career thus far, hitting for a .919 OPS and stealing bases at an 84 percent rate between Single-A and Double-A; last season in Carolina he hit .312 and stole 48 bags in 59 attempts. After winning a divisional championship with the Mudcats, he played in the Arizona Fall League where he was hitting .364 before being sent home with a minor hand injury. Although he's not likely to make the team out of spring training, the front office loves him. He should get his first taste of major league action sometime this season.

Coghlan, a teammate of Raynor's in 2008, isn't far behind him. In his minor league career, the 23-year-old has been a machine in a department in which the Marlins struggled in 2008, OBP, reaching at a .386 clip among four levels. However, if he wants to replace Uggla, the fifth-best glove at the position in the majors last year, he'll need to improve his defense. The Fish can't afford any more bad play in the field, and have worked all offseason to rectify it. In 2008, Coghlan made 23 errors. However, if he gets off to a better start in Double-A this year, the Marlins might explore moving Uggla at the deadline for a hefty return.

Due for a change:

Andrew Miller really hasn't been given a fair shake so far in his young major league career. After being rushed to the majors in 2007 by the Tigers, Miller spent most of his 2008 pitching on an injured push-off leg and running up gaudy numbers before landing on the DL. Never has he gotten to show the potential he used to compile a 2.55 ERA in the minors and before that to strike out 300-plus batters in three seasons at the University of North Carolina. With a healthy Josh Johnson, upstarts Ricky Nolasco and Chris Volstad (who combined to post a 3.20 ERA last year), and Anibal Sanchez pitching in front of him, Miller could shine in the back of the rotation and wind up posting 10-plus wins.

Reasons to be Optimistic:

With a payroll that has increased almost twofold from $22 million last season to more than $40 million this year, the complete rotation they've been waiting

for since Josh Beckett left, and a good mix of power and base hit ability, it's October or bust for the Marlins in 2009. That's especially so after an offseason that resembled the one before the 2003 World Championship year, in which they beat the phrase "small ball" to death by focusing on pitching, speed and defense.

Reasons to be Pessimistic:

GM Larry Beinfest obviously firmly believes that you never can have enough young bullpen help: Most of his offseason signings were mid-20s relievers, but what about veteran bullpen help? Right now, the oldest member of the Florida bullpen is Matt Lindstrom. He's 28. The guy with the most major league experience is Logan Kensing. Last year was his fourth season. Without that veteran presence on a night when a Lindstrom or Nunez just doesn't have it, without someone who can go two or three innings in relief as an Arthur Rhodes or Joe Nelson could, the Florida pen could struggle during the dog days of summer.

Still Left To Do:

Unless something happens at the eleventh hour, it doesn't look like the Marlins are going to acquire catcher Max Ramirez from the Texas Rangers, who have shot down numerous offers. I'm confident in John Baker's future as the everyday starter, but he is going to need a platoon partner this year who can mash left-handed pitching. By signing a veteran such as Toby Hall, who hits lefties at a .283 clip, the Marlins can kill two birds with one stone and allow Hall to mentor the still-developing Baker.

Most Likely Team Outcome:

Playoffs. Yes, I'm talking about playoffs. Carried on the backs of a rotation that is finally 100 percent healthy entering the season and a much-improved bullpen, October baseball will be played in South Florida.

Player Projections

Batters

Alfredo Amezaga (Center Field)

PA	R	H	2B	3B	HR	RBI	SO	BB	SB	CS	BA	OBP	SLG	OPS	3-Year	Fielding	Reliability
390	43	92	14	5	3	31	55	28	8	3	.261	.319	.355	.674	-0.03	B	High

Amezaga's heart is so big it's a wonder that it fits in his chest. Platooning with Cody Ross in center and backing up three different positions, The Amazing One enjoyed his best season as a Marlin last year, hitting .264/.312/.679 with three homers and 32 RBIs. Probably the best utility man in the league, Amezaga will hold the same position with the 2009 Fish.

Robert Andino (Shortstop)

PA	R	H	2B	3B	HR	RBI	SO	BB	SB	CS	BA	OBP	SLG	OPS	3-Year	Fielding	Reliability
406	45	90	16	5	7	38	91	26	9	3	.242	.293	.368	.661	+0.03	D	High

If your name isn't Hanley Ramirez, it's hard to make a name for yourself as a Florida Marlins shortstop. By hitting .201 in 144 major league at-bats and earning the reputation of a journeyman, Andino hasn't done himself any favors. Going on 25, Andino, who is known for his glove but not for his bat, doesn't have much of a future here. The Marlins explored a trade that would have sent Andino to Pittsburgh and will continue to search for a deal.

John Baker (Catcher)

PA	R	H	2B	3B	HR	RBI	SO	BB	SB	CS	BA	OBP	SLG	OPS	3-Year	Fielding	Reliability
417	48	99	21	1	9	46	88	45	1	1	.272	.356	.409	.765	+0.00	D	Average

Many Marlins fans were hoping that GM Larry Beinfest would fill the hole behind the plate in the offseason with one of Texas' big three catching prospects and were disappointed when he didn't. However, in Baker, whom the Marlins claimed off waivers from Oakland, Beinfest may have found the next Dan Uggla (an unknown who came to the team via existential measures and is making a name for himself). After Matt Treanor was forced out of the lineup by a knee injury, Baker entered and, after finding his groove, produced spectacular offensive results, finishing second on the team in OPS in August and third on the team in September. The only knock on Baker's bat is that he struggles against left-handed pitching, but that's nothing a cheap, free agent, southpaw-mashing platoon partner can't fix.

Emilio Bonifacio (Second Base)

PA	R	H	2B	3B	HR	RBI	SO	BB	SB	CS	BA	OBP	SLG	OPS	3-Year	Fielding	Reliability
578	62	135	20	6	3	42	119	34	17	8	.254	.300	.331	.631	+0.05	C	Very High

When he was traded from Arizona to Washington in the Jon Rauch trade, Nats' GM Bowden trumpeted his speed and potential leadoff abilities, comparing him favorably to Luis Castillo. Looking at his minor league stats, I assume he was talking about current-day Castillo.

Jorge Cantu (Third Base)

PA	R	H	2B	3B	HR	RBI	SO	BB	SB	CS	BA	OBP	SLG	OPS	3-Year	Fielding	Reliability
539	68	138	30	2	22	79	98	35	4	1	.280	.334	.484	.818	+0.07	F-	Very High

Cantu returned to his early career form in 2008, hitting .277/.327/.808 with 29 homers and 95 RBIs in 2008 and in turn will earn at least $5 million in arbitration. With a surplus of infielders, Florida shopped Cantu during the offseason. However, it looks like the Fish will retain him and start him at third base in 2009.

Brett Carroll (Center Field)

PA	R	H	2B	3B	HR	RBI	SO	BB	SB	CS	BA	OBP	SLG	OPS	3-Year	Fielding	Reliability
319	38	70	15	2	15	46	79	19	1	2	.241	.298	.461	.759	+0.07	D	High

This guy can't buy a break. As if having your entire minor league career and development halted by injuries wasn't enough, Carroll's best asset, his arm, may now be gone as well after he separated his shoulder last season. It is uncertain if he will be ready for spring training, where he could earn a bench spot.

Christopher Coghlan (Second Base)

PA	R	H	2B	3B	HR	RBI	SO	BB	SB	CS	BA	OBP	SLG	OPS	3-Year	Fielding	Reliability
565	65	120	24	5	7	46	91	55	17	7	.242	.325	.353	.678	+0.06	C	Average

In his first year above Single-A, Coghlan posted a .296/.396/.825 line with the Double-A Mudcats, solidifying himself as Dan Uggla's eventual successor. Coghlan has a great eye and a high contact probability. The only knock scouts have on his offense is that he could lengthen his swing to become more powerful. Coghlan probably won't become a 30-plus home run guy but he could easily post an OBP in the high .300s to low .400s yearly. Coghlan needs to improve his defense but he made great progress last year and he's still only 23.

Wes Helms (Third Base)

PA	R	H	2B	3B	HR	RBI	SO	BB	SB	CS	BA	OBP	SLG	OPS	3-Year	Fielding	Reliability
331	36	77	18	1	7	37	74	25	0	0	.258	.321	.395	.716	-0.02	C	Average

Helms had another good year coming off the bench for the Marlins in 2008, hitting five homers, knocking in 31 runs and scoring 28 in 251 at-bats, earning himself a two-year, $1.9 million deal. He'll assume the same position with the team in 2009.

Jeremy Hermida (Right Field)

PA	R	H	2B	3B	HR	RBI	SO	BB	SB	CS	BA	OBP	SLG	OPS	3-Year	Fielding	Reliability
497	61	118	26	2	16	63	113	47	4	1	.268	.343	.445	.788	+0.03	D	High

Even though he ran a bit low in the patience department, Hermida followed up a great .879 OPS in 2007 with a good .729 OPS in 2008. While he still wasn't the guy the Marlins thought they had after he posted a career .284/.397/.436 minor league line, Hermida is still a bright-eyed 24-year-old who has the experience of a 22-year-old because of injuries. Although Hermida probably had his best season as a pro last year, taking better routes to balls and making more accurate throws, baserunners still took advantage of him, often taking an extra base on base hits. For that reason, Hermida will likely swap positions with Cody Ross, moving from left to right field.

Cameron Maybin (Center Field)

PA	R	H	2B	3B	HR	RBI	SO	BB	SB	CS	BA	OBP	SLG	OPS	3-Year	Fielding	Reliability
478	58	104	16	5	12	49	132	48	12	5	.247	.328	.395	.723	+0.11	D	High

Maybin's cup of coffee at the end of last season couldn't have tasted any better if it had been harvested by Juan Valdez. The prospect who came to South Florida as the centerpiece of the Miguel Cabrera/Dontrelle Willis trade made the most of the 32 at-bats he got with the Fish, hitting .500/.543/1.105, with two homers and nine RBIs. He'll be in center field on Opening Day.

Dallas McPherson (Third Base)

PA	R	H	2B	3B	HR	RBI	SO	BB	SB	CS	BA	OBP	SLG	OPS	3-Year	Fielding	Reliability
402	59	88	17	2	27	72	132	47	6	3	.252	.341	.543	.884	-0.02	C	Average

All right, so the Pacific Coast League is a pure hitters' league, but not everyone does what McPherson did in 2008, pacing it with 42 homers and finishing with the third-highest OPS. After managing to stay healthy for the first time, he'll come into spring training with a good chance of beating out Emilio Bonifacio for the backup job at third base.

Jai Miller (Right Field)

PA	R	H	2B	3B	HR	RBI	SO	BB	SB	CS	BA	OBP	SLG	OPS	3-Year	Fielding	Reliability
542	61	108	22	3	14	56	157	51	12	4	.225	.304	.371	.675	+0.05	C	High

Miller gave up a bright future in both basketball and football at Stanford University to sign with the Marlins. Before 2007, it looked like he had made the wrong decision, but after simplifying his swing, Miller is turning into an attractive piece. He enjoyed the best season of his career last season, posting a .267/.349/.821 line in Triple-A. Eligible at all three outfield positions, Miller, now 23, is worth keeping an eye on as he edges his way toward the big leagues.

Mike Rabelo (Catcher)

PA	R	H	2B	3B	HR	RBI	SO	BB	SB	CS	BA	OBP	SLG	OPS	3-Year	Fielding	Reliability
249	25	54	11	1	4	24	52	16	0	1	.241	.304	.353	.657	-0.02	C	Low

After coming to Florida as a throw-in in the Cabrera/Willis trade, Rabelo was remembered for doing two things in 2008: spiking the baseball on home plate like a wide receiver and forgetting to apply a tag on a runner on an easy play at the plate. Then he went on the 60-day DL with wrist and knee injuries. In his 109 at-bats, he OPSed a meek .550. At 28, Rabelo is nothing more than a career backup.

Hanley Ramirez (Shortstop)

PA	R	H	2B	3B	HR	RBI	SO	BB	SB	CS	BA	OBP	SLG	OPS	3-Year	Fielding	Reliability
624	99	168	36	5	25	89	106	64	34	9	.306	.382	.527	.909	+0.03	D	Very High

In his third year as a pro, Ramirez earned Player of the Month honors in June, an All-Star Game invite in July, access to the 30-30 club in September and a Silver Slugger in November. You'll be telling your grandkids about this guy.

John Raynor (Left Field)

PA	R	H	2B	3B	HR	RBI	SO	BB	SB	CS	BA	OBP	SLG	OPS	3-Year	Fielding	Reliability
505	65	110	21	5	9	45	124	47	26	5	.248	.330	.379	.709	+0.04	—	Average

Raynor has flown through the Marlins' system, posting totals that border on ridiculous at every level. Last year, at Double-A Carolina, he hit .312/.402/.891. He has used his plus speed to steal 123 bags in 144 attempts and is continuing to improve upon an already good eye. His numbers suggest that he has leadoff hitter potential. At 24, Raynor is less than a year away from a big league berth and if conditions permit (an injury to a starter), could see a call-up sometime this year.

Cody Ross (Center Field)

PA	R	H	2B	3B	HR	RBI	SO	BB	SB	CS	BA	OBP	SLG	OPS	3-Year	Fielding	Reliability
419	55	103	24	2	19	63	87	33	4	1	.273	.337	.499	.836	-0.03	D	High

Ross was the breakout position player of the year in 2008, with an OPS over .800 with 22 homers and 73 RBIs, upping his average against right-handed pitchers to .306 and earning a starting spot in 2009. Currently viewed as a better defensive outfielder than Jeremy Hermida, Ross will probably move from right to left field in an attempt to cut down on baserunners taking an extra base on base hits.

Gaby Sanchez (First Base)

PA	R	H	2B	3B	HR	RBI	SO	BB	SB	CS	BA	OBP	SLG	OPS	3-Year	Fielding	Reliability
503	55	104	25	2	12	53	89	51	7	5	.236	.320	.383	.703	+0.01	C	Very High

Sanchez terrorized Double-A pitching in 2008, hitting .314/.404/.917 with 17 homers and 92 RBIs and eventually winning the Southern League MVP before getting his first major league action. Although he got only eight at-bats, the 25-year-old made a good first impression on manager Fredi Gonzalez. Gonzalez will be holding an open competition in spring training for Mike Jacobs' replacement and, barring an injury or a total explosion by one of his competitors, the first base job will be Sanchez's.

Dan Uggla (Second Base)

PA	R	H	2B	3B	HR	RBI	SO	BB	SB	CS	BA	OBP	SLG	OPS	3-Year	Fielding	Reliability
593	77	136	32	3	27	88	141	60	3	2	.262	.345	.491	.836	-0.02	C	Very High

Uggla slowed down in the second half, but after you have the best month in franchise history in May, down is the only way to go. Despite suffering an ankle injury, hitting just .190 in July and barely hitting over .200 in August, he bounced back with a good September and still managed to finish the year with the third-best OBP in baseball. Undoubtedly thanks in part to his gimpy ankle, Uggla's defense fell off a bit in the second half as well but he still wound up ranking 10th overall among second basemen, according to The Fielding Bible. Expect similar production out of Uggla, now 28, in 2009. With Chase Utley out at least a month with a hip injury, another All-Star selection seems imminent.

Pitchers

Burke Badenhop (Starter)

W	L	ERA	TBF	IP	Hit	HR	SO	BB	HBP	3-Year	Reliability
3	7	5.67	398	87	107	13	39	37	6	+0.02	Very High

In the first major league action of his career, Badenhop went 2-3 in eight starts and held a 6.08 ERA in 47.1 innings before being shut down with a shoulder injury. He doesn't have the stuff to make it as a starter, but could suffice in the long reliever/mopup role.

Eulogio De La Cruz (Starter)

W	L	ERA	TBF	IP	Hit	HR	SO	BB	HBP	3-Year	Reliability
7	9	4.89	634	141	149	17	96	74	8	-0.23	Very High

Another type B prospect throw-in in the Cabrera/Willis trade, De La Cruz spent some time with the Marlins and looked extremely hittable, giving up 18 runs in nine innings before being optioned back to Triple-A. He fared pretty well in the hitter-friendly Pacific Coast League, posting a 14-8 record and an ERA in the low 4.00s, but the most he will become is a glorified long reliever. He will try to win that job on this year's team in spring training.

Jesus Delgado (Reliever)

W	L	ERA	TBF	IP	Hit	HR	SO	BB	HBP	3-Year	Reliability
3	4	5.14	301	65	70	7	43	40	4	-0.26	Average

Delgado is a 24-year-old reliever with a dominating fastball. He spent most of 2008 in Double-A, where he posted a 3.45 ERA in 57.1 innings. He also got a cup of coffee with the Marlins in July. Delgado still needs to work on his secondary pitches, but for a guy who missed the 2002 and 2003 seasons due to surgery on his throwing arm, he has made good progress. He'll compete for a bullpen spot.

Josh Johnson (Starter)

W	L	ERA	TBF	IP	Hit	HR	SO	BB	HBP	3-Year	Reliability
7	6	4.08	509	119	121	11	95	44	4	-0.12	High

Johnson got Marlins fans thinking playoffs early in the second half of 2008 when he came back much sooner than expected from Tommy John surgery, throwing 97 mph and not losing any of his first 10 outings. It was the best start to a season of his career. Johnson will most likely be the ace of the staff in 2009.

Logan Kensing (Reliever)

W	L	ERA	TBF	IP	Hit	HR	SO	BB	HBP	3-Year	Reliability
3	4	4.49	283	64	59	8	60	35	3	+0.15	Low

Kensing had a decent season out of the bullpen in 2008, posting a 4.23 ERA in 55 innings, but his bigger accomplishment was being able to stay healthy for a full season for the first time in his career. Now that he's learned how to stay off the DL, Kensing will work on improving his location and walking fewer batters.

Bobby Keppel (Starter)

W	L	ERA	TBF	IP	Hit	HR	SO	BB	HBP	3-Year	Reliability
5	11	6.36	676	145	186	25	62	70	7	+0.24	Very High

Keppel is a 26-year-old righty who has been sub-par at best in the majors. In 2006, he made six starts for the Royals, going 0-4 with a 5.50 ERA before spending a year in the Rockies' organization. After coming to the Marlins as a free agent last year, he spent the year in Albuquerque, where he went 9-11 with a 5.99 ERA. He doesn't have much of a future with Florida.

Matt Lindstrom (Reliever)

W	L	ERA	TBF	IP	Hit	HR	SO	BB	HBP	3-Year	Reliability
3	4	4.19	271	62	63	5	50	26	3	+0.27	Low

With Kevin Gregg gone, Lindstrom will likely be the Marlins' closer in 2009. We got a glimpse of him in the role at the end of 2008. The righty, who occasionally gets his fastball into triple digits, converted all five of his save opportunities.

Jacob Marceaux (Reliever)

W	L	ERA	TBF	IP	Hit	HR	SO	BB	HBP	3-Year	Reliability
2	5	5.85	279	59	66	7	30	42	3	-0.38	Average

In his first season in Double-A, Marceaux struggled, posting a 4.45 ERA with 45 strikeouts and 43 walks in 59 innings. He'll get a look in spring training but is probably still at least a year away.

Ricky Nolasco (Starter)

W	L	ERA	TBF	IP	Hit	HR	SO	BB	HBP	3-Year	Reliability
9	10	4.23	707	168	171	24	134	42	7	+0.15	Very High

Nolasco broke out in a big way in 2008, going from mediocre, injury-prone swing man to Cy Young-worthy starter with one of the lowest BB/9s (1.8) and one of the best K/9s (7.9) in the league. How will he follow up in 2009? Most experts predict very well. Bill James' projection has Nolasco posting a 3.96 ERA, with 7.7 K/9 and a 2.3 BB/9 ratios. The only thing Nolasco has working against him is his health history. Before last year, his previous high in innings pitched in a season was 161.2 in 2005 for Double-A West Tenn.

Renyel Pinto (Reliever)

W	L	ERA	TBF	IP	Hit	HR	SO	BB	HBP	3-Year	Reliability
4	3	4.38	299	67	62	7	59	39	4	+0.12	Average

Pinto, a dynamic lefty, got off to a great start last year, holding an ERA under 2.00 through May. It was such a good start that manager Fredi Gonzalez proceeded to use him in 67 games before shutting him down with arm-falling-off-itis in late September. But, with more than an offseason's rest, Pinto should be ready to anchor the Marlins' pen again in 2009.

Anibal Sanchez (Starter)

W	L	ERA	TBF	IP	Hit	HR	SO	BB	HBP	3-Year	Reliability
5	6	4.72	440	100	103	12	75	46	6	-0.17	High

Sanchez returned way sooner than expected from massive reconstructive shoulder surgery, but may have been better waiting until this year. The lefty got roughed up in his 10 starts, going 2-5 with a 5.57 ERA. Plus, against the team's wishes, Sanchez pitched in the Venezuelan Winter League and didn't fare much better. Sanchez probably isn't coming into the year 100 percent.

Brett Sinkbeil (Starter)

W	L	ERA	TBF	IP	Hit	HR	SO	BB	HBP	3-Year	Reliability
4	10	6.99	598	125	174	22	34	61	8	-0.60	High

Sinkbeil is a 6-foot-4, 185-pound appropriately named sinkerballer with plus velocity out of Missouri State. Before getting hurt in 2006, he was outplaying his Bears teammate, Max Scherzer. After being selected 19th overall in the draft that year, Sinkbeil put together a solid first season as a pro, starting 13 games in A-ball and holding down a respectable 3.63 ERA. Most recently, Sinkbeil got his first taste of Double-A action and tabulated a 5-9 record and a 5.08 ERA in 26 starts. The bad news on Sinkbeil is that he has found it hard to stay healthy, which has stunted his development. As a result, some scouts believe his future as a starter is in doubt. However, Sinkbeil is a hard worker and made great strides improving his change-up last year. His 2009 season in Double-A should give us a pretty good idea of his future.

Taylor Tankersley (Reliever)

W	L	ERA	TBF	IP	Hit	HR	SO	BB	HBP	3-Year	Reliability
3	3	4.53	257	58	54	7	50	32	3	+0.02	Low

Tankersley is a LOOGY who struggled last year, running up an 8.10 ERA before eventually being replaced and optioned to Triple-A. But with Arthur Rhodes gone, Tank will get a chance to win his job back in spring training.

Ryan Tucker (Reliever)

W	L	ERA	TBF	IP	Hit	HR	SO	BB	HBP	3-Year	Reliability
5	8	5.69	526	114	126	16	66	65	7	-0.62	Very High

Tucker had a great season in Double-A last year, going 5-3 with a 1.58 ERA, and was named the organization's Minor League Pitcher of the Year. But, as he proved in his two short stints with the big league club, he is still a bit unpolished. The Marlins hope Tucker can turn into a starter, but he looks destined to be a mid-long reliever. He'll probably begin the year with the Mudcats.

Rick Vanden Hurk (Starter)

W	L	ERA	TBF	IP	Hit	HR	SO	BB	HBP	3-Year	Reliability
5	8	5.55	523	116	121	19	105	61	6	-0.16	Average

After a good spring, Vanden Hurk wound up in the Marlins' rotation, but he lasted only two bad starts before being demoted. The 23-year-old got another call in July and didn't fare much better before returning to the minors to finish out the season. Vanden Hurk has a good foundation (a good cut fastball and a huge 12-6 curve) but control is a serious problem. He'll spend at least another year in the minors.

Christopher Volstad (Starter)

W	L	ERA	TBF	IP	Hit	HR	SO	BB	HBP	3-Year	Reliability
7	10	5.26	705	155	186	14	69	70	8	-0.72	Very High

Volstad was 22 and had never spent a full season above Single-A, so the Marlins were a little wary of purchasing his contract. But after his first three starts, the first of which was an 8.2 inning, one-run outing against the Dodgers, the 6-foot-8 righty had put their minds at ease. Volstad went on to a 6-4 record and a 2.88 ERA, the lowest on the Florida staff. With arguably the best control on the team, he's pegged as the third starter in 2009.

Houston Astros

by Lisa Gray of The Astros Dugout (mvn.com/mlb/astros)

2009 Astros Projections

Record: 80-82
Division Rank/Games Behind: 4th, 9 games back
Runs Scored: 740, 9th in the league
Runs Allowed: 753, 7th in the league
Park Factor: .99, despite its idiosyncrasies

What Happened Last Year:

The Astros had a better year than I expected, thanks to Lance Berkman carrying the team through the first half, and then Carlos Lee and Ty Wigginton picking it up after the All-Star break. As usual, the Astros were better in the second half, going 42-24, unfortunately encouraging the owner to believe that the team was better than it was.

The Astros ended April on a losing note, partly because Roy Oswalt was struggling, partly because Jose Valverde was blowing saves and partly because Michael Bourn and J.R. Towles were significantly underperforming. The Astros had an outstanding May because Berkman couldn't be gotten out and Miguel Tejada and Hunter Pence had their only good months of the year. They lost and lost and lost in June and hit (hahaha) a low point when pitcher Shawn Chacon, uh, shall we say, expressed his displeasure with general manager Ed Wade by punching him.

The manager had clearly lost the team (dissing players to the media is generally not conducive to building a strong working relationship), new catcher Towles had lost his confidence, his swing and his job and new center fielder Bourn was catching balls but not getting on base.

After the All-Star break, as the team started winning, Wade stunned Astros fans by: (1) trading for failed Yankees reliever LaTroy Hawkins, who was installed in the setup role after Doug Brocail ran out of gas and promptly ran off a string of 22 scoreless appearances and, (2) trading for starting pitcher Randy Wolf, who won all but three of his 12 starts.

The Astros responded by winning, especially because Lee upped his game, hitting .371 in July, but he was knocked out for the year on Aug. 9 when a pitched ball broke his pinky. When Wigginton was installed in left, **he** responded by going on the hitting streak of his life,

hitting .369, socking 12 homers and driving in 27 runs until he also was hurt Sept. 5.

In fact, the Astros appeared to be ready to compete for the wild card when disaster hit. A gigantic hurricane headed straight for Houston. Owner Drayton McLane, with at least five days advance knowledge of the direction and scope of the storm, was unwilling to risk losing the gate from three sold-out Cubs games. He delayed rescheduling or relocating them until it was far too late. Commissioner Bud Selig moved the games to Milwaukee (instead of more fan-friendly Arlington, which was available) and the shell-shocked, exhausted, sleep-deprived Astros promptly allowed the Cubs to pitch a no-hitter, then a two-hitter. They lost the last game of the series before heading to Florida and losing three more. That, effectively and permanently, knocked them out of the wild card race.

The Astros' team defense was the third best in the National League and made the fewest errors of any NL team. Both Tejada and Wigginton far outperformed expectations. Berkman looked like J.T. Snow with the glove and Bourn was excellent in center, as were Darin Erstad and Reggie Abercrombie. Lee was, as usual, a cement statue in left, but manager Cecil Cooper had the sense to pull him for Erstad in the late innings if the Astros were ahead.

But sometimes, the whole actually **is** better than the sum of its parts, and the 2008 Astros exemplified that.

Players Lost from Last Year's Team:

Mark Loretta, Ty Wigginton, Randy Wolf, Brad Ausmus, David Newhan

Players Acquired:

Mike Hampton

Management Is:

Overmanaged by McLane and Tal Smith, the president of baseball operations. McLane is infamous for being an interfering owner who is most concerned with signing name free agents to get fans in the ballpark while saying that he wants to be a champion. What he actually wants is for the team to be just competitive enough to make the playoffs to keep fan interest at a maximum. For years, he refused to pay any prospect over slot or to offer arbitration to free agents. He diverted too much money from player development and the farm system essentially disintegrated.

Cecil Cooper was installed as manager (on the recommendation of Bud Selig) at the end of the 2007 season. He doesn't have predecessor Phil Garner's propensity for having position players play as many positions as possible, but other than that, showed little imagination and often bad-mouthed the players to the media. He also had very obvious favorites, and players who get on his bad side stay there.

His inability to elicit cooperation from his players culminated in the Shawn Chacon incident, in which Chacon flagrantly disobeyed Cooper's order to see him in the manager's office. Chacon received overwhelming support from the remainder of the players, which speaks volumes about Cooper's ability to effectively communicate with players. If the players are in open rebellion by midseason, he'll be fired if the team doesn't appear to be able to make its usual second-half run.

Ed Wade was hired as GM because he was the only candidate who agreed to "work with" Tal Smith. He carries a reputation for having built Philadelphia's farm system, but in fact had very little success outside of five first-round picks. I do realize that he was instructed to get rid of most of the players who were traded, and I also know he was instructed to get Tejada, so I don't blame him for those actions. He is, as he always was, obsessed with middle relievers, and he has had good luck with some signings, not so good luck with others. As for his draft, it remains to be seen how successful it will be.

The Minor League System Is:

Ranked No. 30 by every minor league ranking service. The Astros have exactly one good prospect, catcher Jason Castro. They supposedly have a few pitchers who have a chance to make the Astros roster, but they are middle reliever/fifth starter material at best. Astros minor league hitters have little plate discipline, walk seldom and strike out excessively. The Triple-A team is composed of major league rejects and Triple-A lifers who will perform decently and draw crowds to the park, but they offer no real hope for the major league team.

Due For a Change:

I hope Bourn will improve his batting and on-base averages and approach his numbers as a No. 2 hitter, .292/.354.

Reasons to be Optimistic:

Every time I am positive that the Astros are going nowhere, they make one of their patented second-half runs and make it, at the very least, interesting.

Reasons to be Pessimistic:

The team will remain essentially the same and its weaknesses have not been addressed:

1. The rotation consists of Oswalt, Mike Hampton, Wandy Rodriguez, Brian Moehler and Ida Know-Hu. A rotation consisting of one ace, an acceptable third starter when healthy, a 38-year-old who had performed so poorly that he had been relegated to mopup duty before having a decent year last year, and a guy who had been on the DL with one surgery after another for three years doesn't scream "champions" to me.

2. Wigginton, the third-best hitter on the team, is gone and has been replaced by Geoff Blum, who is not good enough with either bat or glove to be a full-time third baseman.

3. Tejada, whose bat was already in severe decline, is even older, and will most likely decline more.

4. Kaz Matsui will spend a third of the year on the DL, as usual, and instead of Mark Loretta/David Newhan filling in, the Astros will have some cheap replacement-level filler like Tomas Perez or Jose Castillo

5. Humberto Quintero, a worse hitter than Brad Ausmus, can't frame a pitch to save his life and will be the main catcher. Neither Oswalt nor Rodriguez appears to like throwing to him.

6. The players do not appear to like playing for the manager. And once again, the manager was not permitted to select his own bench coach. The pitchers do not like pitching coach Dewey Robinson.

7. The four highest-paid players cannot be traded for prospects—three because they have no-trade clauses and one because his contract significantly exceeds his value.

Still Left to Do:

Find a backup catcher and third baseman who can hit and make sure neither costs much more than the minimum. Oh, yeah, and find a fifth starter who won't cost more than the minimum.

Most Likely Team Outcome:

78-84. Yes, I know I said the same last year and I was wrong, but this time, I'm sure this team won't reach .500.

Player Projections

Batters

Reggie Abercrombie (Right Field)

PA	R	H	2B	3B	HR	RBI	SO	BB	SB	CS	BA	OBP	SLG	OPS	3-Year	Fielding	Reliability
394	51	91	19	3	14	48	115	15	19	5	.247	.286	.429	.715	-0.02	B	Average

Abercrombie spent most of the year at Triple-A and, as usual, fielded well and swung mightily. With Houston, he platooned with Michael Bourn in center, flashed good leather, and made the most of his 55 at-bats, going .309/.339/.509 and stealing five bases. Like Bourn, he seldom walks, seldom hits into double plays, won't/can't bunt and strikes out frequently. The Astros non-tendered him, but they want to re-sign him to a minor league contract and give him a shot at the major league roster.

Lance Berkman (First Base)

PA	R	H	2B	3B	HR	RBI	SO	BB	SB	CS	BA	OBP	SLG	OPS	3-Year	Fielding	Reliability
601	88	148	30	2	30	95	107	85	10	2	.293	.398	.538	.936	-0.04	B	Very High

Seems that every year, Berkman outperforms his projections (except for his 2007 BA) and I expect him to do so again. In fact, I see no reason why he wouldn't duplicate his 2008 numbers of .312/.420/.567. In '08, Berkman had a May for the ages with a 1.407 OPS keeping the Astros in the race, meriting a first-half MVP, but he couldn't buy a hit in September as the Astros sank quickly below the waves post-Ike. At age 32 he displayed an excellent glove and superior baserunning. He stole a career-high 18 bases, getting caught only twice.

Geoff Blum (Third Base)

PA	R	H	2B	3B	HR	RBI	SO	BB	SB	CS	BA	OBP	SLG	OPS	3-Year	Fielding	Reliability
380	41	88	20	1	10	45	63	27	1	1	.254	.311	.405	.716	—	C	High

Geoff Blum, the very definition of the replacement player, suddenly has found himself the starting third baseman due to the Astros' decision to non-tender Ty Wigginton. Blum doesn't hit for average or power but he had an uncharacteristically good year fielding (meaning he was somewhat less dreadful than usual). The projections look optimistic, as Blum seldom walks and hasn't hit for an average that high in years. It is possible that the Astros will sign a right-handed hitter to platoon with Blum.

Brian Bogusevic (Outfield)

PA	R	H	2B	3B	HR	RBI	SO	BB	SB	CS	BA	OBP	SLG	OPS	3-Year	Fielding	Reliability
285	36	69	14	1	7	32	55	29	6	2	.279	.357	.428	.785	+0.04	—	Very Low

Bogusevic was the Astros' 2005 first-round pick, a lefty who pitched and hit. The Astros tried unsuccessfully for more than three years to get him to get even A-ball hitters out. Finally, they allowed him to go the Rick Ankiel route and he killed Double-A pitching, hitting .371/.447/.556 over 124 at-bats. He, of course, should face SOME Triple-A pitching before being put on the major league roster. He can, of course, throw, but he played only 31 games in the outfield, so it is difficult to judge his ability to field. He isn't nimble enough to play the vast center field at Minute Maid, and Carlos Lee is cemented (hahahaha) in left, so I would guess that he will spend the year at Triple-A and perhaps earn a September call up.

Michael Bourn (Center Field)

PA	R	H	2B	3B	HR	RBI	SO	BB	SB	CS	BA	OBP	SLG	OPS	3-Year	Fielding	Reliability
433	55	98	11	5	7	34	87	35	27	4	.252	.315	.360	.675	+0.07	A	Average

Bourn was obtained from the Phillies for the Hated Brad Lidge, who went on to have the best season of his career. Eager fans, media and front office personnel expected Bourn to become the second coming of Kenny Lofton but instead, he was Willy Taveras minus all the bunt hits. Bourn was benched for Darin Erstad and Reggie Abercrombie frequently during the second half, but finished the year strongly. He also was expected to be a leadoff hitter, but he did much better in the No. 2 spot, hitting .292/.354 instead of .212/.279. And he's fast—he stole 41 bases. Bourn has been given a much longer leash than any other struggling player on this team would have because the GM's ego is so heavily involved in his success. But if he doesn't start off strongly, I wouldn't be surprised if he is platooned with Erstad and/or Abercrombie.

Jose Castillo (Third Base)

PA	R	H	2B	3B	HR	RBI	SO	BB	SB	CS	BA	OBP	SLG	OPS	3-Year	Fielding	Reliability
408	43	97	22	2	9	46	75	25	1	1	.257	.307	.398	.705	+0.00	D	High

He may be signed to platoon with Geoff Blum at third. He isn't a good hitter, fielder or runner, but so what? He should come dirt cheap.

Darin Erstad (Center Field)

PA	R	H	2B	3B	HR	RBI	SO	BB	SB	CS	BA	OBP	SLG	OPS	3-Year	Fielding	Reliability
354	36	83	16	1	4	32	64	25	3	2	.257	.313	.350	.663	-0.04	C	Low

Erstad was signed last year as a part-time player and he did extremely well, avoiding the injuries that have plagued him throughout his career. He played some center field, some in left as a defensive replacement for Carlos Lee and some in relief of Lance Berkman at first. He had a good year with the bat, probably because he had plenty of rest and wasn't playing hurt. He has little power and seldom walks, but he could exceed the projected BA again.

Christopher Johnson (Third Base)

PA	R	H	2B	3B	HR	RBI	SO	BB	SB	CS	BA	OBP	SLG	OPS	3-Year	Fielding	Reliability
472	46	106	20	1	11	51	98	19	3	2	.239	.274	.362	.636	+0.04	B	Average

Johnson was never designated as a "prospect," but after three mediocre years in A ball he exploded in Double-A, hitting .324/.364/.506. Johnson could find himself in the majors as a platoon partner for Geoff Blum if he excels in spring training.

Carlos Lee (Left Field)

PA	R	H	2B	3B	HR	RBI	SO	BB	SB	CS	BA	OBP	SLG	OPS	3-Year	Fielding	Reliability
525	74	143	30	0	27	88	61	43	8	2	.302	.360	.536	.896	-0.04	D	Very High

Lee is a very good hitter, even if he does ground into 25 or so double plays a year. He hits for average and power and he drives in around 100 runs a year hitting behind on-base machine Lance Berkman. He missed the last month of the season last year because of a broken pinky, but he should be OK for the season. He is a liability with the glove—he seldom catches anything not hit right to him. Any ball hit down the line is an automatic double, and his arm is neither strong nor accurate.

Thomas Manzella (Shortstop)

PA	R	H	2B	3B	HR	RBI	SO	BB	SB	CS	BA	OBP	SLG	OPS	3-Year	Fielding	Reliability
474	43	99	18	3	4	37	91	26	5	4	.227	.274	.309	.583	+0.02	F	High

Manzella has the reputation of being an Adam Everett clone with both bat and glove. He does not have Everett's prowess as a base stealer, however. He hit .299/.346/.446 in Double-A and then was promoted to Triple-A, where he hit .219/.273/.294.

I would prefer to see Miguel Tejada at third and have Manzella and his weak bat at short rather than Geoff Blum at third and Tejada at short. It is doubtful that Blum wil outhit Manzell, and Manzella's glove will save many more runs than his bat will lose.

Kazuo Matsui (Second Base)

PA	R	H	2B	3B	HR	RBI	SO	BB	SB	CS	BA	OBP	SLG	OPS	3-Year	Fielding	Reliability
432	53	107	21	3	5	38	66	34	18	3	.277	.334	.385	.719	-0.04	D	High

Matsui, when not on the DL, hit well in both leadoff and the two-hole and stole 20 bases. However, he made a lot of errors, both booting and missing balls. He did display excellent range and made some very tough plays. When he is healthy, he should repeat his actual numbers from '08 —.293/.354/.427.

Edwin Maysonet (Shortstop)

PA	R	H	2B	3B	HR	RBI	SO	BB	SB	CS	BA	OBP	SLG	OPS	3-Year	Fielding	Reliability
440	41	93	19	2	6	39	84	25	3	2	.232	.281	.334	.615	+0.02	D	High

He outhit Tommy Manzella at Triple-A last year: .271/.343/.379 and he walks more. He has a good chance to replace Mark Loretta as the middle infield utility guy. He doesn't have the power to play third, but then again, neither does Geoff Blum or Jose Castillo.

Hunter Pence (Right Field)

PA	R	H	2B	3B	HR	RBI	SO	BB	SB	CS	BA	OBP	SLG	OPS	3-Year	Fielding	Reliability
573	75	145	31	5	22	82	113	40	8	5	.276	.328	.479	.807	+0.02	C	Very High

Pence suffered the expected sophomore slump, as opposing pitchers discovered he was vulnerable to sliders and fastballs down and away. He has little patience—seldom waits for his pitch, seldom walks. He runs fast, but is not a good baserunner—he was caught stealing on 10 of 21 attempts and made seven significant baserunning blunders which cost the team precious outs. He is an average fielder with an accurate arm whose biggest problem is his first step toward the ball. I am not sure why he has been designated "untouchable" by the organization, but he is being touted as the Next Face Of The Astros—next after Bagwell/Biggio. He just isn't that good.

Humberto Quintero (Catcher)

PA	R	H	2B	3B	HR	RBI	SO	BB	SB	CS	BA	OBP	SLG	OPS	3-Year	Fielding	Reliability
336	34	82	16	1	6	35	57	15	1	1	.265	.308	.382	.690	-0.02	B	Average

Quintero has been designated as the Astros' main catcher for 2009 by default, as J.R. Towles appears to be in their permanent doghouse. He is not a good or patient hitter; his lifetime line over 421 plate appearances is .230/.271/.304. He doesn't have good strike zone judgment and is impatient, garnering only 16 walks over those 421 PA. He should be a backup catcher.

Mark Saccomanno (First Base)

PA	R	H	2B	3B	HR	RBI	SO	BB	SB	CS	BA	OBP	SLG	OPS	3-Year	Fielding	Reliability
504	62	122	26	3	23	77	111	29	2	2	.261	.304	.477	.781	-0.03	—	Very High

Unlike Chris Johnson, Saccomanno has torn the cover off the ball at Triple-A, hitting 33 doubles, three triples and 27 homers over 528 plate appearances. The Astros organization doesn't like him, for some reason, and wasn't happy about having to call him up last fall after Ty Wigginton was hurt. He has a reputation as a butcher at third, so he was put at first. He could at least be a power bat off the bench.

Miguel Tejada (Shortstop)

PA	R	H	2B	3B	HR	RBI	SO	BB	SB	CS	BA	OBP	SLG	OPS	3-Year	Fielding	Reliability
590	70	160	29	1	15	73	70	35	4	2	.295	.343	.435	.778	-0.04	C	Very High

Tejada was obtained before the 2008 season at the cost of three young pitchers and a very good young cheap outfielder. Somehow, the owner and GM were the only people connected with baseball who were shocked to discover that Tejada was two years older than his stated age or that he was, shall we say, rumored to have been a steroid user. For some reason, both the owner and the fans thought that he would hit 40-50 homers and drive in 100 runs. He didn't. His numbers across the board continued their three-year decline, his walks declined, and he grounded into a NL-record 32 double plays. I would not expect him to improve.

Justin Towles (Catcher)

PA	R	H	2B	3B	HR	RBI	SO	BB	SB	CS	BA	OBP	SLG	OPS	3-Year	Fielding	Reliability
385	44	80	15	2	11	43	75	27	5	2	.238	.316	.392	.708	+0.04	B	High

Towles began 2008 as the Astros' top prospect and starting catcher. He showed himself to be an excellent defensive catcher and he hit decently at the start. But between the hitting coach fooling with his swing and the manager's public hostility toward him, Towles was a nervous wreck by the time he headed back to Triple-A, where he resurrected his hitting to the tune of .304/.370/.500. This year, the Astros have not so much as mentioned his name in connection with either starting or backup catching and they even obtained an A-ball catcher in the Rule 5 draft to use as the backup. Unless he hits like Barry Bonds in spring training, he has no chance of making the team.

Pitchers

Brandon Backe (Starter)

W	L	ERA	TBF	IP	Hit	HR	SO	BB	HBP	3-Year	Reliability
6	10	5.65	652	145	164	25	94	65	6	+0.27	High

Backe was supposed to be the No. 2 or No. 3 starter. He wasn't that good, but he was not that far below league average (4.72 ERA) on Aug. 5, when he had a terrible start—he couldn't throw any pitch except a straight fastball and manager Cecil Cooper left him in to give up 11 runs. It happened again a couple of starts later. By the end of August, he was clearly completely out of gas and should have been shut down with a dead arm, but he wasn't. He finished the season with a dreadful 6.05 ERA. He isn't that bad, but it was his first full season back after having Tommy John surgery, and if used judiciously, he should be better next year with an ERA in the high fours. The team has tried very hard to trade him, but it looks as if he'll be competing for the fifth spot in the rotation again.

Doug Brocail (Reliever)

W	L	ERA	TBF	IP	Hit	HR	SO	BB	HBP	3-Year	Reliability
4	4	3.82	287	69	64	8	52	23	2	—	Low

Brocail was signed as the seventh-inning guy, but others faltered and Cecil Cooper used Brocail frequently—15 appearances in April and 14 in May and June. By the All-Star break, Brocail was obviously tired and overworked. Cooper used him more sparingly the remainder of the year, but he wasn't as good or as strong as he had been in the first few months. Brocail will be 42 years old this season and Cooper has learned that he requires rest to stay strong. The eighth-inning duties will be divided among him, LaTroy Hawkins and Geoff Geary.

Tim Byrdak (Reliever)

W	L	ERA	TBF	IP	Hit	HR	SO	BB	HBP	3-Year	Reliability
4	3	4.13	272	63	56	8	56	31	2	—	Very Low

One of GM Ed Wade's good pickups from the scrap heap, Byrdak is a very good lefty whose weakness is walks. His ERA would have been significantly lower had it not been for two bad games. He appeared in 60 games, was sometimes used strictly as a LOOGY, but also pitched multiple innings on 10 occasions.

Jack Cassel (Starter)

W	L	ERA	TBF	IP	Hit	HR	SO	BB	HBP	3-Year	Reliability
5	10	5.74	606	133	170	20	70	50	6	+0.42	Very High

Cassel is a sinkerball pitcher, an extreme groundball pitcher, who strikes out very few. He works quickly and efficiently. He excelled at Triple-A, but wasn't particularly effective at the major league level. I doubt that he will be with the Astros again.

Geoff Geary (Reliever)

W	L	ERA	TBF	IP	Hit	HR	SO	BB	HBP	3-Year	Reliability
4	4	4.25	295	68	71	7	44	25	4	+0.23	Average

The forgotten man in the Brad Lidge trade, Geary proved to be an asset to the bullpen when healthy. He was used as the seventh-inning man, occasionally the setup guy, and sometimes as the high leverage reliever called in when another pitcher left men on base with the game on the line. He cut his hits-per-nine rate by around 40 percent, giving up only 45 hits in 64 innings, with career lows in ERA (2.53), WHIP (1.14) and OPS against (.567). The performance of middle relievers is unpredictable from year to year, but I would expect both his ERA and OPS against to rise a bit.

LaTroy Hawkins (Reliever)

W	L	ERA	TBF	IP	Hit	HR	SO	BB	HBP	3-Year	Reliability
4	3	3.79	269	63	63	6	45	22	2	—	Low

Hawkins was picked off the waiver wire from the Yankees at the trade deadline. He then threw 21 innings over 24 appearances, giving up just one earned run. He was given the job of setup man on Aug. 16 and excelled. He has historically done best as a setup man, which is his projected role with the Astros again.

Brad James (Starter)

W	L	ERA	TBF	IP	Hit	HR	SO	BB	HBP	3-Year	Reliability
4	8	6.50	523	110	143	18	27	59	9	-0.58	High

He just finished his first full year at Double-A, missing about a third of the season because of injuries. James is an extreme groundball pitcher who gives up few home runs and gets few strikeouts. He was placed on the 40-man roster because of his eye-popping numbers in A-ball, but I can't see him on the major-league roster this year, even as a reliever.

Brian Moehler (Starter)

W	L	ERA	TBF	IP	Hit	HR	SO	BB	HBP	3-Year	Reliability
7	8	4.82	598	138	158	21	69	38	5	—	High

Moehler started the year as designated mopup guy, but when Wandy Rodriguez went down with an injury in April, Moehler was put into the rotation and pitched well enough to remain there, even displacing Shawn Chacon later in the year. He started 26 games, threw 142.1 innings, and finished with a 4.43 ERA and a 1.32 WHIP.

I don't know if Moehler will run into the same wall he did in 2006, but it is important to note that when he was a reliever for the Astros in '07, he pitched extremely well in the second half because he was used at least once every 2-4 days instead of sporadically, as he had been in the first half.

Fernando Nieve (Reliever)

W	L	ERA	TBF	IP	Hit	HR	SO	BB	HBP	3-Year	Reliability
3	5	5.47	329	73	80	13	50	34	3	+0.20	Average

Nieve pitched as both a starter and reliever for the Astros in 2006, with an ERA of 4.20 and a WHIP of 1.33. He missed most of 2007 because of Tommy John surgery and hasn't been the same guy since. He threw 72 innings at Triple-A with bad numbers, then threw 10 dreadful innings in the majors. Some guys never regain command after surgery, some never regain velocity and some never regain either. Nieve may improve simply because it's been a year and a half since his operation. I heard that the Astros want to groom him as a closer to replace Jose Valverde, but that remains to be seen.

Bud Norris (Starter)

W	L	ERA	TBF	IP	Hit	HR	SO	BB	HBP	3-Year	Reliability
4	8	5.90	488	106	120	18	80	57	7	-0.26	Low

Norris, like his teammate Brad James, was hurt part of last year at Double-A and threw only 80 innings. Unlike James, he is a strikeout pitcher and, like James, he gives up very few homers. I would be very surprised if he makes the major league roster, as he hasn't pitched in Triple-A and he wasn't exactly ace-like against Double-A hitters.

Roy Oswalt (Starter)

W	L	ERA	TBF	IP	Hit	HR	SO	BB	HBP	3-Year	Reliability
12	9	3.77	789	189	194	19	132	46	7	+0.18	Very High

Oswalt had a simply dreadful April and May, giving up 16 homers over 70 innings and running up an ERA of 5.41. He insisted he wasn't hurt, and had an ERA of 2.98 in June. He **was** injured in July, but came back strong in July and August, posting ERAs of 2.51 and 1.42— in fact, he gave up only five homers after the All-Star break. I would guess he'll at least duplicate his numbers from 2008.

Wandy Rodriguez (Starter)

W	L	ERA	TBF	IP	Hit	HR	SO	BB	HBP	3-Year	Reliability
7	9	4.73	641	147	157	20	117	54	6	+0.47	Very High

Rodriguez is a small lefty who, like many lefties, has taken a while to develop. He has a very good fastball, around 91 mph, and a devastating curve. He has evolved from a Kirk Rueter nibbler, hoping that hitters will hit junk on the edges and ground out, to a strikeout pitcher.

He missed 10 games last year due to injuries (none to his arm/shoulder) and the manager was careful not to stress him when he returned. If he is not hurt, I expect him to significantly outpitch his projection. However, his great weakness is letting his emotions get the better of him on the mound and he doesn't seem to like throwing to designated catcher Humberto Quintero. Perhaps he will end up throwing to the backup.

Chris Sampson (Reliever)

W	L	ERA	TBF	IP	Hit	HR	SO	BB	HBP	3-Year	Reliability
6	6	4.26	447	106	116	13	48	26	4	+0.21	Very High

He's a sinker ball pitcher whose fastball seldom exceeds 88 mph. He also throws a good cut fastball. If his sinker is on, he works quickly, walks few, and needs around 10 pitches per inning. If his sinker doesn't work, he needs to be pulled immediately because his straight fastball is hit like a batting practice pitch. The Astros always wanted him to be a reliever, but two years in a row he pitched his way into the rotation. At the first opportunity last year (the failure of three key relievers) they put him back in the bullpen, where he did very well: 61 innings with a 2.92 ERA, 1.16 WHIP and .225 BAA. He may again start the year as the fifth starter if others fail in spring training.

Jose Valverde (Reliever)

W	L	ERA	TBF	IP	Hit	HR	SO	BB	HBP	3-Year	Reliability
5	3	3.47	299	72	59	8	78	27	3	+0.26	Low

After an extremely shaky start in April, he corrected his delivery and pitched very well for the rest of the year. He has an excellent fastball and splitter. He doesn't seem to have a problem pitching from the stretch, but he does have difficulty stranding other pitchers' runners if called in before the ninth. Owner Drayton McLane is not happy about having to pay Valverde, but he has no cheap alternative now. I wouldn't be surprised if Valverde is signed, then traded.

Randy Wolf (Starter)

W	L	ERA	TBF	IP	Hit	HR	SO	BB	HBP	3-Year	Reliability
8	10	4.78	705	161	170	23	124	63	8	+0.25	High

Randy Wolf is a No. 3 or No. 4 starter pitcher who, for some reason, was highly coveted by GM Ed Wade. He was not re-signed by the Astros only because the owner refused to pay for him. He usually manages to pitch six innings, seldom gives up fewer than two or more than five runs per start.

Wesley Wright (Reliever)

W	L	ERA	TBF	IP	Hit	HR	SO	BB	HBP	3-Year	Reliability
3	4	4.91	279	62	59	9	56	38	4	-0.13	Average

Wright was a Rule 5 pick last year, one of the rare Rule 5 picks who not only makes it onto the major league roster, but merits being retained. He was not used strictly as a LOOGY, but lost effectiveness if asked to pitch more than one inning. His walk rate and homer rate were a bit too high, but were surprisingly good for a guy who had never faced Triple-A hitters.

He has a good fastball with a lot of movement and a decent slider, but not quite the command of the strike zone he will need to stay in the bigs after hitters adjust to him.

Kansas City Royals

by Bradford Doolittle of Upon Further Review (uponfurtherreview.kansascity. com)

2009 Royals Projections

Record: 79-83
Division Rank/Games Behind: 3rd, 7 games back
Runs Scored: 744, 10th in the league
Runs Allowed: 773, 9th in the league
Park Factor: 1.00, neutral

What Happened Last Year:

The 2008 season was another rebuilding year in a very real sense for the Kansas City Royals, both on the field and, well, **around** the field. Third-year general manager Dayton Moore again splurged on the free-agent market, bringing in enigmatic outfielder Jose Guillen for $12 million per annum. The Royals' payroll climbed to a franchise record $58 million. However, because of an orgy of revenue all across the game, that figure still left KC only 24th on the salary ladder.

The expenditures extended to Kauffman Stadium itself, though most of that money was courtesy of a taxpayer subsidy approved in a 2007 election, well before it became common knowledge that the nation's economy was about to be flushed down the toilet. The K featured a gigantic new center field scoreboard, with high-def video and a state-of-the-art sound system. The technology was impressive but, unfortunately, too often the play on the field left the few fans in the stands wishing that the scoreboard was showing the latest episode of Dancing With the Stars. On the hill behind the stadium, the old scoreboard's crown top lay scattered in pieces, while upturned mounds of earth, temporary plywood entrances and lots of scaffolding and plastic promised of a better stadium experience to come.

That may all be well and good, but most Royals fans will tell you that they'd trade a winning season for all the video boards in the world. To that end, the Royals brought in hot-prospect manager Trey Hillman from Japan to shepherd the struggling franchise into a new era of success. Hillman struggled at times, employing techniques that might have worked just fine with the Ham Fighters but weren't as effective with players used to shoe shines and valet service. During the season, whispers abounded that the players were tuning him out, with Guillen, of course, adding to the tempestu-

ous clubhouse atmosphere. In the end, Hillman didn't seem to add much to the mix except for an extra strain of moral fiber. Too often, his in-game style disappointingly fell into the category of manage-by-numbers. Still, Hillman drew nothing but plaudits from the one guy whose opinion matters: Moore.

Going into the season, the Royals figured to be headed for another 65-70 win season, with anything above that a nice bonus. In fact, they finished with 75 victories, their most since 2003. That also means that the Royals have added 19 wins since the 2005 franchise nadir. If you look more closely, KC still seemed to be a squad stuck running in place. The Royals' Pythagorean profile was that of a 72-win team, which is one less than the figure projected in the 2008 *THT Season Preview*. At the same time, a fine second half by young slugger Billy Butler and an 18-8 September convinced many of the Royals faithful that Moore, indeed, finally has the Boys in Blue back on the right path.

Players Lost from Last Year's Team:

Moore entered the offseason facing a gaggle of difficult personnel decisions, since a number of young veterans were entering the arbitration phase of their careers. That left Moore a little hamstrung in terms of payroll. Through the middle of December, that hadn't stopped Moore from remaking the team's roster as best he could. Moore cashed in a couple of bullpen chips in Leo Nunez (to Florida) and Ramon Ramirez (to Boston) in trades to add offense.

He also non-tendered disappointing speedster Joey Gathright, free-agent bust John Bale and journeyman Jason Smith. Second baseman Mark Grudzielanek was offered arbitration, which, as expected, was refused. Grudz will look to spend the golden years of his baseball career with a contender after being a solid performer during his three seasons in Kansas City.

Players Acquired:

During the early portion of the hot stove league, Moore focused on improving a Royals offense that finished 12th in OPS+ in the American League. Right after the World Series, he shipped Nunez to the Marlins for slugger Mike Jacobs, who hit 32 homers last year while posting a sub-.300 OBP. Later, he sent Ramirez to the Red Sox for center fielder Coco Crisp, who is slotted into the leadoff slot in the coming season's lineup.

The bullpen was Moore's next target. He added Doug Waechter and Kyle Farnsworth to serve as righty setup men and added Horacio Ramirez as a swing guy who could get a few turns in the rotation.

Management Is:

Moore seems to be getting a little impatient with some aspects of being the general manager of a small-market franchise but, at the same time, is more resolute than ever to return the Royals to the scenes of former glories. He has steadily added talent at the lower levels of the minors, a process that may not begin to bear fruit until 2010 at earliest. Meanwhile, he is scrambling to get the Royals back on the good side of .500, convinced that the resultant bump in attendance will provide the money KC needs to lock up the likes of Zack Greinke and Alex Gordon for the long term.

Moore did some tweaking in the Royals' front office after the season, shedding long-time scouting director Deric Ladnier and bringing in former Phillies assistant GM Mike Arbuckle after he was passed over as the replacement for Pat Gillick in Philadelphia. Moore's right-hand man, J.J. Picollo, is expected to assume a bigger player-development role with the departure of Ladnier.

The Minor League System Is:

The Royals' affiliates posted an aggregate winning percentage of .478 last year, the worst finish for the organization since 2001. That's not to say that there weren't some encouraging signs for KC, which ranked 24th in Baseball America's preseason talent rankings. First, the system has turned out a nice collection of young talent that has already reached the big leagues. Bill James' young talent rankings slot the Royals fifth in baseball and James says that he wouldn't be surprised if the team wins 85-90 games next season.

It appears that the Royals did well with their selection of Mike Moustakas, who was taken with the second pick of the 2007 draft, one spot after Rays wunderkind David Price. Moustakas was one of the youngest players in the Midwest League last season, yet emerged as one of the best young hitters in the minors during the second half of the season. Despite playing in a pitcher's park in a pitcher's league, Moustakas posted a .321/.392/.557 line after the All-Star break. He was moved from short-stop to third base midway through the season, which eventually could create a logjam at the position at the big-league level.

With the year's first pick in 2008, the Royals took high school slugger Eric Hosmer, whom the team hopes can develop into a left-handed version of Albert Pujols,

with both the glove and the bat. It's hard to know what to make of such things, but when Hosmer took batting practice at Kauffman Stadium after signing in August, several members of the media remarked at his startling power. That's just practice, but Hosmer is the guy to watch in the coming season as the Royals dream of a 2011 heart of the order: Gordon, Butler, Hosmer, Moustakas. In addition, the Royals proved their willingness to invest in the draft, picking and signing righty high school pitcher Tim Melville, a top-10 talent who fell because of perceived signability issues.

Due For a Change:

Keep an eye on Butler, who has flirted dangerously close to becoming pigeonholed into one of the least valued positions you can imagine: DH against lefties. The Royals used Ross Gload as their primary first baseman last season, which on the surface seems inexplicable. In reality, however, KC was attempting to send Butler a message: "If you want to be a starting first baseman in the big leagues, you're going to have to earn it."

Apparently, there was a hint of entitlement in Butler's demeanor and he sometimes would lose focus. A slow start led to Butler being demoted to Triple-A. Upon his return from Omaha, however, Butler began to show some indications that he might be the impact hitter he was once ordained to be. Butler hit .305/.341/.476 in the second half and, for the season, was at .340/.395/.590 against lefties. With Mike Jacobs—an abysmal defender—on board, first base is Butler's position to be had and, let's not forget, the guy doesn't turn 23 years old until April.

Reasons to be Optimistic:

All things considered, the Royals are in a pretty good place. There is young talent on the roster and more of it in the pipeline, some of it possibly in the form of impact bats. Moore has shown a couple of desirable traits you want to see in a GM. First, he refuses to squander top-shelf young talent for short-term gains. And, even more encouraging, he has shown a terrific ability to build a bullpen. This talent, not germane to all GMs, allows him to flip solid but fungible talents like Nunez and Ramirez to fill holes on the rest of the roster. Yet there is no real concern about next year's relief corps because Moore has proven his skill at building a bullpen each season, from scratch if needed.

Reasons to be Pessimistic:

It's an old and tired refrain, but we could be looking at another era of headlines about baseball's economic status, particularly with small-market franchises like the Royals that rely on the massive amounts of dollars they get in MLB's revenue-sharing system. The general economic worries already have had an impact on the NFL and the NBA and are expected to cause the Arena Football League to cancel its 2009 season.

There hasn't been much talk of these problems yet in baseball, where revenues have been climbing ever since the 1994 strike. However, a dearth of fannies in seats might throw a big roadblock in front of whatever momentum Moore's rebuilding efforts has gathered. In a more immediate sense, there has to be some consternation over Zack Greinke's seeming indifference toward signing a long term deal. He's under the Royals' control for a couple of more seasons, but if he's not going to sign on for the duration, Moore may be forced to deal one of baseball's emergent stars.

Still Left to Do:

Moore has likely done enough already to nudge the team toward another incremental improvement. His now-moot pursuit of free agent Rafael Furcal was probably an unnecessary residual from his overwhelming fondness for anything once associated with the Atlanta Braves. The general belief was that to bring Furcal aboard, Moore would have needed to somehow move Jose Guillen. Shockingly, the market for an overpaid, underproductive malcontent isn't too good. Not having Furcal might not be a bad thing, in the end. It would be nice to see what Alberto Callaspo would do with a full season's worth of at-bats.

Most Likely Team Outcome:

While the Royals' 2009 projected lineup might not send many sabermetric hearts a-fluttering, Hillman will nonetheless have a legitimate major league player at all nine spots, with a couple more of the same on his bench. With one of the game's best young closers in Joakim Soria, a top-shelf top of the rotation in Greinke and Gil Meche, and what is shaping up to be a nice corps of middle relievers, a healthy Royals team will make a run at .500. When a team gets to that level, anything is possible. This is not necessarily a make-or-break season for the Moore regime, but it nonetheless could turn out to be the year Royals fans remember as the franchise's watershed campaign.

Player Projections

Batters

Mike Aviles (Shortstop)

PA	R	H	2B	3B	HR	RBI	SO	BB	SB	CS	BA	OBP	SLG	OPS	3-Year	Fielding	Reliability
576	68	155	34	6	12	69	73	25	6	3	.286	.318	.437	.755	+0.01	C	Very High

Aviles entered the 2008 season as a 27-year-old minor leaguer ranked as KC's 29th-best prospect by Baseball America. He finished the season fourth in the voting for AL Rookie of the Year. What happened? When you consider Aviles' age and his line last season (.325/.354/.480 with KC) compared to his minor-league record (.297/.338/.464), it sort of screams "career year!" That's especially so when you consider that, you know, the majors are supposed to be a little more difficult than the minors. Aviles also turned in some shiny numbers with the glove at shortstop, a problem area for the Royals since pretty much forever. It wouldn't be realistic to expect Aviles to repeat last year's numbers, but anything close will give the Royals their best middle infielder in a long time. This is really uncharted territory. Since 1950, only nine players have had more hits than Aviles in a debut season at age 27 or older. Five of those players were Japanese imports from the last decade. None of the others were middle infielders.

John Buck (Catcher)

PA	R	H	2B	3B	HR	RBI	SO	BB	SB	CS	BA	OBP	SLG	OPS	3-Year	Fielding	Reliability
423	46	90	22	1	12	50	92	36	0	2	.239	.315	.399	.714	-0.02	D	High

Buck's development has leveled off, and he is not on a plateau on which you want to be stuck. He's still got some power and still can draw some walks, but his inability to sustain consistent contact has left him hitting in the .220s two years running. He is returning for the 2009 season as little more than a caddie for Miguel Olivo.

Billy Butler (Designated Hitter)

PA	R	H	2B	3B	HR	RBI	SO	BB	SB	CS	BA	OBP	SLG	OPS	3-Year	Fielding	Reliability
563	69	151	31	2	17	75	67	49	0	1	.299	.363	.470	.833	+0.08	C	Very High

The range of possibilities for Butler is wild, elusive, maddening. The early Albert Pujols comparisons have gone by the wayside, but you can't throw in the towel on a player with Butler's minor-league record at the age of 22. The Royals still don't know if Butler is ever going to be able to hold down a position. They don't know if he's a platoon player, a lefty killer who only can play about 40 percent of the time. There is a lot they don't know about Butler and this is the year to find out. As for the range of possibilities, who knows, but it's scary to note that the player holding down the top spot on Butler's list of comps at baseball-reference.com is the immortal Ken Harvey.

Alberto Callaspo (Second Base)

PA	R	H	2B	3B	HR	RBI	SO	BB	SB	CS	BA	OBP	SLG	OPS	3-Year	Fielding	Reliability
352	40	93	18	4	2	33	30	29	2	1	.294	.354	.395	.749	+0.02	D	High

Callaspo had some off-the-field troubles last season that limited his availability. By late August, however, he was playing second base everyday due to an injury to Mark Grudzielanek. From Aug. 23 on, Callaspo hit .319/.371/.407, striking out just five times in 125 plate appearances. Callaspo projects as below-average with the glove, but KC may have found an ideal No. 2 hitter.

Shane Costa (Right Field)

PA	R	H	2B	3B	HR	RBI	SO	BB	SB	CS	BA	OBP	SLG	OPS	3-Year	Fielding	Reliability
381	46	97	24	3	7	42	52	26	7	2	.281	.336	.429	.765	+0.01	C	High

The ship of Costa has pretty much sailed at this point. His minor league record is solid, but in 449 big-league plate appearances, he's been a totally different player, one who doesn't walk or hit for power. He just doesn't have that one standout skill that could help him carve out a niche in the bigs, and the Royals have better options.

Coco Crisp (Center Field)

PA	R	H	2B	3B	HR	RBI	SO	BB	SB	CS	BA	OBP	SLG	OPS	3-Year	Fielding	Reliability
454	55	108	20	3	6	40	66	37	19	4	.267	.329	.376	.705	-0.02	D	Very High

Crisp was a bit of a disappointment for three years in Boston, but he's still a quality player because he's excellent defensively and can hold his own at the plate. He has gap power but can be very streaky. For somebody who doesn't have a big power swing, he strikes out a lot and doesn't draw many walks.

David DeJesus (Center Field)

PA	R	H	2B	3B	HR	RBI	SO	BB	SB	CS	BA	OBP	SLG	OPS	3-Year	Fielding	Reliability
558	68	140	28	6	8	55	72	47	9	3	.284	.355	.413	.768	-0.03	D	Very High

DeJesus was the Royals' best all-around player last season. His numbers were career bests in most categories, but were also remarkably similar to his performances in 2005 and 2006. A few more doubles turned into home runs, though, a trend that will need to continue in 2009 since DeJesus will be manning a corner outfield position due to the acquisition of Coco Crisp. DeJesus may not have the ideal power bat for the corner, but he and Crisp should give the Royals their best outfield defense in years.

Joey Gathright (Center Field)

PA	R	H	2B	3B	HR	RBI	SO	BB	SB	CS	BA	OBP	SLG	OPS	3-Year	Fielding	Reliability
401	51	98	12	2	3	29	59	37	23	7	.283	.361	.355	.716	+0.01	C	High

Gathright had some gaudy numbers in 2007 thanks to an unsustainable batting average, a house of cards which tumbled in 2008. Gathright still has not managed to overcome lackluster instincts to capitalize on his speed. The Royals apparently got tired of waiting: Gathright was non-tendered in December and signed with the Cubs.

Esteban German (Left Field)

PA	R	H	2B	3B	HR	RBI	SO	BB	SB	CS	BA	OBP	SLG	OPS	3-Year	Fielding	Reliability
336	39	80	16	4	2	26	52	31	8	2	.273	.348	.375	.723	-0.04	D	Average

Many have bemoaned German's lack of a real shot as an everyday player with the Royals. Last season, he probably didn't deserve one, hitting .245 without his usual OBP-boosting patience. Nevertheless, the Royals are bringing German back for another go as a utility player.

Ross Gload (First Base)

PA	R	H	2B	3B	HR	RBI	SO	BB	SB	CS	BA	OBP	SLG	OPS	3-Year	Fielding	Reliability
394	42	101	21	2	4	38	46	23	3	3	.278	.323	.379	.702	-0.03	C	Average

Buddy Bell loved Gload; Trey Hillman loves him even more. He does play hard and he does have a fairly consistent line-drive stroke. Still, can any lineup survive a first baseman who hits three home runs in 418 plate appearances?

Alex Gordon (Third Base)

PA	R	H	2B	3B	HR	RBI	SO	BB	SB	CS	BA	OBP	SLG	OPS	3-Year	Fielding	Reliability
541	68	126	33	2	17	69	111	54	8	3	.267	.350	.453	.803	+0.04	D	Very High

Hopes that Gordon would establish himself as the top young third baseman in the game during his sophomore year were dashed by the dazzling season put together by Tampa Bay's Evan Longoria. Gordon did improve, though, and not by a little. His OBP jumped 37 points due to a sharpened batting eye and his SLG jumped a notch as well. Gordon still has some holes in his swing, as his 120 strikeouts will attest, but we've only glimpsed what Gordon can do. As for that OBP, Gordon's .351 mark was the third-best among qualifying AL third basemen—eight points better than Longoria's. Gordon is on the verge of establishing himself as the face of the contemporary Royals.

Mark Grudzielanek (Second Base)

PA	R	H	2B	3B	HR	RBI	SO	BB	SB	CS	BA	OBP	SLG	OPS	3-Year	Fielding	Reliability
425	45	112	24	2	3	40	54	23	2	1	.286	.332	.381	.713	—	C	High

After refusing the Royals' offer of arbitration, Grudzielanek will be moving on. His three years in KC were solid and he's now hit .294 or better six years in a row. Grudzielanek turns 39 next season and while his hands in the field are still dependable, his range is diminished and shrinking by the day.

Jose Guillen (Left Field)

PA	R	H	2B	3B	HR	RBI	SO	BB	SB	CS	BA	OBP	SLG	OPS	3-Year	Fielding	Reliability
554	63	137	30	2	16	70	92	29	3	1	.269	.320	.430	.750	-0.04	D	Very High

Ugh. Guillen drove in 97 runs last season, an unfortunate fact that has people paid to know better thinking that he actually had a good season. Guillen finished with an OBP of an even .300 and is entering the decline phase of his career. He also was a bit of a disaster with the glove and didn't do much to enhance clubhouse harmony. You get the feeling that Guillen doesn't want to be in Kansas City and, deep down, it's doubtful Royals brass really want him to be there, either. But there's $24 million to be paid, too much for another club to take on and too much for the Royals to eat. So the Royals crow that Guillen's "productivity" is essential to improving next year's offense and he will team with Mike Jacobs to form the worst on-base duo in any big-league everyday lineup.

Kila Kaaihue (First Base)

PA	R	H	2B	3B	HR	RBI	SO	BB	SB	CS	BA	OBP	SLG	OPS	3-Year	Fielding	Reliability
488	60	99	18	1	21	65	80	68	1	2	.241	.353	.443	.796	+0.03	B	Very High

Kaaihue caught Royals' brass off-guard last season with his remarkable season in the minors, in which he hit a combined 38 home runs at three different levels. Kaaihue also hit over .300, drew 117 walks and struck out only 69 times. This was well beyond anything he had accomplished before, though, at 24, it's entirely possible that Kaaihue just got better. You'd think that a franchise starving for power and walks would hand Kaaihue an everyday job and see if he could repeat those numbers at the big league level. In the Royals' case, you'd be wrong. Kaaihue is ticketed for Triple-A due to the acquisition of Mike Jacobs.

Chris Lubanski (Left Field)

PA	R	H	2B	3B	HR	RBI	SO	BB	SB	CS	BA	OBP	SLG	OPS	3-Year	Fielding	Reliability
535	58	111	25	6	13	57	143	45	3	3	.232	.299	.391	.690	+0.04	—	Very High

The Royals' first-round pick in 2003 has yet to make his big-league debut. After posting a .306 OBP at Omaha last season, Lubanski—still only 24—appears to be a bust.

Mitch Maier (Center Field)

PA	R	H	2B	3B	HR	RBI	SO	BB	SB	CS	BA	OBP	SLG	OPS	3-Year	Fielding	Reliability
499	57	127	27	4	10	57	80	26	6	2	.276	.317	.417	.734	+0.08	C	Very High

Last season, Maier got his first extended big-league time after a long apprenticeship in the Royals' system. He played hard and played a passable center field. He also drew just two walks and produced just two extra base hits in 97 plate appearances. Probably headed back to Omaha, he'll get back to the big club in the only in the event of an injury to someone better.

Miguel Olivo (Catcher)

PA	R	H	2B	3B	HR	RBI	SO	BB	SB	CS	BA	OBP	SLG	OPS	3-Year	Fielding	Reliability
391	44	94	21	1	13	50	90	13	5	1	.253	.282	.420	.702	-0.02	A	High

Olivo has been named the Royals' starting catcher entering the 2009 season, giving them three players slated to be in the Opening Day lineup likely to post OBPs under .300. Olivo has his virtues, though. For one, he has a career .841 OPS against left handers.

Brayan Pena (Catcher)

PA	R	H	2B	3B	HR	RBI	SO	BB	SB	CS	BA	OBP	SLG	OPS	3-Year	Fielding	Reliability
342	39	89	18	1	6	37	38	22	5	2	.285	.333	.406	.739	+0.08	—	Average

One of the many former Braves prospects brought on board by GM Dayton Moore, Pena posted an .838 OPS with Omaha in 60 games last season. He's battling Matt Tupman to be the organization's third catcher.

Tony Pena (Shortstop)

PA	R	H	2B	3B	HR	RBI	SO	BB	SB	CS	BA	OBP	SLG	OPS	3-Year	Fielding	Reliability
353	33	82	14	3	2	27	61	11	4	2	.245	.272	.323	.595	+0.01	—	Average

We knew that Pena was offensively challenged, but a .169 batting average? That's the second-worst in Royals' history for players with at least 200 at-bats. (The worst? Bob Hamelin. The Hammer!) Pena's glove earned him 225 at-bats but even that won't sustain a big-league job much longer if he continues to struggle to reach a .200 OBP. Still, the Royals have a glut of offense-first middle infielders, so there is a role for Pena to play. Just not with a bat in his hands. He's the neo-Rafael Belliard.

Ryan Shealy (First Base)

PA	R	H	2B	3B	HR	RBI	SO	BB	SB	CS	BA	OBP	SLG	OPS	3-Year	Fielding	Reliability
473	56	109	24	0	19	67	106	42	0	1	.259	.332	.451	.783	-0.02	B	Very High

Shealy has teased Royals fans with a couple of strong stretches in the majors but, at 29, his time is running out. Dayton Moore would like to find a righty-platoon type to pair with Mike Jacobs, but Shealy doesn't hit lefties particularly well. Nevertheless, he is right in the middle of the Butler/Jacobs/Teahen/Gload/Kaaihue quagmire at first base/DH.

Mark Teahen (Right Field)

PA	R	H	2B	3B	HR	RBI	SO	BB	SB	CS	BA	OBP	SLG	OPS	3-Year	Fielding	Reliability
563	69	139	29	5	13	64	114	50	7	2	.275	.341	.429	.770	+0.01	C	Very High

Teahen has everything you'd want in a big-league ballplayer except the productivity. After his breakout 2006 season, Teahen lost his power in 2007. In 2008, he lost his batting average and OBP as well. With no obvious role for him in the 2009 everyday lineup, Teahen is slated for a super-utility role barring a trade.

Pitchers

Brian Bannister (Starter)

W	L	ERA	TBF	IP	Hit	HR	SO	BB	HBP	3-Year	Reliability
8	11	4.92	726	167	185	23	91	53	7	+0.26	Very High

Everything the sabermetrics crowd said about Brian Bannister last season turned out to be right. A well-known follower of baseball science himself, Bannister attempted to counter the anticipated regression in BABIP by striking out more batters. His strikeout rate did indeed increase, but so did almost everything else. Bannister is still a solid control pitcher and innings-eater. He's not the sub-4.00 ERA guy he was in 2007, nor is he the almost-6.00 ERA guy of 2008. He's somewhere in between and that is good enough to be a bona fide member of the back end of somebody's rotation. For now, that back end is the Royals. Wait—that didn't come out right.

Daniel Cortes (Starter)

W	L	ERA	TBF	IP	Hit	HR	SO	BB	HBP	3-Year	Reliability
4	9	6.80	570	120	144	22	71	69	9	-1.05	Very High

Considered the Royals' best pitching prospect, Cortes will be 22 on Opening Day. It's a long shot that he wins a job in spring training, but after posting a solid season last year in the Texas League, he could see big league time in 2009.

Kyle Davies (Starter)

W	L	ERA	TBF	IP	Hit	HR	SO	BB	HBP	3-Year	Reliability
7	10	5.16	676	152	168	19	89	65	5	+0.06	Very High

Another of general manager Dayton Moore's pet Braves, Davies turned in a nice season for the Royals. He sacrificed a few strikeouts for a little bit better control and the result is a pitcher who can be counted upon to provide a decent rate of quality starts. Davies has a good chance to be part of the 2009 rotation.

Brandon Duckworth (Starter)

W	L	ERA	TBF	IP	Hit	HR	SO	BB	HBP	3-Year	Reliability
6	9	5.24	605	135	151	17	73	62	5	+0.26	High

Duckworth is solidly built and still has good stuff, but it doesn't look like he's ever going to harness his command enough to be anything more than a fringe big-leaguer.

Jimmy Gobble (Reliever)

W	L	ERA	TBF	IP	Hit	HR	SO	BB	HBP	3-Year	Reliability
3	4	4.92	284	64	66	7	52	31	2	+0.28	Low

Whatever happened to Jimmy Gobble last season wasn't good. He was unlucky and terrible—a bad combination. After seeming to find a role as a lefty killer in 2007, his ERA ballooned to 7.36 in 2008, though some of that can be attributed to a couple of hairy outings when Gobble was taking one for the team. Despite the struggles, Gobble is headed for another season as a lefty specialist on the big league staff.

Zack Greinke (Starter)

W	L	ERA	TBF	IP	Hit	HR	SO	BB	HBP	3-Year	Reliability
10	9	4.27	728	172	175	20	143	51	6	+0.06	Very High

Greinke has become one of the AL's best starters, a legitimate ace who gives the Royals a good chance to win every time he takes the mound. Last year, at 24, he struck out 183 batters—69 more than his previous career high—and topped 200 innings for the first time in his career, all with a 3.47 ERA. Greinke has become a much more aggressive pitcher. Long gone are the 63 mph curveballs and quick pitches. In their place are a constant stream of well-located, mid-90s fastballs that Greinke hammers batters with despite a motion that looks so free and easy. He'll give up a home run or two—21 last year—but the tradeoff is worth it. Now the Royals just need to get him locked up past his free-agent years, which are still a couple of years away. Royals fans are hoping Greinke is around for a long time.

Ron Mahay (Reliever)

W	L	ERA	TBF	IP	Hit	HR	SO	BB	HBP	3-Year	Reliability
4	3	4.24	286	65	63	6	50	32	2	—	Low

You hate to see so many dollars tied up in middle relievers, but you can't deny that Mahay earned his money in 2008. He isn't strictly a situational lefty, a quality reflected in most of the pitchers GM Dayton Moore tabs for the Royals' pen. Mahay turns 38 next season. In lefty-reliever years, that's 24.

Gil Meche (Starter)

W	L	ERA	TBF	IP	Hit	HR	SO	BB	HBP	3-Year	Reliability
11	10	4.27	796	186	188	20	145	66	6	+0.21	Very High

Two down, three to go. Meche was even better than he was in his Royal debut in 2007, striking out 27 more batters and posting another sub-4.00 ERA. Given the contracts being doled out to the likes of CC Sabathia and A.J. Burnett, the Royals have to be grateful that they have Meche locked up for three more years at $11 million per season. He's worth it and is one of the better No. 2 starters in the American League.

Leo Nunez (Reliever)

W	L	ERA	TBF	IP	Hit	HR	SO	BB	HBP	3-Year	Reliability
3	4	4.33	260	60	60	7	44	22	3	+0.03	Average

Young, skinny Leo Nunez had never been quite as good as his stuff would suggest—till last year. Even so, Nunez's 2.98 ERA wasn't supported by a sparkling set of peripherals. Say what you want about Mike Jacobs, but turning a guy like Nunez into a guy who hit 32 home runs is pretty amazing. Nunez will be in the mix to be a setup guy in Florida but he's done a little starting in the past as well, so don't rule that out.

Joel Peralta (Reliever)

W	L	ERA	TBF	IP	Hit	HR	SO	BB	HBP	3-Year	Reliability
4	4	4.39	302	71	72	9	53	21	2	+0.23	Average

Peralta was overused by Buddy Bell in 2007, logging 87.2 relief innings. The wear and tear showed last year as Peralta's strikeouts plummeted and his ERA soared. KC is not counting on him to be a key component of the 2009 bullpen.

Ramon Ramirez (Reliever)

W	L	ERA	TBF	IP	Hit	HR	SO	BB	HBP	3-Year	Reliability
5	3	3.63	288	68	61	4	63	29	2	+0.18	Low

General manager Dayton Moore flipped erratic starter Jorge de la Rosa to Colorado to land Ramirez. After his service as Trey Hillman's favorite toy in a solid 2008 campaign in a set-up role, Moore has cashed Ramirez in, bringing back a starting center fielder, Coco Crisp, from the Red Sox. This is how the GMing game is supposed to work.

Carlos Rosa (Starter)

W	L	ERA	TBF	IP	Hit	HR	SO	BB	HBP	3-Year	Reliability
4	8	5.77	509	111	134	15	60	52	6	-0.29	Very High

Rosa has steadily climbed the ladder in the Royals' organization as a starter and enters 2009 with an outside shot of winning a spot on the staff. He's got a terrific fastball but his secondary pitches have been slower to develop. As such, it would be nice to let him get his big-league feet warm by pitching out of the bullpen.

Joakim Soria (Reliever)

W	L	ERA	TBF	IP	Hit	HR	SO	BB	HBP	3-Year	Reliability
5	3	3.30	280	68	58	6	67	22	3	+0.04	Very Low

Soria already has moved in behind Dan Quisenberry and Jeff Montgomery as the third-best closer in Royals' history, though there are still some who think his skill set is wasted in that role. The Royals apparently have not completely given up on the idea of moving Soria to the rotation someday, since there is a clause in the contract extension he signed last season that awards piling up the innings. For the time being, the club is hung up on the "psychological advantage" Soria brings to the table, even if he only brings it 70 innings a season.

Robinson Tejeda (Reliever)

W	L	ERA	TBF	IP	Hit	HR	SO	BB	HBP	3-Year	Reliability
4	5	4.67	359	81	77	10	68	43	3	+0.14	High

Tejeda has bounced around for a few years, but certainly seemed to find himself in the Royals' pen last season. He posted 41 strikeouts in 39+ innings with a WHIP of barely 1.00. Nice. The 2009 season could determine the course of the rest of the career for this failed starter.

Yasuhiko Yabuta (Reliever)

W	L	ERA	TBF	IP	Hit	HR	SO	BB	HBP	3-Year	Reliability
4	4	4.71	337	76	81	8	49	33	3	—	Very Low

Yabuta got the boot to Omaha last year after pitching god-awful at the beginning of the season. He never did really recover. He's still in the organization on a minor-league deal, so it looks like another stint at Rosenblatt Stadium for the 36-year-old hurler.

Los Angeles Angels of Anaheim

by Sean Smith of Anaheim Angels All the Way (lanaheimangelfan.blogspot.com)

2009 Angels Projections

Record: 82-80
Division Rank/Games Behind: 1st by 3 games
Runs Scored: 742, 11th in the league
Runs Allowed: 722, 5th in the league
Park Factor: .99, pretty much neutral

What Happened Last Year:

The Angels were expected to win in 2008, and they did not disappoint. Just about everyone picked the Angels for first, though a few people thought the Mariners were not a fluke in 2007, and Eric Bedard would be the extra something they needed. There were even a few people who thought the A's would be a threat.

With John Lackey missing the first month and a half of the season, the pitching wasn't very good to start the year. Ervin Santana and Joe Saunders pitched very well, but Jon Garland was awful (5.94 ERA) for the first month. The Angels hit well enough to slightly outscore the opposition and won enough close games to get off to an 18-11 start, with Frankie Rodriguez saving 11 of those games.

In mid-May, Lackey made a timely return to the rotation, replacing the ineffective Dustin Moseley and inexperienced Nick Adenhart. Lackey was amazing in his first nine starts, not once allowing more than three runs, and heading into July he had an ERA of 1.44. The rest of the rotation followed his lead. Even Garland (1.78 ERA) pitched well in May, his only good month. Santana and Saunders were the constants, pitching well throughout the season, and Jered Weaver had moments of brilliance.

The offense, however, went in the toilet about this time. The Angels were without Chone Figgins and Howie Kendrick for much of that month. Brandon Wood and Sean Rodriguez got their first tastes of regular big league play, and frankly, they hit like pitchers. The Angels would not get any power out of second or third base and sorely missed the singles and walks Figgins provided, as well as the singles and doubles coming off Kendrick's bat. As a team, the Angels hit .232/.300/.346 in May and .252/.305/.362 in June. Rock bottom was reached on June 28, when Weaver combined with Jose Arredondo to no-hit the Dodgers—and lose the game,

1-0. Through it all the Angels still had a 31-23 record for May and June as they kept playing close games and K-Rod kept racking up the saves.

On June 30, the Angels lost to the Oakland A's, and their lead was cut to 3.5 games. Despite the Angels having far more talented players, somehow the A's had both outscored the Angels, and allowed fewer runs. Was this a sign of things to come? Could the Angels' expensive stars really lose to a no-name, minimum wage squad that just takes walks and plays good defense?

It looks silly now, but at the time, the worries were real. They were also short-lived. The next day, the Angels and A's played a tight game. Trailing by one in the bottom of the eighth, the Angels tied it on a Vladimir Guerrero hit and won on Garret Anderson's two-run homer. This was the last time the A's threatened the Angels. A week later the A's traded Rich Harden to Chicago, and a week after that Joe Blanton went to Philadelphia. The A's finished the season 25 games behind the Angels.

The bats heated up in July, thanks to the return of Figgins and Kendrick, as well as great months for Anderson and Juan Rivera, who finally got playing time at the expense of a struggling Gary Matthews Jr. The pitching wasn't quite as sharp, but the Angels played extremely well, and thanks to the magic of close games and K-Rod, their record looked even better at 19-6.

The race was already over when the Angels traded for Mark Teixeira, who hit .358/.449/.632 as the team went 32-22 in the final two months to close out the season with a franchise record and major league-best 100 wins. Teixeira was acquired for the playoffs, and did very well there, hitting .467 with a .550 OBP, though all his hits were singles. It still wasn't enough, as the Angels lost in the first round to Boston, three games to one.

Players Lost from Last Year's Team:

Rodriguez takes his 62 saves to the New York Mets. Darren O'Day, who did a pretty good job on long relief, joins him after being taken in the Rule 5 draft. Anderson and Garland are free agents and not likely to return. Re-signing Teixeira was priority No. 1, but he chose the Yankees' offer instead. He's a tough one to replace, a great hitter and a top-notch defender. There are other good hitters left on the market, but none who offer the all-around game Teixeira did.

Players Acquired:

Brian Fuentes signed a two-year deal to replace K-Rod as the closer. Both pitchers have been closers for the past four seasons, and have similar numbers. K-Rod averaged 11.6 strikeouts and 4.2 walks per nine innings in that span, and Fuentes averaged 10.3 and 3.6. He'll have to learn to point to the sky after his saves, though. Rivera was re-signed to a three-year deal and should get a chance to prove he's an everyday player.

Management Is:

Tony Reagins enters his second season as the general manager. He's earned the nickname "the ninja" on Halos Heaven for his stealth. By the time you know he wants a player, the move has already been made. Last year I had no idea the Angels were even interested in Torii Hunter. The rumors had him going to Texas, or the White Sox, maybe even the Royals or Yankees. Then, on the day before Thanksgiving, we found out he was an Angel. I had no idea Orlando Cabrera was being shopped until he was a White Sock. I'm supposed to give you a team preview, but right now I don't have any idea what the 2009 team will look like.

Manager Mike Scioscia is well respected, a fine leader of men, and one of the best managers in the game. It is rare for a manager to last a decade in the big leagues without wearing out his welcome and making the team think it needs a change. To the best of my knowledge, that's not being contemplated in Anaheim.

Owner Arte Moreno is considered by many to be the game's best owner. He's willing to spend to keep a competitive team, and seems to enjoy being the team's No. 1 fan. He takes responsibility for keeping the rest of the fans happy as well.

The Minor League System Is:

The minor league system is not very good these days. I shouldn't complain too much—being an every-year contender and picking at the end of the draft makes it tough to build that way. The Angels have surrendered most of their recent first-rounders for free agents. In 2005 they lost a pick for signing Cabrera; the pick became Jacoby Ellsbury (with a supplemental pick turning into Jed Lowrie). In 2006, they lost first- and second-round picks for signing Jeff Weaver and Hector Carrasco (though they gained a pick for losing Paul Byrd). In 2007, signing Matthews cost a pretty good pitching prospect in Michael Main, and in 2008 it was Hunter for another pitcher, Carlos Gutierrez. This offseason, the Angels lost two type A free agents, Teixiera and Frankie Rodriguez, and a type B in Garland, so the 2009 draft may be a good one.

The players who put the Angels near the top of Baseball America's prospect lists are now in the majors. Wood and Sean Rodriguez, have not yet established themselves as big leaguers, but they have done everything you can do in Triple-A and are no longer rookies. The Angels system in 2008 was top-heavy, with a good group of offensive-minded infielders at Triple-A Salt Lake City. Wood, Rodriguez, Matt Brown, Kendry Morales and Freddy Sandoval, according to their THT projections, would make a good hitting major league infield. Morales may take over at first base with Teixiera gone, or else compete for at-bats as a DH or left fielder. The rest of the group will have to fight it out for the third base job if Figgins is traded or moved to the outfield.

Outside of immediate infield help, there is little to be excited about in the minors. Adenhart has not progressed well, walking more and striking out fewer at every higher level. His introduction to the major leagues was disastrous (three starts, 9.00 ERA, 13 walks to four strikeouts). There's not much starting pitching at Triple-A or Double-A. The Angels have one minor league starter pitcher who may be good enough to pitch in a big league rotation: Jordan Walden. He throws very hard, but will need to improve his control.

The Angels have no outfield prospects, though speedsters Bradley Coon and Peter Bourjos could fill the Reggie Willits pinch-running role. Hank Conger has a very good bat for a 20-year-old catcher, but he may be more of a first baseman/DH than a catcher. Mark Trumbo finally showed some signs of hitting (32 homers) but his lack of OBP and defense (22 errors at first base) may limit his usefulness. The 2009 Angels may get some relief help from the minors, as Jason Bulger struck out every Triple-A batter he faced and Kevin Jepsen pitched well enough to make his way onto the postseason roster. Walden may wind up in the bullpen, if his control or secondary pitches prevent him from making it as a starter.

Due For a Change:

Wood and Sean Rodriguez are not light-hitting utility infielders, no matter what the big league numbers for 2008 say. I think one of them is going to become a monster in 2009, claim a regular job at one infield position, and blast a bunch of homers. But I can't tell you which one.

Reasons to be Optimistic:

The Angels are a strong organization that will spend what is needed to keep a contending team on the field. The American League West is not a strong division, and even without Teixiera, winning the division with 85 wins is a possibility.

Reasons to be Pessimistic:

They won 100 games, but the runs scored/runs allowed totals say they should have won only 88. Without K-Rod to close out the tight games, the bullpen could struggle to keep those games in the W column. Replacing Teixeira, the Angels could make a Steve Finley/Gary Matthews Jr. kind of mistake, throwing too big a contract in the direction of an aging left fielder with poor defense. (Players meeting that description are in abundance on the free agent market.) An ancient outfield may have trouble covering ground, leading to inflated ERAs for Angels pitchers.

Still Left to Do:

The Angels may add a left field/DH bat such as Bobby Abreu, Adam Dunn or maybe even Manny Ramirez, though the team has denied interest in any of these players. They may add a starting pitcher; this could range anywhere from another ace (dealing youth for Jake Peavy) to a fifth starter type on a one-year deal.

Most Likely Team Outcome:

First place in a weak division, but with fewer than 90 wins. The failure to keep Teixeira hurts. The Angels roster just doesn't have enough talent to keep up last year's winning percentage, but they can be thankful for the competition. Seattle still has no offense, Texas still has no pitching, and while the A's brought in Matt Holliday, they have failed to make other upgrades that would have made them scary. Rafael Furcal staying with the Dodgers was key, as there isn't another shortstop available with the potential to help them as much as he would have.

Player Projections

Batters

Garret Anderson (Left Field)

PA	R	H	2B	3B	HR	RBI	SO	BB	SB	CS	BA	OBP	SLG	OPS	3-Year	Fielding	Reliability
526	60	137	28	2	13	64	76	32	4	2	.281	.323	.426	.749	—	C	Very High

Anderson likely has played his final game as an Angel. He still has an outside shot at 3,000 hits in four years, assuming he can land a regular job. Right now, he's barely good enough to keep a job: His on-base and slugging abilities are below average for a left fielder, and his defense is about average. To get 3,000 hits he'll have to avoid injury and defy the aging process, with no margin for error. Anderson is the most underrated overrated player of our generation. He was legitimately great for two seasons, and for the Angels the timing could not have been better.

Erick Aybar (Shortstop)

PA	R	H	2B	3B	HR	RBI	SO	BB	SB	CS	BA	OBP	SLG	OPS	3-Year	Fielding	Reliability
368	39	91	17	3	3	32	47	18	7	1	.271	.313	.366	.679	+0.03	B	Average

Aybar didn't play much shortstop in the majors before 2008, as Orlando Cabrera was very durable from 2005 to 2007. In the time I saw him play, he looked too erratic. I was pleasantly surprised to see Aybar turn into a top-notch defender. While he made his share of errors, his great range and strong arm allowed him to post a +7.6 Ultimate Zone ranking As a hitter, he made a little progress. He's just a singles hitter, but should hit just enough to make him a useful player, considering his glove.

Matthew Brown (First Base)

PA	R	H	2B	3B	HR	RBI	SO	BB	SB	CS	BA	OBP	SLG	OPS	3-Year	Fielding	Reliability
453	56	111	28	2	18	65	98	31	3	3	.268	.323	.476	.799	+0.07	A	Very High

Brown has played first, second and third, but his defense is viable only at first. Playing third, he looked simply overmatched. He's a bit of a tweener—his bat isn't quite good enough for first unless he surprises us with another round of improvement. He could wind up in Rob Quinlan's role—playing part-time at first, third, DH and corner outfield, mostly against lefties.

Bradley Coon (Center Field)

PA	R	H	2B	3B	HR	RBI	SO	BB	SB	CS	BA	OBP	SLG	OPS	3-Year	Fielding	Reliability
455	48	96	10	4	3	30	80	36	15	7	.236	.304	.302	.606	+0.06	C	High

Coon appears to be, at least by the stats, a poor man's Reggie Willits. He's not likely to have a significant role in the majors.

Chone Figgins (Third Base)

PA	R	H	2B	3B	HR	RBI	SO	BB	SB	CS	BA	OBP	SLG	OPS	3-Year	Fielding	Reliability
509	66	127	20	4	3	36	77	52	31	10	.283	.358	.366	.724	-0.03	B	Very High

By almost all the defensive metrics, Figgins ranked among the best defensive third basemen last year. Perhaps it was due to experience; Figgins seemed to find a home at third instead of moving around the diamond. He's still fast, but not as crazy fast as the guy who hit 18 triples a few years ago. That's probably a combination of turning 30 and having hamstring injuries.

Vladimir Guerrero (Right Field)

PA	R	H	2B	3B	HR	RBI	SO	BB	SB	CS	BA	OBP	SLG	OPS	3-Year	Fielding	Reliability
571	77	155	32	1	23	87	72	51	4	4	.304	.370	.506	.876	-0.03	D	Very High

This future Hall of Famer appears to be in decline. He was 22 batting runs above average, the lowest figure since his rookie season. He played only 99 games in the outfield, seeing increasing time as a DH. He's also in the last year of his contract. If the Guerrero reign is coming to an end, it sure was a good one.

Torii Hunter (Center Field)

PA	R	H	2B	3B	HR	RBI	SO	BB	SB	CS	BA	OBP	SLG	OPS	3-Year	Fielding	Reliability
569	73	143	30	1	21	77	98	43	15	4	.277	.336	.461	.797	-0.05	C	Very High

Hunter was everything the Angels could have expected after signing a five-year deal. He hit well, made spectacular catches, ran the bases well, and delivered in the playoffs. He was the one Angel who hit with runners in scoring position against Boston, and his eighth-inning two-run single in Game 4 of the ALDS temporarily gave the Angels hope. His range is no longer great, but is adequate and Hunter still has a knack for making great plays, running into walls or robbing home runs. And he is an outstanding base runner. He's very smart and takes advantage if the defense lapses for even a second.

Maicer Izturis (Shortstop)

PA	R	H	2B	3B	HR	RBI	SO	BB	SB	CS	BA	OBP	SLG	OPS	3-Year	Fielding	Reliability
373	43	93	17	2	3	33	37	31	10	2	.278	.340	.367	.707	-0.02	C	High

Like a lot of Angels infielders, he just can't seem to stay in the lineup. When he does play, he's a good one, able to provide above-average defense at second, third or short. He gets on base at a good rate and can surprise you with his pop.

Howie Kendrick (Second Base)

PA	R	H	2B	3B	HR	RBI	SO	BB	SB	CS	BA	OBP	SLG	OPS	3-Year	Fielding	Reliability
404	48	114	26	3	6	46	64	15	7	2	.300	.333	.432	.765	+0.02	C	High

We're still waiting for Kendrick to play more than 100 games in a season. He obviously can hit for average, but is unlikely to hit for the .330-.340 range that really would make him an asset unless he can cut down on his strikeouts. His performance in the playoffs, both offensively and defensively, was brutal.

Jeff Mathis (Catcher)

PA	R	H	2B	3B	HR	RBI	SO	BB	SB	CS	BA	OBP	SLG	OPS	3-Year	Fielding	Reliability
398	40	82	20	1	7	38	89	28	5	1	.231	.291	.352	.643	+0.02	C	High

Mathis has some skills. He's very good behind the plate, blocks pitches well, has very good quickness on bunts and loves to try to pick runners off first. As a hitter, he's got about one full season worth of at-bats, and has decent secondary skills, 15 homers and 52 walks. His weaknesses are a tendency to play catch with the center fielder on steal attempts, trouble making contact, and a .241 batting average on balls in play. I think he can correct the first problem and the third one should even out a bit, but he probably just doesn't have the skill to make more contact.

Gary Matthews (Center Field)

PA	R	H	2B	3B	HR	RBI	SO	BB	SB	CS	BA	OBP	SLG	OPS	3-Year	Fielding	Reliability
503	58	117	24	2	10	52	92	46	9	3	.260	.330	.388	.718	-0.05	F	Very High

His free agent signing has proven to be a disaster, but he's not as terrible as he looked in 2008. At least, I hope not. Unless the Angels bring in a free agent bat, he should get a shot at semi-regular playing time in left field, where he'd be below average but better than replacement level.

Kendry Morales (First Base)

PA	R	H	2B	3B	HR	RBI	SO	BB	SB	CS	BA	OBP	SLG	OPS	3-Year	Fielding	Reliability
424	49	114	24	1	12	56	64	22	1	2	.288	.328	.445	.773	+0.02	B	High

I've got a fever, and there's only one cure: More cowbell. Gotta have more Cowbell. Cowbell Morales should finally get a chance to play, either replacing Mark Teixiera at first, as the DH or in left field. As a first baseman, he's got a good glove. As an outfielder, I don't think he's got enough range. The projection looks like the last five years of Garret Anderson. There's nothing wrong with that for a guy making a low baseball salary. It's only wrong when you are paying $12-14 million for it.

Mike Napoli (Catcher)

PA	R	H	2B	3B	HR	RBI	SO	BB	SB	CS	BA	OBP	SLG	OPS	3-Year	Fielding	Reliability
334	47	75	15	1	18	53	79	40	6	2	.264	.361	.514	.875	+0.02	D	High

Had he played full time, Napoli would have led the American League in slugging percentage (.586). Actually, it was all due to a scorching finish, Napoli was hitting .220/.337/.485 as late as September 16. Then he had 18 hits (four homers) in his last 27 at-bats. He's not likely to keep a .273 batting average, probably not even .250, as he swings and misses too much. He doesn't throw well, and depending on how Mathis or Bobby Wilson develops, might wind up at first base or DH. Moving to a less demanding position might let him stay in the lineup more. He's the reincarnation of Mickey Tettleton or Gene Tenace, and possibly my favorite current Angel.

Robb Quinlan (Third Base)

PA	R	H	2B	3B	HR	RBI	SO	BB	SB	CS	BA	OBP	SLG	OPS	3-Year	Fielding	Reliability
265	29	64	11	1	4	26	41	18	4	2	.264	.317	.367	.684	-0.02	F	Low

The Angels surprisingly offered him a new contract. I thought he would have been non-tendered. He'll be 32, had only a .311 slugging percentage last year, and has limited defensive ability. Combine that with a logjam of young infielders, and it should spell non-tender. I don't think he's going to make a lot of money, but the problem is opportunity cost: If he's on the roster, it will prevent a more useful player from getting a chance. Matt Brown has similar skills and is younger and cheaper.

Juan Rivera (Left Field)

PA	R	H	2B	3B	HR	RBI	SO	BB	SB	CS	BA	OBP	SLG	OPS	3-Year	Fielding	Reliability
310	37	78	17	0	12	44	43	20	1	1	.274	.323	.459	.782	-0.02	C	Average

One of the most unusual sights of the 2008 season was watching Rivera play the end of a game at second base after Howie Kendrick and Erick Aybar both got hurt. I got to see it in person, watching from Rev. Halofan's center field seats. Rivera wasn't real fast before the broken leg, but now has very little speed for an outfielder. He's got some power, and rarely strikes out, so the batting average should come back, but inability to walk limits his offensive game. He hits right-handers about as well as lefties.

Sean Rodriguez (Second Base)

PA	R	H	2B	3B	HR	RBI	SO	BB	SB	CS	BA	OBP	SLG	OPS	3-Year	Fielding	Reliability
554	66	123	27	2	20	71	123	41	7	3	.249	.320	.434	.754	+0.05	D	Very High

Sean-Rod has been in the shadow of Brandon Wood for his minor league career. They both were drafted in 2003, but Wood played one level ahead of Rodriguez and grabbed more headlines until last year. At Triple-A, Rodriguez hit .306/.397/.645 in 66 games. Those rate stats are not far off what Tim Salmon did in Triple-A when he was 23. He'll probably start 2009 as a utility player, but if he starts hitting in the majors he'll have plenty of opportunity. He could wind up earning time at second, third or left field.

Hainley Statia (Shortstop)

PA	R	H	2B	3B	HR	RBI	SO	BB	SB	CS	BA	OBP	SLG	OPS	3-Year	Fielding	Reliability
483	44	105	18	4	1	32	58	24	9	4	.239	.279	.305	.584	+0.09	D	High

He's an outstanding defensive shortstop, but no threat at all with the bat. I don't have any problem projecting his offense to be as bad as Adam Everett's. His defense is another question, since minor league fielding reputations do not always translate in the bigs, and the stats are hard to come by. He'll need to field like Everett to overcome his bat and be a major league asset. That's unlikely: You can count the number of players who could field like Adam Everett, over the last 50 years, on one hand.

Mark Teixeira (First Base)

PA	R	H	2B	3B	HR	RBI	SO	BB	SB	CS	BA	OBP	SLG	OPS	3-Year	Fielding	Reliability
601	82	150	34	0	28	95	98	75	1	1	.291	.385	.520	.905	-0.02	B	Very High

As I write this, the Angels say they're no longer trying to sign him. Obviously, he's a great player, a great all-around hitter and Gold Glove quality defender. If he leaves, then trading for him was a waste. The Angels already had virtually clinched the AL West before he played a game. While he played great though August, September and October, his presence still wasn't enough to get the Angels out of the first round. They'll will get two draft picks if he leaves, but I'd rather have Casey Kotchman for 2009-2011 than the picks.

Mark Trumbo (First Base)

PA	R	H	2B	3B	HR	RBI	SO	BB	SB	CS	BA	OBP	SLG	OPS	3-Year	Fielding	Reliability
547	53	112	23	1	18	64	114	21	4	3	.217	.249	.370	.619	+0.09	—	Very High

Trumbo had his best minor league season last year, hitting 32 homers between High-A and Double-A. He's only 22, so there is plenty of time to develop. Trumbo's still a longshot as he's got some weaknesses: doesn't walk, hasn't hit .300 despite good minor league hitters parks, and made the shocking total of 22 errors at first base last year.

Reggie Willits (Center Field)

PA	R	H	2B	3B	HR	RBI	SO	BB	SB	CS	BA	OBP	SLG	OPS	3-Year	Fielding	Reliability
313	36	71	13	1	1	22	50	41	9	3	.274	.374	.343	.717	+0.01	D	Average

His sophomore season was terrible because he started in a slump and never had the playing time to work his way out of it. He has some value in that he should hit .260-.270 if he played enough, with lots of walks and steals, but his complete lack of power means the package doesn't work as a starter unless he's playing good defense in center field. With Torii Hunter around, that's probably not going to happen.

Bobby Wilson (Catcher)

PA	R	H	2B	3B	HR	RBI	SO	BB	SB	CS	BA	OBP	SLG	OPS	3-Year	Fielding	Reliability
359	35	81	19	1	4	33	59	26	1	1	.250	.309	.352	.661	+0.02	C	Average

Wilson doesn't get mentioned among the Angels prospects, but I think this kid can be a pretty good player. He makes good contact, walks just enough and plays excellent defense. As a big leaguer he might hit .270 with a .340 OBP, though probably fewer than 10 homers. He may be more useful than Jeff Mathis. In 62 games at Triple-A he made only two errors, allowed one passed ball, and threw out 43 percent of base stealers. He'll also have a manager who knows a thing or two about developing catchers.

Brandon Wood (Shortstop)

PA	R	H	2B	3B	HR	RBI	SO	BB	SB	CS	BA	OBP	SLG	OPS	3-Year	Fielding	Reliability
572	74	136	31	2	27	88	143	43	8	2	.262	.322	.486	.808	+0.05	F	Very High

Last year I wrote that Wood had not progressed since 2005. His raw numbers declined after the big 43-homer year, but when accounting for level of play, the seasons were almost equal. That's not good; a 20-year-old player should show improvement by ages 22-23. Last year Wood again appeared to be stagnating, but then turned his season around in July, hitting .355/.439/.738. He kept going strong in August, and for the two months hit 18 homers in 198 at-bats, and improved his plate discipline, walking 33 times while striking out 48 times. He spent the next month in the majors and finally showed some promise in the big leagues, hitting .250 and slugging .483 over his last 28 days. With two walks and 16 strikeouts, there is still plenty of room for improvement. He may get a shot at playing third base, where he looks pretty good. At shortstop his range is nowhere near Erick Aybar's.

Pitchers

Nick Adenhart (Starter)

W	L	ERA	TBF	IP	Hit	HR	SO	BB	HBP	3-Year	Reliability
5	11	6.23	689	145	181	18	77	83	9	-0.68	Very High

His prospect status took a hit as he got hit around in Triple-A, and was even worse in three big league starts. Adenhart has a good arm and a fastball with velocity and movement, but he really struggled with his command. He needs at least another season in Triple-A. When he fell behind in the count, his fastball was the only pitch he had any confidence in. Hitters knew it, and he got hammered.

Jose Arredondo (Reliever)

W	L	ERA	TBF	IP	Hit	HR	SO	BB	HBP	3-Year	Reliability
4	4	4.53	316	72	73	8	59	32	3	-0.09	High

The Angels haven't had a rookie reliever this exciting since K-Rod, Brendan Donnelly and Scot Shields all hit the scene in 2002. Arredondo throws hard, throws strikes, and keeps the ball on the ground. What's not to love? He could be the long term answer as the closer, but Shields has more experience and probably deserves first crack at the job.

Jason Bulger (Reliever)

W	L	ERA	TBF	IP	Hit	HR	SO	BB	HBP	3-Year	Reliability
4	3	3.45	262	61	50	4	75	31	3	+0.19	Very Low

At Salt Lake City, he was the most dominant pitcher since Steve Nebraska. In 43 innings he struck out 75 and allowed only three runs. In the majors, he wasn't that good, especially his command. In 34 major league innings over the last few years, his ERA is 6.35, though he has shown the ability to get strikeouts with over one per inning. Now 30 years old, it's time for Bulger to prove he's not just a Triple-A pitcher.

Jon Garland (Starter)

W	L	ERA	TBF	IP	Hit	HR	SO	BB	HBP	3-Year	Reliability
9	11	4.73	788	181	214	19	83	50	6	+0.43	Very High

He's a very frustrating pitcher to watch. He doesn't have the stuff to put batters away and always seems on the verge of getting hammered. But he's good for 200 innings, and even his projected ERA has some value. Garland was offered arbitration but declined, so he'll earn the Angels a supplemental draft pick when he signs somewhere else.

Kevin Jepsen (Reliever)

W	L	ERA	TBF	IP	Hit	HR	SO	BB	HBP	3-Year	Reliability
3	3	5.23	258	56	59	5	40	37	3	-0.19	Low

A big, hard-throwing right hander, 24 years old, he threw a fastball and a curveball in his September call-up. His minor league control record is not very good. He's another pitcher who will get a chance to pitch at the back end of the bullpen, and could develop into something more.

John Lackey (Starter)

W	L	ERA	TBF	IP	Hit	HR	SO	BB	HBP	3-Year	Reliability
10	9	3.92	703	168	167	17	131	45	8	+0.20	Very High

After missing the first month and a half, the first extended injury of his career, Lackey started his season even better than his 2007, when he led the AL in ERA. In the second half he got hit around quite a bit, and allowed 17 gopher balls in 83 innings (more than his season average in over 200 innings from 2005-2007). With the Angels not facing any competition for the division, Lackey may have been coasting, or experimenting with new pitches, or some other convenient excuse. When the Angels needed his pitching again, Lackey pitched two strong games against the Red Sox. Though the team didn't pull those out, Lackey pitched well enough to win.

Dustin Moseley (Starter)

W	L	ERA	TBF	IP	Hit	HR	SO	BB	HBP	3-Year	Reliability
6	10	5.84	665	146	185	22	81	54	7	+0.31	Very High

What an awful year. With the Angels his ERA was 6.79, and in 20 starts at Triple-A he was even worse (6.94). Moseley doesn't do anything above average as a pitcher. His fastball was a bit better in 2007, perhaps because he was used in relief. He might be okay at the back end of the bullpen, but the fewer games he starts in 2009, the better.

Darren O'Day (Reliever)

W	L	ERA	TBF	IP	Hit	HR	SO	BB	HBP	3-Year	Reliability
4	4	4.14	295	68	70	6	46	26	3	+0.11	Low

He was taken by the Mets in the Rule 5 draft. He's a useful pitcher: He throws strikes, keeps the ball on the ground (55 percent) and allowed only two homers in 43 innings. The Angels lost three pitchers in the Rule 5 draft, so maybe the farm system isn't in such bad shape.

Darren Oliver (Reliever)

W	L	ERA	TBF	IP	Hit	HR	SO	BB	HBP	3-Year	Reliability
5	3	3.52	295	71	67	6	49	21	3	—	Average

I didn't expect much when the Angels signed him to a two-year contract before the 2007 season. I thought he'd be a disaster like every other time the Angels try and mix a lefty into the bullpen. Oliver's track record wasn't exactly reliable, and he was no spring chicken either. But Oliver exceeded everyone's expectations. He followed a solid 3.78 ERA in 2007 with an excellent 2.88 last year, cutting his walk rate to two per nine innings. He even earned Type A free agent status and would have gifted the Angels a pair of draft picks. Perhaps sensing a slow market, he accepted arbitration and will be back in the 2009 bullpen.

Francisco Rodriguez (Reliever)

W	L	ERA	TBF	IP	Hit	HR	SO	BB	HBP	3-Year	Reliability
5	3	3.11	293	71	54	6	81	32	2	+0.04	Low

Not sure if anyone noticed, but K-Rod broke an obscure 18-year-old record. He saved just under 90 percent of his opportunities, which is almost the exact same percentage he's had for the last four years as the Angels closer. The big story is that the Angels handing him a record number of chances, a perfect storm for saves. His fastball velocity was down 2 mph from 2007, and 3 mph from 2006. He's throwing the slider less and has developed a really good change-up. Given those trends, he probably won't be the dominant strikeout pitcher that he once was, but he'll likely still be effective and less of an injury risk, as the change-up should be easier on the arm. Frankie, thanks for 2002. I can't blame you for taking the Mets' money, and you'll always be a favorite in Anaheim.

Ervin Santana (Starter)

W	L	ERA	TBF	IP	Hit	HR	SO	BB	HBP	3-Year	Reliability
11	10	4.28	795	188	188	24	165	54	9	+0.16	Very High

Gotta love any pitcher who can strike out 200 while walking fewer than 50. Best case, you are an ace, worst case you're still a solid starter, like Javier Vazquez. Santana has one of the best fastballs in the league, works fast and throws strikes. His great 2008 season is not really a surprise—the real head-scratcher is how a pitcher with Santana's ability pitched so poorly in 2007.

Joe Saunders (Starter)

W	L	ERA	TBF	IP	Hit	HR	SO	BB	HBP	3-Year	Reliability
9	11	4.46	755	176	190	21	101	56	5	+0.22	Very High

You look at his numbers, especially the strikeout rate, and think he's a soft-tossing lefty. He throws pretty hard though, an average fastball of 91 that he can get up to 93-94 on occasion. Don't expect him to win 17 games twice in a row, and his ERA will likely rise because his strikeout rate is not very good. I don't see any reason to think he won't be a solid middle-of-the-rotation starter, though. If he had gone 12-12 with a 4.35 ERA, everyone would think he pitched to his ability and expect him to do it again.

Scot Shields (Reliever)

W	L	ERA	TBF	IP	Hit	HR	SO	BB	HBP	3-Year	Reliability
4	4	3.61	290	69	63	6	64	27	2	+0.22	Average

The Angels avoided overworking Shields last year: He pitched only 63 innings, and remained fresh throughout the season. He hasn't lost any of his stuff, maintaining an average fastball of 92 mph. Shields is one of the better relievers in baseball. He should have no problem handling the closer role if the Angels decide to let him. With a contract paying a bit over $5 million per season over the next two, he'll be a bargain in the ninth inning.

Justin Speier (Reliever)

W	L	ERA	TBF	IP	Hit	HR	SO	BB	HBP	3-Year	Reliability
4	4	4.20	290	68	64	9	56	24	3	—	Low

Speier's second year as an Angel was an ugly one. His role was to pitch the 12th inning, after the good pitchers kept the game tied, and serve up the homer to lose the game. He lost eight games, and allowed 15 home runs in only 68 innings. The good news is that his strikeout rate was still good, and his stuff was not noticeably different than in 2007. He should bounce back and be useful in middle relief.

Jered Weaver (Starter)

W	L	ERA	TBF	IP	Hit	HR	SO	BB	HBP	3-Year	Reliability
9	10	4.29	710	167	171	21	135	48	5	+0.16	Very High

His stuff doesn't appear impressive. It never really has, which is why Weaver had his doubters even when he was dominating in college. He makes up for it with a delivery that's tough to pick up, and knows how to pitch. I'm a fan of pitchers who can post close to a 3/1 strikeout-to-walk ratio. Look for Weaver to take a step forward, as Lackey did in 2005 and Santana and Saunders did last year. Weaver became the first Angel to beat the Red Sox in the playoffs since Doug Corbett.

Los Angeles Dodgers

by Rich Lederer of Baseball Analysts (baseballanalysts.com)

2009 Dodgers Projections

Record: 79-83
Division Rank/Games Behind: 3rd, 6 games back
Runs Scored: 721, 12th in the league
Runs Allowed: 757, 8th in the league
Park Factor: .98, still a pitcher's park, but not like it used to be.

What Happened Last Year:

The Dodgers won the National League West title with an 84-78 record, edging the Arizona Diamondbacks by two games. Los Angeles swept the Chicago Cubs in the NLDS but was beaten by the Philadelphia Phillies in five games in the NLCS.

The NL West champs scored 700 runs and allowed 648, which computes to a Pythagorean win-loss record of 87-75. The team fell short of its expected win total based on run differential due to a 19-24 record in games decided by one run and a 6-12 record in extra-inning contests. Keeping the small sample size in mind, the poor record in close contests is more likely a function of bad luck than any inherent deficiency in the makeup of the club's personnel or management. All else being equal (which it never is), one would expect the Dodgers to win a few more games in 2009 than they did in 2008.

The Dodgers' success was built on run prevention. The club allowed fewer runs than any other team in the NL last year. The pitching staff was fifth in strikeouts (1,205) while giving up the second-fewest walks (480) and the fewest number of home runs (123). More than anything else, it was the latter stat category that separated the Dodgers from the league. The next-closest competitor allowed 20 percent more long balls.

The Dodgers also had a pronounced home/road split, going 48-33 at home and 36-45 on the road. L.A. tied Cincinnati and Colorado for the fourth biggest home and away differential. Look no further than the number of runs allowed at home (3.27 per game) vs. the road (4.73) for the reason why the Dodgers performed so well in Chavez Ravine and so poorly outside of Los Angeles. Amazingly, the team's offense actually scored more runs at home (4.33/game) than on the road (4.31).

All in all, it was a mixed season for the Dodgers. The team, which was 67-70 as it entered the final month of the season, tied the Phillies for the best record in baseball during September (17-8). While it would be easy to point to the acquisition of Manny Ramirez as the reason for the huge improvement, it must be noted that the Dodgers were only 13-16 in August and going nowhere fast. L.A.'s fantastic finish explains why the club spent only 40 days atop the NL West all season long. Arizona, on the other hand, was in first place for 154 days, yet found itself on the outside looking in at the conclusion of the regular season.

Players Lost from Last Year's Team:

Unless the Dodgers don't retain slugger Ramirez, the biggest loss will be Derek Lowe, who averaged 200-plus innings with a FIP under 4.00 during a four-year contract that former GM Paul DePodesta wisely negotiated. The shiny Brad Penny—the one that started the 2007 All-Star Game for the NL—will also be missed. But the tarnished Penny—the one that went 6-9 with a career-high 6.27 ERA in 2008—wasn't worth keeping around. As such, he was tossed in the "take one, leave one" jar.

Takashi Saito was non-tendered and his production over the past three seasons will be difficult, if not impossible, to replace. He has been one of the best and most cost-effective relievers in the majors during his tenure with the Dodgers. Closers like Saito don't fall out of trees or Japan too often. Also missing from last year's outstanding bullpen will be Joe Beimel, Chan Ho Park, and Scott Proctor.

Infielders Jeff Kent (retirement), and Nomar Garciaparra (free agency or retirement) are big names but neither produced as expected last year. Angel Berroa, who was signed last summer to help fill in for the injured Rafael Furcal, was also non-tendered. He is nothing more than a replacement-level player and won't be missed in the least.

Greg Maddux, who announced his retirement on the first day of the winter meetings, will be missed more by the game of baseball than the Dodgers, who picked him up in a waiver deal with the Padres in August, He made just seven starts, going 2-4 with a 5.09 ERA. It was the second time in three years that the four-time Cy Young Award winner had joined the Dodgers during the stretch drive.

Players Acquired:

Mark Loretta was signed as a free agent during the winter meetings at a seemingly attractive cost of $1.25 million plus performance bonuses. The 14-year veteran, a native of Southern California, can play all four infield positions, if necessary, and could wind up playing second base full time if the 23-year-old Blake DeWitt fails to hit or field adequately to hold down this spot.

Management is:

Committed to the organization's best young players. General manager Ned Colletti has listened to assistant GM Logan White, who served as the team's scouting director from 2002-2006, and resisted the temptation to part with the club's top prospects, many of whom now hold starring roles on the Dodgers.

To the extent that management has parted with any of its touted minor leaguers, none of them have paid off for the acquiring clubs yet. Joel Guzman and Andy LaRoche are probably the highest-profile prospects lost and neither has made an impact in the majors, with the former doing his best to stay in the game. However, this could all change if catcher Carlos Santana, the prize in the Casey Blake trade and Cleveland's No. 1 prospect according to Baseball America's latest rankings, continues to progress as he did in the High-A Carolina League last summer (.352/.452/.590 in 126 plate appearances).

The Minor League System:

The Dodgers have fielded one of the best farm systems in baseball for the past several years. Due to a number of players graduating to the big leagues and the trade of Santana, the system is not as strong as it once was, although still more than respectable.

With a strong showing this spring, James McDonald could earn a job at the back of the rotation. The 24-year-old right hander climbed the ladder last year, progressing from Double-A to Triple-A to the major leagues and a spot on the postseason roster.

Former starter Scott Elbert returned from numerous shoulder problems and excelled as a reliever, striking out 46 batters while allowing only 22 hits in 41.1 innings at Double-A Jacksonville. The southpaw earned a late-season promotion to the Dodgers and recorded five Ks in his first 1.2 innings in the bigs.

Ivan DeJesus Jr., the son of the former major league shortstop, finished the season on a 23-game hitting streak for Double-A Jacksonville. The middle infielder, who hit .324/.419/.423 with 76 walks and 81 strikeouts in 128 games, is slated to begin the 2009 campaign at Triple-A Albuquerque and could find time in Los Angeles this summer.

Ethan Martin, the club's No. 1 pick in June, tore the meniscus in his right knee during a fielding drill and did not pitch last summer. He pitched during the instructional league and flashed a 94-mph fastball that projects to touch the upper 90s by the time the 19-year-old right hander reaches the majors.

Due For a Change:

This will be the first spring since 1949 that the Dodgers have not trained in Vero Beach; the team is leaving Dodgertown for Phoenix (or, more specifically, Camelback Ranch-Glendale). The Dodgers will share the new facility with the Chicago White Sox.

One might say that Andruw Jones and Jason Schmidt are also "due for a change," but that doesn't mean either will rebound to his pre-Dodgers performance. Both players are past their peak and coming off injuries. It would be almost impossible for these players to contribute less than they have in Dodger Blue thus far, but I wouldn't bet even Frank McCourt's money on them contributing in a major way this season.

The most likely player on the Dodgers to show year-over-year improvement is Clayton Kershaw, the highly touted left hander with one of the best fastballs and curves in baseball. His upside is extraordinary and it is only a matter of time before he dominates big-league hitters.

Reasons to be Optimistic:

The Dodgers are the best team in a weak division. Moreover, the Diamondbacks, Rockies and Padres are facing financial issues, giving L.A. a competitive advantage over three of their division rivals. Winning 84 games once again may be enough to win the NL West in 2009.

Most of the core talent is in its mid-20s and poised for a couple of breakout seasons that could catapult the team beyond current projections. Despite losing Saito, the bullpen is one of the best in the league. The remaining key members—Jonathan Broxton, Hong-Chih Kuo and Cory Wade—are all back. Broxton and Kuo struck out more than 11 batters per nine while allowing only six home runs in 149 innings.

Reasons to be Pessimistic:

Ownership has more than $42 million tied up this year with former free agent signings Jones, Schmidt and Juan Pierre. Jones was the most overpaid player in the history of baseball last season, Schmidt has all but been forgotten, and Pierre would be the highest-paid fourth outfielder in baseball if not for Gary Matthews, his counterpart 30 miles south on Interstate 5. The first two contracts come off the books after the 2009 season, while the Dodgers will need to live with Pierre through 2011 or eat a large portion of his compensation in a salary dump.

Furthermore, the Blake signing is almost certain to haunt the Dodgers before its expiration in 2011. At nearly $6 million (including a $1.25 million buyout that is unlikely to be exercised) for each of the next three seasons, the 35-year-old Blake could go from adequate in 2009 to subpar in 2010 to "what were we thinking?" in 2011.

Still Left to Do:

They've re-signed shortstop Furcal, solving one problem. In addition to signing Ramirez, the Dodg-ers need to acquire at least one reliable starting pitcher and another reliever capable of pitching at the back end of games. On the contract front, the Dodgers need to lock up Russell Martin and a couple more young studs—such as Andre Ethier, Matt Kemp and/or James Loney—by signing them to new contracts that will buy out a year or two of free agency and keep the young nucleus in Dodger Blue at a discount to what it will cost if the club goes toe-to-toe with these players in arbitration every winter.

Also still left: Find a replacement for Vin Scully. Now 81, the legendary broadcaster will complete his 60th season with the Dodgers in 2009. Charlie Steiner, who was hired away from the Yankees to become the heir apparent, will work exclusively on KABC-AM (790) radio broadcasts for the entire season with former Dodger Rick Monday as his partner. Steiner may revert to TV when Scully retires (dread the thought), but don't be surprised if the next No. 1 comes from outside the organization.

Most Likely Team Outcome:

First place. Thank goodness for being in the NL West.

Player Projections

Batters

Danny Ardoin (Catcher)

PA	R	H	2B	3B	HR	RBI	SO	BB	SB	CS	BA	OBP	SLG	OPS	3-Year	Fielding	Reliability
250	24	52	11	0	4	23	55	20	1	1	.235	.308	.339	.647	-0.04	C	Very Low

A career minor leaguer, the 34-year-old Ardoin has played all or parts of the last 14 seasons in the minors, hitting an undistinguished .254/.344/.393. He has appeared in 165 games in the big leagues spanning five seasons. Ardoin is a cheap option as a backup catcher but nothing more than that.

Angel Berroa (Shortstop)

PA	R	H	2B	3B	HR	RBI	SO	BB	SB	CS	BA	OBP	SLG	OPS	3-Year	Fielding	Reliability
440	45	102	20	0	9	47	75	25	3	1	.255	.307	.373	.680	-0.02	D	High

Berroa is just a guy who can fill in at shortstop in a pinch. He has decent range and sufficient arm strength to handle the job defensively, but his lack of power and discipline at the plate relegate him to the role of a backup. It's hard to believe Berroa was the 2003 American League Rookie of the Year. His career has been heading south ever since.

Casey Blake (Third Base)

PA	R	H	2B	3B	HR	RBI	SO	BB	SB	CS	BA	OBP	SLG	OPS	3-Year	Fielding	Reliability
555	67	133	29	1	19	73	112	48	3	2	.270	.341	.448	.789	—	D	Very High

Blake is a 10-year veteran who didn't start until he was 29. Now 35, he has put up solid counting stats since becoming a starter but his rate stats for a third baseman are pedestrian at best. Blake can play any of the four corners, but adds the most value offensively at third. However, he lacks range at the hot corner and borders on being a defensive liability at that spot.

Blake Dewitt (Third Base)

PA	R	H	2B	3B	HR	RBI	SO	BB	SB	CS	BA	OBP	SLG	OPS	3-Year	Fielding	Reliability
566	61	132	23	2	14	63	90	40	3	2	.255	.310	.389	.699	+0.06	C	Very High

DeWitt surprised everyone by breaking camp as 2008's starting third baseman due to a solid spring and injuries to Andy LaRoche and Nomar Garciaparra. He was optioned to Las Vegas (Triple-A) twice during the season, but started 77 games at third before filling in admirably at second base down the stretch when Jeff Kent went down with an injury. DeWitt is better defensively at third than second, but needs to become more productive at the plate to earn an everyday job.

Andre Ethier (Right Field)

PA	R	H	2B	3B	HR	RBI	SO	BB	SB	CS	BA	OBP	SLG	OPS	3-Year	Fielding	Reliability
533	73	145	30	4	19	78	83	52	3	3	.307	.378	.509	.887	+0.08	D	Very High

Ethier quietly hit .368/.448/.649 in August and September while new teammate Manny Ramirez was getting all the attention. He led the majors with a line-drive rate of 26.6 percent. Ethier struggled against lefties (.243/.325/.368) for the first time and his advanced defensive metrics left a lot to be desired last season. He turns 27 in April and could be poised for a career year in 2009.

Rafael Furcal (Shortstop)

PA	R	H	2B	3B	HR	RBI	SO	BB	SB	CS	BA	OBP	SLG	OPS	3-Year	Fielding	Reliability
371	48	95	16	3	6	36	46	36	15	4	.288	.357	.409	.766	-0.03	C	Very High

Furcal missed nearly five months with a back injury that required surgery. He returned in time to play four games at the end of the regular season. The Dodgers were 18-14 (.563) in the games he started in April and May and 66-64 (.508) the rest of the way. He hit a robust .357/.439/.573 in his 36 games. Furcal runs well and is capable of stealing 25-30 bases over a full season. Last summer, *Baseball America* rated Furcal the third-best defensive shortstop in the NL with the second-best infield arm in the league.

Nomar Garciaparra (Shortstop)

PA	R	H	2B	3B	HR	RBI	SO	BB	SB	CS	BA	OBP	SLG	OPS	3-Year	Fielding	Reliability
333	39	85	16	1	9	41	33	26	2	1	.282	.340	.431	.771	—	F	High

Garciaparra came up so big in 2006 after signing a one-year contract for $6 million that he seduced the Dodgers into giving him a two-year, $18.5 million deal. Now 35 and as prone to injuries as ever (broken right hand, sore calf and sprained MCL last year alone), Nomar is at best a part-time player if he chooses to play in 2009. Remarkably, Garciaparra played twice as many innings at shortstop as he did at first and third combined.

Chin Lung Hu (Shortstop)

PA	R	H	2B	3B	HR	RBI	SO	BB	SB	CS	BA	OBP	SLG	OPS	3-Year	Fielding	Reliability
404	41	95	16	3	5	36	56	23	5	3	.257	.303	.358	.661	+0.03	C	High

A highly regarded prospect, Hu has yet to prove that he can hit big-league pitching. In parts of two seasons, he has hit .193/.250/.290. Hu can handle the leather and has enough arm strength to play shortstop and the footwork to handle second base.

Andruw Jones (Center Field)

PA	R	H	2B	3B	HR	RBI	SO	BB	SB	CS	BA	OBP	SLG	OPS	3-Year	Fielding	Reliability
403	46	80	16	0	16	52	95	45	1	1	.229	.323	.412	.735	-0.02	A	Very High

Jones was a complete bust in his first season as a free agent for the Dodgers. After signing a two-year, $36.2 million contract in December 2007, Jones arrived in Vero Beach overweight and out of shape. He never got untracked, "hitting" .158/.256/.249 in only 75 games while spending part of May, all of June and most of August and September on the disabled list with a bad right knee that required surgery during the middle of the season. Jones hit just three home runs while striking out in nearly one-third of his plate appearances. He will have to earn his playing time by producing at the plate.

Matt Kemp (Center Field)

PA	R	H	2B	3B	HR	RBI	SO	BB	SB	CS	BA	OBP	SLG	OPS	3-Year	Fielding	Reliability
561	78	152	32	5	17	72	124	40	20	4	.297	.348	.478	.826	+0.04	F-	Very High

Kemp, who didn't turn 24 until the last week of the season, is one of the best young talents in the game. At 6-2, 230 pounds, he possesses all five scouting tools. His primary weakness is what many refer to as the sixth tool: plate discipline/pitch recognition. *Baseball America* rated Kemp's arm the third-best among National League outfielders in a poll last summer. He led NL center fielders with 10 assists and added six more as a right fielder.

Jeff Kent (Second Base)

PA	R	H	2B	3B	HR	RBI	SO	BB	SB	CS	BA	OBP	SLG	OPS	3-Year	Fielding	Reliability
480	57	123	27	1	13	61	62	41	1	2	.287	.354	.446	.800	—	F	Very High

Kent may have played the last game in his Hall of Fame-caliber 17-year career. His offense slipped noticeably in 2008: He hit for his lowest average (.280) and OBP (.327) since 1997 and his worst SLG (.418) ever. Kent's defense has slipped even more, trailing all second basemen in the plus/minus system over the past three seasons.

James Loney (First Base)

PA	R	H	2B	3B	HR	RBI	SO	BB	SB	CS	BA	OBP	SLG	OPS	3-Year	Fielding	Reliability
577	72	159	35	4	14	73	83	45	4	2	.303	.358	.465	.823	+0.03	B	Very High

Last year's projection system (.292/.350/.445) nailed Loney's stats (.289/.338/.434) across the board, an impressive feat given his .543 career slugging average heading into the 2008 season. He is an outstanding first baseman, making 58 plays outside of the zone. However, Loney is a below-average baserunner, advancing from first to third on a single only six times in 24 opportunities while getting doubled off or thrown out on the base paths seven times. He doesn't turn 25 until May and his best years should be ahead of him.

Russell Martin (Catcher)

PA	R	H	2B	3B	HR	RBI	SO	BB	SB	CS	BA	OBP	SLG	OPS	3-Year	Fielding	Reliability
579	76	144	29	2	14	66	79	69	15	5	.287	.377	.437	.814	+0.02	C	Very High

Martin is one of the premier catchers in the majors. He has been a workhorse the past two seasons, catching at least 145 games in 2007 and 2008. Martin tired down the stretch once again, hitting .294/.394/.436 in the first half and .260/.371/.336 during the second. Very disciplined at the plate, he had more walks than strikeouts while ranking eighth in BB (90) and 10th in OBP (.385). With a little more rest, Martin could surprise to the upside with his rate stats.

Juan Pierre (Left Field)

PA	R	H	2B	3B	HR	RBI	SO	BB	SB	CS	BA	OBP	SLG	OPS	3-Year	Fielding	Reliability
498	66	132	18	5	2	34	39	27	39	9	.289	.332	.363	.695	-0.04	A	Very High

After not missing a game from 2003-2007, Pierre appeared in only 119 contests for the Dodgers in 2008. He started just 86 times, losing time in the early going to Andruw Jones and later to Manny Ramirez. Pierre hits for a decent average and can bunt and run well, but that's about it when it comes to his positives. Pierre threw out only one runner in 739 innings in left and center field. It's safe to say that the lack of assists is due to his poor throwing arm rather than any respect on the part of baserunners. Now 31, Pierre has three years to go on the five-year, $44 million contract he signed in November 2006.

Manny Ramirez (Left Field)

PA	R	H	2B	3B	HR	RBI	SO	BB	SB	CS	BA	OBP	SLG	OPS	3-Year	Fielding	Reliability
572	82	147	27	1	29	94	109	79	2	0	.305	.406	.545	.951	—	F	Very High

Like him or not, Ramirez is simply one of the best right-handed hitters of all time. He has hit .314/.411/.593 with 527 homers over his career and, based on his two-plus months with the Dodgers last year, doesn't appear to be slowing down one bit. He put up a .396/.489/.743 line in 53 regular season games in Dodger Blue, then went 13-for-25 with four home runs during the postseason. Ramirez is a poor baserunner and a liability in left field, although his advanced defensive metrics at Dodger Stadium weren't nearly as bad as in years past at Fenway Park. But who is paying Manny for his baserunning and defense anyway?

Jason Repko (Right Field)

PA	R	H	2B	3B	HR	RBI	SO	BB	SB	CS	BA	OBP	SLG	OPS	3-Year	Fielding	Reliability
388	46	86	17	2	8	38	80	32	11	3	.252	.330	.384	.714	-0.02	B	Low

The oft-injured Repko is an adequate reserve outfielder when healthy. A good athlete, he can play all three outfield positions but strikes out too much without the corresponding power to get serious consideration as a starter.

Delwyn Young (Right Field)

PA	R	H	2B	3B	HR	RBI	SO	BB	SB	CS	BA	OBP	SLG	OPS	3-Year	Fielding	Reliability
332	39	84	22	1	11	45	69	24	1	1	.279	.334	.468	.802	+0.06	D	High

Coming off a big 2007 in Triple-A in 2007 (.337/.384/.571 with 54 doubles in 536 plate appearances), Young flopped in his rookie season. He spent more time on the bench than the field and was slowed late in the season with a strained oblique. He is coming off arthroscopic surgery on his right elbow and should be fully recovered this spring.

Pitchers

Joe Beimel (Reliever)

W	L	ERA	TBF	IP	Hit	HR	SO	BB	HBP	3-Year	Reliability
4	3	3.83	258	60	60	5	35	24	2	+0.18	Low

The Dodgers didn't offer arbitration to Beimel, a Type B free agent who was a useful left-hander out of the bullpen the past three seasons. Without a strikeout pitch, Beimel lacks upside but gets by with a sinking fastball and a deceptive delivery.

Chad Billingsley (Starter)

W	L	ERA	TBF	IP	Hit	HR	SO	BB	HBP	3-Year	Reliability
11	8	3.69	741	175	158	17	161	74	6	-0.04	Very High

A power pitcher, Billingsley is the emerging ace of the Dodgers staff. However, he slipped on an ice-covered step and broke his left leg during the offseason. The former first-round draft pick had surgery and his health and endurance are the biggest question marks heading into the 2009 campaign. As a 23-year-old, Billingsley ranked seventh in the NL in ERA (3.14), third in K/9 (9.01) and ninth in HR/9 (0.63). At 6-1, 245, the hard-throwing right-hander can dial his fastball up to the mid-90s and possesses a "plus" curveball. He still needs to improve his command and lower his pitch count to work deeper into games and become an even more valuable pitcher.

Jonathan Broxton (Reliever)

W	L	ERA	TBF	IP	Hit	HR	SO	BB	HBP	3-Year	Reliability
6	2	2.76	297	73	56	6	85	27	2	+0.09	Low

The 6-4, 290-pound Broxton throws gas, ranking first in the majors with the most pitches thrown at 100 or more mph (28). His fastball averaged 96.3 mph in 2008, second among all relievers. He also throws a hard slider. Broxton has struck out 306 batters in 241 innings in his three-plus years in the big leagues. At 24, he is one of the best set-up men in the game and enters spring training as the incumbent closer.

Scott Elbert (Reliever)

W	L	ERA	TBF	IP	Hit	HR	SO	BB	HBP	3-Year	Reliability
3	3	4.76	234	52	45	7	48	35	3	-0.12	Average

Elbert was the most highly prized pitching prospect in the organization at one time but shoulder injuries have limited his development and forced him to the bullpen in 2008. The southpaw throws hard but lacks command of his fastball and slider. Only 23, Elbert needs to trust his stuff and learn how to pitch more than anything else.

Clayton Kershaw (Starter)

W	L	ERA	TBF	IP	Hit	HR	SO	BB	HBP	3-Year	Reliability
8	9	4.23	658	151	141	17	130	79	5	-0.58	High

Kershaw jumped from Double-A to the major leagues as a 20-year-old in May. He spent the next four months shuttling between the minors and majors and pitched twice in relief in the NLCS. The seventh overall pick in the 2006 draft, he has a great pitcher's frame and a "plus-plus" fastball and curveball. The southpaw became a YouTube sensation last spring when he struck out Sean Casey with a 12-to-6, shoulders-to-knees bender. Kershaw's potential is limitless if he can cut down on his walks.

Hong-Chih Kuo (Reliever)

W	L	ERA	TBF	IP	Hit	HR	SO	BB	HBP	3-Year	Reliability
5	4	3.28	322	78	65	7	83	30	3	+0.18	Average

Ranking second with a 1.69 relief ERA, Kuo was one of the most effective set-up men in the NL last year. The lefty had a breakout season, whiffing 86 batters while walking only 15 in 69.1 innings as a reliever. When summoned from the bullpen, Kuo throws almost nothing but fastballs that can touch the upper 90s when he is at full strength. He has undergone four surgeries on his elbow and his health is always an issue.

Hiroki Kuroda (Starter)

W	L	ERA	TBF	IP	Hit	HR	SO	BB	HBP	3-Year	Reliability
10	9	4.07	732	173	184	19	101	46	7	+0.23	Low

After an 11-year career in Japan, Kuroda signed a three-year, $35.5 million contract with the Dodgers in December 2007. He lived up to his end of the bargain last year, posting a 3.73 ERA and an even better Fielding Independent ERA (FIP) of 3.59. His FIP ranked ninth in the NL, ahead of such notables as Jake Peavy, Cole Hamels and Roy Oswalt. The veteran has outstanding control and succeeds by pitching to contact early in the count (3.53 pitches per batter, fourth in the NL) and keeping the ball in the yard (0.64 HR/9, 10th in the league).

Derek Lowe (Starter)

W	L	ERA	TBF	IP	Hit	HR	SO	BB	HBP	3-Year	Reliability
12	9	3.40	778	188	190	16	119	49	3	—	Very High

Lowe is a classic sinker/slider pitcher who throws strikes and keeps the ball on the ground and inside the ballpark. The 12-year veteran ranked fourth in the NL in BB/9 (1.92), second in generating ground balls (60.3 percent), and seventh in HR/9 (0.60). His stinginess in allowing walks and home runs allowed him to finish fourth in WHIP (1.13), ninth in ERA (3.24), and third in Fielding Independent ERA (3.24). Now 35, Lowe may not duplicate his fantastic 2008 but should remain successful for the next two or three years.

James McDonald (Starter)

W	L	ERA	TBF	IP	Hit	HR	SO	BB	HBP	3-Year	Reliability
5	10	6.19	610	132	148	26	105	72	9	-0.19	Very High

McDonald worked his way up from Jacksonville (Double-A) to Las Vegas (Triple-A) to the big leagues, where he threw six scoreless innings in relief in September and another 5.1 in the NLCS. Normally a starter, this 6-foot-5 right hander may be given an opportunity to compete for a rotation job this spring. A flyball type, McDonald possesses the standard three-pitch fastball/curve/change arsenal with an average heater and quality secondary offerings.

Chan Ho Park (Reliever)

W	L	ERA	TBF	IP	Hit	HR	SO	BB	HBP	3-Year	Reliability
4	6	4.93	405	92	101	14	66	35	4	—	Very High

A free agent, Park signed a one-year, $2.5 million contract during the offseason with the Phillies. He can earn an additional $2.5 million in performance bonuses. He gives Philadelphia flexibility as a starter or reliever. Although Park worked mostly out of the bullpen for the Dodgers last year, he was 1-0 with a 2.16 ERA in five starts.

Brad Penny (Starter)

W	L	ERA	TBF	IP	Hit	HR	SO	BB	HBP	3-Year	Reliability
7	7	4.55	559	128	144	10	69	45	4	+0.23	Very High

The opening-day starting pitcher for the Dodgers in 2008, Penny won five of his first seven decisions before losing seven in a row and winding up on the disabled list with shoulder tendinitis. He returned after two months, started twice in August, then missed another month, got hit hard twice in relief in September, and found himself on the 60-day DL rather than the club's postseason roster. The Dodgers declined their 2009 team option for $8.75 million and he became a free agent after his worst season ever.

Scott Proctor (Reliever)

W	L	ERA	TBF	IP	Hit	HR	SO	BB	HBP	3-Year	Reliability
3	4	4.33	255	59	55	8	52	28	2	+0.20	Average

A power pitcher, Proctor recorded a 6.05 ERA that defied the fact that he struck out a career-high 25 percent of the batters he faced last season. His downfall? Too many home runs and walks. In five seasons, he has given up 46 homers in 297 innings (equal to an eye-opening rate of 1.4/9 IP).

Takashi Saito (Reliever)

W	L	ERA	TBF	IP	Hit	HR	SO	BB	HBP	3-Year	Reliability
5	2	2.79	246	61	47	5	70	19	2	—	Low

Without a lot of fanfare, Saito has been one of the best relief pitchers in baseball for the past three seasons. He has posted a 1.95 ERA while saving 85 games in 95 opportunities. By changing speeds effectively, he has struck out 245 batters while allowing only 52 walks, 121 hits and nine home runs in 189.2 career innings. Now 39, Saito missed two months with a sprained ligament in his right elbow and struggled down the stretch and in his lone outing in the playoffs.

Eric Stults (Starter)

W	L	ERA	TBF	IP	Hit	HR	SO	BB	HBP	3-Year	Reliability
6	10	5.50	661	147	170	25	102	65	4	+0.53	Very High

Stults threw a four-hit, complete game shutout in his second start of the season last June. He tossed 116 pitches that game and pitched with limited success after that. A southpaw, Stults throws an 88-90 mph fastball along with a curveball and changeup. Look for him to swing back and forth between the majors and minors as well as the rotation and bullpen.

Ramon Troncoso (Reliever)

W	L	ERA	TBF	IP	Hit	HR	SO	BB	HBP	3-Year	Reliability
3	4	4.92	305	67	79	7	45	31	4	+0.02	Average

A career relief pitcher, Troncoso may stick with the big league club for the full season for the first time. He throws a heavy power sinker and an occasional slider, inducing grounders at an extremely high rate—roughly 60 percent of all batted balls. If you're looking for a sleeper in the Dodgers bullpen, Troncoso could be the one.

Cory Wade (Reliever)

W	L	ERA	TBF	IP	Hit	HR	SO	BB	HBP	3-Year	Reliability
3	5	5.29	337	76	85	13	53	27	5	+0.03	High

Wade had a surprisingly productive rookie season, posting a 2.27 ERA in 55 games and 71.1 innings. The 25-year-old right-hander threw strikes (1.89 BB/9) and benefited from a .227 BABIP. He relies on a quality curveball for his "out" pitch as his 89-mph fastball is average at best for a reliever. Look for him to regress in his second year in the majors.

Milwaukee Brewers

by Eric Johnson of Brew Crew Ball (brewcrewball.com/)

2009 Brewers Projections

Record: 79-73
Division Rank/Games Behind: Tied for first
Runs Scored: 807, 3rd in the league
Runs Allowed: 746, 6th in the league
Park Factor: 1.00, perfectly neutral

What Happened Last Year:

The playoffs happened! Well, the playoffs always happen, but they hadn't included the Brewers since 1982. The team spent most of the year chasing the Cubs for the division lead, but a collapse down the stretch for the second straight year led to the firing of manager Ned Yost. A rally under bench coach-cum-interim manager Dale Sveum, who had a little Easter Sunday 1987 magic left, saw the Brewers safely into the playoffs as the wild card.

The player most directly responsible for allowing the team to make the playoffs didn't even begin the year on the club. On July 7, after weeks of rumors, CC Sabathia was acquired by the Brewers from the Indians in exchange for sluggardly prospect Matt LaPorta, hard-throwing young A-baller Rob Bryson, lefty dross Zach Jackson, and a player to be named later, ultimately revealed to be well-regarded Double-A outfielder Michael Brantley. It was a high price to pay, but Sabathia paid the Brewers back in spades, setting off on a run reminiscent of Randy Johnson's 1998 performance for the Astros.

It was expected that Sabathia and Ben Sheets would provide the Brewers with the artillery to go deep into the playoffs, but hopes for riding the two aces to a World Series berth were dashed when Sheets exacerbated an existing muscle tear in his elbow in late September and was done for the year. The Brewers had another trick up their sleeve, however, as young ace-in-training Yovani Gallardo had recovered superhumanly quickly from his May knee surgery, just in time to start the first game of the Division Series, but even that wasn't enough to overcome the eventual World Series champion Phillies.

Though the Brewers didn't make it out of the first round of the playoffs, the season as a whole was a very tasty morsel for a city and fan base that had been hungry for a quarter century.

Players Lost from Last Year's Team:

By far the two biggest names on this list are erstwhile ace Sheets and folk hero Sabathia, who both departed via free agency and will each net the Brewers two high draft picks. The Brewers made an unexpectedly strong run at re-signing Sabathia, and reports indicated that the big fella might have been willing to give the team a substantial discount; however, it was all in vain, for hell hath no fury like a Steinbrenner miss'd the playoffs.

The Brewers also will receive a compensation pick for the departure of LOOGY Brian Shouse; they could have tried for another by offering Eric Gagne arbitration, but they were afraid their $10 million bomb would actually accept. Also departing are relievers Salomon Torres and Guillermo Mota and backups Russell Branyan, Craig Counsell, Ray Durham and Gabe Kapler.

Players Acquired:

The Brewers signed all-time saves leader Trevor Hoffman to a one-year deal as their closer. He's 41, but saved 30 games for San Diego last season.

Jorge Julio will play the role of Mota in 2009 as the hard-throwing relief question mark. R.J. Swindle also was added to the bullpen. Three players who were actually on the team last year really deserve to be listed here as well: Todd Coffey, Mike Lamb and Chris Capuano. The former two were acquired after the Sept. 1 playoff-eligibility deadline, while Capuano missed the entire season recovering from Tommy John surgery.

Management Is:

Beginning a critical phase. Can general manager Doug Melvin retool the team and keep it in the hunt after the loss of its two proven ace starters? Will new manager Ken Macha keep the team on a more even keel and avoid the slumps that plagued the team under Yost and were attributed to his uptightness and anxiety? Will a reassigned Sveum, the new hitting coach, be an improvement over Jim Skaalen, who did not impress? Will Bill Castro, the former bullpen coach who was given a (long-overdue in the eyes of many) promotion to pitching coach, ably fill the shoes of Mike Maddux, who impressed many?

The biggest question of all, though, is whether Bruce Seid and Ray Montgomery can effectively replace Jack Zduriencik and Tony Blengino as head and assistant scouting directors, respectively. Zduriencik, who left to become Seattle's new general manager, bringing Blengino along as his new scouting director, was responsible for drafting most of the Brewers of note currently on the team, including the big three of Prince Fielder, Ryan Braun and Gallardo.

Zduriencik was occasionally criticized for taking too many high-risk prep arms high in the draft, and certainly the burnouts of Mike Jones and Mark Rogers hurt, but he also hit on Gallardo in the second round of the same draft in which he took Rogers, and 2006's choice of Jeremy Jeffress seems like a good one at this point as well. He strictly adhered to taking the player the team considered the best available no matter the position, raising some eyebrows when the Brewers took LaPorta in 2007 despite having nowhere at the major league level to play him; Zduriencik was vindicated when having LaPorta allowed the Brewer to trade for Sabathia. The Brewers hope Seid, the West Coast crosschecker under Zduriencik, was paying attention.

The Minor League System Is:

No longer among the best in the game, but it's still very productive. There aren't any players the caliber of recent graduates Fielder, Braun and Gallardo, but fireballer Jeffress has legitimate ace potential and should be at the very least a late-inning bullpen arm. Alcides Escobar, Mat Gamel and Angel Salome, the system's top three position prospects, all have good chances to be effective major league regulars despite each possessing a significant question mark. Just behind them, toolsy outfielder Lorenzo Cain wowed many observers at the Arizona Fall League and is also close to contributing. Last year's first-round picks Brett Lawrie and Jake Odorizzi provide some high-upside talent to keep an eye on in the low minors.

Helium watch: Former high-profile (for the Brewers, anyway) Dominican signee Wily Peralta is my pick for biggest riser this coming year.

Due For a Change:

This is probably Rickie Weeks' last chance at his established level of play, so he's either due for a change in production or a change of scenery.

Our Favorite Brewers Blogs:

Brew Crew Ball (http://www.brewcrewball.com)

Bernie's Crew (http://community.sportsbubbler.com/blogs/bernies_crew)

Right Field Bleachers (http://www.rightfieldbleachers.com)

The Junkball Blues (http://community.sportsbubbler.com/blogs/the_junkball_blues)

Chuckie Hacks (http://chuckiehacks.com)

Al's Ramblings (http://albethke.blogspot.com)

Reasons to be Optimistic:

Gallardo's knee injuries haven't affected his arm and in fact may be a blessing in disguise, as they kept him from a heavy workload at a critical age. The core of the lineup is young and productive and still has room for growth, while Gamel and Salome provide reasonable contingency plans should either Bill Hall or Jason Kendall go splat.

Reasons to be Pessimistic:

Losing two Cy Young candidates might be a problem.

Still Left to Do:

Finding a quality mid-rotation starter would be nice, and a third baseman who can both hit **and** field would be pretty nifty as well. Also, while this isn't something that can really be addressed by adding a single player, the entire offense, with the exception of Fielder, has below-average plate discipline. There are signs that some players' approaches are maturing—both J.J. Hardy and Braun made encouraging strides in this regard last year—but overall, it's a significant problem.

Most Likely Team Outcome:

A bit of a consolidation year as the team waits for most of its top prospects to work out their remaining kinks in the high minors and searches for a quality starting rotation. Playoff competition is not entirely farfetched; if Gallardo pitches to his ace potential and Manny Parra becomes a consistent second/third starter, the team could make some noise. Still, I foresee a third-place finish and a win total in the low 80s.

Player Projections
Batters

Michael Brantley (Center Field)

PA	R	H	2B	3B	HR	RBI	SO	BB	SB	CS	BA	OBP	SLG	OPS	3-Year	Fielding	Reliability
492	57	119	18	3	4	40	51	49	15	6	.274	.350	.357	.707	+0.13	D	High

After months of drama, Brantley was revealed as the player to be named later in the Sabathia trade. He's an interesting prospect who endeared himself to many followers of the Brewers system over the years with his precociously patient plate approach. However, what's holding him back is an utter lack of power. Very few major leaguers are able to sustain an on-base percentage higher than their slugging percentage, but that's the kind of player Brantley has been in the minors. He'd be a better prospect if was sure to stick as a center fielder, but the Brewers kept finding reasons to play him elsewhere.

Ryan Braun (Left Field)

PA	R	H	2B	3B	HR	RBI	SO	BB	SB	CS	BA	OBP	SLG	OPS	3-Year	Fielding	Reliability
582	85	152	32	4	33	101	117	40	12	4	.286	.339	.548	.887	+0.02	D	Very High

All in all it was a pretty successful sophomore season for the Brauntosaurus. His BABIP, especially his crazy 2007 mark against lefties (.440), regressed to more normal levels, but his walk rate ticked upward ever so slightly and he cut his strikeout rate, evidence of his attempts to rein in his absurdly free-swinging ways. He also made an unexpectedly smooth transition to left field, improving his overall account as he went from defensive liability to contributor. Still, his third-place finish in the MVP voting overstates his value. He'll need to get on base a lot more often to be a legitimate MVP candidate, but our projection sees him staying the course—excellent, but not an MVP.

Mike Cameron (Center Field)

PA	R	H	2B	3B	HR	RBI	SO	BB	SB	CS	BA	OBP	SLG	OPS	3-Year	Fielding	Reliability
525	70	115	26	4	20	68	132	56	15	5	.251	.336	.456	.792	—	C	Very High

Cameron had another vintage Mike Cameron season: a boatload of strikeouts and a low batting average ameliorated by a healthy helping of walks and good center field defense. Don't let the bitching from the hoi polloi that inevitably accompanies his whiffs fool you—as long as his gloveliness doesn't fade, he's worth his $10 million salary. As of this writing, the Brewers are considering trading him to the Yankees for Melky Cabrera and Kei Igawa, a gamble I like from the Brewers' prospective.

Craig Counsell (Shortstop)

PA	R	H	2B	3B	HR	RBI	SO	BB	SB	CS	BA	OBP	SLG	OPS	3-Year	Fielding	Reliability
359	37	72	14	2	2	25	53	43	5	3	.234	.333	.312	.645	—	A	Average

Counsell continued to show that there are exactly two things he can do well: take a walk and play good defense at several infield positions. Unfortunately, he truly cannot hit at all, making it impossible for the Brewers to justify paying him $3 million to continue doing those two things for them in 2009. So endeth Counsell's second go-round with the hometown nine.

Ray Durham (Second Base)

PA	R	H	2B	3B	HR	RBI	SO	BB	SB	CS	BA	OBP	SLG	OPS	3-Year	Fielding	Reliability
460	54	103	23	2	11	50	72	50	7	2	.255	.337	.403	.740	—	F	Very High

Durham came over from the Giants in June to give Rickie Weeks a kick in the ass and did, to the tune of .280/.369/.477. Unfortunately, he was able to play only 41 games for Milwaukee, as he was frequently banged up and unable to go. Overall, the 2008 season was a nice bounce-back from his execrable 2007, but his body may be failing him.

Alcides Escobar (Shortstop)

PA	R	H	2B	3B	HR	RBI	SO	BB	SB	CS	BA	OBP	SLG	OPS	3-Year	Fielding	Reliability
549	59	141	19	5	5	47	91	19	15	7	.272	.299	.357	.656	+0.09	B	High

The legend of Escobar's glove is great and has been landing him on prospect lists for years, but in 2008 his bat finally started catching up. His walk rate, while still below average, increased significantly, and he quadrupled his career high in home runs. He's already better defensively than J.J. Hardy, and if he can sustain or even build on his hitting performance from last year, he could quickly render Hardy obsolete.

Prince Fielder (First Base)

PA	R	H	2B	3B	HR	RBI	SO	BB	SB	CS	BA	OBP	SLG	OPS	3-Year	Fielding	Reliability
617	89	153	32	1	36	107	114	75	2	2	.290	.386	.560	.946	+0.04	D	Very High

Fielder going veggie was received about as enthusiastically as Dylan going electric, but the results weren't nearly as enduring, as Fielder suffered a large slugging dropoff. It's tempting to chalk up the power outage to the diet change, but there's a reason "post hoc ergo propter hoc" is a logical fallacy. Pending further evidence, I'm calling it normal regression to the mean, and both my common sense and our projection expect the Prince to bounce back in 2009.

Mat Gamel (Third Base)

PA	R	H	2B	3B	HR	RBI	SO	BB	SB	CS	BA	OBP	SLG	OPS	3-Year	Fielding	Reliability
570	66	133	29	5	13	64	121	46	4	5	.258	.320	.409	.729	+0.06	D	Very High

Gamel (rhymes with "camel") came on like gangbusters in the first half of the season but was simply a bust in the second half. His monthly slash stats are very dramatic: .379/.448/.680, .387/.438/.669, and .381/.451/.562 in April through June, followed by .243/.288/.350 and .213/.312/.351 in July and August. A sore elbow no doubt contributed to some of his post-break struggles, but he wasn't going to hit like Rogers Hornsby all season no matter what. At the plate, he'll probably be similar to Corey Hart with a little better plate discipline, but his terrible glove is all anyone wants to talk about. The consensus among the scouting community seems to be that Gamel simply won't be able to stick at third. The Brewers, having just moved Ryan Braun off third for similar reasons, will continue to give Gamel chances there, since with Hart and Braun ensconced in the two corner outfield positions and Prince Fielder occupying first there's really nowhere to move him.

Tony Gwynn (Center Field)

PA	R	H	2B	3B	HR	RBI	SO	BB	SB	CS	BA	OBP	SLG	OPS	3-Year	Fielding	Reliability
412	48	102	14	4	5	36	68	30	12	3	.271	.325	.369	.694	+0.08	D	High

Gwynn is a fifth outfielder disguised as a potential starting center fielder because of name recognition. He bunts well, runs fast, and plays a slick center field, but building him up to be something more will just result in disappointment.

Bill Hall (Third Base)

PA	R	H	2B	3B	HR	RBI	SO	BB	SB	CS	BA	OBP	SLG	OPS	3-Year	Fielding	Reliability
470	56	106	27	1	18	64	121	42	4	2	.252	.320	.449	.769	-0.02	C	Very High

The 2006 season seems so long ago, but the Brewers probably wish it were even further in the past at this point, as they still owe Hall $15.7 million on the four-year contract he signed after that peak season. His pop, defensive versatility, and lefty-mashing would make him a useful bench player, but he's increasingly exposed as a starter. Indeed, here's been some talk of dumping his salary off on the Yankees in conjunction with the Mike Cameron-for-Melky Cabrera trade.

J.J. Hardy (Shortstop)

PA	R	H	2B	3B	HR	RBI	SO	BB	SB	CS	BA	OBP	SLG	OPS	3-Year	Fielding	Reliability
538	70	139	26	2	24	83	82	42	3	1	.285	.341	.495	.836	+0.08	B	Very High

Hardy continues to get better each year, raising his performance to legitimately All-Star-caliber in 2008. His walk rate crept up to almost league-average, making him a player with very few holes in his game. He's got to be the slowest athletic-looking guy I've ever seen, but he overcomes his poor foot speed in the field with good positioning. Since he has two full years before he's eligible for free agency, he'll fetch a nice haul on the trade market should the Brewers judge Alcides Escobar ready.

Corey Hart (Right Field)

PA	R	H	2B	3B	HR	RBI	SO	BB	SB	CS	BA	OBP	SLG	OPS	3-Year	Fielding	Reliability
558	79	146	35	5	24	84	104	34	17	5	.286	.335	.516	.851	+0.07	D	Very High

Hart finally got a chance to start from Opening Day with no fear of losing his job, and responded with... a fairly disappointing season. His walk rate, below average to begin with, plummeted, and he failed to display his considerable power consistently. Extremely fast for his size, he steals bases well and plays a better right field than he's given credit for, though his throws home frequently fade up the third-base line. Our projection has him rediscovering his 2007 stroke, but if he doesn't, he'd be wise this time to elide the comments about the fans not being supportive enough.

Gabe Kapler (Center Field)

PA	R	H	2B	3B	HR	RBI	SO	BB	SB	CS	BA	OBP	SLG	OPS	3-Year	Fielding	Reliability
255	29	61	13	1	7	31	43	19	2	1	.264	.323	.420	.743	-0.04	D	Very Low

The Brewers brought Kapler out of retirement and away from a coaching job in the Red Sox system and he rewarded them with a fine season. As long as he can continue to handle center field, he'll make a good platoon player or fourth outfielder for someone.

Jason Kendall (Catcher)

PA	R	H	2B	3B	HR	RBI	SO	BB	SB	CS	BA	OBP	SLG	OPS	3-Year	Fielding	Reliability
537	54	124	24	1	2	41	54	45	6	3	.262	.335	.329	.664	-0.05	B	Very High

Kendall hit poorly, as was to be expected, but his defense made a dramatic recovery. He threw out 41 of 96 baserunners attempting to steal (42 percent), up from a miserable 20 of 131 (15 percent) in 2007. Also, as evidenced by the total attempts dropping by more than 25 percent, teams eventually caught on to the fact that stolen bases weren't gimmes anymore and stopped sending everyone and his mother against him. Early in the year, the Brewers began a bold experiment, correctly determining that a player of Kendall's relatively unusual offensive construction—poor general offense, high ground ball percentage, slow speed, but relatively good on-base skills—would be better served batting ninth, where he could serve as a "second leadoff hitter" and have his tendency to ground into double plays mitigated by immediately succeeding the pitcher. Though the team abandoned the experiment after 46 games, the fact that the Brewers tried it at all is encouraging.

Mike Lamb (Third Base)

PA	R	H	2B	3B	HR	RBI	SO	BB	SB	CS	BA	OBP	SLG	OPS	3-Year	Fielding	Reliability
343	38	81	16	2	7	37	50	31	1	0	.263	.330	.397	.727	-0.04	D	High

Brought in after the Sept. 1 playoff-eligibility deadline for no easily discernible reason, Lamb is likely to be even worse than Bill Hall on offense and is certainly no great shakes on defense. At least Mat Gamel can hit. This team really needs a third baseman.

Lou Palmisano (Catcher)

PA	R	H	2B	3B	HR	RBI	SO	BB	SB	CS	BA	OBP	SLG	OPS	3-Year	Fielding	Reliability
268	28	55	10	1	6	26	54	26	2	1	.233	.315	.360	.675	+0.06	—	Average

Palmisano was taken by the Orioles from the Brewers in the Rule 5 draft and subsequently traded to the Astros. Cap'n Lou, as fans of the Brewers system fondly knew him, excited many in 2003 with his .391/.448/.592 season in the Pioneer League but hasn't come close to matching that production since and also is coming off major knee surgery, never a good sign for a catcher. Still, he's not a complete cipher offensively, so as long his knee allows him to play competent defense, he has a chance to be a decent backup catcher.

Mike Rivera (Catcher)

PA	R	H	2B	3B	HR	RBI	SO	BB	SB	CS	BA	OBP	SLG	OPS	3-Year	Fielding	Reliability
257	29	58	12	0	10	34	48	17	3	2	.246	.300	.424	.724	-0.03	C	Average

Who? Even if you followed the Brewers, you might not have realized Rivera was on the team, given that he received only 69 at-bats despite being on the roster the entire year. Rivera can hit better than most backup catchers and still has just over two years of service time, so he'll be a good option for awhile.

Angel Salome (Catcher)

PA	R	H	2B	3B	HR	RBI	SO	BB	SB	CS	BA	OBP	SLG	OPS	3-Year	Fielding	Reliability
489	56	129	28	2	11	60	75	28	2	2	.285	.328	.428	.756	+0.09	—	High

You really have to see this guy to fully appreciate what people mean when they say that he's built like a bowling ball. He's probably both shorter and heavier than listed, and trust me, it's all muscle; a picture of him flexing with his shirt off was popular among Brewers fans for its that-must-Photoshopped quality. More than just his build is strange; Salome has a bizarre plate approach, stepping in the bucket out of an already-open stance while still somehow covering the plate well. Despite, or because of, all the awkwardness, Salome hit .360/.415/.559 at Double-A Huntsville. What's holding him back at this point is defense. Though he has an excellent arm, poor throwing mechanics have kept his caught-stealing numbers down, and he doesn't block pitches well, leading to a lot of passed balls. Unlike with Gamel, there's no talk of moving Salome anywhere because his unique physique doesn't lend itself to any other position. Since Jason Kendall has a year left on his contract, Salome will get another year in the minors to work on his receiving skills.

Rickie Weeks (Second Base)

PA	R	H	2B	3B	HR	RBI	SO	BB	SB	CS	BA	OBP	SLG	OPS	3-Year	Fielding	Reliability
505	69	111	21	4	17	59	106	60	18	3	.258	.361	.445	.806	+0.07	C	Very High

When Weeks is right at the plate, rifling laser-beam line drives between the gaps, it's hard to believe he could ever hit .235 for a week, let alone two seasons in a row. After all, this is the guy who set the NCAA career batting average record while at Southern. What's going on here? I get the sense that he's never really been quite right since rupturing the sheath of a tendon in his wrist in 2006 while waggling a bat in the dugout, which if true would be a damn shame. He has made significant strides in improving his once-poor defense, but I guarantee you that when he came up in 2005, no one though they'd be looking at his glove as the plus part of his game only a few years later. If he doesn't hit soon, the Brewers will be forced to move on.

Pitchers

Omar Aguilar (Reliever)

W	L	ERA	TBF	IP	Hit	HR	SO	BB	HBP	3-Year	Reliability
3	4	4.64	280	63	57	8	49	40	3	-0.19	Very Low

The Brewers took a flier on Aguilar in the 30th round of the 2005 draft because, though he was recovering from Tommy John surgery, he threw hard. After the surgery, Aguilar threw even harder and can now touch 98 mph. As with many high-velocity pitchers, Aguilar's breaking ball is a work in progress, but when he can find the strike zone with it, he's very good. After pitching well in the Arizona Fall League and being added to the 40-man roster to protect him from the Rule 5 draft, he might be a dark horse candidate to make the bullpen out of spring training. He's surpassed Luis Pena as the best closer prospect in the system.

Dave Bush (Starter)

W	L	ERA	TBF	IP	Hit	HR	SO	BB	HBP	3-Year	Reliability
9	10	4.54	724	171	179	26	107	43	9	+0.45	Very High

Though his season-ending numbers look fine, indeed like he picked up where 2006 left off after a bumpy 2007, Bush struggled so badly to begin the year that he was removed the rotation and actually optioned to Triple-A for a start before being recalled after Yovani Gallardo's injury. The last four months of the season, though, Bush was excellent, and I will forever remember him for being the winning pitcher in the first Brewers playoff game

I ever attended. He can be an effective mid-rotation starter, but his ERA will never quite live up to his excellent WHIPs because of his habit of allowing big innings.

Todd Coffey (Reliever)

W	L	ERA	TBF	IP	Hit	HR	SO	BB	HBP	3-Year	Reliability
4	3	4.22	291	67	70	7	50	26	2	+0.27	Average

Claimed off waivers from Cincinnati too late to make the playoff roster, Coffey nevertheless impressed in his short stint as a Brewer. Gifted with a physique that endears him to the many Brewers fans doing their best to live up to the beer-swilling, brat-downing cheesehead stereotype, Coffey was re-signed and will, probably to his detriment, get a longer look in 2009.

Tim Dillard (Reliever)

W	L	ERA	TBF	IP	Hit	HR	SO	BB	HBP	3-Year	Reliability
4	5	5.13	360	80	92	11	38	35	4	-0.02	Very High

Dillard was an innings-eating control pitcher in the minors, so it was surprising to see him come up as a reliever and consistently hit 95 mph with his fastball. I think the team gave up on him a bit too quickly after he struggled; he could be a valuable member of the bullpen this year.

Eric Gagne (Reliever)

W	L	ERA	TBF	IP	Hit	HR	SO	BB	HBP	3-Year	Reliability
3	3	4.00	247	58	52	7	50	25	2	+0.21	Very Low

So what was wrong with Gagne in 2008? The Hardball Times writer and PITCHf/x guru Josh Kalk determined that his change-up wasn't dropping nearly as much as it did previously, and also that he was throwing it more often. Whether that's fixable is anyone's guess; all I know is that the disparity between the value of his performance and the near-$10 million salary he would have earned had he accepted arbitration caused the Brewers to not even offer it to him, thus forfeiting their chance at the compensation pick Gagne could have netted them. I wonder if Gagne and Derrick Turnbow ever call each other and commiserate.

Yovani Gallardo (Starter)

W	L	ERA	TBF	IP	Hit	HR	SO	BB	HBP	3-Year	Reliability
6	5	4.08	435	102	94	12	98	41	3	-0.26	High

It's tempting to look at the Brewers' playoff run and Gallardo's injury and ask what could have been, but if YoGa had been healthy all year I doubt the Brewers would have gone out and acquired CC Sabathia. While Matt LaPorta's plate discipline would look nice in the middle of the 2009 Brewers' hacktastic lineup, one other potential benefit of Gallardo's injury is that it will keep his arm fresher, an invaluable service both to a young ace and the team relying on him. Gallardo is one of the biggest keys to the Brewers' season; if he can stay healthy and assume the ace mantle, it will go a long way toward stabilizing a rotation suddenly missing its top 40 percent.

Seth McClung (Reliever)

W	L	ERA	TBF	IP	Hit	HR	SO	BB	HBP	3-Year	Reliability
5	6	4.32	438	99	93	11	81	55	4	+0.19	High

McClung was one of the most pleasant surprises for the Brewers in 2008. Acquired from Tampa Bay for Grant Balfour in 2007, McClung had a Nuke LaLoosh reputation for throwing hard without much idea of where it was going. In Milwaukee, Mike Maddux overhauled McClung's mechanics, simplifying them greatly, and McClung experienced the first real success of his career. He was actually more effective as a starter than as a reliever, posting better strikeout and walk rates in the former role, but he had a few legendary relief appearances toward the end of the year where he pitched like a man on fire, a closer being born. It will be interesting to see if McClung can sustain his success now that Maddux has moved on.

Guillermo Mota (Reliever)

W	L	ERA	TBF	IP	Hit	HR	SO	BB	HBP	3-Year	Reliability
4	3	4.21	268	62	60	8	50	26	2	—	Low

A lot of people were left scratching their heads when Doug Melvin traded for him right before the Mets were about to designate Mota for assignment, forcing the Brewers to assume the pitcher's $3.2 million salary, rather than attempting to sign him for much less after his release. Mota, perhaps the most hated Met in recent memory, experienced his share of adversity with the Brewers, at one point struggling so much that the Brewers beat writer, Tom Haudricourt, (wrongly) predicted that the Brewers would designate him for assignment the following day; however, he recovered to pitch well down the stretch. He'll get another chance in 2009, somewhere not in Queens.

Manny Parra (Starter)

W	L	ERA	TBF	IP	Hit	HR	SO	BB	HBP	3-Year	Reliability
8	9	4.55	664	150	157	17	119	70	6	+0.14	High

Parra has the potential to be really good. He had the second-highest fastball velocity for a lefty in all of baseball last year (behind a certain teammate) and throws a nice, hard curveball. Unusually, he also features both a splitter and a change-up. All four of Parra's offerings are, or at least can be, plus pitches, a rarity. If he can avoid the shoulder problems that plagued him in the past and harness his command, he and Gallardo can anchor the top of Milwaukee's rotation for the next few years.

Luis Pena (Reliever)

W	L	ERA	TBF	IP	Hit	HR	SO	BB	HBP	3-Year	Reliability
2	4	5.46	271	58	62	7	42	40	3	0.00	Average

Pena was supposed to be the Brewers' closer by now, but he had a miserable season in Triple-A for a guy with a high-90s fastball and nasty splitter in his repertoire: 6.93 ERA, 2.05 WHIP, 49/47 K/BB in 49.1 innings. Obviously, control is a problem here, but so is the fact that his fastball lacks movement. Pena created a stir in the Triple-A All-Star game when he touched triple digits several times, but the fact that one of those heaters was turned around for a two-run homer tells you all you need to know.

David Riske (Reliever)

W	L	ERA	TBF	IP	Hit	HR	SO	BB	HBP	3-Year	Reliability
3	3	4.78	242	55	56	7	40	26	1	+0.25	Low

Signing non-overpowering relievers to three-year deals is an odd strategy, and it certainly didn't pay off for the Brewers in 2008, as Riske (your pun goes here) was not only bad, but frequently injured. They still owe him almost $9 million over the next two years, so he'll get another prominent role in the 2009 bullpen to try to justify his salary, but he has an excellent chance of becoming the relief version of Jeff Suppan.

CC Sabathia (Starter)

W	L	ERA	TBF	IP	Hit	HR	SO	BB	HBP	3-Year	Reliability
15	9	3.21	867	215	196	20	189	45	7	+0.26	Very High

Sabathia single-handedly fixed the Miller Park roof, extirpated the zebra mussels from Lake Michigan, and solved the city's unemployment problem. Oh yeah, he pitched pretty well too. He hit a home run in his first home start. He threw the Brewers' first no-hitter since 1987 (no matter what the Pittsburgh official scorer says). He pitched the Brewers into the playoffs with a 1.65 ERA over 130.2 innings, encompassing 17 starts, of which an amazing seven were complete games and three of those shutouts. He was more than dominant, he was a force of nature, and the effect he had on the city won't soon be forgotten. In a way, maybe it's good that the Yankees signed him for the gross national product of Swaziland, since even Sabathia himself probably couldn't have lived up to the legend he'd established. In any case, thanks for the run, CC, it was a blast.

Ben Sheets (Starter)

W	L	ERA	TBF	IP	Hit	HR	SO	BB	HBP	3-Year	Reliability
11	8	3.75	719	175	168	20	132	44	2	+0.19	Very High

Sheets had his best season since his magical 2004, managing to stay healthy long enough to log almost 200 innings and even start the All-Star Game. Still, in the end, an injury again defined his year, as he went down with a torn muscle in his elbow in late September, just as the Brewers needed him most for their final push to the postseason. Had Sheets been healthy for the playoffs, who knows how far the Brewers could have gone. From a pure performance standpoint, his rates over the last two years are down significantly from his 2004-'06 heyday, and that combined with his injury history makes me think the Brewers are smart to let him go now.

Brian Shouse (Reliever)

W	L	ERA	TBF	IP	Hit	HR	SO	BB	HBP	3-Year	Reliability
4	2	3.41	244	58	55	4	37	20	2	—	Very Low

In one of Doug Melvin's shrewder deals, Shouse was acquired from the Rangers for Enrique Cruz (who?) in early 2006 and gave the Brewers three seasons of quality LOOGYness. Undoubtedly his greatest gift to Brewers fans, however, was providing the inspiration for the Unofficial Brian Shouse Fan Club (http://www.brianshousefanclub.com), truly a site to behold.

Mitch Stetter (Reliever)

W	L	ERA	TBF	IP	Hit	HR	SO	BB	HBP	3-Year	Reliability
3	3	3.80	236	55	48	5	53	27	2	+0.17	Very Low

Between Triple-A and the majors, Stetter struck out 44 percent of the lefties he faced, making him eminently qualified to inherit Brian Shouse's role as LOOGY. A bane on the sinistral, he wasn't bad against the dextral either, holding them to nearly as low a batting average, though his control, not great to begin with, is much worse against the conventionally handed.

Jeff Suppan (Starter)

W	L	ERA	TBF	IP	Hit	HR	SO	BB	HBP	3-Year	Reliability
8	11	5.04	748	169	197	22	82	62	6	+0.27	Very High

"Ah, that was money well spent," Steve Martin's character in the move "Parenthood" says to his wife after they ask their son where he heard the fecal-oriented song he just sang and he tells them he learned it at summer camp. Suspiciously enough, the characters were coming home from a Cardinals game when that conversation took place. Suppan pitches like a fifth starter, if that, and by all rights should be in danger of losing his job, but the fact that he's still owed $27 million over the next two years by the Brewers will keep him in the rotation for awhile.

Salomon Torres (Reliever)

W	L	ERA	TBF	IP	Hit	HR	SO	BB	HBP	3-Year	Reliability
5	3	3.86	320	75	74	7	51	30	3	—	Average

Torres stepped in as closer after Eric Gagne's flameout and performed admirably. Somewhat surprisingly, he elected to retire after the season, saying he wanted to spend more time with his family and on his faith.

Carlos Villanueva (Reliever)

W	L	ERA	TBF	IP	Hit	HR	SO	BB	HBP	3-Year	Reliability
6	6	4.21	441	104	100	15	82	37	3	+0.03	Very High

Villanueva continued to perform yeoman's work for the Brewers in 2008. After nine mediocre starts to begin the season, he was moved to the bullpen, where all he did was post a 2.12 ERA with a 62/14 K/BB in 59.1 innings. He's been going back and forth between the rotation and pen for a few years now, but seems to have settled in as a reliever and is a potential setup man.

Minnesota Twins

by Parker Hageman of Over the Baggy (overthebaggy.blogspot.com)

2009 Twins Projections

Record: 83-79
Division Rank/Games Behind: 2nd, 3 games back
Runs Scored: 727, 12th in the league
Runs Allowed: 716, 4th in the league
Park Factor: 1.00, and indoors to boot

What Happened Last Year:

Before the 2008 season, as the Central's heavyweight contenders added to their payrolls, the Twins financially downshifted. The Tigers, the monsters of the hot stove, led the way with a 44 percent increase, followed by a 28 percent boost to the 2007 division champion Indians and, finally, an 11 percent increase by the White Sox.

The Twins, on the other hand, shed 20 percent of their total payroll from 2007, putting the bill for their pool of talent $2 million lower than that of the Kansas City Royals. Absent three starting pitchers (Johan Santana, Carlos Silva and Matt Garza), a Gold Glove center fielder (Torii Hunter) and a high-caliber defensive shortstop (Jason Bartlett) and devoid of any obvious successors, it was natural to overlook a team that had more unanswered questions than "Celebrity Jeopardy."

On paper the team lacked scope. The Twins would rely on unproven players in Alexi Casilla and Carlos Gomez to fill vital up-the-middle defensive positions and inserted Nick Blackburn, Kevin Slowey and Glen Perkins into the rotation to throw more innings than they had in their entire careers. First-year general manager Bill Smith plugged the holes in the roster with low-cost, low-reward free agents in Adam Everett, Mike Lamb and Livan Hernandez. Clearly, with Joe Mauer, Justin Morneau and Michael Cuddyer along with the newly acquired Delmon Young, it would be hard to dismiss the team in its entirety. Their presence would give manager Ron Gardenhire virtual permanent fixtures in the three through six slots in the lineup.

Injuries, however, would cost the team Everett and Cuddyer for a substantial chunk of the year. It was these maladies that would present more playing time to the energetic Casilla and force the Twins to recall Denard Span. That duo would give the Twins one of the best table-setting, one-two combinations in the majors. Span displayed great on-base presence while Casilla had the bat control to advance him to scoring position.

It would be left to the highly paid duo of Mauer and Morneau to drive Span home. This scoring methodology gave the Twins the third-highest run-scoring lineup in the American League.

As the season progressed, the Tigers never found their footing and the Indians were spoiled by injuries, leaving the division up for grabs. To the surprise of many, it would be the Twins and the White Sox that would battle for supremacy of the Central. The two teams squared off all season as philosophical contradictions: The White Sox were a team loaded with lumbering sluggers who could lose foot races to glaciers while the Twins were constructed with more Gap shoppers than any lifestyle center in America. The only area where the teams shared a common bond was their affinity for young pitching.

Legendary manager Earl Weaver had an infamous on-air rant describing the differences between the two schools of thought. Paraphrasing for propriety's sake, Weaver opined that the speedy team is more apt to be picked off trying to steal, running itself into outs, and taking runs away from the ballclub. This was the team that the Twins had assembled. They employed liberal use of the sacrifice (52, the most in the AL) and took the extra base when necessary. This, along with an abundance of well-timed hits (.305 BA with RISP) gave the Twins a potent, albeit unorthodox, offense.

It was this manner of play that drove Weaver crazy. Weaver longed for players who could hit the ball out of the park. This, he said, left no room for mistakes. In comparison, the White Sox had hit 234 home runs to the Twins' 111. The 2008 White Sox were the personification of an ideal Weaverian lineup.

Despite the difference in style, the teams were unable to determine who owned the rights to the AL Central after 162 games. One additional meeting would have to be set to determine which team would go after the Rays in the ALDS.

To claim that Game 163 was simply an additional game would be a great injustice. Game 163 transpired on a stage that was more significant than just a runoff baseball contest; it was a case study of what baseball researchers will reference when trying to compile evidence that supports power over speed when nine innings are at stake. One was a franchise that would acquire expensive, aging talent that could hit the ball a ton but couldn't advance on the basepaths without assistance from plate tectonics. The other was a mid-market organization building on homegrown, cheap labor that could gain an extra base and cover acreage in the outfield as the basis of its success.

Power would be the ultimate victor. The White Sox's 235th home run of the season would drop swift justice and eliminate the Twins from the final playoff berth.

In spite of falling one game short of the playoffs, the Twins made massive and unexpected improvements in 2008. The season allowed the organization to provide development time at the major league level to Gomez, Perkins and Blackburn that would not have been available had the team retained Hunter, Santana and Silva. Not only did the Twins make a surprising nine-game swing up from 2007, they were able to do so with a large reduction in the payroll.

Players Lost from Last Year's Team:

Dennys Reyes, Everett, Eddie Guardado. Reyes became expendable when the team acquired Craig Breslow and prospect Jose Mijares emerged as viable options to replace the impeding free agent in the bullpen. Reyes' legacy in Minnesota should be that of a great value acquired during Terry Ryan's tenure as GM. Signed as a minor league free agent in March 2006, Reyes helped stabilize the bullpen for the playoff-bound Twins that year. Before his initial one-year contract of $550,000 expired, Ryan extended it for two more seasons for $2 million. Not only for the small sum of $2.55 million did the Twins received 126.1 innings of work, a 109/51 K/BB ratio and a 2.14 ERA, but they had the added bonus of Elias labeling Reyes a type B free agent. The possibility of a decent compensatory draft pick looms.

Players Acquired:

None.

Management Is:

The front office has produced four division championships since the new millennium by using three critical elements to ensure that the payroll will not fluctuate wildly out of control: (1) Reaping the dividends of a well-stocked farm system, (2) Obtaining inexpensive talent through trades and (3) Signing one or two low-budget free agents to buy time before a prospect or trade can fulfill long-term commitments. This has been the road map for success for the franchise Ryan designed. When Ryan stepped down after 2007, Smith seamlessly transitioned into the general manager's role, continuing the policies of his predecessor and former boss.

Smith did deviate from Ryan's policy of not trafficking young pitching prospects when he flipped Garza

to the Rays, though for the most part Smith followed the guiding principles when constructing his 2008 roster. Smith relied on the internally developed players (Blackburn, Slowey, Casilla), interim free agent signings (Lamb, Everett, Hernandez), and the economical players brought in via trade (Young, Gomez).

The dynamic of how the franchise operates may alter a bit in the next few seasons. With the move to Target Field now just 162 games away, the Twins already have shifted their previous paradigm. Before the 2008 season, Smith locked Morneau, Joe Nathan and Cuddyer into extended contracts that ensure those three core members will remain Twins until 2013, 2012 and 2011, respectively. Mauer, however, is signed through 2010 and certainly will command a healthy raise as the American League's best hitting catcher as well as the face of the franchise. Following Mauer, pitchers like Scott Baker and Francisco Liriano, along with designated hitter Jason Kubel, are ripe for long-term contracts. Will the budget-conscious Twins expand payroll to meet the demands of future contract obligations? The alternative is to shed some of that financial weight through a trade, as dictated by the Ryan blueprint.

The Minor League System Is:

Player development has never been an issue in the Twins organization. Mauer, Morneau, Kubel, Span, Baker, Perkins, Liriano, Slowey and Blackburn all were refined in within the organization's ranks and all were contributing factors in 2008. Minnesota has enough in the pipeline to continue this trend for years to come. Players like Chris Parmalee, Angel Morales, Wilson Ramos and Alexander Soto all show legitimate clout. Luke Hughes and Danny Valencia emerged as potential corner infielders who might be with the club in the near future. Finally the crown jewel of the system, the 2007 first-round draft choice, Ben Revere, hit .379/.433/.497 with a 27/31 BB/K ratio in 83 Midwest League games and was named the organization's Minor League Player of the Year. Overseeing his first draft, Smith and his scouting staff demonstrated keen judgment when they selected Aaron Hicks, Shooter Hunt and Carlos Gutierrez in the first round, adding talent to the lowest echelon of the farm system.

At every step, the Twins have pitching that is progressing nicely. They can churn out control pitchers like Beyonce churns out No. 1 hits. In the immediate future, the team has potential major league-ready pitchers in right-handers Philip Humber and Kevin Mulvey as well as left-handed Brian Duensing. Mulvey is the most likely candidate to contribute to the starting rotation (and has the higher upside of the three), though Humber is out of options and could be a member of the bullpen in 2009. This trio is a testament to the organization's continued cultivation of control artists and, ultimately, proves that pitching will never be a scarce resource for the Minnesota Twins.

Due For a Change:

Cuddyer had an abbreviated, injury-segmented 2008 season. Just five games into the schedule, Cuddyer was sidelined with a thumb injury. Once back, he was slow to rediscover his swing. In a 12-game stretch in June, he settled into a groove by hitting .303/.452/.515 in 42 plate appearances before going on the DL again until September. Give Cuddy time to acclimate himself this spring and if he avoids injuries, 2009 should see a spike in his production. That being said, he is at a precarious stage in his career. In 2009 he will be 30 years old, he has more than $15 million left on his contract through 2010, and perhaps most importantly, he has three younger and more inexpensive players crowding the Twins outfield. Assuming that he is now beginning the downward turn of his aging curve, Cuddyer needs to have a 2009 like his 2006 year if he's to finish his current contract in a Twins uniform.

Reasons to be Optimistic:

The nucleus of the roster is reaching peak playing ages in 2009. At the core of the lineup are a batting champ (Mauer) and an MVP candidate (Morneau), supplemented with a strong supporting cast of Kubel, Cuddyer, Young and Span. The rotation is brimming with arms that have now been road-tested. Baker, Slowey, Perkins and Blackburn were proficient as starters. Liriano will have a full offseason to recoup his arm strength. When healthy, those five combine for a rotation that would make many general managers envious. Finally at the back end of the bullpen is Nathan, who produced numbers equal or better to those of Francisco Rodriguez (save totals notwithstanding), and will preserve the vast majority of leads provided to him.

Reasons to be Pessimistic:

How did a team that hit the fewest home runs in the American League (111) manage to score the third most runs per game (5.09)? The Twins carried a batting average of .279 on the season but somehow managed to hit .305, well above the major league average of .266, when a runner advanced to second or beyond. Individually, the story was the same. The team's RBI leader, Morneau, hit .300, but .048 points higher with runners in scoring

> ### Our Favorite Twins Blogs:
>
> Aaron Gleeman's site (aarongleeman.com) has become virtually synonymous with "Twins" and "blog." His commentary on the team and the sport in general, combined with his Link-o-Ramas that digresses from baseball, keeps his as one of the most popular sites on all of the intertubes and a must visit each morning.
>
> Proprietor of the website SethSpeaks (sethspeaks. net), Seth Stohs, has an unbelievable amount of knowledge and connections to the Twins system from top to bottom. His recent expansion into the multimedia realm of podcasts has supplied a voice to his words. This natural progression of technology has allowed Stohs to provide guests from the organization ranging from set-up man/blogger Pat Neshek to pitching prospect Jeff Manship to former Twins pitcher Grant Balfour.

position. Mauer had a .034 difference between the two averages. Even Gomez had a .038 increase in his average with runners in scoring position. It is hard to imagine that the Twins will be able to sustain this offensive output in 2009.

Still Left to Do:

As in every offseason since Corey Koskie vacated third, the Twins need to find a replacement. Talks with the Mariners for Adrian Beltre and the Rockies for Garrett Atkins proved fruitless. If there is no acquisition by spring training, the position will be filled with a reasonably priced platoon of Brendan Harris and Brian Buscher. With set-up man Pat Neshek out for the season, it appears that the Twins will turn to internal candidates such as Jesse Crain, Boof Bonser and Humber to compete for the role.

Most Likely Team Outcome:

Mark 'em down for 86 wins. The question is whether that will be enough to win the AL Central. It most likely won't. While it never officially lived up to its billing in 2008, the Central is one of the most competitive divisions in baseball. Across the board, the teams showed various levels of improvement: Post-Aug. 1, the Indians went 34-20, leading the American League in victories; After Sept. 1, the Royals finished 18-8—the best winning percentage in baseball. Detroit and Chicago are making offseason adjustments that will guarantee they are contenders. The Twins will have to replicate their offensive output from 2008 to keep pace and, again, it seems like a stretch.

Player Projections

Batters

Brian Buscher (Third Base)

PA	R	H	2B	3B	HR	RBI	SO	BB	SB	CS	BA	OBP	SLG	OPS	3-Year	Fielding	Reliability
471	50	110	20	2	9	49	71	35	2	2	.258	.319	.378	.697	+0.01	D	Very High

Small sample size aside, Buscher put together a decent season by crushing right-handed pitching. That attribute made his second-half partnership with Harris at third relatively productive. His .294 BA overall was inflated by a .335 batting average on balls in play, so anticipate Buscher's average in 2009 to head south. In addition to the strong possibility of statistical regression at the plate, his glove work leaves much to be desired and the Twins probably would like to upgrade to a player who can hit both right- and left-handed pitching.

Alexi Casilla (Second Base)

PA	R	H	2B	3B	HR	RBI	SO	BB	SB	CS	BA	OBP	SLG	OPS	3-Year	Fielding	Reliability
527	55	121	16	3	3	38	66	37	14	6	.257	.315	.323	.638	+0.04	F	Very High

Though it might not be reflected in his overall numbers, Casilla's play made him one of the best table-setters in baseball. His combination of speed and high contact rate made him a very good No. 2 hitter who helped get runners into scoring position through a team-high number of sacrifice bunts (13). Before an injury that took him out of the lineup for a spell midseason, Casilla was having a breakout year, hitting .313/.351/.424 with 19 extra base hits in 273 plate appearances. After his return to the lineup in August, Casilla hit just .225/.302/.289 with just three extra base hits in 164 plate appearances. Our projections suggest that he is somewhere between those two samples for 2009.

Michael Cuddyer (Right Field)

PA	R	H	2B	3B	HR	RBI	SO	BB	SB	CS	BA	OBP	SLG	OPS	3-Year	Fielding	Reliability
414	49	97	21	3	10	47	73	39	4	1	.265	.343	.421	.764	-0.03	D	Very High

The soon-to-be 30-year-old Cuddyer might be having a "Logan's Run" experience, considering the younger Denard Span, Carlos Gomez and Delmon Young are making for a congested outfield. He still has a howitzer of an arm, but cannot monitor the same amount of real estate that Span can. Because the Twins have a pitching staff filled with fly ball creators, the team would benefit more from using Span rather than Cuddyer in right. Cuddyer's destiny is probably that of an expensive DH/part-time outfielder by the time the Twins get to the new stadium.

Carlos Gomez (Center Field)

PA	R	H	2B	3B	HR	RBI	SO	BB	SB	CS	BA	OBP	SLG	OPS	3-Year	Fielding	Reliability
557	65	129	23	6	6	45	120	27	25	5	.252	.299	.356	.655	+0.05	B	High

Miscast as a leadoff hitter for most of the year, Gomez is still learning on the job, particularly at the plate. Just 23 years old in 2009, Gomez has a tendency to swing as if he is being compensated per bat revolution and with enough vigor to create a gale force wind when he misses (which he does quite often). Offense aside, with Gomez patrolling, the Twins possess the best defensive center fielder in the American League. That alone will keep him in the lineup everyday even if he hits near .250 and strikes out in a quarter of his plate appearances.

Brendan Harris (Shortstop)

PA	R	H	2B	3B	HR	RBI	SO	BB	SB	CS	BA	OBP	SLG	OPS	3-Year	Fielding	Reliability
486	53	117	28	2	8	51	93	36	2	1	.269	.329	.397	.726	-0.02	F	High

Harris was the Twins' nomadic infielder, fielding short, second and third providing mediocre defense at all locations. His range at short is subpar and he is a slow double play pivot at second, making third base best suited for his abilities. A terrible month of May (.217/.320/.289) tanked his overall numbers, though his power returned the second half (.434 SLG). By the end of the season, Harris was the right-handed counterpart of the third base platoon with Brian Buscher. If the Twins do not bring in a premier third baseman in 2009, the Harris/Buscher platoon would amount to a passable duo (think Scott Leius/Mike Pagliarulo in 1991).

Luke Hughes (Third Base)

PA	R	H	2B	3B	HR	RBI	SO	BB	SB	CS	BA	OBP	SLG	OPS	3-Year	Fielding	Reliability
421	43	91	16	2	9	43	96	24	3	1	.235	.284	.356	.640	+0.04	D	High

Another Australian product plundered from the Land Down Under, Hughes caught attention in 2008 by slugging over .500 for the first-time and lighting up the Eastern League. But he's a corner infielder/outfielder, and the Twins do not have a slot for Hughes on their roster even if the increase in power is legit.

Jason Kubel (Left Field)

PA	R	H	2B	3B	HR	RBI	SO	BB	SB	CS	BA	OBP	SLG	OPS	3-Year	Fielding	Reliability
476	60	120	24	3	19	68	82	41	2	1	.279	.341	.482	.823	+0.07	D	Very High

After he had a stretch of hitting .322/.391/.610 from June 13 through July 6, when the Twins won 18 of 21 games, Twins fans had a fever and what they needed was more Ku-bel. Kubel finished second on the team with a career-high 20 home runs and drove home 78, which should prove that his knee injury is no longer hindering him at the plate. He is starting to become the polished hitter the team envisioned while he was in the minors and for a brief stretch in 2005. Defensively, he is the fifth-best outfielder on the roster, so he will see little time in the field with the possible exception of playing at a National League park. Slated to be the full-time DH in 2009, Kubel probably will get an occasional reprieve against left-handed pitchers.

Matthew Macri (Shortstop)

PA	R	H	2B	3B	HR	RBI	SO	BB	SB	CS	BA	OBP	SLG	OPS	3-Year	Fielding	Reliability
367	39	80	18	2	11	43	85	20	2	2	.238	.286	.401	.687	+0.06	F	Average

He was a dividend of the Ramon Ortiz trade to Colorado in 2006. Macri's limited performance with the major league club in 2008 may have turned some heads, but he is essentially a high-strikeout, low-walk hitter. Without space at the hot corner for him in 2009, he is to last season what Glenn Williams was to the Twins in 2005.

Joe Mauer (Catcher)

PA	R	H	2B	3B	HR	RBI	SO	BB	SB	CS	BA	OBP	SLG	OPS	3-Year	Fielding	Reliability
550	70	148	30	3	9	62	57	69	2	1	.312	.399	.445	.844	+0.02	B	Very High

No, the home runs didn't make an appearance for Mauer this past season and don't hold your breath that they will in 2009 either. His bread and butter is patience (85 walks in 2008) and driving the ball into vacant areas of the field on a frozen rope. If Mauer gets his pitch, he typically places it wherever he pleases, and if he doesn't, he is satisfied with a walk. That kind of discipline at such a young age is rare. His ability to make contact is uncanny too; he saw 2,545 pitches in 2008 and swung and missed just 85 times (9 percent) making him one of the toughest strikeouts in baseball. His great leap forward was his performance against lefties. He destroyed same-sided pitching (.939 OPS in 205 plate appearances), making the opposing manager's decision to employ a LOOGY on him difficult. Undoubtedly, the batting average will drop in 2009 from his league-leading .328, but his ability to get on base in 40 percent of his plate appearances should remain consistent.

Jose Morales (Catcher)

PA	R	H	2B	3B	HR	RBI	SO	BB	SB	CS	BA	OBP	SLG	OPS	3-Year	Fielding	Reliability
317	29	74	14	1	2	26	50	15	1	1	.251	.291	.325	.616	+0.02	—	Average

Whenever Mike Redmond moves on to whatever his next destination is (coaching?), Morales should be ready to assume the backstop duties. This switch-hitting catcher has improved greatly at the plate in his previous two seasons but has a history of injuries.

Justin Morneau (First Base)

PA	R	H	2B	3B	HR	RBI	SO	BB	SB	CS	BA	OBP	SLG	OPS	3-Year	Fielding	Reliability
623	82	161	35	3	25	94	86	61	0	1	.291	.361	.501	.862	+0.01	D	Very High

The difference between MVP Justin in 2006 and Near League Average First Baseman Justin in 2007 was in the trajectory of the batted ball. In 2006, Morneau laced line drives around the field 23 percent of the time. The following season Morneau's line drive rate dipped to 15 percent and his fly ball tendencies swelled to nearly 40 percent. These were the results of him making efforts to go vertical on virtually every swing. This alteration came at the expense of 30 hits in the same number of plate appearances. After playing in all 163 games for the Twins in 2008, Morneau's batted balls reverted back to his MVP-self. His home run total declined but he bolstered his power numbers by accumulating 74 extra base hits. Now that he is moving into his peak playing years, expect the 2008 production to continue as long as the temptation of the long ball doesn't entice him to elevate.

Jason Pridie (Center Field)

PA	R	H	2B	3B	HR	RBI	SO	BB	SB	CS	BA	OBP	SLG	OPS	3-Year	Fielding	Reliability
545	58	120	18	8	7	45	124	23	16	3	.235	.271	.343	.614	+0.02	C	Very High

Acquired for the second time from the Rays—the first in the 2006 Rule 5 Draft but subsequently returned—Pridie has found himself blocked out by five capable outfielders. His speed and defense will serve some team well as a fourth outfielder, but it doesn't appear that it will happen anytime with the Twins in the near future.

Nick Punto (Shortstop)

PA	R	H	2B	3B	HR	RBI	SO	BB	SB	CS	BA	OBP	SLG	OPS	3-Year	Fielding	Reliability
435	47	97	18	4	1	29	67	39	14	3	.251	.319	.327	.646	-0.03	C	High

After assuming third base in 2006 when the Twins cut Tony Batista, the switch-hitting Punto hit .290/.352/.373 in 459 at-bats. Awarded the starting job in 2007, Punto responded by simply imploding, hitting .210/.291/.271 in 472 at-bats. It was this performance that got Punto booted back to a utility role in 2008. When injuries necessitated Punto's presence in the lineup again, he rebounded to provide numbers closer to his 2006 output. He shows gritty hustle that draws the admiration of managers by making pitchers labor deeper into counts, taking an extra base when needed, and supplying above-average defense at three infield positions. The Twins are rolling the dice that he can continue his 2006 and 2008 output in the next two years at the expense of $8 million.

Randy Ruiz (Designated Hitter)

PA	R	H	2B	3B	HR	RBI	SO	BB	SB	CS	BA	OBP	SLG	OPS	3-Year	Fielding	Reliability
503	56	117	26	2	17	65	131	27	1	1	.253	.304	.428	.732	-0.03	C	Very High

Ruiz in August had 52 plate appearances and hit .320/.370/.420. When Michael Cuddyer returned from the DL in September, however, Ruiz was given just 14 plate appearances the remainder of the season. Rather than sink money in Craig Monroe, the Twins should have considered filling his role with this minor league lifer. On the wrong side of 30 in 2009, Ruiz might provide a franchise with ample and inexpensive power from the right side of the plate. But given the fact that he is a one-dimensional player, he might just fade into obscurity.

Denard Span (Right Field)

PA	R	H	2B	3B	HR	RBI	SO	BB	SB	CS	BA	OBP	SLG	OPS	3-Year	Fielding	Reliability
543	63	128	18	6	4	41	91	46	20	7	.266	.332	.353	.685	+0.03	B	Very High

Span's breakout performance in 2008 made the Twins reassess their outfield situation, reportedly dangling Michael Cuddyer and Delmon Young in front of several teams. A center fielder by trade, his combination with Carlos Gomez gives Twins an alignment in the outfield where fly balls go to die. It is hard to believe he will repeat the offensive numbers he posted in 2008, but he has developed a keen batting eye (thanks to LASIK) and has a quick, short stroke that has increased his line drive rate. Span's patience and speed give the Twins a true leadoff hitter that has not graced the Metrodome since Chuck Knoblauch.

Matt Tolbert (Shortstop)

PA	R	H	2B	3B	HR	RBI	SO	BB	SB	CS	BA	OBP	SLG	OPS	3-Year	Fielding	Reliability
330	36	76	14	3	4	28	50	19	8	3	.252	.298	.358	.656	+0.08	F	Average

Four years Nick Punto's junior, Tolbert is essentially "Punto Nouveau." Like Punto, Tolbert can switch hit, provide above average defense, and he even missed significant time due to a thumb injury. (He did this emulating Punto's trademark headfirst slide into first.) Tolbert has more power than Punto, giving the Twins not just a strong utility player but also a decent pinch hitting option. Some in the organization believe he can be a starting shortstop candidate, although Tolbert still needs plenty of grooming.

Delmon Young (Left Field)

PA	R	H	2B	3B	HR	RBI	SO	BB	SB	CS	BA	OBP	SLG	OPS	3-Year	Fielding	Reliability
592	69	160	30	3	11	66	101	28	10	3	.289	.326	.413	.739	+0.05	—	Very High

Young did not hit his first home run as a Twin until June 7 in 2008, an eternal wait of 253 plate appearances. Built like a prototypical masher—listed at 6-foot-3, 205 pounds—Young didn't have the aerial assault most power hitters feature. The elevation should develop over the next few seasons as he matures. In the field ,Young displays a strong arm in left but often takes short, choppy steps that result in awkward routes to the ball. Keep in mind that Young just turned 23 and has plenty of time to become a finished product at a low cost.

Pitchers

Scott Baker (Starter)

W	L	ERA	TBF	IP	Hit	HR	SO	BB	HBP	3-Year	Reliability
9	9	4.31	694	164	172	21	125	40	5	+0.22	Very High

The de facto ace of the Twins, Baker compiled a strong 2008. This is a great feat for Baker, considering there is nothing about his stuff to recommend him as a front-of-the-rotation starter. What he does is pepper the strike zone and use an effective slider-curve combo to supplement his 90-mph fastball. An increase in strikeout rate (7.36 K/9) and a reduction in the number of hits allowed—thanks to much-improved outfield coverage—led to his sub-4.00 ERA. But logic dictates that his average on balls in play will inflate, resulting in a higher ERA.

Nick Blackburn (Starter)

W	L	ERA	TBF	IP	Hit	HR	SO	BB	HBP	3-Year	Reliability
9	10	4.75	733	170	195	22	75	42	8	+0.16	Very High

Finishing eighth in the Rookie of the Year voting, Nick Blackburn proved that it doesn't make sense to sign a pitcher to an absurd contract who has the same skill set (zone presence, groundball-oriented, etc.) as your own exact same pitcher in the minor league. Blackburn has to improve while on tour (3-8, 5.74 RA on the road), and his almost 200 innings in 2008 cause some concern about the impact of his workload. With a fully healthy staff in 2009, Blackburn should not have to accumulate as many innings and might be more ineffective in turn.

Boof Bonser (Reliever)

W	L	ERA	TBF	IP	Hit	HR	SO	BB	HBP	3-Year	Reliability
7	6	4.26	510	120	121	15	90	40	3	+0.21	Very High

After Bonser's preseason reenactment of The Biggest Loser saw him drop several pounds, Boof Lite proved no better than Boof Supreme. Bonser was vanquished to the bullpen after 12 starts in which he went 2-6 with a 7.08 RA. Because he pitched better than his 5.93 ERA would suggest—as evidenced by his 4.26 FIP—the organization believes Bonser might emerge as a reliever despite several obvious shortcomings: (1) He can't pitch against left-handed batters (a career .896 OPS versus LHB opposed to a .699 OPS versus RHB) and (2) He can't pitch from the stretch (a career .823 OPS with runners on). To avoid being waived, Bonser needs to focus less on the weight issues this offseason and more on the actual pitching issues.

Craig Breslow (Reliever)

W	L	ERA	TBF	IP	Hit	HR	SO	BB	HBP	3-Year	Reliability
3	3	3.75	230	54	49	4	46	22	2	+0.26	Low

Stolen from the Indians at the end of May, Breslow did not allow a run the entire month of June. Given higher leverage situations, Breslow eventually did allow a run, but not many more: just nine in 38.1 innings pitched with the Twins. If the Twins were to limit his usage to same-handed hitters, Breslow would have a phenomenal season, but they probably won't do that, since their right-handed relief options are iffy. He doesn't have lots of velocity, but he does possess a decent slider that the team got him to deploy more frequently.

Jesse Crain (Reliever)

W	L	ERA	TBF	IP	Hit	HR	SO	BB	HBP	3-Year	Reliability
4	3	3.82	266	63	61	6	48	21	2	+0.18	Low

Given that he was recuperating from shoulder surgery, Crain had a decent 2008 season. Yes, August was horrendous (6.35 ERA), but he was reliable in the final month (1.18 ERA). He displayed a fastball in the mid-90s and had the best strikeout rate of his career, but it came at the expense of his control. With Pat Neshek out for 2009 and Matt Guerrier's stock sinking, Crain could see a more substantial role out of the bullpen in the forthcoming season.

Robert Delaney (Reliever)

W	L	ERA	TBF	IP	Hit	HR	SO	BB	HBP	3-Year	Reliability
4	3	4.24	271	64	60	8	52	23	3	-0.08	Very Low

Delaney, an undrafted free agent, tossed 66 innings and posted a 72/11 K/BB ratio with a 1.72 ERA split between two levels of A-ball in 2008. This made him MLB.com's Minor League Relief Pitcher of the Year. Sent to the Arizona Fall League to see if he could be challenged, Delaney was roughed up by the top prospects. That notwithstanding, the Twins will give him a spring audition. He should end up in Double-A.

Brian Duensing (Starter)

W	L	ERA	TBF	IP	Hit	HR	SO	BB	HBP	3-Year	Reliability
6	10	5.43	625	141	170	22	56	48	6	+0.03	Very High

Another control-oriented prospect in the minor leagues, Duensing drew attention in 2007 when he went 15-6 with a 3.07 ERA split between Double-A and Triple-A. His 2008 was not reaffirming of this improvement as he finished a full season at Triple-A with a 5-11 record and a 4.28 ERA. Duensing could find himself deployed as an additional left-handed arm out of the 'pen at some point in the 2009 season.

Eddie Guardado (Reliever)

W	L	ERA	TBF	IP	Hit	HR	SO	BB	HBP	3-Year	Reliability
3	3	4.27	223	52	50	6	36	19	2	—	Very Low

Guardado made 64 appearances in 2008, quite a hefty workload for a 38-year-old who had battled arm injuries while with the Reds. The Twins learned a valuable lesson when they obtained the elder statesman late in the season. Guardado was worn down and opponents made him suffer, lacing line drives around the field. The veteran has enough craftiness to make a serviceable and inexpensive LOOGY—he can still retire his left-handed brethren—but his deployment should be curtailed in order to milk a full season out of him in 2009. Though the peripheral projections seem correct, seeing Guardado throw more than 50 innings would be a push.

Matt Guerrier (Reliever)

W	L	ERA	TBF	IP	Hit	HR	SO	BB	HBP	3-Year	Reliability
4	4	4.12	326	76	76	8	55	28	3	+0.21	Average

Guerrier has had two consecutive late-season collapses. In the first-half of 2008, opponents hit .241/.315/.374; in the last half, they hit .336/.417/.582. There is no clear indication why. The harsh reality is that Guerrier has pitched himself into a lesser role in the bullpen in 2009.

Philip Humber (Starter)

W	L	ERA	TBF	IP	Hit	HR	SO	BB	HBP	3-Year	Reliability
5	9	5.70	570	127	143	23	75	53	7	+0.19	Very High

Out of options, Humber is expected to have a shot at becoming a member of the bullpen, where many in the organization believe his stuff will serve him best.

Bobby Korecky (Reliever)

W	L	ERA	TBF	IP	Hit	HR	SO	BB	HBP	3-Year	Reliability
4	5	4.56	346	79	84	8	48	34	3	+0.36	Average

In 2008, Korecky became just the sixth pitcher to bat in an American League game since the adoption of the designated hitter in 1973—he was the first of the six to get a hit in that at-bat. This did not change the Twins' minds toward Korecky as a pitcher, however. Korecky has displayed good closer stuff in the International League the past three years, but none of the results have enticed the Twins to integrate him into their bullpen. Korecky should get some opportunities in 2009 to demonstrate he can do his stuff in the major leagues.

Francisco Liriano (Starter)

W	L	ERA	TBF	IP	Hit	HR	SO	BB	HBP	3-Year	Reliability
9	8	4.00	665	157	152	17	128	55	4	+0.06	High

The 2006 All-Star Liriano featured a wipeout slider that he relied on nearly 40 percent of the time to harmonize with his 95-mph fastball. It was this pitch that made batters miss 65 percent of the time on pitches outside the zone and provided a groundball rate of 55 percent. It too, some experts claim, was the pitch that was delivered in such a violent motion that it resulted in Tommy John surgery. After sitting out all of 2007, Liriano was back with the club in April 2008. The Twins gave Liriano three starts and 10 innings before he was shipped back to Rochester with an ERA north of 11.00. He regained his control of his fastball and began mixing in a change-up more frequently. Brought back in August, Liriano improved greatly. In his second stint, he went 6-1 while throwing 65 innings and posted 60/19 K/BB ratio. Without his sweeping slider, though, opponents' contact rate on balls out of the zone increased dramatically and he became a pitcher with greater fly ball tendencies (44 percent). For those who haven't officially buried the 2006 version of Liriano, it is time to move on and embrace F-Bomb 2.0.

Joe Nathan (Reliever)

W	L	ERA	TBF	IP	Hit	HR	SO	BB	HBP	3-Year	Reliability
5	3	2.69	279	70	53	5	75	20	2	+0.12	Low

Nathan has been one of the league's most reliable closers since his acquisition in 2004, converting 199 of 219 save opportunities (90.8 percent). Though he has been dominating, a premier closer is often a luxury that a frugal team cannot indulge. Creeping into his mid-30s, one would expect his velocity and his annual strikeout rates to decrease—which it will during the span of his updated contract. This does not mean Nathan will be any less valuable in the coming year, since he can retire batters regularly, but by year four of his extension he might not produce the same results.

Pat Neshek (Reliever)

W	L	ERA	TBF	IP	Hit	HR	SO	BB	HBP	3-Year	Reliability
3	2	3.42	186	45	37	5	49	15	1	+0.25	Low

All of the projections for Neshek's 2009 season are moot: He will be rehabbing from Tommy John surgery all year. After attempts to rehabilitate the partial torn ulnar collateral ligament resulted in a full tear, a lively debate developed regarding the decision to rest and rehab instead of opting for the surgery immediately. Had he undergone the procedure in the spring of 2008, he might have provided a midseason boost to the bullpen in 2009. Lost for the entirety, Neshek will be 29 when he returns to pitch in 2010.

Glen Perkins (Starter)

W	L	ERA	TBF	IP	Hit	HR	SO	BB	HBP	3-Year	Reliability
7	10	5.21	673	153	171	23	84	55	7	+0.06	High

Long a great prospect for the Twins, Perkins has been sidetracked by injuries, most recently sitting out the majority of the 2007 season. The lefty rebounded nicely to provide 151 innings this past season. But what was masked by his winning percentage was that his offense gave him an average of 6.23 runs of support each outing while Perkins was allowing 4.83 runs per game. This will equalize, resulting in fewer victories and a couple more added to the loss column for Perk.

Dennys Reyes (Reliever)

W	L	ERA	TBF	IP	Hit	HR	SO	BB	HBP	3-Year	Reliability
4	2	3.01	231	56	48	3	45	22	2	+0.15	Very Low

You need to get a left-handed batter out and Reyes is as good as anybody. His slider paralyzes his same-sided opponents and has resulted in lots of grounders and strikeouts. Right-handed batters present a challenge for the portly lefty, though; his accuracy wanes under those conditions. In addition, Reyes has had shoulder and control problems that could make a multi-year contract a burden. If his usage is restricted to lefties, he will be effective in 2009.

Kevin Slowey (Starter)

W	L	ERA	TBF	IP	Hit	HR	SO	BB	HBP	3-Year	Reliability
10	8	4.02	668	162	162	22	117	31	6	-0.12	Very High

Slowey is often credited as being a "Thinking Man's Pitcher" (read: lacking overpowering stuff). True, Slowey's fastball does not break 90 mph, but he has three pitches he can place anywhere, anytime, leading to an unbelievable 123/24 K/BB ratio in 2008. Slowey's detriment is that he is a serious flyball pitcher (44 percent) meaning a few fly balls will stray over the fence. However, he was able to greatly decrease that frequency in his second season (1.32 HR/9 in 2008, down from 2.16 in 2007) and stands to have his ERA whittled below 4.00 with the range of his outfielders. With 227 innings at the major league level under his belt, Slowey will show that he can deal in 2009.

Anthony Swarzak (Starter)

W	L	ERA	TBF	IP	Hit	HR	SO	BB	HBP	3-Year	Reliability
5	10	6.43	634	136	170	23	63	63	8	-0.44	Very High

One of the system's top pitching prospects, Swarzak made some scratch their heads with his split in 2008. His record was 3-8 with a 5.67 ERA in Double-A but he went 5-0 and a 1.80 ERA in Triple-A. For the most part, he pitched the same, according to his fielding independent statistics (a 4.42 FIP in Double-A and a 4.40 FIP in Triple-A). The results showed the vast discrepancy in the two defenses. Unless he can demonstrate that he can pitch out of the bullpen in spring training, Swarzak will begin in Triple-A trying to reaffirm the numbers he posted in Rochester last year.

New York Mets

by Eric Simon of Mets Geek (www.metsgeek.com)

2009 Mets Projections

Record: 88-74
Division Rank/Games Behind: 1st by one game
Runs Scored: 830, 2nd in the league
Runs Allowed: 767, 12th in the league
Park Factor: Likely to be a strong pitcher's park.

What Happened Last Year:

Injuries and bad pitching conspired to hand the Mets their second consecutive September meltdown, as well as end the Willie Randolph era at Shea. The Mets lost 916 games to the disabled list from players they expected to be on the active roster on Opening Day. Nine players missed at least 40 team games, including Billy Wagner (49), Moises Alou (139), Ryan Church (56), Orlando Hernandez (162), Luis Castillo (65) and Pedro Martinez (54).

Wagner's protracted absence at the end of the season forced the members of an already mediocre bullpen to assume even greater responsibility. The record will show that they were not up to that challenge, to say the very least. Leads were blown, games were lost, and the Shea Stadium groundskeeping crew was kept busy re-seeding manager Jerry Manuel's well-trodden path between dugout and mound.

Ryan Church was the team's best player well into May, but his second concussion of the year cost him most of the summer and he wasn't quite the same once he finally returned to the lineup. Martinez left his first start of the season with a hamstring injury, spent the next two months recuperating, and the subsequent four months pitching dreadfully. In the first year of a four-year contract that seemed onerous even at its inception, Castillo struggled with assorted leg ailments en route to his worst season as a pro. The 41-year-old Alou made it onto the field for just 92 innings, which was 92 more than the of-indeterminate-origin Hernandez, who spent most of the season wearing a doctor-prescribed physical therapy boot.

Injuries aside, the Mets' pitching staff couldn't get out of its own way long enough to establish any kind of consistency over a grueling 162-game season. Mets starting pitchers were in the bottom 10 in Fielding Independent Pitching for the first two months of the season, but they turned things around in June and were one of the best staffs in baseball the rest of the way.

The bullpen was equally inconsistent, but took things a step further by swinging wildly performance-wise from month to month. The relievers were middle of the pack in April, then alternated solid and wretched months before putting together back-to-back stinkers in August and September. Those last two months of horrendous relief work, as much as anything, were responsible for the Mets falling short of the NL East title for the second straight year.

Players Lost from Last Year's Team:

Training room regulars Alou and Hernandez, Luis Ayala, Damion Easley and, at press time, Oliver Perez and Martinez, were all "lost" to free agency. Aaron Heilman, Joe Smith and cult hero Endy Chavez were dealt away in the J.J. Putz trade. Scott Schoeneweis was similarly traded to the Diamondbacks.

Players Acquired:

Putz was brought in to set up new closer Francisco Rodriguez. Reliever Sean Green and outfielder Jeremy Reed came aboard in the Putz deal, and reliever Connor Robertson was acquired from Arizona in exchange for Schoeneweis.

Management Is:

Off the field, general manager Omar Minaya has a penchant for the big move, signing Martinez, Wagner and Carlos Beltran in his first offseason and trading for Carlos Delgado in his second. He orchestrated a block-buster deal for Johan Santana in his third winter, and has already signed Rodriguez and traded for Putz this winter. Big New York money helps with these things, so some credit goes to owner Fred Wilpon for opening his check-book and generally keeping his nose out of the baseball operations department. Minaya also has shown a knack for turning lead into gold, as he did in acquiring starters John Maine and Perez essentially as throw-ins in deals for Jorge Julio and Roberto Hernandez, respectively.

It hasn't always come up roses for Minaya, however. Recent free agent signings of Alou and Castillo have not worked out, as Alou appeared in just 102 games over two seasons while Castillo missed almost half of 2008 and is under contract for another three seasons. The three-year deal given to Schoeneweis after the 2006 season wasn't one of his brightest moments, either. He (somewhat) famously left catching prospect Jesus Flores unprotected in 2006, only to watch the Nationals pluck him from the Mets in the Rule 5 draft.

153

Minaya also seemingly caved to player and media pressure by hastily shipping Lastings Milledge out of town last November. Perhaps his biggest mistakes as GM of the Mets—especially so considering the team's bullpen failures late in 2007 and 2008—were trading four young relievers over a five-day span in November 2006 (Heath Bell and Royce Ring to the Padres, Matt Lindstrom and Henry Owens to the Marlins) and getting back nothing of substance.

All told, though Minaya occasionally loses sight of the forest for the trees, he usually makes keen use of his financial resources and, when a deal he wants isn't quite to his liking, he has the patience to wait for circumstances to turn in his favor.

On the field, manager Manuel is fairly run-of-the-mill and unimaginative by most standards. He manages by the book almost exclusively. He is an entertaining postgame interview, a welcome departure from the incessant "battling" of Art Howe and the unapologetic sugarcoating by Willie Randolph. Given a set lineup and well-defined bullpen, Manuel will put the pieces where they belong and generally keep from embarrassing himself.

Given some question marks, a possible platoon situation or a patchwork bullpen, Manuel can manage his team right out of ballgames. He doesn't seem especially statistically inclined, and often ignores his relievers' glaring platoon splits. He's not afraid to give young guys a shot (Daniel Murphy, Nick Evans) or demote a struggling veteran (Castillo), but he also has a tendency to stick with players far beyond the point of rationality (Marlon Anderson).

The Minor League System Is:

Not in great shape. A farm system that improved considerably following some inspired international free agent signings in 2007 was subsequently depleted by last offseason's trade for Johan Santana, partially restocked by a decent 2008 draft, and then taken down a half-notch by December's trade for Putz. The Mets have some potential impact talent in their low minors, with 17-year-old shortstop Wilmer Flores (the highlight of that 2007 international class) and 2008 draftee Brad Holt, a right-handed pitcher, turning heads (as well as sleeper third baseman Jefry Marte). Outside of Fernando Martinez and Jon Niese (and catcher Josh Thole, a personal favorite), the upper levels are practically bereft of young talent, and a big winter dipping into the free agent market could leave the Mets twiddling their thumbs in the early rounds of the 2009 draft.

Due For a Change:

Believe it or not, David Wright could get a whole lot better. He struggled with runners in scoring position in 2008, so a reversal of that trend would make him even more dangerous. He's still a couple of years short of his prime, and is said to be working on his explosiveness this offseason, so don't be surprised if he hits 40 home runs in 2009.

Reasons to be Optimistic:

The team's biggest weakness over the past two seasons has been (seemingly) addressed and, while there were always areas of potential improvement, a decent bullpen in 2007 and 2008 would have all but assured NL East titles in both. The core of Wright, Beltran, Jose Reyes and Santana is still there, still young, and still amazingly good. Each is among the very best in baseball at his respective position, and at least Wright and Reyes stand a good chance of actually getting better in 2009. Mike Pelfrey had a breakthrough season in 2008 and is also a good candidate to improve even more this year.

Reasons to be Pessimistic:

As of press time, the Mets are still two starters short of a full rotation, and even the best bullpens will eventually wear down from overuse. Church may never recover from his concussion problems and, absent an everyday left fielder, a Fernando Tatis/Dan Murphy platoon might provide insufficient offense at a position that demands serious clout. Delgado could book a return trip to Stinkville, the last exit on the Precipitous Career Regression Turnpike, leaving the Mets with few desirable options at first base.

Still Left to Do:

Find a left fielder, possibly a right fielder, and a starting pitcher or two. The bench could also use some TLC.

Most Likely Team Outcome:

The Phillies are the team to beat, but if the Mets stay healthy and their bullpen is as strong as it appears to be, no one should be surprised if they finally wind up on top of the NL East.

Player Projections

Batters

Moises Alou (Left Field)

PA	R	H	2B	3B	HR	RBI	SO	BB	SB	CS	BA	OBP	SLG	OPS	3-Year	Fielding	Reliability
248	30	55	12	0	9	32	29	19	6	17	.299	.366	.511	.877	—	C	Average

Alou played in just 15 games in 2008 (after playing in 87 in 2007), hitting .347 with no power in such limited action. The Mets took a chance by signing him in the first place, and the concerns about his health turned out to be reasonable. He turned 42 in July and it's not clear if he can hold his body together to be even remotely useful to a big league team. When healthy, the man can still hit and hit well. He's painful to watch playing the field, and he can't run much anymore, but he knows how to swing a bat.

Marlon Anderson (Left Field)

PA	R	H	2B	3B	HR	RBI	SO	BB	SB	CS	BA	OBP	SLG	OPS	3-Year	Fielding	Reliability
237	27	55	11	1	5	26	40	19	3	1	.259	.320	.391	.711	-0.03	B	Low

Anderson is a weird guy: He could be a perfectly useful pinch-hitter and occasional starter, as he was for the Mets in the second half of 2007, or he could be beyond useless and an offensive sinkhole who sucks up at-bats and spits back outs, as he was for the Mets throughout 2008. The Mets have him signed for 2009, and if I had any money to bet I'd put it all on "useless sinkhole."

Carlos Beltran (Center Field)

PA	R	H	2B	3B	HR	RBI	SO	BB	SB	CS	BA	OBP	SLG	OPS	3-Year	Fielding	Reliability
612	89	146	33	3	29	91	98	76	19	2	.277	.368	.516	.884	-0.03	B	Very High

He isn't flashy and he rarely gets his name in the papers, but year after year Beltran is one of the most valuable players in baseball. He doesn't do anything poorly, and does almost everything well or extraordinarily so. He hits for decent power, he draws walks, he steals bases frequently and efficiently, and he does it all at a position where offense is typically an afterthought—center field—that he just-so-happens to play about as well as anyone alive. As much as you can say about anyone making $17 million a year, Carlos Beltran is a bargain.

Luis Castillo (Second Base)

PA	R	H	2B	3B	HR	RBI	SO	BB	SB	CS	BA	OBP	SLG	OPS	3-Year	Fielding	Reliability
450	52	108	14	2	2	32	46	47	16	4	.276	.355	.338	.693	-0.04	D	Very High

Castillo historically has been a dependable on-base guy with good stolen base numbers and solid-if-unspectacular defense at second base. He never has hit for much power and never will, but his patient-to-the-point-of-passivity approach at the plate has allowed him to remain a useful middle infielder. Knee and mild weight problems have limited his defensive range in recent years, though he has vowed to get in better shape for 2009. All of which begs the question: Why not just **be** in shape instead of having to **get** in shape?

Ramon Castro (Catcher)

PA	R	H	2B	3B	HR	RBI	SO	BB	SB	CS	BA	OBP	SLG	OPS	3-Year	Fielding	Reliability
240	30	57	12	0	11	37	54	21	0	0	.266	.334	.475	.809	-0.02	C	Very Low

It's a little surprising that Castro hasn't been given an opportunity to be a starting catcher somewhere by now. He has above-average plate discipline for the position and has more power than most backstops in the league. Back injuries and general lethargy have cost him significant playing time over the past few seasons, and he probably has a tough time shaking that "career backup" label he's been saddled with after having been, well, a backup for his entire career. He could be a top-10 catcher given health and regular playing time, though neither of those assumptions can reasonably be considered a safe bet.

Ryan Church (Right Field)

PA	R	H	2B	3B	HR	RBI	SO	BB	SB	CS	BA	OBP	SLG	OPS	3-Year	Fielding	Reliability
419	51	98	23	1	14	55	92	42	2	2	.266	.347	.448	.795	-0.02	C	High

Church was a throw-in in the deal that landed the Mets Brian Schneider before the 2008 season but also cost them Lastings Milledge. Church's defense was better than advertised, and he was arguably their best offensive player in the early going before his second concussion of the season cost him most of the summer. He contributed very little after his late-August return, hitting just .219/.305/.307 over the last five weeks of the season.

Carlos Delgado (First Base)

PA	R	H	2B	3B	HR	RBI	SO	BB	SB	CS	BA	OBP	SLG	OPS	3-Year	Fielding	Reliability
598	77	140	29	1	30	93	115	63	1	1	.268	.353	.500	.853	—	C	Very High

Delgado looked washed-up during the latter part of May, OPS-ing .650 amid swirling rumors that the Mets might cut him outright. At that point, perhaps sensing that his career was on the brink, something clicked, though it's still not clear what. Maybe he was finally healthy; or he fixed a problem with his swing; or he made a pact with our Dark Lord. Whatever the case, Delgado was reborn, mashing to the tune of .291/.371/.581 over his final 116 games and garnering quite a bit of MVP support. There's still a sense among some folks that Delgado could return to being useless at a moment's notice, though that group is considerably smaller than it once was.

Damion Easley (Second Base)

PA	R	H	2B	3B	HR	RBI	SO	BB	SB	CS	BA	OBP	SLG	OPS	3-Year	Fielding	Reliability
344	38	81	13	1	8	38	47	25	1	1	.263	.327	.389	.716	—	F	Average

Easley is a decent bat off the bench, good for the occasional walkoff home run, and has historically walked enough and hit for enough power to remain useful. He is passable defensively almost anywhere but behind the plate, though he'll be 39 this year and looked in 2008 like he didn't have a whole lot left in the tank.

Nick Evans (First Base)

PA	R	H	2B	3B	HR	RBI	SO	BB	SB	CS	BA	OBP	SLG	OPS	3-Year	Fielding	Reliability
514	56	113	26	3	15	62	106	34	2	1	.240	.294	.403	.697	+0.09	C	Very High

Evans and Dan Murphy were both recalled from the minors in 2008, though Evans, a year younger, is the less impressive hitter of the two. Evans was quite good against lefties—.319/.380/.514—but couldn't hit a lick in limited action against righties, which could pose problems for his long-term viability as a big leaguer. If the Mets can't find him at-bats as a platoon outfielder in 2009, Evans would be best served getting regular playing time at Triple-A.

Fernando Martinez (Center Field)

PA	R	H	2B	3B	HR	RBI	SO	BB	SB	CS	BA	OBP	SLG	OPS	3-Year	Fielding	Reliability
449	47	103	19	3	8	45	88	27	4	2	.249	.301	.367	.668	+0.13	D	Average

Martinez, the Mets' top prospect for a few years now, has missed some time the past two seasons due to nagging injuries. He just turned 20, and 2009 will be a very important year in his development. He had a terrific stint in the Arizona Fall League, and will begin the season with Triple-A Buffalo. He has skated by to this point on his age and by holding his own at each level, while failing to dominate at any single stop. His power hasn't developed as many predicted it would, but he also has been among the youngest hitters in each league he has played. A good start this season could land him at Citi/Taxpayer Field by mid-summer.

Daniel Murphy (Second Base)

PA	R	H	2B	3B	HR	RBI	SO	BB	SB	CS	BA	OBP	SLG	OPS	3-Year	Fielding	Reliability
568	62	129	28	3	12	60	88	44	7	4	.251	.313	.388	.701	+0.05	C	High

A rash of injuries led to Murphy's call-up in early August and he put on a hitting clinic for the next month. His bat cooled off a bit in September, but he showed an advanced approach at the plate for a kid with just four plate appearances above Double-A. The Mets sent him to Arizona this fall to get some playing time at second base, where his bat would be even more valuable. The Mets insist that they still view Murphy as a corner outfielder, but he was primarily a third baseman in the minors so it's not out of the question that he could be a viable option at second. Look for him to get at least the occasional rep there in 2009.

Angel Pagan (Left Field)

PA	R	H	2B	3B	HR	RBI	SO	BB	SB	CS	BA	OBP	SLG	OPS	3-Year	Fielding	Reliability
241	28	54	11	2	5	23	43	19	6	1	.249	.310	.387	.697	+0.00	B	Low

With Moises Alou on the disabled list early (and late, as it turned out), Pagan saw an opportunity for significant playing time evaporate when he injured his shoulder in early May. Pagan has enough talent and tools to be a useful bench player, but he's a bit of a reach as an everyday outfielder. His oxymoronic appellative is sure to delight area headline writers for as long as Pagan stays around.

Jeremy Reed (Center Field)

PA	R	H	2B	3B	HR	RBI	SO	BB	SB	CS	BA	OBP	SLG	OPS	3-Year	Fielding	Reliability
474	56	118	25	3	10	53	63	34	7	4	.275	.330	.417	.747	+0.01	C	High

For years a major disappointment, Reed may have blown his last chance at ever being a regular with his feeble 2008. While he's a perfectly adequate defensive center fielder, he's not so good that he can skip the whole hitting thing, and he's just never been able to recover the level swing he had five years ago. Now 27, Reed might've been worth one final flier from a rebuilding team with time to spare, but instead he's off to New York, where he should settle in as a career fourth outfielder who always makes people wonder what could've been.

Argenis Reyes (Second Base)

PA	R	H	2B	3B	HR	RBI	SO	BB	SB	CS	BA	OBP	SLG	OPS	3-Year	Fielding	Reliability
479	46	103	11	3	5	36	75	25	11	4	.235	.280	.309	.589	+0.07	C	High

Reyes has a decent glove at second but proved barely capable of hitting his own weight in 2008. He has little power and no plate discipline to speak of, and isn't even qualified to be a utility infielder since he has only negligible experience at shortstop. The Mets are probably in serious trouble if Reyes gets another 120 plate appearances in 2009.

Jose Reyes (Shortstop)

PA	R	H	2B	3B	HR	RBI	SO	BB	SB	CS	BA	OBP	SLG	OPS	3-Year	Fielding	Reliability
666	103	173	31	12	14	67	76	59	52	13	.291	.354	.454	.808	+0.02	C	Very High

Very few players are capable of .300/20/80 with 60-plus stolen bases, and this one plays shortstop. Though Reyes seems destined for greatness, to this point he and the Mets have had to settle for very-goodness. At times, Reyes looks like an MVP candidate (who doesn't?), but at other times he seems to lose some focus and get jumpy at the plate. He has a cannon arm and looks slick with the glove, but defensive metrics haven't been impressed with him of late. All of that said, it's easy to forget that he'll be just 26 in 2009 and is still a couple of years shy of his prime.

Brian Schneider (Catcher)

PA	R	H	2B	3B	HR	RBI	SO	BB	SB	CS	BA	OBP	SLG	OPS	3-Year	Fielding	Reliability
424	44	94	17	1	7	41	63	45	1	0	.254	.336	.362	.698	-0.04	B	High

Schneider isn't a great catcher. He's probably not even a good catcher, but the reality is that there simply aren't a whole lot of good catchers, period, let alone ones who might be readily available. Schneider has above-average plate discipline and will hit a modest number of home runs—typically in bunches—but his batting average is uninspiring and his counting stats are nothing to write home about. Oh, he's also on the wrong side of 30. Nevertheless, Schneider is a "proven veteran" and "calls a good game" and "at one time wasn't terrible," so the Mets' best hope is that Ramon Castro stays healthy enough to take some at-bats away from him.

Fernando Tatis (Left Field)

PA	R	H	2B	3B	HR	RBI	SO	BB	SB	CS	BA	OBP	SLG	OPS	3-Year	Fielding	Reliability
464	58	110	22	2	17	63	87	45	3	2	.268	.343	.455	.798	-0.04	B	Very High

Tatis was one of the great comeback stories of 2008. His only big league action since 2003 had come in 64 plate appearances with the Orioles in 2006. The Mets signed him to a minor league deal, and he proceeded to mash the ball with Triple-A New Orleans before a mid-May promotion brought him up to the big club for good. When injuries derailed the seasons of Moises Alou and Ryan Church, Tatis stepped in to provide well-above-average offense when nobody expected him to. For a guy who looked washed up at 28, Tatis has resurrected his career and figures to get plenty of playing time with the Mets in 2009, either in a corner outfield platoon or as a super-sub.

David Wright (Third Base)

PA	R	H	2B	3B	HR	RBI	SO	BB	SB	CS	BA	OBP	SLG	OPS	3-Year	Fielding	Reliability
641	100	176	37	2	32	104	106	78	19	3	.319	.404	.567	.971	+0.07	A	Very High

Once considered one of the best young players in the game, Wright has shed the youthful qualifier and can now be counted among the game's elite regardless of age. He hits for average, he hits for power, he has terrific plate discipline, he steals some bases, he plays above-average defense at a tough position. Wright's biggest weakness may be that he works **too** hard, often putting undue pressure on himself to perform in the biggest situations. Like Reyes, Wright will turn 26 this season, and will similarly be a big part of any pennant run the Mets make. If he can loosen up a little bit, there's no reason he can't win an MVP or two before his days are done.

Pitchers

Pedro Feliciano (Reliever)

W	L	ERA	TBF	IP	Hit	HR	SO	BB	HBP	3-Year	Reliability
4	3	3.49	266	63	56	5	53	28	3	+0.19	Low

Omar Minaya rescued Feliciano from Japanese ball and he rewarded the Mets by pitching impressively against most comers in 2006 and 2007. Last year, however, Feliciano devolved back into a LOOGY and rarely pitched as much as a full inning. He was bitten by the longball more than in earlier seasons; a little more luck and consistent strategic use against only southpaws could allow him to remain a useful reliever for years to come.

Nelson Figueroa (Starter)

W	L	ERA	TBF	IP	Hit	HR	SO	BB	HBP	3-Year	Reliability
5	9	5.29	557	125	137	21	78	54	6	+0.17	High

Figueroa hadn't made a big league appearance since 2004 before the Mets gave him a few spot starts in 2008. Those went better than expected, but a few more spot starts revealed why Figueroa pitched all over the globe—everywhere but MLB—over the preceding four seasons. A switch to the bullpen ceded decent results, so it's conceivable that Figgy could find a spot in that role with the Mets or some other team in 2009.

Aaron Heilman (Reliever)

W	L	ERA	TBF	IP	Hit	HR	SO	BB	HBP	3-Year	Reliability
5	4	3.83	334	78	72	6	64	32	4	+0.20	Average

Heilman was dreadful in 2008, but he was mostly very good in the two years prior and his peripherals remained mostly solid despite his ERA going into the tank. His HR/FB rate spiked, which was his biggest problem above all else. He'll take the ball almost every day and, even if he doesn't dominate lefties the way he once did, he is still a perfectly viable seventh- or eighth-inning guy.

Brandon Knight (Reliever)

W	L	ERA	TBF	IP	Hit	HR	SO	BB	HBP	3-Year	Reliability
4	4	4.00	298	70	62	9	67	30	3	+0.22	Very Low

Knight probably isn't good enough to start anywhere, but he could be serviceable as a soft middle-innings or mop-up guy.

John Maine (Starter)

W	L	ERA	TBF	IP	Hit	HR	SO	BB	HBP	3-Year	Reliability
8	9	4.22	647	151	142	20	122	64	5	+0.21	Very High

The Mets were counting on Maine to help anchor their rotation in 2008, but a bone spur led to a drop in control and ultimately an early end to the season. Talk of him returning to close games in September never materialized, so the Mets are left to cross their fingers and hope that Maine returns to good health (and good form) in time for spring training. Maine looked like a burgeoning star when the curtains went down on 2007, as a lively fastball that snuck into the mid-90s fooled hitters league-wide. There's plenty of talent—and surprisingly few innings—in that young arm, so if Maine can get past the problems with his pitching shoulder he could still be one of the better No. 3 starters in the National League.

Pedro Martinez (Starter)

W	L	ERA	TBF	IP	Hit	HR	SO	BB	HBP	3-Year	Reliability
6	8	4.67	536	124	128	18	94	43	6	—	High

Martinez hurt his hamstring in the second game of the season and missed the next two months on the shelf. He returned to action at the beginning of June but was never able to establish any kind of consistency. He tossed the occasional gem, but more often his outings were mediocre or worse. His strikeout, walk and home run rates were all career lows since he became a full-time starter in 1994. At times he looked like a serviceable mid-rotation starter. At others he looked entirely washed-up and not even worthy of a make-good contract at the league minimum.

Carlos Muniz (Reliever)

W	L	ERA	TBF	IP	Hit	HR	SO	BB	HBP	3-Year	Reliability
3	4	4.95	267	61	61	10	42	27	3	+0.24	Low

The 27-year-old Muniz spent most of 2008 on the shuttle between New York and their Triple-A affiliate, New Orleans. A late-round draft pick in 2003, Muniz surprised many by posting good numbers at almost every stop on his way up the minors. Still, he's not a young man anymore, and much of his minor league success came from a low home run rate despite flyball tendencies. Muniz doesn't figure prominently in the Mets' plans in 2009, so another season on the shuttle seems to be in order.

Jonathon Niese (Starter)

W	L	ERA	TBF	IP	Hit	HR	SO	BB	HBP	3-Year	Reliability
6	11	5.38	695	153	173	21	90	76	8	-0.58	Very High

Niese has good stuff all around. He keeps the ball on the ground and inside the park, strikes out enough and doesn't walk too many. He's not especially dominant in any one area, but as a lefty with a hammer curve and the aforementioned peripheral skills, and at just 21 years old, Niese has plenty of upside. He made three September starts with the Mets last year, getting roughed up in two and tossing eight shutout innings in the third. The Mets say they're comfortable handing him the fifth starter spot in 2009, but even if they find a veteran to fill that role, Niese will give them plenty of depth should one of the regulars go absent for any period of time.

Bobby Parnell (Starter)

W	L	ERA	TBF	IP	Hit	HR	SO	BB	HBP	3-Year	Reliability
5	10	6.38	642	136	165	23	71	80	10	-0.37	Very High

One of the few major-league-ready pitchers in the Mets' system, Parnell is something of a divisive prospect. He's got some quality stuff—a power sinker and a good slider—but he's never put together a dominant season in the minor leagues. His strikeout and walk numbers aren't fantastic, and he'll likely need to better his groundball rate (a ground ball rate of 46 percent in 2008) to succeed in the majors. Even if he doesn't, he has a chance to contribute in the bullpen at some point in 2009 and down the line.

Mike Pelfrey (Starter)

W	L	ERA	TBF	IP	Hit	HR	SO	BB	HBP	3-Year	Reliability
9	10	4.48	743	169	185	15	96	65	12	-0.26	Very High

Through his first 26 big league starts, Pelfrey had a 5.48 ERA and 1.08 strikeouts per walk and looked like a Quad-A pitcher who could dominate the minor leagues but couldn't hack it in the majors. Over his next 23 starts he posted a 3.20 ERA and more than doubled his strikeout-to-walk ratio, and now he looks like a viable No. 2 starter. The remarkable turnaround was part confidence and part stuff, as Pelfrey started throwing his hard sinker more often, got a bunch of ground balls, and finally started to experience some success. He still walks a few too many batters, and a few more strikeouts wouldn't hurt, but he's finally on the right track and he figures to be an important part of the Mets' rotation for the foreseeable future.

Oliver Perez (Starter)

W	L	ERA	TBF	IP	Hit	HR	SO	BB	HBP	3-Year	Reliability
9	10	4.75	763	173	165	26	151	88	9	+0.23	Very High

If Perez could ever get a handle on his control problems, he would be one of the most dominant pitchers in the game. He does manage to get it in check a few times a year, and you just watch as opposing hitters flail away uselessly at his rising mid-90s fastball and devastating slider. Far more often, though, Perez is as inconsistent as they come, alternating three-strikeout innings with three-walk ones. He loses focus and confidence easily, and occasionally will bring nothing with him to the mound and wind up hitting the showers after just an inning or two. He's still young enough to figure things out. Randy Johnson didn't get his walks under control until he was 29, and Perez is about to play his age 27 season. None of this is to say that Perez will follow Johnson's career arc, just that for some talented pitchers, the light flicks on later.

Duaner Sanchez (Reliever)

W	L	ERA	TBF	IP	Hit	HR	SO	BB	HBP	3-Year	Reliability
4	2	3.73	249	58	54	5	43	23	3	+0.28	Very Low

Sanchez returned to action after missing all of 2007 (and part of 2006) following shoulder surgery to repair damage caused in a taxicab accident just before the 2006 July trade deadline. It was clear early on that Sanchez was a different pitcher, though, having lost nearly 4 mph on his fastball and allowing home runs nearly twice as often as before surgery. Sanchez still induced plenty of ground balls, and given another year of post-surgery good health and a nominal improvement in velocity, he could still contribute meaningfully to the Mets' bullpen in 2009.

Johan Santana (Starter)

W	L	ERA	TBF	IP	Hit	HR	SO	BB	HBP	3-Year	Reliability
13	10	3.47	836	206	180	26	189	55	5	+0.30	Very High

Santana's only problem in 2008 was his inability to throw complete games every time out. Given a little more run and bullpen support, 20 wins and a Cy Young award wouldn't have been out of the question. Wins and losses are largely the domain of capricious baseball events and beyond the control of pitchers, but on matters within his grasp Santana was his usual dominant self. He led the National League in innings pitched, was second in strikeouts and seventh in strikeouts per walk, and almost pitched the Mets into the playoffs with a three-hit shutout on the season's penultimate day. He didn't miss quite as many bats as in years past and his fastball velocity dropped about a half-tick from 2007, but he was exactly what the Mets thought they were getting when they emptied their farm system to acquire him the prior offseason.

Scott Schoeneweis (Reliever)

W	L	ERA	TBF	IP	Hit	HR	SO	BB	HBP	3-Year	Reliability
3	4	4.69	267	60	65	7	36	27	3	—	Low

Schoeneweis gets plenty of ground balls and is a perfectly useful LOOGY when limited to that role. He ran into trouble because Mets manager Jerry Manuel seemed to think Schoeneweis was also competent at retiring righties. He was not (.520 OPS vs LHB, .955 OPS vs RHB). His groundball-edness will serve him well in Arizona, so long as Bob Melvin learns from Manuel's mistakes and doesn't extend Schoeneweis beyond his skill set.

Joseph Smith (Reliever)

W	L	ERA	TBF	IP	Hit	HR	SO	BB	HBP	3-Year	Reliability
4	3	3.68	268	62	59	4	50	29	4	-0.09	Very Low

Smith is a submarine-style righty who does exactly the things you'd expect from a submarine-style righty: He gets tons of ground balls and dominates right-handed batters but can't get lefties out to save his life. Despite his stark platoon splits, a groundball machine who owns righties can make a pretty nice career for himself (see: Bradford, Chad).

Brian Stokes (Starter)

W	L	ERA	TBF	IP	Hit	HR	SO	BB	HBP	3-Year	Reliability
6	9	5.17	613	137	154	19	79	59	6	+0.49	Very High

After a rough outing in his only start as a Met, Stokes was moved to the bullpen and had pretty good success down the stretch. His fastball touched 95 mph and his peripherals were solid across the board. His platoon splits were very dramatic (.618 OPS vs RHB, .899 OPS vs LHB), which will have to change if he wants to have any kind of career as a big league pitcher since ROOGYs aren't exactly in high demand these days (or any days, for that matter).

Tobi Stoner (Starter)

W	L	ERA	TBF	IP	Hit	HR	SO	BB	HBP	3-Year	Reliability
5	10	6.19	601	131	158	24	63	60	7	-0.37	High

Despite a phenomenal name and some good minor league numbers, there's an excellent chance Tobi Stoner never becomes more than organizational filler.

Claudio Vargas (Starter)

W	L	ERA	TBF	IP	Hit	HR	SO	BB	HBP	3-Year	Reliability
5	7	4.71	473	109	114	16	74	39	4	+0.23	Very High

Vargas saw only limited time in the majors in 2008. Signed by the Mets in April after a surprising release from the Brewers, Vargas failed to make much of an impression on management during a handful of emergency starts and long relief appearances in May and June. Vargas is capable of posting solid, if unspectacular, strikeout and walk ratios, but troubles with the home run should continue to limit his effectiveness as a major-league starter.

Billy Wagner (Reliever)

W	L	ERA	TBF	IP	Hit	HR	SO	BB	HBP	3-Year	Reliability
4	3	3.04	244	60	49	6	63	19	2	—	Low

Wagner was the Mets' best reliever in the early going, striking out many and walking few. Unfortunately, he blew out his elbow and missed the second half of the season, including the resplendent bullpen implosion in August and September that cost the Mets a playoff spot. Elbow surgery is likely to keep Wagner out for the entire 2009 season, with a remote chance that he'll recover in time to pitch in September. The Mets have him under contract, but he likely has pitched his last game for them.

New York Yankees

by Larry Mahnken of The Hardball Times

2009 Yankees Projections

Record: 100-62
Division Rank/Games Behind: 1st by two games
Runs Scored: 884, 1st in the league
Runs Allowed: 702, 2nd in the league
Park Factor: Likely to be a neutral park

What Happened Last Year:

Much as in recent seasons, the Yankees started out slowly. Unlike recent seasons, they didn't turn it around.

Early on they'd win one, lose one; win three, lose three; win two, lose three. For much of the first two months they were in last place, albeit only a game or two out of third. Every time they seemed on the cusp of getting back into the race, they started losing games, usually to inferior teams. An eight-game winning streak coming out of the All-Star break got them into a tie with Boston for the wild card, but they immediately went 6-13, killing any realistic chance of a postseason berth.

Their last real surge came with the final home stand at Yankee Stadium, where they won eight of their last nine games, pushing back elimination until the final week of the season (and coming tantalizingly close to a scenario in which they could have forced a one-game playoff for the wild card with a sweep of Boston to end the regular season).

The immediate reason the Yankees missed the playoffs was the emergence of the Rays as a competitive team. Had the Rays merely improved to become an 88-win team, the Yankees would have won the wild card again.

The second reason they missed out was injuries. Jorge Posada's shoulder rendered him unable to catch, forcing them to play one of the worst hitters in the league behind the plate for lack of a better option. Chien-Ming Wang went down for the season on a freak base running injury at Houston in June, Phil Hughes pitched ineffectively with a cracked rib early in the season, and Joba Chamberlain was knocked from the rotation with shoulder tendinitis in August just as he was establishing himself as an ace. At one point, their rotation consisted of Mike Mussina, Carl Pavano, Sidney Ponson, Darrell

Rasner, and a clearly worn-down Andy Pettitte. It was no surprise the Yankees fell apart.

As the season wound down, the team started playing for milestones that in previous years would have been secondary. Derek Jeter passed Lou Gehrig to set the all-time Yankee Stadium hits record, Mussina finally won 20 games, and the Yanks closed out the Stadium with a win. It wasn't how they had planned on finishing their stay in the House that Ruth Built, but all good things come to an end someday. The team heads into 2009 hoping to start a new postseason streak, and christen the new ballpark with a World Championship of its own.

Players Lost from Last Year's Team:

Bobby Abreu, Wilson Betemit, Jason Giambi, Mussina, Pettitte, Carl Pavano, Darrell Rasner, Ivan Rodriguez

Players Acquired:

A.J. Burnett, CC Sabathia, Nick Swisher, Mark Teixeira

Management Is:

Hank Steinbrenner has all the bluster of his father during his '70s glory days, but his brother Hal—the one you never read about in the papers—has just as much power and is much more level-headed. Hal Steinbrenner thinks more like Brian Cashman, who is loathe to part with young talent and determined to stick with his long-term plans, even when short-term setbacks seem to turn all of New York against him.

The manager, Joe Girardi, is entering his second season in the Bronx. A control freak, Girardi banned sweets from the clubhouse, much to the chagrin of his veteran players, and established a strict conditioning regimen in spring training that didn't appear to have much positive effect on the team. The Yankees' younger players almost all had significantly worse seasons under Girardi than predecessor Joe Torre, and his almost daily shakeup of the lineup early in the season disrupted the team's sense of stability as it tried to put together a strong run. As Torre made the playoffs in Los Angeles (although in a very weak division and with a worse record than New York), Girardi became the first Yankees manager since the '94 strike to not lead his team to the playoffs.

The Minor League System Is:

Still fairly weak in major league-ready talent. There are promising players in the low minors, led by Austin Jackson, but he won't be ready until 2010, at least. If the Yankees had been better the last two seasons, they probably wouldn't have called up Chamberlain, Hughes or Ian Kennedy yet, so it's not like they've failed to produce young talent. It's just not likely you'll see any new faces make an impact this season.

Due For a Change:

There are several older players in the Yankees' lineup, any or all of whom could collapse completely. Johnny Damon had one of his best offensive seasons, so a regression is likely there, and Xavier Nady is likely to drop back to his old level after a fantastic first two-thirds of 2008. Robinson Cano and Swisher had such brutal seasons that they're probably locks to improve, but who knows if they'll go back to what they were in 2007? How much they improve will go a long way toward deciding the team's fate. Jeter had his worst offensive season despite hitting .300, mostly because of an injury early on. If healthy, he'll rebound somewhat.

Reasons to be Optimistic:

The Yankees may have the best rotation in baseball, and if Hughes were to break out and fulfill all the promise of 2007, the team could have four legitimate aces. With Hughes, Alfredo Aceves and Kennedy lined up as the fifth through seventh starters, the Yankees would need three pitchers to go down at once before they got into Ponson territory again. The signing of Teixeira gives the team a second big bat to complement Rodriguez and mitigates the loss of Abreu and Giambi on offense—a healthy season by Jorge Posada and strong rebound seasons by Cano, Jeter and Swisher could give them one of the best offenses in baseball to support that strong rotation.

Reasons to be Pessimistic:

Their offensive prowess depends a lot on the return of their aging catcher from surgery on his throwing shoulder, significant rebounds by multiple players and no significant declines by their many older players. The bullpen is lacking established arms before the ninth inning, and many of the guys who were so good in '08 can't yet be relied on to repeat that in '09. As deep and talented as the rotation is, there are some health and consistency concerns there, too.

Still Left to Do:

By adding Teixeira, the lineup is better able to absorb an offensive sinkhole like Melky Cabrera was in 2008, but while the team is hoping for improved production from Cabrera and Brett Gardner in '09, a more reliable bat and glove in center field would relieve the last significant worry for the team, outside of Posada's ability to catch regularly. A veteran fifth starter, though unnecessary, would protect the team against disaster in the case of multiple injuries and give the Yankees more reliable production at the back of the rotation, but would also block a potential breakout season by one of their young starters.

Most Likely Team Outcome:

Not last. The top three teams in the division are pretty close in talent, so you can't project a playoff spot for the Yankees even if things go right. Barring injuries, they should be in contention all year, and are more likely than not to make the playoffs again. Once in October, that rotation could make them a favorite to win their 27th World Championship.

Player Projections

Batters

Bobby Abreu (Right Field)

PA	R	H	2B	3B	HR	RBI	SO	BB	SB	CS	BA	OBP	SLG	OPS	3-Year	Fielding	Reliability
618	82	153	34	3	14	68	104	76	18	5	.286	.374	.439	.813	-0.05	F	Very High

He's not a good defensive player anymore, doesn't have as much home run and doubles power, and merely gets on base at a "very good" clip, rather than his old "great" clip. But even in decline, Abreu was an extremely valuable player for the Yankees. They saved a few million by cutting him loose, but they'll miss his bat in the lineup. Wherever he ends up, the lineup will be better.

Melky Cabrera (Center Field)

PA	R	H	2B	3B	HR	RBI	SO	BB	SB	CS	BA	OBP	SLG	OPS	3-Year	Fielding	Reliability
525	61	131	22	3	8	51	66	41	11	3	.277	.338	.387	.725	+0.04	C	Very High

Not really a failed prospect, Cabrera just never had the pure talent to develop into a consistently good player. If he hits over .280 he can get on base enough to be a reasonable solution for most teams in center, but even that seems like a stretch at times, and he doesn't seem likely to develop much power, either. He might be able to make a career out of being a fourth or fifth outfielder, but unless he surprises a whole lot of people, his day in the sun has passed.

Robinson Cano (Second Base)

PA	R	H	2B	3B	HR	RBI	SO	BB	SB	CS	BA	OBP	SLG	OPS	3-Year	Fielding	Reliability
576	73	164	34	3	18	82	68	30	3	2	.306	.346	.481	.827	+0.08	D	Very High

Except for a month and a half from the All-Star break until late August, Cano had a terrible, terrible year, and was one of the biggest reasons the team missed the playoffs for the first time since Cano was a preteen. The Yankees will need him to rebound to have a realistic chance to contend, even with their offseason acquisitions. We project that he will.

Justin Christian (Left Field)

PA	R	H	2B	3B	HR	RBI	SO	BB	SB	CS	BA	OBP	SLG	OPS	3-Year	Fielding	Reliability
386	41	85	14	3	4	29	59	20	15	3	.237	.281	.327	.608	-0.02	C	High

A late bloomer, Christian is ready to surprise everyone with an epic power surge. OK, he's not going to do that, but I figure the only reason anyone will read this capsule is because he did just that and they want to know who the heck he is and how he did it. I don't know, either, buddy.

Johnny Damon (Left Field)

PA	R	H	2B	3B	HR	RBI	SO	BB	SB	CS	BA	OBP	SLG	OPS	3-Year	Fielding	Reliability
573	74	140	26	3	13	61	80	59	22	5	.276	.352	.417	.769	—	A	Very High

In desperate need of a center fielder in 2004, the Yankees decided to sign Carl Pavano and Jaret Wright, and trade for Randy Johnson rather than sign a discount-offering Carlos Beltran. A year later they brought in Damon. They got essentially nothing out of Pavano and Wright, Johnson was a bust, and while Damon had good offensive seasons in 2006 and 2008, he can't play center field anymore. If Damon can repeat his 2008 season, then the contract wasn't a bad one, but with better decision making in the 2004-05 offseason, they never would have had to sign it.

Shelley Duncan (Right Field)

PA	R	H	2B	3B	HR	RBI	SO	BB	SB	CS	BA	OBP	SLG	OPS	3-Year	Fielding	Reliability
386	48	81	17	0	19	57	88	40	3	1	.239	.322	.457	.779	-0.03	C	Very High

A big goofy-looking guy with a personality to match, Duncan has enough power to hit a home run into the old Yankee Stadium from the new one, which sounds even more impressive when you know where the new stadium is located. Unfortunately for Shelley, he blew his big shot to stick in the majors when he couldn't buy a hit as the regular first baseman, a role the Yankees probably let him hold for too long. You'll see him again, but he'll probably never get another chance to start.

Brett Gardner (Center Field)

PA	R	H	2B	3B	HR	RBI	SO	BB	SB	CS	BA	OBP	SLG	OPS	3-Year	Fielding	Reliability
506	63	110	15	7	2	30	96	56	31	5	.252	.339	.332	.671	+0.02	C	High

Gardner will never hit home runs, and may never even hit 20 doubles. But if he can beat out enough ground balls to hit closer to .300 than .250, and if his plate discipline translates from his days in the minors, he'll be worth be worth sticking in center field for the Yankees or some other team for a few years, until he loses a step. If he never hits, he'll always find a spot somewhere as a pinch-runner. Dude is **fast**.

Jason Giambi (First Base)

PA	R	H	2B	3B	HR	RBI	SO	BB	SB	CS	BA	OBP	SLG	OPS	3-Year	Fielding	Reliability
488	66	101	20	1	26	75	97	69	1	1	.251	.375	.500	.875	—	D	Very High

Even if you take out the first two years before the BALCO revelations, Jason Giambi had a good run with the Yankees. He didn't hit for average like he did in Oakland, but he got on base 40 percent of the time and hit with excellent power—and often at crucial times. He was popular with his teammates and fans, and the fact is that the team will realize sometime this summer that they probably should have given him at least a one-year deal after declining his option. The lineup will be much, much less dangerous without him.

Austin Jackson (Center Field)

PA	R	H	2B	3B	HR	RBI	SO	BB	SB	CS	BA	OBP	SLG	OPS	3-Year	Fielding	Reliability
530	57	121	26	4	8	49	108	35	10	4	.250	.303	.369	.672	+0.12	—	Very High

The Yankees expect great things from this kid, but with Phil Hughes and Ian Kennedy hitting speedbumps in 2008, management might start looking at players like Jackson as trade bait again. That's not likely to happen this season, but even if it does, don't expect Jackson to be dealt: the Yankees hope he can compete for the starting center field job in 2010, and there don't appear to be any better options on the market.

Derek Jeter (Shortstop)

PA	R	H	2B	3B	HR	RBI	SO	BB	SB	CS	BA	OBP	SLG	OPS	3-Year	Fielding	Reliability
616	75	166	29	2	8	63	88	50	13	4	.303	.369	.407	.776	-0.05	F	Very High

Poor Derek Jeter. For the first time since he was 20, he didn't have anything to do in October. He must have suffered through many a sleepless night this winter, and not the usual "sleepless" nights he's had with hot models in the past. Though the hot models were there with him … on his giant pile of money. Okay, maybe it's not easy to feel sorry for Jeter, but 2008 was an awful year for him. In addition to missing the playoffs, he had probably his worst offensive season ever. But he was playing through an injury early, and was red-hot at the end of the season, so there's good reason to expect him to exceed that projection and return to his previous established level. If he can do that, it goes a long way toward getting him back to his accustomed place in the playoffs.

Hideki Matsui (Left Field)

PA	R	H	2B	3B	HR	RBI	SO	BB	SB	CS	BA	OBP	SLG	OPS	3-Year	Fielding	Reliability
426	52	105	20	1	13	54	57	47	1	1	.282	.364	.446	.810	-0.06	B	High

Once a guy who never missed a game, Matsui has missed almost half of the Yankees' games since getting hurt in May 2006. If he's healthy and productive in 2009, it'll go a long way toward making up for the losses of Abreu and Giambi.

Chad Moeller (Catcher)

PA	R	H	2B	3B	HR	RBI	SO	BB	SB	CS	BA	OBP	SLG	OPS	3-Year	Fielding	Reliability
239	22	49	11	0	3	21	50	17	0	1	.227	.293	.320	.613	-0.03	C	Very Low

When Jorge Posada was trying to play through his shoulder injury, the Yankees kept Moeller as their third catcher, losing a spot they could have used on the roster, out of fear he'd be claimed on waivers if they tried to send him to Scranton. In a related story, Moeller was cut by the Nationals in spring training so they could keep Wil Nieves. Tip: If you own a major league baseball team and your GM claims Chad Moeller on waivers, fire him.

Jose Molina (Catcher)

PA	R	H	2B	3B	HR	RBI	SO	BB	SB	CS	BA	OBP	SLG	OPS	3-Year	Fielding	Reliability
320	29	70	18	0	4	29	60	16	1	1	.241	.288	.344	.632	-0.04	A+	Low

He's a perfectly OK solution for a backup catcher who plays every fifth or sixth game, but the Yankees faced their worst nightmare when Molina became their regular catcher after Jorge Posada injured his shoulder. Although pitchers liked working with him and he was good at throwing out baserunners, those talents cover up only so much suck with the bat. And yet somehow he hit the last home run ever at Yankee Stadium, one of a whopping 19 in his career.

Xavier Nady (Right Field)

PA	R	H	2B	3B	HR	RBI	SO	BB	SB	CS	BA	OBP	SLG	OPS	3-Year	Fielding	Reliability
530	65	137	28	1	21	77	99	32	2	1	.283	.336	.475	.811	-0.03	D	Very High

Nady was having a career year with the Pirates when he was dealt to New York, and for a couple of weeks he was performing even better in pinstripes. He collapsed down the stretch and his overall numbers with the Yankees looked pretty much like his career numbers. He'll be an acceptable and fairly cheap solution for the team in right field, but there remains the question: why does a team with a $200 million payroll settle for "acceptable and fairly cheap?"

Jorge Posada (Catcher)

PA	R	H	2B	3B	HR	RBI	SO	BB	SB	CS	BA	OBP	SLG	OPS	3-Year	Fielding	Reliability
362	45	88	20	1	10	46	65	42	1	1	.282	.373	.449	.822	—	C	High

If Jorge Posada can catch regularly and meet our projection, that improvement might be enough on its own to get the Yankees back into the playoffs. If he can't catch, they're in big trouble. Jose Molina is that bad. Most importantly, the Yankees need to make sure they don't get a good first baseman, because they need a spot to put Posada when he can't catch or hit anymore.

Cody Ransom (Third Base)

PA	R	H	2B	3B	HR	RBI	SO	BB	SB	CS	BA	OBP	SLG	OPS	3-Year	Fielding	Reliability
479	58	102	24	1	20	65	118	42	9	3	.239	.310	.440	.750	-0.02	C	Very High

Personal story here: On Aug. 17 my parents made their last visit to Yankee Stadium, and saw Ransom homer in his first plate appearance as a Yankee. About a week later I was working in Baltimore and Ransom came to the plate in the ninth inning after replacing Jason Giambi in the field. I turned to the reporter next to me and joked about his 1.000/1.000/4.000 line on the scoreboard, "this guy hits a home run every time up." Ransom hit a three-run homer to left center, and I turned to the reporter and said, "See?"

Alex Rodriguez (Third Base)

PA	R	H	2B	3B	HR	RBI	SO	BB	SB	CS	BA	OBP	SLG	OPS	3-Year	Fielding	Reliability
577	89	146	27	0	34	99	111	69	15	4	.297	.394	.559	.953	-0.04	B	Very High

Until A-Rod carries the Yankees to a World Championship, he'll never be truly appreciated in New York. Our projection would be an outstanding, MVP-caliber season, and is perfectly reasonable. Yankees fans would consider a season like that from Rodriguez a flop. They expect him to repeat 2007 ever year. And maybe he will have another 2007, but it would be nice to get some awe in return for it.

Ivan Rodriguez (Catcher)

PA	R	H	2B	3B	HR	RBI	SO	BB	SB	CS	BA	OBP	SLG	OPS	3-Year	Fielding	Reliability
461	50	119	22	2	7	48	76	21	6	2	.275	.310	.384	.694	—	A	Very High

Jose Molina clearly wasn't a viable solution behind the plate, so at the trade deadline the Yankees snagged Pudge Rodriguez for Kyle Farnsworth, who they had been desperate to get rid of ever since they realized they had signed Kyle Farnsworth. Getting Molina out of the lineup would be a huge boost to a team trying to surge its way back into the playoffs … which is why Rodriguez started fewer than half of the Yankees' games the rest of the way. To be fair, that was because Mike Mussina and Andy Pettitte wanted to throw to Molina, and to be fairer, Rodriguez hit only .219/.257/.323 the rest of the season. Of course, Pettitte had an ERA of 5.43 throwing to Molina his last 10 starts, and Molina hit .192/.234/.342 the rest of the way, so that doesn't exactly justify starting Molina.

Regardless of that bad decision, Pudge is done. That's not surprising, considering he's in his late 30s and has been catching in the majors since he was a teenager. Still, he'll stick as a starter somewhere, because a stathead and a manager would look at that projection and see completely different things.

Richie Sexson (First Base)

PA	R	H	2B	3B	HR	RBI	SO	BB	SB	CS	BA	OBP	SLG	OPS	3-Year	Fielding	Reliability
400	46	83	18	0	17	54	92	42	1	1	.236	.320	.432	.752	-0.05	C	Very High

As soon as Sexson started to lose his bat speed, it was all over for him. If he connects with one he can hit it a long way, but he can't connect with them as often as he used to, and pitchers aren't afraid to challenge him.

Nick Swisher (Center Field)

PA	R	H	2B	3B	HR	RBI	SO	BB	SB	CS	BA	OBP	SLG	OPS	3-Year	Fielding	Reliability
565	70	120	25	1	23	76	121	78	3	2	.252	.362	.454	.816	-0.02	D	Very High

For Swisher, it was a disastrous short stay with the White Sox. He finished the season with a .219/.332./.419 batting line, but that isn't to say he can't rebound. Based on the work of Chris Dutton and Peter Bendix on BABIP, Swisher was one of the unluckiest hitters of 2008, with a 0.49 differential between his expected and actual BABIP. He still took of ton of walks last season, hit for power and showed good versatility playing all three outfield positions and first base while holding his own defensively. Assuming he rebounds, the trade with the White Sox is going to pay off greatly for the Yankees.

Pitchers

Chris Britton (Reliever)

W	L	ERA	TBF	IP	Hit	HR	SO	BB	HBP	3-Year	Reliability
4	3	3.74	260	62	54	7	48	24	2	+0.13	Low

If you're a great big fat right-handed pitcher who throws in the upper 80s, you pretty much have to be flawless for a major league manager to not dismiss you. Sure, that sleek lefty with the 98 mph heater gets bombed all the time, but look at that stuff! And from the left side, too! It's not fair, but who said life is fair. Britton has never done anything that would indicate he can't succeed as a major league relief pitcher, particularly that time in 2006 where he succeeded as a major league relief pitcher.

Non-tendered in December, he's still a young guy, so he'll have plenty more opportunities to get unfairly passed over.

Brian Bruney (Reliever)

W	L	ERA	TBF	IP	Hit	HR	SO	BB	HBP	3-Year	Reliability
3	3	3.76	215	50	41	5	46	26	2	+0.11	Very Low

After nobody in the entire 6,000 years of human existence had ever suffered a "Lisfranc fracture," the Yankees lost two pitchers to the injury in 2008. The first was Brian Bruney, who was presumed lost for the season but instead decided to rehab and came back in August. Bruney actually pitched ridiculously well in 2008, so I guess in hindsight he was justified in acting kind of dickish when getting cut in 2007.

Joba Chamberlain (Reliever)

W	L	ERA	TBF	IP	Hit	HR	SO	BB	HBP	3-Year	Reliability
7	4	3.17	413	100	82	8	111	39	4	+0.04	Low

Yankees fans think it's idiotic for Joba Chamberlain to be a starter for three reasons: (1) the average sports fan is pretty stupid, (2) they haven't figured out that it's not 1999 anymore, when the only question about their rotation was who their fifth starter would be, and (3) they overestimate the importance of Mariano Rivera in winning for World Championships—he was important, but the depth of their rotation was more important. And if Rivera had been able to go through a lineup three times without getting hit hard the second and third time around, he would have been a starter. Chamberlain was a spectacular success in the rotation after the Yankees made the move, and only a bout of tendinitis in August reignited the controversy.

In Chamberlain, the Yankees have a pitcher capable of making CC Sabathia their No. 2 starter, and it would be absolutely foolish to throw that opportunity away. He should start until it's clear he can't handle the workload or simply isn't that great as a starter.

Phil Coke (Reliever)

W	L	ERA	TBF	IP	Hit	HR	SO	BB	HBP	3-Year	Reliability
5	9	5.39	558	123	138	18	76	60	5	+0.18	Very High

It wasn't anything like Jobamania, but the 26-year-old lefty thrilled Yankees fans as a relief pitcher in September, and earned a shot at the bullpen in 2009. As a reliever, he's got a decent shot to outperform that projection, but he's not going to be as good as he looked in September.

Dan Giese (Reliever)

W	L	ERA	TBF	IP	Hit	HR	SO	BB	HBP	3-Year	Reliability
5	6	4.41	425	99	102	12	68	33	4	+0.21	Average

The career reliever got a shot as a starter last season, and while the Yankees lost all three games he started, he actually pitched very well in two of them. He's not going to be a starter with the Yankees unless several guys get hurt, but he'll get some looks in the bullpen.

Kei Igawa (Starter)

W	L	ERA	TBF	IP	Hit	HR	SO	BB	HBP	3-Year	Reliability
6	10	5.54	635	143	157	27	90	58	6	+0.54	High

Igawa's MLB ERA is 6.66. What that says depends on whether you're a Yankees fans or a Yankees hater. At some point the Yankees are going to trade Igawa for a nothing prospect, pick up most or all of his salary, and watch him win 15 games the next season.

Damaso Marte (Reliever)

W	L	ERA	TBF	IP	Hit	HR	SO	BB	HBP	3-Year	Reliability
4	3	3.70	275	65	56	6	64	28	3	+0.21	Low

The first couple of weeks of Damaso Marte's Yankees career were nothing less than disastrous: He gave up nine runs in nine relief appearances. He was as good the rest of the way as he was bad before that, and the Yankees re-signed him after the season. The Yankees have been desperate for a reliable lefty ever since Mike Stanton left after 2002. Marte might finally fill that role.

Mike Mussina (Starter)

W	L	ERA	TBF	IP	Hit	HR	SO	BB	HBP	3-Year	Reliability
11	9	4.05	742	178	191	19	125	35	6	—	Very High

Moose retired in the offseason after winning 20 games for the first time by beating the Red Sox on the last day of the season.

Mussina could have hung around for two or three more years to win 300 games and get a plaque in Cooperstown, but as he said, why should he be judged solely on what he did at the end of his career? Mussina was not Pedro or Maddux or Clemens, but he was one of the best pitchers of his era. He should have won the Cy Young in 2001, and he probably would have won 20 games two times if not for the '94 strike. It won't be a travesty if he doesn't make it into the Hall of Fame, but he also fits in just fine with the guys who are already in there. The unappreciated ace of his generation, the Moose will be missed.

Carl Pavano (Starter)

W	L	ERA	TBF	IP	Hit	HR	SO	BB	HBP	3-Year	Reliability
5	6	4.99	442	101	110	16	56	35	6	+0.25	Very Low

Shockingly, Carl Pavano wasn't the other Yankees pitcher to go down to a Lisfranc fracture. Even more shockingly, Pavano actually pitched for the Yankees in 2008. Not at all shockingly, he was very, very bad.

Andy Pettitte (Starter)

W	L	ERA	TBF	IP	Hit	HR	SO	BB	HBP	3-Year	Reliability
11	10	4.23	800	187	204	19	130	57	4	—	Very High

Pettitte was cruising along until July 31, when he got bombed by the Angels at Yankee Stadium, giving up nine runs in 5.1 innings. The team had entered the game tied in the loss column with the Red Sox for the wild card, but Pettitte's struggles the rest of the way and Joba Chamberlain's injury a few days later sounded the death knell of the Yankees' playoff hopes. The Yankees had relied on Pettitte to be their No. 1 or No. 2 starter in 2008, a role he probably can't fill anymore. If he pitches for the Yankees in 2009, it will be as their fourth- or fifth-best starter, a role in which he should be able to help them.

Sidney Ponson (Starter)

W	L	ERA	TBF	IP	Hit	HR	SO	BB	HBP	3-Year	Reliability
7	9	5.01	623	141	163	17	63	54	6	+0.26	High

Apparently forgetting how well it worked out for them in 2006, the Yankees signed Ponson last season when they were really, really desperate for warm bodies in the rotation. As Ponson's body stays warm even in Arctic climates, he seemed a good fit. This capsule is the only place on earth where you will find the words "Ponson" and "fit" in the same sentence.

Edwar Ramirez (Reliever)

W	L	ERA	TBF	IP	Hit	HR	SO	BB	HBP	3-Year	Reliability
4	3	3.89	262	62	53	7	71	27	3	+0.21	Very Low

Ramirez can be a dominating reliever when he's able to set up his change-up with his fastball, but if he can't, it's like he's throwing batting practice. He had stretches of both in 2008, but overall had a pretty solid season that earned him a spot in the majors to start 2009.

Mariano Rivera (Reliever)

W	L	ERA	TBF	IP	Hit	HR	SO	BB	HBP	3-Year	Reliability
6	2	2.48	279	71	58	4	68	13	3	—	Low

There have been a lot of closers just as dominating as Mariano Rivera. Except they're that dominating for three or four years, and either flame out or become much more ordinary for the rest of their careers. Mariano Rivera has been as good or better than any other reliever for 13 seasons. He has the highest ERA+ for any pitcher with 1,000 or more innings. He has the lowest ERA for any pitcher since the deadball era. This isn't a guy playing out the string—his age 38 season may have been his best one. In 40 save situations, he gave up 25 baserunners, and just three runs.

Jose Veras (Reliever)

W	L	ERA	TBF	IP	Hit	HR	SO	BB	HBP	3-Year	Reliability
4	3	3.81	281	66	58	6	66	29	3	+0.27	Low

Apart from one really awful outing against the Red Sox in late August, Veras had a great season out of the bullpen. He's got the stuff to repeat that, and doing so goes a long way to determining the quality of the Yankees 'pen in 2009.

Chien-Ming Wang (Starter)

W	L	ERA	TBF	IP	Hit	HR	SO	BB	HBP	3-Year	Reliability
8	7	3.83	562	132	141	9	64	42	4	+0.28	Very High

He doesn't strike guys out, he doesn't dominate, all he's done is win. An ace, but not a stopper, Wang is best suited heading a deep rotation or as the No. 2 behind a dominating starter. In 2009, he fits into the latter role. Wang's Lisfranc fracture rounding third base in Houston June 15 was the irreplaceable injury. The rotation had no margin for error after that, and when Joba got hurt and Pettitte lost effectiveness, they were done. They won't be relying on him quite as much in '09 with CC Sabathia and A.J. Burnett in the mix, but a healthy, effective Wang will go a long way toward getting the Yankees back to the top of the standings.

Oakland Athletics
by Sal Baxamusa of The Hardball Times

2009 Athletics Projections
Record: 79-83
Division Rank/Games Behind: 2nd, 3 games back
Runs Scored: 781, 8th in the league
Runs Allowed: 789, 10th in the league
Park Factor: .98, a pitcher's park

What Happened:

The A's continued their rebuilding project in earnest, trading both Joe Blanton and Rich Harden midseason. With an eye to the future, the A's handed everyday jobs to the kids. Carlos Gonzalez, Ryan Sweeney and Daric Barton became everyday players. Greg Smith and Dana Eveland were slotted into the rotation almost immediately, and Sean Gallagher joined them as soon as he was acquired from the Cubs.

It was in general a trying summer, and unless you had a rooting interest, kind of a boring one, too. The most entertaining part of the year was watching two of Oakland's best players, Jack Cust and Mark Ellis, go about their business. Their warts are extremely prominent. In Cust's case, it's the strikeouts, particularly the called ones, and the embarrassingly bad glove; in Ellis' case it's the uninspiring offense and a lack of flashy plays in the field.

But both contributed about three wins above replacement last year. Cust's walks and Herculean power mitigate the strikeouts and help make up for the glove. Ellis may not make the highlight show, but his range and hands are outstanding and he was, per usual, one of the best defenders in the AL. Even for a losing cause, both Cust and Ellis were joys to watch.

Players Lost from Last Year's Team:

Huston Street, Smith, Gonzalez, Blanton, Harden, Alan Embree, Frank Thomas, Emil Brown, Mike Sweeney, Donnie Murphy, Chad Gaudin, Keith Foulke, and some roster filler. Good golly, that's a quarter of the 40-man roster. A's fans better be prepared for a lot of "who the hell is this guy?" moments.

Players Acquired:

Matt Holliday, Chris Schroder, Yung Chi Chen, Joe Dillon, Ben Copeland. Holliday is the only one who will be consequential, although Schroder might find a role in the bullpen. Gallagher, Josh Outman, Eric Patterson and Matt Murton all came into the Oakland organization last year midseason.

Management Is:

Reversing course. This time last year, the A's had committed themselves to a lengthy rebuilding project. The trades of Nick Swisher and Dan Haren were particularly telling, since they were signed to team-friendly contracts for several years. If the A's planned to rebuild quickly, Swisher and Haren could certainly have served as ready-made centerpieces for a 2010 contender.

But the A's decided to go the long route, which is a defensible move, and started shipping out anybody with value. Then, just as quickly, they reversed course this offseason by dealing for Holliday. They parted with a lot of present and future value in Gonzalez and Street. But if they hope to capitalize on the Holliday prior to his free agency after 2009, they now have to shop for free-agent solutions in the infield and the rotation.

The conventional wisdom is that the A's must think that the Angels can be had this year and are gunning for a division title. It's not a crazy notion. The Angels have great pitching, but they will be bringing back most of the hitters that were collectively about 20 runs below average on offense. With the Angels failing to re-sign Mark Teixiera, they're likely to have a below-average offense. It's possible that they slip just enough that the A's could compete.

That's far from a certainty—it's not even likely—and there is a fair amount of wishcasting involved from the A's perspective. But all signs point to this being the plan. If you assume that the A's are shooting for the postseason this year, wouldn't it have been made more sense to do so with Swisher and Haren, not to mention Blanton and particularly Harden in the fold?

That's not a simple question. Think about it this way: if you assume the A's were punting 2008, the Haren trade breaks down to Haren and Street for Aaron Cunningham, Brett Anderson, Eveland and Holliday. That's not a slam-dunk win for the A's given the equity built into Haren and Street vis-à-vis their contracts, but which set of players do you think will accrue more wins in 2009?

But viewed from that perspective, the Blanton and Harden trades still don't make sense, and it's an open question whether Gio Gonzalez and Ryan Sweeney contribute enough in 2009 to make the A's forget about Swisher. The simpler explanation behind the Holliday trade is that the A's saw an opportunity to acquire a superstar for players they didn't value and pulled the trigger. If having a superstar on your team is a problem, then it's a good kind of problem to have. Having Holliday will help the A's win games, there's always the possibility of trading him at the deadline, and at worst you get a year of Holliday and a couple of draft picks.

Oakland's aggressive, though ultimately failed, pursuit of Rafael Furcal need not be related to the Holliday acquisition. The A's offered the most lucrative deal and Furcal turned them down and opted to return to Los Angeles. The episode proves, if nothing else, that the A's are serious about getting a long-term shortstop, not merely some guy who will complement Holliday for a year.

It ought to be no surprise that the A's are looking to land a shortstop—Bobby Crosby is a complete bust at this point and there aren't any appealing internal options. Even if you believe that Crosby might still turn it around—and he won't—he will be a free agent after 2009. In 2010, the free agent shortstop class will be headlined by Khalil Greene and an aging Miguel Tejada. Furcal made a ton of sense for the A's and they put in their best effort. And if the downside to finding a shortstop a year early was a shot at winning a few games in 2009, well, that wouldn't have hurt either.

Finally, there is another reason to build a winner for 2008: the new stadium. Owner Lew Wolff is still trying to build support for his plan to build a new stadium in Fremont, and that's easier to do when you are building a team rather than tearing one apart. It's not that rebuilding was a bad idea, but getting a fan base to buy into the idea of losing is … well, that's not really what fans root for, is it? Making baseball decisions with an eye on public relations hasn't been the modus operandi for the A's since the Haas era, and while that policy has served them well, some flexibility may be called for in this instance.

The Minor League System Is:

One of the deepest in the major leagues. Just off the top of my head, the A's have eight of the top 100 prospects in baseball: Trevor Cahill, Brett Anderson, Gio Gonzalez, James Simmons, Vincent Mazzaro, Chris Carter, Adrian Cardenas, and Aaron Cunningham. You can add Michel Inoa to the list if you want to project a 16-year old to make the majors (I wouldn't). Having a system that deep isn't a problem in and of itself, but there are some things not to like.

The first issue is that most of those guys are pitchers. That's a good thing given the attrition rate for young pitchers, but this is a team badly in need of some position players. The second, and related, problem is that apart from Cahill and Anderson, the system strength comes from its depth. There aren't any premium position-player prospects.

The top position players in the minors are Carter, Cardenas and Cunningham. Each has his warts: Carter is terrible defensively (his listing as a third baseman on some prospect lists is plain silly), Cardenas has yet to put it all together, and Cunningham has limited upside. Last summer's draftee Jemile Weeks could rise through the system quickly, but it's too soon to know.

To complete their rebuilding process, the A's may need to sign or trade for a premium free agent position player. If the A's can make Holliday fall in love with the Bay Area, then he might be that guy. In fact, looking at the 2010 free agent class, he'd **better** be that guy.

Due For a Change:

Brad Ziegler and Joey Devine won't combine for a sub-1.00 ERA again, but they should still be top-flight bullpen arms. Justin Duchscherer isn't going to be an ace again either. Even though all three will likely perform worse, they will still be assets to the team. A lot of their projected decline has a lot to do with regression to the mean and little to do with actually pitching worse. Along those lines, Barton and Travis Buck are good bets to hit better. I'm high on both Gallagher and Gio Gonzalez—strikeouts can atone for many sins—and although their projections agree that they'll be better than last year, they're not expected to be above average.

I'm most curious about Ellis. His peripherals looked fine last year: he upped his walk rate and struck out less frequently and his power was right in line with his career averages. But a career-worst .233 batting average led to a sub-.700 OPS.

Ellis has been more or less a league-average hitter over his career and in most cases I'd be inclined to call this a fluke-BABIP season. Indeed, his .248 BABIP ranked third from worst in the AL last year. But Ellis hasn't lost a step. In fact, he stole a career-high 14 bases last year and was caught only twice. He also legged out three triples. So that .248 BABIP has got to be a fluke, right?

Maybe not. Fully one-quarter of Ellis' fly balls were infield popups. Nobody hits popups that frequently; since 2004 the nearest to that mark has been Vernon Wells in 2005 with a 21.7 percent mark. All those popups explain the low BABIP. Ellis' low BABIP wasn't a case of bad luck; it resulted directly from his batted-ball profile.

The real question is whether he'll continue that. Ellis' 2008 season was cut short by torn cartilage in his right shoulder. The shoulder has since been operated upon, and by all accounts he is recovering well. But, for a right-handed hitter, the torn cartilage may have made it painful or difficult for Ellis to lift his back shoulder properly during his swing. And what happens when you drop your back shoulder during a swing? Popups.

Reasons to be Optimistic:

The key issue facing the franchise is its long-term home. Wolff already has made clear that he intends to get the team out of the Coliseum, and for the past few years the A's have been preparing to build a stadium in nearby Fremont. It's not Oakland, but it is the Bay Area, which is where the A's belong. Moving the A's to a new stadium is a reason to be optimistic if it leads to new revenue streams, whether due to increased attendance, corporate sponsorships, or more lucrative media contracts resulting from the buzz. Of course, that optimism is only warranted if ownership invests that money back into the baseball team.

Reasons to be Pessimistic:

The plan for a new stadium in Fremont is in flux. Wolff, a real estate developer, was planning to develop retail and housing in the area surrounding the new ballpark in Fremont. But—and you may have heard about this—the economy is kind of in the tank right now, so it's unclear whether that plan is still viable. Moreover, Wolff is apparently frustrated by the slow-moving process surrounding the required Environmental Impact Report.

Some fans would like nothing better for the Fremont plan to fall apart and for the team to remain in Oakland. But the flip side is that Commissioner Bud Selig recently

> **Our Favorite Athletics Blogs:**
> Athletics Nation (http://www.athleticsnation.com)
> Catfish Stew (http://catfishstew.baseballtoaster.com)
> Marine Layer's New Ballpark (http://newballpark.blogspot.com/). Marine Layer in particular assisted in fact-checking the new stadium.

gave Wolff the okay to look outside of Fremont "in the event that (he is) not able to promptly assure the implementation of the desired ballpark in Fremont." The worst-case scenario is that the A's leave the state, and that's a reason to be pessimistic.

The alternative plan at this point is San Jose. The Giants own the territorial rights to San Jose, but *San Jose Mercury-News* columnist Mark Purdy recently wrote, "(The Giants) do not control those territorial rights. Major League Baseball does. And if enough team owners vote to allow the A's into Santa Clara County, those territorial rights would vanish." Selig and Wolff are buddies from their days together as fraternity brothers in Wisconsin, and there are rumblings that Selig could make this vote happen if necessary.

Still Left to Do:

Get a long-term shortstop and a short-term starting pitcher.

Most Likely Team Outcome:

The A's could win the AL West, but a lot would have to go right. Young players would have to improve, everybody would have to stay healthy, and Cahill, Anderson or both would need to make a second-half splash. The most likely outcome is that the A's finish behind the Angels.

Player Projections

Batters

Daric Barton (First Base)

PA	R	H	2B	3B	HR	RBI	SO	BB	SB	CS	BA	OBP	SLG	OPS	3-Year	Fielding	Reliability
556	63	120	26	4	10	56	94	68	2	2	.253	.349	.388	.737	+0.06	B	Very High

His batting average was dragged down by bad luck, and the projection has him making up for it somewhat. It's still nowhere near what a first baseman needs to do. What's troubling is that his upside has always been limited by his lack of power, and the best-case scenario was always a .400 OBP/40 doubles hitter. His terrible year last year and this projection both suggest that he may not reach even that plateau.

Rob Bowen (Catcher)

PA	R	H	2B	3B	HR	RBI	SO	BB	SB	CS	BA	OBP	SLG	OPS	3-Year	Fielding	Reliability
200	20	41	10	0	5	21	51	18	1	1	.234	.310	.377	.687	-0.01	C	Very Low

He's a switch-hitter, can take a walk, doesn't make much money, and might even pop a double every now and then. Do you really expect much more from a backup catcher?

Emil Brown (Left Field)

PA	R	H	2B	3B	HR	RBI	SO	BB	SB	CS	BA	OBP	SLG	OPS	3-Year	Fielding	Reliability
447	48	102	20	1	9	47	73	32	5	2	.250	.307	.370	.677	-0.05	C	Very High

He's not good, he's not even average, and he was nicknamed "DFA" by bloggers at Athletics Nation. While the terrible hitting is enough to drive you crazy, his boneheaded moves in the field and on the basepaths are truly maddening. In the first game of the season, the A's were trailing the Red Sox by two in the bottom of the 10th. With one out, Brown hit a clutch double to drive in a run, but—in a baserunning display that would embarrass even Jack Cust—took a big turn coming around second and was tagged out in a 7-4-3-5-6-3 rundown. The next two batters reached base, and Brown likely would have scored to tie the game. Instead, the A's lost by a single run. As Brown took the walk of shame back to the dugout, manager Bob Geren had a look on his face that said, "Man, I have to deal with **this** all year?" My wife will tell you I had the same look on my face, and it stayed there until the end of the season.

Travis Buck (Right Field)

PA	R	H	2B	3B	HR	RBI	SO	BB	SB	CS	BA	OBP	SLG	OPS	3-Year	Fielding	Reliability
387	44	88	21	3	7	41	73	36	4	1	.256	.331	.396	.727	+0.03	A	Average

Shin splits, concussions, thumb injuries, wrist problems, you name it. Buck just can't stay healthy. His lack of power is troubling for a corner outfielder, but he's hit for average and gotten on base at every stop save for the first month of 2008. While I'd never advocate throwing out that fact, it stands in such stark contrast to his established level of performance that it's worth wondering whether there was something physically wrong with him last April.

Adrian Cardenas (Second Base)

PA	R	H	2B	3B	HR	RBI	SO	BB	SB	CS	BA	OBP	SLG	OPS	3-Year	Fielding	Reliability
502	48	108	17	3	3	36	85	31	10	2	.234	.284	.303	.587	+0.13	—	Average

I don't see it, but then I've never seen him play. There's something in his performance that piques the THT projection system's interest; it aggressively projects him to improve over the next three years. By the time he arrives in Oakland, there should be openings at second, short and third, so he's got some wiggle-room, organizationally speaking, to slide around the infield.

Eric Chavez (Third Base)

PA	R	H	2B	3B	HR	RBI	SO	BB	SB	CS	BA	OBP	SLG	OPS	3-Year	Fielding	Reliability
283	33	61	14	1	10	35	53	30	2	1	.244	.325	.428	.753	-0.02	D	High

You think I'm going to say something bad about my favorite player? I'm rooting hard for him to get back to where he was just a few years ago. A few offseason surgeries later, he may do just that. (Astute readers will note that I just copied and pasted what I wrote for last year's preview.)

Yung Chi Chen (Second Base)

PA	R	H	2B	3B	HR	RBI	SO	BB	SB	CS	BA	OBP	SLG	OPS	3-Year	Fielding	Reliability
298	30	67	12	2	2	24	42	17	6	1	.246	.293	.327	.620	+0.03	D	Low

Once an interesting prospect at second base, Chen has been ripped apart by injuries. His shoulder cost him all of 2007 and his knee cost him half of 2008, and at 25 years old, he's starting to look like a longshot. The talent's still in there somewhere, but unless he's able to recover some of his lost power while finding a way to stay on the field, he's never going to make it. Off to Oakland, his upside at this point is as a reserve.

Bobby Crosby (Shortstop)

PA	R	H	2B	3B	HR	RBI	SO	BB	SB	CS	BA	OBP	SLG	OPS	3-Year	Fielding	Reliability
504	50	108	25	0	8	46	85	39	7	2	.235	.294	.341	.635	-0.02	C	High

His defense has regressed from good to average; while it may have been a one-year blip, I'm inclined to think the back problems have sapped him of his range. Combined with the ugly projected hitting you see above, you've got yourself a replacement-level player.

Aaron Cunningham (Center Field)

PA	R	H	2B	3B	HR	RBI	SO	BB	SB	CS	BA	OBP	SLG	OPS	3-Year	Fielding	Reliability
550	65	129	25	5	13	60	120	37	11	5	.260	.319	.410	.729	+0.09	D	Very High

Athletics Nation regular Paul Thomas calls him the Rodney Dangerfield of prospects. In other words, he don't get no respect. Guys with his profile tend to get overlooked. He's a strong defensive outfielder, but isn't a speed burner. More than a third of his hits go for extra bases, but he's not a particularly big guy. He knows how to take a free pass, but he strikes out a lot, too. He's major league ready, but he doesn't have projectable tools.

His minor league line was .311/.384/.496. Carlos Gonzalez hit .286/.340/.473. Cunningham is six months younger than Gonzalez, and Cunningham has sustained his success in the high minors while Gonzalez had most of his success in the low minors. They're not mutually exclusive prospects by any means, and Gonzalez is a tools monster with huge upside. But trading the uber-prospect and counting on Cunningham … well, maybe he's getting some respect after all.

Jack Cust (Left Field)

PA	R	H	2B	3B	HR	RBI	SO	BB	SB	CS	BA	OBP	SLG	OPS	3-Year	Fielding	Reliability
556	76	113	21	1	29	84	162	104	0	1	.253	.394	.499	.893	-0.03	D	Very High

Cust was something like three wins above replacement last year, horrendous defense and all. That was better than Bobby Abreu, better than Adam Dunn, and about even with Pat Burrell. Cust's offensive projection for next season is, by OPS, better than Abreu and Burrell. And his fielding is grade D, which is not only a passing grade but exceeds the grade for those other three guys. If Cust found himself on the open market today, do you think he'd command as much cash as any of those other guys? No? Then sabermetrics ain't dead yet. Yeah, he strikes out a lot. Don't look at that projection. Do you want to know the terrifying truth about his strikeouts or do you want to watch him sock a few dingers?

Rajai Davis (Center Field)

PA	R	H	2B	3B	HR	RBI	SO	BB	SB	CS	BA	OBP	SLG	OPS	3-Year	Fielding	Reliability
325	41	76	13	2	2	22	50	20	25	5	.256	.307	.333	.640	0.00	C	Average

Let's say you had never seen him play, but you saw his stats from last year. He picked up only 200 plate appearances despite appearing in 100 games. He stole 25 bases and scored 28 runs despite reaching base fewer than 60 times of his own accord. He hit more triples (four) than home runs (three). You could easily write up a scouting report: "Little guy, poor swing, fast as hell, best used as defensive replacement and pinch-runner. Fifth outfielder on a contender." And you'd be right.

Mark Ellis (Second Base)

PA	R	H	2B	3B	HR	RBI	SO	BB	SB	CS	BA	OBP	SLG	OPS	3-Year	Fielding	Reliability
512	59	115	24	2	12	55	73	43	9	1	.253	.323	.394	.717	-0.03	A	Very High

Did you know that Mark Ellis is a star? Analyst Mitchel Lichtman, creator of the highly regarded Ultimate Zone Rating defensive metric, has Ellis at +23, +12, +26, and +21 runs above average on defense. The word to describe that kind of defense is "otherwordly." His glove alone is probably worth 15 runs. That projection is about league average offense, give or take. Throw in positional adjustment and missed time, and you've got yourself a three-win player, at least. That makes him a certifiable star, on par with Justin Morneau.

Given that, it's unusual that he re-signed with Oakland for $11 million over two years. He would have to fall off a cliff offensively and defensively **and** miss significant time for the A's to come out behind on this deal. He left tens of millions of dollars on the table to re-sign with an organization that stood by him when he suffered a potentially career-ending injury in 2005. Noble or stupid? Either way, A's fans ought to be ecstatic that he's sticking around for a few more years.

Jack Hannahan (Third Base)

PA	R	H	2B	3B	HR	RBI	SO	BB	SB	CS	BA	OBP	SLG	OPS	3-Year	Fielding	Reliability
498	54	106	24	1	10	51	118	60	3	2	.247	.342	.378	.720	-0.02	B	Very High

He's a stopgap, nothing more, and the A's had better hope that Eric Chavez is both healthy and productive in the coming year. Hannahan gets on base just enough to justify his existence.

Matt Holliday (Left Field)

PA	R	H	2B	3B	HR	RBI	SO	BB	SB	CS	BA	OBP	SLG	OPS	3-Year	Fielding	Reliability
589	84	156	36	2	23	86	104	56	16	3	.300	.374	.509	.883	-0.02	C	Very High

The question people ask about Matt Holliday is how his skills will translate now that he no longer plays half his games in the Mile High City, but instead in the sea level smogbowl that is Oakland's McAfee Coliseum. As a clearly biased fan, I suspect a lot of smart baseball analysts are underestimating him. Holliday's a unique talent, a multidimensional offensive force who will continue to hit at an elite level anyplace he plays. On the bad side—and it hurts to write this about a player who generally leaves everything on the field—I think he gave up on the Rockies at the end of 2008. I doubt he will for Oakland in a walk year, but let this be a warning to whoever winds up with him in 2010.

Matt Murton (Left Field)

PA	R	H	2B	3B	HR	RBI	SO	BB	SB	CS	BA	OBP	SLG	OPS	3-Year	Fielding	Reliability
414	46	99	21	2	6	41	54	38	4	1	.268	.339	.384	.723	+0.02	B	High

He gives the A's what they've been missing since Bobby Kielty skipped town: a lefty-masher with orange hair. Granted, that's a very specific role, but Murton is going to have to be a role player in the majors. Murton didn't impress after coming over from the Cubs in the Rich Harden trade and he's going to be 27 next year. In a crowded A's outfield, he might make a good platoon partner or pinch hitter. But he might just be a right-handed Graham Koonce, too.

Eric Patterson (Second Base)

PA	R	H	2B	3B	HR	RBI	SO	BB	SB	CS	BA	OBP	SLG	OPS	3-Year	Fielding	Reliability
480	56	111	20	5	8	44	89	33	17	4	.253	.305	.376	.681	+0.01	D	Very High

He's not a prospect anymore, and it's hard to figure out why he ever was considered one. The only big minor-league numbers he ever put up were as a 22-year old in the Midwest League and last year, as a 25-year old repeating Triple-A. Given that his infield defense has never been impressive and he doesn't have projectable tools, it's hard to know what made him so attractive. Probably a utility guy.

Kurt Suzuki (Catcher)

PA	R	H	2B	3B	HR	RBI	SO	BB	SB	CS	BA	OBP	SLG	OPS	3-Year	Fielding	Reliability
519	54	120	24	1	7	50	70	43	1	2	.260	.331	.362	.693	+0.02	C	Very High

For fans still scarred by the Jason Kendall Experience, Kurt Suzuki is a breath of fresh air. A league average hitter at **the** premium defensive position on the diamond? I'll take two, please. The stereotypical catcher has some raw physical power, but doesn't get on base much. Suzuki is the opposite; he has a tidy OBP but little power. That he is, by all appearances, a durable kid, is a bonus. During his cost-controlled years, a player like Suzuki gives you good production and lets you overpay for production, if necessary, elsewhere on the diamond.

Ryan Sweeney (Right Field)

PA	R	H	2B	3B	HR	RBI	SO	BB	SB	CS	BA	OBP	SLG	OPS	3-Year	Fielding	Reliability
528	59	127	24	3	8	51	84	45	8	2	.268	.333	.383	.716	+0.05	B	High

The good news is that, despite having been on the radar seemingly forever, he's only 23 and he might develop the power that would suit his big frame. I'm guessing it's his size that makes the THT projection system sanguine on his chances for improvement over the next three years. But I wouldn't bet on it; his swing is unimpressive and it's hard to imagine that he'll ever hit more than 10 or 15 homers in a season. He has to keep his batting average up to maintain his value, and for a guy who makes such weak contact, it's easy to imagine things getting ugly in a hurry. He's average defensively in center and he'd better stay that way if he wants a career as a starter.

Frank Thomas (Designated Hitter)

PA	R	H	2B	3B	HR	RBI	SO	BB	SB	CS	BA	OBP	SLG	OPS	3-Year	Fielding	Reliability
413	51	91	17	0	17	57	70	54	0	1	.259	.361	.453	.814	—	—	Very High

His return to Oakland was met with palpable excitement, and the team's 11-2 victory that day invigorated the fan base. He hit a nifty .319/.417/.516 for a month, hit the DL, and was terrible for the remainder of the year. He'll be hard-pressed to find work this season; if so, he might as well start working on his Hall of Fame induction speech. Highlight of the year: Frank Thomas legging out a triple against the Angels, his first since 2002.

Pitchers

Jerry Blevins (Reliever)

W	L	ERA	TBF	IP	Hit	HR	SO	BB	HBP	3-Year	Reliability
4	3	3.96	286	67	65	7	58	24	3	+0.03	Low

He's 6-foot-6, but tips the scales at 180 pounds. There's not much to dislike about his performance to date: lots of strikeouts, not a lot of walks, very few home runs. Look for him to become a key late-inning reliever over the next few years. If fantasy leagues used WPA as a category, he'd be a nifty snag in the late rounds.

Dallas Braden (Starter)

W	L	ERA	TBF	IP	Hit	HR	SO	BB	HBP	3-Year	Reliability
6	7	4.49	509	118	124	15	82	41	4	+0.03	High

Braden's major league FIP is 4.70. He's projected for a 4.49 ERA next year. He's dominated the minors for the past few years. He's going to be 25 in 2009. He may not be much to look at—his fastball sits at 87-89 mph and he really only has two secondary pitches—but he at least deserves a shot. He should get one this year, and he's one of the favorites for the fifth spot in the rotation.

Andrew Brown (Reliever)

W	L	ERA	TBF	IP	Hit	HR	SO	BB	HBP	3-Year	Reliability
3	3	3.96	229	53	47	5	44	27	2	+0.19	Low

Brown is a human benchmark: If you can construct a relief corps where Brown is your worst option, then you've done a good job. If he's one of your eighth-inning relievers, then you've got problems.

Trevor Cahill (Starter)

W	L	ERA	TBF	IP	Hit	HR	SO	BB	HBP	3-Year	Reliability
7	7	4.26	545	124	117	12	88	64	8	-0.64	Average

He's Oakland's other top prospect, along with Brett Anderson, and easily one of the top pitching prospects in the minors. There's a lot to like about Cahill: He's got a heavy sinker (60 percent ground ball rate last year), he misses bats (9.5 K/9), and he keeps the ball in the park (0.35 HR/9). He could cut down on the walks, but even as it stands, the free passes shouldn't be a problem. He posted a 3.26 FIP in Double-A next year, and while he'll probably spend all of this year in the minors, he could crack the 2010 rotation. As with Anderson, he's only 21, so he comes with the standard "if healthy" caveats.

Santiago Casilla (Reliever)

W	L	ERA	TBF	IP	Hit	HR	SO	BB	HBP	3-Year	Reliability
4	3	3.93	261	61	56	6	51	26	2	+0.28	Low

If he cuts down on the walks, he will almost immediately become an elite reliever; you could say that about any generic hard-throwing fastball-slider pitcher.

Joey Devine (Reliever)

W	L	ERA	TBF	IP	Hit	HR	SO	BB	HBP	3-Year	Reliability
4	2	3.08	223	54	42	4	55	22	2	+0.02	Very Low

Joey Devine was a revelation last year, striking out loads of batters and not giving up any home runs. The latter will certainly change, but that projection is the 10th best ERA among relievers. That the A's got anything for a broken-down Mark Kotsay is impressive; that they got Devine is—well, I won't say "divine." But I want to.

Justin Duchscherer (Starter)

W	L	ERA	TBF	IP	Hit	HR	SO	BB	HBP	3-Year	Reliability
8	6	3.82	542	130	125	14	90	36	5	+0.17	Average

His fastball is unimpressive, but the movement on his cutter is outstanding and his curveball is just devastating. After an outstanding run in the bullpen, credit the A's for giving him a chance in the rotation. He's bound to regress, but it's not every day you can find a mid-rotation starter hanging out in your bullpen. Duke is one of the few non-superstar pitchers that fans of any team should tune in to watch: he works quickly, doesn't give up a lot of walks, and the Bugs Bunny curveball is the cherry on top.

Alan Embree (Reliever)

W	L	ERA	TBF	IP	Hit	HR	SO	BB	HBP	3-Year	Reliability
4	3	4.32	281	65	66	8	54	26	2	—	Low

He can still chuck the baseball, and despite the poor year, he can help a bullpen. At age 38, he regularly dialed that fastball up to 93 mph. If he retains his velocity, there's no reason why he can't pitch a few more years.

Dana Eveland (Starter)

W	L	ERA	TBF	IP	Hit	HR	SO	BB	HBP	3-Year	Reliability
9	9	4.01	689	159	155	13	108	68	9	+0.04	High

He had a nice start to 2008, but from late June to early August, he hit a seven-start rough patch and walked 20 batters while striking out only 23 over 35 innings. He was demoted for a few weeks to Triple-A, where he was asked to rework his delivery. He did so, came back up in late August, and walked fewer than three batters per nine over his last seven starts. Obviously, those samples are too small to know anything conclusively, but they support the narrative. THT's projection really likes him, and I see no reason not to, either.

Keith Foulke (Reliever)

W	L	ERA	TBF	IP	Hit	HR	SO	BB	HBP	3-Year	Reliability
3	2	4.18	191	45	42	6	33	16	1	—	Very Low

If he wants to play, there's no reason why he wouldn't fit into the back of somebody's bullpen. I still have an irrational hatred of Foulke, and here's why: In Game 4 of the thrilling 2003 ALDS, Foulke came in to protect a 4-3 Oakland lead against Boston. But David Ortiz doubled off Foulke to drive in two runs, the A's lost the game and eventually lost the series. In a "can't-beat-'em-join-'em" moment, he turned around and signed with Red Sox after the season. Meanwhile, Oakland's plan B closer, Tom Gordon, was snatched away by the Yankees. Thus was born the disastrous Arthur Rhodes experiment. In the last game I attended in Oakland, Rhodes blew a save against the Yankees, ruining what I had hoped would be a sweet final memory in Oakland. Then I moved to Boston just in time to watch Foulke win a World Series with insanely clutch postseason pitching.

Sean Gallagher (Starter)

W	L	ERA	TBF	IP	Hit	HR	SO	BB	HBP	3-Year	Reliability
8	8	4.49	628	143	138	16	105	69	8	-0.17	Very High

His major league strikeout rate is below his minor league numbers, and his walk rate is higher. I suspect that's normal, but the degree to which this phenomenon has affected Gallagher seems abnormal. Considering that he's only 23, I'd say that he's got a bright long-term outlook as a mid-rotation starter. The Triple-A FIPs look great (sub-3.00 in both 2007 and 2008).

Gio Gonzalez (Starter)

W	L	ERA	TBF	IP	Hit	HR	SO	BB	HBP	3-Year	Reliability
7	9	5.09	656	147	142	23	120	84	7	-0.14	Very High

The strikeouts are great, but the walks are just appalling. Watching a guy with a curveball that good pitch so poorly is torturous; the control problems have been with him throughout the minors and they seem unlikely to go away. It's not to say that he won't be a good pitcher one day, but he's on a team that might have better options in 18 months. His stay in Oakland might be short.

Vincent Mazzaro (Starter)

W	L	ERA	TBF	IP	Hit	HR	SO	BB	HBP	3-Year	Reliability
6	11	5.68	684	149	177	17	58	71	13	-0.72	Very High

Although his ERAs in A-ball never looked shiny, he always had a nice strikeout/groundball combination. Last year, he slashed his walk rate from 4.2 to 2.4 per nine innings while moving up to Triple-A. Let's wait to see if he sustains that improvement into 2009; if so, he could slot in very nicely behind Brett Anderson and Trevor Cahill.

Henry Alberto Rodriguez (Starter)

W	L	ERA	TBF	IP	Hit	HR	SO	BB	HBP	3-Year	Reliability
5	7	5.41	523	112	114	12	85	82	5	-0.77	Average

Here's a cautionary tale for prospect-rankers. In 2007, Rodriguez pitched almost 100 innings for Class A Kane County with 9.6 K/9 and 5.2 BB/9. Trevor Cahill in 2007 at Class A Kane County chucked 105 innings with 10 K/9 and 3.4 BB/9. Cahill had the better numbers, but Rodriguez was lighting up radar guns with a high-90s fastball. You'd forgive prospect hounds, then, for ranking them as near-equivalents going into 2008. A year later, Cahill is one of the best prospects in baseball and Henry Rodriguez is unlikely to crack many top-100 lists. Flameout or flamethrower? Neither is out of the question, although his future is likely in the bullpen.

Huston Street (Reliever)

W	L	ERA	TBF	IP	Hit	HR	SO	BB	HBP	3-Year	Reliability
5	3	3.68	285	68	62	7	68	22	2	+0.04	Low

The problem with closers is that, no matter how minor, their struggles—or bad luck—are magnified because late leads, and therefore games, are lost. Street's FIP for the last four years: 2.62, 2.61, 2.70, 3.32. Last year was the first year that he really struggled, and he wasn't all that bad. He went through a rough patch last year that coincided with a period where his slider didn't have its typical bite. Correlation isn't causation, but it was a data point nevertheless. In any event, the slider was back by the end of the year, and that's a strong projection. A word of caution: Street is entering arbitration, and arbitrators tend to view closers separately from relievers. While H's a good value right now, he may not be in a few years.

Brad Ziegler (Reliever)

W	L	ERA	TBF	IP	Hit	HR	SO	BB	HBP	3-Year	Reliability
4	4	4.41	328	75	81	8	36	29	4	+0.28	High

A submariner who induces grounder after grounder, Ziegler had a run of bad luck to start his career: He was drafted and then cut by the Phillies, pitched in an independent league, signed with the A's, fractured his skull, converted from traditional overhand pitcher to submarine freakshow, and fractured his skull again. Finally called up to the majors last year, he got some national press when he registered 39 consecutive scoreless innings to start his career, shattering the record of 25. The projection is obviously not a fan of his, but his groundballing tendencies dovetail nicely with Oakland's infield defense. Like most submariners, he struggles against opposite-handed batters.

Philadelphia Phillies

by Eric Seidman of Fangraphs (fangraphs.com)

2009 Phillies Projections

Record: 87-75
Division Rank/Games Behind: 2nd by one game
Runs Scored: 841, 1st in the league
Runs Allowed: 794, 14th in the league
Park Factor: 1.02, a hitter's park

What Happened Last Year?

What happened with the Phillies in 2008? Hmm... well, they won their first World Series since 1980. That happened! The 2008 team, for the most part, stayed incredibly healthy, losing only a few players for a short period of time. The Charlie Manuel Gang also bore witness to the resurrection of Brad Lidge, who recorded 41 saves in 41 opportunities. Though the task of winning a second division title did not prove easy, everyone on the team contributed—even So Taguchi—making it possible for the Phillies to edge out the Mets once more.

Offensively, the Phillies were stellar, led by Chase Utley, Pat Burrell and Ryan Howard, and featuring nice under-the-radar performances from Jayson Werth and Shane Victorino. Jimmy Rollins missed time to an injury and was league average offensively, but he was statistically rated the best shortstop in baseball defensively. Utley ranked atop all second baseman in the defensive metrics, giving the Phillies the best gloves up the middle in the league. Only the Rays, the team they would later play in the World Series, were better defensively, all told.

The starting rotation struggled at times, but Cole Hamels delivered another great year. Jamie Moyer proved incredibly consistent and durable, putting together his best season in a while. And post-demotion Brett Myers looked untouchable. Acquiring Joe Blanton allowed the team to move Kyle Kendrick and Adam Eaton out of the rotation, which is arguably more productive than the performance of Blanton himself. And the bullpen ... well, as John Walsh showed in the *2008 THT Annual*, the sextet of Lidge, Ryan Madson, J.C. Romero, Chad Durbin, Clay Condrey, and Rudy Seanez vastly outperformed their projections to become the best in the bigs.

The 2008 Philadelphia Phillies combined extremely solid defense with some career years and luck in the health department en route to a championship. Sometimes those three factors can be more important to a team's chances than pure talent and ability.

Players Lost:

Remarkably, only an Alfonseca-handful of players were not under contract or control at the season's end, and half of these players were not major contributors. Tom Gordon, Seanez, Taguchi, Moyer, Scott Eyre and Burrell all became free agents. The team had no intentions of bringing back Gordon, Seanez or Taguchi, so these are not considered tough losses. Eyre quickly resigned a one-year deal following the season. Moyer resigned to the tune of for two years, leaving Burrell as the only truly productive player not under contract who will be missed in 2009.

Players Acquired:

With 80 percent of the team returning, there were not many holes to fill in the offseason. The first two trades of the Ruben Amaro Jr. era were fringe moves. First, he traded Greg Golson to the Rangers for John Mayberry, and he followed that up by swapping Jason Jaramillo for Ronny Paulino of the Pirates. Seanez was then replaced with Chan Ho Park, leaving only Burrell's spot vacant. The team did not offer Pat the Bat arbitration, given that his likely salary would vastly exceed his fair market value, but then replaced him with Raul Ibanez. While Ibanez is a nice hitter, Amaro's reasoning dealt with improving defensively at the position. Via several defensive metrics, Burrell and Ibanez have been the two worst left fielders defensively over the last three seasons.

Management Is:

When Pat Gillick took over the reins as GM in 2006, many expected an immediate firing of Charlie Manuel. After all, Uncle Charlie did not seem to be too smart a manager and, with Gillick's authoritative way of running the show, bringing in his own guy made sense. Gillick stuck with Manuel, the ultimate player's manager, who ended up fitting his style perfectly. While the impact of a manager on a team likely is not as important as many make it out to be, the players absolutely love playing for Manuel. So, after the Phils won the division in 2007, Gillick signed Manuel to a two-year extension through the 2009 season. Following a championship in 2008, he got an extension on the previous deal, keeping him in red pinstripes through 2011.

Manuel is an excellent handler of personalities and his in-game strategies leave little to be desired. With Ibanez now in the fold, it will be interesting how he assembles his lineup. Realistically, the only right-handed threat is Werth, making a potential lineup of Rollins, Victorino, Utley, Howard and Ibanez a left-handed heavy No. 1-5. Rollins and Victorino are switch-hitters, but against a right hander, this gives the Phillies five lefties to start the game.

Gillick retired following the championship win, handing the title to Amaro, a former player and assistant to both him and Ed Wade. Amaro competed with scout extraordinaire Mike Arbuckle for the position. After that decision, Arbuckle left for a more prominent role in Kansas City.

After Amaro's first two moves, small victories in acquiring Mayberry and Paulino, he angered many Phillies fans by not offering arbitration to Burrell. This seemed like the first of many slaps in the face to Burrell, whose consistent offensive production over the last four seasons from the right side of the plate has been important. Amaro said he wanted to improve defensively at the position, which is understandable, but then completely thrown out the window when considering he replaced Burrell with Ibanez. Via Ultimate Zone Rating, from 2006-2008, Burrell is the third worst left fielder; Ibanez is the second worst.

Otherwise, how Amaro and the team handle the potential for 10 or more prominent players eligible for arbitration will be interesting to see. Hamels should be locked up to a long-term deal and Howard should not be; both have been linked to such negotiations. The Phillies won the World Series in 2008, and should field a decent team once more in 2009, but the Amaro era did not get off to a blistering start.

The Minor League System Is:

One of the trademarks of a Gillick team is talented veterans at the major league level and a barren farm system, mostly from dealing prospects for veterans. Gillick resisted this urge while in Philadelphia, leaving the average farm system mostly intact. Carlos Carrasco, a right-handed pitcher with a plus fastball, is considered the team's best prospect, and could have been used to net the Phils many a talented player at the trading deadline last season. Carrasco should compete for the fifth starter's spot in spring training with fellow prospect J.A. Happ, but if the past examples of the Phillies poorly handling their prospects is any indication, Carrasco could spend the whole year in Triple-A.

Catcher Lou Marson is widely considered the team's next best prospect. With Carlos Ruiz, Chris Coste and Paulino competing for two catching spots, it seems likely that Marson, too, will begin the year in the minor leagues—another questionable decision. There is absolutely no reason Ruiz should be guaranteed a starting job while Marson has no idea about his status.

After these two, and middle infielder Jason Donald, the system is still pretty barren. Arbuckle may have done well drafting from 1997-2002, but he has largely missed lately. Rounding out the top five, though, are Kyle Drabek—son of former major league pitcher Doug—and outfielder Michael Taylor. The Phillies' farm system is not anything to get overly excited about.

Due For a Change:

The 2008 Phillies did not necessarily overly benefit from lucky performances, but rather from health. Virtually nobody missed extended periods of time, which kept Manuel from having to play replacement players. One example of a breakout season bound for regression is Lidge's. He was a perfect 41 for 41 in save opportunities last season, but looked capable of faltering in at least half of them. He rarely throws his slider for strikes, and if hitters lay off the pitch, they can wait for a 94-mph fastball that is not anything they have not seen before. Given the propensity for home runs at Citizen's Bank Park and his extremely low HR/FB percentage in 2008, it is safe to say that he will not produce another amazing season. This is not to say that Lidge could not be effective—I fully expect him to be—but the late-inning dominance of last season should be slightly diminished.

Another example is Chad Durbin, who went from below-average starter to bullpen savior last season, posting a 2.87 ERA in 71 games. Durbin began to struggle toward the end of the year, as he wore down. The projections for 2009 are not terribly optimistic for Durbin, and as we saw the last two seasons, an effective and stable bullpen can be the difference between the division title and a flight home in October. The Phillies should not experience extreme regressions on offense, or even in the rotation, but several members of their bullpen overachieved in 2008 and should come back down to Earth in 2009.

Reasons to be Optimistic:

Virtually the entire team that won the World Series will be returning, and, with the exception of Burrell, no major contributors to that success were lost to free agency. The Phillies still have the best fielding shortstop-second base combo in baseball, and Pedro Feliz, one of the best fielding third basemen over the last four years. In the outfield, Ibanez is a poor defender, but Victorino is a fantastic player still improving in CF and

Werth will have a full season's worth of plate appearances to build on his 20-20 season. Offensively, the Phillies have been potent in the recent past and this looks to continue in 2009. Howard will likely improve a bit, but the real question will be if Ibanez really can replace Burrell's offensive production.

The Phils didn't upgrade the rotation to the level of CC Sabathia, A.J. Burnett, or Derek Lowe, but the team will start the year with four guaranteed durable starters in Hamels, Myers, Moyer, and Blanton, with the fifth spot open to Happ, Kendrick, Carrasco or Park.

With most of the same players returning next season, the confidence factor will loom large as well. Many players said that now that they knew they could win, it was easier and less stressful to play.

Reasons to be Pessimistic:

Utley and Feliz underwent offseason surgery, with their timetables indefinite. Utley could return in May, or not until June or July if complications persist. Losing one of the 10 best players in the sport for any amount of time will hurt the team. The Phillies have struggled in April over the last four or five seasons, and while it is not realistic to replace Utley's contributions, they need to mitigate the loss if they want to be competitive after the season's first month. Otherwise, the only real reason for this fan to be pessimistic is wondering how Manuel will handle this year's team: Will he bat lefty after lefty after lefty? Will he realize Ibanez, like Burrell, needs a defensive replacement in the late innings? Will Ruiz be pulled if he stinks offensively, as he did last season?

Our Favorite Phillies Blogs:

Crashburn Alley (http://www.crashburnalley.com)
Beer Leaguer (http://beerleaguer.typepadcom)
The Good Phight (http://www.thegoodphight.com)
Todd Zolecki's Philadelphia Inquirer blog, The Phillies Zone (http://www.philly.com/philly/blogs/phillies_zone)

Still Left to Do:

Amaro said he's finished shopping this winter, and with virtually an entire team assembled, there is not realistically anything left to do. Adding another starting pitcher would be nice, given the relative uncertainty surrounding the fifth spot and given pitchers' susceptibility to injuries.

Most Likely Team Outcomes:

Utley is probably the most underrated and underappreciated player in baseball, and his time lost in April will loom large on the Phillies' success in 2009. Back in 2007, Tadahito Iguchi filled in admirably while Utley missed time, but he was not even good enough to hold down a major league job the next year, and the other replacements are an untested Donald and the below-average-hitting Eric Bruntlett. With that in mind, the Phillies are probably an 84-87 win team. With Utley in the lineup, the Phillies are bumped up to an 88-90 win team. If he misses two months, it is not likely that the team is going to be playoff-bound. Utley is the key component to the team, and his time absent will determine its fate.

Player Projections

Batters

Eric Bruntlett (Shortstop)

PA	R	H	2B	3B	HR	RBI	SO	BB	SB	CS	BA	OBP	SLG	OPS	3-Year	Fielding	Reliability
329	37	72	14	2	3	25	54	33	11	1	.251	.332	.345	.677	-0.03	C	Average

Bruntlett is the prototypical no-hit, above-average-fielding utility player. He served as Pat Burrell's late-inning replacement most of the season and filled in when Jimmy Rollins went down with an injury. His only true fantasy value will occur if Chase Utley misses significant time; he is likely heading the pack of potential replacements.

Pat Burrell (Left Field)

PA	R	H	2B	3B	HR	RBI	SO	BB	SB	CS	BA	OBP	SLG	OPS	3-Year	Fielding	Reliability
574	77	123	27	1	29	88	124	93	0	1	.260	.382	.505	.887	-0.03	F	Very High

A three-true-outcomes hitter (one with a high percentage of walks, strikeouts, and home runs), Burrell has another one or two good years left before his skills vastly decline. He has been incredibly consistent over the past four seasons, making his projected OBP and SLG all the more attractive. One has to wonder, though, if playing away from the friendly confines of Citizens Bank Park will affect his offensive output.

Chris Coste (Catcher)

PA	R	H	2B	3B	HR	RBI	SO	BB	SB	CS	BA	OBP	SLG	OPS	3-Year	Fielding	Reliability
360	38	85	17	0	9	42	60	20	1	1	.259	.311	.393	.704	—	D	Average

Coste, otherwise known as "The 33-Year-Old-Rookie," has become a popular figure in Philadelphia over the last two seasons. He is not a great defender and his offense declined last season as well. With Lou Marson waiting in the wings and the acquisition of Ronny Paulino, Coste's playing time likely will not meet his projections.

Greg Dobbs (Third Base)

PA	R	H	2B	3B	HR	RBI	SO	BB	SB	CS	BA	OBP	SLG	OPS	3-Year	Fielding	Reliability
334	41	86	17	2	10	44	59	24	3	0	.282	.336	.449	.785	-0.01	D	Average

The best pinch-hitter in baseball, Dobbs looks to build on his 2008 success, perhaps with an extended role. This may come in the form of a quasi-platoon at third base with Pedro Feliz. It is not likely that this righty-masher will become a full-time starter, but if Feliz goes down with an injury, Dobbs is an excellent bet to replace and exceed his production.

Jason Donald (Shortstop)

PA	R	H	2B	3B	HR	RBI	SO	BB	SB	CS	BA	OBP	SLG	OPS	3-Year	Fielding	Reliability
459	53	103	18	4	11	50	101	38	6	3	.251	.321	.395	.716	+0.04	D	Average

Donald exploded onto the scene at the Olympics, making other major league teams take notice. At shortstop, he has a significant roadblock in front of him in the form of Jimmy Rollins, but he could prove to be a useful role player. With Chase Utley's surgery, Donald could garner some starts at the beginning of the season, despite his below-average projection.

Pedro Feliz (Third Base)

PA	R	H	2B	3B	HR	RBI	SO	BB	SB	CS	BA	OBP	SLG	OPS	3-Year	Fielding	Reliability
494	54	116	23	2	17	64	70	31	1	1	.255	.301	.426	.727	-0.06	B	Very High

What Feliz may lack in offensive production he more than makes up for with the glove. His primary value comes on the defensive end, which is why most consider any offense he adds to be a bonus. His back injury this offseason could hinder his availability or force him into a platoon with Greg Dobbs.

Gregory Golson (Center Field)

PA	R	H	2B	3B	HR	RBI	SO	BB	SB	CS	BA	OBP	SLG	OPS	3-Year	Fielding	Reliability
554	57	122	20	4	13	56	156	19	13	3	.233	.262	.361	.623	+0.04	C	High

The Phillies unloaded Golson, once thought to have five-tool potential, to the Rangers this offseason for John Mayberry Jr. Golson seems to be another Chris Roberson or Michael Bourn: a speedster who plays decent defense but cannot hit a lick. If he does anything in 2009, it will involve replacing an outfielder late in the game or pinch-running for a slowpoke.

Ryan Howard (First Base)

PA	R	H	2B	3B	HR	RBI	SO	BB	SB	CS	BA	OBP	SLG	OPS	3-Year	Fielding	Reliability
618	93	147	26	1	45	120	174	85	1	0	.281	.384	.592	.976	-0.03	D	Very High

Howard is one of the more curious players in the game, capable of masking flaws with a barrage of home runs. His 2009 projection, in terms of OBP/SLG, looks a lot like the 2008 season of Ryan Ludwick. If Howard can produce like that, he would vastly exceed his 2008 campaign's value and hop back up amongst the elite, perhaps even justifiably earning MVP votes. His slumps will annoy the heck out of you, but he has proven himself as a 45-plus homer run hitter and there are, well, just about none of them left.

Tadahito Iguchi (Second Base)

PA	R	H	2B	3B	HR	RBI	SO	BB	SB	CS	BA	OBP	SLG	OPS	3-Year	Fielding	Reliability
420	48	99	19	1	7	41	79	39	9	1	.265	.335	.377	.712	-0.05	C	High

Iguchi filled in admirably for Chase Utley in 2007, though he did not receive much playing time after rejoining the team in 2008. He was then optioned to the Phillies' Triple-A affiliate, where he will likely spend most of the year. With Utley's injury and indefinite timetable for recovery, Iguchi may end up as the starting keystone cornerman on Opening Day, but he seems to be at the end of his career.

Jason Jaramillo (Catcher)

PA	R	H	2B	3B	HR	RBI	SO	BB	SB	CS	BA	OBP	SLG	OPS	3-Year	Fielding	Reliability
461	49	104	18	1	11	50	87	37	1	1	.251	.318	.379	.697	+0.07	—	High

Jaramillo seemingly has been in the farm system forever, and with Lou Marson ahead of him on the depth chart, was not going anywhere. So, the team sent Jason to the Pirates for Ronny Paulino. Jaramillo never will be a superstar, but he could earn major league playing time with a rebuilding team like the Bucs.

Geoff Jenkins (Right Field)

PA	R	H	2B	3B	HR	RBI	SO	BB	SB	CS	BA	OBP	SLG	OPS	3-Year	Fielding	Reliability
401	47	95	19	1	14	53	89	33	2	1	.264	.332	.439	.771	-0.05	C	High

The original reasoning behind signing Geoff Jenkins last year involved platooning him in right field with Jayson Werth. When Werth established himself as a dynamite player and full-time regular, Jenkins was relegated to the bench. As a bench player, and one with injuries to boot, Jenkins was not terribly effective in 2008. The acquisition of Raul Ibanez will further diminish his playing time, meaning 360 at-bats as a Phillie is not likely.

Lou Marson (Catcher)

PA	R	H	2B	3B	HR	RBI	SO	BB	SB	CS	BA	OBP	SLG	OPS	3-Year	Fielding	Reliability
498	52	111	20	2	6	45	98	54	2	3	.254	.340	.351	.691	+0.09	C	High

He's the top hitting prospect in the Phillies system, and many fans are calling for Marson to be the new starting catcher. This job likely still will belong to Carlos Ruiz come Opening Day, but a competent team would have Marson on the roster. If Ruiz starts to struggle, Marson could earn himself some serious playing time. Known more for his patience than power (.433 OBP/.416 SLG in 2008), Marson is not going to smash too many long balls but he should find himself on base much more than any other catching options for the team.

Jimmy Rollins (Shortstop)

PA	R	H	2B	3B	HR	RBI	SO	BB	SB	CS	BA	OBP	SLG	OPS	3-Year	Fielding	Reliability
610	90	157	33	9	17	71	66	47	35	3	.285	.344	.471	.815	-0.02	C	Very High

Injuries slowed Rollins in 2008 on the heels of his MVP season. The .285/.344/.470 projection seems dead on, which makes him extremely valuable since shortstop is a premium position. Add in the potential for 10 triples, 20 home runs and 35 stolen bases, and there are not going to be many more valuable fantasy shortstops than Jimmy Rollins next season. His defense is equally stellar; he ranks as the top shortstop in 2008 via the plus/minus system.

Carlos Ruiz (Catcher)

PA	R	H	2B	3B	HR	RBI	SO	BB	SB	CS	BA	OBP	SLG	OPS	3-Year	Fielding	Reliability
414	46	95	20	1	8	44	52	41	3	2	.264	.344	.391	.735	-0.03	C	High

Ruiz, while developing a reputation for being a solid defender and handling a pitching staff well, had a putrid year with the bat in 2008. With several options available for the Phillies at the position, Ruiz's leash may be rather short. He will start the season as the everyday catcher, but if his offense does not rebound, expect to see someone else serving as the Phillies' backstop.

Matt Stairs (Left Field)

PA	R	H	2B	3B	HR	RBI	SO	BB	SB	CS	BA	OBP	SLG	OPS	3-Year	Fielding	Reliability
395	49	94	18	1	15	55	76	43	1	1	.272	.355	.460	.815	—	D	High

Forever entrenched in Phillies lore for his mammoth home run against Jonathan Broxton, Stairs will return as a lefty power threat off the bench. His playing time is going to be limited with Dobbs ahead of him on the bench depth chart. He will be a valuable member of the Phillies bench, but if he gets significant playing time, it will be as a DH if a team pries him from the Phillies near the deadline.

So Taguchi (Right Field)

PA	R	H	2B	3B	HR	RBI	SO	BB	SB	CS	BA	OBP	SLG	OPS	3-Year	Fielding	Reliability
263	29	63	12	1	2	23	35	20	6	2	.271	.334	.357	.691	—	B	Low

Taguchi was brought in to serve as a defensive replacement and pinch-runner. He proved to be nothing special on the basepaths and took poor routes on balls in the outfield. Therefore, it came as no surprise that the Phillies decided not to bring him back. At 39 and lacking the skills that once made him effective, it is time for Taguchi to hang up the cleats.

Chase Utley (Second Base)

PA	R	H	2B	3B	HR	RBI	SO	BB	SB	CS	BA	OBP	SLG	OPS	3-Year	Fielding	Reliability
619	90	165	37	4	27	95	99	54	11	2	.305	.383	.538	.921	-0.03	A+	Very High

The best offensive second baseman in baseball? Check. The best defensive second baseman over the last three years via UZR? Check. You get the picture. Chase Utley is one of the top 10 most valuable players in the sport, and looks to produce another extremely stellar campaign in 2009. Unfortunately, the raw numbers might not be all that spectacular given his offseason surgery and indefinite recovery timetable. He may not be in action until May or June, but he is still the best second baseman in the game.

Shane Victorino (Center Field)

PA	R	H	2B	3B	HR	RBI	SO	BB	SB	CS	BA	OBP	SLG	OPS	3-Year	Fielding	Reliability
542	73	139	25	5	11	56	65	38	26	5	.286	.346	.425	.771	-0.03	A	Very High

Before the 2008 postseason, Shane Victorino was not a household name outside of Philadelphia and perhaps New York. After setting the Phillies' postseason record for RBIs, however, it comes as no surprise that the phones have been ringing inquiring about his services. He is a fantastic defender with a great arm, an excellent baserunner, and even a hitter with some pop in his bat to boot. His switch-hitting makes him even more valuable, and, at 28, he still has a few more solid years in him.

Jayson Werth (Right Field)

PA	R	H	2B	3B	HR	RBI	SO	BB	SB	CS	BA	OBP	SLG	OPS	3-Year	Fielding	Reliability
437	61	104	18	2	19	61	105	52	13	2	.275	.364	.484	.848	-0.03	A	Average

Werth, a first-round draft pick in 1997, finally broke out in 2008 as an everyday player. He absolutely demolishes lefties, and is steadily improving against righties as well. After he established himself as a 20-20 player in 2008, there is little reason to think he could not repeat the feat. Playing a full year in right field, without platooning, 25-25 would be a reasonable expectation for Werth. Chase Utley may be the most underrated player in baseball, but Werth may be the most under-the-radar.

Pitchers

Joe Blanton (Starter)

W	L	ERA	TBF	IP	Hit	HR	SO	BB	HBP	3-Year	Reliability
10	10	4.56	788	183	206	23	109	53	5	+0.37	Very High

The "big" midseason pickup for the Phillies in 2008, Blanton, for the most part, failed to live up to his innings-eating moniker. His performance improved in September and October, but Blanton's issues all seemingly stem from control. He is not going to strike out many hitters, but if he limits free passes, there is no reason he could not amass 200 innings of 4.30 ERA baseball again.

Clay Condrey (Reliever)

W	L	ERA	TBF	IP	Hit	HR	SO	BB	HBP	3-Year	Reliability
4	4	4.56	304	69	80	7	34	23	3	+0.25	Average

One of the better mop-up men of the 2008 season, Condrey will return in a similar role in 2009. His playing time largely depends on where Chan Ho Park ends up on the team. If Park earns the fifth rotation spot, expect Condrey to see plenty of long relief outings. Should Park be relegated to the bullpen, he would likely get those, leaving Condrey's pitching limited to blowouts.

Chad Durbin (Reliever)

W	L	ERA	TBF	IP	Hit	HR	SO	BB	HBP	3-Year	Reliability
4	6	4.71	374	86	90	12	54	34	4	+0.21	Very High

Durbin pitched himself to a career year in 2008. He will be back as the seventh-inning pitcher for the Phillies, likely platooning with either Scott Eyre or J.C. Romero in his role. Though Durbin's BABIP in 2008 did not portend too much luck on balls in play, his 77 percent rate of stranding runners is very likely to regress. He probably will not revert to the pre-2008 Durbin, but his performance moving forward will be a bit different than what Phillies fans saw last season.

Adam Eaton (Starter)

W	L	ERA	TBF	IP	Hit	HR	SO	BB	HBP	3-Year	Reliability
5	10	5.93	613	134	165	24	72	55	8	+0.26	Very High

Few people understood why Adam Eaton was given the lucrative three-year deal he received prior to 2007. Even more people are struggling to grasp why he is still taking up an active roster spot. His bright spots have been few and far between, and with four rotation spots committed, the fifth likely will go to either J.A. Happ, Kyle Kendrick or Carlos Carrasco. This leaves Eaton out of the loop, and with the Phils' full and effective bullpen, he's out of luck with this team.

Scott Eyre (Reliever)

W	L	ERA	TBF	IP	Hit	HR	SO	BB	HBP	3-Year	Reliability
3	2	4.18	202	47	44	6	45	22	2	—	Low

While the Joe Blanton move near the trading deadline garnered publicity in Philadelphia, the more important move involved acquiring Scott Eyre from the Cubs. That allowed J.C. Romero to become more of one-and-two-batter specialist, stabilizing the bullpen. Eyre will be the lefty responsible for longer outings out of the Phillies bullpen. He may not be pitching too much longer, but his projection makes him a pretty valuable reliever.

Tom Gordon (Reliever)

W	L	ERA	TBF	IP	Hit	HR	SO	BB	HBP	3-Year	Reliability
3	2	4.19	211	49	47	6	40	20	2	—	Very Low

Tom Gordon's tenure in Philadelphia did not go as planned. Injuries and spurts of ineffectiveness kept him from contributing at the level he would have preferred. He will not be returning to the Phillies, and at 38 and with his injury history, he will be lucky to latch on elsewhere. He could be a good bargain; he can still bring the heat and would not cost much.

Cole Hamels (Starter)

W	L	ERA	TBF	IP	Hit	HR	SO	BB	HBP	3-Year	Reliability
12	9	3.88	791	192	183	27	166	50	4	+0.06	Very High

Fresh off his NLCS and World Series MVP wins, the 24-year old lefty phenom will look to build upon his past success in 2009. He couples a 92-mph fastball with a filthy change-up, occasionally mixing in some curveballs. Toward the end of the season, he even unveiled a two-seam fastball, according to the PITCHf/x data. All that could prevent him from continued greatness is injuries, something he has dealt with his entire career.

J.A. Happ (Starter)

W	L	ERA	TBF	IP	Hit	HR	SO	BB	HBP	3-Year	Reliability
7	9	5.19	642	144	149	24	127	72	5	+0.19	Very High

After a brief albeit unsuccessful spot start in 2007, Happ dominated the minor leagues in 2008, earning another shot. In eight appearances, four of which were starts, he looked poised and posted some nice numbers. He'll be part of the battle for the fifth spot of the Phillies' rotation. With his mix of experience and better peripherals than Kyle Kendrick, he has a more than solid chance.

Kyle Kendrick (Starter)

W	L	ERA	TBF	IP	Hit	HR	SO	BB	HBP	3-Year	Reliability
7	10	5.54	704	157	191	24	63	55	9	-0.40	Very High

After a deceivingly good rookie season, Kendrick severely regressed in 2008. He doesn't strike hitters out, issues too many free passes, and gives up long balls with the greatest of ease. This is not a recipe for success. If Kendrick can learn a new pitch to complement the sinker, he could experience some more success in the major leagues, but until then, it is unlikely he will be on the major league team.

Brad Lidge (Reliever)

W	L	ERA	TBF	IP	Hit	HR	SO	BB	HBP	3-Year	Reliability
5	3	3.55	297	70	59	7	82	32	3	+0.20	Low

Make no mistake about it: The Phillies do not win the World Series in 2008 without Brad Lidge. By holding down the fort in the last stages, Lidge basically ensured that the Phillies were playing eight-inning games. His home run rate should regress and he isn't going to go another full season without blowing a save, but with the number of wins the Phillies are projected to have, he is a good bet to have another solid year.

Ryan Madson (Reliever)

W	L	ERA	TBF	IP	Hit	HR	SO	BB	HBP	3-Year	Reliability
4	4	4.30	328	76	81	8	57	27	3	+0.33	High

Madson always has had potential, but down the stretch in 2008, he seemed to harness his abilities into something special. He pitched his way into a permanent eighth-inning setup role, somehow began throwing 96-97 mph, and is now being compared to a young Mariano Rivera by agent Scott Boras. Lidge and Madson will be linked, as Madson will hold the key to how many save opportunities Lidge receives. If Madson can continue to throw as hard as he did during September and October, there is no reason he should not crush his projection.

Jamie Moyer (Starter)

W	L	ERA	TBF	IP	Hit	HR	SO	BB	HBP	3-Year	Reliability
9	11	4.73	775	179	197	26	102	56	7	—	Very High

Fresh off his best season since 2003, Moyer inked a two-year deal with the Phillies that will keep him employed until the age of 48. His 2008 campaign was somewhat luck-enhanced, and Moyer's success from here on largely hinges on the plate umpires. If he does not get borderline calls, as he did in the NLDS and NLCS, Moyer does not have the stuff to stay in the game. He will provide some stability to the rotation, but is definitely a risk.

Brett Myers (Starter)

W	L	ERA	TBF	IP	Hit	HR	SO	BB	HBP	3-Year	Reliability
9	10	4.42	736	172	177	25	143	60	5	+0.35	Very High

Brett Myers in 2008 can be broken up into two segments: pre-demotion and post-demotion. Before being sent to the minor leagues, Myers was the definition of replacement level, if not worse. Upon returning, he seemed virtually unhittable, even outpitching teammate Hamels for a stretch. At 28, the time he has to turn his potential into full-on success is diminishing, but perhaps the confidence he gained after the demotion will carry over, full force, into 2009.

J.C. Romero (Reliever)

W	L	ERA	TBF	IP	Hit	HR	SO	BB	HBP	3-Year	Reliability
4	3	3.82	270	62	55	5	48	37	3	+0.21	Low

Romero has always struggled with walking hitters, and always will, but using him in small doses can be very effective. The acquisition of Scott Eyre relegated Romero to a one- or two-batter specialist role, as opposed to extended seventh- inning duty. He has a filthy slider and a plus fastball, and as long as Eyre remains effective, Romero can remain a specialist. If Eyre falters, he will be pressed into a larger role, which could inflate his numbers.

Rudy Seanez (Reliever)

W	L	ERA	TBF	IP	Hit	HR	SO	BB	HBP	3-Year	Reliability
3	3	4.30	246	57	56	7	44	25	2	—	Low

Martial arts enthusiast Rudy Seanez proved to be a great under-the-radar pickup by Pat Gillick in 2008. He did not pitch in high leverage situations, but proved to be a much better back-end-of-the-bullpen pitcher than other teams have. He is not going to return to the team in 2009, and at 38, may not have much left.

Pittsburgh Pirates

by Pat Lackey of Where Have You Gone, Andy Van Slyke? (whygavs.com)

2009 Pirates Projections

Record: 72-90
Division Rank/Games Behind: Last, by 15 games
Runs Scored: 687, 15th in the league
Runs Allowed: 779, 13th in the league
Park Factor: .98, a pitcher's park

What Happened Last Year:

For the first time in a long while, the Pirates mustered some offense in the first half of 2008, led by one of the best slugging outfield combinations in the National League in Nate McLouth, Jason Bay and Xavier Nady. Unfortunately, the pitching was terrible (the Pirates' 884 runs allowed were the worst in the National League by a good measure) and when Bay and Nady were dealt in a rebuilding effort, the Pirates suffered through a disastrous August and September. In the end, they won 67 games—exactly the number they've won in three of the past four seasons (the other year they won 68).

Players Lost from Last Year's Team:

Bay, Nady and Damaso Marte were lost at last year's trade deadline; Jason Michaels, Luis Rivas and Doug Mientkiewicz are likely gone to free agency; and to this point, general manager Neal Huntington has spent most of his offseason trying to trade Jack Wilson.

Players Acquired:

Andy LaRoche, Brandon Moss, Craig Hansen, Jeff Karstens, Daniel McCutchen and Ross Ohlendorf all were acquired around the trade deadline last year. Ramon Vazquez was signed as a utility man shortly after the winter meetings.

Management Is:

Attempting to sift through the wreckage of the Dave Littlefield era. The common joke in Pittsburgh is that the Pirates have been rebuilding since 1993 and the trades of Bay and Nady indicate another rebuilding phase. The truth is that since about 1998, the Pirates' front office has been content to shoot for 70-75 wins each year and avoid the embarrassment of losing 100 games, rather than actually trying to rebuild the franchise into a winner.

In his first year, Huntington made some serious strides toward actually rebuilding the farm system that had atrophied badly under Littlefield. This sort of thing is never fun and Huntington took a considerable amount of flak for the Bay and Nady trades, but he does seem to at least have the right idea, especially when it comes to the draft and signing players from Latin America.

The Minor League System Is:

Getting better. At this point last year, Steve Pearce was arguably the Pirates' second-best prospect. In a year, Huntington has added Jose Tabata (who bounced back nicely in Double-A after the Pirates traded for him) and Pedro Alvarez. Combined with Andrew McCutchen, that makes a very nice trio at the top of the Pirates' prospect list. Perhaps even more encouragingly, Huntington paid out above-slot bonuses to sign several late round picks (Wesley Freeman, Robbie Grossman, Quinton Miller) in June's draft.

Due For a Change of Scenery:

Guys like Wilson, Freddy Sanchez, John Grabow and Adam LaRoche won't be around long enough to see Huntington's plan come to fruition, which means they're all possible trade targets. Wilson and Grabow are almost certain to go at some point. Nate McLouth and Paul Maholm are drawing interest from other teams, but Huntington doesn't seem likely to move them unless he gets an offer close to what he thinks they're worth.

Reasons to be Optimistic:

In terms of the 2009 season, the pitching staff simply can't be worse than it was in 2008. Ian Snell and Tom Gorzelanny are both much better than they pitched in 2008, while the addition of Ohlendorf, Karstens and Daniel McCutchen to the mix gives the Pirates enough depth. That means they can avoid giving 25 starts to pitchers as bad as the disastrous quartet of Phil Dumatrait, John Van Benschoten, Yoslan Herrera and Matt Morris.

Joe Kerrigan replaced Jeff Andrews as pitching coach and immediately hunkered down with videotape to get to know his new staff. He's indicated that his emphasis will be on teaching the young staff how to prepare for games and set hitters up. Essentially, he seems to focus on how to "pitch" instead of "throw." This sort of help may be invaluable for a pitcher like Snell. With a big drop in offensive production expected, an improved pitching staff will be vital if the Pirates want to avoid 100 losses.

Beyond 2009, there are more reasons to be optimistic. As mentioned, Huntington has worked hard to rebuild the minor league system. The team spent in the neighborhood of $9 million on its 2008 draft, went to bat with Scott Boras to get Alvarez signed, is putting the finishing touches on a new baseball academy in the Dominican Republic, and spent more money last year on Latin American signings than ever. All of these seem like common-sense ways for a bad team to get better, but they were sadly ignored in the Littlefield years. Huntington's staff has gone so far as to sign players from South Africa and India in its global search for talent. It's too early to tell if any of these changes are going to result in better players in Pittsburgh, but they're all movements in the right direction.

Reasons to be Pessimistic:

The 2009 Pirates are going to be terrible. After the trade deadline they went 17-37 with the same group that will be taking the field for most of 2009. As a team, they scored only 82 runs in the month of August. Without Bay and Nady, the Pirates are going to need superhuman contributions from the LaRoches to avoid a truly atrocious offense. It's never easy for fans to go into a season with little or no hopes of winning, but that's the situation the Pirates are in again in 2009.

Still Left to Do:

The new front office made some serious strides in its first year, but there's still a long way to go to get the minor league system to the point that it needs to be for the Pirates to be a viable franchise. That road is fraught with plenty of places to misstep, and the Pirates

are going to continue to compile losing seasons. As that happens, attendance will continue to drop precipitously and the fans who remain will likely be very vocal with their displeasure. Whether Bob Nutting will apply pressure from the owner's box to appease the fans with useless free agent signings remains to be seen. All of this is simply to say that the Pirates are still a ways away from where they need to be and there's much that can go wrong on their way there.

Most Likely Team Outcome:

The Pirates are close to a mortal lock for their 17th consecutive losing season, which will set a record for most consecutive losing years by a North American sports franchise. In the past four years, they've won 67, 67, 68 and 67 games. I don't see much of a deviation from that in 2009.

Instead of focusing on the win-loss column, Pirates fans should be keeping an eye on Snell and Gorzelanny to see how they bounce back, on how Andy LaRoche develops after a disastrous 2008, and whether recently acquired players like Moss, Ohlendorf, Karstens and Daniel McCutchen can break through and turn into something other than the disposable bit players they were in the eyes of the Yankees and Red Sox.

Player Projections

Batters

Brian Bixler (Shortstop)

PA	R	H	2B	3B	HR	RBI	SO	BB	SB	CS	BA	OBP	SLG	OPS	3-Year	Fielding	Reliability
491	55	107	16	4	8	42	131	35	14	4	.246	.316	.356	.672	+0.06	D	High

Bixler is probably a career utility infielder who will be miscast as a starting shortstop if Jack Wilson is traded. His projection nails his problem perfectly: He still strikes out a ton. There are also a lot of concerns about his glove and the team seems to like Luis Cruz more.

Luis Cruz (Shortstop)

PA	R	H	2B	3B	HR	RBI	SO	BB	SB	CS	BA	OBP	SLG	OPS	3-Year	Fielding	Reliability
524	46	112	27	1	7	47	64	19	3	3	.229	.261	.331	.592	+0.04	C	Very High

For his first 3,000 minor league plate appearances, Luis Cruz seemed like a guy with no clue at the plate. Suddenly, when promoted to Triple-A by the Pirates toward the end of last year, he exploded to a .325/.347/.483 line. As of this writing, he's hitting nicely in Mexico this winter, but I'd still be willing to wager that the ugly .592 OPS projection is about what he'd do if given a full year in the majors.

Ryan Doumit (Catcher)

PA	R	H	2B	3B	HR	RBI	SO	BB	SB	CS	BA	OBP	SLG	OPS	3-Year	Fielding	Reliability
416	53	112	26	1	15	60	66	29	3	2	.298	.356	.492	.848	0.00	D	Average

After struggling with a slew of injuries and the Pirates' bull-headed refusal to give him significant playing time, Doumit won the starting catching job from Ronny Paulino last spring and produced for the Bucs with his .318/.357/.501 line. His health will always be a big question mark, but if he can stay healthy in 2009 there's no reason to think those numbers will tail off.

Adam LaRoche (First Base)

PA	R	H	2B	3B	HR	RBI	SO	BB	SB	CS	BA	OBP	SLG	OPS	3-Year	Fielding	Reliability
537	68	130	32	2	23	80	116	52	1	1	.272	.343	.492	.835	-0.03	C	Very High

LaRoche very quietly went about having a very good year last year. After his annual April struggle (he had a .505 OPS on the month), he crushed the ball in July and September, slugging over .800 in July and .690 in September. He struggled with injuries all year and played in only 136 games. That kept his counting stats down, but his rate stats showed that 2008 was the second-best year of his career. If he ever figures out how to hit in April, the Pirates might actually have the first baseman they traded for two years ago.

Andy LaRoche (Third Base)

PA	R	H	2B	3B	HR	RBI	SO	BB	SB	CS	BA	OBP	SLG	OPS	3-Year	Fielding	Reliability
435	52	98	19	1	13	53	64	53	3	1	.262	.358	.423	.781	+0.01	B	Very High

After coming to Pittsburgh as the centerpiece of the Jason Bay/Manny Ramirez deal, this LaRoche was putrid. Still, his minor league numbers (especially his K/BB ratio to go with his pretty OPS) indicate that he's going to figure things out eventually. Most projection systems, including this one, seem to agree. At the trade deadline, I would've been horrified at the thought of a .780 OPS from LaRoche next year. Now, I think that'd be a huge step in the right direction.

Andrew McCutchen (Center Field)

PA	R	H	2B	3B	HR	RBI	SO	BB	SB	CS	BA	OBP	SLG	OPS	3-Year	Fielding	Reliability
560	65	132	24	3	9	53	94	46	17	6	.262	.326	.375	.701	+0.09	C	Very High

McCutchen's a small guy but he's got a great swing that should translate well to the big leagues when he gets there. He'll probably start 2009 in Triple-A, but August was his second-best month last year and if he starts well in Indy next April, he'll likely find himself in PNC Park sooner rather than later.

Nate McLouth (Center Field)

PA	R	H	2B	3B	HR	RBI	SO	BB	SB	CS	BA	OBP	SLG	OPS	3-Year	Fielding	Reliability
534	74	129	31	4	19	71	83	49	19	1	.275	.351	.480	.831	+0.01	F	Very High

After years of sharing time in center field with the likes of Chris Duffy and Rajai Davis and Nyjer Morgan, McLouth was given a chance to start and had a breakout season. Because he put up similarly impressive numbers over part of the summer in 2007, it wouldn't be wise to dismiss him as a flash in the pan. I see that his projection is looking for a dip in home run power, but he's quite good at taking aim at the short right field wall in PNC Park and I wouldn't be surprised to see him approach 30 homers again.

Jason Michaels (Right Field)

PA	R	H	2B	3B	HR	RBI	SO	BB	SB	CS	BA	OBP	SLG	OPS	3-Year	Fielding	Reliability
371	40	86	19	1	8	40	69	29	2	1	.257	.317	.392	.709	-0.03	C	High

Jason Michaels quietly had an awful season in Pittsburgh in 2008. I say quietly because he managed 44 RBIs with only 52 hits, which gave the impression that he was hitting better than he was. He signed with Houston as a free agent, but shouldn't be counted on to be anything more than a fourth or fifth outfielder.

Doug Mientkiewicz (First Base)

PA	R	H	2B	3B	HR	RBI	SO	BB	SB	CS	BA	OBP	SLG	OPS	3-Year	Fielding	Reliability
345	38	82	20	1	4	34	43	38	1	1	.273	.357	.387	.744	-0.05	A	Average

Mientkiewicz is well-known for his good glove and as long as he stays at first base (and not at third or in the outfield where the Pirates often played him), that's still true. At this point in his career, though, he might be more valuable for being a cheap, decent bat off of the bench (his OPS has been above league average the last two years). He's a free agent again and while the Pirates seem interested in bringing him back, it seems likely he'll head for greener pastures in 2009.

Nyjer Morgan (Left Field)

PA	R	H	2B	3B	HR	RBI	SO	BB	SB	CS	BA	OBP	SLG	OPS	3-Year	Fielding	Reliability
463	55	110	15	4	0	27	78	26	29	6	.263	.316	.318	.634	-0.02	B	High

Nyjer Morgan is fast. He has no power, he needs his speed to make up for poor judgment in the outfield, and he doesn't have a very good eye at the plate. Still, his speed has the Pirates talking like he's going to start in a corner outfield spot in 2009, which is terrifying. Help us, Andrew McCutchen, you're our only hope.

Brandon Moss (Left Field)

PA	R	H	2B	3B	HR	RBI	SO	BB	SB	CS	BA	OBP	SLG	OPS	3-Year	Fielding	Reliability
475	54	110	25	3	12	55	116	39	3	2	.256	.318	.412	.730	+0.02	B	Very High

Moss was an interesting acquisition in the Bay trade if only because his left-handed swing seems to have the opportunity to develop some power at PNC Park. He still strikes out too much and his on-base skills aren't great, but it's worth the Pirates' time to give him some at-bats and see what happens. He may miss the early part of 2009 recovering from knee surgery, and how that affects him remains to be seen.

Ronny Paulino (Catcher)

PA	R	H	2B	3B	HR	RBI	SO	BB	SB	CS	BA	OBP	SLG	OPS	3-Year	Fielding	Reliability
369	41	93	20	0	8	43	69	29	1	1	.278	.336	.409	.745	+0.01	B	High

I was once told you could judge how well-liked a person was by the number of affectionate nicknames they have. Ronny Paulino had several nicknames in Pittsburgh, but none of them were affectionate. Some called him "Joggin' Ronny" because of the way he generally runs the bases. Other called him "Ronny Ballgame," mocking Jim Tracy's constant proclamations that he was a "gamer." Mostly, everyone's just happy he's been traded somewhere else now, even if the Pirates got precious little from the Phillies in return for a guy who hit .310 as a rookie in 2006.

Steven Pearce (Right Field)

PA	R	H	2B	3B	HR	RBI	SO	BB	SB	CS	BA	OBP	SLG	OPS	3-Year	Fielding	Reliability
533	62	121	29	2	19	69	97	33	8	3	.249	.304	.434	.738	+0.02	C	Very High

After a huge year spanning three minor league levels in 2007, Pearce never settled in at Triple-A in 2008, hitting only 12 home runs and slugging .417. This seemed to turn the front office off of him, with guys like Nyjer Morgan getting playing time in Pittsburgh ahead of him all year. After Brandon Moss's injury, he got some regular playing time and did seem to perk up down the stretch. All four of his big league homers came in September, but he'll likely need a big spring to be considered for a starting spot in the Pittsburgh outfield if Brandon Moss is healthy.

Luis Rivas (Second Base)

PA	R	H	2B	3B	HR	RBI	SO	BB	SB	CS	BA	OBP	SLG	OPS	3-Year	Fielding	Reliability
330	33	73	12	2	5	29	50	21	5	3	.242	.296	.345	.641	-0.03	D	Average

Hell is watching Luis Rivas try to play shortstop.

Freddy Sanchez (Second Base)

PA	R	H	2B	3B	HR	RBI	SO	BB	SB	CS	BA	OBP	SLG	OPS	3-Year	Fielding	Reliability
571	63	159	35	2	8	64	65	27	1	1	.302	.338	.421	.759	-0.03	C	Very High

It's worth noting that despite his huge drop in production, Freddy Sanchez's line-drive percentage went up in 2008. Just as the prediction suggests, that means there's probably a good chance his average, and the rest of his offensive stats accordingly, will go up a bit in 2009.

Jose Tabata (Right Field)

PA	R	H	2B	3B	HR	RBI	SO	BB	SB	CS	BA	OBP	SLG	OPS	3-Year	Fielding	Reliability
476	49	111	18	2	4	39	79	27	9	2	.254	.307	.332	.639	+0.13	C	Average

He started off 2008 in a disastrous fashion for the Yankees' Double-A affiliate in Trenton, which was bad enough to get him shipped to Pittsburgh with three pitchers in the Nady/Marte deal in July. Once he was sent to Altoona, he came alive, reminding people why he was such a highly touted prospect. In 22 games with the Curve, he had 11 extra base hits, only one fewer than in his 79 games with the Thunder. He probably won't see Pittsburgh in 2009, but acquiring him may end up being the steal of the 2008 trade deadline by Neal Huntington.

Ramon Vazquez (Third Base)

PA	R	H	2B	3B	HR	RBI	SO	BB	SB	CS	BA	OBP	SLG	OPS	3-Year	Fielding	Reliability
390	43	89	18	3	6	38	74	41	2	1	.263	.344	.388	.732	-0.04	C	Average

Vazquez brought a career batting line of .251/.319/.343 into 2008, whereupon he inexplicably became competent at the plate. Some disciples of Texas hitting coach Rudy Jaramillo (like Mark DeRosa) have retained their grandeur upon leaving Texas, while others (like Gary Matthews Jr.) have collapsed. Pittsburgh banked on the former and signed him to a two-year contract. Vazquez is an adequate 5th infielder, a stopgap as the strong side of a platoon, and absolutely overstretched as a regular. Versatile but not strong defensively, he'd be a significant step down even from light-hitting Jack Wilson.

Neil Walker (Third Base)

PA	R	H	2B	3B	HR	RBI	SO	BB	SB	CS	BA	OBP	SLG	OPS	3-Year	Fielding	Reliability
556	59	121	27	3	13	59	110	34	7	4	.237	.286	.378	.664	+0.05	B	High

In his first full year at Triple-A, Walker managed only a .280 OBP and showed few signs of adjusting to the level as the year wore on. He's still young, but he's fallen in favor and is likely behind both Pedro Alvarez and Andy LaRoche on the third base prospect depth chart. Even if he does hit in Triple-A this year, another position change may be in his future.

Jack Wilson (Shortstop)

PA	R	H	2B	3B	HR	RBI	SO	BB	SB	CS	BA	OBP	SLG	OPS	3-Year	Fielding	Reliability
419	44	107	22	1	5	42	45	25	2	2	.281	.330	.384	.714	-0.03	C	Very High

Wilson's still got a great glove, but his offense slipped back to his career levels in 2008 after a good year in 2007. He's also seeing a pretty steady decline in games played, as injuries are becoming more and more of a problem for Wilson as he ages. As of this writing, the Pirates are trying hard to trade him, but it's looking unlikely that they're going to find a suitor.

Pitchers

Jimmy Barthmaier (Starter)

W	L	ERA	TBF	IP	Hit	HR	SO	BB	HBP	3-Year	Reliability
5	9	5.99	603	129	155	19	80	72	8	-0.27	Very High

Grabbed after being put on waivers by Houston, Barthmaier had a nice year split between Double-A and Triple-A for the Pirates in 2008. He was a good prospect just a few years ago for the Astros, so the Pirates are hoping to salvage something here. The few starts he did get with the Pirates, though, were disastrous.

T.J. Beam (Reliever)

W	L	ERA	TBF	IP	Hit	HR	SO	BB	HBP	3-Year	Reliability
4	4	4.66	332	76	78	10	51	31	3	+0.36	Average

Beam was decent out of the bullpen for the Pirates in '08, but he walked nearly as many hitters as he struck out. That generally hasn't been the case for him in the minors and if he can rein his walks in, he may prove to be a useful reliever.

Sean Burnett (Reliever)

W	L	ERA	TBF	IP	Hit	HR	SO	BB	HBP	3-Year	Reliability
3	5	5.17	322	71	78	8	38	39	2	+0.17	High

After his career was derailed by multiple arm injuries, Burnett returned to Pittsburgh in 2008 as a reliever. He was mostly used as a long reliever, though his true usefulness is as a LOOGY, as righties teed off on him for a .980 OPS against while he held lefties to a .171/.238/.276 line.

Matt Capps (Reliever)

W	L	ERA	TBF	IP	Hit	HR	SO	BB	HBP	3-Year	Reliability
4	3	3.50	261	64	60	7	47	13	2	+0.02	Average

Capps is a beast. Even missing two months with an injury last year, he threw 53.2 innings. His control is approaching urban legend status. Through three years, he's struck out 163 batters and walked 33, with 15 of those walks intentional. His shoulder injury wasn't serious, so there's no reason to think he won't continue along the path of being an insanely accurate, 80-inning monster out of the bullpen.

Jesse Chavez (Reliever)

W	L	ERA	TBF	IP	Hit	HR	SO	BB	HBP	3-Year	Reliability
3	5	5.02	333	75	83	10	60	32	3	+0.06	Average

Like many of the Pirates' pitchers, Chavez is a hard thrower who's found success in the minors but struggled in his short stint in the majors. Unlike some of the other guys in the system, his control seems to be decent and it took him a year or so to adjust to Triple-A. Once he did so, he struck out a batter an inning and earned his call to Pittsburgh. The Pirates hope he has a similar learning curve in the majors.

Zach Duke (Starter)

W	L	ERA	TBF	IP	Hit	HR	SO	BB	HBP	3-Year	Reliability
8	11	4.83	737	168	208	18	71	45	5	+0.07	Very High

Duke's biggest problem is that he gets hit hard. In his last two full seasons as a starter, he's given up 255 and 230 hits. Part of that is due to the Pirates generally awful defense, but Duke will never be more than a fringe starter if he can't figure out how to induce some more swings and misses. He'll likely be challenged for the fourth or fifth slot in the rotation this spring by Dan McCutchen, Ross Ohlendorf and anyone else Huntington might acquire before camp starts.

Phil Dumatrait (Starter)

W	L	ERA	TBF	IP	Hit	HR	SO	BB	HBP	3-Year	Reliability
4	7	5.60	442	96	112	14	51	49	4	+0.31	Very High

Pulling him off the scrap heap after the Reds released him, the Pirates actually got a few decent starts out of Dumatrait before he started having shoulder problems, which cost him the second half of the season. As is often the case with shoulder issues, he's been slow to recover and a move to the bullpen seems likely in 2009.

Tom Gorzelanny (Starter)

W	L	ERA	TBF	IP	Hit	HR	SO	BB	HBP	3-Year	Reliability
7	10	4.70	657	149	157	18	94	65	6	+0.19	Very High

The Pirates never openly admitted Tom Gorzelanny was hurt last year, but they kept him on a very tight leash during his demotion to Triple-A. His walk rate also doubled and he looked uncomfortable on the mound all year. The Pirates hope a winter's rest and Joe Kerrigan will get him back on track, as he was one of the more promising pitching prospects the Pirates have had in recent years before the 2008 debacle.

John Grabow (Reliever)

W	L	ERA	TBF	IP	Hit	HR	SO	BB	HBP	3-Year	Reliability
4	4	3.91	304	71	67	7	55	31	2	+0.20	Average

Grabow's ERA and WHIP were very good last year, though his strikeout and walk rates didn't change much from 2007 to 2008. This would indicate we'll see some regression for him in 2009. He'll probably inherit Damaso Marte's role as lefty set-up man out of John Russell's pen, though it's worth noting that there's not much of a platoon split against him. Still, as an effective lefty reliever facing free agency after 2009, he's almost certain to finish this year wearing a different uniform.

Craig Hansen (Reliever)

W	L	ERA	TBF	IP	Hit	HR	SO	BB	HBP	3-Year	Reliability
3	4	4.33	292	65	65	4	45	39	3	-0.01	Average

In 16 appearances with the Pirates, Hansen walked 20 batters and struck out only seven. Batters hit only .200 against Hansen while he was in Pittsburgh, but put up an OBP of .421. Neal Huntington loves live arms and that's likely why he was included as part of the Jason Bay trade, but if he can't find some way to rein in his control, it's hard to imagine there can be a spot for him on any major league roster.

Jeff Karstens (Starter)

W	L	ERA	TBF	IP	Hit	HR	SO	BB	HBP	3-Year	Reliability
5	9	5.27	551	125	144	20	65	43	5	+0.19	Very High

In his second start with the Pirates, Karstens took a perfect game into the eighth inning against the Arizona Diamondbacks, forever endearing himself to Pirate fans. Karstens has good command of the strike zone and seemed to pitch some well thought-out games in his short stint with the Pirates last year, but he doesn't have great stuff and that's likely to be his downfall.

Paul Maholm (Starter)

W	L	ERA	TBF	IP	Hit	HR	SO	BB	HBP	3-Year	Reliability
10	10	4.25	767	178	194	19	110	59	7	+0.14	Very High

After cutting his walk rate down in 2007, Maholm added some strikeouts last year and became a very effective starter for the Pirates. He was one of the few pitchers in recent years to actually benefit from the Pirates' defense, as he keeps the ball on the ground much more than the other starters on the staff and the Pirates' infield defense was fairly strong in 2008. He'll likely regress a bit in 2009 and if/when Jack Wilson is traded, it's possible that he'll be the pitcher who suffers the most.

Daniel McCutchen (Starter)

W	L	ERA	TBF	IP	Hit	HR	SO	BB	HBP	3-Year	Reliability
6	10	5.65	645	145	169	27	85	52	6	+0.22	High

Though he was old to be making his Triple-A debut last year, McCutchen's pro career didn't start until after his 23rd birthday. In that context, his numbers last year are slightly more interesting and he should be given a shot to win a rotation spot in the spring.

Evan Meek (Reliever)

W	L	ERA	TBF	IP	Hit	HR	SO	BB	HBP	3-Year	Reliability
3	4	5.16	304	66	75	7	44	37	3	0.00	High

Meek was terrible in a short stint with the Pirates after being picked in the Rule 5 draft (13 innings, 10 earned runs, three homers, 12 walks), but Neal Huntington liked him enough to pay Tampa Bay to keep him after the Pirates sent him down. He got his act together and pitched very well in both Double-A and Triple-A. The key for him, like so many other Pirates pitchers, is control. If he can bring the control he found in the minors last year to the majors, he could be a very effective reliever.

Ross Ohlendorf (Starter)

W	L	ERA	TBF	IP	Hit	HR	SO	BB	HBP	3-Year	Reliability
5	9	5.28	556	124	147	17	81	46	6	+0.18	Very High

After his trade to the Pirates, he was sent to Triple-A to stretch his arm out for the rotation and pitched very well in Indianapolis, flashing a fastball that topped out in the high 90s and sporting a nice 5/1 K/BB ratio in seven starts. When he came to Pittsburgh, he was mostly crushed in five starts and he walked more batters in 22.2 innings with the Pirates than he did in 46.2 with Indianapolis. The Pirates will try him as a starter, but his true home is probably in the bullpen, where he can lean more on his big fastball.

Romulo Sanchez (Reliever)

W	L	ERA	TBF	IP	Hit	HR	SO	BB	HBP	3-Year	Reliability
3	4	5.17	289	64	71	8	33	30	4	-0.30	Average

After struggling with his control the first two years of his Pirate career, Sanchez found the strike zone in 2007 in Double-A and emerged as a real relief prospect. He didn't do anything in Triple-A to diminish that status. To this point he's gotten two short stints in the Pirates' bullpen the last two years, but he may get a longer look in 2009.

Ian Snell (Starter)

W	L	ERA	TBF	IP	Hit	HR	SO	BB	HBP	3-Year	Reliability
8	10	4.98	738	166	185	21	126	70	4	+0.27	Very High

With Tom Gorzelanny, Snell was one of the most disappointing Pirates last year. He struggled with minor elbow problems early and didn't get things together until August, when he claimed that watching CC Sabathia pitch taught him to set batters up with his fastball. I suspect this incident is why pitching coach Jeff Andrews was fired. Whatever actually happened, Snell's last nine starts were more in line with what the Pirates expected from him in 2008 and they hope he can carry that into 2009.

John Van Benschoten (Starter)

W	L	ERA	TBF	IP	Hit	HR	SO	BB	HBP	3-Year	Reliability
4	7	5.60	478	103	117	13	65	59	6	+0.44	High

It's worth noting that John Van Benschoten's career 9.20 ERA is the worst in history among pitchers who have thrown more than 75 career innings, so this 5.59 projection is positively peachy. Van Benschoten is White Sox property now. I have no idea what they intend to do with him.

Tyler Yates (Reliever)

W	L	ERA	TBF	IP	Hit	HR	SO	BB	HBP	3-Year	Reliability
4	4	3.92	310	72	67	6	59	35	2	+0.19	Low

You know the drill by now: "Yates is a hard throwing reliever with control problems." He had a seemingly solid start to 2007, but his 12/18 K/BB ratio betrayed his 2.91 ERA after 21.2 innings. He flamed out from mid-May to mid-August (a 6.88 ERA in 34 innings), then dominated down the stretch, giving up only two runs and striking out 18 hitters (with only two walks) over his last 12 appearances. In fact, 39 of his 41 walks came through Aug. 18. I doubt he can replicate that kind of control over a full season, but it was awfully tantalizing to see what his 96-plus mph fastball looks like when he knows where it's going.

San Diego Padres
by Geoff Young of The Hardball Times

2009 Padres Projections
Record: 73-89
Division Rank/Games Behind: Last, 12 games back
Runs Scored: 695, 14th in the league
Runs Allowed: 759, 10th in the league
Park Factor: .92, an extreme pitcher's park

What Happened Last Year:

Everything that could go wrong did go wrong. Jake Peavy and Chris Young got hurt, and the stellar bullpen of 2007 turned into a disaster area. On the offensive side, the Padres received zero production out of the catcher, second base and shortstop positions. As a result, they were out of the race before it even began and fell about 20 wins short of most projections. Fans grew weary and stopped showing up at the ballpark. Principal owners John and Becky Moores filed for divorce, leaving the franchise's future direction up in the air and San Diegans in a state of "heightened awareness."

Management's current plan involves slashing payroll in a big way. The good news is, the last time the Padres did this (1993), they reached the World Series five years later. The bad news is, fans suffered through some pretty miserable seasons before seeing their team reach the top again and there's no guarantee that the suffering will be followed by glory again.

Players Lost from Last Year's Team:

Catchers Josh Bard and Michael Barrett, infielder Khalil Greene, outfielder Paul McAnulty, pitchers Kevin Cameron, Brian Corey, Shawn Estes, Charlie Haeger, Dirk Hayhurst, Clay Hensley, Trevor Hoffman and Mark Prior

Players Acquired:

Infielders Everth Cabrera and Travis Denker, pitchers Chris Britton, Ivan Nova and Mark Worrell

Management Is:

General manager Kevin Towers, the self-proclaimed "sludge merchant," actively works the waiver wire (Scott Linebrink was one of his prizes a few years ago) and has a knack for making trades that benefit his team more than his trading partner's (e.g., Adam Eaton and Akinori Otsuka for Adrian Gonzalez and Chris Young). Towers didn't make any huge deals in 2008, but he did sign Jody Gerut to a minor-league contract just before spring training. Gerut, who hadn't played in the big leagues since 2005, responded by taking Jim Edmonds' spot in the lineup and emerging as one of the most productive center fielders in baseball.

Towers prefers to fill holes via trade rather than free agency. When he does sign free agents, it's often in the form of short-term, incentive-laden deals to veterans undervalued by the market—Mike Piazza, Greg Maddux and Randy Wolf are a few recent examples.

Manager Bud Black is calm and patient, measuring his words and actions. When he questions an umpire's call, he does so in the same manner that he might, say, chat with a neighbor while watering his lawn. Black's cool demeanor fits well with the city in which he manages and complements the analytical approach taken by the front office. Everything about him says, "Wait, let's talk about this first."

On the field, Black's in-game tactics are fairly vanilla. The former big-league pitcher and pitching coach sometimes leaves his starter on the mound for a few too many batters, but other than that, nothing about his managerial style stands out. The one big questionable move Black made in 2008 was leaving Bard in to catch all 22 innings of a game in April, after which Bard's season unraveled.

The Minor League System Is:

Still improving. After a few poor drafts, culminating in the 2004 debacle that saw the Padres take local high school shortstop Matt Bush over Stephen Drew and Jered Weaver to save a few bucks, the team brought in Sandy Alderson as CEO to help revamp the process. This past season, the Padres saw their first returns from the 2005 draft in the forms of Josh Geer, Chase Headley, Nick Hundley and Will Venable.

From the 2006 draft, Matt Antonelli and Wade LeBlanc made September cameos and figure to see material time in 2009. The early returns on 2007—Mitch Canham, Drew Cumberland, Kellen Kulbacki, Eric Sogard—are promising. The same is true for 2008, with James Darnell, Jaff Decker, and Allan Dykstra.

Add in guys like Kyle Blanks, Cedric Hunter and Mat Latos, and the high-profile international signings spawned by their new Dominican facility, and the Padres are moving in the right direction. Not all of these players will reach their potential, of course, but with a larger pool of better talent than they've had in recent years, the Padres are at least giving themselves a chance to develop from within, which is crucial for a mid-market team.

Due For a Change:

Greene's poor 2008 came out of nowhere; he's an excellent bet to improve, although that no longer will benefit the Padres. Assuming Young can stay healthy, he will put up better numbers. Headley should improve a little with experience, and Kevin Kouzmanoff has room to grow if he can tighten his strike zone.

Brian Giles isn't getting any younger. Despite his breakout 2008 campaign, Gerut remains something of an unknown quantity. I guess one of the good things about everything going wrong in a given year is that it's unlikely that many individuals will do worse the following season.

Reasons to be Optimistic:

A team that slips 25 1/2 games in the standings from Year 1 to Year 2 is unlikely to fall even further in Year 3. Almost by definition, the Padres have to improve in 2009. The team has a solid nucleus of good, relatively young hitters in Gerut, Gonzalez, Scott Hairston, Headley and Kouzmanoff. The front office has demonstrated the ability in years past to assemble usable talent at reasonable prices. The farm system is finally starting to bear fruit again.

Reasons to be Pessimistic:

The pitching staff is a mess. Fans aren't buying into management's strategy and vision. The tenuous ownership situation and faltering economy have forced the Padres to slash payroll. Even if the team improves, there is the distinct possibility that nobody will care. The Padres were unable to capture San Diegans' hearts

> **Our Favorite Padres Blogs:**
> Ducksnorts (http://ducksnorts.com/blog)
> Friar Forecast (http://friarforecast.com/)
> Gaslamp Ball (http://www.gaslampball.com/)
> It Might Be Dangerous... You Go First (http://itmightbedangerous.blogspot.com/)
> Sacrifice Bunt (http://thesacrificebunt.com/)

during the unprecedented run of success from 2004 to 2007. With the Petco Park honeymoon phase drawing to a close, the memory of a 99-loss season looming large in the public's collective mind, and fans' mistrust of the current administration – particularly its recent handling of Hoffman (who got into some "he said, she said" with the front office by way of the local media) and Peavy – there is a lot more to sell here than the promise of winning baseball games. The fan base has grown disillusioned, and the Padres need to work some serious public relations magic if they are to repair their relationship with the citizens of San Diego and thrive going forward.

Still Left to Do:

The Padres need to find a shortstop, add pitching depth, and figure out how to regain the confidence and trust of their fan base. They also may need to find a new owner.

Most Likely Team Outcome:

Expectations couldn't be much lower, which might work to the club's advantage. With or without Peavy, the Padres will be better in 2009. I'll say 75 wins, and that may be too conservative.

Player Projections

Batters

Matt Antonelli (Second Base)

PA	R	H	2B	3B	HR	RBI	SO	BB	SB	CS	BA	OBP	SLG	OPS	3-Year	Fielding	Reliability
586	63	115	18	4	11	51	109	65	8	4	.226	.319	.342	.661	+0.05	D	High

Antonelli suffered through a horrendous season at Triple-A Portland, hitting just .215/.335/.322. The good news is, he maintained his strong plate discipline and came on toward the end, batting .290/.391/.473 in August. This was Antonelli's second full pro season and his second season playing second base, where he is still learning the nuances. It's way too early to give up on him.

Josh Bard (Catcher)

PA	R	H	2B	3B	HR	RBI	SO	BB	SB	CS	BA	OBP	SLG	OPS	3-Year	Fielding	Reliability
315	36	79	21	1	4	32	45	30	3	2	.282	.351	.406	.757	-0.03	F-	Average

Bard caught all 22 innings of a game on April 17 and never really recovered. He hit .169/.239/.246 after that game and made two trips to the disabled list. When healthy, he possesses a smooth line-drive stroke from both sides of the plate and calls a good game behind it. Bard doesn't throw runners out and probably is best suited to a reserve role at this stage of his career.

Michael Barrett (Catcher)

PA	R	H	2B	3B	HR	RBI	SO	BB	SB	CS	BA	OBP	SLG	OPS	3-Year	Fielding	Reliability
274	29	62	12	1	6	30	44	20	1	1	.250	.309	.379	.688	-0.05	F-	Average

It would be difficult to contribute any less than Barrett did during his brief tenure in San Diego.

Travis Denker (Second Base)

PA	R	H	2B	3B	HR	RBI	SO	BB	SB	CS	BA	OBP	SLG	OPS	3-Year	Fielding	Reliability
510	52	102	25	2	8	46	108	52	4	2	.227	.309	.345	.654	+0.05	C	High

An interesting prospect: Denker's built more like a catcher than a second baseman and has delivered power and strike zone discipline for several years in the minors. He must be considered a long shot, but one to keep an eye on.

Jody Gerut (Center Field)

PA	R	H	2B	3B	HR	RBI	SO	BB	SB	CS	BA	OBP	SLG	OPS	3-Year	Fielding	Reliability
477	62	119	22	4	16	63	74	43	8	4	.279	.345	.461	.806	-0.03	D	Low

Gerut took over the starting center field job in mid-May and thrived in his first big-league action since 2005. He hit .316/.365/.534 from June 1 to Sept. 19, when his season ended prematurely because of a sprained finger. Gerut proved to be a capable defender, covering the vast NL West outfields with ease and displaying a right fielder's arm.

Brian Giles (Right Field)

PA	R	H	2B	3B	HR	RBI	SO	BB	SB	CS	BA	OBP	SLG	OPS	3-Year	Fielding	Reliability
581	68	137	29	2	10	60	59	75	2	2	.275	.370	.402	.772	—	B	Very High

Last year in this space I said that "Giles is good for no more than 12-15 homers these days, but if he's healthy, expect a slight rebound." Well, he hit 12 home runs, stayed healthy, and enjoyed more than a slight rebound. The Padres picked up Giles' option for 2009. He'll slip a little but still provide good production near the top of the lineup.

Adrian Gonzalez (First Base)

PA	R	H	2B	3B	HR	RBI	SO	BB	SB	CS	BA	OBP	SLG	OPS	3-Year	Fielding	Reliability
625	85	163	34	2	32	104	125	61	1	1	.294	.367	.536	.903	+0.07	C	Very High

Among all big leaguers, only Philadelphia's Ryan Howard has hit more road homers than Gonzalez over the past two seasons. Gonzalez hits everything hard to all fields, has few weaknesses as a hitter (he struggled against southpaws in 2008 and occasionally chases fastballs up around his eyes), and won his first Gold Glove at first base. He is young, cheap, a local product, and real good—in other words, a player around whom the Padres can and should build.

Edgar V Gonzalez (Second Base)

PA	R	H	2B	3B	HR	RBI	SO	BB	SB	CS	BA	OBP	SLG	OPS	3-Year	Fielding	Reliability
464	51	110	20	2	8	47	90	38	4	4	.263	.328	.378	.706	-0.02	D	High

Adrian's older brother got his first taste of The Show after eight years in the minors. He started off strong (.328/.373/.466 through July 22) before fading (.199/.268/.272 from July 23 to end of season). This Gonzalez isn't quick enough to play the middle infield regularly and lacks the power expected of a corner guy. His 2008 season made for a nice story locally, but his big-league future is far from assured.

Scott Hairston (Left Field)

PA	R	H	2B	3B	HR	RBI	SO	BB	SB	CS	BA	OBP	SLG	OPS	3-Year	Fielding	Reliability
382	47	87	18	2	17	55	81	34	3	0	.257	.327	.472	.799	-0.02	C	High

After nearly propelling the Padres into the playoffs in 2007, Hairston entered the season with high expectations but got off to a slow start before catching fire in June. He hit .309/.390/.610 from June 1 to Aug. 15 and then tore a ligament in his left thumb two weeks later, causing him to miss the rest of the season. Hairston is the rare hitter who isn't intimidated by Petco Park. He hit .271/.333/.514 at home and also destroyed left-handers (.280/.316/.580). He played a strong left field and a reasonable center field when needed.

Chase Headley (Left Field)

PA	R	H	2B	3B	HR	RBI	SO	BB	SB	CS	BA	OBP	SLG	OPS	3-Year	Fielding	Reliability
570	66	128	28	3	17	68	140	56	3	1	.255	.335	.424	.759	+0.03	B	Very High

Headley didn't set the world on fire in his rookie season, but he did hold his own, although he could stand to make better contact. A third baseman playing left field, Headley teammates would benefit from a return to the infield, where he is less likely to injure himself or someone else.

Nick Hundley (Catcher)

PA	R	H	2B	3B	HR	RBI	SO	BB	SB	CS	BA	OBP	SLG	OPS	3-Year	Fielding	Reliability
449	45	91	18	1	15	53	97	31	0	1	.222	.279	.380	.659	+0.02	C	High

Hundley, no relation to former big-leaguers Randy and Todd, took over as starting catcher late in the season and figures to be the starter in 2009. He is easily the best defender among the lot who donned the tools of ignorance in San Diego last year and should provide enough offense to be useful in a Jason LaRue kind of way.

Kevin Kouzmanoff (Third Base)

PA	R	H	2B	3B	HR	RBI	SO	BB	SB	CS	BA	OBP	SLG	OPS	3-Year	Fielding	Reliability
563	70	142	28	2	21	79	109	31	7	1	.275	.325	.459	.784	+0.01	C	Very High

What a strange season for "Kouz." He swung at everything, stopped hitting right handers, and saw his overall production slide a bit from his rookie year. At the same time, his defense improved dramatically. Kouzmanoff's fielding percentage rose from .932 to .974, his range factor rose from 2.38 to 2.64, and he led all big-league third basemen with 34 double plays turned. Despite "minor" shoulder surgery in November, he is expected to be ready for spring training.

Paul McAnulty (Left Field)

PA	R	H	2B	3B	HR	RBI	SO	BB	SB	CS	BA	OBP	SLG	OPS	3-Year	Fielding	Reliability
396	48	92	19	2	12	49	79	48	0	1	.270	.361	.442	.803	+0.01	C	High

McAnulty is old for someone still trying to establish himself in the big leagues, and he doesn't really look like a ballplayer. What he does is spray line drives all over the field, draw walks and knock the occasional home run. McAnulty is now with the Red Sox, who may have a better idea how to use him than the Padres did.

Luis Rodriguez (Shortstop)

PA	R	H	2B	3B	HR	RBI	SO	BB	SB	CS	BA	OBP	SLG	OPS	3-Year	Fielding	Reliability
323	32	75	13	2	2	26	31	25	2	1	.261	.322	.341	.663	-0.02	D	Low

Rodriguez took over at shortstop when Greene's season ended early and did a surprisingly good job in limited duty. He is a capable defender who hit a very empty .287. With Greene now gone, and few other options on the horizon, Rodriguez could see a lot of playing time in 2009. Don't expect much.

William Venable (Center Field)

PA	R	H	2B	3B	HR	RBI	SO	BB	SB	CS	BA	OBP	SLG	OPS	3-Year	Fielding	Reliability
555	59	121	18	4	12	55	116	40	7	2	.241	.302	.364	.666	+0.07	C	Very High

Venable, son of former big-league outfielder and current Padres minor-league hitting instructor Max Venable, made huge strides in 2008. The former Princeton hoopster is a terrific athlete who possesses gap power and strong baserunning instincts. Despite having little experience at the position, he also is a solid defender in center field. Venable is a bit old for a prospect and he does expand the strike zone at times, but he could have a reasonably productive career in the mold of, say, Gary Matthews Jr.

Pitchers

Mike Adams (Reliever)

W	L	ERA	TBF	IP	Hit	HR	SO	BB	HBP	3-Year	Reliability
4	3	3.69	285	67	63	6	63	27	2	+0.20	Very Low

A prototypical Kevin Towers pickup, Adams became the Padres' most reliable reliever in 2008 despite having missed most of the previous three seasons due to injury. True to form, Adams had shoulder surgery in October and is expected to be out until at least June 2009.

Cha Seung Baek (Starter)

W	L	ERA	TBF	IP	Hit	HR	SO	BB	HBP	3-Year	Reliability
7	8	4.33	582	136	140	18	81	43	5	+0.35	Very High

In a Sept. 10 game against the Dodgers, Baek made Manny Ramirez look helpless in consecutive at-bats. This served as a cruel reminder that the Korean-born right hander possesses front-line stuff. The rest of his time in a Padres uniform served as a reminder that stuff doesn't matter if you nibble constantly and refuse to attack hitters.

Josh Banks (Starter)

W	L	ERA	TBF	IP	Hit	HR	SO	BB	HBP	3-Year	Reliability
6	9	5.18	599	138	156	25	70	42	5	+0.20	Very High

Claimed off waivers from Toronto in late May, Banks got off to a brilliant start (1.62 ERA in 33.1 innings through June 19) before the league caught up with him (6.75 ERA in 52 IP thereafter). Banks didn't display the impeccable control that was his hallmark in the minors. With eight pitches in his repertoire, perhaps he would do well to focus on three or four and make those even better.

Heath Bell (Reliever)

W	L	ERA	TBF	IP	Hit	HR	SO	BB	HBP	3-Year	Reliability
5	4	2.96	318	77	65	5	74	27	3	+0.15	Average

On the heels of his breakout 2007 campaign, Bell again served as manager Bud Black's eighth-inning guy. The results were mixed. Before the All-Star break, Bell had a 2.15 ERA over 50.1 innings and held opponents to a .209/.269/.291 line. In the second half, though, those numbers ballooned to a 6.18 ERA over 27.2 innings and a .264/.355/.415 line. Bell was worked very hard in 2007. It's hard to say how much of his late-season fade may have been due to this, and whether any ill effects might linger into 2009 and beyond.

Joshua Geer (Starter)

W	L	ERA	TBF	IP	Hit	HR	SO	BB	HBP	3-Year	Reliability
6	12	5.83	744	165	204	28	72	59	10	+0.08	Very High

Geer is an extreme finesse pitcher who succeeds by keeping the ball around the plate and changing speeds. His lack of dominance at any level makes him a risky long-term investment. The frayed ligament found in his elbow after the season makes him a risky short-term investment as well.

Justin Hampson (Reliever)

W	L	ERA	TBF	IP	Hit	HR	SO	BB	HBP	3-Year	Reliability
3	3	4.10	228	53	52	5	35	21	2	+0.31	Average

As he had the previous season, Hampson pitched well in 2008 while nobody was looking. There is nothing special about his game, but he makes a capable 10th or 11th man on most staffs.

Clay Hensley (Reliever)

W	L	ERA	TBF	IP	Hit	HR	SO	BB	HBP	3-Year	Reliability
4	7	5.47	433	95	110	13	55	48	4	+0.49	Very High

Hensley worked almost exclusively out of the bullpen in his return from September 2007 shoulder surgery. The results weren't pretty, but he got his work in and could be ready to contribute this year, although for whom and in what role remain uncertain.

Trevor Hoffman (Reliever)

W	L	ERA	TBF	IP	Hit	HR	SO	BB	HBP	3-Year	Reliability
4	2	3.26	235	58	49	6	48	16	2	—	Low

On the heels of two high-profile blown saves to end 2007, Hoffman faced the usual predictions of his imminent demise. When he got off to a slow start, the pundits congratulated themselves for finally have been proven right after years of waiting. On June 1, Hoffman's ERA stood at 5.68 and opponents were hitting .276/.329/.434 against him. From that point forward, those numbers were 2.39 and .181/.206/.362. Still, his margin for error has all but disappeared. Baseball's all-time career saves leader needs to have perfect command to succeed, and perfection is a lot to ask of anyone.

Wade Leblanc (Starter)

W	L	ERA	TBF	IP	Hit	HR	SO	BB	HBP	3-Year	Reliability
6	10	5.03	639	145	151	25	112	61	7	-0.16	High

LeBlanc shot through the system, reaching San Diego at the end of his second full pro season. He took his lumps at Triple-A Portland in 2008 but maintained strong K/9 and K/BB rates before getting pounded with the big club in September. LeBlanc won't be a front-line starter, and as a pitcher who relies heavily on his changeup, he may encounter more rough patches before settling in at the back of a big-league rotation.

Cla Meredith (Reliever)

W	L	ERA	TBF	IP	Hit	HR	SO	BB	HBP	3-Year	Reliability
5	3	3.10	308	74	74	4	50	21	3	-0.03	Average

Meredith is a solid innings eater who serves up an insane number of ground balls. He may never recapture the form he showed as a rookie, but he can be a useful reliever if used properly. His control wasn't as sharp in 2008 as in the previous season, and he hasn't fared well in high-leverage situations over the past two years (.364/.408/.523 in 2007, .333/.372/.500 in 2008).

Jake Peavy (Starter)

W	L	ERA	TBF	IP	Hit	HR	SO	BB	HBP	3-Year	Reliability
11	8	3.50	713	172	154	17	163	56	5	+0.19	Very High

The best starting pitcher in Padres history added to his legacy in 2008 with another fine season marred only by his team's inability to score runs on his behalf and a month-long stint on the disabled list. Right handers hit .194/.271/.299 against him last year, which is actually a step back from 2007, when they hit just .174/.228/.251. Because of the Padres' tenuous ownership situation, Peavy may end up elsewhere in 2009, although he has to approve any trade.

Joe Thatcher (Reliever)

W	L	ERA	TBF	IP	Hit	HR	SO	BB	HBP	3-Year	Reliability
4	4	3.59	290	68	64	6	56	27	3	+0.16	Low

Perhaps being counted on to carry too much of the load in a revamped bullpen, Thatcher couldn't get anyone out in 2008 and ended up back at Triple-A for much of the season.

Chris Young (Starter)

W	L	ERA	TBF	IP	Hit	HR	SO	BB	HBP	3-Year	Reliability
8	7	3.91	561	133	112	17	117	57	4	+0.34	Very High

For the second straight year, Young battled injuries that kept him from pitching up to his ability. In 2007, a strained oblique plagued him for most of the second half. Last year a deviated septum in May (thank you, Albert Pujols) kept him out of action for two months, and a strained right forearm caused him to miss time in August. Young remains one of the least efficient pitchers in baseball, but assuming he stays healthy, he should re-establish himself as a front-line starter for the Padres.

San Francisco Giants

by Steve Treder of The Hardball Times

2009 Giants Projections

Record: 79-83
Division Rank/Games Behind: 3rd, six games back
Runs Scored: 680, last in the league
Runs Allowed: 700, 1st in the league
Park Factor: 1.01, just about neutral

What Happened Last Year:

All in all, things went just about as well as could have been hoped for the Giants in 2008. But when the result of things going just about as well as could have been hoped is a 72-90 record, well, the talent base is modest indeed.

Obviously the big story was the sensational breakout performance by Cy Young Award winner Tim Lincecum, in just his first full year in the big leagues. Overshadowed by Lincecum, fellow young starter Matt Cain was also quite good, for the second straight season vastly better than his won-lost record. A few of the Giants' make-do veteran regulars were solid: catcher Bengie Molina, right fielder Randy Winn and center fielder Aaron Rowand. But a couple of other veterans counted upon in key roles were disastrous: starting pitcher Barry Zito and shortstop Omar Vizquel.

As expected, the offense was feeble, and the bullpen problematic, and it added up to a noncompetitive ball club. The silver lining, perhaps, was that at long last the Giants allowed some space to experiment with young players in the infield, but the only one looking particularly interesting was 21-year-old third baseman-catcher Pablo Sandoval.

Players Lost from Last Year's Team:

Vizquel and pitchers Kevin Correia, Tyler Walker, Brad Hennessey and Vinnie Chulk. Infield supersub Rich Aurilia is unsigned as of this writing, and he was the one of this crew making a substantial contribution in '08.

Players Acquired:

Shortstop Edgar Renteria, starting pitcher Randy Johnson, and relievers Jeremy Affeldt and Bobby Howry. First baseman Josh Phelps has been signed to a minor league contract.

Management Is:

The Giants are under new ownership in 2009, with Bill Neukom taking over from Peter Magowan. But longtime GM Brian Sabean remains in place, and it remains to be seen whether he will operate differently under a new boss. After having been a clever and dynamic acquirer of talent in the late 1990s and early 2000s, for the past several years Sabean's approach has distinctly regressed into a virtual parody of risk-averse timidity, with comical reliance on "proven veterans" and short-term stopgaps. With Barry Bonds let go in 2008, the team at long last began to get younger, but it hasn't (yet) undergone a full-scale rebuilding. Sabean's free agent signings of this offseason of modest placeholders Renteria, Affeldt and Howry don't indicate a departure from the treadmill; Randy Johnson is likely better than a modest placeholder, but at the age of 45 he's about as short-term as it gets.

Field manager Bruce Bochy reflects the no-drama style, with a colorless personality and a careful, steady manner. He did give playing time to a very long list of rookies in 2008, but primarily in secondary roles. In particular, the decisions Sabean and Bochy make at third base, second base and first base in 2009 will be interesting, since as of this writing there's no one on the roster with extensive major league experience at any of these positions.

The Minor League System Is:

For years, the Giants have been maligned for their near-total inability to produce position players of quality, while their record in sprouting young pitchers has been strong. Their drafts of the past couple of years have received generally positive reviews, and opportunities for system-developed talent to step forward are ample.

But the organization's most intriguing position-player prospects (catcher Buster Posey, third baseman Conor Gillaspie and first baseman Angel Villalona) are all at least a year away from the majors. Sandoval is the only non-pitching youngster with star potential likely to get significant big league time in 2009; all the rest project as varying degrees of journeyman.

Of course, pitchers are players too, and the Giants deserve significant credit for coming up with Lincecum and Cain, and several other impressive young arms.

Due For a Change:

It sure would be nice if Zito could bounce back to something resembling his Oakland form, but don't count on it. Aside from him, no Giant still on the roster had an off year in 2008, nor did anyone appear to be performing over his head.

Reasons to be Optimistic:

They say that starting pitching is the cornerstone of a championship ball club, and no one can boast a more intriguing cornerstone in that regard than the Giants, with Lincecum and Cain, and The Big Unit to boot. Furthermore, there's … well, if … um …

Okay, how about this: The NL West was by far the worst division in baseball in 2008. If that status holds, any team bubbling up with 80-85 wins emerges as a contender. That many wins would be a leap forward for the Giants, but it isn't beyond the realm of possibility. Well, maybe not too far beyond the realm of possibility.

Reasons to be Pessimistic:

In six words: Bengie Molina is still batting cleanup.

It's difficult to imagine Lincecum performing much better than he did in 2008, and with arguably the best pitcher in the majors logging 227 innings this team still lost 90 games. The addition of Renteria shores up the weakness at shortstop, Johnson is a boon to the rotation,

and Affeldt and Howry probably will help the bullpen, but none of them is anything special. Run production will remain a huge problem.

Still Left to Do:

Well, acquiring big-time bats at first base and corner outfield would be a great idea, but doesn't appear to be happening. Realistically, the major questions remaining are to find out if Sandoval can handle third base on a regular basis, and to sort out who among the uninspiring list of candidates will emerge at second base and first base.

Most Likely Team Outcome:

Fourth place again. The Giants are probably better than the Padres, but that's it.

Player Projections

Batters

Eliezer Alfonzo (Catcher)

PA	R	H	2B	3B	HR	RBI	SO	BB	SB	CS	BA	OBP	SLG	OPS	3-Year	Fielding	Reliability
286	32	71	16	1	8	36	65	13	1	1	.267	.309	.425	.734	-0.03	D	Average

Some pop in his bat is the only positive. He's backup catcher material at best.

Rich Aurilia (First Base)

PA	R	H	2B	3B	HR	RBI	SO	BB	SB	CS	BA	OBP	SLG	OPS	3-Year	Fielding	Reliability
431	48	108	22	2	9	49	58	30	1	1	.274	.325	.408	.733	—	B	High

After an injury-slowed 2007, Aurilia gave the Giants what they were looking for in 2008: a useful supersub contribution. Of course, the fact that he got as much playing time as he did is an indicator of how weak the 2008 Giants were at first and third base, but if healthy, Aurilia still can help a good team in a utility role.

Brian Bocock (Shortstop)

PA	R	H	2B	3B	HR	RBI	SO	BB	SB	CS	BA	OBP	SLG	OPS	3-Year	Fielding	Reliability
492	45	88	17	3	2	27	120	38	17	6	.202	.269	.268	.537	+0.05	D	Low

Bocock got the chance to fill in as the Giants' starting shortstop in early 2008, but was so not ready for prime time. If he has a big league future, it will be as a backup.

John Bowker (Left Field)

PA	R	H	2B	3B	HR	RBI	SO	BB	SB	CS	BA	OBP	SLG	OPS	3-Year	Fielding	Reliability
478	53	112	22	5	11	54	99	27	3	2	.253	.300	.400	.700	+0.02	C	Very High

Bowker leapfrogged past Triple-A straight into the Giants' starting first base job early in 2008, and for a while he made some noise. Then, shall we say, reality set in. He has no business being a regular, but Bowker could emerge as a useful first base/corner outfield role player.

Emmanuel Burriss (Shortstop)

PA	R	H	2B	3B	HR	RBI	SO	BB	SB	CS	BA	OBP	SLG	OPS	3-Year	Fielding	Reliability
516	57	120	15	4	2	34	63	30	24	8	.255	.306	.317	.623	+0.05	D	Average

Burriss landed in the majors in 2008 after skipping both Double-A and Triple-A, and didn't perform badly at all. He has no power, but makes reliable contact, runs extremely well and appears defensively competent at either short or second. He will be a major league utilityman if not a regular.

Brett Harper (First Base)

PA	R	H	2B	3B	HR	RBI	SO	BB	SB	CS	BA	OBP	SLG	OPS	3-Year	Fielding	Reliability
393	48	102	22	2	16	58	82	18	1	1	.277	.313	.478	.791	0.00	C	Average

He's a career minor leaguer with power, but not enough else to be a legit prospect.

Stephen Holm (Catcher)

PA	R	H	2B	3B	HR	RBI	SO	BB	SB	CS	BA	OBP	SLG	OPS	3-Year	Fielding	Reliability
284	30	60	13	1	7	30	51	27	1	1	.240	.322	.384	.706	-0.03	D	Average

Holm, a career minor leaguer, performed soundly for the Giants as a backup catcher in 2008. He has no upside beyond that.

Brian Horwitz (Left Field)

PA	R	H	2B	3B	HR	RBI	SO	BB	SB	CS	BA	OBP	SLG	OPS	3-Year	Fielding	Reliability
387	42	96	17	2	5	38	54	30	2	2	.275	.335	.378	.713	+0.09	C	High

He's a good hitter for average, but a corner outfielder without power or speed. This is the sort of "prospect" that has long made one wonder what the Giants are thinking.

Travis Ishikawa (First Base)

PA	R	H	2B	3B	HR	RBI	SO	BB	SB	CS	BA	OBP	SLG	OPS	3-Year	Fielding	Reliability
491	59	110	25	3	19	66	116	41	4	2	.250	.317	.449	.766	+0.02	C	High

After appearing to be toast after back-to-back poor years in 2006-2007, Ishikawa suddenly lit up Double-A and Triple-A in '08, and didn't embarrass himself with the big club down the stretch. Ishikawa's combination of limited upside and inconsistency isn't encouraging. Only if his improvement is genuine will a future as a platoon first baseman materialize.

Fred Lewis (Left Field)

PA	R	H	2B	3B	HR	RBI	SO	BB	SB	CS	BA	OBP	SLG	OPS	3-Year	Fielding	Reliability
474	62	112	21	8	9	48	103	48	14	4	.266	.342	.419	.761	-0.02	B	High

Lewis made the most of the opportunity the Giants provided. Still, playing as well as could be expected, what Lewis produced was modest for a full-time left fielder. He's a legit big leaguer, but should be a fourth outfielder.

Bengie Molina (Catcher)

PA	R	H	2B	3B	HR	RBI	SO	BB	SB	CS	BA	OBP	SLG	OPS	3-Year	Fielding	Reliability
515	59	139	27	1	15	69	50	22	0	0	.288	.323	.442	.765	-0.05	A	Very High

This Molina has been steady and remarkably durable, providing everything the Giants could have hoped for, including his strongest defensive performance in several years in 2008. Molina's offense isn't nearly as effective as his triple-crown stats indicate; he's the quintessential better-in-Fantasy-than-in-real-life hitter.

Ivan Ochoa (Shortstop)

PA	R	H	2B	3B	HR	RBI	SO	BB	SB	CS	BA	OBP	SLG	OPS	3-Year	Fielding	Reliability
412	47	99	17	3	6	38	77	28	10	4	.268	.328	.380	.708	+0.07	D	Average

He's your standard, garden-variety utility infielder.

Dan Ortmeier (Center Field)

PA	R	H	2B	3B	HR	RBI	SO	BB	SB	CS	BA	OBP	SLG	OPS	3-Year	Fielding	Reliability
333	37	74	17	2	6	33	71	21	7	2	.242	.295	.370	.665	+0.02	F	High

A modest talent who was given a shot at the Giants' wide-open 1B job in 2008, Ortmeier got hurt and hit dreadfully in both the majors and minors. An extreme long shot.

Edgar Renteria (Shortstop)

PA	R	H	2B	3B	HR	RBI	SO	BB	SB	CS	BA	OBP	SLG	OPS	3-Year	Fielding	Reliability
528	62	139	28	2	8	57	72	43	7	2	.291	.348	.408	.756	-0.05	C	Very High

The Tigers not only declined their option on Renteria heading into the 2009 season but they chose not to take the chance of even offering him arbitration after a subpar year. Renteria had a solid second half at the plate (.296/.343/.469 after the break) but that didn't make up for diminished range in the field. Renteria somehow managed to cash in, though, and he signed a two-year deal to be the Giants' starting shortstop.

Dave Roberts (Left Field)

PA	R	H	2B	3B	HR	RBI	SO	BB	SB	CS	BA	OBP	SLG	OPS	3-Year	Fielding	Reliability
309	40	73	12	5	0	19	43	32	18	4	.269	.346	.351	.697	—	A	Average

Spent half of 2008 on the DL, and made a marginal utility-role contribution when he played. Has turned in a nice little career, but it's over, and everyone but his $6.5 million contract knows it.

Ryan Rohlinger (Third Base)

PA	R	H	2B	3B	HR	RBI	SO	BB	SB	CS	BA	OBP	SLG	OPS	3-Year	Fielding	Reliability
502	48	95	19	2	10	47	89	34	3	2	.210	.275	.327	.602	+0.02	B	High

For some reason, the Giants thought it would be a good idea to have this grade-B prospect skip Triple-A and spend the final month and a half of 2008 in the majors. He was completely overmatched. He projects as a scrubeenie at best.

Aaron Rowand (Center Field)

PA	R	H	2B	3B	HR	RBI	SO	BB	SB	CS	BA	OBP	SLG	OPS	3-Year	Fielding	Reliability
561	66	140	33	2	14	68	107	39	4	2	.278	.343	.434	.777	-0.03	F	Very High

The okay-but-nothing-special performance he delivered in 2008 was in line with Rowand's career norms. As he enters his 30s, he must at least sustain this level for his contract to become anything but an albatross. It might be meaningless, but this can't be a good sign: In September, Rowand hit .217/.286/.253, with one RBI in 91 plate appearances.

Pablo Sandoval (Catcher)

PA	R	H	2B	3B	HR	RBI	SO	BB	SB	CS	BA	OBP	SLG	OPS	3-Year	Fielding	Reliability
554	63	148	33	4	13	69	78	18	2	1	.281	.307	.433	.740	+0.09	C	Very High

Oh, yeah. Watching this guy is the sort of thing that makes being a baseball fan glorious. He's a roly-poly switch-hitter who spent 2008 converting every pitch "strike, ball, or wild" into a line drive. Sandoval's body type is born-to-be-catcher, but he's played some third base, and if the Giants can get mileage out of him there for a few years it will enhance his value. There's talk of playing him full time at first, but he won't generate enough offense for that to make sense.

Nate Schierholtz (Right Field)

PA	R	H	2B	3B	HR	RBI	SO	BB	SB	CS	BA	OBP	SLG	OPS	3-Year	Fielding	Reliability
475	63	130	28	7	14	64	75	22	7	3	.293	.331	.482	.813	+0.04	C	Very High

Probably the best of the many corner outfield/first base types the Giants organization has produced, Schierholtz will likely forge a major league career, but there isn't great upside. He's a very good line-drive hitter, but has yet to deliver the kind of home run power you'd like to see from a guy his size. He has zilch strike zone discipline, average-at-best speed, and limited defensive aptitude.

Clay Timpner (Center Field)

PA	R	H	2B	3B	HR	RBI	SO	BB	SB	CS	BA	OBP	SLG	OPS	3-Year	Fielding	Reliability
467	47	109	19	4	3	36	73	28	8	5	.254	.301	.338	.639	+0.01	D	High

He's a nice defensive center fielder, but there's no way he'll hit well in the majors.

Eugenio Velez (Second Base)

PA	R	H	2B	3B	HR	RBI	SO	BB	SB	CS	BA	OBP	SLG	OPS	3-Year	Fielding	Reliability
460	60	112	19	10	8	43	81	24	21	8	.261	.303	.408	.711	+0.07	D	High

Velez provides excellent speed and helpful defensive versatility, but overall his talent doesn't project beyond utilityman. He's the sort of player who's handy to have on your bench, but if you find him in the lineup on a regular basis, you've got problems.

Omar Vizquel (Shortstop)

PA	R	H	2B	3B	HR	RBI	SO	BB	SB	CS	BA	OBP	SLG	OPS	3-Year	Fielding	Reliability
417	43	97	16	3	1	29	41	33	9	4	.262	.321	.329	.650	—	B	Very High

Vizquel hit .344 in September, moving an injury-marred season all the way up from "horrendous" to merely "lousy." He wants to play in 2009, but if he does, it had better be in a strict backup role.

Randy Winn (Right Field)

PA	R	H	2B	3B	HR	RBI	SO	BB	SB	CS	BA	OBP	SLG	OPS	3-Year	Fielding	Reliability
598	71	153	33	2	9	60	82	48	14	2	.283	.342	.401	.743	-0.05	B	Very High

At age 34, Winn gave the Giants another solid season—to which the appropriate response might be, "So what?" Like Fred Lewis in left field, Winn is the classic tweener—lacking the range to be satisfactory as a regular center fielder, and lacking the bat to be satisfactory as a regular corner. And his too-rich contract has inhibited the Giants' ability to trade Winn to a contender that could make sensible use of him as a role player.

Adam Witter (Catcher)

PA	R	H	2B	3B	HR	RBI	SO	BB	SB	CS	BA	OBP	SLG	OPS	3-Year	Fielding	Reliability
454	51	93	18	3	16	55	103	45	2	3	.231	.309	.410	.719	+0.01	—	Average

He's been too old at each level to be a serious prospect, but Witter is a lefty-hitting catcher with some power, a combination that could get him major league exposure at some point.

Pitchers

Matt Cain (Starter)

W	L	ERA	TBF	IP	Hit	HR	SO	BB	HBP	3-Year	Reliability
11	10	4.04	812	191	176	19	155	77	5	-0.08	Very High

It's easy to forget that Cain is younger than Tim Lincecum. While Cain hasn't made the tremendous leap forward Lincecum did in 2008, he doesn't really need to: With decent run support, Cain would have snagged 15-plus wins in both '07 and '08, and would be widely acclaimed as the fine young star he is. And if Cain does achieve a breakthrough in command, his stuff is such that he'll be a Cy Young candidate in his own right.

Vinnie Chulk (Reliever)

W	L	ERA	TBF	IP	Hit	HR	SO	BB	HBP	3-Year	Reliability
3	4	4.56	276	63	65	8	45	25	2	+0.22	Low

He was a blah component in the Giants' blah 2008 bullpen. Yawn.

Kevin Correia (Starter)

W	L	ERA	TBF	IP	Hit	HR	SO	BB	HBP	3-Year	Reliability
5	8	5.13	522	117	134	15	71	46	4	+0.43	High

A guy who'd spent a few years seeming on the verge of busting out as a solid major leaguer, 2008 was his big chance. But he suffered an oblique injury early in the season, and when he came back had nothing resembling his former velocity. He slogged through the rest of the season getting his brains beaten out.

The Giants have given up on him, but he's worth some sort of shot, someplace.

Brad Hennessey (Starter)

W	L	ERA	TBF	IP	Hit	HR	SO	BB	HBP	3-Year	Reliability
5	11	6.05	642	141	177	24	58	54	6	+0.53	Very High

He was putting together a decent little career and then, wham: 2008. Hennessey encountered a low-grade illness, attempted to play through it, and encountered ghastly results. His career is at the proverbial crossroads.

Alexander Hinshaw (Reliever)

W	L	ERA	TBF	IP	Hit	HR	SO	BB	HBP	3-Year	Reliability
3	3	4.81	258	57	52	7	58	38	4	+0.17	Low

A slightly odd case: He arrived in the majors in 2008 at the age of 25, but with fewer than 150 minor league innings. Hinshaw was immediately effective, then faded; if he improves his control, he could emerge as a first-rate reliever.

Tim Lincecum (Starter)

W	L	ERA	TBF	IP	Hit	HR	SO	BB	HBP	3-Year	Reliability
12	8	3.45	766	183	159	16	200	71	5	+0.06	High

By working 227 innings in 2008, Lincecum more than doubled his professional total. Think about that. His sudden and spectacular big league success is of a sort seen only a handful of times in history; bagging a Cy Young Award with fewer than 60 major league appearances under his belt is a feat previously achieved only by Vida Blue and Fernando Valenzuela. The only concern at this point is the one that applies to every young pitcher: Will he stay healthy? If the answer is "yes," then hang on tight, because we're in for quite a ride.

Patrick Misch (Starter)

W	L	ERA	TBF	IP	Hit	HR	SO	BB	HBP	3-Year	Reliability
6	8	5.31	562	126	148	19	74	46	7	+0.24	Very High

Last season was his big opportunity, getting a crack at the starting rotation, and Misch flopped big time. With excellent control but quite homer-prone, his future is probably in the bullpen.

Jonathan Sanchez (Starter)

W	L	ERA	TBF	IP	Hit	HR	SO	BB	HBP	3-Year	Reliability
8	8	4.49	636	145	144	15	134	68	7	+0.18	High

A big-time enigma: This guy's stuff compares with anyone's, but he has yet to pull all the pieces together. Through the first half of 2008 Sanchez appeared to have found the formula, cruising at 8-4 with a 3.79 ERA, but then he fell apart and went 1-8, 7.23 the rest of the way. The good news is that his K rate remained healthy through his godawful struggles. It's prudent to consider Sanchez still a "buy."

Jack Taschner (Reliever)

W	L	ERA	TBF	IP	Hit	HR	SO	BB	HBP	3-Year	Reliability
3	4	4.53	259	59	59	6	49	28	2	+0.23	Low

Here's a LOOGY who's never been much good at retiring left-handed batters. What's wrong with this picture?

Merkin Valdez (Reliever)

W	L	ERA	TBF	IP	Hit	HR	SO	BB	HBP	3-Year	Reliability
2	2	4.48	171	38	38	4	29	20	2	+0.20	Very Low

Valdez has a world of stuff, but can't stay off the DL.

Tyler Walker (Reliever)

W	L	ERA	TBF	IP	Hit	HR	SO	BB	HBP	3-Year	Reliability
4	2	3.70	241	57	52	5	47	23	2	+0.20	Very Low

He made it back from Tommy John surgery to deliver a so-so performance in 2008. Nothing special, but he can help fill out a bullpen.

Brian Wilson (Reliever)

W	L	ERA	TBF	IP	Hit	HR	SO	BB	HBP	3-Year	Reliability
4	3	3.84	280	65	59	5	58	31	3	+0.11	Low

Give the Giants credit for this much: Since getting third-degree burns from the Armando Benitez contract, they've demonstrated a grasp of the concept that just about anyone can pile up lots of saves in the closer role. That includes, for example, this completely ordinary and quite inexpensive reliever. It remains to be seen whether the Giants understand the related concept—that a gaudy save total does not equal effective pitching at the top of the bullpen.

Keiichi Yabu (Reliever)

W	L	ERA	TBF	IP	Hit	HR	SO	BB	HBP	3-Year	Reliability
4	4	4.09	309	71	70	6	49	30	4	—	Very Low

A nice story: Japanese ultra-veteran persuades the Giants to give him a whirl, and he delivers a very solid year of mop-up relief.

Barry Zito (Starter)

W	L	ERA	TBF	IP	Hit	HR	SO	BB	HBP	3-Year	Reliability
9	10	4.85	765	171	181	21	108	84	5	+0.24	Very High

The steadily bloating ERA is bad enough, but it's the relentlessly rotting BB/K underlying it that stinks the worst. Regaining his peak form is completely out of the question; the only issue left to resolve is just how high Zito's contract will rate on the list of all-time disasters.

Seattle Mariners

by Jeff Sullivan of Lookout Landing (lookoutlanding.com)

2009 Mariners Projections

Record: 73-89
Division Rank/Games Behind: Last by nine games
Runs Scored: 682, Last in the league
Runs Allowed: 747, 6th in the league
Park Factor: .97, pitcher's park

What Happened Last Year:

Dumping the farm system to land Erik Bedard and dumping $48 million to land Carlos Silva, the Seattle Mariners were built to win in 2008. And they did win—61 times. Unfortunately the front office forgot about the other 101 games and everyone got fired.

Trying to build this team to win in the short term was already a grave miscalculation—Bill Bavasi surrendered way too much in constructing a roster that was never as good as the Angels in the first place. But while the winter leading up to the season was misguided, the season itself took even the most modest of goals and stomped them to little bits. Erik Bedard got hurt in the first game. J.J. Putz got hurt in the second. From there it was all downhill, and by Memorial Day the Mariners were 16 games under .500 and 12.5 games back in the division.

Nothing went right all year long, and a team that many predicted to win around 85 games wound up narrowly avoiding the worst record in baseball. And it was every bit as ugly as it sounds. The DH position put up a combined OPS of .608. The starting first baseman got cut in July and replaced by Miguel Cairo. The everyday catcher was rewarded with a three-year extension when he was batting .197. I've had nightmares before, but I almost never remember them in the morning. This one I did remember. Every morning. For six months. Even as someone who never bought into the 2008 Mariners as a legitimate contender, this season broke me.

Players Lost from Last Year's Team:

Raul Ibanez, Willie Bloomquist and Miguel Cairo all filed for free agency, with Ibanez already signing with Philadelphia and neither of the other two expected to return. Putz, Sean Green and Jeremy Reed were shipped off to New York. Luis Valbuena was sent to Cleveland in the first trade of Jack Zduriencik's GM career. Jamie Burke was non-tendered. R.A. Dickey was outrighted off the 40-man roster. Jake Woods, Eric O'Flaherty and Jared Wells are also gone, but then nobody cares. If I write "Jarrod Washburn" in here enough times, I wonder if it'll come true.

Players Acquired:

The offseason started kind of slowly, with Zduriencik content to make a couple of minor league additions while overhauling the coaching staff, but then things picked up with the signings of Russell Branyan and Chris Shelton and the big three-way Putz trade that netted the organization seven players, including Aaron Heilman, Franklin Gutierrez, Endy Chavez and Mike Carp. The Mariners also snagged infielder Reggie Corona and reliever Jose Lugo in the Rule 5 Draft. That's all that's been done at this writing, but more is likely to come.

Management Is:

Brand new. At long last, the Mariners shook things up and got rid of a front office that crashed the team into the ground, put it back together with spit and Scotch tape, and crashed it into the ground again. Bavasi's long gone, and his interim understudy Lee Pelekoudas is out of the main chair. Taking over is Zduriencik, a former assistant and director with Milwaukee who's the only non-GM to be named Baseball America Executive of the Year.

Zduriencik has a terrific eye for talent, and it's hard to find a current Brewer of significance he didn't have a hand in acquiring. As candidates to help this organization rebuild are concerned, I'm not sure the M's could've made a better pick. In a few short months he's already demonstrated an understanding of both freely available talent and the value of defense, which—well, if you paid attention to the Mariners before, this is a little bit mind-blowing.

Coming with Zduriencik from Milwaukee are Tom McNamara and Tony Blengino. McNamara essentially replaces the beloved Bob Fontaine, bringing over some of the drafting magic responsible for making the Brewers such a strong organization. And Blengino, the new assistant GM, is exciting because he has a SABR background and intends to create a research group to help inform decisions at every level. Zduriencik's is hardly the first name to come to mind when you think about new and potential GMs with stathead inclinations, but the eagerness with which the new front office seems prepared to blend excellent scouting with strong statistical knowledge is something Mariners fans haven't experienced. It's an incredible turnaround from the horrors of the previous administration, and it portends well for the future.

Management change hasn't occurred only in the front office. While Jim Riggleman said all the right things during his brief stint with the team, he and the rest of his staff were shown the door after the season, with Don Wakamatsu being brought in from Oakland as the new manager. That the Mariners would even consider hiring someone away from the A's is something I'm not sure we would've seen under Bavasi. Wakamatsu brings with him a strong record of not being Don Baylor, which scores him major points.

Ownership is still the same, but while I loathe them and occasionally wish ill on their families, they did make the call to bring in Zduriencik, so for the time being I'm easing off. They've earned a brief respite.

The Minor League System Is:

Okay, but not real big on impact talent. There is but a single potential superstar in the system, and that's Carlos Triunfel, the 18-year-old "middle infielder" who held his own in high-A. Triunfel's bat is still a work in progress, and his body may force him to a corner before he hits 20, but he makes good contact, his power is developing, and his offensive ceiling may not even exist. I know, I know, High Desert is High Desert, but Triunfel just picked up more extra-base hits than Miguel Cabrera had at the same age. He is unquestionably the guy to watch going forward.

Outside of Triunfel, you've got a handful of guys who look like solid future regulars. Jeff Clement's unlikely to stick behind the plate, but he's going to hit no matter where he plays. Wladimir Balentien will never be a star, but he and Carlos Lee aren't really too different. Carp could be a worse defensive Lyle Overbay. Adam Moore, Matt Tuiasosopo and Michael Saunders are on the way. And so on and so forth. There's talent here. Bavasi sacrificed a lot of the future to build his failure of a team, but he didn't sacrifice all of it.

You'll notice, though, that I didn't mention a single pitcher. That's because you have to reach pretty deep to find a good one. Phillippe Aumont's hanging around, but he's still in A ball. The same with Juan Ramirez, Maikel Cleto and Michael Pineda. Losing Tony Butler and Chris Tillman did a number on the organization's pitching depth, and this is a well that needs to be replenished. Being able to develop pitching internally helps prevent mistakes like the Bedard trade and the Silva signing. In that regard, this system needs help. Fortunately, ownership hired the right people to provide it. In the coming years, look for this particular section of the *THT Season Preview* to become way more optimistic.

Due For a Change:

Without a doubt, the biggest candidate for change is Kenji Johjima. His 2008 was so bad teammates started to resent him for getting a contract extension he didn't deserve, but while his power disappeared, he also put up a BABIP of just .233 despite a career-high line drive rate. Odds are he's going to recover a chunk of his batting average and look like a decent catcher next season.

I also have to believe that Silva will bounce back, if only because it takes some concentration to sustain such an awesome level of bad. As for the rest of the team, Yuniesky Betancourt should see a little jump in his numbers, and both Clement and Balentien should begin to hit like actual major leaguers now that they've gotten their feet wet for a few hundred at-bats. Clement's more likely to get going first. Washburn should benefit greatly from the new outfield defense if he doesn't get traded first. Gutierrez's offense should climb a bit higher.

I don't see any good candidates to get worse, mainly because pretty much everyone was awful last year. I suppose Roy Corcoran probably isn't long for a low-3's ERA. Oh no! It's also an open question as to whether Jose Lopez continues to improve or if he regresses from his standout 2008.

Reasons to be Optimistic:

New front office. And Felix Hernandez. New front office and Felix Hernandez. The Mariners were mismanaged for so long that it's hard to believe there's anything left, but there are a few building blocks still sticking around, and when you combine that with a big budget and the guys who helped turn Milwaukee's system into a talent pipeline, things don't seem quite as bad as they did in September. There's hope. For the first time in years and years, the Seattle Mariners and the fans who follow them have hope, and just because that hope is predicated around the entire organization being rebuilt doesn't negate its validity.

Fans have wanted to see this organization start over for a long time. Now they're getting that chance, and the people in charge seem to have a pretty good idea of what they're doing. It's a long road back to being a powerhouse, but today we can say with a reasonable degree of confidence that the team's actually on the right path.

Reasons to be Pessimistic:

I guess it really boils down to two reasons: (1) this team right now doesn't have enough talent, and (2) we still don't know if the new front office will live up to its billing.

211

I don't think the former needs very much explanation. This team doesn't have very many legitimately good players, and right now the farm system is in position to be of only limited help. It's a tough project to take on. If this team's going to contend within the next couple of years, the front office is going to have to make an awful lot of good decisions. All that hope for the future – that's for a long ways away. In the short term, this team looks bad to mediocre, with an upside of half-decent.

As for the latter—I don't know if "pessimistic" is the right word, but it's certainly a reason to be cautious. The fact is that we don't have a great idea of what Zduriencik and company will be like, and we won't know much until they've actually made more than a handful of moves. For all we know, they could just end up being a different kind of wrong. I don't think that'll be the case, mind you, as I was rather fond of their hiring and I like the moves so far, but it wouldn't be out of the question for further damage to be wrought by purported winds of change. If that happens, expect this chapter to be written by someone else next year, as I will have killed myself.

Still Left to Do:

Almost everything. The front office needs to continue figuring out which players it wants to keep around so the rest of them can be sent packing for prospects and money. Is Lopez a part of the future? If not, trade him. Is Betancourt a part of the future? If not, trade him. Is Adrian Beltre a part of the future? If not, trade him. Etc. It's complicated. The Putz trade got things off to a good start.

Rebuilding is neither easy nor easily predictable, so it's kind of hard to speak in anything but the most general of terms, but when I say "almost everything," I mean it. In making this team its own, the front office needs to evaluate every single player in the system and make moves to hasten the long march back to respectability. This process has only just begun.

In the short term, I imagine the team would like to add both a DH and a utility infielder while exploring a few bullpen options and trying to find room in the rotation for everyone the front office wants to see start.

Most Likely Team Outcome:

With the moves the team already has made, the Mariners are better now than they were at any point last season. While any number of things could change by spring training, as of now the offense is in line to be below average but substantially improved, and Gutierrez and Chavez should do wonders for what was recently a pretty bad defensive unit. The team's taken a significant step forward. However, it's still a roster with a bunch of flaws and a bigger bunch of questions, so with that in mind, I'm prepared to become more familiar with the basement. I already know it pretty well, but the more time you spend with something, the more you find out about it. In this corner, the mold kind of looks like Jesus. The Orioles are passed out somewhere near the washing machine.

Player Projections

Batters

Wladimir Balentien (Center Field)

PA	R	H	2B	3B	HR	RBI	SO	BB	SB	CS	BA	OBP	SLG	OPS	3-Year	Fielding	Reliability
510	62	111	25	2	22	71	119	46	5	3	.244	.314	.452	.766	+0.03	F	Very High

Balentien was billed by supporters of the Erik Bedard trade as the young outfielder who would make Mariners fans everywhere forget about Adam Jones. Thrust into a regular role after the release of Brad Wilkerson, he instead came up, didn't hit, went down, hit, came back up a month and a half later, and didn't hit again. The argument could be made that he was even worse following the second promotion than he was after the first. Over 71 games in Seattle last year, Balentien didn't do anything right. Wlad's obviously not as bad as he looked during the summer, but his performance raised legitimate questions about his future. He makes limited contact, and while his power is good, it's not extraordinary, and he doesn't have a very good eye. Throw in the fact that he's not a plus defender and you've got a guy who needs a lot of things to go his way in order to be a real asset. Balentien's skill set is not one of a future star. It's one of a guy who could earn a lot of money down the road if he develops a little more, since the market loves to pay slugging corner outfielders who don't play much defense, but in terms of actual value, he's no Adam Jones, and he'll probably never be close.

Adrian Beltre (Third Base)

PA	R	H	2B	3B	HR	RBI	SO	BB	SB	CS	BA	OBP	SLG	OPS	3-Year	Fielding	Reliability
575	72	142	31	2	21	79	93	42	9	2	.271	.327	.458	.785	-0.02	A	Very High

Despite my best efforts, Beltre remains one of the most underappreciated players in baseball. Playing with a torn ligament in his thumb on 2008, Beltre put up another season of above-average offensive numbers that, were it not for a little bad luck, should have been even better—he was absolutely stinging the ball, and his .279 BABIP didn't do justice to his elevated line drive rate. To go along with his annual solid production at the plate, Beltre also routinely places near the top of the defensive leader boards, to the tune of being worth +10 or +15 runs in the field. He's an excellent all-around asset and a bargain at $12 million. I think it would be better had 2004 never happened, because Beltre doesn't deserve to be viewed as a disappointment; he deserves to be viewed as the legitimate star player he really is. This is one Mariner that I will be sad to see leave.

Yuniesky Betancourt (Shortstop)

PA	R	H	2B	3B	HR	RBI	SO	BB	SB	CS	BA	OBP	SLG	OPS	3-Year	Fielding	Reliability
543	62	150	31	3	11	65	50	19	5	4	.293	.318	.429	.747	+0.08	D	Very High

Yuni's never going to hit very much. He just doesn't have it in him. He can make frequent contact and run pretty fast, but players who don't walk or hit for power have low offensive ceilings. With that in mind, it would seem that Betancourt's value is tied to his ability to play good defense. The problem is that he doesn't. Where Yuni was once regarded by observers as a range-happy magician, his defense has slipped with almost unprecedented speed to the point at which it's become a significant problem. Now, a guy who can't hit or field isn't a guy you want in your everyday lineup. So the Mariners need to hope that Yuni can work himself back into shape and recover some of what he's lost, because if he doesn't, he's just not a player worth playing anymore.

Willie Bloomquist (Shortstop)

PA	R	H	2B	3B	HR	RBI	SO	BB	SB	CS	BA	OBP	SLG	OPS	3-Year	Fielding	Reliability
273	30	61	8	1	1	18	44	25	12	3	.253	.328	.306	.634	-0.03	C	Low

It's always been funny to me how baseball's version of a jack-of-all-trades is, generally speaking, a jack of none of them. Bloomquist does a lot of different things, but he doesn't do any of them particularly well. I don't think anybody ever dreams of growing up to be a major league baseball player whose scouting report reads "Alfredo Amezaga without the defense."

Russell Branyan (Third Base)

PA	R	H	2B	3B	HR	RBI	SO	BB	SB	CS	BA	OBP	SLG	OPS	3-Year	Fielding	Reliability
330	45	74	16	1	19	55	90	39	3	1	.259	.349	.521	.870	-0.03	D	Average

Another year, another ridiculous projection for Russell the Muscle. Branyan made a triumphant return to the Brewers, seemingly the only organization in baseball willing to give him even half a chance, just as Bill Hall was faltering. He proceeded to launch a bunch of tape-measure home runs and then got injured and was pretty much forgotten about. GM Jack Zduriencik brought Branyan with him to Seattle to back up Adrian Beltre.

Jamie Burke (Catcher)

PA	R	H	2B	3B	HR	RBI	SO	BB	SB	CS	BA	OBP	SLG	OPS	3-Year	Fielding	Reliability
229	23	54	12	0	3	23	31	14	0	1	.260	.314	.362	.676	—	C	Low

An old backup catcher with a heartwarming story, Burke has his uses. It just so happens that many of those uses involve being nice to coaches and teammates and few of those uses involve playing baseball. Burke makes contact and goes to all fields, and you can't really ask for much more from someone in his position, but he doesn't do anything that distinguishes him from the rest of his peer group, so he's not a noteworthy player. He's just a good guy. And who knows, that might be enough to keep him employed.

Miguel Cairo (Second Base)

PA	R	H	2B	3B	HR	RBI	SO	BB	SB	CS	BA	OBP	SLG	OPS	3-Year	Fielding	Reliability
297	30	64	14	2	0	19	44	21	8	2	.242	.302	.310	.612	-0.03	C	Low

Why The 2008 Seattle Mariners Lost 101 Games In 25 Words Or Less: Miguel Cairo was signed as a pinch-runner. He started 37 games at first base.

Mike Carp (First Base)

PA	R	H	2B	3B	HR	RBI	SO	BB	SB	CS	BA	OBP	SLG	OPS	3-Year	Fielding	Reliability
541	58	117	23	1	13	58	100	50	1	2	.246	.327	.380	.707	+0.09	D	Very High

Carp is interesting enough to remain a fringe prospect. He has good plate discipline and a nice left-handed stroke, but he struggles against southpaws and hasn't yet hit for enough power to project him as any kind of major league first baseman. This is an important season for Carp: Either he'll experience a surge in the power department and possibly emerge from the margins of prospect-dom, or he'll just remain a decent left-handed bat at a position that demands considerably more than decency.

Endy Chavez (Outfield)

PA	R	H	2B	3B	HR	RBI	SO	BB	SB	CS	BA	OBP	SLG	OPS	3-Year	Fielding	Reliability
326	35	81	14	3	1	25	38	20	8	2	.275	.321	.353	.674	-0.02	A+	Average

Chavez might be the best defensive outfielder in baseball, but he has numerous offensive shortcomings: No power, little plate discipline, and just so-so base-stealing ability despite very good speed. Even with all of that working against him, his glove is so good that he'd probably be something like an average all-around center fielder if only the Mets had a need for one.

Jeff Clement (Catcher)

PA	R	H	2B	3B	HR	RBI	SO	BB	SB	CS	BA	OBP	SLG	OPS	3-Year	Fielding	Reliability
447	53	101	24	2	15	59	90	43	0	1	.257	.340	.443	.783	+0.02	D	High

Jeff Clement's summer didn't really go much better than Wladimir Balentien's, all things considered. He terrorized Triple-A with two of the best offensive months in Tacoma history, but upon getting promoted to the big leagues he left his eye, power and contact ability behind, and the hitter we saw in Seattle looked nothing like the hitter we expected. In addition, he didn't blow anyone away with his work behind the plate. It's this last bit that's probably the biggest issue going forward. Clement's still a good bet to hit pretty well once he's adjusted, but whether he's doing it as a catcher, first baseman or DH has yet to be determined. The latter two would obviously take quite a bit of shine off the apple, although since's he's a homegrown lefty with power, I'm sure the fans would be willing to overlook a position switch as long as he could sock a few dingers.

Victor Diaz (Left Field)

PA	R	H	2B	3B	HR	RBI	SO	BB	SB	CS	BA	OBP	SLG	OPS	3-Year	Fielding	Reliability
487	58	111	24	1	19	67	140	36	5	2	.251	.313	.439	.752	+0.01	D	High

Over a two-month stint with the Rangers in 2007, Diaz hit nine home runs and drew one walk. He's the classic slow corner outfielder who swings from the heels at every other pitch regardless of what it is or where it's going, and while that can make watching him a memorable experience, I don't think anyone's in a particular rush to bring him to a major league stadium near you. Now 27, he's as good as he's ever going to get.

Franklin Gutierrez (Right Field)

PA	R	H	2B	3B	HR	RBI	SO	BB	SB	CS	BA	OBP	SLG	OPS	3-Year	Fielding	Reliability
450	51	105	23	2	11	50	95	31	9	3	.258	.316	.406	.722	+0.01	A+	High

Gutierrez had the unfortunate luck to be an outstanding center fielder on a team with Grady Sizemore. Because he didn't hit consistently enough to play on a corner, he ended the season as a reserve outfielder. Now he'll get an opportunity to play center for Seattle; even if he doesn't hit, his range and arm alone make him a productive player.

Tim Hulett (Shortstop)

PA	R	H	2B	3B	HR	RBI	SO	BB	SB	CS	BA	OBP	SLG	OPS	3-Year	Fielding	Reliability
460	55	102	21	4	9	46	93	49	9	3	.256	.339	.397	.736	+0.01	D	Very High

Hulett's .518 SLG in Triple-A showed more power than we expected from the little dude. He's not armed with a ton of defensive versatility, and as the patient sort he can end up behind in a lot of pitcher's counts, but as a capable middle infielder who can work a walk and hit the occasional home run, Hulett's a good bet to carve himself out a career as a major league reserve. Not entirely unlike his father, really. Turns out "utility player" is genetic.

Raul Ibanez (Left Field)

PA	R	H	2B	3B	HR	RBI	SO	BB	SB	CS	BA	OBP	SLG	OPS	3-Year	Fielding	Reliability
620	76	155	33	3	20	82	101	56	1	2	.279	.345	.457	.802	—	D	Very High

I imagine everybody expects me to use this space to talk about how Ibanez's poor defense negates a huge chunk of his offensive productivity. But I'm not going to. Not me. I'm not that predictable. Why would I want to talk about how Ibanez's poor defense negates a huge chunk of his offensive productivity? The fact that Ibanez's poor defense negates a huge chunk of his offensive productivity isn't that interesting. I'd like to think that I'm capable of coming up with something newer and fresher than just repeating the same old stuff about how Ibanez's poor defense negates a huge chunk of his offensive productivity.

Kenji Johjima (Catcher)

PA	R	H	2B	3B	HR	RBI	SO	BB	SB	CS	BA	OBP	SLG	OPS	3-Year	Fielding	Reliability
448	47	110	22	0	9	50	45	20	1	1	.266	.311	.384	.695	-0.03	B	Very High

Kenji Johjima's 2008 was as unlucky as it was disappointing—among 314 players who came to the plate at least 250 times, Johjima's .233 BABIP ranked third-lowest despite a line drive rate as healthy as ever. That's completely unsustainable, and a little regression takes his batting average way back up into more palatable territory. Unfortunately, bad luck with BABIP doesn't account for a power outage, and last year Johjima hit half as many home runs as he did the year before. And at 32, that power may never come back. So while Johjima's average doesn't reflect how he was hitting the ball, he did still begin to decline, and his three-year extension is only now kicking in. Whoops. He could be okay in 2009, but after that, who knows?

Rob Johnson (Catcher)

PA	R	H	2B	3B	HR	RBI	SO	BB	SB	CS	BA	OBP	SLG	OPS	3-Year	Fielding	Reliability
450	46	106	23	1	6	44	75	29	5	4	.257	.306	.361	.667	+0.02	D	High

Always a guy with a sterling defensive reputation, Johnson added a little punch in 2008, hitting the ball on more of a line and pulling his average above .300 for the first time in his career. It wasn't a particularly jaw-dropping season, but for a guy many people didn't think would be able to hit, it represented an encouraging step forward. While Johnson's no prize, he's ready to be a backup right now, and if another team acquired him in the hopes of turning him into a starter down the road, it wouldn't be the stupidest thing ever. He could be all right for a season or three around his peak.

Bryan LaHair (First Base)

PA	R	H	2B	3B	HR	RBI	SO	BB	SB	CS	BA	OBP	SLG	OPS	3-Year	Fielding	Reliability
507	57	118	28	1	15	64	124	45	1	2	.259	.326	.424	.750	+0.06	B	Very High

Only under the Bill Bavasi administration could Bryan LaHair ever be considered a prospect. A slap-hitting first baseman with little power and a mediocre eye, LaHair kept his head above water in Tacoma but got exposed in the big leagues, where pitchers took advantage of every hole in his swing and left him with Miguel Cairo's batting line. He's not a good player now, and he doesn't have the skill set to be a good player down the road. His only real hope is that someday he gets invited to camp with an NL ballclub and one of the coaches double dog dares one of the executives to do something stupid.

Jose Lopez (Second Base)

PA	R	H	2B	3B	HR	RBI	SO	BB	SB	CS	BA	OBP	SLG	OPS	3-Year	Fielding	Reliability
593	66	157	29	3	13	69	67	26	4	2	.284	.318	.418	.736	+0.02	B	Very High

You'd be hard-pressed to find a more contentious Seattle Mariner than Jose Lopez. Lopez rebounded in a big way from a disastrous 2007 with a strong 2008 that saw him blow his previous numbers out of the water. Now 25, in theory he seems primed to take off, but memories of prior seasons still linger, and it's unclear whether he'll continue to improve or regress back to something in between his last two years. With his defensive ability in question, Lopez needs it to be the former in order to be a valuable player. The good news is that there are a number of positive indicators aside from his age, like his increased strength and reduced strikeout rate, but there's still no guarantee. Watch Lopez closely. What he does in 2009 will in large part serve to shape the rest of his career.

Adam Moore (Catcher)

PA	R	H	2B	3B	HR	RBI	SO	BB	SB	CS	BA	OBP	SLG	OPS	3-Year	Fielding	Reliability
453	45	97	19	1	11	49	93	27	0	1	.236	.295	.367	.662	+0.04	—	High

It would've been easy to write off Moore's surprising 2007 as a High Desert mirage, but then he came right back and did the same thing again in Double-A last season, establishing himself as a legitimate prospect and potential future starting catcher. He still has a lot of hurdles to overcome before he enters any big league discussions, like carrying his success into Triple-A and polishing his game behind the plate, but there's a lot of gap power ability in his bat that could take him pretty far should he continue to develop. You don't see too many backstops collect 35-40 doubles, but Moore has a chance.

Michael Saunders (Center Field)

PA	R	H	2B	3B	HR	RBI	SO	BB	SB	CS	BA	OBP	SLG	OPS	3-Year	Fielding	Reliability
507	56	107	22	4	9	48	133	43	9	6	.239	.310	.366	.676	+0.08	C	High

Saunders has always kind of flown under the radar a little bit, but it's about time for that to stop. Only 22, he's not likely to stick in center as he fills out, but he looks like a plus defensive corner outfielder with an ability to hit for average, draw a walk, and find the gaps. USS Mariner's David Cameron has been calling Saunders "Shin-soo Choo without the accent" for a while, now, and Choo's certainly worked out pretty well. Saunders is an underrated little prospect. He doesn't have Balentien's light tower power, but he has a more well-rounded skill set and the higher career ceiling of the two. His arrival doesn't look very far off.

Ichiro Suzuki (Right Field)

PA	R	H	2B	3B	HR	RBI	SO	BB	SB	CS	BA	OBP	SLG	OPS	3-Year	Fielding	Reliability
659	85	187	20	6	3	52	67	45	32	4	.310	.360	.378	.738	—	A+	Very High

Ichiro's offensive dropoff in 2008 had nothing to do with a decline in talent and everything to do with a decline in BABIP. Every single one of his macroscopic and microscopic indicators remained remarkably stable, but his BABIP dropped 53 points, pulling the rest of his numbers down with it. Ichiro lost six hits due to bad luck with grounders and he lost nine hits due to bad luck on liners. There's no reason to believe that he's gotten slower or developed a tendency to hit weaker line drives, so the only sensible conclusion is that he was just the victim of some lousy breaks. Expect things to end up somewhere in between his 2007 and 2008. He's still an unparalleled player.

Jose Vidro (Designated Hitter)

PA	R	H	2B	3B	HR	RBI	SO	BB	SB	CS	BA	OBP	SLG	OPS	3-Year	Fielding	Reliability
428	44	106	18	0	5	40	49	34	1	1	.274	.334	.360	.694	-0.04	C	Very High

An obvious candidate for a little BABIP regression after a lucky 2007, Vidro got the crap regressed out of it in 2008, and as a result found himself out of a job in early August. Witness everything that was wrong with the Bill Bavasi era in Seattle, all tied up in one fat little package. A below-average hitter in each of his final two seasons in Washington, Vidro was acquired specifically for his bat and nothing else, and—surprise!—he was bad. Over two years with the Mariners he batted .285/.344/.374 as a designated hitter, all for the low, low cost of $12 million, and if that doesn't seem awful to you, then how the hell did you ever find this book in the first place?

Pitchers

Miguel Batista (Reliever)

W	L	ERA	TBF	IP	Hit	HR	SO	BB	HBP	3-Year	Reliability
6	8	4.94	562	125	135	13	75	62	5	—	Very High

Evidently it's bad when a pitcher loses his ability to throw strikes, miss bats and keep the ball on the ground. The worst starting pitcher in baseball last year, Batista can always choose to blame injuries for his ineffectiveness, but he has a long, long way to climb back before he's even close to being respectable again. Batista's become almost exclusively a fastball/cutter guy over the years, so at this point, given his lousy results and limited repertoire, he should probably just accept that he'll be living out his days in the bullpen.

Erik Bedard (Starter)

W	L	ERA	TBF	IP	Hit	HR	SO	BB	HBP	3-Year	Reliability
8	6	3.57	528	126	112	12	126	48	5	+0.30	Very High

One of the most talented players to ever don a Mariners uniform, Bedard hurt his hip in his first game of the season, hurt his shoulder in his second, and shut things down in early July. A little while later he went under the knife. It wasn't exactly the debut season that Bill Bavasi was looking for. The good news is that Bedard's on track to be all better by spring training, so while his personality rubbed a lot of fans and journalists the wrong way last year, not all hope is lost, and he may yet be able to show the world just why Bavasi was so insistent on bringing him in. As recently as 2007, Bedard was the best starter in baseball, and when he's healthy, he still has that same terrifying hammer that befuddles lefties and righties alike. He's a good pitcher. Correction: He's a good pitcher when he's banged up. He's a great pitcher when he's peaches. Root for him. It's the right thing to do.

Roy Corcoran (Reliever)

W	L	ERA	TBF	IP	Hit	HR	SO	BB	HBP	3-Year	Reliability
4	4	3.93	336	76	73	4	50	43	4	+0.24	Average

Among pitchers who threw at least 40 innings last year, Roy Corcoran's 70 percent groundball rate was the highest in baseball. He doesn't miss many bats and he doesn't pound the zone, but you can get away with an awful lot when you don't let people hit the ball in the air. Corcoran's going to regress a little bit, because a 10 percent line drive rate isn't sustainable, but even so, he's a groundball machine, and as such, he'll always stand as another example of why it's foolish to pay any kind of big money to a middle reliever. Corcoran's virtually a carbon copy of Sean Green before Sean Green went sidearm.

R.A. Dickey (Starter)

W	L	ERA	TBF	IP	Hit	HR	SO	BB	HBP	3-Year	Reliability
6	10	5.21	632	142	158	21	65	61	7	+0.17	Very High

It was the right idea, anyway. Dickey threw nearly 70 percent knuckleballs last season over 112 innings, mixing up speeds to try to keep the batters off balance. Batters hit over .300 against it. I'd be perfectly happy to see the organization keep Dickey around in Triple-A to let him try to perfect the pitch, because the potential is there for him to be useful, but right now, the knuckler isn't good enough for him to survive in the major leagues.

Ryan Feierabend (Starter)

W	L	ERA	TBF	IP	Hit	HR	SO	BB	HBP	3-Year	Reliability
5	9	5.64	582	129	153	19	69	52	7	-0.37	Very High

Feierabend's changeup remains both a good weapon and his strongest offering, but it's also his only offering that's even close to being major league caliber. Neither his curve nor his slider has any kind of consistency, and his 85-88 mph fastball is missing a few ticks from where it was a couple years ago. A quarter of the time he's throwing something good and 75 percent of the time he's throwing something bad. Feierabend's always been young for his level, and he's still only 23, but he's running out of time to strengthen his arsenal. Odds are he never makes it. His ceiling is low, even if he does.

Sean Green (Reliever)

W	L	ERA	TBF	IP	Hit	HR	SO	BB	HBP	3-Year	Reliability
5	4	3.59	332	77	74	4	53	35	4	+0.23	Average

Green's career has taken off since he lowered his arm angle two years ago. Where once he was a groundballer, now he's a groundballer who misses bats, which elevates his status from useful to valuable. As a sidearmer, he'll always have trouble keeping lefties off base, but righties get tied in knots by Green's sinking fastball and frisbee slider. He deserves more credit for the work he did in Seattle. Part of the J.J. Putz blockbuster, Green's tendency to wear down at the end of the year should fit in great with the Mets.

Felix Hernandez (Starter)

W	L	ERA	TBF	IP	Hit	HR	SO	BB	HBP	3-Year	Reliability
12	9	3.61	774	185	177	16	160	61	6	-0.28	Very High

While his ERA won't show it, 2008 actually represented a bit of a step back for Felix, as his strike rate dropped from 65 to 64 percent, his swinging strike rate dropped from 10 to 9 percent, and his groundball rate dropped from 60 to 51 percent. It's the last bit that's the most disconcerting; while 51 percent is excellent, it's far more human and far less Felix than that to which we became accustomed. Nevertheless, he is a 22-year-old power arm with four A or B-level pitches, and the occasional bumps in the road are par for the course. He's still one of the most valuable assets in baseball. Watch to see if a change in pitching coaches changes Felix's approach—if he starts throwing fewer fastballs, the sky's the limit.

Cesar Jimenez (Reliever)

W	L	ERA	TBF	IP	Hit	HR	SO	BB	HBP	3-Year	Reliability
4	4	4.19	302	70	68	7	54	30	3	-0.12	Average

A lefty reliever whose best pitch is a slow change, Jimenez has a repertoire ill-suited for situational work, which is either a good thing or a bad thing for him, depending on how you look at it. On the one hand, he's less likely to get pigeonholed, but on the other, he's also less likely to stick around the big leagues if the rest of his stuff doesn't get any better. With the way the Mariner bullpen looks as of this writing, 2009 may be the best chance Jimenez ever gets to establish himself.

Mark Lowe (Reliever)

W	L	ERA	TBF	IP	Hit	HR	SO	BB	HBP	3-Year	Reliability
3	4	4.29	273	63	61	6	52	28	3	+0.04	Very Low

Coming back from unusual surgery on his elbow, Lowe did a good job of staying healthy and a bad job of pitching well. Still, though, being able to avoid the DL was a pretty big deal for a guy in his position, so his season has to be considered a success. His arsenal is more or less intact from 2006, although he's lost a mile or two and reduced his slider frequency, presumably in an attempt to protect his arm. And that arsenal gives him a whole lot of upside. Lowe has plus velocity and three solid pitches. There's no guarantee that he'll ever be able to refine his command or avoid getting injured, but the stuff is definitely there for him to excel.

Brandon Morrow (Reliever)

W	L	ERA	TBF	IP	Hit	HR	SO	BB	HBP	3-Year	Reliability
5	5	4.25	377	87	75	10	90	47	3	0.00	Low

We already knew that Brandon Morrow has an outstanding fastball. What we didn't know was that he could learn to control it while simultaneously developing some killer secondary weapons. Morrow dominated out of the bullpen before getting stretched out in the minors and coming back to one-hit New York in his ML starting debut. The rest of his time as a starter was up and down, but all the while he flashed an interesting change-up, a sharp but inconsistent slider, and a curveball with splitter movement that has the potential to make Morrow a superstar. Whether he continues to start or returns to the bullpen has yet to be determined, but the stuff Morrow flashed in September makes him one of the most exciting pitchers Seattle's ever had. Suddenly, I don't feel the same draft regret that I felt a year ago.

Eric O'Flaherty (Reliever)

W	L	ERA	TBF	IP	Hit	HR	SO	BB	HBP	3-Year	Reliability
2	3	4.41	191	43	45	4	34	20	3	-0.18	Low

O'Flaherty was supposed to be the team's go-to lefty last year, but he wound up allowing 15 runs in 14 days on the roster and getting shipped back to Triple-A, where he missed the second half of the season with a bad back. A surprising cut by the Mariners, O'Flaherty's still young enough to have a productive major league future, but the haste with which he was dropped from Seattle's 40-man roster suggests that his back may not be where he'd like it to be.

J.J. Putz (Reliever)

W	L	ERA	TBF	IP	Hit	HR	SO	BB	HBP	3-Year	Reliability
5	2	2.82	255	63	48	5	71	23	2	+0.14	Low

J.J. Putz was J.J. Putz for one game in 2008. In the second game, he hurt his rib, blew a save, took a loss, and sent his season spiraling out of control. Costochondritis and a hyperextended right elbow took their toll, and while he put up a 2.96 ERA over 27 appearances in the second half, he never fully recovered the same command or stuff that he had before getting injured. The Mets are taking a big chance with him. For two years he was one of the best relievers in baseball, but relievers are volatile, and now he's got some health issues to worry about. Neither the most optimistic nor the most pessimistic 2009 forecast coming true would be much of a surprise.

Ryan Rowland-Smith (Starter)

W	L	ERA	TBF	IP	Hit	HR	SO	BB	HBP	3-Year	Reliability
6	6	4.43	482	111	109	13	80	49	5	+0.03	Average

Although effective as a reliever, Rowland-Smith never really belonged in the bullpen, as he's always possessed a broad repertoire that seemed better suited to starting. The Mariners gave him that chance in 2008, and he responded by allowing 30 runs over 72 innings in the rotation. He's not quite that good, and he's never going to blow anyone away, but he provides everything you get from Jarrod Washburn for a fraction of the price. RRS' effective change, biting slider and lollipop curve are good enough to make up for his mediocre fastball and keep him a reasonable asset at the back of the rotation.

Carlos Silva (Starter)

W	L	ERA	TBF	IP	Hit	HR	SO	BB	HBP	3-Year	Reliability
7	11	5.03	698	161	197	24	71	36	5	+0.41	Very High

Signed to a big contract because he was "the best starter on the market," Silva got pounded, got hurt, and got sent home after the season with an order to lose weight. There's no saving this one. Silva's stuff sucks and he barely even counts as a groundballer. He's like Bill Bavasi's way of saying "you can fire me now, but you'll remember me for years."

Jarrod Washburn (Starter)

W	L	ERA	TBF	IP	Hit	HR	SO	BB	HBP	3-Year	Reliability
8	9	4.70	681	157	168	21	86	52	7	+0.16	Very High

If I'm Jarrod Washburn, and I see my employer go out and get Franklin Gutierrez and Endy Chavez in a trade, I tell my wife to start packing her things, because I'm about to get a new home. Just because Washburn hasn't been a good pitcher since 2002 doesn't mean other people have to know that.

Sean White (Starter)

W	L	ERA	TBF	IP	Hit	HR	SO	BB	HBP	3-Year	Reliability
4	9	6.66	566	119	162	17	33	57	7	+0.36	High

White looked like a decent Rule 5 grab at the time, being a guy with a fastball in the 90s and a bunch of ground balls, but last year everything fell apart and White wound up getting outrighted off the 40-man roster at the end of the season. The ground balls were still there, and anyone capable of keeping the ball out of the air stands a chance of getting a break, but if White was a long shot in 2007, he's now staring at nearly impossible odds.

St. Louis Cardinals

by Larry Borowsky of Viva El Birdos (vivaelbirdos.com)

2009 Cardinals Projections
Record: 81-81
Division Rank/Games Behind: 3rd, 8 games back
Runs Scored: 757, 7th in the league
Runs Allowed: 758, 9th in the league
Park Factor: .98, a slight pitcher's park

What Happened Last Year:

The Cardinals gave opportunities to a number of players trying to establish their careers; nearly all played well, making the Cards into surprise contenders. Of course, Albert Pujols' MVP season also had a thing or two to do with their unexpected success. The Cardinals hiked their scoring total by 54 runs, posted their best team batting average since the 1930s, and led the league handily in park-adjusted OPS.

Just as important, they tightened up a defense that bled runs profusely in 2007. Replacing aged, ineffective fielders in center (Jim Edmonds) and at shortstop (David Eckstein) saved the Cards at least 30 runs. Adam Kennedy bounced back from a knee injury to play stellar defense up the middle. After yielding 88 unearned runs in 2007, they gave away just 46 in 2008.

The Cardinals' rotation was more stable, too. The five pitchers in their Opening Day rotation made 143 starts, the highest total since the 100-win season of 2005; for the first time since that year, the Cardinals didn't get any starts from a DFA'd pitcher. Unfortunately, they got three only starts from the one midseason addition they'd most counted on: Chris Carpenter. He looked terrific in three August starts, his first after 16 months on the DL; then a nerve in Carpenter's elbow acted up, and he threw only one inning the rest of the way.

But even without Carpenter, the 2008 Cardinal rotation logged 66 more innings than the prior year's version, while yielding 71 fewer runs. The rotation, lineup, and defense improved by enough to carry the Cardinals to the playoffs—and they would have pulled it off if not for a disastrous collapse by the bullpen. The Cardinals lost 14 games they led after seven innings; they had a run differential of plus 86 in innings one through eight, but minus 32 from the ninth inning on. Most painful of all, the Cardinal blew two ninth-inning leads to the Brewers; on two other occasions they blew eighth-inning leads of three runs. St. Louis' win expec-

tancy exceeded 90 percent in all four of those games; if they'd merely won three of them, they would have finished ahead of the Brewers and tied with the Mets for the wild card.

Players Lost from Last Year's Team:

Braden Looper, Cesar Izturis, Felipe Lopez, Aaron Miles, Ron Villone, Russ Springer, Randy Flores, Jason Isringhausen, Mark Worrell

Players Acquired:

Khalil Greene

Management Is:

Still in transition. John Mozeliak did a commendable job in his first year as GM. Inheriting an old, injury-prone, top-heavy roster riddled with bad contracts, he managed to clear away a lot of deadweight and create room for some promising new growth. The Cards gained youth and flexibility while remaining competitive—no small feat.

The trick now will be to capitalize on the opportunity and further reshape the roster to restore it to the NL elite. So far, Mozeliak hasn't figured out how to do that. Will he be able to cash in some of the farm system's talent for a player (or players) like Mark McGwire, Edmonds and Scott Rolen, a la Walt Jocketty? Will he sell high on players like Rick Ankiel or Ryan Ludwick to add young players to the Cards' improving farm system? Maybe he'll do some of both?

As of this writing, it's still not clear what type of GM Mozeliak is. We know he has a knack for picking up pretty good players on the cheap (e.g., Troy Glaus, Khalil Greene, Kyle Lohse in '08, Lopez), but those were all stay-afloat moves—they plugged leaks in the hull but didn't add new boilers to the engine room. We also know that Mo has twice squandered some of his hard-won maneuverability by overpaying for mid-rotation pitchers (Joel Pineiro, Lohse in '09). If they hadn't dropped $40 million on Lohse, the Cardinals might have had the money to compete for a potential difference-maker such as Ben Sheets, Derek Lowe or A.J. Burnett.

Mozeliak has built a roster that's pretty solid everywhere but excellent nowhere, except in the person of Pujols. That'll keep you in the race most of the time, get you to the playoffs sometimes, maybe even get you deep into the playoffs if you get really lucky—as the Cardinals did in 2006. Is that the lesson the organization learned from its last championship—surround Pujols with serviceable pros and hope for the best? I hope not.

The Minor League System Is:

Exerting itself more forcefully. Four Cardinals regulars in 2009 were completely homegrown products—Yadier Molina, Pujols, Skip Schumaker, and Ankiel—and by year's end the bullpen was populated mainly by St. Louis draftees. The same transformation is occurring at the upper rungs of the farm system. The dead-end veterans who filled the Triple-A roster toward the end of Jocketty's regime have been replaced by actual prospects. *Baseball America* ranked five Cardinals farmhands among the top 20 prospects in the Pacific Coast League.

Under Jeff Luhnow, the Cardinals have largely taken a play-the-percentages approach to the draft. They select a lot of polished, "safe" players (mostly college pitchers) who are perceived as having low ceilings but can reach those ceilings relatively quickly. Seven players from the 2006 and 2007 drafts sped to Triple-A by the end of 2008, and more than a dozen reached Double-A. And four players drafted since 2005—Mitchell Boggs, Jaime Garcia, Nick Stavinoha and Chris Perez—graduated to the big leagues in 2008. At least one more (Colby Rasmus) is destined to arrive in 2009.

By drafting polished players and advancing them rapidly, the Cardinals have amassed a large pool of homegrown replacement-level talent—and the hope is that a few of these players will beat expectations and become big-league regulars. They're not counting on Boggs, Clay Mortensen, Jess Todd, Adam Ottavino and P.J. Walters all to develop into league-average starting pitchers, but they're betting that one of them will. Luhnow and Co. have built up similar positional depth at shortstop, third base, outfield and closer within the last four drafts. Has the depth reached a critical mass? If it's not there yet, it's getting close.

The knock on the system is that it lacks star power: Aside from Rasmus and Brett Wallace, there aren't any players in the organization who project as outstanding big leaguers. For now, the Cardinals seem content with that. If the farm system can supply enough average ballplayers who are cost-controlled, the Cards will gain enough payroll flexibility to buy their stars on the open market.

Due For a Change:

1. Greene: Sometimes a talented but struggling player just needs a hug, and there's no better place for that than St. Louis. Darryl Kile, Edmonds, Rolen and Carpenter are just some of those who came to the Cardinals in

Our Favorite Cardinals Blogs:
Viva El Birdos (http://www.vivaelbirdos.com): Now under new management, but hasn't skipped a beat.
Future Redbirds (http://futureredbirds.com): Terrific coverage of the Cardinal minor-league system.
Bird Land (http://www.stltoday.com/blogzone/bird-land/): A great beat-reporter blog by the Post-Dispatch's Derrick Goold.

their late 20s and bounced back from down seasons. Not coincidentally, all those players were pending free agents when they got to St. Louis—as is Greene. He is not quite the caliber of player as the aforementioned, but he doesn't have to be a star to make the Cards a whole lot better. If he just returns to his 2004-2007 level of play, he makes the Cards about three wins better.

2. Ludwick: He's a good hitter, but 37 homers? A more realistic level is probably 25, with maybe 80 RBIs. Gary Ward had a breakout season in 1982, and while he remained a solid performer he never regained his '82 plateau. I doubt Ludwick will ever recapture the magic of 2008—but he's still got plenty of value.

3. Lohse: For the first year or two of his new contract, Lohse is a reasonable bet to earn his salary. He might even win 15 games again, especially if the Cardinals solve their bullpen question. But I wouldn't expect an ERA under 4.00.

Reasons to be Optimistic:

First and foremost: Pujols. As long as they have him, the Cardinals will always have a chance to contend.

Second: Carpenter will be 20 months post-Tommy John by Opening Day, and his nerve issues are believed (as of January) to be manageable. Even if he makes only half his starts, he probably improves the Cardinals by two games.

Third: The bullpen can't possibly suck that bad two years in a row. Between better personnel and dumb luck, the Cards ought to gain a couple of wins (at least) in the late innings.

Fourth: Greene eliminates a hole in the St. Louis offense and shores up the Cardinals' weakness against lefties.

Fifth: Should they need to plug a hole midseason, the Cardinals will have depth from which to trade.

Sixth: With the defections from Milwaukee's pitching staff, only one team in the division is clearly better than the Cardinals on paper: the Cubs.

Reasons to be Pessimistic:

Main reason: Nearly every Cardinals regular and starting pitcher performed above his established level of ability in 2008; the number who regress to the mean in 2009 probably will be higher than the number who maintain or surpass their 2008 performance. Other reasons: The Cardinals still have a woeful lack of left-handed pitching. They are planning to give 30 starts to Pineiro. All three of their best starting pitchers (Adam Wainwright, Todd Wellemeyer and Carpenter) spent, or should have spent, time on the DL last year

Still Left to Do:

After the winter meetings, the Cardinals still had a surplus in the outfield and a lack of depth in the rotation and middle infield. They need to trade one or more outfielders to gain depth in an area of need—preferably young depth with upside.

Most Likely Team Outcome:

87 wins, second place.

Player Projections

Batters

Rick Ankiel (Center Field)

PA	R	H	2B	3B	HR	RBI	SO	BB	SB	CS	BA	OBP	SLG	OPS	3-Year	Fielding	Reliability
490	66	119	21	2	28	83	104	39	3	2	.269	.331	.515	.846	-0.02	D	High

What a marvel—and he's just learning how to hit. Against Triple-A pitching in 2007, he only walked once per 16 plate appearances; last year, against big-league pitching, he improved that rate to one walk per 11 plate appearances. Ankiel still has plenty to work on—he's too streaky, he can't hit to the opposite field, he's got poor situational splits—but the guy finished 5th in VORP among NL center fielders last year, despite starting only 107 games. He's playing for a new contract and being pushed by top prospect Colby Rasmus, and Ankiel hasn't always responded well to pressure; fantasy players beware. But whether he continues his remarkable metamorphosis or gets exposed as a hitter with too many holes, this guy won't be boring. In April he took a 17-pitch at-bat against Carlos Villanueva (he walked); in a May game at Colorado he made two 300-foot on-the-fly pegs to nail baserunners at third base. A good player, not a great one—but a great entertainer, and a phenomenal story.

Brian Barden (Shortstop)

PA	R	H	2B	3B	HR	RBI	SO	BB	SB	CS	BA	OBP	SLG	OPS	3-Year	Fielding	Reliability
453	49	108	20	3	8	46	82	34	2	2	.264	.325	.386	.711	0.00	D	High

Barden got to Triple-A in 2004 and has been at that level since, logging 558 games and more than 2,200 at-bats there. He had a nice year with the bat last season and played for the U.S. Olympic team in Beijing. The Cardinals had him playing mostly shortstop, hoping he'd gain the versatility necessary to compete for a big-league utility-infield role. He's 28 years old and has logged a grand total of 44 major-league at-bats so far.

Brian Barton (Left Field)

PA	R	H	2B	3B	HR	RBI	SO	BB	SB	CS	BA	OBP	SLG	OPS	3-Year	Fielding	Reliability
387	45	88	13	2	10	42	90	30	6	3	.260	.339	.399	.738	+0.06	C	High

There's a lot to like—great speed, good range afield, good plate discipline and pitch recognition, sufficient pop. But Barton swings and misses way too often; he can't handle a decent big-league fastball. Probably won't ever be an everyday player, but does enough things well to stick for a few years as a sub.

Chris Duncan (Left Field)

PA	R	H	2B	3B	HR	RBI	SO	BB	SB	CS	BA	OBP	SLG	OPS	3-Year	Fielding	Reliability
363	46	84	16	1	15	52	86	43	2	1	.265	.353	.465	.818	+0.02	D	High

While still recovering from the sports hernia that derailed him in 2007, Duncan was hit with a more serious injury in 2008: a herniated disk in his neck. He had surgery in August and it reportedly went well, but the procedure has never before been performed on a baseball player. Despite all his ailments, Duncan maintained his plate discipline and posted a .346 OBP (.371 vs right-handed pitchers). Health permitting, he probably still is capable of posting good numbers. He'll turn 28 in May.

David Freese (Third Base)

PA	R	H	2B	3B	HR	RBI	SO	BB	SB	CS	BA	OBP	SLG	OPS	3-Year	Fielding	Reliability
483	56	110	20	3	17	61	106	35	3	1	.251	.313	.427	.740	+0.02	B	High

He made the leap from Single-A to Triple-A look easy, posting an MLE line of .271/.322/.484. The Cardinals are high on him; Troy Glaus has the everyday job for 2009, but Freese is a player to keep tabs on.

Troy Glaus (Third Base)

PA	R	H	2B	3B	HR	RBI	SO	BB	SB	CS	BA	OBP	SLG	OPS	3-Year	Fielding	Reliability
552	71	126	26	0	25	81	105	73	0	2	.268	.368	.483	.851	-0.04	C	Very High

Early in the year, Glaus was plagued by a severe case of hay fever; he even removed himself from one May game because his eyes got so watery he couldn't see the baseball. Before Memorial Day, Glaus slugged only .380 with two dingers; thereafter he launched 25 bombs and slugged .538. He also posted the second-highest batting average and OBP of his career while turning in a surprisingly effective season with the glove. The Cardinals have high hopes for some of their minor-league 3B talent; they'll have to be thrilled if any of those guys can match the production Glaus supplied in 2008.

Khalil Greene (Shortstop)

PA	R	H	2B	3B	HR	RBI	SO	BB	SB	CS	BA	OBP	SLG	OPS	3-Year	Fielding	Reliability
471	54	109	26	2	15	60	94	29	4	1	.252	.302	.425	.727	-0.03	C	Very High

At age 28, without warning or explanation, Greene saw his offensive game collapse. Never blessed with good, or even passable, plate discipline, Greene's calling card is above-average power for a shortstop. When that disappeared in 2008, he became Neifi Perez without the batting average. On June 30, Greene broke his hand punching a storage cabinet in frustration, ending his season. From 2004 to 2007, he hit .280/.334/.511 on the road. Now with St. Louis, Greene should enjoy not having to play half his games at Petco Park.

Cesar Izturis (Shortstop)

PA	R	H	2B	3B	HR	RBI	SO	BB	SB	CS	BA	OBP	SLG	OPS	3-Year	Fielding	Reliability
418	45	103	16	2	2	32	28	26	13	2	.269	.320	.337	.657	-0.03	B	Average

With another 20 points of OBP, he would have been a very useful two-way player. But the Cardinals still had to be pleased with what they got from Izturis, whose defense probably saved them 30 runs over 2007. His offensive numbers, though feeble, were near the top of Izturis' range. The Cards didn't make a serious effort to bring him back.

Adam Kennedy (Second Base)

PA	R	H	2B	3B	HR	RBI	SO	BB	SB	CS	BA	OBP	SLG	OPS	3-Year	Fielding	Reliability
390	42	93	18	3	3	32	52	29	8	3	.263	.321	.357	.678	-0.05	A	High

Hardly anyone noticed, but Kennedy in 2008 did almost exactly what he was signed to do: His offensive numbers were near league-average for a second baseman (and near his own career norms), and he was superlative with the glove. On balance, he was an asset. Kennedy buried himself with a terrible May (.417 OPS in 62 at-bats), but from June 1 forward he hit .304/.335 /.430 in 207 at-bats. The Cards are overpaying him, but Kennedy isn't such an awful player.

Jason LaRue (Catcher)

PA	R	H	2B	3B	HR	RBI	SO	BB	SB	CS	BA	OBP	SLG	OPS	3-Year	Fielding	Reliability
268	28	54	11	1	6	27	49	24	1	0	.232	.315	.365	.680	-0.06	C	Low

When batting .213 represents a major comeback season, it says a lot about how your career is going … LaRue's numbers in 2008 were almost identical to his numbers the previous year for Kansas City, except he hit 10 additional singles last year. He does have one of the best mustaches in baseball.

Ryan Ludwick (Right Field)

PA	R	H	2B	3B	HR	RBI	SO	BB	SB	CS	BA	OBP	SLG	OPS	3-Year	Fielding	Reliability
538	74	135	31	2	29	91	128	47	3	3	.282	.352	.538	.890	-0.03	C	Very High

Ludwick's 16th-place finish in the MVP voting was an insult. He ranked second in the league in slugging, fourth in homers and OPS, and sixth in RBI; also 10th in VORP and ninth in WSAB. He and Albert Pujols formed the Cardinals' first-ever pair of 1-2 finishers in slugging. Fluke? Sort of—Ludwick's not a true .600 slugger. But he has been healthy for three seasons in a row and posted slugging averages (either actual, or MLE) above .500 in all three years. His true ability level probably lies in the .280/.340/.500 range; i.e., solidly above average.

Joe Mather (Right Field)

PA	R	H	2B	3B	HR	RBI	SO	BB	SB	CS	BA	OBP	SLG	OPS	3-Year	Fielding	Reliability
448	58	102	21	1	23	70	85	36	5	1	.256	.327	.487	.814	+0.07	C	Very High

Mather's defense was a revelation; in only 18 starts as a corner outfielder, he was worth half a win with the glove. He's got very good secondary offensive skills and makes contact at acceptable levels. If he does all that while hitting .270 (and that's within his range), Mather is a pretty useful package. He will turn 27 in July.

Aaron Miles (Second Base)

PA	R	H	2B	3B	HR	RBI	SO	BB	SB	CS	BA	OBP	SLG	OPS	3-Year	Fielding	Reliability
431	44	113	17	2	2	37	44	28	3	1	.286	.333	.354	.687	-0.03	D	High

He had a genuinely good year with the bat but probably won't repeat it. He held his own defensively; he had to pitch only one inning in 2008…

Yadier Molina (Catcher)

PA	R	H	2B	3B	HR	RBI	SO	BB	SB	CS	BA	OBP	SLG	OPS	3-Year	Fielding	Reliability
457	51	119	22	0	11	54	43	34	0	2	.288	.344	.421	.765	+0.08	C	High

He had the best offensive season by a Cardinals catcher in 25 years while winning a Gold Glove. I wouldn't expect Yadi to hit .300 again, but .280 with a decent OBP isn't too much to hope for—and he still has some untapped power potential. He'll turn 27 this year.

Albert Pujols (First Base)

PA	R	H	2B	3B	HR	RBI	SO	BB	SB	CS	BA	OBP	SLG	OPS	3-Year	Fielding	Reliability
590	92	163	34	1	33	106	59	87	4	3	.330	.431	.603	1.034	-0.03	A+	Very High

As of late July, Pujols was on pace for 27 homers and fewer than 90 RBIs. His rate stats were MVP-caliber, but his counting stats seemed to rule him out as a serious candidate for the award. Over the Cards' last 57 games, though, Albert hit .377 with 19 homers and 60 RBI to finish in the top four in all three Triple Crown categories and claim his second MVP. He also established new career highs in OPS, OBP and walks, then became the third Cardinal to receive the Roberto Clemente Award for community service (Ozzie Smith and Lou Brock are the others). Little-noticed fact: Pujols nearly halved his GIDP total last year, finishing with just 16; for only the second time in his career, he ranked outside the league's top 10 in that category.

Colby Rasmus (Center Field)

PA	R	H	2B	3B	HR	RBI	SO	BB	SB	CS	BA	OBP	SLG	OPS	3-Year	Fielding	Reliability
511	63	112	23	4	16	60	100	51	11	2	.250	.330	.426	.756	+0.09	D	Very High

Rasmus spent the first few weeks of the schedule pouting that he didn't make the St. Louis roster out of spring training, where he slugged .515 in 33 at-bats. But after two months at Triple-A, he was slugging only .348 in 207 at-bats. He rebounded with a very strong June, but a knee injury in July cut his year short. His final line was .251/.346/.396. For all the struggles, he was named the No. 1 prospect in the PCL by *Baseball America*. Expect him to see significant playing time in St. Louis this year.

Brendan Ryan (Shortstop)

PA	R	H	2B	3B	HR	RBI	SO	BB	SB	CS	BA	OBP	SLG	OPS	3-Year	Fielding	Reliability
403	46	96	17	2	6	38	61	28	12	2	.264	.319	.371	.690	+0.08	D	Average

He's an above-average defender at shortstop, so if he could reliably post a .675 OPS he'd have a chance to start somewhere in the big leagues. He hasn't established that he can hit that well, and he's now 27 years old.

Skip Schumaker (Center Field)

PA	R	H	2B	3B	HR	RBI	SO	BB	SB	CS	BA	OBP	SLG	OPS	3-Year	Fielding	Reliability
517	59	139	22	3	6	51	62	38	5	2	.295	.348	.393	.741	-0.02	D	Very High

He's a legitimately good hitter against right-handed pitchers—.340/.393/.468 in 461 plate appearances last year—but an automatic out against lefties, who held him to a .423 OPS in 133 plate appearances. It all added up to a terrific value for the Cardinals, who got the same production out of Schumaker they'd been getting from Juan Encarnacion—but for $5 million a year less. I wouldn't expect Schumaker to improve on his 2008 performance, but he could have a useful career as a platoon player.

Pitchers

Mitchell Boggs (Starter)

W	L	ERA	TBF	IP	Hit	HR	SO	BB	HBP	3-Year	Reliability
5	11	5.86	660	142	172	20	65	74	8	-0.38	Very High

Boggs didn't show much in his short stint with St. Louis—22 walks, just 13 strikeouts in 34 innings—but led the Pacific Coast League in ERA. His rise through the Cardinals system has been steady but unspectacular. Boggs isn't likely to ever be more than a fourth or fifth starter. If he's in St. Louis in 2009, it probably will be as a relief pitcher.

Chris Carpenter (Starter)

W	L	ERA	TBF	IP	Hit	HR	SO	BB	HBP	3-Year	Reliability
5	3	3.45	295	71	70	6	50	18	3	+0.21	Average

For all intents and purposes, he has missed two entire years due to injury. You can count on one hand the number of guys who've returned to form after a rehab that long. There's been talk of using Carpenter as a closer to protect his arm, but that's probably all it is, talk. More likely the Cards will try to wring as many starts out of him as they can between DL stints. If they get more than 15, hurrah; if they make the postseason and have Carpenter available in October, hallelujah.

Ryan Franklin (Reliever)

W	L	ERA	TBF	IP	Hit	HR	SO	BB	HBP	3-Year	Reliability
4	4	4.24	325	76	80	8	44	25	3	—	Average

Franklin always has been miscast as a late-inning reliever; he got the role only because the Cards had no one else to turn to in early 2007. Yes, he excelled at it for a few months, but (what a shock!) it didn't last. Now that they have at least three better options—Chris Perez, Kyle McClellan and Jason Motte —will Tony La Russa and Dave Duncan keep sending Franklin out there to hold eighth-inning leads? He'd probably serve the team best as a spot-starter/long-reliever.

Jason Isringhausen (Reliever)

W	L	ERA	TBF	IP	Hit	HR	SO	BB	HBP	3-Year	Reliability
4	2	3.72	248	58	52	5	45	27	2	—	Low

Izzy was even worse last year than in 2006, when he pitched on one leg for five months. He's a courageous player—but it takes more than guts to get hitters out.

Kyle Lohse (Starter)

W	L	ERA	TBF	IP	Hit	HR	SO	BB	HBP	3-Year	Reliability
9	11	4.41	761	176	195	18	100	52	7	+0.22	Very High

The Cardinals have long believed Lohse might be a good fit in St. Louis, and 2008 proved them right. Pitching in a non-DH league with good defensive support and a strong coach to guide him, Lohse had his best season and cashed it in for a four-year, $40 million deal. The Cardinals overpaid rather badly; Lohse maxed out his upside last year and is almost certain to regress. He'll deliver league-average innings in bulk, but he's not a difference-maker.

Braden Looper (Starter)

W	L	ERA	TBF	IP	Hit	HR	SO	BB	HBP	3-Year	Reliability
9	10	4.31	739	173	190	20	83	46	6	+0.14	Very High

In his second year as a starter, Looper increased his K rate, lowered his walk rate, and didn't miss a turn in the rotation. His line was virtually identical to that of his teammate, Kyle Lohse, but while the Cardinals rewarded Lohse with a four-year, $40 million deal, Looper didn't get so much as an arbitration offer. He's more useful than that. At 34 years old, he ought to stick around for awhile as a reliable low-walk, high-ground ball, keep-you-in-the-game type for the back of somebody's rotation.

Kyle McClellan (Reliever)

W	L	ERA	TBF	IP	Hit	HR	SO	BB	HBP	3-Year	Reliability
4	4	3.79	307	72	71	6	53	25	3	-0.11	Very Low

The kid just ran out of gas. Through his first 57 appearances (63.2 innings) he had an ERA of 2.69, a K/BB of 3:1, and an opponent line of .255/.314/.360. In his last 11 appearances (12 innings) he had an ERA of 11.25, a K/BB of 1:1, and an opponent OPS of .925. Dave Duncan thinks McClellan has the repertoire to start. Given the depth of the Cardinals' relief corps (especially from the right side), that might be the best use of this pitcher's talents. His role will get sorted out in spring training.

Jason Motte (Reliever)

W	L	ERA	TBF	IP	Hit	HR	SO	BB	HBP	3-Year	Reliability
4	3	3.88	276	64	56	6	74	30	3	+0.15	Very Low

He has one pitch, a 98-mph fastball; he may not need another. He struck out 40 percent of the big-league batters who faced him in an 11-inning trial at St. Louis; at Triple-A, in a much larger sample, he fanned 38 percent of the batters he saw. Tony La Russa and Dave Duncan aren't real keen on pure power pitchers, but they like Motte's makeup. He has a good chance to be pitching late in games for St. Louis this year.

Christopher Perez (Reliever)

W	L	ERA	TBF	IP	Hit	HR	SO	BB	HBP	3-Year	Reliability
4	3	3.97	278	64	51	7	67	38	4	-0.02	Low

Perez serves to illustrate the disconnect that still exists between the Cardinals front office and the dugout. The front office drafted Perez, a college closer, in the first round of the 2006 draft with a view toward having him close in St. Louis. The kid closed in A-ball, Double-A, and Triple-A; he closed for Team USA in the fall of 2007. And when given the chance to close in St. Louis late last summer, he converted seven saves in nine tries. All according to the plan—so he's the closer heading into 2009, right? You would think so... but this off-season Tony La Russa and Dave Duncan pushed general manager John Mozeliak hard to acquire an established closer. The Cardinals pursued K-Rod, Brian Fuentes and J.J. Putz (before he was dealt to the Mets), and even discussed bringing Jason Isringhausen back. As they did with Anthony Reyes, La Russa and Duncan are trying to teach Perez to keep the ball down.

Joel Pineiro (Starter)

W	L	ERA	TBF	IP	Hit	HR	SO	BB	HBP	3-Year	Reliability
7	9	4.94	631	145	172	19	75	42	4	+0.24	Very High

In mid-2007 the Red Sox DFA'd this player; two months later the Cardinals guaranteed him two years and $14 million. Which valuation seems more accurate?

Russ Springer (Reliever)

W	L	ERA	TBF	IP	Hit	HR	SO	BB	HBP	3-Year	Reliability
4	3	3.52	249	60	51	6	51	21	2	—	Low

He turned 40 in November. During his two years in St. Louis, he held right-handed hitters to a .166 batting average with an OPS in the .450 range. But lefties stung him for an .848 OPS last year.

Brad Thompson (Reliever)

W	L	ERA	TBF	IP	Hit	HR	SO	BB	HBP	3-Year	Reliability
5	5	4.73	404	92	106	11	40	29	5	+0.16	High

In 2008, he saw his ERA increase for the third consecutive year.

Ron Villone (Reliever)

W	L	ERA	TBF	IP	Hit	HR	SO	BB	HBP	3-Year	Reliability
3	4	4.18	267	61	55	6	50	35	2	—	Average

At 39, Villone still can do his primary job: get left-handers out. They hit .176/.311/.318 against him last year.

Adam Wainwright (Starter)

W	L	ERA	TBF	IP	Hit	HR	SO	BB	HBP	3-Year	Reliability
8	8	4.02	610	143	150	13	92	44	5	+0.23	Very High

Wainwright doesn't quite have "ace" stuff, but he does have the mentality. With competent bullpenning, he might have gone 14-3 last year; the Cardinals' closers cost him three wins with blown saves. Wainwright lowered his walk rate and opponent average while improving his strikeout rate slightly, and the Cards have every reason to believe he's fully recovered from the finger injury that sidelined him for 10 weeks: He went 5-0, 3.35 after returning from the DL in late August.

Todd Wellemeyer (Starter)

W	L	ERA	TBF	IP	Hit	HR	SO	BB	HBP	3-Year	Reliability
9	9	4.39	690	160	160	20	105	62	6	+0.22	High

Wellemeyer compiled a 2.93 ERA in his first 13 starts last year and a 2.97 mark over his last 12. But over the seven starts in the middle (from June 13 through July 24) he had a 7.00 ERA. Welley should have been on the DL during that span with a sore elbow, but the Cardinals asked him to pitch through it because other injuries had depleted the staff. He finished strong, surpassing 110 pitches in five of his last 10 starts without ill effect. Wellemeyer throws very hard and has always been uncomfortable to hit against; now that he has mastered the strike zone, he has a chance to be very good. But it remains to be proven that his elbow can withstand regular starting duty.

Mark Worrell (Reliever)

W	L	ERA	TBF	IP	Hit	HR	SO	BB	HBP	3-Year	Reliability
3	4	4.09	273	63	55	7	64	31	3	+0.05	Low

I can guarantee you've never seen a delivery like this guy's. Picture somebody trying to hurl a bowling ball over the pins. But hey, it worked at Triple-A, where Worrell posted outstanding numbers two years in a row. I have no idea whether he can hold down a big-league job, but I really hope so, just so everybody gets a fair chance to see that freaky delivery. He's no relation to former Cardinals closer Todd Worrell.

Tampa Bay Rays

by Cork Gaines of Rays Index (raysindex.com)

2009 Rays Projections

Record: 90-72
Division Rank/Games Behind: 3rd, 10 games back
Runs Scored: 806, 5th in the league
Runs Allowed: 706, 3rd in the league
Park Factor: .99, pretty much neutral

What Happened Last Year:

While many thought the Rays would be improved in 2008, almost nobody envisioned how far this team would go. Despite the addition of Evan Longoria and the maturation of their young core, the Rays actually scored eight fewer runs in 2008 (774) than they did the year before. But with a new-found emphasis on pitching and defense, the addition of Jason Bartlett and Matt Garza and a revamped bullpen, the Rays allowed 273 fewer runs in 2008, an improvement of 28.9 percent.

And with that, a team that never had won more than 70 games, and had finished last in nine of the team's 10 years of existence, jumped all the way to 97 wins and the AL East championship. Despite a couple of late-season runs by the Red Sox, the Rays held first place every day in the second half. And the Yankees were never closer than three games after the All-Star break.

The Rays rode their first AL East championship to an easy first round win over the White Sox in four games. But that was just the appetizer for the American League Championship Series: The Rays were able to shut down the Red Sox in Game 7 for the their first AL pennant, with the last five outs being recorded by David Price, making only his eighth major league appearance.

Players Lost from Last Year's Team:

The strengths of the Rays, beyond the talent, are the age of the players, the depth of the organization and the ability of the front office to sign the youngsters to long-term deals at below-market cost. All eight position players projected to be in the Opening Day lineup are under team control through at least the 2010 season. Even more amazing, all five of the starting pitchers projected to be in the rotation are under team control through at least the 2012 season.

Because of this stability, the Rays can pick which players are "lost" after each season. Following the 2008 season, the Rays chose not to pick up the 2009 options on Trever Miller, Cliff Floyd and Rocco Baldelli. The only free agent lost was Eric Hinske. Edwin Jackson was traded to the Tigers for Matt Joyce. The move was deemed necessary to open a spot for rookie of the year candidate Price.

Players Acquired:

The Rays made their single biggest free agent acquisition since the days of the Hit Parade. In Pat Burrell, the Rays instantly upgrade two of their biggest offensive weaknesses, DH and the ability to hit left-handed pitchers. Because he's 32 and signed to a two-year deal, the Rays are safe from the decline that will inevitably hit Burrell later in his career.

The first player added in the offseason by Andrew Friedman and Co. was Joyce, acquired from the Tigers for Edwin Jackson. Joyce represents the kind of player the Rays covet. He is young (24), cheap (three years before arbitration), excellent defensively and above-average offensively. With his struggles against lefties, there is some feeling that Joyce will begin the year in the minors. Whenever his career with the Rays begins, you can pencil Joyce's name into right field for the next six years.

Just before the new year, the Rays added right-handed reliever Joe Nelson, who was effective with the Marlins last season.

Management Is:

While Friedman received all the glory, the Rays' front office is really a two-headed organization with Friedman and former Astros GM Gerry Hunsicker. The wonder-twins use a mix of statistics and player evaluations, and in just three years have constructed an organization that will contend for years with a minimal payroll.

Defense is the Rays' "Moneyball" trait. While Billy Beane's A's targeted high-OBP players as those who would be undervalued (at the time) by other organizations, the Rays target great defense as a trait undervalued by others. The additions of Bartlett and Carlos Pena, the promotion of Longoria and the moves of B.J. Upton and Aki Iwamura to new positions gave the Rays one of the best defenses in baseball in 2008 and were a large factor in the improved pitching staff.

The best trait of the front office is its ability to land specific players through trades that meet the needs of the team, with Joyce being the perfect example. Most teams appear to target star players and difference-makers in trades and fill the rest of the holes from within.

The Minor League System Is:

Even with the promotions of Longoria and Price, the Rays may still have the best minor league system in baseball. Mitch Talbot and Wade Davis would be in the majors in 2009 with many organizations. With the Rays, there is a good chance neither will see the majors for another season. Jeremy Hellickson, whom the Rays refused to move at the trading deadline, is right behind those two. And a little further down, pitchers Nick Barnese and Matt Moore will start showing up on top prospect lists soon. And that does not include Jake McGee, who was lost to Tommy John surgery in 2008. Most organizations would have a hard time recovering from the loss of such a prized pitching prospect. The Rays won't miss a beat.

Offensively, the system is not as deep, but the Rays still have Reid Brignac and two athletically gifted outfielders in Fernando Perez and Desmond Jennings. Jennings would be one of the top prospects in baseball if he could stay healthy.

With their pitching depth, the Rays will be able to target bullpen roles for certain pitchers whom other organizations could not afford to move from starter status. Offensively, the Rays are set for at least the next two seasons, so there is time for the talent to develop.

Due For a Change:

This team is built not only to win in 2009, but to compete year-in and year-out, with only minor changes.

Reasons to be Optimistic:

The biggest reason is that, on paper at least, the 2009 Tampa Bay Rays will actually be better than the team that won the toughest division in baseball and the American League pennant. And with the experience of the pennant chase and the World Series run, this young squad is already pressure tested.

During the offseason, the Rays addressed each of their biggest needs by adding Joyce and Burrell. With Nelson, they have a pitcher who's tough against lefties and righties and once again will give the Rays seven proven pitchers in the bullpen.

The four top starting pitchers are back, and there is no reason to think they cannot at least duplicate their performance from the 2008 season. In fact, Scott Kazmir, the youngest member of the rotation, missed April with a sore elbow and never seemed to find his groove. It is not a stretch to think that he will be better

in 2009. In addition, the Rays traded away their fifth starter, Edwin Jackson, whose 14 wins belied his true performance. He will most likely be replaced by Price, whose performance in the postseason hinted at his potential dominance.

Offensively, the Rays should be much improved over their 2008 performance. Last season, the Rays posted an OPS of .762, eighth in the American League, without a single player posting a career season. In fact, several players were well off their statistical norms and seven of the regulars missed significant time due to injury, totaling over 130 games. Upton played most of the season with a tear in his labrum (shoulder) that limited his power.

Defensively, the Rays may be the best in baseball. All four infielders play Gold Glove-caliber defense and Bartlett should rebound to his Minnesota days after battling multiple injuries in 2008. With Joyce joining Upton and Carl Crawford in the outfield, the Rays may have the best defensive outfield in baseball. Behind the plate, Dioner Navarro is much improved.

It is not too much of a stretch to think the Rays' pitching staff can maintain the same pace established last season. Nor is it a stretch to think the Rays will score more runs in 2009, leading to an improvement on their plus-103 run differential.

Reasons to be Pessimistic:

The biggest question about the 2009 Rays is how the long 2008 season and deep postseason run will affect the young arms on the pitching staff. Of the four starters returning from the 2008 roster, Garza and James Shields each showed a significant increase in innings pitched over the 2007 season.

Shields is only a minor concern, with an 11.6 percent increase (including postseason), since he only had one start with at least 110 pitches. Garza, though, increased his innings pitched by 21.8 percent over the 2007 season and had seven starts with at least 110 pitches. With the shorter offseason, there is concern that Garza could suffer from a tired arm in 2009.

The other question is whether the bullpen's 2008 season is repeatable. One year after fielding a bullpen that was statistically one of the worst in the last 50 years, the Rays relievers jumped to the head of the class.

The biggest question marks are J.P. Howell and Grant Balfour. Howell, in his first full season as a relief pitcher, developed into one of manager Joe Maddon's go-to guys in late-inning, game-saving situations. Balfour is an even bigger enigma. After failing to make the team in spring training, Balfour emerged with one of the most dominating seasons ever by any relief pitcher. In

2008, he became just the fourth pitcher to strike out more than 11 batters per nine innings, give up less than a base runner per inning and post an ERA below 1.70 (minimum 40 innings).

If Howell and Balfour are unable to repeat their 2008 performances, the Rays will struggle in the late innings and won't duplicate their 24 wins when trailing in the seventh inning or later.

Of course the biggest reason to be concerned about the 2009 season is the Rays' division. Last year's AL East was the first American League division since the implementation of the current format (in 1994) with four teams with winning records. The East should only be better in 2009. The Red Sox, Yankees and Rays are all legitimate playoff contenders and the Blue Jays are on the cusp. Only one team is a guaranteed a spot in the playoffs, and at least two of those teams will be home in October. It is easy to envision a 2009 Tampa Bay Rays baseball club that is better than the 2008 version and yet doesn't make the playoffs.

Still Left to Do:

A team never has too much of something until it has much of it at the major league level. The Rays now have too much pitching on the big club and must find homes for all the arms, whether it be in the rotation, the bullpen, the minors or another organization.

With nine starting pitchers who are major league-ready, and five pieces already in the rotation under team control for at least four years, players like Talbot, Jeff Niemann and Jason Hammel will compete for bullpen jobs. If they lose out, the Rays will most likely deal those pieces off, which will only add more talent to the organization. And with Davis and Hellickson right around the corner, the Rays will face the same questions late in 2009 or early 2010. Certainly, it is a nice problem to have.

Our Favorite Rays Blogs:

Her Rays (http://herraysbaseball.com/) takes a more light-hearted approach to covering the Rays, yet it is never difficult to detect the emotional attachment to the team.

Rays Prospects (http://www.raysprospects.com/) is an invaluable resource for keeping tabs on the best minor league system in baseball.

David Chalk of Bugs and Cranks (http://www.bugsandcranks.com/author/david-chalk/) brings an emotional level to Rays coverage rarely seen in a baseball blog. The only person in the world to predict the Rays' run to the World Series, Chalk is as old school as a Rays fan can get and refuses to acknowledge the organization's name change.

Most Likely Team Outcome:

It is easy to see this team outperforming its 2008 AL East title run. The offense not only can repeat, but should be better. And with the addition of Price and a healthy Kazmir, the pitching staff should be just as good.

But it is also easy to see this team struggling in the toughest division in baseball. The Red Sox will be back and the Yankees added the two biggest free agent starting pitchers. The Rays play 36 games against two of the top teams in baseball. And with the Blue Jays and the Orioles, the AL East lacks a punching bag and occasional breather that contenders in other divisions enjoy. If the Rays win the division, they will have earned it … again.

This team is built to win 92-97 games. That number could win the division. Or that number might be good enough for only third place. Look for the Rays to finish 95-67 and make the playoffs as the wild card team.

Player Projections

Batters

Willy Aybar (Third Base)

PA	R	H	2B	3B	HR	RBI	SO	BB	SB	CS	BA	OBP	SLG	OPS	3-Year	Fielding	Reliability
337	40	81	17	1	9	40	44	30	2	1	.271	.342	.424	.766	+0.02	C	Average

After missing all of 2007, Aybar had an up-and-down season but had a bit of a coming-out party in the final two months of the season. With Evan Longoria spending a month on the DL, Aybar started 40 games, posting a .797 OPS in August and September. Aybar's biggest strength, positional flexibility, will keep him from being a starter, but should net him plenty of playing time. A starter at all four infield spots in 2008, he could become a regular contributor in right field and DH in 2009. Depending on injuries, Aybar could start 100 games in 2009 without a regular position.

Rocco Baldelli (Right Field)

PA	R	H	2B	3B	HR	RBI	SO	BB	SB	CS	BA	OBP	SLG	OPS	3-Year	Fielding	Reliability
227	28	54	11	1	9	30	49	14	3	1	.261	.318	.454	.772	0.00	C	Low

From 2005 through 2007, Baldelli played in 127 of the Rays' 486 games (26.1 percent). Before the 2008 season, Baldelli was diagnosed with a rare mitochondrial disorder that reduces his energy level and keeps him from recovering normal from exercise. With the condition now under control, if not cured, Baldelli did return late in the year and appeared in 28 games. At this point, Baldelli is best-suited as a part of a DH platoon and backup outfielder. Under those conditions, Baldelli could appear in 100 games.

Jason Bartlett (Shortstop)

PA	R	H	2B	3B	HR	RBI	SO	BB	SB	CS	BA	OBP	SLG	OPS	3-Year	Fielding	Reliability
503	57	123	23	4	2	39	70	32	16	3	.270	.327	.351	.678	-0.03	B	Very High

Bartlett's value lies in his glove and even that took a small step back last season as he battled a shoulder injury early in the season and a leg injury late in the year. His range may also have been hindered by the Gold Glove-caliber defense of Evan Longoria, who gets to balls in the hole that Bartlett feasted on in previous years. Offensively, Bartlett gets on base just enough (.329) and steals just enough bases (20) to be serviceable as a bottom-of-the-order hitter.

Reid Brignac (Shortstop)

PA	R	H	2B	3B	HR	RBI	SO	BB	SB	CS	BA	OBP	SLG	OPS	3-Year	Fielding	Reliability
515	55	111	27	4	11	54	118	32	6	2	.235	.286	.378	.664	+0.09	D	Very High

Between 2006 and 2008, Reid Brignac has become a completely different ball player, for good and bad. In 2006, Brignac was on his way to the California League MVP, hitting .321/.376/.539 with 61 extra-base hits. But in the field he committed 32 errors, leaving many to wonder if he would ever be a major league shortstop. Two years later, Brignac has improved his defense to the point that he was named the best defensive shortstop of the International League. Unfortunately, now the doubts lie in his bat; he hit .250/.299/.412 at Triple-A. Brignac will be back at Durham in 2009 and will need to show marked improvement in his swing or he could soon become an afterthought.

Carl Crawford (Left Field)

PA	R	H	2B	3B	HR	RBI	SO	BB	SB	CS	BA	OBP	SLG	OPS	3-Year	Fielding	Reliability
509	74	137	22	8	11	53	76	32	32	7	.292	.340	.444	.784	+0.01	B	Very High

Once upon a time, Crawford was The Perfect Storm. He was young, talented and signed to a team-friendly long-term deal. Fast forward a couple of seasons and Crawford will be 27 in 2009 and his numbers seem to have plateaued. Add to that his '09 salary of $8.25 million on a deal that expires after 2010 and Crawford is no longer the envy of many teams. Crawford has yet to develop the power that many envisioned and he has made it clear that the turf in Tropicana Field has caused his legs to wear down late in seasons. Crawford is still a great talent entering the prime of his career, but he is no longer the MVP threat many believed he could be.

Jonny Gomes (Left Field)

PA	R	H	2B	3B	HR	RBI	SO	BB	SB	CS	BA	OBP	SLG	OPS	3-Year	Fielding	Reliability
371	45	75	18	1	14	46	96	36	8	2	.231	.318	.422	.740	-0.02	D	High

Is Jonny Gomes the latest Kevin Maas? Gomes is a one-dimensional player, and that one dimension (power) is streaky at best. After hitting a home run every 16.6 at-bats his rookie season, that number slipped to once every 19.3, 20.5 and 19.3 at-bats the last three years. His career .979 OPS against lefties and his below-average defense suggest that Gomes is best suited to be part of a DH platoon.

Gabe Gross (Right Field)

PA	R	H	2B	3B	HR	RBI	SO	BB	SB	CS	BA	OBP	SLG	OPS	3-Year	Fielding	Reliability
359	45	80	17	2	12	45	74	42	3	1	.257	.346	.439	.785	-0.03	B	Average

Gross is serviceable as the left-handed half of a right field platoon. But even then, his .256/.352/.434 split against righties is far below-average for a right fielder. The Rays would like to see Matt Joyce develop into the most-days right fielder as he offers a similar skill-set to Gross, only Joyce is younger, cheaper and has a higher upside. However, if Joyce is not ready early in 2009, Gross will continue to start in right field against right handers.

Akinori Iwamura (Second Base)

PA	R	H	2B	3B	HR	RBI	SO	BB	SB	CS	BA	OBP	SLG	OPS	3-Year	Fielding	Reliability
596	69	141	24	7	5	51	109	59	9	6	.268	.344	.369	.713	-0.03	C	High

With a .349 OBP and only eight steals, Iwamura is not an ideal leadoff hitter, but with a lack of better options, manager Joe Maddon will continue to pencil his name in the top spot. The best you can say is that he is dependable. He will consistently provide .280/.350/.400. But with an OPS+ near 100, you would like more. Defensively, Iwamura has the glove to win a Gold Glove, but may never get recognized as long as he plays for the Rays.

John Jaso (Catcher)

PA	R	H	2B	3B	HR	RBI	SO	BB	SB	CS	BA	OBP	SLG	OPS	3-Year	Fielding	Reliability
455	46	93	16	2	7	40	65	49	2	1	.235	.324	.338	.662	+0.02	C	High

The only thing keeping Jaso from being one of the top prospects in baseball is his defense and a lack of home run power. His career 255/251 strikeout to walk ratio in the minors, along with his .381 OBP, suggest that he will be a productive hitter at the major league level. While his defense has progressed, there is still work to do. If he could add a little lift to his swing, and develop 20 home run power, he could be a very attractive catcher in 2010.

Matthew Joyce (Left Field)

PA	R	H	2B	3B	HR	RBI	SO	BB	SB	CS	BA	OBP	SLG	OPS	3-Year	Fielding	Reliability
491	53	96	21	4	16	57	120	44	2	3	.219	.294	.394	.688	+0.03	C	Very High

When the Tigers gave up on Jacque Jones, Matt Joyce was called up to take his place as another left-handed bat in the lineup. He got off to a nice start, but it looks like the pitchers figured him out: He finished with a .252/.339/.492 line. Joyce was dealt during the winter meetings to the Tampa Bay Rays for Edwin Jackson so he'll have to fight for a job with the defending AL champions this spring.

Evan Longoria (Third Base)

PA	R	H	2B	3B	HR	RBI	SO	BB	SB	CS	BA	OBP	SLG	OPS	3-Year	Fielding	Reliability
545	73	132	30	2	25	83	121	49	6	1	.273	.347	.499	.846	+0.06	B	Very High

Is there a more valuable position player in baseball right now? Evan Longoria will be 23 in 2009 and already has a season with a 125 OPS+ at a position where it is not easy to find great offense. And he is signed through 2016 to a team-friendly deal. In the fourth year of the deal, Longoria will make $2 million. David Wright, another young third baseman, signed long-term, was paid $5 million in his fourth season. In years five, six and seven Wright will make $31.5 million total, while the Rays will pay $18 million. And like Wright, The Dirtbag has the talent to be a perennial MVP candidate.

Dioner Navarro (Catcher)

PA	R	H	2B	3B	HR	RBI	SO	BB	SB	CS	BA	OBP	SLG	OPS	3-Year	Fielding	Reliability
444	49	110	23	1	9	49	55	37	1	2	.277	.340	.408	.748	+0.03	B	High

Dioner Navarro is finally living up to the promise of his prospect status from his time in the Yankees organization and proved that his second-half line from 2007 (.285/.340/.475) was no fluke. The Fat Catcher will never hit 30 home runs, but he is a line drive hitting machine (23.5 percent last year). If he could run a little better he has the swing to hit .330, but he will never benefit from the occasional infield hit. Still, .300/.360/.450 every year, coupled with his much-improved defense and age (25 in 2009), will make Navi one of the top catchers in baseball for the next five years.

Carlos Pena (First Base)

PA	R	H	2B	3B	HR	RBI	SO	BB	SB	CS	BA	OBP	SLG	OPS	3-Year	Fielding	Reliability
549	76	118	23	2	31	88	134	81	2	1	.260	.379	.524	.903	-0.03	B	Very High

Before the 2008 All-Star break, a time that included a month on the DL, Pena posted a .236/.340/.438 line. He rebounded with .260/.418/.561 in the second half, which was much closer to his breakout 2007 season (.282/.411/.627). In the first half, Pena pulled everything down the first base line. Pena has enough power to use the entire field and when he takes the ball to center and left-center he is a much better player. If he can stay away from his pull-everything mentality, Pena should continue to crank 35-40 home runs and OPS .950+.

Fernando Perez (Center Field)

PA	R	H	2B	3B	HR	RBI	SO	BB	SB	CS	BA	OBP	SLG	OPS	3-Year	Fielding	Reliability
562	65	118	14	7	4	36	142	55	25	8	.239	.318	.320	.638	+0.01	C	Very High

Perez caught the eye of manager Joe Maddon during a late-season call-up, but it might not be enough to earn a roster spot in 2009. Still learning how to switch-hit, Perez struggles with contact from the left side, striking out once every 2.8 at-bats as a lefty (one every 4.6 as a RHB). If Perez does start the season in the minors, he will be the first option when an outfielder is needed at the big league level.

Shawn Riggans (Catcher)

PA	R	H	2B	3B	HR	RBI	SO	BB	SB	CS	BA	OBP	SLG	OPS	3-Year	Fielding	Reliability
258	27	59	12	1	6	29	52	15	1	1	.252	.306	.389	.695	-0.02	D	Low

Consistently near an .800 OPS his last three seasons in the minors, Riggans can be a decent hitting catcher in the majors and is serviceable as a backup. Unfortunately, he is not good enough defensively to play every day and doesn't hit well enough to play a different position.

Justin Ruggiano (Right Field)

PA	R	H	2B	3B	HR	RBI	SO	BB	SB	CS	BA	OBP	SLG	OPS	3-Year	Fielding	Reliability
430	57	101	21	3	14	53	114	36	15	4	.263	.333	.442	.775	+0.06	B	High

Ruggiano is a five-tool player, except all five tools are just above-average. He is solid, if not spectacular defensively. At the plate, his career minor league OBP of .393 bodes well, but his 66 home runs in five minor league seasons are not enough production for a corner outfielder. Unfortunately for Ruggiano, they now test for steroids, because at age 27, he is not likely to experience a power surge and is a fourth outfielder at best, and more likely a journeyman minor leaguer.

B.J. Upton (Center Field)

PA	R	H	2B	3B	HR	RBI	SO	BB	SB	CS	BA	OBP	SLG	OPS	3-Year	Fielding	Reliability
571	78	132	26	3	13	57	121	73	31	7	.271	.368	.416	.784	+0.03	D	Very High

Projection systems cannot account for a player who played an entire season with a torn labrum in his shoulder. B.J. Upton admitted late in the season that the injury took away his power and made him hesitant to swing at certain pitches that he would normally drive. When healthy, Upton has one of the quickest bats in baseball and will hit 30 home runs and steal 40 bases in an average season. His strikeout rate (288 Ks in 274 games since 2007) is easy to tolerate when he is getting on base at a .380-plus clip. But one has to be a little concerned—Upton is only 23 and already has two shoulder surgeries on his resume.

Ben Zobrist (Shortstop)

PA	R	H	2B	3B	HR	RBI	SO	BB	SB	CS	BA	OBP	SLG	OPS	3-Year	Fielding	Reliability
392	46	87	16	3	9	41	66	42	6	2	.255	.341	.399	.740	+0.02	D	High

Ben Zobrist will receive plenty of playing time in 2009 even without a regular position. Joe Maddon likes to rotate his bench in frequently and Zobrist will see time at several different positions. The only question will be which Zobrist will show up. Will it be the on-base machine who posted a .429 OBP in five minor league seasons, or the Zorilla who slugged .505 in 198 at-bats with the Rays last season?

Pitchers

Grant Balfour (Reliever)

W	L	ERA	TBF	IP	Hit	HR	SO	BB	HBP	3-Year	Reliability
5	3	3.18	298	72	52	6	90	33	3	+0.17	Very Low

In 2008, Balfour posted one of the most dominating seasons by a relief pitcher in baseball history. The Mad Australian became just the fourth pitcher to post 11 strikeouts per nine innings, with a WHIP below 1.00 and a sub-1.70 ERA (minimum 40 innings pitched). The other three on the list are a who's who of dominating closer performances: Eric Gagne (2003), Billy Wagner (1999) and Joe Nathan (2006). The only difference between their seasons and Balfour's was the number of saves. Balfour would be a dominating closer on most teams, and would be on the Rays also if Maddon played by the book. But Maddon prefers to use his best relief pitchers in the most important points of a game. Balfour did log 90.2 innings in 2008. That marks a 33 percent increase over 2007. If Balfour pitches for Australia in the World Baseball Congress, he may be a candidate for a tired arm in 2009.

Chad Bradford (Reliever)

W	L	ERA	TBF	IP	Hit	HR	SO	BB	HBP	3-Year	Reliability
4	3	3.52	269	64	67	3	29	19	3	+0.13	Low

Chad Bradford is the relief pitcher every team loves to have in September and October but nobody wants from March through August. The lack of love is due mostly to his $3.5 million price tag. With two-thirds of batted balls resulting in ground balls, Bradford is the ultimate late-inning, double-play specialist.

Wade Davis (Starter)

W	L	ERA	TBF	IP	Hit	HR	SO	BB	HBP	3-Year	Reliability
6	10	5.62	665	145	157	20	91	81	12	-0.29	Very High

Davis would be in the rotation of most major league teams in 2009. But with the Rays, Davis is no better than ninth on the depth chart. He, Jeff Niemann and Mitch Talbot will get first crack at the rotation should a need arise. Still, we have to think that, at age 23, Davis will make his major league debut at some point in the '09 season, even if it is as a September call-up.

Matt Garza (Starter)

W	L	ERA	TBF	IP	Hit	HR	SO	BB	HBP	3-Year	Reliability
9	10	4.37	728	169	171	19	121	61	9	+0.03	Very High

Those who watch the Rays regularly will tell you that Matt Garza has the best "stuff" of any pitcher on the staff. After a June scrape with catcher Dioner Navarro in the dugout, Garza began seeing a sports psychologist and finally seemed to overcome the one thing that was holding him back, his emotions. After that, Garza threw two shutouts and a third complete game in which he allowed one run on one hit and won the ALCS MVP.

However, Garza is the one Rays pitcher who may be at risk for a down season due to the long season. Including the postseason, Garza threw 213.1 innings, a 22 percent increase over his 2007 total. He also had seven starts with at least 110 pitches. The coaching staff will be cautious with Garza's arm in the spring and early in the year, but one has to worry about the threat of pitching in 2009 with a tired arm.

Jason Hammel (Reliever)

W	L	ERA	TBF	IP	Hit	HR	SO	BB	HBP	3-Year	Reliability
4	6	4.97	394	89	96	11	58	39	4	+0.18	Very High

Hammel is a victim of the talent level that is now found at the major league level for the Rays. Hammel would be a league-average fifth starter with potential on many teams. But with the emergence of Andy Sonnanstine and the next wave of starters now ready for the big leagues, Hammel was relegated to the bullpen in 2008 and may not find a spot even there in 2009. A 95 mph fastball and the ability to eat innings may make him an attractive option in another organization.

Jeremy Hellickson (Starter)

W	L	ERA	TBF	IP	Hit	HR	SO	BB	HBP	3-Year	Reliability
6	9	5.43	611	138	155	25	99	50	8	-0.76	High

How high are the Rays on Jeremy Hellickson? Despite having nine legitimate major league starting pitchers, the Rays deemed Hellickson "untouchable" before the trade deadline last season. Why? 9.6 strikeouts per nine innings and an astronomical 8:1 strikeout-to-walk ratio between High-A and Double-A in 2008. A power pitcher with command of the strike zone at age 21 is a rare entity indeed, and the Rays are not about to let him go easily. With their pitching depth, the Rays can afford to be patient. Hellboy won't even sniff the big leagues until 2010.

J.P. Howell (Reliever)

W	L	ERA	TBF	IP	Hit	HR	SO	BB	HBP	3-Year	Reliability
6	4	3.86	387	91	85	9	83	36	5	+0.03	Very High

In his first season as a relief pitcher, J.P. Howell teamed with Grant Balfour to be the Rays' middle inning "closers." Howell's 89.1 innings were the most by a left-handed reliever in the last 10 years, and most of those innings were used during the most crucial moments of games. Howell did tire toward the end of the year, and needed some extended breaks. With the deep postseason run, Howell will need to be watched closely to see if he suffers a hangover in 2009.

Edwin Jackson (Starter)

W	L	ERA	TBF	IP	Hit	HR	SO	BB	HBP	3-Year	Reliability
7	11	5.46	721	160	187	21	99	71	4	+0.06	Very High

Jackson, now a Tiger, has a dominating fastball and a ton of upside. But despite his 14 wins in 2008, Jackson is still far from dominant—his peripheral numbers suggest something less. He needs to further develop his slider and change-up, and cut back on his walk rate (3.8 per nine innings) before he can be a dependable starter. If he can develop just the slider, he could be groomed into an effective closer with his 98 mph fastball.

Scott Kazmir (Starter)

W	L	ERA	TBF	IP	Hit	HR	SO	BB	HBP	3-Year	Reliability
9	9	4.01	670	158	140	20	171	66	6	+0.06	Very High

Kazmir never looked "right" in 2008. He missed all of April recovering from a strained elbow and battled his mechanics and pitch counts for most of the season. In his last 19 starts, Kazmir worked into the seventh inning once and yet seven of his 27 starts featured at least 110 pitches. The key is entering 2009 healthy. In 2008 Kazmir threw his slider only 11 percent of the time, down from 16 percent in 2007. This seemed to be directly related to his preseason elbow injury. If Kazmir is healthy, he should be able to rely on his dominating slider once again and reestablish himself as one of the best young pitchers in baseball.

Jacob McGee (Starter)

W	L	ERA	TBF	IP	Hit	HR	SO	BB	HBP	3-Year	Reliability
5	7	5.51	490	107	111	16	76	65	5	-0.49	High

How deep is the pitching talent in the Rays' system? McGee, one of the top prospects in baseball, was lost to Tommy John surgery and it was barely noticed. McGee should recover fully, but will miss most of 2009. There was some rumbling before the injury that the lefty would be better suited as a dominant reliever, and the injury may force that move. Joe Maddon has said he sees McGee in much the same role as David Price was used in the postseason.

Jeff Niemann (Starter)

W	L	ERA	TBF	IP	Hit	HR	SO	BB	HBP	3-Year	Reliability
7	8	4.82	612	139	139	19	101	64	9	+0.04	High

Niemann did not take the step forward in 2008 that many hoped for, which leaves many wanting just a little more. His K-rate was nearly identical (8.7 in 2008, 8.5 in 2007) as was his walk rate (3.4 in 2008, 3.2 in 2007). He did lower his hit rate (9.9 per nine innings in 2007, 6.8 in 2008) but he is still not dominant. If not for concerns over the amount of time it takes Niemann to warm up, he might be destined to be a closer. Whether he is a starter or a reliever, Niemann needs to stick someplace in 2009; he is out of minor league options. With David Price lurking, the bullpen may be Niemann's only option.

Troy Percival (Reliever)

W	L	ERA	TBF	IP	Hit	HR	SO	BB	HBP	3-Year	Reliability
3	3	4.02	235	56	46	7	46	25	2	—	Very Low

When Percival was healthy in 2008 he was a dependable closer, blowing only four saves. However, he was never faced with a tough save opportunity (tying run already on base), and injuries to his back and legs limited him late in the season. At this point of Percival's career, he must battle his age and his weight. When right, he still can be effective. But unfortunately, he is more likely to face multiple trips to the DL in 2009.

David Price (Starter)

W	L	ERA	TBF	IP	Hit	HR	SO	BB	HBP	3-Year	Reliability
7	7	4.08	556	129	127	14	95	53	7	-0.16	Very Low

The first overall pick in the 2007 draft, Price had quite a season last year. He threw his first professional pitch in May, rocketed through the system and made it all the way to the major leagues in September. He was impressive enough that the Rays decided to add him to the postseason roster, where Price dominated on a national stage, striking out eight in 5.7 innings and posting a 1.59 ERA. Price's projection is already pretty good, but given his 94 mile-per-hour fastball and 87 mile-per-hour slider, his upside is limitless.

James Shields (Starter)

W	L	ERA	TBF	IP	Hit	HR	SO	BB	HBP	3-Year	Reliability
11	10	3.99	788	189	192	23	144	40	10	+0.21	Very High

One major concern for the Rays is the toll of a deep playoff run on the arms of their young pitching staff. Shields threw 240 innings in 2008 (including the playoffs), an 12 percent increase over 2007. The coaches will take care with his arm this offseason and will limit his innings in the spring. He does have a history of being a workhorse and in 2008 he posted only one start with at least 110 pitches. As a pitcher with a dominant change-up, he may actually be more effective when his arm is tired as it keeps him from overthrowing his change. As he enters his prime seasons, he should be good for 32-plus starts, a 3.50 ERA and 15-19 wins every season. If he gets on a run, he is capable of contending for a Cy Young award.

Andrew Sonnanstine (Starter)

W	L	ERA	TBF	IP	Hit	HR	SO	BB	HBP	3-Year	Reliability
10	10	4.49	755	178	191	25	114	42	8	+0.06	Very High

Sonnanstine is like a Volvo, safe and dependable, but you wouldn't want to pick a girl up in one. With 48 different pitches and 78 different release points, a batter never knows what he is going to get. But from the point of view of the front office, with Sonnanstine, what you have is a poor man's Greg Maddux. He will win 12-15 games with a 4.00-4.50 ERA every year. A team could do worse at the back end of a rotation.

Mitch Talbot (Starter)

W	L	ERA	TBF	IP	Hit	HR	SO	BB	HBP	3-Year	Reliability
7	10	5.05	694	155	177	18	93	63	12	+0.01	Very High

Much like Jeff Niemann, Mitch Talbot could be a victim of numbers. A starting pitcher at the major league level in many organizations, Talbot will likely have to wait in Triple-A. Talbot will never be a dominating pitcher, but with a plus-change, and a 4:1 strikeout-to-walk ratio in Triple-A, he should be a very effective back-of-the-rotation starter if he gets a shot.

Dan Wheeler (Reliever)

W	L	ERA	TBF	IP	Hit	HR	SO	BB	HBP	3-Year	Reliability
4	4	3.82	285	68	60	8	59	24	3	+0.18	Average

In 2008, Wheeler struggled as the closer in the absence of Troy Percival. In the seventh and eighth innings, Wheeler allowed hitters an OPS of .439 (162 plate appearances). In the ninth inning, that number jumped to .776. Joe Maddon prefers to use his best relievers in the toughest situations, which usually means J.P. Howell or Grant Balfour. Outside of those, Wheeler will continue to receive the bulk of the eighth-inning duty and the occasional ninth-inning save opportunity when Percival is not available.

Texas Rangers

by Scott Lucas of The Ranger Rundown (rangers.scottlucas.com)

2009 Rangers Projections

Record: 77-85
Division Rank/Games Behind: 3rd, five games back
Runs Scored: 813, 4th in the league
Runs Allowed: 865, 13th in the league
Park Factor: 1.03, a hitter's park

What Happened Last Year:

In a repeat of 2007, the Rangers began the season by digging a hole. Their 7-16 start included seven straight at Boston and Detroit during which they were outscored 67-24. Manager Ron Washington came within an inch of losing his job, but the Rangers saved him by taking series against the Royals and Twins, then winning nine of 13 consecutive games against Oakland and Seattle.

From May through July, Texas never strayed more than four games from .500. In early August, rookie Matt Harrison bested New York's Andy Pettitte, and the 60-54 Rangers trailed Boston by only five games for the wild card. Alas, the Rangers have a long and sordid history of summer collapses, and they weren't really that good. Only Kansas City and Seattle had inferior run differentials at the time. Texas promptly lost 13 of 16 and fell from contention. A catastrophic 19-17 loss at Boston on Aug. 12 sealed their fate. Texas trailed 10-0 after the first, retook a 16-14 lead in the sixth, and squandered it in the eighth. The Rangers would score four runs in their next three games, all losses. They played .500 ball in September.

Texas led the league in runs scored and most runs allowed for the first time since 1991. The Rangers used a team-record 30 pitchers, including 15 starters. Among the 14 tossing at least 30 innings, only Frank Francisco had a run average below 5.24. Bad though it was, the pitching was undercut further by terrible defense. Texas was worst in errors and defensive efficiency, and at or near the bottom in several other defensive measures. On the plus side, Texas had the best offense in the league (even after adjusting for its hitter-friendly park), outscoring second-place Boston by 56.

Players Lost from Last Year's Team:

Milton Bradley, Gerald Laird, Kameron Loe, Ramon Vazquez, Jamey Wright. Only Bradley is a significant loss. Some combination of catchers Taylor Teagarden,

Jarrod Saltalamacchia and Max Ramirez should replace Laird's production. Loe moved to Japan.

Texas also traded or released Eddie Guardado, Sidney Ponson, Ben Broussard and Chris Shelton during the season.

Players Acquired:

Texas largely sat out the offseason. Of those acquired for Laird, only 25-year-old pitcher Guillermo Moscoco might contribute in 2009.

Management Is:

After barely surviving last April, Washington maintains a tenuous hold on his employment. For the second consecutive season, the Rangers came out of the gate flat and sloppy, a poor reflection on their leader. Washington's boundless enthusiasm wilted in the Texas heat as he constantly trudged to the mound to replace whoever was getting pummeled that night. Some of his ideas—thinking Broussard could hit lefties, batting slugger Davis ninth specifically because he was a rookie while letting equally green Joaquin Arias bat second—don't hold up to even mild scrutiny. He's still learning on the job.

Texas fired Washington's ostensible mentor, Art Howe, and replaced him with 69-year-old Jackie Moore, who managed Nolan Ryan's Round Rock squad for several years. This was definitely not Washington's idea. Although Texas isn't playing to win the division, Washington won't survive a third disappointing start.

General manager Jon Daniels is entering his fourth season. Daniels and his staff have quickly upgraded the farm system to one of baseball's best. In particular, the 2007 draft and trades of Mark Teixeira, Eric Gagne and Kenny Lofton yielded nine of Texas's top 20 prospects plus outfielder David Murphy. While Daniels and company have excelled at acquiring talent, successfully developing it and keeping the right players have often evaded them.

The losses of Chris Young and John Danks in previous trades can be chalked off as learning experiences, but they'll continue to haunt the franchise for years. Last winter, Texas waived and then traded C-level prospect Armando Galarraga to Detroit for some nonentity to make room for Jason Jennings. Jennings pitched horribly before succumbing to injury. As if by some horrible curse, Galarraga immediately flourished outside the Rangers system. Daniels' trade of Edinson Volquez to the Reds for Josh Hamilton has worked exceptionally well for both teams, but it's also another starter lost. Contemplate those pitchers, and then contemplate the Texas rotation's league-worst 869 innings and 607 runs allowed in 2008.

Now, Texas essentially has declared its best prospects untouchable in trades. That's fine for now, but if the club finds itself in contention in 2010-2011, which it should, it probably will need to move some of its "bright futures" for players who'll make an immediate impact. Management's performance at that juncture will be a watershed event.

Daniels answered directly to owner Tom Hicks until last year, when Ryan became the team's president. Ryan focused on business and mostly just observed the baseball side during 2008. After the season, he asserted his views by publicly berating the fitness of the minor league pitchers. Texas will institute a tougher conditioning program and call for longer outings and less reliance on pitch counts in the majors and upper minors. Coincidentally or not, the minor league pitching coordinator departed to become Seattle's pitching coach. Ryan also brought in Moore and new pitching coach Mike Maddux, another Round Rock alumnus.

Amidst these and previous management shakeups is owner Hicks. Though not impetuous in the manner of vintage-period George Steinbrenner, Hicks seems to institute a new five-year plan every other year or so. Some examples:

1. Fired GM Doug Melvin two years after Texas won its third division title in four seasons, by far its most successful era.
2. Signed Alex Rodriguez to a 10-year deal, then traded him three years later.
3. Gave former GM John Hart license to spend freely after 2001, then instituted an aggregate payroll cut of more than $30 million that lasts to this day.
4. Fired assistant GM Grady Fuson two years and nine months into a three-year "internship" for the GM spot.
5. Gave manager Buck Showalter a three-year extension following 2004, then fired him before it kicked in.
6. Hired a 30-year-old Ivy Leaguer as GM, then hired the older, old-school Nolan Ryan as his boss two years later.

The Minor League System Is:

Texas boasts one of the deepest and most formidable systems in baseball, especially at pitcher (believe it or not). Management has worked tirelessly on all fronts—the draft, overseas, and through trades—to supply the

Rangers with better and cheaper talent. The team's 2006 fifth-rounder, Davis, made the biggest splash among rookies in '08, and several others showed potential, if not results. Homegrown catcher Teagarden and pitcher Eric Hurley (both still technically rookies) have the best chance of contributing this season.

Others could make bigger impacts down the road. Top prospects Neftali Feliz (a right-handed pitcher acquired for Teixeira) and lefty Derek Holland (25th round, 2006) both jumped from low-A to Double-A last year. Feliz can surpass 100 mph. His offspeed pitches aren't there yet, but he could make his debut this season. Holland doesn't throw quite as hard (only 97 or so) and has slightly more refined secondary offerings.

Switch-hitting 1B Justin Smoak somehow fell to 11th in the 2008 draft, and Texas eagerly nabbed him despite having Davis in house. Smoak signed late but made impressive showings in low-A and the Arizona Fall League. Considered the superior defender, he could push Davis to a DH role as soon as 2010.

Shortstop Elvis Andrus (another Teixeira return) held his own in Double-A as a 19-year-old. Already a terrific defender, Andrus has the speed but hasn't shown a bat worthy of a leadoff spot. Still, before long, Texas will have to decide where to move Michael Young.

Due For a Change:

The pitching staff as a whole should improve, if only because it can't be that bad again. While the Rangers haven't switched to "win now" mode, the youngsters will be expected to produce results, not just valuable learning experiences. Veterans Kevin Millwood and Vicente Padilla are pitching for their eight-digit 2010 paychecks. Even without that incentive, they're better than what they've shown. Brandon McCarthy can't be any worse.

Young batted .284/.339./402 with a broken finger and other injuries. He's uncommonly durable and a good bet to hit .300 again. Nelson Cruz may have finally established his major league credentials, but he's not going to repeat 2008's .330/.421/.609 performance.

Reasons to be Optimistic:

Notwithstanding Hicks' strategic reversals listed above, the owner has shown admirable patience with Daniels' development plan. He has willingly paid "above slot" money to draft picks and paid for the rejuvenation of Texas's scouting and development in Latin America. The Rangers should have a steady infusion of talent for years to come (even if Daniels himself isn't around to enjoy it).

A promising showing in 2009 should impel a concerted effort toward making the postseason. Most of the team's core, especially on offense, is under team control at a reasonable cost for several years.

Reasons to be Pessimistic:

Per-game attendance fell 17 percent to a 20-year low in 2008, under two million total. Record gas prices, $12 parking, and soul-crushing heat played their parts, but fans will tolerate all of that and more to see a winning team. In 2009, the worst economic conditions in several decades portend even lower attendance, possibly constraining Texas' ability to retain its best players and sign free agents.

Location in baseball's only four-team division hasn't helped Texas reach the playoffs this decade. Los Angeles has strong management and an owner with the deep pockets and the desire to spend heavily. Oakland has a farm system to match Texas' plus Billy Beane. Seattle canned Bill Bavasi and appears headed back toward reality-based evaluations of potential free agent signings and its own players. Though the Angels won't repeat their 100 wins, none of Texas's divisional rivals can rightfully be described as declining.

The Rangers are 80 games under .500 with just one winning season this decade. That's not bad luck. During the past 11 seasons, only one pitcher drafted or originally signed by Texas has pitched 162 innings in a season for the Rangers: Doug Davis in 2001. Texas'

division rivals have combined for 49 such seasons from 16 pitchers during that span.

Still Left to Do:

Texas doesn't appear compelled to take on the Angels for the postseason in 2009, so any moves will likely be minor. Texas is weakest at third base. If Hank Blalock can't play there, none of the other internal options at third base inspires confidence. Practically everyone earning significant money is available in trade as Texas builds for a playoff run in 2010 and beyond.

Most Likely Team Outcome:

Texas should finish at or near 81 wins. The Rangers won't upend Los Angeles and will struggle to retain second place against a suddenly present-minded Athletics squad, but they ought to improve slightly on their 2008 record.

When and how the Rangers achieve those wins could decide the future of their manager and general manger. Another bad start will cost Washington his job, and another sub-.500 season may cost Daniels his. If they're axed, it's Ryan's show.

Player Projections

Batters

Joaquin Arias (Second Base)

PA	R	H	2B	3B	HR	RBI	SO	BB	SB	CS	BA	OBP	SLG	OPS	3-Year	Fielding	Reliability
439	51	111	19	7	5	40	61	17	12	2	.270	.301	.386	.687	+0.04	C	Average

Though he's only 24, Arias' future hangs by a thread. A shoulder injury wiped out 2007 and forced him to second base rather than short for most of 2008. Therein lies the problem. Arias doesn't offer much at the plate beyond contact and won't hit enough to warrant a full-time job. If healthy, he may yet evolve into a capable utility player. If not, he's nothing but a slap-hitting second baseman.

Hank Blalock (First Base)

PA	R	H	2B	3B	HR	RBI	SO	BB	SB	CS	BA	OBP	SLG	OPS	3-Year	Fielding	Reliability
351	43	88	19	2	11	47	55	28	2	1	.277	.336	.453	.789	-0.01	B	High

The Rangers know they owe Blalock $6.2 million in 2008. All else is in question. During the past two years, he's hit much better than in his dreadful 2006 season but missed more than 200 games because of injuries that may prevent him from playing third. Texas might give him one more try there if Travis Metcalf or German Duran don't cut it. If not, he'll DH and spell Chris Davis at first. No telling how he'll perform with the bat. The most likely scenario involves better health and reduced production compared to 2007-2008.

Brandon Boggs (Left Field)

PA	R	H	2B	3B	HR	RBI	SO	BB	SB	CS	BA	OBP	SLG	OPS	3-Year	Fielding	Reliability
435	50	86	19	4	11	46	109	48	5	2	.227	.316	.385	.701	+0.01	B	High

Pressed into service after spending 2007 in the minors, Boggs had a respectable MLB debut. His approach is patient to the extreme: No Ranger swung at a lower percentage of pitches. This led to a terrific walk rate and a ton of strikeouts. A switch-hitter, Boggs didn't hit righties well. He could maintain a major league career as a backup or the wrong end of a platoon, but might begin 2009 in Triple-A.

Milton Bradley (Right Field)

PA	R	H	2B	3B	HR	RBI	SO	BB	SB	CS	BA	OBP	SLG	OPS	3-Year	Fielding	Reliability
439	62	109	21	2	18	63	86	58	6	2	.292	.392	.504	.896	-0.02	B	High

Bradley enjoyed a career year and was a model citizen, notwithstanding an overblown incident in Kansas City. Alas, he also (barely) achieved 500 plate appearances for only the second time in the eight years since his rookie season, and he batted an unsustainable .388 on balls in play. In Texas, he DH'ed 80 percent of the time yet still missed 32 games. Thus, no matter how potent his bat, signing him to a multi-year deal entails significant risk, so Texas understandably offered nothing beyond arbitration. That said, he's easily Texas's biggest offseason loss.

Marlon Byrd (Center Field)

PA	R	H	2B	3B	HR	RBI	SO	BB	SB	CS	BA	OBP	SLG	OPS	3-Year	Fielding	Reliability
484	60	124	25	4	12	58	81	40	5	3	.288	.357	.448	.805	-0.03	B	Very High

Byrd seemed primed for a letdown after batting .363 on balls in play in 2007. Though his BABIP did fall to .330, he compensated with career bests in walks and extra-base hits. He also defends every outfield spot capably. Unless he falters, which is possible but not highly probable, Byrd will justify a multi-year contract as a free agent. Not bad for a guy signed to a minor-league deal after washing out with the lowly Nationals.

Frank Catalanotto (Left Field)

PA	R	H	2B	3B	HR	RBI	SO	BB	SB	CS	BA	OBP	SLG	OPS	3-Year	Fielding	Reliability
361	40	88	21	2	5	36	40	30	2	1	.277	.348	.403	.751	-0.06	D	High

The former .300-hitting "super utility" player hasn't aged gracefully. Cat's bat won't suffice at first and he's devolved into the type of left fielder best kept under glass, to be used only in an emergency. On a squad with Chris Davis, Hank Blalock, and up to five competent defensive outfielders, he fills no role. He wouldn't be part of the discussion if not for money: Texas owes him $4 million in 2009. Jon Daniels will entertain all offers.

Nelson Cruz (Right Field)

PA	R	H	2B	3B	HR	RBI	SO	BB	SB	CS	BA	OBP	SLG	OPS	3-Year	Fielding	Reliability
529	78	136	25	2	30	90	119	50	12	4	.290	.361	.543	.904	-0.02	B	Very High

Cruz hit bottom last spring when he went unclaimed on waivers. Rather than press or sulk, he earned the Pacific Coast League's MVP award with 37 homers and a .342 average. Still, he'd flopped in two previous MLB trials, so expectations were guarded when he received one last chance at age 28 in Texas. Happily for Cruz and the Rangers, he finally carried his minor-league success with him and has staked a claim on right field in 2009. Goodness knows how he'll hit this time, but the prognosis is positive.

Christopher Davis (First Base)

PA	R	H	2B	3B	HR	RBI	SO	BB	SB	CS	BA	OBP	SLG	OPS	3-Year	Fielding	Reliability
569	81	152	35	3	34	105	141	34	4	3	.289	.334	.561	.895	+0.08	B	High

Davis may one day lead the majors in home runs. He's blasted 76 during the past two seasons, including 17 in his half-season MLB debut. Davis' swing is powerful yet compact enough to generate a pleasingly high average. Even more than most hitters, Davis is an absolute terror in favorable counts and mouse-like when behind. If he can quit thinking of every pitch as a potential homer, he'll draw more positive counts and more walks. Davis played some third base with Texas and right field in the minors. He's suited for neither.

German Duran (Shortstop)

PA	R	H	2B	3B	HR	RBI	SO	BB	SB	CS	BA	OBP	SLG	OPS	3-Year	Fielding	Reliability
371	39	84	16	3	9	40	65	17	3	1	.246	.285	.390	.675	+0.03	D	High

Duran didn't make a strong impression with his bat or glove in his rookie season. He has a shot a winning the third base job, but Texas envisions him more as a super-utility player. In the minors, he's been neither bad nor great at anything, just solidly above average in all respects.

Josh Hamilton (Center Field)

PA	R	H	2B	3B	HR	RBI	SO	BB	SB	CS	BA	OBP	SLG	OPS	3-Year	Fielding	Reliability
549	78	146	28	4	26	87	103	51	6	2	.299	.368	.532	.900	+0.00	D	High

Twenty-six-year-old center fielders who bat .290 with power aren't normally considered high-risk acquisitions, but Hamilton's injury-shortened rookie season and checkered past raised two huge red flags. Hamilton continued to walk the straight and narrow, amassed 700 plate appearances, and hit just as well as in 2007. He also added a page to sports history with his epic Home Run Derby performance. Concerns allayed and potential fully realized, Hamilton should contend for MVP honors for the next several years. Why the Hallmark Channel hasn't already filmed his biopic is beyond me.

Ian Kinsler (Second Base)

PA	R	H	2B	3B	HR	RBI	SO	BB	SB	CS	BA	OBP	SLG	OPS	3-Year	Fielding	Reliability
531	77	142	30	3	21	75	71	47	20	2	.303	.370	.514	.884	+0.07	C	Very High

Kinsler made the jump from good second baseman to MVP candidate. His endless barrage of line drives recalled teammate Michael Young's 2005. Though lacking blazing speed, Kinsler has proven an astonishingly gifted runner, swiping 60 bases versus only eight caught over three seasons. One serious injury each year has limited him to a maximum 130 games, but calling him injury prone would be inaccurate. Kinsler's defense is adequate, if maddeningly erratic. Until Texas calls up or acquires a more prototypical leadoff hitter, Kinsler will remain in the No. 1 slot.

Travis Metcalf (Third Base)

PA	R	H	2B	3B	HR	RBI	SO	BB	SB	CS	BA	OBP	SLG	OPS	3-Year	Fielding	Reliability
408	42	88	19	1	12	48	93	27	1	1	.235	.288	.388	.676	+0.07	C	High

Unless Hank Blalock returns to the hot corner, Metcalf is the internal frontrunner for the starting job. Adept with the glove, Metcalf's offensive growth stalled in Double-A. His swing-from-the-heels approach generates some pop but a low average. It's even money that he won't maintain a .300 OBP. It's also third or bust for Metcalf, who doesn't have the bat for first or the range to play anywhere else.

David Murphy (Right Field)

PA	R	H	2B	3B	HR	RBI	SO	BB	SB	CS	BA	OBP	SLG	OPS	3-Year	Fielding	Reliability
477	56	114	26	4	11	54	81	36	6	1	.262	.318	.416	.734	+0.01	C	Very High

Murphy's all-out style recalls fond memories of Rusty Greer, the apotheosis of grit from Texas' late-'90s glory days. Murphy also imitated Greer by missing a third of the season after a home-plate collision. Though lacking Greer's patience or contact skills, he's an excellent fourth outfielder and borderline regular, capable of left, center or right. As long as he sits against lefties, he's a net positive.

Maximiliano Ramirez (Catcher)

PA	R	H	2B	3B	HR	RBI	SO	BB	SB	CS	BA	OBP	SLG	OPS	3-Year	Fielding	Reliability
382	45	85	15	2	12	47	82	41	2	2	.255	.343	.421	.764	+0.05	C	High

Texas' most promising offensive backstop receives only passing mention in the conversation about Texas' catcher of the future. Ramirez received only eight plate appearances during September while Texas was playing out the string. Questions persist about whether he can stick behind the plate. His (very generously) listed height of 5-foot-11 makes him a less-than-ideal first baseman, and he lacks the range to play elsewhere. He might be best suited to DH. A delightful blend of contact, power and patience, he might also hit enough to justify it.

Jarrod Saltalamacchia (Catcher)

PA	R	H	2B	3B	HR	RBI	SO	BB	SB	CS	BA	OBP	SLG	OPS	3-Year	Fielding	Reliability
489	54	105	23	2	13	56	127	49	1	1	.243	.323	.396	.719	+0.05	D	High

Just 23 on Opening Day 2009, Saltalamacchia has more MLB experience and is younger than competitors Taylor Teagarden and Max Ramirez. He's still working on fulfilling his enormous potential. Over parts of two major league seasons, he's displayed impressive contact, power and patience, but never simultaneously. He's also inferior to Gerald Laird defensively, though improving, and not guaranteed Texas' primary catcher spot despite Laird's departure. Both Atlanta and Texas played Saltalamacchia at first base in 2007 just to get his bat in the lineup. Chris Davis' emergence has terminated that experiment.

Michael Young (Shortstop)

PA	R	H	2B	3B	HR	RBI	SO	BB	SB	CS	BA	OBP	SLG	OPS	3-Year	Fielding	Reliability
633	73	169	35	2	9	67	99	46	8	1	.292	.345	.406	.751	-0.04	C	Very High

A broken finger and other nagging injuries resulted in six-year lows in average, OBP and slugging percentage. He should rebound, but even if healthy, he's not the .331/.385/.513-hitting marvel of 2005. In a strange coincidence, he won a Gold Glove just as discussion of a potential move to a less demanding position heated up. Young is popular, works tirelessly, leads by example and supplies intangibles by the bushel. Unfortunately, he's also 32, not that far above average at this point, and just beginning a five-year, $80 million extension signed in 2007.

Pitchers

Joaquin Benoit (Reliever)

W	L	ERA	TBF	IP	Hit	HR	SO	BB	HBP	3-Year	Reliability
4	3	4.16	263	61	54	6	58	30	2	+0.20	Average

Offseason shoulder soreness plagued Benoit all season, ruining the chance of repeating his breakout 2007. He was disabled or otherwise incapacitated at three different parts of the season. When available, he often found himself entering low-leverage situations. The right hander has dominated lefties and scuffled against righties for the last two years. He can regain a prominent setup role with a good spring.

Scott Feldman (Starter)

W	L	ERA	TBF	IP	Hit	HR	SO	BB	HBP	3-Year	Reliability
7	8	5.19	621	139	158	18	70	56	9	+0.03	High

Though the statistics indicate otherwise, Feldman performed heroically in 2008. Converted to a starting role the previous winter and shed of his sidearm delivery, he made only two minor-league starts before injuries to others thrust him into the Texas rotation. He eventually threw 83 more innings than any previous year because Texas had no one to take his place. Admirable, yes, but he wasn't much better than replacement level and may suffer a hangover from the dramatically increased workload. He's highly unlikely to survive the year unscathed.

Frank Francisco (Reliever)

W	L	ERA	TBF	IP	Hit	HR	SO	BB	HBP	3-Year	Reliability
4	3	3.78	270	64	53	6	66	29	2	+0.32	Very Low

After an impressive 2004 rookie campaign, Francisco lost nearly two years to Tommy John surgery and another to wildness. Finally, in 2008, he returned to form. Francisco mows down lefties and righties alike with a 95 mph fastball, a splitter, and a curve. He still occasionally loses the strike zone and dabbles with questionable pitch selections. Though not a particularly safe bet to maintain his recent effectiveness, Francisco will battle C.J. Wilson for the closer role unless Texas acquires a "name" third party.

Kason Gabbard (Starter)

W	L	ERA	TBF	IP	Hit	HR	SO	BB	HBP	3-Year	Reliability
5	7	4.94	499	111	120	14	70	58	6	+0.14	Very High

Gabbard's assortment of off-speed pitches (even his fastball is off-speed) induces an amazing number of ground balls. He needs pinpoint control to succeed, but his control has failed him at the major league level. Batters wait for a good count and tee off, or don't swing at all; they managed a .496 OBP against Gabbard if his first pitch missed the strike zone. After beginning 2008 in the rotation, he's now reduced to fighting for a long relief role.

Matt Harrison (Starter)

W	L	ERA	TBF	IP	Hit	HR	SO	BB	HBP	3-Year	Reliability
2	8	7.60	430	86	118	15	32	59	7	+0.28	Very High

Harrison took his rookie lumps. His first seven starts resulted in 19 walks, only seven strikeouts, and a 7.07 ERA. Thereafter, he posted a 4.31 ERA in 48 innings that included a shutout of Oakland and eight scoreless frames against Tampa Bay. Harrison entered pro ball out of high school with an advanced feel for three pitches and has added a slider to his repertoire. He won't strike out many batters, but displayed good control and an aptitude for avoiding homers in the minors. He has a pretty good shot at making the Opening Day rotation and the potential of league-average inning-chewing.

Eric Hurley (Starter)

W	L	ERA	TBF	IP	Hit	HR	SO	BB	HBP	3-Year	Reliability
5	9	6.25	556	122	141	27	81	55	7	-0.28	Very High

Arguably Texas's top pitching prospect entering 2008, Hurley had a passable major league debut cut short by shoulder trouble (with an aborted final start that sabotaged his ERA). Hurley relies heavily on a slider and mixes in a fastball touching 93-94 with a still-developing change-up. To date, he's been unwilling or unable to eschew his predilection for pitching up in the zone, as evidenced by the 20 homers allowed in fewer than 100 innings. He's a decent starter if he makes that adjustment, but he'll likely have to prove himself in Triple-A first.

Warner A. Madrigal (Reliever)

W	L	ERA	TBF	IP	Hit	HR	SO	BB	HBP	3-Year	Reliability
4	4	4.67	303	69	68	9	56	33	2	-0.10	Very Low

A converted outfielder, Madrigal reached the majors after only 109 minor-league innings. Among Rangers, only Frank Francisco imparted more velocity on his fastball. He allowed six runs in his debut but pitched effectively thereafter, with slightly better control but far fewer strikeouts than in the minors. Just 25 and with all three options still available, Madrigal might have to bide his time in Triple-A while Texas sorts through its older, option-free personnel.

Brandon McCarthy (Starter)

W	L	ERA	TBF	IP	Hit	HR	SO	BB	HBP	3-Year	Reliability
4	6	5.16	400	90	99	13	56	37	3	+0.06	Average

Acquired for John Danks, McCarthy missed most of 2008 with elbow trouble and pitched more innings on rehab assignment than for the Rangers. Adding insult to injury, he earned a full year of major league service and is arbitration-eligible for the first time. Nolan Ryan personally assisted with an overhaul of McCarthy's delivery during his lengthy rehab, to modestly encouraging results, but his strikeout rate remained alarmingly low. You'll need a calculator with scientific notation to calculate his odds of ever having one season as good as Danks' 2008.

Luis Mendoza (Starter)

W	L	ERA	TBF	IP	Hit	HR	SO	BB	HBP	3-Year	Reliability
4	8	6.42	520	111	150	16	43	45	9	+0.08	Very High

That Mendoza lacked a strikeout pitch was understood. That he lacked ground out and fly out pitches resulted in an staggeringly awful season even by Rangers standards. Opponents batted .343/.405/.523 against Mendoza, akin to Ian Kinsler with 30 points of batting average tacked on. He's not truly that bad and was intermittently effective, but of course he's completely out of the discussion for a mop-up role, much less a spot in the rotation. Mendoza will gather himself in Triple-A and hope for another chance.

Kevin Millwood (Starter)

W	L	ERA	TBF	IP	Hit	HR	SO	BB	HBP	3-Year	Reliability
9	10	4.78	730	167	191	19	114	51	6	+0.17	Very High

Highly erratic in the past, Millwood has established a dejecting consistency by failing to reach 180 innings or post a sub-5.00 ERA in consecutive seasons. If the former happens again, he forfeits his $12 million option for 2010. His 2007 peripherals indicated a better future, but, once more, he was simply very, very hittable. Questionable fitness, a plague of minor injuries, and general inconsistency have made a mockery of his ace status. Expect modest improvement.

Vicente Padilla (Starter)

W	L	ERA	TBF	IP	Hit	HR	SO	BB	HBP	3-Year	Reliability
8	10	4.94	712	161	176	21	110	63	10	+0.23	Very High

Unlike Kevin Millwood, the taciturn Padilla partially returned to form after a lousy and injury-filled 2007, gracing his employer with a sub-5.00 ERA and just enough innings to qualify for the ERA title. Padilla relies on his fastball (in the 92-94 mph range) more than almost any starter in the majors. Just for giggles, he also occasionally hits batters deliberately and tosses an eephus curve. Padilla can be an effective pitcher but is five years removed from his last outstanding season. Playing for his $12 million team option or his next contract elsewhere should provide ample incentive.

Josh Rupe (Reliever)

W	L	ERA	TBF	IP	Hit	HR	SO	BB	HBP	3-Year	Reliability
4	4	4.83	329	73	79	8	44	35	5	+0.14	Low

Can a pitcher with a 5.14 ERA be an unsung hero? Josh Rupe ranked fourth on the team in innings, most of them cleaning up rotational spills. He doesn't have great control and faded badly down the stretch, but he at least offered a mundane stability in contrast to the bullpen's many failures. He'll fulfill the same role in 2009.

C.J. Wilson (Reliever)

W	L	ERA	TBF	IP	Hit	HR	SO	BB	HBP	3-Year	Reliability
4	2	4.03	253	58	54	6	50	28	3	+0.25	Low

Wilson wants badly to be the closer and certainly doesn't lack for confidence, but he's not a lock to regain his ninth-inning role after missing the final two months with elbow problems. In 2007, the nascent closer struggled against righties. Last year, he struggled against everyone. The peripherals indicate he didn't pitch much worse, and he should rebound. That said, Wilson again fared poorly when pitching without a day off, calling into question his viability as a closer or even a setup man. He can be an effective pitcher, but in what role?

Toronto Blue Jays

by John Brattain of The Hardball Times

2009 Blue Jays Projections

Record: 73-89
Division Rank/Games Behind: 4th, 17 games back
Runs Scored: 698, 13th in the league
Runs Allowed: 769, 4th in the league
Park Factor: 1.02, a bit of a hitter's park

What Happened Last Year:

The offense of 2008 was a testament to Murphy's Law: If something could go wrong, it most assuredly did. The hitters got off to a horrendous start, especially with runners in scoring position. There was a major power outage up and down the lineup and all too many rallies were short-circuited by double plays, Lyle Overbay and Alex Rios being the most notable culprits.

General manager J.P. Ricciardi attempted to give the lineup a spark by picking up Brad Wilkerson and Kevin Mench and hoping that they could recover past success (they couldn't). Frank Thomas was released after a slow start. Vernon Wells was on and off the disabled list. Matt Stairs got off to a decent start but went into a season-long malaise after mid-May with only a few spurts here and there.

The costs were catastrophic: the Blue Jays had 20 losses when holding the other side to three or fewer runs—among those were 12 games that could be described as outstanding Toronto pitching efforts (defined as two or fewer runs over nine innings or three or fewer in extra innings). The Jays lost two 10-inning games while holding the opposition to three runs, and had 12-inning losses in which they allowed one and three runs. Seven other times they were beaten by two or fewer runs. Ten of the 19 losses were inflicted by the clubs just ahead of them in the standings: the Rays (5), the Yankees (3) and the Red Sox (2).

Although the offense perked up after manager John Gibbons was fired (as well as hitting coach Gary Denbo) and Cito Gaston and Gene Tenace were brought back, it was too little too late. A 10-game winning streak got the Jays to the fringes of the wild card race, but it wasn't enough. The pitching and defense were pennant caliber, but there just wasn't enough offense to get it done.

Players Lost From Last Year's Team:

A.J. Burnett, David Eckstein, Stairs, Hector Luna, Wilkerson, Mench, Shannon Stewart, Gregg Zaun, Thomas

Players Acquired:

Matt Clement, Angel Sanchez, Kelvin Jimenez

Management is:

Ricciardi is known for attempting the creative solution rather than going for the obvious one (who needs a Barry Bonds or an Adam Dunn when Wilkerson or Jose Bautista are available!). While Ricciardi is very good at identifying undervalued relief pitching talent, he struggles to find quality starting pitching and seems to have a fondness of players who remind him of himself (light hitting infielders). He also is overly concerned with clubhouse issues, preferring a character guy (also known as "scrappy outmakers") to a controversial star, although his criteria always seem to be in flux depending on the mood of the moment.

Ricciardi also lives for the future, never considering whether the club is set to compete in a given year. He is always talking about "protecting the future" and not "mortgaging the future," never specifying when the future is. He's still deeply involved in his "five-year plan" to get the Jays into contention (he is now in year four—eight in human years—of the plan, hoping to contend in 2010 ... stay tuned). He is also prone to blame the team's failures on everything but himself, even though he is slow to rectify obvious problems.

At trade deadlines, he never commits the Jays as being buyers or sellers. He has lost the confidence of large segments of the fan base. It has gotten so bad that some misguidedly long for the Gord Ash years (ouch).

Gaston is known for using a set lineup and sticking with players who have earned his trust. He lets both his starting and relief pitchers work out of jams rather than bringing in a fresh arm. He is an advocate of intelligent aggression at the plate: The batter is expected to swing, but only at a hittable pitch and to go up to the plate with a plan in mind about what pitch he wants.

The minor league system is:

Although not highly ranked, there is talent there: In recent seasons, the best in the bushes have cracked the varsity in the persons of Shaun Marcum, Dustin McGowan, Aaron Hill, Rios, etc. The next group

(Travis Snider, Brian Jeroloman, J.P. Arencibia, Ricky and Davis Romero, David Purcey, Brett Cecil, Brad Mills, etc.) hasn't had a chance to establish itself in the big leagues yet. There is talent due to arrive in the next two-three years, but it'll be hard to judge until these prospects get a chance to prove themselves. It's a lot better than the perception by many pundits. The reason for it being underrated isn't clear.

Due for a change:

Rios has yet to have a full season in which his production remained consistent in both halves. In 2006, a staph infection cooled a hot start, in 2007 his power again waned in the second half and last season he struggled under the Gibbons/Denbo approach but caught fire after they were replaced by Gaston and Tenace. Rios seems comfortable under Gaston and will be 28 next season. Expect a superstar performance from the Jays' right fielder.

Reasons for Optimism:

Gaston has a knack for working with hitters and several are due for big improvements. Not only Rios, but Wells flourished once Gaston came on board. Adam Lind will man left field and Overbay's power should improve now that his hand is back to full strength. The Jays will have Hill back and Snider may be ready to mash at the big league level.

With the above enjoying Gaston's tutelage since last June, the offense should be much improved and will likely be a bit better than league average. The AL's best bullpen will have back several key parts missing from last season and there is a decent chance that from among Purcey, Cecil, and Davis and Ricky Romero will emerge two starters who will step up alongside Roy Halladay and Jesse Litsch.

The Jays have enough in-house pitching options that they should be able to cobble together a service-able rotation behind Halladay and can count on top-notch bullpen and defensive support. The kiddie corps shouldn't feel undue pressure as they get their feet wet at the big league level.

Reasons for Pessimism:

When your management talks about 2010 even before 2009 begins, you know you're in trouble. The lineup lacks a pure masher and leadoff man and you cannot lose 60 percent of your elite starting rotation—especially when they're your 2-3-4 starters—and expect not to see a significant dropoff in quality. (Burnett signed with the Yankees; Marcum and McGowan are lost to injury.)

Even if the team manages to contend, will there be money in the budget to add a contract at the trading deadline? And even if money is available, will Ricciardi get what is needed or try to impress us with the genius that brought the Jays Wilkerson and Mench as offensive upgrades rather than get the big ticket item? Of course, being in the same division as three quality teams built and focused to win right now while Ricciardi continues to plan for the future doesn't inspire optimism.

Still left to do:

A backup catcher, possibly a DH, a shortstop, leadoff hitter and another starting pitcher. Don't be surprised of all these are filled from within the organization.

Most likely team outcome:

84-78, fourth place.

> **Our Favorite Blue Jays Blogs:**
> Drunk Jays Fans (http://drunkjaysfans.blogspot.com/)
> The Tao of Stieb (http://taoofstieb.blogspot.com/)
> Batters Box (www.battersbox.ca/)
> Mockingbird (http://bjays.wordpress.com/)

Player Projections

Batters

Rod Barajas (Catcher)

PA	R	H	2B	3B	HR	RBI	SO	BB	SB	CS	BA	OBP	SLG	OPS	3-Year	Fielding	Reliability
357	38	80	20	1	10	43	61	24	0	1	.247	.306	.407	.713	-0.05	C	Average

Barajas is as streaky as they come. Unfortunately, those hot streaks are fairly infrequent. It was a hot streak between mid-May and late June (.337/.390/.609) that wrested the starting job from incumbent Gregg Myers, but outside of that torrid spell he hit a mere .218/.260/.339. If he can avoid another season of a reverse-platoon split (.204/.239/.352 vs. LHP) he could be more of an asset offensively. Defensively, pitchers enjoy working with him and he keeps base runners honest—key with some of the starting staff being less than adept at keeping potential thieves close to first base.

Jose Bautista (Third Base)

PA	R	H	2B	3B	HR	RBI	SO	BB	SB	CS	BA	OBP	SLG	OPS	3-Year	Fielding	Reliability
475	53	100	23	2	14	56	98	46	2	1	.242	.322	.409	.731	-0.02	F-	Very High

Late season acquisition Bautista may be the solution to Lyle Overbay's sudden inability to hit lefties. Although he manned the hot corner for the Pittsburgh Pirates, his future may be at the other side of the infield where his .263/.366/.500 mark against southpaws the last three seasons would look might good alongside Overbay's work against RHP. The only downside to this arrangement is that he looked very inelegant at the position in the five games he played there.

Aaron Hill (Second Base)

PA	R	H	2B	3B	HR	RBI	SO	BB	SB	CS	BA	OBP	SLG	OPS	3-Year	Fielding	Reliability
394	47	103	23	2	9	48	57	27	3	2	.290	.342	.442	.784	+0.08	B	Very High

Hill is a major question mark coming into 2009. Will he suffer from post-concussion syndrome after his tete-a-tete with David Eckstein? Can he hit in the early part of the season? How much rust does he have in his swing? The tools are there for him to be a solid contributor. In 2007, he hit 47 doubles and 17 homers (and would've had 19 had he not been robbed in back-to-back games by Joey Gathright in Kansas City), while providing defense that helps fans forget the days of Roberto Alomar and Orlando Hudson. The Blue Jays will be watching Hill closely in spring training.

Joe Inglett (Second Base)

PA	R	H	2B	3B	HR	RBI	SO	BB	SB	CS	BA	OBP	SLG	OPS	3-Year	Fielding	Reliability
449	52	110	19	7	4	40	66	33	8	4	.274	.333	.387	.720	-0.02	C	High

The good news is that Mighty Joe Inglett acquitted himself rather well in his first taste of semi-regular work, all the more impressive when one considers that he played every position but catcher and first base in 2008. He hit almost .300, coaxed enough walks to goose his OBP to a respectable .355 and flashed occasional extra base power good for an OPS+ of 103. He was competent against lefties (.276/.364/.345) and was an absolute beast with the bases loaded (.438/.471/.750). He swiped the odd base and kept the double plays to a minimum. If Aaron Hill struggles in his return, Inglett is option 1A. If Hill is sound and Marcos Scutaro and John McDonald open the year as the starting shortstops, then Inglett takes over the role Scutaro had last season as supersub. The Jays would gratefully take league average offense from him.

Adam Lind (Left Field)

PA	R	H	2B	3B	HR	RBI	SO	BB	SB	CS	BA	OBP	SLG	OPS	3-Year	Fielding	Reliability
519	62	132	27	3	16	69	105	33	2	2	.276	.324	.446	.770	+0.02	C	Very High

The education of Adam Lind is ongoing. After returning from Syracuse about the same time Cito Gaston returned from managerial oblivion, Lind was feasting on opposing pitching to the tune of .329/.362/.600. Word got around quickly that the kid could murder a fastball and maybe it was time to give him something else at which to swing. The pitchers adjusted and Lind hit a "Wilkerson being himself-eque" .255/.287/.292 the remainder of the season (35 games) and the ball never left the yard in fair territory. Now it is time to see if Lind can adjust. He'll turn 26 in July and this could be the year in which he establishes himself as a regular or a platoon (.253/.303/.385 vs. LHP in 2008) player. If he hits well, he could become the Jays' first baseman if Overbay is dealt.

John McDonald (Shortstop)

PA	R	H	2B	3B	HR	RBI	SO	BB	SB	CS	BA	OBP	SLG	OPS	3-Year	Fielding	Reliability
306	28	66	14	2	1	22	44	16	4	1	.238	.285	.314	.599	-0.05	A	Low

The aptly named (by Drunk Jays Fans) Prime Minister of Defense, McDonald wasn't as brilliant defensively as he was in 2007 but then again, he ain't as young as he used to be; nevertheless he figures to be in the shortstop mix for 2009. As difficult as it may sound, he regressed offensively last season and should ideally start only against lefties (.250/.304/.319) and be used as a late-inning defensive replacement. Regardless, he's always good for a few days of snappy hitting. They are when it's really fun to root for the little guy.

Lyle Overbay (First Base)

PA	R	H	2B	3B	HR	RBI	SO	BB	SB	CS	BA	OBP	SLG	OPS	3-Year	Fielding	Reliability
550	64	131	32	2	14	65	99	58	1	1	.271	.350	.432	.782	-0.04	B	Very High

Overbay was the Blue Jays' answer to Dr. Jekyll and Mr. Hammer-the-hide in 2008, his hitting swinging from one extreme to the other. Still recovering from a broken hand suffered in 2007, Overbay's power finally started to return in the second half. While valuable defensively, he struggled against lefties (.215/.285/.255) for the first time in his career and struggled in big spots: In the seventh inning or later (10 PA) Overbay was .143/.300/.143 with three GiDP, and the 24 double plays his bat started were three short of the AL lead. With his hand fully healed, Overbay should return to 115-120 OPS+ territory, although that could be higher if he is platooned.

Alex Rios (Right Field)

PA	R	H	2B	3B	HR	RBI	SO	BB	SB	CS	BA	OBP	SLG	OPS	3-Year	Fielding	Reliability
606	83	159	38	6	18	77	101	43	21	6	.287	.340	.475	.815	+0.00	A	Very High

Rios under Gary Denbo: .270/.328/.372; Rios under Gene Tenace and Cito Gaston: .308/.343/.533. That pretty much sums it up. Whatever was happening in 2008 with Rios' slow start, it was cleared up after the firing of John Gibbons (and Denbo) and the enigmatic young talent played in the manner many expected of him. He is still a work in progress as evidenced by hitting .200/.250/.309 over the last 15 games with the Jays in the fringe of the wild card race. However, he has a ton of talent and is playing under a coaching staff suited to his talents. Expect a big year from Rios in 2009, especially if he returns to his lefty-mashing ways.

Scott Rolen (Third Base)

PA	R	H	2B	3B	HR	RBI	SO	BB	SB	CS	BA	OBP	SLG	OPS	3-Year	Fielding	Reliability
466	55	108	30	2	12	55	74	43	4	1	.262	.339	.433	.772	-0.06	A+	Very High

Scott Rolen's 2009 will depend mostly on health: If he is ouchie-free he should be a productive member of the Blue Jays' infield; if he's less than sound, expect a repeat of 2008. Granted, a 107 OPS+ from a stellar defensive hot corner man is nothing at which to turn up one's nose, but when he was hot, he was very hot, when he was sore … in the 67 games leading up to his final DL stint Rolen was batting .232/.337/.359. There is cause for optimism, however, if you can avoid being distracted by sample size issues. After returning to the lineup and following a physical therapist's advice to keep his hands below shoulder level when swinging, he hit .298/.350/.532 over his final 100+ plate appearances.

Marco Scutaro (Shortstop)

PA	R	H	2B	3B	HR	RBI	SO	BB	SB	CS	BA	OBP	SLG	OPS	3-Year	Fielding	Reliability
500	54	117	22	2	6	46	64	48	4	2	.266	.341	.366	.707	-0.05	B	High

It overstates the case when people refer to Scutaro as the Blue Jays' most valuable player, but that shouldn't detract from what he did bring to the club in 2008. He provided defensive versatility, a better-than-league average OBP, and a solid clutch stick (.296/.403/.400; with two out .278/.443/.315). It was that useful enough amount of offense coupled with solid glove work that won him Cito Gaston's confidence and the starting shortstop job at season's end and, barring a transaction, in 2009. While it's unreasonable to expect improvement at his age, he should remain a useful player despite a lack of pop.

Travis Snider (Left Field)

PA	R	H	2B	3B	HR	RBI	SO	BB	SB	CS	BA	OBP	SLG	OPS	3-Year	Fielding	Reliability
538	63	123	29	3	19	71	145	45	2	2	.254	.320	.444	.764	+0.11	D	High

At age 20, Snider was the Blue Jays' "baby boomer" and gave the fans optimism for the coming years. When the club went into Fenway for a four-game set and in a position to really get into the wild card race, he banged out a double and a homer, driving in five in the first game of a doubleheader in mid-September. Despite his inexperience, he didn't embarrass himself against left-handed pitchers, batting .286/.375/.357 and will be given a long look in spring training. If he can't make the club as a starter, he will be sent back to Syracuse, where he will continue to develop as a big part of the future.

Shannon Stewart (Left Field)

PA	R	H	2B	3B	HR	RBI	SO	BB	SB	CS	BA	OBP	SLG	OPS	3-Year	Fielding	Reliability
343	38	85	14	1	5	33	40	29	5	1	.275	.339	.375	.714	-0.05	B	Average

Stewart's second stint with the Blue Jays will never be forgiven him, since he cost the team fan favorite Reed Johnson (who went on to a very decent year with the NL Central champion Chicago Cubs). While Stewart couldn't provide speed, power or defense, he was a big part of the double-play machine (almost half of his at-bats resulted in a ground ball) that was the Toronto Blue Jays of the Gary Denbo era. An ankle injury mercifully ended his season and tour of duty in Canada.

Vernon Wells (Center Field)

PA	R	H	2B	3B	HR	RBI	SO	BB	SB	CS	BA	OBP	SLG	OPS	3-Year	Fielding	Reliability
507	64	128	28	2	18	70	67	37	7	2	.277	.331	.462	.793	-0.02	F-	Very High

Wells missed a big 2008 due to injury. Despite being limited to 108 games, he led the team in homers with 20, was the only everyday player to bat .300 (on the nose) and the only one to come within shouting distance of slugging .500 (.496). His defense is no longer drawing the rave reviews of times past, but he has been working intensively during the offseason to improve all aspects of his game. A healthy Wells should be capable of returning to his 2006 levels of offensive production, although the Jays' brass would cheerfully take a repeat of 2008 provided it comes with 150-plus games played.

Brad Wilkerson (Right Field)

PA	R	H	2B	3B	HR	RBI	SO	BB	SB	CS	BA	OBP	SLG	OPS	3-Year	Fielding	Reliability
367	42	75	16	2	12	43	89	39	4	2	.235	.319	.410	.729	-0.03	C	High

Love conquers all—even really awful hitting. For years, J.P. Ricciardi lusted after Wilkerson, and when he was cut loose from the Seattle Mariners for offensive infidelity, the Jays' GM knew that this was the man to solve Toronto's hitting woes. He approached Wilkerson on bended knee and promised to love him through better and worse and while the fans hoped he'd get better, his hitting only became worse. After Cito Gaston came on board, the offense perked up but Wilkerson hit a Ruthian (Westheimer) .172/.259/.280 from that point through the end of the season (108 plate appearances).

Gregg Zaun (Catcher)

PA	R	H	2B	3B	HR	RBI	SO	BB	SB	CS	BA	OBP	SLG	OPS	3-Year	Fielding	Reliability
355	40	76	18	1	8	38	50	42	2	1	.249	.341	.393	.734	—	D	High

Zaun remains a useful player. Switch-hitting catchers with good batting eyes don't come along every day. However, his lack of power caused him to lose the starting job to Rod Barajas and while he remains a solid defensive backstop (despite problems with base thieves) he needs to hit to play regularly. His bat has only "slider speed" and the only time he can get around on fastballs is if he guesses right and starts his swing early. Still, he won't get himself out and walked as often as he struck out (38—which will be his age in April). He remains a serviceable extra piece on a club but is no longer suited to fulltime duty.

Pitchers

Jeremy Accardo (Reliever)

W	L	ERA	TBF	IP	Hit	HR	SO	BB	HBP	3-Year	Reliability
3	2	3.99	183	43	43	4	32	15	2	+0.18	Low

In 2007, Accardo stepped into the breach when B.J. Ryan needed Tommy John to visit his left elbow. In 2008, the roles were reversed, although Accardo's forearm didn't require surgical intervention. In 2007, he converted 30 of 37 save chances and absolutely owned lefties with his fastball-split finger combo. He has solid command, and if he's back up to speed will give the Jays an absolutely sick relief corps.

A.J. Burnett (Starter)

W	L	ERA	TBF	IP	Hit	HR	SO	BB	HBP	3-Year	Reliability
12	9	3.80	796	189	174	19	176	70	9	+0.19	Very High

Burnett is an enigma —terrific raw stuff but prone to cold streaks and injury. He is awe-inspiring to watch throwing in the high 90s with seemingly little effort and when he can get his curve over for strikes is close to unhittable. Every season he'll have a run of at least a dozen starts of dominance. Burnett does have the unfortunate inability to put a bad call, an error or some other misfortune out of his mind and concentrate on the task at hand. Nevertheless, if he's healthy, odds are good that he'll throw seven quality innings.

Jesse Carlson (Reliever)

W	L	ERA	TBF	IP	Hit	HR	SO	BB	HBP	3-Year	Reliability
3	4	4.98	267	61	63	9	51	25	4	+0.43	Low

It took him six years and four organizations to reach The Show but once there southpaw Carlson didn't disappoint. He handled lefty and righty hitters with equal aplomb, walked just over three per nine innings pitched, struck out almost a batter per frame and kept the ball in the park (a HR/9 of .9). His 2.25 ERA was not a fluke as evidenced by his tidy 1.033 WHIP. The only question is: Can he do it again?

Scott Downs (Reliever)

W	L	ERA	TBF	IP	Hit	HR	SO	BB	HBP	3-Year	Reliability
5	3	3.36	288	69	62	5	58	28	3	+0.19	Low

Lefty Downs was superb in 2007, and managed to be even better in 2008. He gave the Jays their most reliable eighth-inning reliever since Duane Ward set up for Tom Henke. As good as his season's totals were, he was much better than they show, since he wore down toward the end, his ERA rising from 1.23 to 1.78. There is talk that the Jays want him to try starting again, but "Snakeface" has made it known he enjoys working out of the bullpen.

Jason Frasor (Reliever)

W	L	ERA	TBF	IP	Hit	HR	SO	BB	HBP	3-Year	Reliability
4	2	4.05	252	58	53	6	55	28	2	+0.19	Low

Frasor is a great pitcher provided it's not a big situation. He has an electric arm and can throw in the mid-90s but has absolutely no faith in his ability to get hitters out. When the pressure is on, he simply stops challenging hitters. In low-leverage situations he allows an OOBP of .305, in medium leverage situations it rises to .355, in high leverage spots it spikes at .406.

Roy Halladay (Starter)

W	L	ERA	TBF	IP	Hit	HR	SO	BB	HBP	3-Year	Reliability
14	9	3.31	845	207	204	17	147	40	7	+0.16	Very High

Halladay is among the best starting pitchers in baseball. In recent seasons he began to eschew going for the strikeout to focus on getting batters out with as few pitches as possible. Although he has been snake-bit at times (a Kevin Mench line drive ended one season; appendicitis took a chunk out of another and a third was cut short as a precaution after he had surgery) he can be counted on for a ton of quality innings. Assuming a healthy 2009, look for Doc to be in the Cy Young discussion and be among the league leaders in IP, WHIP, complete games, BB/9 and ERA+. He is a staff ace in the truest sense of the word and if he has five or six more Halladay-type seasons, it will be time to begin speaking of him in Hall of Fame terms.

Brandon League (Reliever)

W	L	ERA	TBF	IP	Hit	HR	SO	BB	HBP	3-Year	Reliability
4	3	3.66	284	66	66	4	48	25	4	-0.03	Low

One of Cito Gaston's best projects was converting underachieving flamethrower League from enigmatic mop up man to future closer—a role once projected for him. It looked like he was ready for stardom after a solid 2006, but a poorly constructed offseason weightlifting program ruined his velocity and his command (a BB/9 of 6.67 for 2007-Aug. 9, 2008). Gaston slowly increased the leverage of his use and in his last 18 appearances of the season League struck out 16 in 16.1, innings, walking just one. This could be the year League finally meets expectations.

Jesse Litsch (Starter)

W	L	ERA	TBF	IP	Hit	HR	SO	BB	HBP	3-Year	Reliability
10	9	4.43	742	174	188	21	99	48	10	-0.28	Very High

Litsch is not impressive to watch; indeed he seems completely hittable when he is on the mound. Yet he gets outs, gets through innings and logs a fair share of them and when all is said and done sports an ERA that is not insignificantly better than league average. How does he do it? The old fashioned way—he keeps the free passes to a minimum (1.99 BB/9 in 2008), throws a lot of ground balls (GB/FB of 1.3) and keeps the ball in the park (1.02 HR/9). He is again proof of the adage that if you don't beat yourself, teams will have a hard time beating you. His K/9 rate continues to grow and he'll be just 24 on Opening Day. He should be good to be at least league average and probably a good bit better.

Dustin McGowan (Starter)

W	L	ERA	TBF	IP	Hit	HR	SO	BB	HBP	3-Year	Reliability
8	7	4.17	578	135	133	14	108	53	5	+0.14	Very High

McGowan has been a tease. Opposing hitters compare his raw stuff to Roy Halladay's, but he's had a difficult time staying healthy. He has already endured the Tommy John procedure and last season had a frayed labrum repaired. He's not expected back until May or June, and it would be naive to expect him to be up to full speed right out of the gate. First-pitch strikes will be key to his success—his command improved from 2007-'08, but that was the biggest obstacle he had to getting established when he was a prospect.

John Parrish (Starter)

W	L	ERA	TBF	IP	Hit	HR	SO	BB	HBP	3-Year	Reliability
6	7	4.46	513	117	115	13	90	57	5	+0.20	Low

Lefty Parrish has two problems: finishing off hitters and staying on top of his breaking stuff. He throws a lot of pitches per inning, often getting to strike two quickly but lacking the raw stuff to get the third pitch past the hitter, resulting into lots of balls fouled off and deep counts. Further, even on the TV screen it is easy to see when Parrish releases his pitches from the side of the ball rather than the top. It's even easier to see the results: The breaking pitches become very tempting to the batter. Still, he has decent command, is left-handed and will be useful as a swing man. If he finds a way to finish off hitters more quickly, he could be a decent end-of-rotation starter.

David Purcey (Starter)

W	L	ERA	TBF	IP	Hit	HR	SO	BB	HBP	3-Year	Reliability
7	10	5.16	674	152	157	23	126	69	10	+0.19	Very High

Purcey pitched a lot better than his pitching line would indicate. His first two major league starts revealed a bad case of jitters, but once he was given a regular starting job he pitched pretty well. When recalled in late July, he averaged almost six innings per start, gave up about a hit per inning pitched, struck out close to a batter per inning and walked fewer than three per nine innings pitched. Generally, when a pitcher does that, he'll do quite well. In 2008, he pitched a total of 182 professional innings, striking out 179 while walking 63—and 11 of those bases on balls came in his first two major league starts about a month apart. Subtract that and Purcey had a BB/9 of 2.68. Don't be surprised to see 170-plus innings of league-average work.

B.J. Ryan (Reliever)

W	L	ERA	TBF	IP	Hit	HR	SO	BB	HBP	3-Year	Reliability
4	3	3.33	248	60	48	5	60	25	2	+0.20	Very Low

Considering that Ryan had Tommy John surgery on his left elbow less than 12 months before he made his 2008 debut, he enjoyed a remarkable season, converting 32 of 37 saves, striking out a man per inning and posting a sub-3.00 ERA. However, Blue Jays fans will tell you that he made ninth innings that put the drunk in Drunk Jays Fans. Only in 21 of his 60 appearances did he face just three batters and 23 times he faced five or more. Regardless, command is generally the last thing to return to pitchers undergoing the procedure, and Ryan figures to be improved in that department in 2009. Expect him to return to elite status.

Brian Tallet (Reliever)

W	L	ERA	TBF	IP	Hit	HR	SO	BB	HBP	3-Year	Reliability
4	3	4.09	271	63	59	6	50	28	3	+0.20	Low

Forgotten lefty Tallet is an enigma—some days he's the southpaw version of Jason Frasor only to go on extended streaks of being almost unhittable. In 2007, he ran off 21.2 innings in which he gave up nine hits and an earned run. Last season he opened with 23 innings in which he gave up just three earned runs. The key is throwing strikes and getting ahead of hitters, since he lacks the raw velocity and stuff to come back when he falls behind. When he gets into one of his hot streaks, the manager is well served to keep going back to him until he finally implodes and then use him carefully until he finds his groove again.

Brian Wolfe (Reliever)

W	L	ERA	TBF	IP	Hit	HR	SO	BB	HBP	3-Year	Reliability
4	4	4.43	303	71	73	9	45	24	3	+0.29	Average

A once-promising starter in the Minnesota organization, Wolfe has been used often in relief with mixed success. With a potentially depleted starting rotation, the Blue Jays may stretch out Wolfe to see if he can return to rotation duty. In 2002, he went 13-8, 2.81 ERA (and a cool WHIP of 1.00) for the Quad City River Bandits in 160 innings, so who knows? While not overpowering as a reliever, he keeps base runners to a minimum (BB/9 of 2 and a H/9 of 7.2 in 2007-08), keeps the ball in the park (.94 HR/9) and throws a lot of ground balls (GB/FB of 1.62 in 2008) but has trouble finding regular work. His peripherals suggest he'd be better suited to starting, so he'll be one to keep an eye on in Dunedin this spring.

Washington Nationals

by Chris Needham, formerly of Capitol Punishment (dcbb.blogspot.com)

2009 Nationals Projections

Record: 66-96
Division Rank/Games Behind: Last by 22 games
Runs Scored: 721, 13th in the league
Runs Allowed: 858, last in the league
Park Factor: 1.01, pretty much neutral

What Happened Last Year:

Remember that Ryan Zimmerman walk-off on that first Sunday night of the season? Well, when the year's highlight happens before the calendar flips to April, you know you've had a terrible season.

Every spring, fans and managers (field and general) play the "if-this'n-that" game. It's that list of about 20 things a team needs to go right to have a successful season. For a team like the Nats, the list is a lot longer than that of the Red Sox, but if they hit, say, 25 out of 28, they're printing up playoff tickets for their first-round loss. It's that dreaming that gives fans of lousy teams hope. Invariably what happens is that only 14 of those 28 things go right, and the team muddles right around realistic rational expectations.

Then there's the 2008 Washington Nationals.

Just as hitting 25 of 28 is improbable, so is hitting just three of 30, which is exactly what happened to the Nationals. The list of things that worked out goes something like: Cristian Guzman showed that '07 wasn't a fluke and Elijah Dukes didn't kill anyone. If you need a third, how about Johnny Lannan showing that he's a pretty good middle-of-the-rotation pitcher?

The list of things that went wrong for the Nats is nearly innumerable: Nick Johnson broke down earlier than expected; Zimmerman didn't recover from his hamate problems, then went down with injury; Wily Mo Pena put up one of the worst OPS+ numbers of any semi-regular left fielder in baseball history before mercifully breaking down; Chad Cordero threw about ten 74-mph pitches before ripping his labrum; Aaron Bleepin' Boone had more innings at first base than any other Nat. Get the picture?

Meanwhile, they broke in a new park that plays fairly, unlike the cavernous RFK Stadium. Fans seemed to enjoy it, even if some had some small gripes. But the other side of that story is how few came through its gates, and the corresponding dismal TV ratings.

A midseason report showed that only about 9,000 people were watching the team's television broadcasts, a number that seems fishy but is so low that even if it were off by 300 percent, the Nats still would be in the league's cellar.

On the field and off the field, it was a season to forget. Except for Zimmerman's homer.

Players Lost from Last Year's Team:

Felipe Lopez, yay! Emilio Bonifacio, yay! Paul Lo Duca, yay! Johnny Estrada, yay! Dmitri Young is set to ply his wares in Syracuse. Tim Redding, Boone and Odalis Perez are free agents, and the Nats seem mildly interested in re-signing them all.

Players Acquired:

Scott Olsen and Josh Willingham came over from the Marlins and while neither is a championship-level performer, they represent upgrades at their respective positions. The Nationals hope ex-Oriole Daniel Cabrera finally can pitch to his potential.

Management Is:

Manny Acta's pretty popular among the statheads for his choice quotes about bunting and stealing, but if you watch him more closely, he can be aggravating. There are times where he takes the strategy too far, refusing to bunt late in games or with good bunters at the plate. He rides his bullpen hard, and his stubborn insistence on using Luis Ayala, even past the point it was clear that his stuff had diminished, cost the team a few games. Still, he did well with the patchwork bullpen late in the season, and there were certain decisions—like all the time Boone saw at first—that he was forced into by terrible roster construction.

This could be a make or break season for Acta. General manager Jim Bowden is rarely a patient man, and there's a sense that with another poor season, Acta could be on the outs in D.C., which would be a shame, especially if he wound up in New York, reunited with Omar Minaya.

Bowden gets a bum rap sometimes. He's not a great GM, and on his best days, he's only good. But he's not Syd Thrift/Dave Littlefield terrible. He's done reasonably well at times in the Nats' system, where strong ownership and the heavy hand of Stan Kasten have helped to temper some of his biggest weaknesses. He's brought in some excellent baseball people, and oversaw the building of a dramatically improved scouting and player development operation. And last off-season's acquisitions of Dukes and Lastings Milledge brought in a ton of young talent at very little expense.

Still, there are the annoying aspects to him. He's given out a few unwise contract extensions, including the one to Young, who promptly ate himself out of the league. He's terribly impatient, and sometimes seems to make rash decisions. He hasn't given Acta the authority to hire and fire his coaches, which led to a lame duck hitting coach pointlessly hanging around at the end of the season. This offseason's talk of Willy Taveras shows that his infatuation with speed continues. And despite his "pitching, pitching, pitching" mantra, he hasn't added any notable pitching from outside the organization, other than one-year stop-gaps like Perez. Still, to his credit, the team has developed Lannan, and Jordan Zimmermann is on the cusp of breaking through.

The Minor League System Is:

It's better than it was a few years ago, but it doesn't look as improved as it did last season. The Nats' prospects had a tough year. Last year's top pick, Ross Detwiler, struggled all season. Chris Marrero, their top offensive prospect, missed half the season after blowing out his ankle in a play at the plate.

But there are a few interesting names. Zimmermann took over as the team's top pitching prospect, dominating batters in his second year in the minors. He's got a good chance to break camp with the Nats; they're really high on him. Incidentally, he was one of the picks the Nats got when they lost Alfonso Soriano to the Cubs, something those who like to sneer at the Nats' ineptitude never consider. Michael Burgess has impressive raw power, but he's going to have to pick up the contact ability to make an impact. One name to watch a bit lower is Derek Norris. He's a catcher who's played only short-season ball, but he's shown a pretty solid batting eye, and hits for solid power for someone so young.

The Nats flubbed last year's No. 1 pick, failing to sign Aaron Crow, even though they knew he'd have exorbitant demands when they drafted him. This year's going to be a huge chance for them, with the No. 1 overall pick and a compensatory pick at about No. 10 for Crow. The Nats are going to need two round-trippers with their picks, especially in terms of their financial outlay. Even the casual Nats fan already knows the name Stephen Strasburg, and they'll be watching.

Due For a Change:

All of 'em. There's a school of thought that hitting and pitching coaches don't matter. For the most part, I agree. But I look at it as more of a bell-curve kinda thing. Most are in the middle and are fairly interchangeable.

Our Favorite Nats Blogs:

Nationals Farm Authority extensively covers the minor league system for the Nats: (http://www.farm-authority.dcsportsnet.com/)

Nats320 does more original first-hand coverage of the team than almost any other baseball blog: (http://nats320.blogspot.com/)

Oleanders and Morning Glories uses stats smartly, with just the right amount of cynicism this team deserves: (http://mvn.com/oleanders/)

Then there are the extremes. For every Walt Hriniak, there's a Lenny Harris. Harris' reign of terror ended in the offseason, but in his time with the Nats, batter after batter stagnated or regressed. His hitting philosophy involved making contact with strikes, regardless of quality, hitting to the opposite field, and Dr. Phil-style aphorisms. The Nats hired Rick Eckstein, and even if he's one of those hitting coaches who's a blob in the middle of the bell curve, that's worth a few extra runs next season.

Along those lines, this better be the year that Ryan Zimmerman takes the step forward. He entered the season coming off hamate surgery, which often robs batters of power. After taking some time off with shoulder problems, he came back strongly, hitting .306/ .370/ .455 post-DL. Free from injury, and with more distance from the hamate surgery, this could be the season Nats fans have been waiting for.

Reasons to be Optimistic:

Most of the Nats performed under expectations last year, so if they just play to their averages, they'll be improved. It's also a very young team. Ryan Zimmerman, Jesus Flores, Milledge and Dukes are all under 25 and any or all could be capable of a breakout season.

Reasons to be Pessimistic:

Two seasons ago, the Nats fended off predictions that they'd be "historically bad" by cobbling together a free-talent starting rotation that greatly exceeded expectations. Rather than building upon that, the Nats have viewed that as a model for all future staffs, and this year's rotation appears to be as shaky as any others have been. Lannan is set to front it, along with 22-year-old Collin Balester. Newly acquired Cabrera and Olsen fill two of the other spots, though Cabrera is consistently inconsistent and questions about Olsen's declining stats and attitude make him no sure thing. Other than that, there's not much. The team hopes that this is the year (HA!) that Shawn Hill's finally healthy. They think that one of their minor leaguers, such as Jordan Zimmermann, can fill one of the slots. But there's little depth beyond that. If one or more of those players is injured or is terribly ineffective, there aren't many options. In the past, the Nats have done fairly well at picking out a veteran arm to eat innings right before spring training. They're going to need to do the same this year. Otherwise, whatever gains they make offensively will be wiped out by worse run prevention.

Still Left to Do:

Beyond filling out a starting rotation, Bowden's immediate concern has been finding a big bat for the middle of the order. They were hot and heavy in the Mark Teixeira sweepstakes, but Adam Dunn seems as likely a possibility, filling in at left field or taking over at first when the inevitable Johnson injury occurs.

As constructed, the Nats are loaded with outfielders, and with the team's unhappiness with Milledge's mediocre defense in center, they may be looking for more help. With Willingham, Dukes, Milledge, Austin Kearns and Willie Harris all fighting for time, how the logjam gets resolved (trade perhaps?) will be one of the key questions for the coming season.

Most Likely Team Outcome:

Despite the terrible season, I think bad luck and bad instruction played a large role in the team's misfortune. There was enough talent on that team to win in the low 70s. It just didn't work out that way. In many ways, the Nats are returning that same level of talent, and that same low- to mid-70s win total is a reasonable goal.

Player Projections

Batters

Ronnie Belliard (Shortstop)

PA	R	H	2B	3B	HR	RBI	SO	BB	SB	CS	BA	OBP	SLG	OPS	3-Year	Fielding	Reliability
426	48	107	23	1	9	49	63	33	2	1	.278	.337	.413	.750	-0.04	F	Very High

He's given the Nats what they've asked for and has been a capable sub, filling in at all the infield spots, and providing Nats fans with another big memory—his walk-off blast against Peter Angelos' Orioles. He's lost a step on defense, and if he's thrust into full-time duty, the Nats (especially their pitchers!) are sure to be disappointed.

Rogearvin Bernadina (Center Field)

PA	R	H	2B	3B	HR	RBI	SO	BB	SB	CS	BA	OBP	SLG	OPS	3-Year	Fielding	Reliability
517	58	112	16	5	4	35	109	41	22	8	.242	.306	.325	.631	+0.03	D	High

He got an early and surprising call-up to the majors from Double-A. While he didn't have any success, he took it out on the International League's pitchers, combining solid defense with a .351/.404/.513 line that gives him an outside chance at another promotion this season.

Aaron Boone (First Base)

PA	R	H	2B	3B	HR	RBI	SO	BB	SB	CS	BA	OBP	SLG	OPS	3-Year	Fielding	Reliability
317	35	72	15	1	7	35	62	25	1	1	.255	.327	.390	.717	—	C	Average

That he played more games at first base than any other Nat should not be held against Manny Acta, but against Jim Bowden, and his assistant GM, Bob Boone. Hey, wait a minute. Those two have the same last name! I wonder if that has something to do with why they considered re-signing him. Hmmm.

Kory Casto (Left Field)

PA	R	H	2B	3B	HR	RBI	SO	BB	SB	CS	BA	OBP	SLG	OPS	3-Year	Fielding	Reliability
418	45	87	17	2	9	43	89	44	2	2	.236	.319	.367	.686	+0.01	C	Very High

Are two chances enough? Once he was the team's top offensive prospect, which was as much a comment on the quality of the team's farm system as it was about Casto's prospecthood. Now, he's a longshot to break camp as a four-corners fill-in. With this team's injury history, even if he doesn't break camp he's got a good chance to see if the third's the charm.

Elijah Dukes (Right Field)

PA	R	H	2B	3B	HR	RBI	SO	BB	SB	CS	BA	OBP	SLG	OPS	3-Year	Fielding	Reliability
348	47	76	15	2	13	44	70	47	8	3	.259	.368	.456	.824	+0.04	C	Average

It's kind of refreshing that the big question surrounding him doesn't involve when he's going to assault someone, but whether he can stay on the field enough to be the team's big hitter. He had a sensational season that surpassed everyone's expectations on and off the field, but he played only 81 games because of various leg and knee injuries. When healthy, he was the lone National to actually have a plan at the plate, waiting for his pitch instead of merely swinging at the first strike he could get the bat on. It's an approach that served him well.

Jesus Flores (Catcher)

PA	R	H	2B	3B	HR	RBI	SO	BB	SB	CS	BA	OBP	SLG	OPS	3-Year	Fielding	Reliability
383	40	84	19	1	11	45	90	22	1	1	.240	.295	.394	.689	+0.03	C	Average

As much potential as he's shown, he's still got work to do; the sum of the individual impressions of him has been greater than the sum total of his stat line. You can see the talent in flashes: the strength of his swings, the patience he sometimes shows, the plus throwing ability, etc. He just needs to take that extra step to become the player we all think he is. For one, he could use a strong backup to help take some of those at-bats against tough righties. After two seasons, he's hitting just .232/.282/.347 against them, while looking like an All-Star against lefties. Still, the Nats aren't afraid to throw him in the thick of things—he batted fourth, fifth or sixth for them in the majority of his games.

Cristian Guzman (Shortstop)

PA	R	H	2B	3B	HR	RBI	SO	BB	SB	CS	BA	OBP	SLG	OPS	3-Year	Fielding	Reliability
477	56	132	24	4	7	51	56	26	5	2	.298	.340	.418	.758	-0.03	D	Average

So maybe seeing the ball really does affect how well one hits! Guzman put up another decent season, and he was rewarded with a trip to the All-Star Game (where he made some pretty nifty plays in the field to keep the game tied) and with a new two-year deal. No Nats fan who lived through 2005 could've envisioned a scenario where a two-year deal would be viewed as a decent move.

But after laser eye surgery and surgery to repair tears in his shoulders, he's been a bit of a different player. He doesn't walk much, but his physical health allows him to drive the ball a bit better, leading to what appears to be a fairly sustainable increase in his BABIP over what he had done the previous few seasons.

Willie Harris (Left Field)

PA	R	H	2B	3B	HR	RBI	SO	BB	SB	CS	BA	OBP	SLG	OPS	3-Year	Fielding	Reliability
423	53	94	17	5	8	41	70	44	13	4	.255	.338	.393	.731	-0.02	A+	High

When you factor in his amazing defense, you can make a solid argument that he was one of the top half dozen or so left fielders in the league. Scary stuff! Harris's career year earned him a two-year extension at a team-friendly salary, making him a bargain even if he returns to the super-sub role he filled at the start of the season. His sudden power outburst nearly tripled his career homer total, but even if the power recedes a bit, he's still the perfect NL bench guy.

Anderson Hernandez (Shortstop)

PA	R	H	2B	3B	HR	RBI	SO	BB	SB	CS	BA	OBP	SLG	OPS	3-Year	Fielding	Reliability
553	58	130	22	5	7	49	92	31	9	5	.254	.297	.357	.654	+0.08	D	Very High

Nicknamed IPOR by Mets fans for the almost automatic "In Play, Outs Recorded" line that'd show up on MLB.com's Gameday application, Nats fans were spoiled by his outrageous batting line last season. He's clearly not a .333 hitter; we've got 3,500 minor league at-bats (at a .260ish clip) to demonstrate that. And he doesn't do enough other things well to be anything other than a backup/stopgap at the position. Despite that, he appears penciled in as the starter at second base for next season, in part because of the raves about his defense. I don't see it. But I'm not sure that seeing Ron Belliard waddle back out to the keystone works either.

Nick Johnson (First Base)

PA	R	H	2B	3B	HR	RBI	SO	BB	SB	CS	BA	OBP	SLG	OPS	3-Year	Fielding	Reliability
248	33	55	14	0	9	33	43	43	2	1	.277	.412	.483	.895	-0.04	B	Average

We know what he's capable of when he's healthy. This line above, combined with his typical plus defense would put him among the top third of MLB first basemen. But counting on him being healthy is ridiculous. It isn't just that he gets all sorts of wacky injuries, it's that he heals more slowly than a Molina runs to first. This latest injury—a tear of the tendon sheath in his right wrist—is especially worrisome. Johnson had wrist problems while in the minors, which kept him out for a significant period, and this injury, which occurred on a swing, happened in mid-May and was supposed to keep him out for only a month or two. Even if he's ready for spring training, given his injury history, the location of the injury, and how it happened in the first place, can you really count on many games or any production at all?

Austin Kearns (Right Field)

PA	R	H	2B	3B	HR	RBI	SO	BB	SB	CS	BA	OBP	SLG	OPS	3-Year	Fielding	Reliability
458	52	103	22	1	12	52	83	49	2	2	.259	.350	.410	.760	-0.03	B	Very High

Great defense or no, there's no making up for a corner-man with a .316 slugging average. Worse, the stubbornly patient Manny Acta batted him cleanup or fifth in almost every one of his starts. After two disastrous months, he went on the DL with elbow problems—the number of loose bodies floating around in his elbow surprised even his surgeons. When he came back, he wasn't much better, struggling to slug Dmitri Young's weight. His season mercifully ended in late August with a broken foot. What to expect this season? Nats fans would be happy with the projection. But with the crowded outfield situation, he's going to have to start strong and earn his plate appearances. If you've watched him swing, it's pretty clear that he needs someone to completely rebuild it. If he makes the adjustments, he'll be the player the Nats thought they had when they gave him the big- dollar extension. Otherwise, we're looking at the league's most expensive defensive replacement.

Ryan Langerhans (Center Field)

PA	R	H	2B	3B	HR	RBI	SO	BB	SB	CS	BA	OBP	SLG	OPS	3-Year	Fielding	Reliability
384	45	79	17	3	7	36	93	51	7	2	.242	.346	.377	.723	-0.01	D	Average

With the league's increasing emphasis on defense, I'm kind of surprised that the Nats were able to send him down to the minors and re-sign him without someone else nabbing him. A tremendous defensive outfielder, his offense improved once he took a crack at the minors and the Nats' hitting coach there (now the major league hitting coach), Rick Eckstein. If he hits this projection, he's an asset in the outfield. But like the other guys on this team, he's going to have to battle for playing time. Right now, he's sixth or seventh on the depth chart, rightly or wrongly.

Lastings Milledge (Center Field)

PA	R	H	2B	3B	HR	RBI	SO	BB	SB	CS	BA	OBP	SLG	OPS	3-Year	Fielding	Reliability
546	71	136	26	3	14	63	90	41	15	5	.281	.351	.434	.785	+0.06	F-	High

There's a lot to like about the enthusiasm with which he plays and the potential he shows, but two things stick in my mind about his season. First, he was terrible in center field, especially his reaction time. He always seemed to be a step behind, and the team has grumbled enough about it to make me think that he's not going to be there long (or possibly with the team at all). The second is his base running. He might be the worst baserunner I've ever seen, constantly trying to take the extra base with little success in situations where trying to stretch it out makes little or no sense. It might be my faulty memory, but I swear he was retired on 6-5 putouts about 42 times this season. He was just aggressive to the point of stupidity. Worse, he showed little improvement in either category all season.

Luke Montz (Catcher)

PA	R	H	2B	3B	HR	RBI	SO	BB	SB	CS	BA	OBP	SLG	OPS	3-Year	Fielding	Reliability
441	43	82	17	1	11	45	99	37	1	1	.207	.277	.338	.615	+0.03	C	High

When Columbus' season ended, Montz drove home to Louisiana during Hurricane Gustav. Almost immediately, he got a phone call calling him up to the majors when Jesus Flores sprained his ankle. He got that first homer out of the way pretty quickly, but is likely on the outside looking in, barring another injury. He's shown some flashes of power in the minors, but he's going to need to do the same at Triple-A to make it back to Washington.

Wil Nieves (Catcher)

PA	R	H	2B	3B	HR	RBI	SO	BB	SB	CS	BA	OBP	SLG	OPS	3-Year	Fielding	Reliability
275	25	61	11	1	2	22	39	16	1	0	.243	.289	.318	.607	-0.02	D	Low

The team loves his energy, and when you watch him play, you can sorta feel it through the screen. But that doesn't excuse the lack of offense. After he hit the most improbable walk-off homer you'll ever see (a high fly ball to the opposite field that just kept floating forever), he batted just .248/.290/.318 over his final 61 games—about what you'd expect given his record, and practically a dead ringer for this projection.

Pete Orr (Second Base)

PA	R	H	2B	3B	HR	RBI	SO	BB	SB	CS	BA	OBP	SLG	OPS	3-Year	Fielding	Reliability
365	39	80	14	6	1	24	73	22	12	2	.241	.292	.328	.620	-0.03	C	Low

Everyone's favorite scrappy Canadian, Orr became a bit of a fan favorite because of the way he hustles. But on a team of Felipe Lopezes, even Dmitri Young sometimes looks like he's hustling.

Wily Mo Pena (Left Field)

PA	R	H	2B	3B	HR	RBI	SO	BB	SB	CS	BA	OBP	SLG	OPS	3-Year	Fielding	Reliability
302	35	72	13	1	11	41	76	22	0	1	.262	.321	.437	.758	+0.06	D	Average

The less said the better: a disaster in the field and at the plate. The only thing that kept Nats fans from storming the field and carrying him away was that they were beaten to it by his season-ending injury, tears to his rotator cuff and labrum. He exercised his $2 million option for next season, and is set to fight his way into the Nats crowded outfield. But with Josh Willingham penciled in as the left fielder, the at-bats aren't just going to be given to him as Manny Acta did last season over and over and over and over and over again.

Dmitri Young (First Base)

PA	R	H	2B	3B	HR	RBI	SO	BB	SB	CS	BA	OBP	SLG	OPS	3-Year	Fielding	Reliability
313	36	78	16	1	7	37	52	32	0	0	.282	.358	.423	.781	—	C	Average

Oh, how the heavy have fallen. With a new two-year extension in his pocket, after having had his career left for dead, Dmitri showed up to camp fatter than ever. He rapidly broke down, spraining his back in the first week of the season. After coming back, he played passably, but then his diabetes flared up to the point where he was even unable to travel. At the end of the season, he was outrighted to Syracuse, and faces a long road back if he's going to make it to the majors again.

Ryan Zimmerman (Third Base)

PA	R	H	2B	3B	HR	RBI	SO	BB	SB	CS	BA	OBP	SLG	OPS	3-Year	Fielding	Reliability
520	65	135	31	2	17	72	84	43	3	2	.287	.348	.470	.818	+0.04	A	Very High

He was one of the Nats most affected by injury last year, and while this projection seems like a big step forward to him, it's probably about where he could've been last season barring those injuries. He entered the season coming off surgery to remove the hamate bone in his wrist. That's been known to sap players of their power. He slugged just .427 through the first half before missing time with a separate injury to the labrum in his left shoulder. After coming back from that, he failed to hit a homer over his next 120-plus ABs. But once he connected, he was back to his old self, finishing the season with a .325/.381/.553 stretch that filled Nats fans with hope. Even though nobody expects that level of performance over the season, it shows what he's capable of when he's fully healthy and focused.

Pitchers

Collin Balester (Starter)

W	L	ERA	TBF	IP	Hit	HR	SO	BB	HBP	3-Year	Reliability
6	10	5.61	667	148	169	24	84	62	9	-0.58	Very High

Balester is a favorite to break camp with the team, but given his moderate minor-league success, he's going to need to improve dramatically to stay there. He doesn't get nearly enough ground balls to strike out as few as he does, and he's going to need to improve his command. Still, he's 23. What were you doing when you were that old?

Jason Bergmann (Starter)

W	L	ERA	TBF	IP	Hit	HR	SO	BB	HBP	3-Year	Reliability
7	10	5.05	654	149	160	23	100	55	5	+0.29	Very High

In some ways, I feel bad for Bergmann. Jerked in and out of the rotation, demoted to the pen, berated by the general manager: he takes a lot of crap sometimes. But when you see him pitch when he's on, you see why there's so much frustration surrounding him. He has an awesome riding fastball, and sharp breaking pitches, diving down, changing the plane of the batter's swing. But too often, he's not fully healthy, so he loses bite on those breaking pitches, or command of the fastball. When that happens, he's walking the park, or turning into a pitching machine. The best thing for him might be a full-time slot in the pen; he really does seem to have endurance problems, struggling way too many times in the fifth inning.

Matt Chico (Starter)

W	L	ERA	TBF	IP	Hit	HR	SO	BB	HBP	3-Year	Reliability
4	7	5.16	420	95	104	15	52	38	4	+0.06	Very High

The unsung hero of the 2007 staff, Chico's mediocre arm didn't hold up last year either. He had Tommy John surgery in July, and the chances of him contributing anything this season are slim.

Tyler Clippard (Starter)

W	L	ERA	TBF	IP	Hit	HR	SO	BB	HBP	3-Year	Reliability
6	9	5.61	629	138	147	22	96	74	8	-0.25	Very High

Clippard, who came over from the Yankees for a middle reliever, mostly provided depth at Columbus. He didn't get much of a chance in Washington, and it's pretty clear he's way down on the depth chart of the Nats' plans. He's got marginal stuff, and doesn't throw hard, which means he's going to have to overwhelm with other stats if he's going to be a regular.

Jesus Colome (Reliever)

W	L	ERA	TBF	IP	Hit	HR	SO	BB	HBP	3-Year	Reliability
4	4	4.39	298	68	66	7	46	32	3	+0.20	Low

Even lousy teams need mopup men, and Colome was the canary in the coal mine for Nats fan. If you turned the game on and he was pitching, you knew you could just turn the game off. The outcome sure wasn't in doubt.

Joel Hanrahan (Reliever)

W	L	ERA	TBF	IP	Hit	HR	SO	BB	HBP	3-Year	Reliability
4	5	4.56	368	83	78	10	71	46	4	+0.22	Very High

Hanrahan was thrust into the closer role when Chad Cordero's injury and Jon Rauch's trade left the Nats' pen with nuttin'. He did well in the role, as it appeared that he started to learn how to harness that big mid-90s fastball. His Ks were up, the BBs were down, and given the Nats' low-budget ways, the chances of them bringing in a big-name closer to supplant him are slim.

Shawn Hill (Starter)

W	L	ERA	TBF	IP	Hit	HR	SO	BB	HBP	3-Year	Reliability
6	6	4.46	453	104	117	10	57	32	5	+0.23	Average

He's on the verge of winning the John Patterson Award. He just hopes that it doesn't come with the spring training release that Patterson got last year when he proved that he wasn't healthy enough to pitch in the majors. He has had a litany of arm injuries, and it's pretty clear that his arm just can't hold up to the rigors of pitching. Last season, he tried muddling through, but the lack of command, especially on his breaking pitches, was noticeable. All the line drives whistling past his ears certainly told him.

Michael Hinckley (Reliever)

W	L	ERA	TBF	IP	Hit	HR	SO	BB	HBP	3-Year	Reliability
2	8	7.60	430	86	118	15	32	59	7	+0.28	Very High

It's been a long, strange trip for Hinckley. The organization's former top left-handed starting prospect, injury and attrition turned him into a big ol' bust. After flaming out, being knocked off the 40-man and just about out of baseball, he wound up in the 'pen, where he remade himself as a LOOGY. If 13.2 innings in the majors are any judge, it's worked. It was enough so that his name was penciled in next year's bullpen.

John Lannan (Starter)

W	L	ERA	TBF	IP	Hit	HR	SO	BB	HBP	3-Year	Reliability
8	10	4.78	714	161	175	20	85	73	7	-0.28	Very High

When he's on—which is more often than not—he's a delight to watch. He's really started to master command of his breaking pitches, and is even able to spot them on the inside corner. He attacks the zone, keeping hitters off balance, giving him a combination of pitches that's superior to any individual pitch. While his peripherals aren't overwhelming, his command, and his ability to induce grounders, compensate for a portion of that. The projection system doesn't really like him, but I'd bet the under on that.

Charlie Manning (Reliever)

W	L	ERA	TBF	IP	Hit	HR	SO	BB	HBP	3-Year	Reliability
4	3	4.33	297	67	63	7	56	38	3	+0.29	Average

While it's true that no LOOGY is ever going to face only left-handed batters, a manager does have a certain amount of control in seeing that they will in high-leverage situations, saving a good chunk of appearances against RHB for mopup appearances. In Manning's case, his struggles were due to Manny Acta letting him face too many righties. He was effective enough against left-handers.

Shairon Martis (Starter)

W	L	ERA	TBF	IP	Hit	HR	SO	BB	HBP	3-Year	Reliability
6	9	5.68	610	134	150	20	76	65	7	-0.97	Very High

Martis threw a no-hitter in the last World Baseball Classic, no doubt aided by his decent low-90s fastball. His minor league stats aren't overwhelming, but he's like any number of young pitchers: If one more thing clicks, he could break through. Not allowing two homers a game would be a good place to start.

Garrett Mock (Starter)

W	L	ERA	TBF	IP	Hit	HR	SO	BB	HBP	3-Year	Reliability
6	8	5.11	558	124	135	17	91	56	8	+0.05	High

Mock looked like he started putting it together last season. He's always struck out a decent number of batters, but gave up an ungodly number of hits when they did make contact, usually the sign of a pitcher who's got decent stuff, but doesn't have polished command, especially of the breaking pitches. The Nats used him primarily out of the 'pen, and there was talk that that's where he's going to remain. His stuff was decent enough, but the walks jumped way up, and if he's going to succeed, he's going to have to refine that command even more.

Odalis Perez (Starter)

W	L	ERA	TBF	IP	Hit	HR	SO	BB	HBP	3-Year	Reliability
8	9	4.71	678	156	174	19	93	52	6	+0.22	Very High

There was a collective sigh when he was named the starter for the first game at Nationals Park—as if Jason Bergmann would've been a better choice. Perez had a perfectly cromulent season, pitching just well enough to keep the Nats in most of his starts. He succeeded by dramatically upping his K rate, thanks to more reliance on a solid cut fastball. If his improvement holds, he's a solid back-of-the-rotation starter for any number of teams.

Tim Redding (Starter)

W	L	ERA	TBF	IP	Hit	HR	SO	BB	HBP	3-Year	Reliability
8	11	4.99	737	167	186	24	95	64	7	+0.24	Very High

You know your pitching stinks when fans complain about the non-tendering of Tim Redding. His near-five ERA and barely five innings of fury are replaceable. Redding was humming along with a respectable first half (3.85) ERA, but collapsed in the second half. While offseason foot surgery could explain some of that, fatigue on his arm is as likely as any other—his average fastball velocity was up a tick last year, but I bet a graph of his seasonal velocity would be sloping down.

Saul Rivera (Reliever)

W	L	ERA	TBF	IP	Hit	HR	SO	BB	HBP	3-Year	Reliability
5	4	3.97	347	79	82	5	53	35	3	+0.19	Average

Rivera's about the perfect middle reliever. He's got a rubber arm, allowing him to pitch an inning or more seemingly every game. And when you think back on the last season, you don't really recall anything specific he did. In short, that means he did his job, getting the ball to the big boys at the end of the game without gacking it away. Manager Acta's going to rely on it even more, as the loss of Chad Cordero and Jon Rauch moves him from the sixth-seventh innings to the eighth. If something happens to Hanrahan, he could even find himself closing, despite stuff that's not really overwhelming.

Fantasy Values

On the following four pages, you'll find the projected fantasy dollar value of each player, based on our projections. We have only listed players with positive value projections, but you can find values for all players on our download page (see the Glossary in the Introduction for more information about downloads). The dollar values given are meant to be used for a traditional 12-team mixed leagues with 5x5 categories (AVG, HR, RBI, R, SB, ERA, WHIP, W, K, SV) with these positions (2 C, 1B, 2B, 3B, SS, MI, CI, 5 OF, 9 P). Although this is the unofficial industry standard, your league could very well vary, and the dollar values (and possibly even the ordinal rankings) will vary along with it.

To derive these values, Alex Patton's Standings Gain Points method was used in combination with replacement level theory. Please also note that projected playing time has been taken into consideration, but future off-season and spring training events could change these values accordingly.

Hitters are listed first, and positions are listed as OF (outfield), CI (corner infield: first base and third base), MI (middle infield: second base and shortstop), C (catcher) or DH (designated hitter). Pitchers are next, and they are listed as SP (starting pitcher), MR (middle reliever) or CL (closer).

Hitters

Name	Team	POS	Price
Jose Reyes	NYN	MI	$46.16
Hanley Ramirez	FLO	MI	$45.61
Jimmy Rollins	PHI	MI	$37.57
Chase Utley	PHI	MI	$35.60
Ryan Braun	MIL	OF	$34.98
Grady Sizemore	CLE	OF	$33.70
David Wright	NYN	CI	$33.70
Alex Rodriguez	NYA	CI	$32.11
Alfonso Soriano	CHN	OF	$30.76
Carlos Beltran	NYN	OF	$29.97
Brian McCann	ATL	C	$29.90
Ryan Howard	PHI	CI	$29.60
Ian Kinsler	TEX	MI	$29.55
Albert Pujols	STL	CI	$29.05
Geovany Soto	CHN	C	$28.83
Carlos Lee	HOU	OF	$26.83
Russell Martin	LA	C	$26.41
David Ortiz	BOS	DH	$25.77
Matt Holliday	OAK	OF	$24.99
Miguel Cabrera	DET	CI	$24.98
Lance Berkman	HOU	CI	$24.89
Joe Mauer	MIN	C	$24.74
Carl Crawford	TAM	OF	$23.79
Mike Napoli	LAA	C	$23.10
Brian Roberts	BAL	MI	$23.08
Josh Hamilton	TEX	OF	$21.83
Dustin Pedroia	BOS	MI	$21.38
Prince Fielder	MIL	CI	$21.17
Ryan Doumit	PIT	C	$20.91
Vladimir Guerrero	LAA	OF	$20.63
Brandon Phillips	CIN	MI	$20.56

Name	Team	POS	Price
Matt Wieters	BAL	C	$20.31
Matt Kemp	LA	OF	$19.49
Chris Iannetta	COL	C	$19.43
Jay Bruce	CIN	OF	$19.32
Victor Martinez	CLE	C	$18.98
Robinson Cano	NYA	MI	$18.50
Christopher Davis	TEX	CI	$18.09
Kelly Johnson	ATL	MI	$17.67
Kazuo Matsui	HOU	MI	$17.44
B.J. Upton	TAM	OF	$17.33
Chipper Jones	ATL	CI	$17.08
Curtis Granderson	DET	OF	$17.03
Corey Hart	MIL	OF	$16.87
Jack Cust	OAK	DH	$16.86
Nate McLouth	PIT	OF	$16.80
Mark Teixeira	NYA	CI	$16.74
Nick Markakis	BAL	OF	$16.39
Adrian Gonzalez	SD	CI	$16.14
Joey Votto	CIN	CI	$16.09
Brad Hawpe	COL	OF	$15.92
Jorge Posada	NYA	C	$15.79
Jermaine Dye	CHA	OF	$15.52
Ryan Ludwick	STL	OF	$15.45
Alex Rios	TOR	OF	$15.39
Bengie Molina	SF	C	$15.22
Jason Bay	BOS	OF	$14.98
Derek Jeter	NYA	MI	$14.94
Aubrey Huff	BAL	DH	$14.93
Carlos Pena	TAM	CI	$14.90
Dan Uggla	FLO	MI	$14.24
Rafael Furcal	LA	MI	$14.24

Name	Team	POS	Price
J.J. Hardy	MIL	MI	$14.17
Shane Victorino	PHI	OF	$14.16
Magglio Ordonez	DET	OF	$14.10
Alexei Ramirez	CHA	MI	$13.87
Juan Pierre	LA	DH	$13.69
Jayson Werth	PHI	OF	$13.20
Dallas McPherson	FLO	CI	$13.15
Chris Young	ARI	OF	$13.08
Jim Thome	CHA	CI	$12.86
Shin-Soo Choo	CLE	DH	$12.85
Nelson Cruz	TEX	OF	$12.76
Pablo Sandoval	SF	C	$12.47
Rick Ankiel	STL	OF	$12.43
Cody Ross	FLO	OF	$11.73
Evan Longoria	TAM	CI	$11.64
Ichiro Suzuki	SEA	OF	$11.60
Travis Hafner	CLE	DH	$11.11
Miguel Tejada	HOU	MI	$10.99
Howie Kendrick	LAA	MI	$10.92
Rickie Weeks	MIL	MI	$10.85
Torii Hunter	LAA	OF	$10.54
Milton Bradley	CHN	OF	$10.40
Carlos Delgado	NYN	CI	$10.25
Hunter Pence	HOU	OF	$10.21
Paul Konerko	CHA	DH	$10.17
Chris Dickerson	CIN	OF	$10.06
Jhonny Peralta	CLE	MI	$9.89
Carlos Quentin	CHA	OF	$9.78
Garrett Atkins	COL	CI	$9.77
Aramis Ramirez	CHN	CI	$9.69
Troy Tulowitzki	COL	MI	$9.55
Johnny Damon	NYA	OF	$9.45
Justin Morneau	MIN	CI	$9.39
Chris Snyder	ARI	C	$9.18
Felipe Lopez	ARI	MI	$9.06
Stephen Drew	ARI	MI	$8.69
Andre Ethier	LA	OF	$8.61
Mark DeRosa	CLE	MI	$8.02
Luke Scott	BAL	OF	$7.95
Kevin Youkilis	BOS	CI	$7.60
Jacoby Ellsbury	BOS	OF	$7.50
Chone Figgins	LAA	CI	$7.46
Willy Taveras	CIN	OF	$7.44
Ramon Hernandez	CIN	C	$6.87
Dioner Navarro	TAM	C	$6.85
Josh Bard	BOS	C	$6.80
Russell Branyan	SEA	CI	$6.61
Adam Jones	BAL	OF	$6.60

Name	Team	POS	Price
Michael Young	TEX	MI	$6.59
Vernon Wells	TOR	OF	$6.58
Delmon Young	MIN	DH	$6.28
Conor Jackson	ARI	CI	$6.02
Billy Butler	KC	DH	$5.83
Cristian Guzman	WAS	MI	$5.79
A.J. Pierzynski	CHA	C	$5.59
James Loney	LA	CI	$5.46
Placido Polanco	DET	MI	$5.45
Hideki Matsui	NYA	DH	$5.30
Jason Giambi	OAK	CI	$5.26
Lastings Milledge	WAS	OF	$5.16
Adrian Beltre	SEA	CI	$4.98
Adam LaRoche	PIT	CI	$4.89
Edgar Renteria	SF	MI	$4.88
Aaron Hill	TOR	MI	$4.77
Coco Crisp	KC	OF	$4.53
Juan Rivera	LAA	DH	$4.46
Ryan Zimmerman	WAS	CI	$4.29
Yadier Molina	STL	C	$4.17
J.D. Drew	BOS	OF	$3.85
John Baker	FLO	C	$3.83
Alex Gordon	KC	CI	$3.78
Carlos Guillen	DET	CI	$3.69
Mark Reynolds	ARI	CI	$3.44
Ramon Castro	NYN	C	$3.19
Freddy Sanchez	PIT	MI	$3.17
Geoff Blum	HOU	MI	$2.94
Josh Anderson	ATL	OF	$2.84
Asdrubal Cabrera	CLE	MI	$2.54
Carlos Ruiz	PHI	C	$2.48
Adam Lind	TOR	OF	$2.46
Derrek Lee	CHN	CI	$2.38
Marcus Thames	DET	OF	$2.21
Matt Diaz	ATL	OF	$2.17
Yunel Escobar	ATL	MI	$2.17
Edwin Encarnacion	CIN	CI	$1.77
Steve Pearce	PIT	OF	$1.69
Elijah Dukes	WAS	OF	$1.69
Josh Willingham	WAS	OF	$1.59
Pat Burrell	TAM	OF	$1.15
Nick Swisher	NYA	OF	$0.99
Ryan Church	NYN	OF	$0.87
Yuniesky Betancourt	SEA	MI	$0.82
Clint Barmes	COL	MI	$0.74
Travis Snider	TOR	OF	$0.61
Seth Smith	COL	OF	$0.57
Khalil Greene	STL	MI	$0.46

Name	Team	POS	Price
Scott Hairston	SD	OF	$0.39
Kurt Suzuki	OAK	C	$0.21
Troy Glaus	STL	CI	$0.19
Alberto Callaspo	KC	MI	$0.15

Name	Team	POS	Price
Ryan Spilborghs	COL	OF	$0.11
J.R. Towles	HOU	C	$0.08
Raul Ibanez	PHI	OF	$0.06

Pitchers

Name	Team	POS	Price
CC Sabathia	NYA	SP	$36.15
Roy Halladay	TOR	SP	$34.60
Johan Santana	NYN	SP	$32.63
Cole Hamels	PHI	SP	$24.94
Mariano Rivera	NYA	CL	$24.68
Jonathan Papelbon	BOS	CL	$23.54
Tim Lincecum	SF	SP	$23.28
Jake Peavy	SD	SP	$22.61
Erik Bedard	SEA	SP	$22.46
Felix Hernandez	SEA	SP	$21.91
Javier Vazquez	ATL	SP	$21.29
Hong-Chih Kuo	LA	SP	$20.66
Joe Nathan	MIN	CL	$20.49
Joba Chamberlain	NYA	MR	$20.13
Brandon Webb	ARI	SP	$19.63
Jonathan Broxton	LA	MR	$18.96
Josh Beckett	BOS	SP	$18.94
Derek Lowe	ATL	SP	$18.69
James Shields	TAM	SP	$18.52
Justin Duchscherer	OAK	MR	$17.92
Roy Oswalt	HOU	SP	$16.78
J.J. Putz	NYN	CL	$16.38
Francisco Rodriguez	NYN	CL	$16.12
Trevor Hoffman	MIL	CL	$14.79
Kevin Slowey	MIN	SP	$14.38
Heath Bell	SD	MR	$14.07
Scott Kazmir	TAM	SP	$13.59
Jose Valverde	HOU	CL	$13.22
Bobby Jenks	CHA	CL	$13.07
Matt Capps	PIT	CL	$13.06
A.J. Burnett	NYA	SP	$13.06
Rich Harden	CHN	SP	$12.75
Kerry Wood	CLE	CL	$12.17
Joakim Soria	KC	CL	$12.12
Joey Devine	OAK	MR	$12.09
Dan Haren	ARI	SP	$12.07
Chad Billingsley	LA	SP	$11.81
Brian Fuentes	LAA	MR	$11.71
Brad Lidge	PHI	CL	$11.40
Yovani Gallardo	MIL	SP	$11.13

Name	Team	POS	Price
John Lackey	LAA	SP	$10.94
B.J. Ryan	TOR	CL	$10.56
Max Scherzer	ARI	SP	$10.48
Carlos Marmol	CHN	MR	$10.40
Huston Street	COL	CL	$10.39
Randy Johnson	SF	SP	$10.25
Chris Carpenter	STL	SP	$10.04
Francisco Cordero	CIN	CL	$10.00
Mike Gonzalez	ATL	MR	$9.83
Rafael Soriano	ATL	CL	$9.79
Adam Wainwright	STL	SP	$9.69
Fernando Rodney	DET	MR	$9.16
Chris Young	SD	SP	$8.91
Matt Cain	SF	SP	$8.87
Cliff Lee	CLE	MR	$8.59
Justin Verlander	DET	SP	$8.00
Ryan Dempster	CHN	SP	$7.89
Frank Francisco	TEX	MR	$7.87
Ervin Santana	LAA	SP	$7.86
Troy Percival	TAM	CL	$7.47
Aaron Harang	CIN	SP	$7.26
John Maine	NYN	SP	$6.64
Chad Qualls	ARI	MR	$6.39
Grant Balfour	TAM	MR	$6.16
Ted Lilly	CHN	SP	$5.66
Brett Myers	PHI	SP	$5.09
Matt Thornton	CHA	MR	$4.86
Rafael Betancourt	CLE	MR	$4.84
Rafael Perez	CLE	MR	$4.81
Carlos Zambrano	CHN	SP	$4.79
Francisco Liriano	MIN	SP	$4.32
Octavio Dotel	CHA	MR	$4.06
Hiroki Kuroda	LA	SP	$3.87
Brian Wilson	SF	CL	$3.84
Andy Sonnanstine	TAM	SP	$3.67
Jered Weaver	LAA	SP	$3.52
Takashi Saito	BOS	CL	$3.52
Pedro Feliciano	NYN	MR	$3.50
Bob Howry	SF	MR	$3.48
Edinson Volquez	CIN	SP	$3.45

Name	Team	POS	Price
Matt Garza	TAM	SP	$3.44
Dan Wheeler	TAM	MR	$3.16
Aaron Heilman	SEA	MR	$2.92
Scott Downs	TOR	MR	$2.85
Scott Baker	MIN	SP	$2.84
Dana Eveland	OAK	SP	$2.61
Cla Meredith	SD	MR	$2.57
Jeremy Bonderman	DET	SP	$2.56
Edwar Ramirez	NYA	MR	$2.49
Duaner Sanchez	NYN	MR	$2.37
Chris Perez	STL	MR	$2.37
Hideki Okajima	BOS	MR	$2.32
Chien-Ming Wang	NYA	SP	$2.29
Kyle McClellan	STL	MR	$2.10

Name	Team	POS	Price
Zack Greinke	KC	SP	$1.87
Jair Jurrjens	ATL	SP	$1.79
Daisuke Matsuzaka	BOS	SP	$1.76
Mike Adams	SD	MR	$1.69
Carlos Villanueva	MIL	SP	$1.09
J.P. Howell	TAM	SP	$0.86
Manny Delcarmen	BOS	MR	$0.51
Gil Meche	KC	SP	$0.38
Ryan Rowland-Smith	SEA	MR	$0.37
Joel Zumaya	DET	MR	$0.36
Santiago Casilla	OAK	MR	$0.31
John Danks	CHA	SP	$0.03
Joe Blanton	PHI	SP	$0.02

Career Milestone Projections

by David Gassko

In last year's *Season Preview*, I introduced a system for projecting career totals. Bill James devised his own system a long time ago—he called it "The Favorite Toy"—but I've found that his projections are usually too optimistic. So I developed my own approach.

To develop my system, I put together a database of all major league players who had debuted after World War II and retired by 2006. I then found every string of three consecutive seasons for every hitter in my database and every string of two consecutive seasons for every pitcher (a third season proved to be unnecessary). I grouped the players by age and found how many home runs, hits, or wins they had remaining in their career at a given age. Then I ran a regression trying to predict that number based on the number of hits, home runs, or wins they had in the previous few seasons. For very young or old players, only more recent seasons proved to be significant, so that's all I used. Players younger than 20 or older than 40 in their most recent season were excluded because of the miniscule sample sizes.

Let's use Justin Morneau as an example. Morneau is going to be 28 years old this season. He's hit 23, 31, and 34 home runs each of the past three years, respectively. We apply our formula for 28 year olds to calculate the number of home runs we think he'll hit in the rest of his career: $3.475*23 + 1.239*31 + 0.939*34 = 150$ home runs remaining. He already has 133 career home runs, so in total, we think he'll hit $133 + 150 = 283$ career home runs.

Okay, but what is the probability that he does much better and hits, say, 500 home runs? I developed a way of calculating standard errors around our predicted totals, which can then be converted to probabilities. In Morneau's case, the standard error around our prediction is about 91. For Morneau to reach 500, he would have to be $(500 - 283)/91 = 2.38$ standard deviations better than our prediction—statistically, there's about a 4.9 percent chance that he'll do just that.

Using this methodology, we've listed probabilities of individual hitters reaching 3,000 hits, 500 home runs and 763 home runs, and of pitchers reaching 300 wins. These projections were developed for fun. So enjoy.

Hitters

Name	Hits	HR	3000 %	500 %	763 %
A.J. Pierzynski	1563	143	1.5%	0.3%	0.1%
Aaron Rowand	1458	162	1.6%	0.5%	0.1%
Adam Dunn	1560	480	2.2%	43.0%	3.5%
Adam LaRoche	1295	239	1.6%	2.9%	0.5%
Adrian Beltre	2226	352	8.9%	8.7%	0.8%
Adrian Gonzalez	1652	315	5.3%	9.2%	1.3%
Albert Pujols	2424	511	17.6%	54.1%	4.3%
Alex Gordon	1142	174	1.9%	1.8%	0.4%
Alex Rodriguez	2870	667	37.5%	100.0%	16.9%
Alexis Rios	1741	165	5.4%	1.2%	0.2%
Alfonso Soriano	1776	363	1.7%	8.7%	0.7%
Andre Ethier	1341	157	2.7%	1.3%	0.3%
Andruw Jones	1910	410	0.8%	7.0%	0.2%
Aramis Ramirez	2000	363	5.0%	10.1%	0.9%
Aubrey Huff	1819	279	3.2%	3.2%	0.4%
Austin Kearns	1179	162	0.8%	0.6%	0.1%
B.J. Upton	1658	168	6.9%	1.6%	0.3%
Bengie Molina	1483	163	1.0%	0.3%	0.1%
Bill Hall	1137	188	0.9%	1.4%	0.2%
Bobby Abreu	2382	286	9.1%	1.2%	0.1%
Brad Ausmus	1590	82	0.0%	0.0%	0.0%
Brad Hawpe	1129	201	1.1%	1.9%	0.3%
Brandon Phillips	1410	200	2.6%	2.0%	0.4%
Brian Giles	2135	303	2.6%	0.2%	0.0%

Name	Hits	HR	3000 %	500 %	763 %
Brian McCann	1781	260	8.4%	4.7%	0.7%
Brian Roberts	1752	97	3.4%	0.1%	0.0%
Carl Crawford	1966	135	6.9%	0.5%	0.1%
Carlos Beltran	2142	363	6.1%	9.3%	0.8%
Carlos Delgado	2321	535	5.1%	68.8%	2.0%
Carlos Guillen	1536	141	1.0%	0.2%	0.0%
Carlos Lee	2052	368	3.6%	8.9%	0.7%
Carlos Pena	1054	260	0.5%	2.8%	0.4%
Carlos Quentin	1013	246	1.4%	4.3%	0.7%
Casey Blake	1233	176	0.6%	0.4%	0.1%
Chase Utley	1575	256	3.0%	3.4%	0.5%
Chipper Jones	2597	450	13.4%	18.2%	0.3%
Chris Young	1375	291	3.4%	8.4%	1.3%
Cliff Floyd	1611	255	0.2%	0.1%	0.0%
Cody Ross	771	152	0.6%	1.2%	0.2%
Corey Hart	1339	184	2.8%	1.8%	0.4%
Corey Patterson	1324	156	1.0%	0.4%	0.1%
Cristian Guzman	1699	74	2.1%	0.0%	0.0%
Curtis Granderson	1419	195	2.8%	1.9%	0.4%
Damion Easley	1514	173	0.2%	0.0%	0.0%
Dan Uggla	1176	246	1.5%	3.5%	0.6%
Darin Erstad	1873	130	0.7%	0.0%	0.0%
David Ortiz	1665	373	1.1%	9.1%	0.7%
David Wright	2184	380	16.6%	20.4%	2.8%

267

Name	Hits	HR	3000 %	500 %	763 %
Delmon Young	2249	166	27.0%	1.7%	0.3%
Derek Jeter	2983	232	48.3%	0.2%	0.0%
Derrek Lee	2083	314	5.4%	2.5%	0.2%
Dmitri Young	1517	184	0.2%	0.0%	0.0%
Dustin Pedroia	1824	150	10.6%	1.3%	0.3%
Edgar Renteria	2480	158	11.4%	0.1%	0.0%
Edwin Encarnacion	1361	242	2.8%	3.7%	0.6%
Eric Chavez	1398	263	0.2%	0.5%	0.1%
Eric Hinske	1025	166	0.3%	0.6%	0.1%
Evan Longoria	1100	217	2.1%	3.2%	0.6%
Felipe Lopez	1533	108	2.5%	0.1%	0.0%
Garret Anderson	2675	299	17.2%	0.4%	0.0%
Garrett Atkins	1600	206	3.7%	2.0%	0.4%
Gary Sheffield	2729	520	9.2%	75.2%	0.1%
Geoff Jenkins	1499	253	0.3%	0.4%	0.0%
Grady Sizemore	2000	353	11.1%	15.5%	2.1%
Hank Blalock	1248	196	0.7%	1.0%	0.2%
Hanley Ramirez	2145	360	19.0%	21.3%	3.9%
Hunter Pence	1305	194	2.8%	2.2%	0.4%
Ian Kinsler	1367	170	2.9%	1.5%	0.3%
Ichiro Suzuki	2340	86	9.9%	0.0%	0.0%
Ivan Rodriguez	2827	308	25.8%	0.1%	0.0%
J.D. Drew	1440	243	0.6%	0.9%	0.1%
J.J. Hardy	1502	234	4.1%	3.4%	0.6%
Jack Cust	596	168	0.2%	1.3%	0.3%
Jacque Jones	1392	169	0.1%	0.0%	0.0%
James Loney	1484	159	4.6%	1.5%	0.3%
Jason Bay	1433	272	1.9%	3.9%	0.5%
Jason Giambi	1994	441	0.9%	15.9%	0.4%
Jason Kendall	2273	77	4.2%	0.0%	0.0%
Jason Kubel	1036	154	1.3%	1.3%	0.3%
Jason Varitek	1337	185	0.2%	0.1%	0.0%
Jay Bruce	1372	278	4.5%	9.3%	1.7%
Jeff Francoeur	1901	204	10.4%	2.2%	0.4%
Jeremy Hermida	1338	203	2.9%	2.4%	0.5%
Jermaine Dye	2055	376	3.5%	9.1%	0.6%
Jhonny Peralta	1687	225	5.1%	2.7%	0.5%
Jim Edmonds	2001	407	0.4%	2.9%	0.1%
Jim Thome	2247	595	2.1%	100.0%	2.9%
Jimmy Rollins	2195	215	9.4%	1.7%	0.3%
Joe Crede	1014	195	0.3%	1.0%	0.2%
Joe Mauer	1842	120	8.1%	0.6%	0.1%
Joey Votto	1129	173	2.0%	1.8%	0.4%
Johnny Damon	2669	220	20.1%	0.4%	0.1%
Jorge Cantu	1396	208	2.7%	2.3%	0.4%
Jorge Posada	1500	230	0.1%	0.0%	0.0%
Jose Cruz	1182	205	0.0%	0.0%	0.0%
Jose Guillen	1864	243	2.8%	1.1%	0.2%
Jose Lopez	2141	179	18.6%	1.8%	0.4%
Jose Reyes	2361	188	22.8%	1.9%	0.4%
Jose Vidro	1787	145	1.0%	0.0%	0.0%
Josh Hamilton	1062	186	1.4%	1.9%	0.4%
Juan Pierre	2043	16	4.4%	0.0%	0.0%
Juan Uribe	1310	172	0.9%	0.7%	0.1%
Justin Morneau	1731	283	5.3%	4.9%	0.7%
Justin Upton	1607	267	8.6%	8.1%	1.5%
Ken Griffey	2868	644	28.9%	100.0%	2.7%
Kevin Kouzmanoff	1198	172	2.1%	1.6%	0.3%
Kevin Millar	1467	198	0.4%	0.3%	0.0%
Kevin Youkilis	1229	157	1.5%	1.1%	0.2%
Khalil Greene	1072	157	0.7%	0.8%	0.2%
Lance Berkman	1966	381	3.9%	11.1%	0.8%
Lastings Milledge	1275	154	2.9%	1.4%	0.3%
Luis Castillo	1908	33	1.0%	0.0%	0.0%
Magglio Ordonez	2280	321	7.1%	2.5%	0.2%
Manny Ramirez	2741	591	23.4%	100.0%	3.6%
Marcus Thames	538	167	0.1%	0.9%	0.2%
Mark Grudzielanek	2160	95	1.0%	0.0%	0.0%
Mark Kotsay	1839	123	1.4%	0.0%	0.0%
Mark Loretta	1826	82	0.4%	0.0%	0.0%
Mark Reynolds	1088	257	1.7%	5.2%	0.9%
Mark Teixeira	1816	366	5.0%	12.4%	1.2%
Matt Holliday	1752	274	5.0%	4.4%	0.6%
Matt Kemp	1688	201	8.1%	2.5%	0.5%
Melky Cabrera	1560	109	5.2%	0.7%	0.2%
Melvin Mora	1546	195	0.6%	0.3%	0.1%
Michael Young	2109	153	6.6%	0.2%	0.0%
Miguel Cabrera	2343	451	20.4%	38.1%	6.3%
Miguel Tejada	2341	304	7.9%	0.7%	0.1%
Mike Cameron	1710	292	0.7%	1.6%	0.2%
Mike Jacobs	1009	231	1.0%	3.0%	0.5%
Mike Lowell	1742	243	1.1%	0.6%	0.1%
Mike Napoli	540	158	0.2%	1.3%	0.3%
Mike Sweeney	1518	205	0.1%	0.0%	0.0%
Milton Bradley	1221	173	0.7%	0.8%	0.2%
Nate McLouth	1214	186	2.1%	1.9%	0.4%
Nick Markakis	2020	251	15.1%	4.4%	0.7%
Nick Swisher	1154	248	1.2%	3.4%	0.5%
Nomar Garciaparra	1822	243	0.3%	0.1%	0.0%
Orlando Cabrera	2130	125	5.4%	0.0%	0.0%
Pat Burrell	1583	358	1.3%	9.2%	0.8%
Paul Konerko	1854	371	1.5%	7.9%	0.5%
Pedro Feliz	1122	164	0.4%	0.3%	0.1%
Placido Polanco	2035	102	4.8%	0.0%	0.0%
Prince Fielder	1884	475	10.9%	46.9%	20.3%
Rafael Furcal	1650	111	1.0%	0.1%	0.0%

Name	Hits	HR	3000 %	500 %	763 %
Ramon Hernandez	1391	179	0.7%	0.3%	0.1%
Randy Winn	2015	129	3.6%	0.1%	0.0%
Raul Ibanez	1733	223	1.4%	0.5%	0.1%
Ray Durham	2256	203	2.2%	0.0%	0.0%
Rich Aurilia	1759	200	0.6%	0.0%	0.0%
Richie Sexson	1457	344	0.2%	1.9%	0.1%
Rickie Weeks	1163	160	1.6%	1.3%	0.3%
Robinson Cano	1879	186	8.8%	1.8%	0.3%
Ron Belliard	1535	130	0.6%	0.1%	0.0%
Russell Branyan	543	168	0.0%	0.2%	0.0%
Russell Martin	1518	154	4.4%	1.3%	0.3%
Ryan Braun	1476	390	4.5%	31.6%	8.5%
Ryan Howard	1329	428	2.0%	30.4%	3.8%
Ryan Ludwick	770	157	0.4%	1.1%	0.2%
Ryan Zimmerman	1903	226	11.5%	3.1%	0.5%

Name	Hits	HR	3000 %	500 %	763 %
Scott Rolen	1935	298	1.4%	0.4%	0.0%
Sean Casey	1745	132	0.6%	0.0%	0.0%
Shannon Stewart	1789	121	0.3%	0.0%	0.0%
Stephen Drew	1489	169	4.3%	1.6%	0.3%
Todd Helton	2178	330	2.0%	0.3%	0.0%
Tony Clark	1235	255	0.0%	0.0%	0.0%
Torii Hunter	1832	281	2.5%	2.3%	0.3%
Travis Hafner	933	190	0.2%	0.4%	0.1%
Troy Glaus	1704	393	1.8%	12.8%	0.8%
Troy Tulowitzki	1358	156	3.3%	1.4%	0.3%
Ty Wigginton	1165	198	0.7%	1.4%	0.2%
Vernon Wells	1792	268	3.2%	2.8%	0.4%
Vladimir Guerrero	2632	473	20.5%	36.8%	1.4%
Xavier Nady	1241	181	1.3%	1.3%	0.2%

Pitchers

Name	Wins	300 %
A.J. Burnett	136	3.0%
Aaron Cook	105	2.4%
Aaron Harang	96	1.0%
Aaron Laffey	50	1.1%
Adam Eaton	86	0.6%
Adam Wainwright	86	2.3%
Andrew Miller	58	1.4%
Andy Pettitte	250	14.4%
Andy Sonnanstine	83	2.4%
Armando Galarraga	57	1.3%
Arthur Rhodes	82	0.2%
Barry Zito	160	2.9%
Bartolo Colon	159	0.9%
Ben Sheets	135	2.9%
Bobby Howry	56	0.4%
Brad Penny	121	1.3%
Brad Thompson	52	0.9%
Braden Looper	91	1.2%
Brandon Backe	61	0.8%
Brandon Webb	167	7.5%
Brett Myers	108	1.7%
Brett Tomko	98	0.3%
Brian Bannister	66	1.3%
Brian Moehler	94	0.7%
Bronson Arroyo	113	2.0%
C.C. Sabathia	195	10.3%
Carl Pavano	76	0.4%
Carlos Silva	83	0.8%

Name	Wins	300 %
Carlos Villanueva	52	1.0%
Carlos Zambrano	163	5.8%
Casey Fossum	52	0.3%
Chad Billingsley	135	6.6%
Chad Gaudin	79	1.8%
Chan Ho Park	126	0.6%
Chien-Ming Wang	104	2.2%
Chris Carpenter	100	0.2%
Chris Volstad	68	2.1%
Chris Young	71	0.9%
Claudio Vargas	61	0.4%
Clayton Kershaw	82	3.0%
Cliff Lee	144	4.7%
Cole Hamels	123	4.9%
Daisuke Matsuzaka	110	3.9%
Dana Eveland	54	1.2%
Daniel Cabrera	85	1.3%
Danny Haren	135	4.5%
Darren Oliver	112	0.6%
Dave Weathers	74	0.3%
David Bush	85	1.5%
Derek Lowe	162	2.9%
Dontrelle Willis	83	0.5%
Doug Davis	102	0.8%
Dustin McGowan	59	1.1%
Edinson Volquez	92	3.0%
Edwin Jackson	92	2.8%
Erik Bedard	76	0.9%

Name	Wins	300 %
Ervin Santana	128	4.6%
Esteban Loaiza	126	0.2%
Fausto Carmona	99	3.2%
Felix Hernandez	122	4.7%
Freddy Garcia	118	0.3%
Garrett Olson	53	1.2%
Gavin Floyd	101	3.6%
Gil Meche	127	2.7%
Glen Perkins	67	1.8%
Glendon Rusch	73	0.3%
Hideo Nomo	123	0.2%
Horacio Ramirez	54	0.4%
Huston Street	64	1.3%
Ian Snell	69	1.2%
Jair Jurrjens	109	4.8%
Jake Peavy	141	3.6%
Jake Westbrook	69	0.3%
James Shields	98	2.9%
Jamey Wright	97	0.7%
Jarrod Washburn	113	0.7%
Jason Jennings	62	0.2%
Jason Johnson	56	0.1%
Jason Marquis	122	2.2%
Javier Vazquez	171	4.1%
Jeff Francis	83	1.1%
Jeff Suppan	156	2.1%
Jered Weaver	96	2.6%
Jeremy Bonderman	85	0.9%

Name	Wins	300 %
Jeremy Guthrie	52	0.9%
Jesse Litsch	100	3.7%
Joe Blanton	97	1.8%
Joe Saunders	98	2.9%
Joel Pineiro	99	1.0%
Johan Santana	169	5.6%
John Danks	92	3.2%
John Lackey	144	3.5%
John Lannan	67	1.8%
John Maine	83	1.8%
Johnny Cueto	76	2.4%
Jon Garland	158	4.2%
Jon Lester	99	3.2%
Jon Lieber	133	0.4%
Jonathan Sanchez	56	1.2%
Jorge de la Rosa	67	1.3%
Jorge Sosa	60	0.6%
Jose Arredondo	54	1.2%
Jose Contreras	82	0.6%
Josh Beckett	151	4.7%
Josh Fogg	80	0.6%
Josh Johnson	53	0.9%
Julian Tavarez	85	0.2%
Justin Duchscherer	64	1.0%
Justin Verlander	110	3.2%
Kent Mercker	76	0.2%
Kerry Wood	88	0.5%
Kevin Millwood	166	2.1%
Kevin Slowey	74	2.0%
Kip Wells	76	0.4%

Name	Wins	300 %
Kyle Davies	79	1.9%
Kyle Kendrick	96	3.4%
Kyle Lohse	130	3.0%
LaTroy Hawkins	65	0.3%
Livan Hernandez	181	3.6%
Manny Parra	57	1.3%
Mariano Rivera	77	0.4%
Mark Buehrle	175	5.2%
Mark Hendrickson	63	0.4%
Mark Mulder	103	0.2%
Mark Redman	69	0.2%
Matt Cain	88	2.3%
Matt Garza	76	2.0%
Matt Harrison	76	2.4%
Matt Morris	125	0.4%
Micah Owings	50	1.0%
Miguel Batista	104	0.7%
Mike Hampton	147	0.6%
Mike Pelfrey	78	2.2%
Nate Robertson	76	0.8%
Odalis Perez	98	1.0%
Oliver Perez	112	2.8%
Paul Byrd	137	1.7%
Paul Maholm	76	1.5%
Pedro Martinez	221	2.4%
Randy Wolf	126	1.9%
Rich Harden	76	1.2%
Ricky Nolasco	95	2.9%
Ron Villone	56	0.1%
Roy Halladay	192	7.8%

Name	Wins	300 %
Roy Oswalt	190	7.5%
Ryan Dempster	112	1.7%
Ryan Franklin	65	0.4%
Salomon Torres	55	0.3%
Scot Shields	62	0.5%
Scott Baker	79	1.8%
Scott Elarton	57	0.2%
Scott Kazmir	121	4.2%
Scott Olsen	86	2.1%
Shaun Marcum	73	1.6%
Shawn Chacon	54	0.3%
Shawn Estes	104	0.3%
Sidney Ponson	109	0.8%
Steve Trachsel	148	0.6%
Ted Lilly	140	3.1%
Tim Hudson	180	3.6%
Tim Lincecum	109	4.3%
Tim Redding	67	1.0%
Todd Jones	66	0.3%
Todd Wellemeyer	62	1.2%
Tom Gordon	148	0.8%
Tom Gorzelanny	63	1.2%
Tony Armas	58	0.2%
Trevor Hoffman	62	0.3%
Ubaldo Jimenez	74	2.0%
Vicente Padilla	133	2.8%
Wandy Rodriguez	71	1.1%
Zach Duke	54	0.8%
Zack Greinke	101	3.0%

Injury Risk Considerations

by Chris Neault

The 2008 season was full of injuries to some of the baseball's best players. Fantasy baseball managers felt the wrath of these injuries as they altered lineups in order to field a full, competitive team.

This season will be no different. While any player can be injured in any season, the aim of this article is to target players who are especially at risk, to give some insight on why each player may or may not be worth selecting in the upcoming draft, and to project their production in 2009.

Out for the Year – Take Off Your Draft Lists

- Tim Hudson, SP, Atlanta (Tommy John surgery)
- Shaun Marcum, SP, Toronto (Tommy John surgery)
- Billy Wagner, RP, New York Mets (Tommy John surgery)
- Pat Neshek, RP, Minnesota (Tommy John surgery)

May Return Late in Season – Possible Free Agent Pickups

- Jose Contreras, SP, Chicago White Sox (Achilles surgery)
- Jake Westbrook, SP, Cleveland (Tommy John/hip surgeries)
- Sergio Mitre, SP/RP, New York Yankees (Tommy John surgery)
- Kelvim Escobar, SP, Los Angeles Angels (Labrum surgery)

Might Retire

- Curt Schilling, SP
- Tom Glavine, SP
- Juan Encarnacion, OF
- Jason Isringhausen, RP
- Frank Thomas, DH
- Moises Alou, OF

A.L. East

Josh Beckett | SP | Boston

I watched Beckett during the 2008 playoffs against the Rays, and as a Sox fan I can truly say that his stuff was simply not there. His fastball was mostly between 89-91 mph, and his curve did not seem to have its normal bite. He struggled with numbness in his fingers and hand last season, which usually means a pitcher is experiencing nerve irritation at the medial elbow, which means inflammation of the ulnar nerve. My gut tells me that Beckett pitched through pain last year, while my heart wants the Beckett of old to return for '09. I am going to avoid drafting him as my top starting pitcher in all fantasy leagues. Instead, I will try to nab him as my second or third starter. I will hedge my bets and project his games started at 24.

Brad Penny | SP | Boston

Recently signed to a one-year, $5 million contract (with incentives), Penny is an insurance policy for the Red Sox in the event that Tim Wakefield gets hurt, or if Clay Buchholz is not ready to be a full-time part of the rotation. Penny is a big injury risk due to his lengthy history of biceps injuries, as well as shoulder, forearm and back strains. His '08 season was cut short by bouts of what had been diagnosed as numerous things (tendinitis, bursitis, inflammation and scar tissue formation). I am not sold that his shoulder problems are past him.

Penny typically has struck out six to seven batters per game, but the past two seasons that number has dropped to around four to five. His walk rates and home run rates have also increased. Steer clear, and add him only in the late rounds of your mixed league drafts as a flier. If he ends up on your waiver wire and he lands a spot in the rotation during spring training, add him and hope for the best. Remember, he will not be pitching in a friendly home stadium any longer. He will probably end up in the 4.25-4.50 ERA range, and he will be detrimental in the WHIP department—likely in the 1.35-1.45 area.

Mike Lowell | 3B | Boston

He is rehabilitating his right hip following arthroscopic debridement of a labrum tear, removal of bone spur formation, and surgical release of one of the adductor (groin) muscles. AL-only owners can rest assured that he will be a productive third baseman for fantasy purposes but mixed leaguers probably won't want to have him as a starting third baseman. He is going to produce as a solid utility player for mixed league owners: He should provide a solid average, a respectable power game and helpful RBI totals. With the bone spurs and torn labrum now removed, his right hip joint will be able to flex and internally rotate more freely, allowing him to bend down to field, as well as pivot on his back leg as he swings a bat. The main focus of his rehabilitation will be to restore full range of motion and strength about

271

the hip. He is progressing well, and is on pace to be set for Opening Day. Expect Lowell to flirt with .290, 20 homers, and 80 RBI in 2009 – definitely a serviceable member of your fantasy team.

David Ortiz | 1B/DH | Boston

The health of Big Papi's left wrist tendon sheath will certainly be a huge determining factor in who ends up winning the AL East this season, as well as fantasy leagues in '09. Remember, he did not have surgery to repair the tissue, and he did not seem to be playing like his typical self toward the end of the season or in the postseason. Perhaps part of this was due to the departure of Manny Ramirez, but Ortiz's swing seemed slow, inconsistent and without force. The long offseason should help heal any remaining defects in the tendon sheath, so I would expect a much different Papi in '09. I would be happy with a .280/30/105 season, with anything additional being gravy. Sadly, the days of 47 to 54 home runs are probably gone, but the mid-to-high 30s is not out of the question.

Jorge Posada | C | New York

Posada is bouncing back after undergoing a repair to his right glenoid labrum, and, at 37, is set to be behind the plate for most of the season; newly acquired Kevin Cash will spell him. To keep his bat in the lineup, the Yankees will have to DH him on occasion since they signed first baseman Mark Teixeira. I expect Posada to continue to be a defensive liability, and he will need to be rested often. Likely he'll catch 100-120 games this season and DH the remaining games he plays in. While he should end up with a batting average in the .270-.280 range, his power should drop. I would not expect more than 15-18 homers.

CC Sabathia | SP | New York

When you are reported to be weighing in the 290-pound range, there will obviously be concerns about your durability. The hefty lefty has pitched 494 innings over the last two seasons, with 10 complete games last year alone. Problems that I usually see with heavier athletes include cartilage issues at the knee (meniscus tears) and hip (acetabular labrum), as well as back pain. His past workload is also a red flag for potential breakdown at the shoulder and/or elbow. It is important to note that Sabathia did pass a physical before signing with the Yankees, so there is nothing currently awry with him. He is a must-draft, top-tier starting pitcher, regardless of his recent workload and weight issues.

B.J. Upton | OF | Tampa Bay

His left (non-throwing) shoulder was surgically repaired in November, and he is expected to be in the starting lineup on Opening Day. He may be a bit rusty early on, as he works on regaining his swing pattern, but once he does, there should be no issues. After a step back in the power department during the regular season, Upton amassed seven postseason home runs. I would not be shocked to see the breakout year we have all been waiting for.

Troy Percival | RP | Tampa Bay

The aging closer will probably slide into a lesser role this season while younger, healthier options like Grant Balfour, Dan Wheeler, and J.P. Howell battle to be Tampa's next closer. Pass on Percival unless you have a thing for nostalgia.

Dustin McGowan | SP | Toronto

He underwent surgery late in July 2008 to debride fraying in the labrum. He did not have his rotator cuff repaired, which bodes well for his ability to return with some success in 2009. Right now, indications are that McGowan probably will return in early May. Do not overpay for him or draft him in the middle or early rounds this season. He is a perfect late-round addition in any format.

Others of Note: Phil Hughes, SP, New York; A.J. Burnett, SP, New York; Tim Wakefield, SP, Boston; Chris Ray, RP, Baltimore; Aaron Hill, 2B, Toronto; J.D. Drew, OF, Boston

A.L. West

Howie Kendrick | 2B | Los Angeles

His history of hamstring injuries is well known, and he struggled to get right last season. He always has been a slow healer for some reason, but when he's healthy, he is a great talent. He is safe to be drafted as a middle-tier second baseman, but make sure you also have a serviceable replacement who at least provides a good batting average. Hamstring injuries never seem to go away, especially for those who have repeated strains.

John Lackey | SP | Los Angeles

After three consecutive seasons with more than 200 innings pitched—and the past five seasons over 190—Lackey finally had some elbow issues last season and ended up with the smallest workload of his career (minus his 18-start rookie campaign). While Lackey is considered a bulldog on the mound, he is only human, and the innings totals are beginning to pile up for the 30-year-old ace. He allowed an astounding 26 home runs in just 163.1 innings in 2008, while having allowed only 45 in three seasons prior. Expect a decline in production this season with his first ERA over 4.00 since 2004.

Eric Chavez | 3B | Oakland

You simply cannot draft Chavez as your starting third baseman in mixed leagues. AL-only managers should not expect more than a .270 average and 20 HR. He is apparently making great progress following surgery to repair a moderately damaged labrum in his right shoulder. He also had a biceps tendon transposition, called a tenodesis, where the biceps is actually anchored to the humerus instead of the scapula. This is the procedure that Curt Schilling had. The optimistic view has him improving to the tune of .270/20/80, while it may be more realistic to expect a .260 average and closer to 15 homers.

Justin Duchscherer | SP | Oakland

Two years, two hip surgeries. A career relief pitcher-turned-starter. You do the math. He is risky, no doubt, but when healthy he has been lights-out. I am banking on a nice rebound for The Duke in '09, but I will also be anticipating a late-season hip flare-up.

Erik Bedard | SP | Seattle

Bedard's 2008 season began with high expectations, but quickly shifted to disappointment as he dealt with left hip pain. He has had a history of such hip pain. The nature of this injury seemed to point to involvement of the acetabular labrum, though this was never reported to be the exact cause of his pain. He then developed shoulder pain, went to the DL, and eventually had his season cut short. Offseason shoulder surgery revealed no major damage, simply a benign cyst that was removed, and he also had some debridement performed at the labrum. He should be set to return by Opening Day. He has been cleared to throw already, indicating that he has regained most—if not all—of his range of motion, as well as a good deal of shoulder strength. He should be able to produce solid No. 2 or 3 starting pitcher stats this year.

Hank Blalock | 3B/1B/DH | Texas

It is anyone's guess where Blalock will end up in the Rangers lineup, but one thing is for certain—he is an injury risk in '09 and beyond. The Rangers probably would be best off with Blalock at DH or even trading him. I was expecting a huge bounce-back season for Blalock in 2008, but injuries to his hamstrings and shoulder were continual problems. Unless he dedicated himself to rehabilitating these problem areas in the offseason, you can expect two or three DL stints for various nagging problems.

Others of Note: Jarrod Saltalamacchia, C, Texas; Scot Shields, RP, Los Angeles; Kevin Millwood, SP, Texas; Bobby Crosby, SS, Oakland; Santiago Casilla, RP, Oakland

A.L. Central

Fausto Carmona | SP | Cleveland

He went from 74-plus innings in 2006 to more than 215 in 2007. He followed up in 2008 with just over 120 innings, after having spent a good part of the middle of the season on the DL with a left hip strain that took much longer than expected to recover from. His strikeout rates were noticeably lower than in previous years, while his control was erratic and his walk rates increased. It is anyone's guess whether this was due to the injury, but I would keep a close eye on his spring training performance before spending a pick on him in the first half of your drafts. He does not seem like the same pitcher who wowed everyone in 2007.

Travis Hafner | 1B/DH | Cleveland

He is not likely to return to the days of 40-plus home runs, but the 20- to 25-homer range is not out of the question. He had arthroscopic debridement of his right shoulder, so this should clear up much of the source of his pain and limitation on the follow-through of his swing. The surgery lasted only 45 minutes, and addressed "chronic changes" in the shoulder. This likely means it was a basic "clean-up," which typically involves removing scar tissue, cleaning up fraying of the rotator cuff, and in some cases, decompressing bone spur formation. He should be an average starting first baseman-utility player for mixed leaguers in 2009.

Victor Martinez | C/DH/1B | Cleveland

He tried to play through what must have been quite a painful elbow injury—one that eventually required surgery. He had loose bodies (bone fragments) moving around in his elbow joint. Once those were removed, he was able to work on restoring mobility and strength about the elbow. He missed most of June, all of July, and most of August. He was more like the V-Mart we all know and love after that, with a September split of .288/.358/.475. I expect Martinez to bounce back nicely in 2009 and be one of the top three catchers in the game and in fantasy baseball.

Carlos Guillen | OF | Detroit

Fantasy owners will want to avoid Guillen this year if possible. He is moving to yet another defensive position (left field), and with his history of injuries (back, knee, hamstring, groin, shoulder, abdominal, etc.), you can bet he will hit the DL at least once or twice. It did not sound like the disc bulge in his lower back was fully resolved at the end of last season, so this is obviously still a cause for concern. The fact that he was having weakness and pain in his right foot and leg in addition to back spasms means that the disc involvement was pretty bad.

Joel Zumaya | RP | Detroit

He somehow sustained a stress fracture on his coracoid process, which is a bony prominence on the front of the shoulder blade that serves as a site of attachment for many muscles and ligaments. This is proof to me that he either has horrible mechanics or some sort of instability in the front of his shoulder. Overusing the short head of the biceps, pectoralis mino, and coracobrachialis muscles could create a stress fracture here over time. While we cannot prove this, one thing is for certain: Zumaya's delivery looks painful. He probably will provide his owners with brief stretches of nice K/9 ratios, but his lack of control and his inability to stay healthy remain barriers to his ultimate success as a possible closer in Detroit. Look for Fernando Rodney to be the guy to shut the door on Tigers wins this year.

Francisco Liriano | SP | Minnesota

As more time passes, Liriano should continue to recover from his Tommy John surgery. He pitched well in August, but became more hittable in September as he was likely tiring. This could be the year that Liriano arrives for good, as long as the Twins are careful not to overwork him and keep him fresh. Twelve to 15 wins, a 3.80 ERA, and a K/9 over 9.0 seems about right.

Others of Note: Octavio Dotel, RP, Chicago; Michael Cuddyer, OF, Minnesota; Jim Thome, DH, Chicago; Anthony Reyes, SP, Cleveland; Gary Sheffield, DH, Detroit; Jeremy Bonderman, SP, Detroit

N.L. East

J.J. Putz | RP | New York

The Mets were convinced that the elbow hyperextension that hindered his production last season was not anything major, and decided to make him a highly paid setup man to the newly acquired K-Rod. There are some questions about whether he will be able to replicate his dominant 2007 season, especially as a setup man, and elbow problems tend to have a way of resurfacing. K-Rod owners would be wise to draft Putz as a handcuff, and if your league counts holds, he is likely to be among the league leaders while also providing a stellar K/9 ratio.

Chase Utley | 2B | Philadelphia

Utley's hip surgery is the biggest draft day ordeal for 2009 fantasy leagues. While it was initially felt that he would miss the first month or two of the season, Utley's recent comments that he could be ready to go on Opening Day are certainly encouraging. He had surgery on Nov. 24, and after having used crutches for just under two weeks, he is now walking briskly and without a limp. This indicates that the involvement of the hip was not as bad as initially feared, and should cut down the rehab length.

If no setbacks or major issues arise in the rehab process, I would expect Utley to return fully and without any major limitations. It is not uncommon for patients who undergo this type of surgery to have residual discomfort in the anterior (front) of the hip or groin region during recovery.

From a production standpoint, turning and exploding out of a lead from first base may be difficult with an uncomfortable hip, so his stolen base totals could suffer early in the year. His ability to pull his hits to right field for power may initially be hindered, as he gets acclimated to rotating rapidly and forcefully over his front hip. My projections below are what I feel will be his baseline output, with greater totals possible if he starts the season on time.

Projections: 138 games, 514 AB, .292/.374/.520, 23 HR, 96 RBI, 9 SB

With numbers like this (and possibly higher), you have to consider taking him in the second or third round, but if word gets out that he will make it to the starting lineup on Day 1, you should bump him up to late first round or early second round status.

Rafael Soriano | RP | Atlanta

Combine his seemingly weekly bout of elbow soreness/pain/inflammation with his long history of right medial elbow pain and Tommy John surgery in 2004, and Soriano is a headache if you own him in fantasy leagues. He had an ulnar nerve transposition and a small bone spur removed from his right elbow in August, so there may be some hope for a semi-productive 2009. Soriano posts some excellent numbers when healthy, so if he is okay at the beginning of the season, feel free to add him to bolster your WHIP and strikeout categories. Understand, however, that another elbow flare-up is just around the corner.

Josh Johnson | SP | Florida

Following a dominant 2006 season, Johnson started four games in '07 but was terribly hittable and had control issues. He then underwent Tommy John surgery and ended his season. He returned late last season – well ahead of his rehabilitation schedule—and pitched very effectively, snagging a 7-1 record with 77 strikeouts in 87.1 innings. He is one of my favorite mid- to late-round targets this season in all league formats. He makes an excellent No. 4 or No. 5 starting pitcher for fantasy teams this year. Expect an ERA around 3.50-3.80 with nearly a strikeout per inning.

Ricky Nolasco | SP | Florida

He emerged as one of Florida's best pitchers last season after a forgettable 2007 that had him start only four games due to shoulder surgery. He is penciled in at the top of the Marlins rotation for '09, and could be a huge sleeper this year—especially in NL-only leagues.

Ryan Church | OF | New York

It is widely felt that his concussion situation was mishandled by the Mets last year, and as a result, he is now a huge injury risk. Those who suffer concussions are always more vulnerable to having additional ones. He plays blue-collar baseball and runs the bases hard, so he will always be in danger's path. As long as he avoids contact to his head, he will be fine, but it is possible that even a minor collision could put him on the DL for an extended period of time. He is a great late-round target to fill out your bench spots.

Ryan Zimmerman | 3B | Washington

The franchise player for the Nationals was limited greatly in 2008 by a torn glenoid labrum. Though he was able to return from a DL stint to finish out the regular season, he never produced to the level that was expected of him. The tear in his shoulder was small, so plenty of rest and strengthening could be enough to have him rebound in 2009. Expect Zimmerman to improve on his 2008 production, though diving and falling on an outstretched left arm could put him at risk for injury. It was encouraging that he hit .306 after the All-Star break, and hit five home runs in September alone. A 25-homer season should happen this season.

Others of Note: Chipper Jones, 3B, Atlanta; Mike Gonzalez, RP, Atlanta; Elijah Dukes, OF, Washington; Luis Castillo, 2B, New York; Anibal Sanchez, SP, Florida; Carlos Delgado, 1B, New York; Nick Johnson, 1B, Washington

N.L. West

Eric Byrnes | OF | Arizona

He opted against having surgery for his significantly torn hamstring, so this could be an ongoing saga that extends into '09. Because hamstrings are long, thin, biarticular muscles (they cross more than one joint), they are susceptible to strains and are easily aggravated. For a player like Byrnes, an all-out hustler who tends to be reckless with his body, having a serious hamstring injury is not a recipe for continued good health. If you draft him, expect a relapse of this hamstring tear.

Rafael Furcal | SS | Los Angeles

He had a disc herniation that required surgery during the middle of last season, but he is apparently in good health now. He played fairly well in the Dodgers' postseason run, but he did not steal a single base following his return. He probably will be limited in the base stealing department as the Dodgers attempt to keep their shortstop healthy. The risk of re-injury following this procedure is not too substantial, though a strict conditioning regimen of trunk stabilization exercise will be needed to keep his back healthy. With shortstop such a shallow position for fantasy purposes, drafting Furcal is essential, despite the injury risk.

Jason Schmidt | SP | Los Angeles

The Dodgers are expecting Schmidt to return as their No. 3 starter, but I would not be surprised if he logs no more than 10-15 starts this year. He is coming back from right shoulder surgery to repair the labrum—a very difficult surgery to bounce back from. He also had a secondary surgery to remove excessive scar tissue formation in the joint and clean up an arthritic acromioclavicular (AC) joint. I need to see Schmidt on the mound against major leaguers before I add him to my roster.

Randy Johnson | SP | San Francisco

He is susceptible to the occasional sore and achy lower back due to his age, but he managed to put together a nice season in 2008. As long as his back holds up, he will put up respectable numbers, but the chances of him landing on the DL this season are pretty good. Eight to 10 wins and just under a strikeout per inning seem to be reasonable expectations.

Todd Helton | 1B | Colorado

The aging first baseman has a chronic, degenerative back condition that's likely to linger for the rest of his career. He has lost his power stroke, and probably will be just a source of respectable batting average. He can be ignored in most mixed leagues, though if your league counts on-base percentage, he can be useful, since he draws quite a few walks.

Others of Note: Jeff Francis, SP, Colorado; Noah Lowry, SP, San Francisco; Huston Street, RP, Colorado; Andruw Jones, OF, Los Angeles; Chris Young, SP, San Diego

N.L. Central

Roy Oswalt | SP | Houston

His innings totals have regressed each year since 2005, so you could project him to be just under 200 innings this season for the first time since 2003. His stubborn nature and unwillingness to admit to pain probably will cost him at some point. He struggled with a left hip strain last season and attempted to return to the mound too early and aggravated the injury, causing him to miss more time. His demeanor will likely keep him on the mound for at least 185 innings, if not more. I'm concerned that his HR rate of 0.99 was substantially higher in 2008 than it had been since 2003.

Aaron Harang | SP | Cincinnati

Harang had a sprained elbow ligament in his pitching arm during the 2004 season, so for him to have had a major forearm strain last season is a concern. Not only that, but his walk rate increased to 2.44 BB/9 last season, compared to 2.17, 2.15 and 2.02 in 2005, 2006 and 2007, respectively. There could be more going on here. Three straight seasons of more than 211 innings pitched could have been what tipped his forearm over the edge. Would it surprise anyone if he lasted only 160-180 innings this season? I didn't think so.

Albert Pujols | 1B | St. Louis

He proved all of the doubters wrong last season and put together another very healthy, productive, MVP season. There will always be worries about his chronic elbow ligament tear, but as long as he is playing first base, the elbow will be preserved. The act of throwing would be the main irritating factor to his elbow ligament, so as long as he limits his volume and intensity of throwing, he should be good to go. His plantar fascia issue probably will pop up again at some point unless he has addressed that through custom orthotics and/or physical therapy. Draft him in the first round and enjoy mammoth production—he is the best hitter in the game.

Adam Wainwright | SP | St. Louis

Last season, he missed nearly the entire month of June, all of July and most of August after injuring his right middle finger during his start on June 7. He actually tore one of the annular pulleys in the finger, connective tissue that holds the flexor tendons in place. This tissue heals very slowly and very poorly, but does form a lot of scar tissue. When the pulley is torn, the muscles become inefficient in contraction due to the poor alignment of the tendons as they course through the finger. Wainwright didn't have surgery, and he was able to return in late August. He pitched fairly well in his remaining games, but did have some control issues, which is normal given this type of injury. The offseason should have allowed some good healing, so I would not expect this to be a problem for Wainwright in '09. However, if you see that his control is off during spring training, you can figure that his finger is still not right.

Chris Carpenter | SP/RP | St. Louis

He attempted to come back last season after having Tommy John surgery, but had setbacks early in his return. Carpenter has had numerous pitching arm injuries over the past five seasons, including surgery to repair a torn labrum, the Tommy John procedure, nerve compressions and tendinitis and shoulder strains. Clearly, he is one of the highest injury risks in baseball, and this trend will likely continue. While he should be stronger and more effective than he was late last season, he seems to be predisposed to nerve irritation due to compression. For mixed league owners, I would avoid Carpenter altogether, but NL-only managers will want to add him to the back end of their rotation.

Carlos Zambrano | SP | Chicago

The workload has to catch up to him at some point, right? The bouts of shoulder tendinitis he went through last season may have made him realize that he should work more diligently in the offseason on his strengthening and conditioning. He did acknowledge that this is a problem area and he promised Cubs fans that he would work harder in preparation for the '09 season. I am still confident that he can be a No. 1 starting pitcher in all fantasy leagues, but his injury risk remains.

Rich Harden | SP | Chicago

He was successful last season after being shipped to Chicago, but do not be fooled—this is the same pitcher with the same injury history (back, oblique, shoulder and elbow injuries). I hope that I am wrong here, but until he puts together a stellar season without much in the way of injuries, you simply have to draft with caution. He remains—and will always be—the biggest high-upside injury risk in baseball.

Others of Note: Chris Capuano, SP, Milwaukee; Rickie Weeks, 2B, Milwaukee; Ian Snell, SP, Pittsburgh; Ryan Doumit, C, Pittsburgh; Edinson Volquez, SP, Cincinnati

Rookies to Watch in 2009

by Derek Carty

One of my favorite fantasy strategies is to select high-upside players late in the draft. If the player reaches his upside, you've received a ton of value at very little cost. If the player doesn't reach his upside, you can subsequently drop him and scan the waiver wire for someone comparable to one of the safer late-round picks you passed over. It's a low-risk, high-reward strategy I will use in most leagues.

While rookies sometimes end up going too early if their hype machine cranks into high gear in the preseason, you can get many high-upside rookies late in the draft. Last year, that meant guys like Evan Longoria, Edinson Volquez, Geovany Soto, Kosuke Fukudome, Alexei Ramirez, Joey Votto, Jay Bruce, Chris Davis, Clayton Kershaw and Hiroki Kuroda. Let's see if we can find the 2009 players who have the greatest chance of breaking out they way those players did.

To do this, we need to consider two primary factors: skill and opportunity. A player can be the best prospect in baseball, but the major league team has to have a spot for him if he's to have fantasy value. Triple-A stats don't count. If Longoria had been on the Mets, he could have spent the year in the minors behind David Wright. Of course, if a player has the opportunity, he also must have the skill. It does fantasy owners no good if Bryan LaHair is starting at first base for the Mariners if he's hitting only .250 with no steals and a home run every 50 at-bats.

This being said, let's look at the prospects with the best combination of skills and opportunity for the 2009 season.

Hitters

Matt Wieters | BAL | C

Perhaps the top prospect in baseball. I'm sure you've heard all about Wieters by now. He's rocketing through the Orioles' system, and with the trade of Ramon Hernandez this offseason, Wieters could be starting in Baltimore as early as Opening Day. If he doesn't start the season with the team, expect him by the end of May, at the latest. He has monster power for a catcher and also is capable of posting a solid batting average (with upside) thanks to a 79 percent aggregate MLE (Major League Equivalent) contact rate last year.

2009 Projection: .291 AVG/25 HR/1 SB

Travis Snider | TOR | OF

Snider has some work to do, but he still could be a valuable fantasy asset in 2009. He began 2008 at high-A ball and finished the year at the major league level, batting .301 with homers 73 at-bats. He strikes out way too much (67 percent MLE contact rate), but he has nice raw power, and the opportunity is there for him to begin 2009 as the Blue Jays' DH. He might spend more time in the minors, but if he does well, an early season call-up could be in the cards. Temper expectations, but all it would take is some BABIP luck and a decent spot in the order for Snider to have mixed-league value.

2009 Projection: .254 AVG/19 HR/2 SB

Cameron Maybin | FLA | OF

Maybin might be an afterthought to some fantasy leaguers at this point after the Tigers pushed him too hard in 2007 and he fell flat. The Marlins let him spend the entire 2008 season at Double-A, though, and now it appears he could have the starting center field gig out of spring training.

Maybin is similar to Snider in that he strikes out *waaay* too much. As a result, his MLE average was similar at just .228 last year. Still, he has an appealing power/speed combo and lots of raw ability. If Michael Bourn was drafted in the teen rounds last year, Maybin in the end-game seems like a solid pick, especially since he has greater upside than Bourn. The only hurdle right now for Maybin to have legitimate mixed league value is the average.

2009 Projection: .247 AVG/12 HR/12 SB

Andrew McCutchen | PIT | OF

McCutchen likely could have played in the majors in 2008, but the team opted to keep him at Triple-A for his age 21 season. He doesn't have great power yet and didn't post a great MLE batting average (.250), but both have upside, and the batting average could get there in 2009—it isn't low as a result of strikeouts (80 percent MLE contact rate) as it is with Snider and Maybin. The biggest plus with McCutchen, though, is his speed.

He'll get plenty of steals, and if he leads off, he would have a lot of value with all those runs scored.

Nate McLouth will own one outfield spot going into 2009, and McCutchen will battle with Nyjer Morgan, Brandon Moss and Steven Pearce for the final two spots. Pearce is a solid player, but McCutchen likely deserves it over the rest. Like Wieters, if he doesn't win a spot outright, he could be up shortly.

2009 Projection: .262 AVG/9 HR/17 SB

Chris Dickerson | CIN | OF

Dickerson isn't as hyped but is perhaps more advanced than the three outfield prospects I've discussed. Like Maybin, he has an intriguing power/speed combo but might not hurt you as much in batting average. It should be noted, though, that his contact rate was just about the same (68 percent) as Maybin's and his average was propped up by a .363 BABIP. Furthermore, his path to a starting gig would be blocked if the Reds sign another outfielder, as is being rumored, and his path to the lead-off spot might already be cut off with the signing of Willy Taveras. I probably like his power the best of any of these guys, though, so he might be worth a flier.

2009 Projection: .250 AVG/18 HR/19 SB

Kila Ka'aihue | KC | 1B

He absolutely mashed in 2008. His MLE says that he would hit 45 home runs in 550 at-bats. That is huge for a guy who gets such little attention. Unfortunately, the Kansas City trade for Mike Jacobs this offseason pushes

him even further down the depth chart. With Jacobs, Billy Butler, Ryan Shealey and Ross Gload all first basemen/designated hitters, the likelihood of Ka'aihue getting enough at-bats to have value in 2009 is somewhat low. He deserves at-bats, though, and could post a 2007 Carlos Pena-like season if he finds his way into a starting job. Here's hoping for a big spring training.

2009 Projection: .241 AVG/21 HR/1 SB

Alcides Escobar | MIL | SS

Not much power yet and not nearly as well-known as the other guys I've talked about, but Escobar's speed and position make him someone for fantasy owners to watch. He should be able to post a good batting average because he keeps an above-average contact rate (84 percent MLE). He's currently blocked by J.J. Hardy, but there's a decent chance the Brewers will trade Hardy at some point, which would leave the job open for Escobar. That he's supposed to be a defensive wizard makes it all the more likely the Brewers make room for him.

2009 Projection: .272 AVG/5 HR/15 SB

Mat Gamel | MIL | 3B

Gamel made himself known in 2008, belting 19 homers and hitting .329 at Double-A. Unfortunately, he isn't great defensively, and all the positions he'd be capable of playing are filled in Milwaukee. He may be close to establishing himself as a top-notch talent, but it would take an injury or a trade of someone like Bill Hall for him to see any time in the majors in 2009.

2009 Projection: .258 AVG/13 HR/4 SB

Starting Pitchers

Max Scherzer | ARI | SP

Scherzer misses rookie status by six innings, but I need to mention him anyway. He blows hitters away with a combination of a 94 mph fastball, a solid slider, and a ridiculous change-up that is 9 mph slower than the fastball and is capable of getting screwball action on a good day. He made strides with his control in 2008 and could be poised for a huge 2009 season. Great late-round selection.

2009 Projection: 9.7 K/G – 4.2 BB/G – 46% GB

David Price | TB | SP

Price is getting all the hype now, but I'm not buying into all of it. His PITCHf/x data isn't super-impressive, and neither are his MLEs. Even his raw totals (8.7 K/9,

2.5 BB/9 at Double-A) weren't what you would expect out of a supposed phenom. He was being drafted as early as round 11 in early mock drafts, but I'm not touching him that soon. He'll be solid, and the potential is there, but that is far too high, especially since it's not quite guaranteed he'll be the Rays' fifth starter.

2009 Projection: 6.5 K/G – 3.8 BB/G – 50% GB

Dave Huff | CLE | SP

Huff might not crack the Opening Day rotation for the Tribe, but he probably should. He doesn't have tremendous "stuff," but he has impeccable control, gets ground balls, and his MLE strikeout rate was still above average (and well above Price's, for that matter). He probably doesn't have No. 1 upside, but he could wind up as a poor man's James Shields. With a number of marginal pitchers in Cleveland's projected rotation (some worse than marginal), there's a pretty good chance we'll be seeing Huff before the All-Star break.

2009 Projection: 6.4 K/G – 3.2 BB/G – 47% GB

J.A. Happ | PHI | SP

Happ doesn't excel in any one area, like Scherzer with strikeouts or Huff with control, but he's solid all around and could go overlooked in your draft. He's a bit of a fly ball pitcher and doesn't throw very hard, but his 2008 MLE K/G is the second highest of any 2009 rookie starter (third if you count Scherzer). Right now he'd be the favorite for the fifth spot in the Phillies' rotation, although he could get bumped if they acquire another starter. In that case, Happ would likely be the first called up, though, and could make you a nice profit.

2009 Projection: 7.9 K/G – 4.5 BB/G – 38% GB

Guillermo Moscoso | TEX | SP

Moscoso is 25 years old already, but he's a young 25; He doesn't have a lot of innings on his arm (although this comes at the expense of an injury history). He strikes out tons of batters and has solid control, though there are a couple of drawbacks. The first is that he is an extreme—**extreme**—fly ball pitcher, which limits his potential (especially now that he's on the Rang-

ers), and his 26 percent groundball rate could even get worse once his 12 percent line drive rate normalizes. The second is that he has pitched just 34.2 innings at Double-A, so despite a very poor Texas rotation and his nice MLEs, we might not be seeing him for most of 2009.

However, his MLEs were too good not to mention. Texas traded for him for a reason, and the Rangers could have the worst rotation in baseball, so keep an eye on him. If he pitches well at Triple-A in the first couple of months, there is a chance we'll see him.

2009 Projection: 8.4 K/G – 3.2 BB/G – 26% GB

Brett Anderson | OAK | SP

While the Athletics' rotation is far from set, Anderson is still probably too raw to earn an Opening Day spot. If there's room at the All-Star break, though, Anderson could get called up. His MLE K/G is depressed because he spent half the year at Single-A, but he could be a strikeout threat as he matures. He also gets a lot of ground balls and already is solid with his control. He's likely just a deep AL-only pick, but he's someone to watch. The same goes for fellow A's prospect Trevor Cahill, though his numbers have been a little less impressive and he still has some control issues.

2009 Projection: 6.1 K/G – 3.3 BB/G – 53% GB

Relief Pitchers

Chris Perez | STL | RP

Perez, who had time in the majors at the end of 2008, is currently slated to close for the Cardinals and is therefore an attractive fantasy option. It must be noted, though, that Cards manager Tony La Russa has made it known that he'd like the team to acquire a proven closer. He doesn't seem to have much faith in Perez, so if he struggles, he could get pulled from the role quickly. While he has the skills to succeed, there will likely be better options on draft day.

2009 Projection: 9.4 K/G – 5.3 BB/G – 43% GB

Cesar Jimenez | SEA | RP

Many analysts are saying to avoid the Mariners' closing situation, but that might not be necessary. While he throws just 90 mph, Jimenez's MLEs suggest he would be plenty capable of holding down the job, and he may get the chance if both Brandon Morrow and Aaron Heilman start the year in the rotation. Even if one starts out closing (or if someone else does), Jimenez would still make a solid speculative pick, especially in AL-only leagues.

2009 Projection: 6.9 K/G – 3.9 BB/G – 42% GB

Charts

I could cover only some of the prospects who could have an impact in 2009. The following charts include a lot more players (though it certainly isn't exhaustive) who could have 2009 fantasy value.

Note: The 1-5 scales on these charts aren't precise. They are intended to help you see how prospects stack up to each other. Furthermore, a player's "opportunity score" is subject to change based on offseason moves, spring training battles, and the like.

Opening Day Possibilities

Opportunity	Skill				
	1	2	3	4	5
5	Josh Outman, Daryl Thompson	Jon Niese, Scott Lewis, Clayton Richard	Gio Gonzalez, Ross Ohlendorf	David Price, Andrew McCutchen, Cameron Maybin, Travis Snider	Max Scherzer, Matt Wieters
4		James McDonald, Dan Murphy, Tommy Hanson, Jeff Niemann	Michael Bowden, Garrett Mock, Steven Pearce, Taylor Teagarden	David Huff, J.A. Happ, Max Ramirez, Cesar Jimenez, Chris Dickerson	Chris Perez
3	Nick Adenhart				Jason Motte, James Hoey
2				Adam Miller	Kila Ka'aihue, Joseph Koshansky
1			Eric Patterson		

Midseason Possibilities

Opportunity	Skill				
	1	2	3	4	5
5		Jordan Schafer, Jack Egbert	Jordan Zimmerman, Trevor Cahill	Colby Rasmus, Brett Anderson, Gordon Beckham	
4		Brett Cecil, Chris Tillman		Dayan Viciedo, Mark DiFelice	Guillermo Moscoso
3		Carlos Carrasco	Matt LaPorta	Alcides Escobar, Brandon Wood	
2				Mat Gamel	
1	Eddie Kunz		Nolan Reimold		

An Intro to Risk Management

by Victor Wang

Sabermetricians have come a long way in projecting player statistics. Multiple projection systems, many of which are free, are available online. They seem to produce fairly similar results, with the top projection systems usually just barely ahead.

Most projection systems start with the same basic procedure, which involves taking a weighted average of a player's past few seasons. The projection system then regresses that weighted average to a mean, and adjusts for age. Systems differ on what statistics to regress and what mean various statistics are regressed to.

Some systems take more advanced steps. For example, PECOTA, developed by Nate Silver of *Baseball Prospectus*, generates a list of comparable players and adjusts a player's projected statistics based on how his comparable players performed.

Despite the varying complexity of forecasting systems, the level of accuracy remains pretty similar. In fact, I'd bet that the most accurate projection you could achieve among currently available resources would be an average of, say, the top five projection systems. Why? Because I think we are at a point of diminishing returns on projection systems, at least with the way projection systems are currently designed.

I think the next big forecasting breakthrough will come in the area of risk management and analysis. You may have heard this term before, specifically in the finance area. Risk management is basically a way to identify and treat various risks. In the fantasy baseball setting, this will be most applicable to your draft or auction. Risk management is a relatively new area within sabermetrics, with just a little past work. I'm going to use this article to introduce readers to how risk management can be applied to baseball. First, I'll define risk, going over various tools that can be used to identify it, and then we'll see how you can apply risk to evaluate players.

Defining Risk

Risk was first properly defined by University of Chicago economist Frank Knight. He defined risk as something that was random but whose probabilities were knowable. He made a distinction between risk and uncertainty, which was defined as something that was random but whose probabilities were unknowable. Many people mix up risk and uncertainty and talk about risk when they should be talking about uncertainty and vice versa.

Risk generally brings with it a negative connotation. For example, when people hear "risk," they often think of things like a heart attack or cancer or the stock market crashing. In a fantasy baseball setting, risk is also usually perceived negatively. That's fair, so I will define risk, for fantasy baseball players, as the chances of an unwanted event occurring. This could be the chance that your ace pitcher needs Tommy John surgery or your starting first basemen stops hitting home runs. However, I still want to emphasize the distinction between risk and uncertainty. Risk involves known chances while uncertainty does not. Given this, I also feel it is best to split risk up into two categories.

The first is performance risk. That's the risk that a player suffers an unwanted variation from his expected performance; for example, your first baseman stops hitting home runs or the batting champion from last year hits only .250. When this occurs, not only is a player not performing up to expectations, but he is also at risk of getting decreased playing time.

The second category is injury risk; e.g., a pitcher needing Tommy John surgery. The tricky thing with injury risk is that not all injuries are made known to the public. If a player is performing poorly, it may be because of injury, but a fantasy owner would have no way of knowing this if an injury is not made known.

Measuring Risk

So, how do you measure a player's performance and injury risk? Well, first you should try to figure out your own risk preference. How tolerant are you to risk and what attitude do you take when faced with a chance situation?

For example, suppose I were to offer you this gamble: I flip a coin, and if it lands heads you get double your yearly salary. However, if it lands tails you get nothing. If we just consider expected value, you'd be indifferent to this gamble. Obviously, though, almost no one in real life would be indifferent. Most people would require an upfront payment to take the gamble over their salary. The exact amount depends on a person's risk preference.

A person can have three different risk preferences. We can describe these preferences using the coin flip example again, changing some of the parameters. We'll say that if the coin lands heads, you receive $1,000 but if it lands tails you receive nothing. The expected value of this coin flip is $500. However, before you flip the coin you can choose to receive an upfront payment.

A person is risk-averse if he would accept an upfront payment of less than $500 over the coin flip. A person is risk neutral if he is indifferent between receiving an upfront payment of $500 and taking the coin flip. A person is risk-seeking if he would rather take the coin flip than receive an upfront payment of $500 or less.

Thinking over your risk preference before your draft or auction would be very beneficial. But how do you go about it?

First, think in terms of dollar values for players, even if you're in a draft league. You can then ask yourself questions like this: Suppose there is one player, player X, who has a 50 percent chance of being a $40 player and a 50 percent chance of being a $0 player. How many certain dollars would a player need to be worth to make me indifferent between that player and player X? In other words, would you rather take player X or a player who was guaranteed to produce $20? Player X or a player who produces $15? By asking yourself questions like this, you can come up with your general risk preference.

If you are risk-averse, you would take a player who produces a certain value of $20 over player X. If you are risk-neutral, you are indifferent between player X and a player who always produces $20. If you are risk-seeking, you would take player X over a player who produces a certain value of $20.

Of course, your risk preference doesn't necessarily have to stay the same in all situations. Instead, I would recommend determining your risk preference for these three situations:

1. $30-plus players/first third of your draft: Many owners prefer to be more risk-averse in this situation as these players are going to be your biggest investments. However, if you feel you are at disadvantage against other owners, perhaps because they have superior keepers, it could help you to be risk-seeking in this situation.
2. $11-$30 players/middle third of your draft: This is where you can best mold your risk strategy. Most owners will be risk-averse at the beginning of a draft and risk-seeking at the end of a draft. In the middle of a draft, though, you start to see differing player evaluations. This is where you'll have to decide how high, or if, you want to go for your breakout picks.
3. $1-$10 players/last third of your draft: It makes a lot of sense to be risk-seeking in this situation. For example, you would rather have a player who's

worth $20 five percent of the time and $0 the other 95 percent than a player who is worth $1 all the time, since you can easily replace the $1 player.

Now, once you have your risk preference determined for various situations, you'll actually have to go about measuring risk for certain players. A few tools can help you.

PECOTA Beta Score:

This measure was introduced with the 2008 PECOTA forecasts. It measures the volatility in a player's forecast, with one being average, below one being less risky, and above one being more risky.

Pros:
1. Measures volatility of a player's forecast in simple number.
2. Adjusts risk for a player's expected playing time (a player won't be more risky just because he's slated for less playing time).

Cons:
1. Generated based on a player's comparable player list, so will be unreliable for players with few comparables.
2. Has not been empirically tested.
3. Assumes future variance can be projected from past variance.

Baseball HQ Reliability Scores:

This measures a player's risk on a scale from 0-100. Scores are based on a player's past playing time, injury history, age, and variance in performance.

Pros:
1. Another risk measure available in a simple, handy number.
2. Accounts for a number of factors that would seem to relate to risk.

Cons:
1. Like PECOTA, assumes future variance can be projected from past variance.
2. Not useful for rookies or players with little time in the majors.

Will Carroll Team Health Reports:

Carroll grades each player's injury risk on a red, yellow, green scale.

Pros:
1. Only injury projection model.
2. Easy-to-use scale.

Cons:
1. Measures only probability, does not measure impact.
2. Empirical study showed system struggled with "green" and "red" hitters and green pitchers.

Qualitative Risk Measurement System

I introduced a risk measurement system that measures various risk factors using qualitative judgments and combines them into an overall risk score.

Pros:
1. Since judgments are qualitative, allows user to predict future risk rather than rely on past data.
2. Assesses probability and impact.

Cons:
1. Entirely subjective
2. You need a ton of free time to create risk scores for all players.

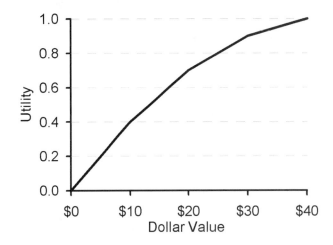

The hardest part is using these risk tools to come up with a range of outcomes for players, while some forecast systems, PECOTA and CHONE for example, provide a range of outcomes in their forecasts. Let's say we do know the risk and range of outcomes of a player. Perhaps you estimate using a combination of the risk measurement tools available or use one of the projection systems. How do we convert that into something meaningful for fantasy? We use something called a utility curve, which measures the relative satisfaction one receives as a variable changes. We can use fantasy dollar values as the variable in this situation.

Here's an example. Let's say the highest dollar value you project for any one player is $40. So a player who generates $40 would give you a utility of one. Meanwhile, a player who produces $0 of value produces zero utility. These are the end points on your utility curve.

Now let's find the rest of your points. We'll start with what it would take to get .5 utility. If you were risk-neutral, a player who produces $20 would be worth .5 utility, since 20 is halfway between 0 and 40. However, if you are not risk-neutral, your answer will be different.

To figure out what dollar value is worth .5 utility for you, you have to ask yourself how many certain dollars would make you indifferent between a player who is worth $0 half the time and $40 the other half. Let's say you would be indifferent between a player who always produces $15 and a player who produces $0 half the time and $40 the other half. Then a $15 player will be worth .5 utiles for you.

You continue this process for other points on your utility curve until you can draw it out. Let's say your utility curve turns out something like the graph on the next column. (The x-axis is a player's dollar value, and the y-axis is the utility the dollar values generate.)

Here's how you can use this utility curve to create a risk-adjusted dollar value. Let's say there is a player worth $20 on average, but you know that half the time he will produce $10 and the other half he will produce $30. First, multiply the probability of each dollar value times the utility of each dollar value. To find the utility of a dollar value, mark the desired dollar value with your finger on the x-axis. Drag your finger up until you hit the utility curve and move your finger to the left to the y-axis. The number you land on is the utility of the dollar value. So using our example we get:

- Utility of $10 = .4
- Probability of $10 = .5
- Utility of $30 = .9
- Probability of $30 = .5
- Total Utility = (.4)(.5) + (.9)(.5) = .65

We now need to convert this utility value into dollar values again. To do this, mark the utility value on the y-axis at the point where it equals the total utility. Drag your finger until you hit the utility curve and drag down from that point to the x-axis. What you land on is the risk adjusted dollar value. In our example, that is about $18. This is your risk adjusted dollar value given our simulated risk preference and the range of outcomes for our imaginary player.

I don't expect anyone to have the time to do this sort of analysis for every player for a draft or auction, but I do think the thought process is useful. I hope that someday you will be able to plug in your risk preference and range of outcomes for a player and have a dollar value pop out. While this does not exist now, I do think knowing about this process can be helpful with adjusting dollar values for risk and finding your own risk preference.

In conclusion, while there are a few systems available, risk measurement systems are still a ways behind the status of forecasting systems. Given that there's no one magic system you can use to forecast risk, what can you do to account for risk in your draft or auction? Here are a few suggestions:

- Use the tools available, but don't be trapped by them. Don't be afraid to mix qualitative judgment with any quantitative measurements you decide to use. In fact, I wouldn't put blind faith in any current quantitative risk measurement tools.

- Decide on your risk preference before your draft or auction. You don't want to be changing your strategy during the heat of the battle. I also prefer to set a dollar limit, an exit strategy of sorts, on players before going into an auction. I prefer to do this before an auction because I find it can be hard to stay rational at times and make rapid decisions in the middle of an auction.

- If you're uncomfortable with projecting the risk of a certain player, ignore him and go with players you're more comfortable with. For example, say you're deciding whether to draft CC Sabathia but aren't sure if he can handle the heavy workload he's had the past few seasons and don't have any confidence in projecting his health. If you're in a situation like this with no confidence, I would ignore Sabathia and go with someone you're more comfortable with.

- If you feel you don't have much time to prepare a risk strategy, look up various plans that exist already. Popular plans include the LIMA plan, spread the risk or stars and scrubs, and the Labadini plan.

What's Next

You likely have thought about these types of things before with draft or auction preparation. However, I hope I have brought to your attention how useful and important risk management can be. In the future, I believe, risk projection systems will be just as important as the player projection systems we have right now. If you're looking for a leg up on the competition, risk analysis is a good place to start. I hope to be providing risk advice and research during the 2009 season via THT Fantasy Focus.

Good luck with your season.

Sources

1. *Risk, Uncertainty, and Profit* by Frank Knight
2. *Diamond Dollars* by Vince Gennaro
3. http://baseballprospectus.com/glossary/index.php?mode=viewstat&stat=467
4. *Baseball Forecaster 2008* by Ron Shandler
5. http://www.hardballtimes.com/main/fantasy/article/player-risk-profile-tulowitzki/
6. *The Black Swan* by Nassim Taleb
7. *Readings in Decision Analysis* by Ronald Howard
8. http://www.insidethebook.com/ee/index.php/site/comments/forecasting_injuries/

Player Index

Following is a list of all the players with projections and comments in the *Season Preview*, and the team section each one is listed within.

Name	Team
Aardsma, David	Boston Red Sox
Abercrombie, Reggie	Houston Astros
Abreu, Bobby	New York Yankees
Accardo, Jeremy	Toronto Blue Jays
Acosta, Manny	Atlanta Braves
Adams, Mike	San Diego Padres
Adenhart, Nick	Los Angeles Angels
Affeldt, Jeremy	Cincinnati Reds
Aguilar, Omar	Milwaukee Brewers
Albers, Matt	Baltimore Orioles
Alfonzo, Eliezer	San Francisco Giants
Allen, Brandon	Chicago White Sox
Alou, Moises	New York Mets
Amezaga, Alfredo	Florida Marlins
Anderson, Brian	Chicago White Sox
Anderson, Garret	Los Angeles Angels
Anderson, Josh	Atlanta Braves
Anderson, Marlon	New York Mets
Andino, Robert	Florida Marlins
Ankiel, Rick	St. Louis Cardinals
Antonelli, Matt	San Diego Padres
Ardoin, Danny	Los Angeles Dodgers
Arias, Joaquin	Texas Rangers
Armas, Tony	New York Mets
Arredondo, Jose	Los Angeles Angels
Arroyo, Bronson	Cincinnati Reds
Ascanio, Jose	Chicago Cubs
Atkins, Garrett	Colorado Rockies
Aubrey, Michael	Cleveland Indians
Aurilia, Rich	San Francisco Giants
Aviles, Mike	Kansas City Royals
Aybar, Erick	Los Angeles Angels
Aybar, Willy	Tampa Bay Rays
Backe, Brandon	Houston Astros
Badenhop, Burke	Florida Marlins
Baek, Cha Seung	San Diego Padres
Bailey, Homer	Cincinnati Reds
Bailey, Jeff	Boston Red Sox
Baker, Jeff	Colorado Rockies
Baker, John	Florida Marlins
Baker, Scott	Minnesota Twins
Bako, Paul	Cincinnati Reds
Baldelli, Rocco	Tampa Bay Rays
Balentien, Wladimir	Seattle Mariners
Balester, Collin	Washington Nationals

Name	Team
Balfour, Grant	Tampa Bay Rays
Banks, Josh	San Diego Padres
Bannister, Brian	Kansas City Royals
Barajas, Rod	Toronto Blue Jays
Bard, Josh	San Diego Padres
Barden, Brian	St. Louis Cardinals
Barfield, Josh	Cleveland Indians
Barmes, Clint	Colorado Rockies
Barrett, Michael	San Diego Padres
Barthmaier, Jimmy	Pittsburgh Pirates
Bartlett, Jason	Tampa Bay Rays
Barton, Brian	St. Louis Cardinals
Barton, Daric	Oakland A's
Bass, Brian	Baltimore Orioles
Batista, Miguel	Seattle Mariners
Bautista, Jose	Toronto Blue Jays
Bay, Jason	Boston Red Sox
Beam, T.J.	Pittsburgh Pirates
Beckett, Josh	Boston Red Sox
Bedard, Erik	Seattle Mariners
Beimel, Joe	Los Angeles Dodgers
Belisle, Matt	Cincinnati Reds
Bell, Heath	San Diego Padres
Belliard, Ronnie	Washington Nationals
Beltran, Carlos	New York Mets
Beltre, Adrian	Seattle Mariners
Bennett, Jeff	Atlanta Braves
Benoit, Joaquin	Texas Rangers
Bergesen, Bradley	Baltimore Orioles
Bergmann, Jason	Washington Nationals
Berkman, Lance	Houston Astros
Bernadina, Rogearvin	Washington Nationals
Berroa, Angel	Los Angeles Dodgers
Betancourt, Rafael	Cleveland Indians
Betancourt, Yuniesky	Seattle Mariners
Betemit, Wilson	Chicago White Sox
Bierd, Randor	Baltimore Orioles
Billingsley, Chad	Los Angeles Dodgers
Bixler, Brian	Pittsburgh Pirates
Blackburn, Nick	Minnesota Twins
Blake, Casey	Los Angeles Dodgers
Blalock, Hank	Texas Rangers
Blanco, Gregor	Atlanta Braves
Blanco, Henry	Chicago Cubs
Blanton, Joe	Philadelphia Phillies

285

Name	Team
Blevins, Jerry	Oakland A's
Bloomquist, Willie	Seattle Mariners
Blum, Geoff	Houston Astros
Bocock, Brian	San Francisco Giants
Boggs, Brandon	Texas Rangers
Boggs, Mitchell	St. Louis Cardinals
Bogusevic, Brian	Houston Astros
Bonderman, Jeremy	Detroit Tigers
Bonifacio, Emilio	Florida Marlins
Bonine, Eddie	Detroit Tigers
Bonser, Boof	Minnesota Twins
Boone, Aaron	Washington Nationals
Borowski, Joe	Cleveland Indians
Bourgeois, Jason	Chicago White Sox
Bourn, Michael	Houston Astros
Bowden, Michael	Boston Red Sox
Bowen, Rob	Oakland A's
Bowker, John	San Francisco Giants
Boyer, Blaine	Atlanta Braves
Braden, Dallas	Oakland A's
Bradford, Chad	Tampa Bay Rays
Bradley, Milton	Texas Rangers
Brantley, Michael	Milwaukee Brewers
Branyan, Russell	Seattle Mariners
Braun, Ryan	Milwaukee Brewers
Bray, Bill	Cincinnati Reds
Breslow, Craig	Minnesota Twins
Brignac, Reid	Tampa Bay Rays
Britton, Chris	New York Yankees
Broadway, Lance	Chicago White Sox
Brocail, Doug	Houston Astros
Brown, Andrew	Oakland A's
Brown, Emil	Oakland A's
Brown, Matthew	Los Angeles Angels
Broxton, Jonathan	Los Angeles Dodgers
Bruce, Jay	Cincinnati Reds
Bruney, Brian	New York Yankees
Bruntlett, Eric	Philadelphia Phillies
Buchholz, Taylor	Colorado Rockies
Buck, John	Kansas City Royals
Buck, Travis	Oakland A's
Buckner, Billy	Arizona Diamondbacks
Buehrle, Mark	Chicago White Sox
Bulger, Jason	Los Angeles Angels
Burke, Chris	Arizona Diamondbacks
Burke, Jamie	Seattle Mariners
Burnett, A.J.	Toronto Blue Jays
Burnett, Sean	Pittsburgh Pirates

Name	Team
Burrell, Pat	Philadelphia Phillies
Burres, Brian	Baltimore Orioles
Burriss, Emmanuel	San Francisco Giants
Burton, Jared	Cincinnati Reds
Buscher, Brian	Minnesota Twins
Bush, Dave	Milwaukee Brewers
Butera, Drew	Minnesota Twins
Butler, Billy	Kansas City Royals
Bynum, Freddie	Baltimore Orioles
Byrd, Marlon	Texas Rangers
Byrd, Paul	Boston Red Sox
Byrdak, Tim	Houston Astros
Byrnes, Eric	Arizona Diamondbacks
Cabrera, Asdrubal	Cleveland Indians
Cabrera, Daniel	Baltimore Orioles
Cabrera, Jolbert	Cincinnati Reds
Cabrera, Melky	New York Yankees
Cabrera, Miguel	Detroit Tigers
Cabrera, Orlando	Chicago White Sox
Cahill, Trevor	Oakland A's
Cain, Matt	San Francisco Giants
Cairo, Miguel	Seattle Mariners
Callaspo, Alberto	Kansas City Royals
Cameron, Mike	Milwaukee Brewers
Campillo, Jorge	Atlanta Braves
Cano, Robinson	New York Yankees
Cantu, Jorge	Florida Marlins
Capps, Matt	Pittsburgh Pirates
Cardenas, Adrian	Oakland A's
Carlson, Jesse	Toronto Blue Jays
Carlyle, Buddy	Atlanta Braves
Carmona, Fausto	Cleveland Indians
Carp, Mike	Seattle Mariners
Carpenter, Chris	St. Louis Cardinals
Carrasco, D.J.	Chicago White Sox
Carroll, Brett	Florida Marlins
Carroll, Jamey	Cleveland Indians
Casey, Sean	Boston Red Sox
Cash, Kevin	Boston Red Sox
Casilla, Alexi	Minnesota Twins
Casilla, Santiago	Oakland A's
Cassel, Jack	Houston Astros
Castillo, Jose	Houston Astros
Castillo, Luis	New York Mets
Castillo, Wilkin	Cincinnati Reds
Casto, Kory	Washington Nationals
Castro, Juan	Baltimore Orioles
Castro, Ramon	New York Mets

Name	Team
Catalanotto, Frank	Texas Rangers
Cedeno, Ronny	Chicago Cubs
Chamberlain, Joba	New York Yankees
Chavez, Endy	Seattle Mariners
Chavez, Eric	Oakland A's
Chavez, Jesse	Pittsburgh Pirates
Chen, Yung Chi	Oakland A's
Chico, Matt	Washington Nationals
Choo, Shin-Soo	Cleveland Indians
Christian, Justin	New York Yankees
Chulk, Vinnie	San Francisco Giants
Church, Ryan	New York Mets
Cintron, Alex	Baltimore Orioles
Clark, Tony	Arizona Diamondbacks
Clement, Jeff	Seattle Mariners
Clippard, Tyler	Washington Nationals
Coffey, Todd	Milwaukee Brewers
Coghlan, Christopher	Florida Marlins
Coke, Phil	New York Yankees
Colome, Jesus	Washington Nationals
Colon, Bartolo	Boston Red Sox
Condrey, Clay	Philadelphia Phillies
Contreras, Jose	Chicago White Sox
Cook, Aaron	Colorado Rockies
Coon, Bradley	Los Angeles Angels
Cora, Alex	Boston Red Sox
Corcoran, Roy	Seattle Mariners
Cordero, Francisco	Cincinnati Reds
Cormier, Lance	Baltimore Orioles
Corpas, Manny	Colorado Rockies
Correia, Kevin	San Francisco Giants
Cortes, Daniel	Kansas City Royals
Costa, Shane	Kansas City Royals
Costanzo, Michael	Baltimore Orioles
Coste, Chris	Philadelphia Phillies
Cotts, Neal	Chicago Cubs
Counsell, Craig	Milwaukee Brewers
Crain, Jesse	Minnesota Twins
Crawford, Carl	Tampa Bay Rays
Crede, Joe	Chicago White Sox
Crisp, Coco	Kansas City Royals
Crosby, Bobby	Oakland A's
Crowe, Trevor	Cleveland Indians
Cruz, Juan	Arizona Diamondbacks
Cruz, Luis	Pittsburgh Pirates
Cruz, Nelson	Texas Rangers
Cuddyer, Michael	Minnesota Twins
Cueto, Johnny	Cincinnati Reds

Name	Team
Cunningham, Aaron	Oakland A's
Cust, Jack	Oakland A's
Damon, Johnny	New York Yankees
Danks, John	Chicago White Sox
D'Antona, James	Arizona Diamondbacks
Davies, Kyle	Kansas City Royals
Davis, Christopher	Texas Rangers
Davis, Doug	Arizona Diamondbacks
Davis, Rajai	Oakland A's
Davis, Wade	Tampa Bay Rays
De La Cruz, Eulogio	Florida Marlins
De La Rosa, Jorge	Colorado Rockies
DeJesus, David	Kansas City Royals
Delaney, Robert	Minnesota Twins
Delcarmen, Manny	Boston Red Sox
Delgado, Carlos	New York Mets
Delgado, Jesus	Florida Marlins
Dellucci, David	Cleveland Indians
Dempster, Ryan	Chicago Cubs
Denker, Travis	San Diego Padres
DeRosa, Mark	Chicago Cubs
Devine, Joey	Oakland A's
Dewitt, Blake	Los Angeles Dodgers
Diaz, Matt	Atlanta Braves
Diaz, Victor	Seattle Mariners
Dickerson, Chris	Cincinnati Reds
Dickey, R.A.	Seattle Mariners
Dillard, Tim	Milwaukee Brewers
Dobbs, Greg	Philadelphia Phillies
Donald, Jason	Philadelphia Phillies
Donnelly, Brendan	Cleveland Indians
Dotel, Octavio	Chicago White Sox
Doumit, Ryan	Pittsburgh Pirates
Downs, Scott	Toronto Blue Jays
Drew, J.D.	Boston Red Sox
Drew, Stephen	Arizona Diamondbacks
Duchscherer, Justin	Oakland A's
Duckworth, Brandon	Kansas City Royals
Duensing, Brian	Minnesota Twins
Duke, Zach	Pittsburgh Pirates
Dukes, Elijah	Washington Nationals
Dumatrait, Phil	Pittsburgh Pirates
Duncan, Chris	St. Louis Cardinals
Duncan, Shelley	New York Yankees
Dunn, Adam	Arizona Diamondbacks
Duran, German	Texas Rangers
Durbin, Chad	Philadelphia Phillies
Durham, Ray	Milwaukee Brewers

Name	Team
Dye, Jermaine	Chicago White Sox
Easley, Damion	New York Mets
Eaton, Adam	Philadelphia Phillies
Eckstein, David	Arizona Diamondbacks
Edmonds, Jim	Chicago Cubs
Egbert, Jack	Chicago White Sox
Elbert, Scott	Los Angeles Dodgers
Ellis, Mark	Oakland A's
Ellsbury, Jacoby	Boston Red Sox
Embree, Alan	Oakland A's
Encarnacion, Edwin	Cincinnati Reds
Erstad, Darin	Houston Astros
Escobar, Alcides	Milwaukee Brewers
Escobar, Yunel	Atlanta Braves
Ethier, Andre	Los Angeles Dodgers
Evans, Nick	New York Mets
Eveland, Dana	Oakland A's
Everett, Adam	Detroit Tigers
Eyre, Scott	Philadelphia Phillies
Fahey, Brandon	Baltimore Orioles
Farnsworth, Kyle	Detroit Tigers
Feierabend, Ryan	Seattle Mariners
Feldman, Scott	Texas Rangers
Feliciano, Pedro	New York Mets
Feliz, Pedro	Philadelphia Phillies
Fielder, Prince	Milwaukee Brewers
Fields, Josh	Chicago White Sox
Figgins, Chone	Los Angeles Angels
Figueroa, Nelson	New York Mets
Flores, Jesus	Washington Nationals
Floyd, Gavin	Chicago White Sox
Fogg, Josh	Cincinnati Reds
Fontenot, Mike	Chicago Cubs
Fossum, Casey	Detroit Tigers
Foulke, Keith	Oakland A's
Fowler, Dexter	Colorado Rockies
Fox, Jake	Chicago Cubs
Francis, Jeff	Colorado Rockies
Francisco, Ben	Cleveland Indians
Francisco, Frank	Texas Rangers
Francoeur, Jeff	Atlanta Braves
Franklin, Ryan	St. Louis Cardinals
Frasor, Jason	Toronto Blue Jays
Freel, Ryan	Baltimore Orioles
Freese, David	St. Louis Cardinals
Fuentes, Brian	Colorado Rockies
Fukudome, Kosuke	Chicago Cubs
Fuld, Sam	Chicago Cubs

Name	Team
Furcal, Rafael	Los Angeles Dodgers
Gabbard, Kason	Texas Rangers
Gagne, Eric	Milwaukee Brewers
Galarraga, Armando	Detroit Tigers
Gallagher, Sean	Oakland A's
Gallardo, Yovani	Milwaukee Brewers
Gamel, Mat	Milwaukee Brewers
Garcia, Freddy	Detroit Tigers
Garciaparra, Nomar	Los Angeles Dodgers
Gardner, Brett	New York Yankees
Garko, Ryan	Cleveland Indians
Garland, Jon	Los Angeles Angels
Garza, Matt	Tampa Bay Rays
Gathright, Joey	Kansas City Royals
Gaudin, Chad	Chicago Cubs
Geary, Geoff	Houston Astros
Geer, Joshua	San Diego Padres
German, Esteban	Kansas City Royals
German, Franklyn	Chicago White Sox
Gerut, Jody	San Diego Padres
Getz, Christopher	Chicago White Sox
Giambi, Jason	New York Yankees
Giese, Dan	New York Yankees
Gil, Jerry	Cincinnati Reds
Giles, Brian	San Diego Padres
Glaus, Troy	St. Louis Cardinals
Glavine, Tom	Atlanta Braves
Gload, Ross	Kansas City Royals
Gobble, Jimmy	Kansas City Royals
Golson, Gregory	Philadelphia Phillies
Gomes, Jonny	Tampa Bay Rays
Gomez, Carlos	Minnesota Twins
Gomez, Chris	Pittsburgh Pirates
Gonzalez, Adrian	San Diego Padres
Gonzalez, Carlos	Colorado Rockies
Gonzalez, Edgar	Arizona Diamondbacks
Gonzalez, Edgar V	San Diego Padres
Gonzalez, Gio	Oakland A's
Gonzalez, Mike	Atlanta Braves
Gordon, Alex	Kansas City Royals
Gordon, Tom	Philadelphia Phillies
Gorzelanny, Tom	Pittsburgh Pirates
Grabow, John	Pittsburgh Pirates
Granderson, Curtis	Detroit Tigers
Green, Sean	Seattle Mariners
Greene, Khalil	St. Louis Cardinals
Greinke, Zack	Kansas City Royals
Griffey, Ken	Chicago White Sox

Name	Team
Grilli, Jason	Colorado Rockies
Gross, Gabe	Tampa Bay Rays
Grudzielanek, Mark	Kansas City Royals
Guardado, Eddie	Minnesota Twins
Guerrero, Vladimir	Los Angeles Angels
Guerrier, Matt	Minnesota Twins
Guillen, Carlos	Detroit Tigers
Guillen, Jose	Kansas City Royals
Guthrie, Jeremy	Baltimore Orioles
Gutierrez, Franklin	Seattle Mariners
Guzman, Cristian	Washington Nationals
Guzman, Freddy	Detroit Tigers
Gwynn, Tony	Milwaukee Brewers
Hafner, Travis	Cleveland Indians
Hairston, Jerry	Cincinnati Reds
Hairston, Scott	San Diego Padres
Hall, Bill	Milwaukee Brewers
Hall, Toby	Chicago White Sox
Halladay, Roy	Toronto Blue Jays
Hamels, Cole	Philadelphia Phillies
Hamilton, Josh	Texas Rangers
Hammel, Jason	Tampa Bay Rays
Hammock, Robby	Arizona Diamondbacks
Hampson, Justin	San Diego Padres
Hanigan, Ryan	Cincinnati Reds
Hannahan, Jack	Oakland A's
Hanrahan, Joel	Washington Nationals
Hansen, Craig	Pittsburgh Pirates
Happ, J.A.	Philadelphia Phillies
Harang, Aaron	Cincinnati Reds
Harden, Rich	Chicago Cubs
Hardy, J.J.	Milwaukee Brewers
Haren, Dan	Arizona Diamondbacks
Harper, Brett	San Francisco Giants
Harrell, Lucas	Chicago White Sox
Harris, Brendan	Minnesota Twins
Harris, Willie	Washington Nationals
Harrison, Matt	Texas Rangers
Hart, Corey	Milwaukee Brewers
Hart, Kevin	Chicago Cubs
Hatteberg, Scott	Cincinnati Reds
Hawkins, LaTroy	Houston Astros
Hawpe, Brad	Colorado Rockies
Headley, Chase	San Diego Padres
Heilman, Aaron	New York Mets
Hellickson, Jeremy	Tampa Bay Rays
Helms, Wes	Florida Marlins
Helton, Todd	Colorado Rockies

Name	Team
Hennessey, Brad	San Francisco Giants
Hensley, Clay	San Diego Padres
Hermida, Jeremy	Florida Marlins
Hernandez, Anderson	Washington Nationals
Hernandez, David	Baltimore Orioles
Hernandez, Felix	Seattle Mariners
Hernandez, Livan	Colorado Rockies
Hernandez, Luis	Baltimore Orioles
Hernandez, Ramon	Baltimore Orioles
Herrera, Daniel	Cincinnati Reds
Hill, Aaron	Toronto Blue Jays
Hill, Koyie	Chicago Cubs
Hill, Shawn	Washington Nationals
Hinckley, Michael	Washington Nationals
Hinshaw, Alexander	San Francisco Giants
Hirsh, Jason	Colorado Rockies
Hoffman, Trevor	San Diego Padres
Hoffpauir, Micah	Chicago Cubs
Holliday, Matt	Oakland A's
Holm, Stephen	San Francisco Giants
Hopper, Norris	Cincinnati Reds
Horwitz, Brian	San Francisco Giants
Howard, Ryan	Philadelphia Phillies
Howell, J.P.	Tampa Bay Rays
Howry, Bob	Chicago Cubs
Hu, Chin Lung	Los Angeles Dodgers
Hudson, Orlando	Arizona Diamondbacks
Hudson, Tim	Atlanta Braves
Huff, Aubrey	Baltimore Orioles
Huff, David	Cleveland Indians
Hughes, Luke	Minnesota Twins
Hulett, Tim	Seattle Mariners
Humber, Philip	Minnesota Twins
Hundley, Nick	San Diego Padres
Hunter, Torii	Los Angeles Angels
Hurley, Eric	Texas Rangers
Iannetta, Chris	Colorado Rockies
Ibanez, Raul	Seattle Mariners
Igawa, Kei	New York Yankees
Iguchi, Tadahito	Philadelphia Phillies
Infante, Omar	Atlanta Braves
Inge, Brandon	Detroit Tigers
Inglett, Joe	Toronto Blue Jays
Ishikawa, Travis	San Francisco Giants
Isringhausen, Jason	St. Louis Cardinals
Iwamura, Akinori	Tampa Bay Rays
Izturis, Cesar	St. Louis Cardinals
Izturis, Maicer	Los Angeles Angels

Name	Team
Jackson, Austin	New York Yankees
Jackson, Conor	Arizona Diamondbacks
Jackson, Edwin	Tampa Bay Rays
Jackson, Zach	Cleveland Indians
James, Brad	Houston Astros
James, Chuck	Atlanta Braves
Janish, Paul	Cincinnati Reds
Jaramillo, Jason	Philadelphia Phillies
Jaso, John	Tampa Bay Rays
Jenkins, Geoff	Philadelphia Phillies
Jenks, Bobby	Chicago White Sox
Jepsen, Kevin	Los Angeles Angels
Jeter, Derek	New York Yankees
Jimenez, Cesar	Seattle Mariners
Jimenez, Ubaldo	Colorado Rockies
Johjima, Kenji	Seattle Mariners
Johnson, Christopher	Houston Astros
Johnson, Jim	Baltimore Orioles
Johnson, Josh	Florida Marlins
Johnson, Kelly	Atlanta Braves
Johnson, Nick	Washington Nationals
Johnson, Randy	Arizona Diamondbacks
Johnson, Reed	Chicago Cubs
Johnson, Rob	Seattle Mariners
Jones, Adam	Baltimore Orioles
Jones, Andruw	Los Angeles Dodgers
Jones, Brandon	Atlanta Braves
Jones, Chipper	Atlanta Braves
Joyce, Matthew	Tampa Bay Rays
Kaaihue, Kila	Kansas City Royals
Kapler, Gabe	Milwaukee Brewers
Karstens, Jeff	Pittsburgh Pirates
Kazmir, Scott	Tampa Bay Rays
Kearns, Austin	Washington Nationals
Kemp, Matt	Los Angeles Dodgers
Kendall, Jason	Milwaukee Brewers
Kendrick, Howie	Los Angeles Angels
Kendrick, Kyle	Philadelphia Phillies
Kennedy, Adam	St. Louis Cardinals
Kensing, Logan	Florida Marlins
Kent, Jeff	Los Angeles Dodgers
Keppel, Bobby	Florida Marlins
Keppinger, Jeff	Cincinnati Reds
Kershaw, Clayton	Los Angeles Dodgers
Kinsler, Ian	Texas Rangers
Knight, Brandon	New York Mets
Kobayashi, Masahide	Cleveland Indians
Konerko, Paul	Chicago White Sox

Name	Team
Korecky, Bobby	Minnesota Twins
Koshansky, Joseph	Colorado Rockies
Kotsay, Mark	Boston Red Sox
Kouzmanoff, Kevin	San Diego Padres
Kubel, Jason	Minnesota Twins
Kuo, Hong-Chih	Los Angeles Dodgers
Kuroda, Hiroki	Los Angeles Dodgers
Lackey, John	Los Angeles Angels
Laffey, Aaron	Cleveland Indians
LaHair, Bryan	Seattle Mariners
Laird, Gerald	Detroit Tigers
Lamb, Mike	Milwaukee Brewers
Lambert, Chris	Detroit Tigers
Langerhans, Ryan	Washington Nationals
Lannan, John	Washington Nationals
Larish, Jeff	Detroit Tigers
LaRoche, Adam	Pittsburgh Pirates
LaRoche, Andy	Pittsburgh Pirates
LaRue, Jason	St. Louis Cardinals
League, Brandon	Toronto Blue Jays
Leblanc, Wade	San Diego Padres
Ledezma, Wilfredo	Arizona Diamondbacks
Lee, Carlos	Houston Astros
Lee, Cliff	Cleveland Indians
Lee, Derek	Chicago Cubs
Lester, Jon	Boston Red Sox
Lewis, Fred	San Francisco Giants
Lewis, Jensen	Cleveland Indians
Lidge, Brad	Philadelphia Phillies
Lieber, Jon	Chicago Cubs
Lilly, Ted	Chicago Cubs
Lincecum, Tim	San Francisco Giants
Lincoln, Mike	Cincinnati Reds
Lind, Adam	Toronto Blue Jays
Lindstrom, Matt	Florida Marlins
Linebrink, Scott	Chicago White Sox
Link, Jon	Chicago White Sox
Liriano, Francisco	Minnesota Twins
Litsch, Jesse	Toronto Blue Jays
Liz, Radhames	Baltimore Orioles
Logan, Boone	Chicago White Sox
Lohse, Kyle	St. Louis Cardinals
Loney, James	Los Angeles Dodgers
Longoria, Evan	Tampa Bay Rays
Looper, Braden	St. Louis Cardinals
Lopez, Aquilino	Detroit Tigers
Lopez, Felipe	Arizona Diamondbacks
Lopez, Javier	Boston Red Sox

Name	Team
Lopez, Jose	Seattle Mariners
Lowe, Derek	Los Angeles Dodgers
Lowe, Mark	Seattle Mariners
Lowell, Mike	Boston Red Sox
Lowrie, Jed	Boston Red Sox
Lubanski, Chris	Kansas City Royals
Ludwick, Ryan	St. Louis Cardinals
Lugo, Julio	Boston Red Sox
Lyon, Brandon	Arizona Diamondbacks
MacDougal, Mike	Chicago White Sox
Macri, Matthew	Minnesota Twins
Madrigal, Warner A.	Texas Rangers
Madson, Ryan	Philadelphia Phillies
Mahay, Ron	Kansas City Royals
Maholm, Paul	Pittsburgh Pirates
Maier, Mitch	Kansas City Royals
Maine, John	New York Mets
Majewski, Gary	Cincinnati Reds
Manning, Charlie	Washington Nationals
Manzella, Thomas	Houston Astros
Marceaux, Jacob	Florida Marlins
Markakis, Nick	Baltimore Orioles
Marmol, Carlos	Chicago Cubs
Marquis, Jason	Chicago Cubs
Marshall, Sean	Chicago Cubs
Marson, Lou	Philadelphia Phillies
Marte, Andy	Cleveland Indians
Marte, Damaso	New York Yankees
Martin, Russell	Los Angeles Dodgers
Martinez, Fernando	New York Mets
Martinez, Pedro	New York Mets
Martinez, Victor	Cleveland Indians
Martis, Shairon	Washington Nationals
Masset, Nick	Cincinnati Reds
Masterson, Justin	Boston Red Sox
Mastny, Tom	Cleveland Indians
Mather, Joe	St. Louis Cardinals
Mathis, Jeff	Los Angeles Angels
Matos, Osiris	San Francisco Giants
Matsui, Hideki	New York Yankees
Matsui, Kazuo	Houston Astros
Matsuzaka, Daisuke	Boston Red Sox
Matthews, Gary	Los Angeles Angels
Mauer, Joe	Minnesota Twins
Maybin, Cameron	Florida Marlins
Maysonet, Edwin	Houston Astros
Mazzaro, Vincent	Oakland A's
McAnulty, Paul	San Diego Padres

Name	Team
McCann, Brian	Atlanta Braves
McCarthy, Brandon	Texas Rangers
McClellan, Kyle	St. Louis Cardinals
McClung, Seth	Milwaukee Brewers
McCrory, Bob	Baltimore Orioles
McCutchen, Andrew	Pittsburgh Pirates
McCutchen, Daniel	Pittsburgh Pirates
McDonald, James	Los Angeles Dodgers
McDonald, John	Toronto Blue Jays
McGee, Jacob	Tampa Bay Rays
McGowan, Dustin	Toronto Blue Jays
McLouth, Nate	Pittsburgh Pirates
McPherson, Dallas	Florida Marlins
Meche, Gil	Kansas City Royals
Meek, Evan	Pittsburgh Pirates
Mendoza, Luis	Texas Rangers
Meredith, Cla	San Diego Padres
Metcalf, Travis	Texas Rangers
Michaels, Jason	Pittsburgh Pirates
Mickolio, Kameron	Baltimore Orioles
Mientkiewicz, Doug	Pittsburgh Pirates
Miles, Aaron	St. Louis Cardinals
Millar, Kevin	Baltimore Orioles
Milledge, Lastings	Washington Nationals
Miller, Corky	Atlanta Braves
Miller, Jai	Florida Marlins
Miller, Jim	Baltimore Orioles
Millwood, Kevin	Texas Rangers
Miner, Zach	Detroit Tigers
Misch, Patrick	San Francisco Giants
Mock, Garrett	Washington Nationals
Moehler, Brian	Houston Astros
Moeller, Chad	New York Yankees
Molina, Bengie	San Francisco Giants
Molina, Jose	New York Yankees
Molina, Yadier	St. Louis Cardinals
Montanez, Luis	Baltimore Orioles
Montz, Luke	Washington Nationals
Moore, Adam	Seattle Mariners
Mora, Melvin	Baltimore Orioles
Morales, Jose	Minnesota Twins
Morales, Kendry	Los Angeles Angels
Morgan, Nyjer	Pittsburgh Pirates
Morillo, Juan	Colorado Rockies
Morneau, Justin	Minnesota Twins
Morrow, Brandon	Seattle Mariners
Moseley, Dustin	Los Angeles Angels
Moss, Brandon	Pittsburgh Pirates

Player Index

Name	Team
Mota, Guillermo	Milwaukee Brewers
Motte, Jason	St. Louis Cardinals
Moyer, Jamie	Philadelphia Phillies
Muniz, Carlos	New York Mets
Murphy, Daniel	New York Mets
Murphy, David	Texas Rangers
Murton, Matt	Oakland A's
Mussina, Mike	New York Yankees
Myers, Brett	Philadelphia Phillies
Nady, Xavier	New York Yankees
Napoli, Mike	Los Angeles Angels
Nathan, Joe	Minnesota Twins
Navarro, Dioner	Tampa Bay Rays
Nelson, Christopher	Colorado Rockies
Neshek, Pat	Minnesota Twins
Niemann, Jeff	Tampa Bay Rays
Niese, Jonathon	New York Mets
Nieve, Fernando	Houston Astros
Nieves, Wil	Washington Nationals
Nix, Jayson	Colorado Rockies
Nolasco, Ricky	Florida Marlins
Norris, Bud	Houston Astros
Nunez, Leo	Kansas City Royals
Ochoa, Ivan	San Francisco Giants
O'Day, Darren	Los Angeles Angels
O'Flaherty, Eric	Seattle Mariners
Ohlendorf, Ross	Pittsburgh Pirates
Ohman, Will	Atlanta Braves
Ojeda, Augie	Arizona Diamondbacks
Okajima, Hideki	Boston Red Sox
Oliver, Darren	Los Angeles Angels
Olivo, Miguel	Kansas City Royals
Olson, Garrett	Baltimore Orioles
Omogrosso, Brian	Chicago White Sox
Ordonez, Magglio	Detroit Tigers
Orr, Pete	Washington Nationals
Ortiz, David	Boston Red Sox
Ortmeier, Dan	San Francisco Giants
Oswalt, Roy	Houston Astros
Outman, Joshua	Oakland A's
Overbay, Lyle	Toronto Blue Jays
Owens, Jerry	Chicago White Sox
Owings, Micah	Cincinnati Reds
Padilla, Vicente	Texas Rangers
Pagan, Angel	New York Mets
Palmisano, Lou	Milwaukee Brewers
Papelbon, Jonathan	Boston Red Sox
Park, Chan Ho	Los Angeles Dodgers
Parnell, Bobby	New York Mets
Parra, Manny	Milwaukee Brewers
Parrish, John	Toronto Blue Jays
Patterson, Corey	Cincinnati Reds
Patterson, Eric	Oakland A's
Pauley, David	Boston Red Sox
Paulino, Ronny	Pittsburgh Pirates
Pavano, Carl	New York Yankees
Payton, Jay	Baltimore Orioles
Pearce, Steven	Pittsburgh Pirates
Peavy, Jake	San Diego Padres
Pedroia, Dustin	Boston Red Sox
Pelfrey, Mike	New York Mets
Pena, Brayan	Kansas City Royals
Pena, Carlos	Tampa Bay Rays
Pena, Luis	Milwaukee Brewers
Pena, Tony	Arizona Diamondbacks
Pena, Tony	Kansas City Royals
Pena, Wily Mo	Washington Nationals
Pence, Hunter	Houston Astros
Penn, Hayden	Baltimore Orioles
Pennington, Cliff	Oakland A's
Penny, Brad	Los Angeles Dodgers
Peralta, Jhonny	Cleveland Indians
Peralta, Joel	Kansas City Royals
Percival, Troy	Tampa Bay Rays
Perez, Christopher	St. Louis Cardinals
Perez, Fernando	Tampa Bay Rays
Perez, Odalis	Washington Nationals
Perez, Oliver	New York Mets
Perez, Rafael	Cleveland Indians
Perkins, Glen	Minnesota Twins
Petit, Yusmeiro	Arizona Diamondbacks
Pettit, Christopher	Los Angeles Angels
Pettitte, Andy	New York Yankees
Phillips, Brandon	Cincinnati Reds
Pie, Felix	Chicago Cubs
Pierre, Juan	Los Angeles Dodgers
Pierzynski, A.J.	Chicago White Sox
Pignatiello, Carmen	Chicago Cubs
Pineiro, Joel	St. Louis Cardinals
Pinto, Renyel	Florida Marlins
Podsednik, Scott	Colorado Rockies
Polanco, Placido	Detroit Tigers
Ponson, Sidney	New York Yankees
Posada, Jorge	New York Yankees
Prado, Martin	Atlanta Braves
Pridie, Jason	Minnesota Twins

Name	Team
Proctor, Scott	Los Angeles Dodgers
Pujols, Albert	St. Louis Cardinals
Punto, Nick	Minnesota Twins
Purcey, David	Toronto Blue Jays
Putz, J.J.	Seattle Mariners
Qualls, Chad	Arizona Diamondbacks
Quentin, Carlos	Chicago White Sox
Quinlan, Robb	Los Angeles Angels
Quintanilla, Omar	Colorado Rockies
Quintero, Humberto	Houston Astros
Quiroz, Guillermo	Baltimore Orioles
Rabelo, Mike	Florida Marlins
Raburn, Ryan	Detroit Tigers
Ramirez, Alexei	Chicago White Sox
Ramirez, Aramis	Chicago Cubs
Ramirez, Edwar	New York Yankees
Ramirez, Hanley	Florida Marlins
Ramirez, Horacio	Chicago White Sox
Ramirez, Manny	Los Angeles Dodgers
Ramirez, Maximiliano	Texas Rangers
Ramirez, Ramon	Kansas City Royals
Ramirez, Wilkin	Detroit Tigers
Ransom, Cody	New York Yankees
Rasmus, Colby	St. Louis Cardinals
Rauch, Jon	Arizona Diamondbacks
Raynor, John	Florida Marlins
Redding, Tim	Washington Nationals
Redman, Mark	Colorado Rockies
Reed, Jeremy	New York Mets
Register, Steven	Colorado Rockies
Reimold, Nolan	Baltimore Orioles
Renteria, Edgar	San Francisco Giants
Repko, Jason	Los Angeles Dodgers
Reyes, Anthony	Cleveland Indians
Reyes, Argenis	New York Mets
Reyes, Dennys	Minnesota Twins
Reyes, Jo-Jo	Atlanta Braves
Reyes, Jose	New York Mets
Reynolds, Gregory	Colorado Rockies
Reynolds, Mark	Arizona Diamondbacks
Richard, Clayton	Chicago White Sox
Riggans, Shawn	Tampa Bay Rays
Rios, Alex	Toronto Blue Jays
Riske, David	Milwaukee Brewers
Rivas, Luis	Pittsburgh Pirates
Rivera, Juan	Los Angeles Angels
Rivera, Mariano	New York Yankees
Rivera, Mike	Milwaukee Brewers

Name	Team
Rivera, Saul	Washington Nationals
Roberts, Brian	Baltimore Orioles
Roberts, Dave	San Francisco Giants
Robertson, Nate	Detroit Tigers
Rodney, Fernando	Detroit Tigers
Rodriguez, Alex	New York Yankees
Rodriguez, Francisco	Los Angeles Angels
Rodriguez, Henry Alberto	Oakland A's
Rodriguez, Ivan	New York Yankees
Rodriguez, Luis	San Diego Padres
Rodriguez, Sean	Los Angeles Angels
Rodriguez, Wandy	Houston Astros
Roenicke, Joshua	Cincinnati Reds
Rohlinger, Ryan	San Francisco Giants
Rolen, Scott	Toronto Blue Jays
Rollins, Jimmy	Philadelphia Phillies
Romero, J.C.	Philadelphia Phillies
Rosa, Carlos	Kansas City Royals
Rosales, Adam	Cincinnati Reds
Rosales, Leonel	Arizona Diamondbacks
Ross, Cody	Florida Marlins
Ross, David	Atlanta Braves
Rowand, Aaron	San Francisco Giants
Rowland-Smith, Ryan	Seattle Mariners
Ruggiano, Justin	Tampa Bay Rays
Ruiz, Carlos	Philadelphia Phillies
Ruiz, Randy	Minnesota Twins
Rupe, Josh	Texas Rangers
Rusch, Glendon	Colorado Rockies
Russell, Adam	Chicago White Sox
Ryan, B.J.	Toronto Blue Jays
Ryan, Brendan	St. Louis Cardinals
Ryan, Dusty	Detroit Tigers
Sabathia, C.C.	Milwaukee Brewers
Saccomanno, Mark	Houston Astros
Sadler, Billy	San Francisco Giants
Saito, Takashi	Los Angeles Dodgers
Salazar, Jeff	Arizona Diamondbacks
Salazar, Oscar	Baltimore Orioles
Salome, Angel	Milwaukee Brewers
Saltalamacchia, Jarrod	Texas Rangers
Samardzija, Jeff	Chicago Cubs
Sampson, Chris	Houston Astros
Sanchez, Anibal	Florida Marlins
Sanchez, Duaner	New York Mets
Sanchez, Freddy	Pittsburgh Pirates
Sanchez, Gaby	Florida Marlins
Sanchez, Jonathan	San Francisco Giants

Player Index

Name	Team
Sanchez, Romulo	Pittsburgh Pirates
Sandoval, Pablo	San Francisco Giants
Santana, Ervin	Los Angeles Angels
Santana, Johan	New York Mets
Santiago, Ramon	Detroit Tigers
Sardinha, Dane	Detroit Tigers
Sarfate, Dennis	Baltimore Orioles
Saunders, Joe	Los Angeles Angels
Saunders, Michael	Seattle Mariners
Schafer, Jordan	Atlanta Braves
Schierholtz, Nate	San Francisco Giants
Schneider, Brian	New York Mets
Schoeneweis, Scott	New York Mets
Schumaker, Skip	St. Louis Cardinals
Scott, Luke	Baltimore Orioles
Scutaro, Marco	Toronto Blue Jays
Seanez, Rudy	Philadelphia Phillies
Seay, Bobby	Detroit Tigers
Sexson, Richie	New York Yankees
Shealy, Ryan	Kansas City Royals
Sheets, Ben	Milwaukee Brewers
Sheffield, Gary	Detroit Tigers
Shell, Steven	Washington Nationals
Sherrill, George	Baltimore Orioles
Shields, James	Tampa Bay Rays
Shields, Scot	Los Angeles Angels
Shoppach, Kelly	Cleveland Indians
Shouse, Brian	Milwaukee Brewers
Silva, Carlos	Seattle Mariners
Sinkbeil, Brett	Florida Marlins
Sizemore, Grady	Cleveland Indians
Skelton, James	Detroit Tigers
Slaten, Doug	Arizona Diamondbacks
Slowey, Kevin	Minnesota Twins
Smith, Joseph	New York Mets
Smith, Seth	Colorado Rockies
Smoltz, John	Atlanta Braves
Snell, Ian	Pittsburgh Pirates
Snider, Travis	Toronto Blue Jays
Snyder, Chris	Arizona Diamondbacks
Snyder, Kyle	Boston Red Sox
Sonnanstine, Andrew	Tampa Bay Rays
Soria, Joakim	Kansas City Royals
Soriano, Alfonso	Chicago Cubs
Soriano, Rafael	Atlanta Braves
Soto, Geovany	Chicago Cubs
Sowers, Jeremy	Cleveland Indians
Span, Denard	Minnesota Twins

Name	Team
Speier, Justin	Los Angeles Angels
Speier, Ryan	Colorado Rockies
Spilborghs, Ryan	Colorado Rockies
Springer, Russ	St. Louis Cardinals
Stairs, Matt	Philadelphia Phillies
Statia, Hainley	Los Angeles Angels
Stetter, Mitch	Milwaukee Brewers
Stewart, Ian	Colorado Rockies
Stewart, Shannon	Toronto Blue Jays
Stokes, Brian	New York Mets
Stoner, Tobi	New York Mets
Street, Huston	Oakland A's
Stults, Eric	Los Angeles Dodgers
Suppan, Jeff	Milwaukee Brewers
Suzuki, Ichiro	Seattle Mariners
Suzuki, Kurt	Oakland A's
Swarzak, Anthony	Minnesota Twins
Sweeney, Ryan	Oakland A's
Swisher, Nick	New York Yankees
Tabata, Jose	Pittsburgh Pirates
Taguchi, So	Philadelphia Phillies
Talbot, Mitch	Tampa Bay Rays
Tallet, Brian	Toronto Blue Jays
Tankersley, Taylor	Florida Marlins
Taschner, Jack	San Francisco Giants
Tatis, Fernando	New York Mets
Taveras, Willy	Colorado Rockies
Teahen, Mark	Kansas City Royals
Teixeira, Mark	Los Angeles Angels
Tejada, Miguel	Houston Astros
Tejeda, Robinson	Kansas City Royals
Terrero, Luis	Baltimore Orioles
Thames, Marcus	Detroit Tigers
Thatcher, Joe	San Diego Padres
Theriot, Ryan	Chicago Cubs
Thomas, Clete	Detroit Tigers
Thomas, Frank	Oakland A's
Thome, Jim	Chicago White Sox
Thompson, Brad	St. Louis Cardinals
Thompson, Daryl	Cincinnati Reds
Thornton, Matt	Chicago White Sox
Timlin, Mike	Boston Red Sox
Timpner, Clay	San Francisco Giants
Tolbert, Matt	Minnesota Twins
Torrealba, Yorvit	Colorado Rockies
Torres, Salomon	Milwaukee Brewers
Towles, Justin	Houston Astros
Tracy, Chad	Arizona Diamondbacks

Name	Team
Troncoso, Ramon	Los Angeles Dodgers
Trumbo, Mark	Los Angeles Angels
Tucker, Ryan	Florida Marlins
Tulowitzki, Troy	Colorado Rockies
Uggla, Dan	Florida Marlins
Upton, B.J.	Tampa Bay Rays
Upton, Justin	Arizona Diamondbacks
Uribe, Juan	Chicago White Sox
Utley, Chase	Philadelphia Phillies
Valaika, Chris	Cincinnati Reds
Valbuena, Luis	Cleveland Indians
Valdez, Merkin	San Francisco Giants
Valentin, Javier	Cincinnati Reds
Valverde, Jose	Houston Astros
Van Benschoten, John	Pittsburgh Pirates
Vanden Hurk, Rick	Florida Marlins
Vargas, Claudio	New York Mets
Varitek, Jason	Boston Red Sox
Vazquez, Javier	Chicago White Sox
Vazquez, Ramon	Pittsburgh Pirates
Velez, Eugenio	San Francisco Giants
Venable, William	San Diego Padres
Veras, Jose	New York Yankees
Verlander, Justin	Detroit Tigers
Victorino, Shane	Philadelphia Phillies
Vidro, Jose	Seattle Mariners
Villanueva, Carlos	Milwaukee Brewers
Villone, Ron	St. Louis Cardinals
Vizcaino, Luis	Colorado Rockies
Vizquel, Omar	San Francisco Giants
Volquez, Edinson	Cincinnati Reds
Volstad, Christopher	Florida Marlins
Votto, Joey	Cincinnati Reds
Wade, Cory	Los Angeles Dodgers
Wagner, Billy	New York Mets
Wainwright, Adam	St. Louis Cardinals
Wakefield, Tim	Boston Red Sox
Walker, Jamie	Baltimore Orioles
Walker, Neil	Pittsburgh Pirates
Walker, Tyler	San Francisco Giants
Wang, Chien-Ming	New York Yankees
Ward, Daryle	Chicago Cubs
Washburn, Jarrod	Seattle Mariners
Wassermann, Ehren	Chicago White Sox
Watson, Sean	Cincinnati Reds
Weathers, David	Cincinnati Reds
Weaver, Jered	Los Angeles Angels
Webb, Brandon	Arizona Diamondbacks

Name	Team
Weeks, Rickie	Milwaukee Brewers
Wellemeyer, Todd	St. Louis Cardinals
Wells, Randy	Chicago Cubs
Wells, Vernon	Toronto Blue Jays
Werth, Jayson	Philadelphia Phillies
Westbrook, Jake	Cleveland Indians
Wheeler, Dan	Tampa Bay Rays
White, Sean	Seattle Mariners
Wieters, Matt	Baltimore Orioles
Wilkerson, Brad	Toronto Blue Jays
Willis, Dontrelle	Detroit Tigers
Willits, Reggie	Los Angeles Angels
Wilson, Bobby	Los Angeles Angels
Wilson, Brian	San Francisco Giants
Wilson, C.J.	Texas Rangers
Wilson, Jack	Pittsburgh Pirates
Wilson, Michael	Seattle Mariners
Wimberly, Corey	Colorado Rockies
Winn, Randy	San Francisco Giants
Wise, Dewayne	Chicago White Sox
Witter, Adam	San Francisco Giants
Wolf, Randy	Houston Astros
Wolfe, Brian	Toronto Blue Jays
Wood, Brandon	Los Angeles Angels
Wood, Kerry	Chicago Cubs
Worrell, Mark	St. Louis Cardinals
Wright, David	New York Mets
Wright, Wesley	Houston Astros
Wuertz, Michael	Chicago Cubs
Yabu, Keiichi	San Francisco Giants
Yabuta, Yasuhiko	Kansas City Royals
Yates, Tyler	Pittsburgh Pirates
Youkilis, Kevin	Boston Red Sox
Young, Chris	Arizona Diamondbacks
Young, Chris	San Diego Padres
Young, Delmon	Minnesota Twins
Young, Delwyn	Los Angeles Dodgers
Young, Dmitri	Washington Nationals
Young, Eric	Colorado Rockies
Young, Michael	Texas Rangers
Zambrano, Carlos	Chicago Cubs
Zaun, Gregg	Toronto Blue Jays
Ziegler, Brad	Oakland A's
Zimmerman, Ryan	Washington Nationals
Zito, Barry	San Francisco Giants
Zobrist, Ben	Tampa Bay Rays
Zumaya, Joel	Detroit Tigers

Also Available from ACTA Sports

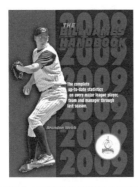

THE BILL JAMES HANDBOOK 2009
BILL JAMES
and BASEBALL INFO SOLUTIONS

Every year, thousands of avid baseball fans eagerly await **The Bill James Handbook**— the best and most complete annual baseball guide available. Full of exclusive stats, this book is the most comprehensive resource of every hit, pitch and catch in Major League Baseball's 2008 season. Key features include the Fielding Bible Awards, the Young Talent Inventory, and Career Data with more statistical categories than any other book.

$23.95, 520 pages, paperback
$28.95, 520 pages, spiral-bound

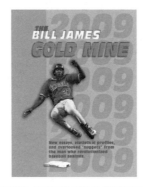

THE BILL JAMES GOLD MINE 2009
BILL JAMES

Starting in the 1970s, a night watchman from Kansas forever changed the way that many people view baseball analysis and ultimately the game itself. In his latest work, Bill James continues that tradition with **The Bill James Gold Mine 2009**—a groundbreaking collection of original essays, statistical profiles, and hidden "nuggets" of information worth their weight in gold.

$23.95, 320 pages, paperback

THE FIELDING BIBLE—VOLUME II
JOHN DEWAN
and BASEBALL INFO SOLUTIONS

First published in 2006, *The Fielding Bible* completely changed the entire perception of fielding statistics in Major League Baseball. Using the revolutionary Plus/Minus approach to fielding analysis previously available exclusively to Major League Baseball teams, John Dewan and Baseball Info Solutions have moved the conversation forward on this important and often overlooked part of the game.

$23.95, 240 pages, paperback

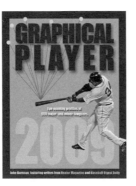

GRAPHICAL PLAYER 2009
JOHN BURNSON and WRITERS
FROM *HEATER* MAGAZINE

In **Graphical Player**, John Burnson offers a new approach to ballplayer analysis: visually analyzing charts and graphs to uncover trends and tendencies among players. With full profiles of 900 major and minor league players, key features include daily game logs (now for three years), support for point leagues (including yearly and weekly trends), and the Graphical Minors— profiles of baseball's top prospects. Burnson and his team of writers won the 2008 CBS Sportsline Fantasy Baseball League of Experts.

$21.95, 300 pages, paperback

THE HARDBALL TIMES
BASEBALL ANNUAL 2009
THE HARDBALL TIMES WRITERS

This is the most complete annual collection of brand new baseball commentary, analysis, and historical baseball writing by some of the best writers working today. **The Hardball Times Baseball Annual 2009** reports on some of the hottest issues in baseball, helps fantasy gamers look ahead to underrated players for 2009, and recaps the 2008 season in detail.

$21.95, 382 pages, paperback